Strategic Paper P3

MANAGEMENT ACCOUNTING RISK AND CONTROL STRATEGY

For exams in May 2005

Study Text

In this July 2004 new edition

- A new user-friendly format for easy navigation
- Targeted topic coverage, directly linked to CIMA's new learning outcomes and syllabus content
- Regular fast forward summaries emphasising the key points in each chapter
- Exam focus points showing you what the examiner will want you to do
- Questions and quick quizzes to test your understanding
- Exam question bank containing exam standard questions with answers
- A full index

BPP's **i-Pass** product also supports this paper.

FOR EXAMS IN MAY 2005

First edition July 2004

ISBN 0 7517 1686 3

British Library Cataloguing-in-Publication Data
A catalogue record for this book
is available from the British Library

Published by

BPP Professional Education
Aldine House, Aldine Place
London W12 8AW

www.bpp.com

Printed in Great Britain by W M Print
45-47 Frederick Street
Walsall, West Midlands
WS2 9NE

We are grateful to the Chartered Institute of Management Accountants for permission to reproduce past examination questions and questions from the pilot paper. The suggested solutions in the exam answer bank have been prepared by BPP Professional Education.

Contents

Page

Introduction

The BPP Study Text – The BPP Effective Study Package – Help yourself study for your CIMA exams – Syllabus and learning outcomes – The exam paper – What the examiner means

Part A Management control systems

1 Control systems: underlying concepts ... 3
2 Controlling people ... 33
3 Control and the organisation ... 69
4 Management accounting control systems ... 99

Part B Risk and internal control

5 Risks and risk management ... 131
6 Risk measurement ... 151
7 Internal control systems ... 179
8 Corporate governance ... 197

Part C Review and audit of control systems

9 Internal audit ... 233
10 Audit evidence and techniques ... 251
11 Risk and analytical review ... 281
12 Planning and control of internal audits ... 301
13 Testing the accounting systems ... 323
14 Types of audit ... 355
15 Fraud ... 377
16 Ethics ... 391

Part D Management of financial risk

17 Financial and international risk ... 413
18 Currency risk I ... 431
19 Currency risk II ... 461
20 Interest rate risk ... 483

Part E Risk and control in information systems

21 Information requirements and strategy ... 519
22 Information systems ... 543
23 Organising the information technology function ... 557
24 Information technology risks and controls ... 579
25 Systems development controls ... 609

Appendix 1: International terminology ... 629
Appendix 2: Mathematical tables and exam formulae ... 635

Exam question bank ... 643
Exam answer bank ... 659

Index ... 717
Review form and free prize draw
Order form

Computer-based learning products from BPP

For **self-testing**, try **i-Pass,** which offers a large number of **objective test questions**, particularly useful where objective test questions form part of the exam.

See the order form at the back of this text for details of these innovative learning tools.

Virtual Campus

The Virtual Campus uses BPP's wealth of teaching experience to produce a fully **interactive** e-learning resource **delivered via the Internet**. The site offers comprehensive **tutor support** and features areas such as **study**, **practice**, **email service**, **revision** and **useful resources**.

Visit our website www.bpp.com/virtualcampus/cima to sample aspects of the campus free of charge.

Learning to Learn Accountancy

BPP's ground-breaking **Learning to Learn Accountancy** book is designed to be used both at the outset of your CIMA studies and throughout the process of learning accountancy. It challenges you to consider how you study and gives you helpful hints about how to approach the various types of paper which you will encounter. It can help you **get your studies both subject and exam focused**, enabling you to **acquire knowledge**, **practise and revise efficiently and effectively**.

The BPP Study Text

Aims of this Study Text

To provide you with the knowledge and understanding, skills and application techniques that you need if you are to be successful in your exams

This Study Text has been written around the **Management Accounting Risk and Control Strategy** syllabus.

- It is **comprehensive**. It covers the syllabus content. No more, no less.
- It is written at the **right level**. Each chapter is written with CIMA's precise learning outcomes in mind.
- It is targeted to the **exam**. We have taken account of the pilot paper, guidance the examiner has given and the assessment methodology.

To allow you to study in the way that best suits your learning style and the time you have available, by following your personal Study Plan (see page (viiii))

You may be studying at home on your own until the date of the exam, or you may be attending a full-time course. You may like to (and have time to) read every word, or you may prefer to (or only have time to) skim-read and devote the remainder of your time to question practice. Wherever you fall in the spectrum, you will find the BPP Study Text meets your needs in designing and following your personal Study Plan.

To tie in with the other components of the BPP Effective Study Package to ensure you have the best possible chance of passing the exam (see page (vi))

Recommended period of use	Elements of the BPP Effective Study Package
From the outset and throughout	**Learning to Learn Accountancy** Read this invaluable book as you begin your studies and refer to it as you work through the various elements of the BPP Effective Study Package. It will help you to acquire knowledge, practice and revise, efficiently and effectively.
Three to twelve months before the exam	**Study Text** Use the Study Text to acquire knowledge, understanding, skills and the ability to apply techniques.
Throughout	**Virtual Campus** Study, practise, revise and take advantage of other useful resources with BPP's fully interactive e-learning site with comprehensive tutor support.
Throughout	**Big Picture Posters** Display these posters where you're studying and give yourself a feel for the overall shape of the paper and the connections between syllabus areas. Examiners have stressed that you will need to be able to link up different areas when you take the exam. The visual stimulation the posters provide will help you remember the key areas of the syllabus.
Throughout	**i-Pass** **i-Pass**, our computer-based testing package, provides objective test questions in a variety of formats and is ideal for self-assessment.
One to six months before the exam	**Practice & Revision Kit** Try the numerous examination-format questions, for which there are realistic suggested solutions prepared by BPP's own authors. Then attempt the two mock exams.
From three months before the exam until the last minute	**Passcards** Work through these short, memorable notes which are focused on what is most likely to come up in the exam you will be sitting.
One to six months before the exam	**Success CDs** The CDs cover the vital elements of your syllabus in less than 90 minutes per subject. They also contain exam hints to help you fine tune your strategy.

Help yourself study for your CIMA exams

Exams for professional bodies such as CIMA are very different from those you have taken at college or university. You will be under **greater time pressure before** the exam – as you may be combining your study with work. There are many different ways of learning and so the BPP Study Text offers you a number of different tools to help you through. Here are some hints and tips: they are not plucked out of the air, but **based on research and experience**. (You don't need to know that long-term memory is in the same part of the brain as emotions and feelings - but it's a fact anyway.)

The right approach

1 **The right attitude**

Believe in yourself	Yes, there is a lot to learn. Yes, it is a challenge. But thousands have succeeded before and you can too.
Remember why you're doing it	Studying might seem a grind at times, but you are doing it for a reason: to advance your career.

2 **The right focus**

Read through the Syllabus and learning outcomes	These tell you what you are expected to know and are supplemented by Exam focus points in the text.
Study the Exam Paper section	The pilot paper is likely to be a reasonable guide to what you should expect in the exam.

3 **The right method**

The whole picture	You need to grasp the detail - but keeping in mind how everything fits into the whole picture will help you understand better. • The **Introduction** of each chapter puts the material in context. • The **Syllabus content, Learning outcomes** and **Exam focus points** show you what you need to **grasp**. BPP's Big Picture Posters will help you see the links here.
In your own words	To absorb the information (and to practise your written communication skills), it helps to **put it into your own words**. • **Take notes.** • Answer the **questions** in each chapter. You will practise your written communication skills, which become increasingly important as you progress through your CIMA exams. • Draw **mindmaps**. • Try **'teaching' a subject** to a colleague or friend.
Give yourself cues to jog your memory	The BPP Study Text uses **bold** to **highlight key points**. • Try **colour coding** with a highlighter pen. • Write **key points** on cards.

4 **The right review**

Review, review, review	It is a **fact** that regularly reviewing a topic in summary form can **fix it in your memory**. Because **review** is so important, the BPP Study Text helps you to do so in many ways. • **Chapter roundups** summarise the 'fast forward' key points in each chapter. Use them to recap each study session. • The **Quick quiz** is another review technique you can use to ensure that you have grasped the essentials. • Go through the **Examples** in each chapter a second or third time.

Developing your personal Study Plan

BPP's **Learning to Learn Accountancy** book emphasises the need to prepare (and use) a study plan. Planning and sticking to the plan are key elements of learning success.
There are four steps you should work through.

Step 1 **How do you learn?**

First you need to be aware of your style of learning. The BPP **Learning to Learn Accountancy** book commits a chapter to this **self-discovery**. What types of intelligence do you display when learning? You might be advised to brush up on certain study skills before launching into this Study Text.

BPP's **Learning to Learn Accountancy** book helps you to identify what intelligences you show more strongly and then details how you can tailor your study process to your preferences. It also includes handy hints on how to develop intelligences you exhibit less strongly, but which might be needed as you study accountancy.

Are you a **theorist** or are you more **practical**? If you would rather get to grips with a theory before trying to apply it in practice, you should follow the study sequence on page (ix). If the reverse is true (you like to know why you are learning theory before you do so), you might be advised to flick through Study Text chapters and look at examples, case studies and questions (Steps 8, 9 and 10 in the **suggested study sequence**) before reading through the detailed theory.

Step 2 **How much time do you have?**

Work out the time you have available per week, given the following.

- The standard you have set yourself
- The time you need to set aside later for work on the Practice & Revision Kit and Passcards
- The other exam(s) you are sitting
- Very importantly, practical matters such as work, travel, exercise, sleep and social life

		Hours
Note your time available in box A.	A	

Step 3 **Allocate your time**

• Take the time you have available per week for this Study Text shown in box A, multiply it by the number of weeks available and insert the result in box B.	B	
• Divide the figure in box B by the number of chapters in this text and insert the result in box C.	C	

Remember that this is only a rough guide. Some of the chapters in this book are longer and more complicated than others, and you will find some subjects easier to understand than others.

Step 4 **Implement**

Set about studying each chapter in the time shown in box C, following the key study steps in the order suggested by your particular learning style.

This is your personal **Study Plan**. You should try and combine it with the study sequence outlined below. You may want to modify the sequence a little (as has been suggested above) to adapt it to your **personal style**.

BPP's **Learning to Learn Accountancy** gives further guidance on developing a study plan, and deciding where and when to study.

Suggested study sequence

It is likely that the best way to approach this Study Text is to tackle the chapters in the order in which you find them. Taking into account your individual learning style, you could follow this sequence.

Key study steps	Activity
Step 1 **Topic list**	Each numbered topic is a numbered section in the chapter.
Step 2 **Introduction**	This gives you the big picture in terms of the context of the chapter, the content you will cover, and the learning outcomes the chapter assesses. In other words, it sets your objectives for study.
Step 3 **Knowledge brought forward boxes**	In these we highlight information and techniques that it is assumed you have 'brought forward' with you from your earlier studies. If there are topics which have changed recently due to legislation for example, these topics are explained in more detail.
Step 4 **Fast forward**	Fast forward boxes give you a quick summary of the content of each of the main chapter sections. They are listed together in the roundup at the end of each chapter to provide you with an overview of the contents of the whole chapter.
Step 5 **Explanations**	Proceed methodically through the chapter, reading each section thoroughly and making sure you understand.
Step 6 **Key terms and Exam focus points**	• Key terms can often earn you *easy marks* if you state them clearly and correctly in an appropriate exam answer (and they are highlighted in the index at the back of the text). • Exam focus points give you a good idea of how we think the examiner intends to examine certain topics.
Step 7 **Note taking**	Take brief notes, if you wish. Avoid the temptation to copy out too much. Remember that being able to put something into your own words is a sign of being able to understand it. If you find you cannot explain something you have read, read it again before you make the notes.
Step 8 **Examples**	Follow each through to its solution very carefully.
Step 9 **Case studies**	Study each one, and try to add flesh to them from your own experience. They are designed to show how the topics you are studying come alive (and often come unstuck) in the real world.
Step 10 **Questions**	Make a very good attempt at each one.
Step 11 **Answers**	Check yours against ours, and make sure you understand any discrepancies.
Step 12 **Chapter roundup**	Work through it carefully, to make sure you have grasped the significance of all the fast forward points.
Step 13 **Quick quiz**	When you are happy that you have covered the chapter, use the Quick quiz to check how much you have remembered of the topics covered and to practise questions in a variety of formats.
Step 14 **Question(s) in the Exam question bank**	Either at this point, or later when you are thinking about revising, make a full attempt at the Question(s) suggested at the very end of the chapter. You can find these at the end of the Study Text, along with the Answers so you can see how you did. We highlight those that are introductory, and those which are of the standard you would expect to find in an exam.

Short of time: Skim study technique?

You may find you simply do not have the time available to follow all the key study steps for each chapter, however you adapt them for your particular learning style. If this is the case, follow the **skim study** technique below (the icons in the Study Text will help you to do this).

- Study the chapters in the order you find them in the Study Text.
- For each chapter:
  - Follow the key study steps 1-3
  - Skim-read through step 5, looking out for the points highlighted in the fast forward boxes (step 4)
  - Jump to step 12
  - Go back to step 6
  - Follow through steps 8 and 9
  - Prepare outline answers to questions (steps 10/11)
  - Try the Quick quiz (step 13), following up any items you can't answer
  - Do a plan for the Question (step 14), comparing it against our answers
  - You should probably still follow step 7 (note-taking), although you may decide simply to rely on the BPP Passcards for this.

Moving on...

However you study, when you are ready to embark on the practice and revision phase of the BPP Effective Study Package, you should still refer back to this Study Text, both as a source of **reference** (you should find the index particularly helpful for this) and as a way to **review** (the Fast forwards, Chapter roundups and Quick quizzes help you here).

And remember to keep careful hold of this Study Text – you will find it invaluable in your work.

More advice on Study Skills can be found in BPP's **Learning to Learn Accountancy** book.

Syllabus and learning outcomes

Paper P3 Management Risk and Control Strategy

The syllabus comprises:

Topic and Study Weighting

A	Management Control Systems	15%
B	Risk and Internal Control	20%
C	Review and Audit of Control Systems	15%
D	Management of Financial Risk	30%
E	Risk and Control in Information Systems	20%

Learning aims

Students should be able to:

- Evaluate and advise on management and internal control systems for a range of risks
- Plan a review process, including an internal audit, of such systems
- Evaluate alternatives and advise on the management of financial risks
- Advise on the development of information systems that support the risk control environment

Learning outcomes and Syllabus content

A – Management Control Systems – 15%

Learning outcomes		**Covered in chapter**
On completion of their studies students should be able to:		
(i)	Evaluate and recommend appropriate control systems for the management of organisations	1, 3
(ii)	Evaluate the control of activities and resources within the organisation	1, 2
(iii)	Recommend ways in which the problems associated with control systems can be avoided or solved	1, 3
(iv)	Evaluate the appropriateness of an organisation's management accounting control systems and make recommendations for improvements	4
Syllabus content		
(1)	The ways in which systems are used to achieve control within the framework of the organisation (eg contracts of employment, policies and procedures, discipline and rewards, reporting structures, performance appraisal and feedback)	1, 2, 3
(2)	The application of control systems and related theory to the design of management accounting control systems and information systems in general (ie control system components, primary and secondary feedback, positive and negative feedback, open- and closed-loop control)	1

		Covered in chapter
(3)	Structure and operation of management accounting control systems (eg identification of appropriate responsibility and control centres within the organisation, performance target setting, avoiding unintended behavioural consequences of using management accounting controls)	1, 4
(4)	Variation in control needs and systems dependent on organisational structure (eg extent of centralisation versus divisionalisation, management through strategic business units)	3
(5)	Assessing how lean the management system is (eg extent of the need for detailed costing, overhead allocation and budgeting, identification of non-value adding activities in the accounting function.	4
(6)	Cost of quality applied to the management accounting function and 'getting things right first time'	4

B – Risk and internal Control – 20 %

Learning outcomes

On completion of their studies students should be able to:

(i)	Define and identify risks facing an organisation	5, 17
(ii)	Explain ways of measuring and assessing risks facing an organisation, including the organisation's ability to bear such risks	5, 6
(iii)	Discuss the purposes and importance of internal control and risk management for an organisation	5
(iv)	Evaluate risk management strategies	5, 17
(v)	Evaluate the essential features of internal control systems for identifying, assessing and managing risks	7
(vi)	Evaluate the costs and benefits of a particular internal control system	7
(vii)	Discuss the principles of good corporate governance for listed companies, particularly as regards the need for internal controls	8

Syllabus content

(1)	Types and sources of risk for business organisations: financial, commodity price, business (eg fraud, employee malfeasance, loss of product reputation), technological, external (eg economic an political), and corporate reputation (eg from environmental and social performance) risks	5, 17
(2)	Risks associated with international operations (eg from cultural variations and litigation risk to loss of goods in transit and enhanced credit risk). (Note no specific real country will be tested)	5, 17
(3)	Quantification of risk exposures (impact if an adverse event occurs) and their expected values, taking account of likelihood	5, 6
(4)	Minimising the risk of fraud (eg fraud policy statements, effective recruitment policies and good internal controls, such as approval procedures and separation of functions, especially over procurement and cash).	15
(5)	Fraud related to sources of finance (eg advance fee fraud and pyramid schemes)	15

		Covered in chapter
(6)	Minimising political risk (eg by gaining government funding, joint ventures, local finance)	17
(7)	The principle of diversifying risk (Note. Numerical questions will not be set)	5
(8)	Purposes of internal control (eg safeguarding of shareholders' investment and company assets, facilitation of operational effectiveness and efficiency, contribution to the reliability of reporting)	7
(9)	Issues to be addressed in defining management's risk policy	5
(10)	Elements in internal control systems (eg control activities, information and communication processes, processes for ensuring continued effectiveness etc)	7
(11)	Operational features of internal control systems (eg embedding in company's operations, responsiveness to evolving risks, timely reporting to management)	7
(12)	The pervasive nature of internal control and the need for employee training	7
(13)	Costs and benefits of maintaining the internal control system	7
(14)	The principles of good corporate governance for listed companies (the Combined Code) (eg separation of Chairman and CEO roles, appointment of non-executive directors, transparency of directors' remuneration policy, relations with shareholders, the audit committee). Examples of recommended good practice may include the King Report on Corporate Governance for South Africa, Sarbanes-Oxley Act in the USA, the Smith and Higgs Reports in the UK, etc)	8
(15)	Recommendations for internal control (eg the Turnbull Report)	8

C –Review and Audit of Control Systems – 15%

Learning outcomes

On completion of their studies students should be able to:

(i)	Explain the importance of management review of controls	12
(ii)	Evaluate the process of internal audit	9-10, 12-14
(iii)	Produce a plan for the audit of various organisational activities including management, accounting and information systems	10-15
(iv)	Analyse problems associated with the audit of activities and systems, and recommend action to avoid or solve those problems	12, 15
(v)	Recommend action to improve the efficiency, effectiveness and control of activities	14
(vi)	Discuss the principles for good corporate governance for listed companies, for conducting reviews of internal controls and reporting on compliance	12
(vii)	Discuss the importance of exercising ethical principles in conducting and reporting on internal reviews	16

Syllabus content

(1)	The process of review (eg regular reporting to management on the effectiveness of internal controls over significant risks) and audit of internal controls	9, 12, 13
(2)	Major tools available to assist with such a process (eg audit planning, documenting systems internal control questionnaires, sampling and testing)	10, 12
(3)	Detection and investigation of fraud	15

		Covered in chapter
(4)	Role of the internal auditor and relationship of the internal audit to the external audit	9
(5)	Operation of internal audit, the assessment of audit risk and the process of analytical review including different types of benchmarking, their use and limitations	11, 12
(6)	The principles of good corporate governance for listed companies for the review of the internal control system and reporting on compliance	12
(7)	Relationship of the above to other forms of audit (eg value-for-money audit, management audit, social and environmental audit)	14
(8)	Particular relevance of the fundamental principles in CIMA's Ethical Guidelines to the conduct of an impartial and effective review of internal controls	16
(9)	Applications of CIMA's Ethical Guidelines on the resolution of ethical conflicts in the context of discoveries made in the course of internal review	16

D – Management of Financial Risk – 30%

Learning outcomes

On completion of their studies students should be able to:

(i)	Identify and evaluate financial risks facing an organisation	17, 18, 20
(ii)	Identify and evaluate appropriate methods for managing financial risks	17-20
(iii)	Evaluate the effects of alternative methods of risk management and make recommendations accordingly	18-20
(iv)	Calculate the impact of differential inflation rates on forecast exchange rates	18
(v)	Explain exchange rate theory	18
(vi)	Recommend currency risk management strategies	18,19

Syllabus content

(1)	Sources of financial risk, including those associated with international operations (eg hedging of foreign investment value) and trading (eg purchase prices and sales values)	17, 18
(2)	Transaction, translation, economic and political risk	18
(3)	Minimising political risk (eg gaining government funding, joint ventures, obtaining local finance)	17
(4)	Quantification of risk exposures and their expected values	18
(5)	Operation and features of the more common instruments for managing interest rate risk: swaps, forward rate agreements, futures and options. (Note. Numerical questions will not be set involving FRA's, futures or options. See the note below relating to the Black Scholes model)	20
(6)	Illustration and interpretation of simple graphs depicting cap, collar and floor interest rate options	20
(7)	Theory and forecasting of exchange rates (eg interest rate parity, purchasing power parity and the Fisher effect)	18
(8)	Operation and features of the more common instruments for managing currency risk: swaps, forward contracts, money market hedges, futures and options. (Note. The Black Scholes option pricing model will not be tested numerically, however, an understanding of the variables which will influence the value of an option should be appreciated)	18, 19

		Covered in chapter
(9)	Principles of valuation of financial instruments for management and financial reporting purposes (IAS 39), and controls to ensure that the appropriate accounting method is applied to a given instrument.	20
(10)	Internal hedging techniques (eg netting and matching)	18

E – Risk and Control in Information Systems– 20%

Learning outcomes

On completion of their studies students should be able to:

(i)	Evaluate and advise managers on the development of IM, IS and IT strategies that support management and internal control requirements	21, 25
(ii)	Identify and evaluate IS/IT systems appropriate to an organisation's need for operational and control information	22
(iii)	Evaluate benefits and risks in the structuring and organisation of the IS/IT function and its integration with the rest of the business	23
(iv)	Evaluate and recommend improvements to the control of information systems	24
(v)	Evaluate specific problems and opportunities associated with the audit and control of systems which use information technology	24, 25

Syllabus content

(1)	The importance and characteristics of information for organisations and the use of cost-benefit analysis to assess its value	21, 22, 25
(2)	The purpose and content of IM, IS and IT strategies, and their role in performance management and internal control	21, 25
(3)	Data collection and IT systems that deliver information to different levels in the organisation (eg transaction processing, decision support and executive informative systems)	22, 25
(4)	The potential ways of organising the IT function (eg the use of steering committees, support centres for advice and help desk facilities, end user participation)	23
(5)	The arguments for and against outsourcing	23
(6)	The criteria for selecting outsourcing/Facilities Management partners and for managing ongoing relationships service level agreements, discontinuation/change of supplier, hand-over considerations	23
(7)	Methods for securing systems and data back-up in case of systems failure and/or data loss	24
(8)	Minimising the risk of computer-based fraud (eg access restriction, password protection, access logging and automatic generation of audit trail)	24
(9)	Risks in IS/IT systems: erroneous input, unauthorised usage, imported virus infection, unlicensed use of software, theft, corruption of software	24
(10)	Risks and benefits of Internet ad Intranet use by a organisation	24
(11)	Control which can be designed into an information system, particularly one using information technology (eg security, integrity and contingency controls	24

		Covered in chapter
(12)	Control and audit of system development and implementation	25
(13)	Techniques available to assist audit in a computerised environment (computer-assisted audit techniques eg audit interrogation software)	10

Notes on syllabus

Paper P3 Management Accounting Risk and Control Strategy does not closely correspond to any of the previous syllabus papers. The closest correspondence is probably with the pre 2000 syllabus Paper 16 *Management Accounting Control Systems,* although Paper P3 is more focused on risk than Paper 16 was and is also intended to be more practical.

Although Paper P3 has been matched for the purposes of the transitional rules with Paper 14 *Management Accounting Information Strategy* different sections of the syllabus include topics that were previously covered in Paper 10 *Systems and Project Management* and Paper 13 *Management Accounting Financial Strategy.*

The examiners have emphasised the importance of the learning outcomes, as the exam is focusing on principles rather than details. The syllabus may not be fully indicative of what might be examined.

Section A *Management control systems* contains various elements from Paper 10 Section (iii) *Control of activities and resources.* However the scope of Section A is wider than the equivalent section in Paper 10, and students will be expected to cover issues such as the operation of control systems, the impact of organisational structure and cost and quality issues. The examiners have stated that the exam may cover control systems other than management accounting control systems; students must be able to understand the problems and limitations of these systems.

Section B *Risk and control systems* expands significantly on topics in various areas of Paper 13, particularly Section iii *Risk management.* Candidates will have to use their previous knowledge of various techniques such as expected values for quantifying risk. The emphasis this section places on internal controls and corporate governance has more in common with the pre 2000 Paper 16 than any of the 2000 syllabus papers.

Section C *Review and audit of control systems* is closest to old syllabus Paper 10 Section (iv) *Audit of activities and systems.* The main differences are that Paper P3 covers a wider range of audits including social and environmental audits, and links in corporate governance requirements, particularly the requirement for management to regularly review controls. Paper P3 also links audit work to CIMA's Ethical Guidelines.

Section D *Management of financial risk* is very similar to Paper 13 Section iii *Risk management.* On interest rate risk the syllabus has gone back to the pre May 2004 situation on Paper 13 with only interest rate swaps being examinable numerically. The one significant addition compared with the old syllabus is principles of valuation of financial instruments based round IASs 32 and 39. Candidates will be expected to have some knowledge of these standards and be aware in particular of how an organisation's activities and systems may be affected by them.

Section E *Risk and control in information systems* contains a number of elements of Paper 10 and Paper 14, particularly from Section (iii) *Control of activities and resources* from Paper 10 and Section (iii) *Planning and implementation of IS/IT strategies* from Paper 14. However the syllabus for P3 clearly emphasises the risks faced by computer systems; although knowledge of risks were required for Papers 10 and 14, they were not highlighted to the same extent in the old syllabuses.

The exam paper

Format of the paper Strategic papers

		Number of marks
Section A:	A compulsory scenario-based question with up to 4 parts	50
Section B:	2 out of 4 questions, 25 marks each	50
		100

Time allowed: 3 hours

The examiners have stated that credit will be given for focusing on the right principles and making practical evaluations and recommendations in a variety of different business scenarios, including manufacturing, retailing and financial services. A likely weakness of answers is excessive focus on details. Plausible alternative answers could be given to many questions, so model answers should not be regarded as all-inclusive.

Candidates must demonstrate a risk-based perspective, focusing on wider issues. They must be able to classify and map risks in different environments and identify major risks in a variety of scenarios. Governance and control are also key topics for this paper.

The paper is likely to have about a 25% numerical content, mainly in questions relating to Section D *Financial risk*. Financial risk hedging will be covered in the majority of papers. Calculations may also be set involving expected values and exposure to other sorts of risk. Questions may also include the interpretation of data.

Questions in *both* sections of the paper may cover more than one syllabus area, see for example Question 4 on the Pilot paper.

Candidates should also bring in their knowledge from other Strategic level papers. One aim of this paper is to prepare candidates for the TOPCIMA exam.

Pilot paper

Section A

1 Importance of risk management; analysis of risks; identification and quantification of risks; components of management control system and control recommendations

Section B

2 IM, IS and IT strategy; ERPS and EIS; improvements in budgetary allocations for IT and evaluation of ERPS and EIS

3 Types of financial risk; quantification of transaction risk; hedging and derivatives

4 Expected values of expansion; risks of franchising; managing and minimising the risks of making loans

5 Role and responsibilities of board; role and responsibilities of audit committee; disclosure of corporate governance arrangements

What the examiner means

The table below has been prepared by CIMA to help you interpret exam questions.

Learning objective	Verbs used	Definition
1 Knowledge What you are expected to know	• List • State • Define	• Make a list of • Express, fully or clearly, the details of/facts of • Give the exact meaning of
2 Comprehension What you are expected to understand	• Describe • Distinguish • Explain • Identify • Illustrate	• Communicate the key features of • Highlight the differences between • Make clear or intelligible/state the meaning of • Recognise, establish or select after consideration • Use an example to describe or explain something
3 Application How you are expected to apply your knowledge	• Apply • Calculate/ compute • Demonstrate • Prepare • Reconcile • Solve • Tabulate	• To put to practical use • To ascertain or reckon mathematically • To prove with certainty or to exhibit by practical means • To make or get ready for use • To make or prove consistent/compatible • Find an answer to • Arrange in a table
4 Analysis How you are expected to analyse the detail of what you have learned	• Analyse • Categorise • Compare and contrast • Construct • Discuss • Interpret • Produce	• Examine in detail the structure of • Place into a defined class or division • Show the similarities and/or differences between • To build up or compile • To examine in detail by argument • To translate into intelligible or familiar terms • To create or bring into existence
5 Evaluation How you are expected to use your learning to evaluate, make decisions or recommendations	• Advise • Evaluate • Recommend	• To counsel, inform or notify • To appraise or assess the value of • To advise on a course of action

Part A
Management control systems

1

Control systems: underlying concepts

Introduction

This chapter provides an overview of the theory of control, in order to open your mind to how control is exercised – or not! – at all levels of the organisation, and the many types of control that exist. The theory of control also rests on certain basic assumptions about how people behave and how systems behave, and we shall briefly question these assumptions.

The overall syllabus, of course, covers risk and control, perhaps with a focus on financial risks and controls. It is worth bearing in mind, though, the wider context so that control does not become a box ticking exercise, and so that you can see its broader purpose and problems.

Topic list	Learning outcomes	Syllabus references	Ability required
1 The context of control	A (i), (ii), (iii)	A (1), (2), (3)	Evaluation
2 Control and systems theory	A (i), (ii), (iii)	A (1), (2), (3)	Evaluation
3 Subsystems	A (i), (ii), (iii)	A (1), (2), (3)	Evaluation
4 Open and closed systems	A (i), (ii), (iii)	A (1), (2), (3)	Evaluation
5 Control systems and cybernetics	A (i), (ii), (iii)	A (1), (2), (3)	Evaluation
6 Feedback and control systems	A (i), (ii), (iii)	A (1), (2), (3)	Evaluation
7 Problems with cybernetic control systems	A (i), (ii), (iii)	A (1), (2), (3)	Evaluation
8 Hard and soft systems	A (i), (ii), (iii)	A (1), (2), (3)	Evaluation
9 Problems in enforcing goal congruence	A (i), (ii), (iii)	A (1), (2), (3)	Evaluation
10 Structuration theory	A (i), (ii), (iii)	A (1), (2), (3)	Evaluation
11 Conclusion	A (i), (ii), (iii)	A (1), (2), (3)	Evaluation

1 The context of control

FAST FORWARD

Control matters at all levels of an organisation, from its **overall governance**, to the **details of its operating practices**. The purpose and types of control at each level will differ and even the best intentioned controls can be undermined by human action.

1.1 The context of governance: macro level

You are expected to evaluate and recommend appropriate control systems to the management of an organisation. This is easier said than done, and it is easy to get fixated on one particular model of control. We start with a case study to give you some idea as to context. We shall revisit this example at the end of the chapter.

Case Study

Enron Corporation

A major corporate scandal of recent years has been Enron, the American energy supplier, which had promised to revolutionise energy businesses. Enron was a US-based energy supply company, with global activities. For example, it owned power plants in India, but the terms of the ownership were controversial.

As well as operating physical power plants, Enron also supported the liberalisation of energy trading markets and the introduction of competition. Many countries saw the injection of competition into the power supply industry as a means of reducing prices for consumers (in the developed world), or providing additional capacity to support economic growth (in the developing world).

At the heart of Enron's business strategy was the belief that it could be a big energy company without owning all the power plants, ships, pipelines and other facilities. Instead, it could use contracts to control the facilities in which other companies had invested. Deregulation had destroyed the integrated production and distribution operations, and users could buy energy from different sources. In this free market, Enron acted as an intermediary, buying and selling energy (and other assets such as Internet bandwidth).

This business model is not valueless or fraudulent in itself. UBS Warburg, the merchant bank, has acquired Enron's energy trading operations, including 635 employees. UBS Warburg believed that, scandals aside, the trading operations were profitable (The Economist, 20 April 2002).

However, Enron's business practices and accounting issues raised a number of issues.

1 **Non-consolidated affiliates**

Enron set up about 3,500 affiliates, which effectively removed assets and liabilities from Enron's balance sheet (effectively additional debt of $1.2bn). Some of these affiliated partnerships were run by Enron's directors and managers who are alleged to have profited from this, including the Chief Financial Officer, Andrew Fastow. (As accountants, you are doubtless aware of what this means in terms of 'off balance sheet finance' or even 'related party transactions'.)

Many small investors did not know of the extent of off balance sheet financing although it is estimated that $27bn of $60bn assets were treated in this way. It is suggested that Enron's directors and advisers were well aware of the position. Enron did not have to report them and chose not to.

The share price rose from $30 to $90 between 1998 and 2000, as sales increased from $31 billion to more than $100 billion. In 2001, Enron had to restate its profits. The share price fell by 90 percent in 2001. In October 2001, Enron reported a third-quarter loss of $618 million. The company's massive debt was downgraded to near junk-bond status, and the CEO and CFO left the company. Shareholders sued and the (US) Securities and Exchange Commission (SEC) launched an investigation.

Enron capitalised these affiliates not with cash but with its own shares: if the shares were rising these investments appeared well-capitalised, but once Enron's shares began to fall, the company had to inject more shares to keep its side of the agreement with the affiliates. These affiliates were used to draw in money from outside investors.

These arrangements were justified on the basis that the investments offered little in the short term. By taking them off balance sheet, Enron could raise more money for other investments and enhance its corporate earnings.

2 **Accounting**

It is possible that such ventures were perfectly legal under US GAAP (Generally Accepted Accounting Principles) which is more rule-bound than the approach adopted in the UK and elsewhere. (There is a wider issue about ethics here: rules or principles and how these apply to corporate codes of practice.)

There is little doubt however that many shareholders were seriously misled about the financial position of the company. Enron's profits had to be restated.

Enron's accountants, Arthur Andersen, and its lawyers endorsed the accounting treatment. Arthur Andersen is alleged to have destroyed large number of documents relating to its dealings with Enron when these matters were finally investigated.

An internal management report revealed the following accounting treatments (Financial Times, 4 February 2002).

(a) **Inflate profits and revenues**. Book income immediately on contracts that could take years complete, and count trades made through online subsidiaries as revenues

(b) **Offload debt**. Transfer it to 'off-balance-sheet' partnerships, some managed by Enron officers.

(c) **Massage quarterly figures**. Transactions were timed for the end of accounting periods to flatter earnings and balance sheet.

(d) **Avoid taxes**. Use offshore vehicles and other methods to minimise tax bill.

(e) **Do deals**. Mask poor performance by buying, selling and trading assets rapidly.

(f) **Use derivatives**. Hide speculative losses, bury debts and inflate asset values with complex financial instruments.

3 **Enron's directors and employees**

As mentioned above, many of Enron's employees had their personal wealth tied up in Enron shares, now worthless. They were actively discouraged from selling them. Many of Enron's directors, however, sold the shares when they began to fall, potentially profiting from them. It is alleged that the Chief Financial Officer, Andrew Fastow, concealed the gains he made from his involvement with affiliated companies.

4 **Enron's political influence**

Like many firms, Enron actively lobbied legislators and government agencies for government contracts or for legislation favourable to its commercial interests. Indeed, Enron's directors advised the new Republican administration on energy policy. Such lobbying is hardly rare. Enron paid money to support the re-election campaigns of many American legislators of both main parties. So Enron's activities fed into a far wider debate on campaign finance reform in the US.

Enron and Arthur Andersen also had contacts with the Labour government in the UK. The extent to which Enron benefited from these arrangements is debatable, however, and is subject to much speculation.

5 **Enron's customers and market behaviour**

In 2001, California faced an energy crisis. Power supply was open to competition, but prices were fixed, and capacity was limited. Unable to cope with increasing prices which they could not pass on to consumers, a number of local power companies faced financial ruin.

Eventually, a political solution was found, and Enron became a significant beneficiary by selling power to California. It has been alleged that Enron overcharged California for the energy supplied by systematically manipulating the power trading system.

It might have been difficult to criticise the company's actions at the time on grounds that they were actually harmful to individuals. Indeed, Enron was highly praised by external experts for its innovative approach to financial strategy, and the shareholders were very happy. However, the firm's alleged exploitation of the letter of the accounting rules, in defiance of their spirit, suggests that legality, rather than, ethicality, was the only yardstick of behaviour

Criminal proceedings have now begun.

The point about introducing this example near the beginning of a 'risk and control' book is to introduce some of the wider issues of the syllabus, and it is worth drawing out some lessons.

Who 'controlled' Enron?	Clearly, something went wrong with Enron's corporate governance, in other words the overall guidance mechanism of the company. There was a **failure of oversight**. The audit committees did not have enough information on which to make judgments: the management system interfered with the running of the formal 'control' system.
Financial performance	In this case, accounting standards were followed to the letter, most of the time, but the overall effect was to inflate Enron's apparent performance. Performance measurement systems – as we shall see an important part of control – were clearly measuring something, but not everything. After all, 'off balance sheet finance' exists **precisely** because it does not have to be reported as a liability.
Incentive schemes	Everyone benefited from the rocketing share price: employers, managers and shareholders. So few had an interest in telling the truth.
Performance appraisal and **reward systems**	Enron was notorious for **aggressive human resource management**, with the bottom 'performers', as defined by management being sacked regularly.
Culture, ethics and targets	The culture of the company encouraged **aggressive accounting** and **over booking of revenues**. It was more important to report meeting targets than to meet them in fact.

It is clear then that many of the structures that are supposed to manage and control corporate behaviour failed. Enron was a sophisticated business operation, with talented people, innovative business models, and the whole panoply of audit committees. Yet the rot set in from the top, and a lot of the controls that are supposed to protect shareholders from potentially rapacious management failed in this instance. Enron is, unlike some other companies, not simply a case of simple fraud, as lot of what it did was technically legal.

The context of control in this case is, therefore:

- **Market expectations** set targets for the company to achieve
- **Reporting of financial performance**
- **Management and organisation** structures (with many partnerships, divisions and related companies)
- **Human resources management**

1.2 The context of control at operational level

Of course, risk and control do not only matter at the corporate level as described above. Control systems are built into the detailed operating technologies and procedures of a company. Many of the procedures for processing accounting transactions – control accounts, reconciliations, variance analysis, authorisation procedures and so on – are specifically designed for control. Companies can fail for example, through failure to manage their receivables properly – this is not matter of wrong doing, just poor control.

Other procedures exist to control the organisation's behaviour. Procedures for recruitment, selection and reward must be designed to ensure compliance with the law (eg against discrimination), and monitored.

2 Control and systems theory

FAST FORWARD

Control is often discussed in the **context of systems theory**. An organisation is a type of system, and a control system is a type of system.

Most systems have **inputs, processes and outputs** and are separated from the environment by a **boundary** that can be physical, social, legal, or all three.

Exam focus point

The syllabus is ambiguous about the examinability of control theory. However, the syllabus content does identify 'the application of control systems and related theory' and identifies components such as 'primary and secondary feedback, positive and negative feedback, open and closed loop control). The syllabus also explicitly brings in control within the framework of the organisation.

2.1 What do we mean by system?

Key terms

A **system** is set of interacting components that operate together to accomplish a purpose.

A **business system** is a collection of people, machines and methods organised to accomplish a set of specific functions.

The systems approach to organisation defines the organisation as a type of system. The word **system** has a number of meanings and is used in many contexts: you may have heard of 'social system', 'the capitalist system', 'information system'. The following are examples of systems.

(a) Technical systems (eg motor car production lines)

(b) Information systems

(c) Social systems (eg a household): a social system is made up of people, and so an organisation - such as a business - is a type of social system.

An understanding of the concepts of systems theory is relevant to the design of **financial and management accounting systems.** The application of systems theory may:

(a) Create an awareness of **subsystems** (the different parts of an organisation), each with potentially conflicting goals which must be brought into line with each other.

(b) Help in the design and development of **information systems** to help **decision makers** ensure that decisions are made for the benefit of the organisation as a whole.

(c) Help identify the effect of the **environment** on systems. The external factors that affect an organisation may be wide-ranging. For example, the government (in all its forms), competitors, trade unions, creditors and shareholders all have an interactive link with an organisation.

(d) Highlight the **dynamic aspects** of the business organisation, and the factors which influence the growth and development of all its subsystems.

2.2 System objectives

An organisation generally exists for purpose, to which its activities are directed. **Hospitals exist** to cure the **sick** for example

Other systems also have objectives, for example, an air conditioning system is designed to maintain a set temperature; a management accounting system is designed to produce information for management control

The **objectives of systems** will often be **conflicting**, so that some form of compromise or **trade-off** between them must be reached. A system will not operate as efficiently as it should if these compromises are not reached in a satisfactory or optimal manner. A wish to reduce production costs, for example, must be measured against health and safety conditions at work, the treatment of waste and effluence from production, the quality of goods produced, and spending on new technology or research and development.

Question — System objectives

Learning outcome: A(iii)

You work in a credit control department of a large organisation which runs a number of different accounts for business clients. Sales people are encouraged to maximise sales, and your job is to maximise debt recovery. Sales people are paid on commission and there is an increasing problem with bad debts. What might be the problems with the objectives to the systems and how would you correct them?

Answer

Clearly, all sales have to be profitable sales in which the debt is fully recovered, as soon as possible. There are number of different solutions.

(a) You can introduce new controls over credit accounts, so that any credit sale must be approved.

(b) You can, more radically, change the salespersons' objectives and reward: instead of focusing on sales, the objective can be set on cash recovery, for example if sales person's commission is not paid until the cash is received. Of course, this has the effect of making sales people into credit controllers, and the ultimate conflict, between maximising headline sales turnover and recovering cash is resolved, uncomfortably, in the sales person's head.

2.3 The component parts of a system

A system has three component parts: inputs, processes and outputs. Other key characteristics of a system are the environment and the system boundary - as shown in the following diagram.

An organisation is sometimes described as a system of transformation. The diagram below shows. In order to make profits businesses obtain **inputs** (resources from the environment), transform them in some way into **outputs** to the environment.

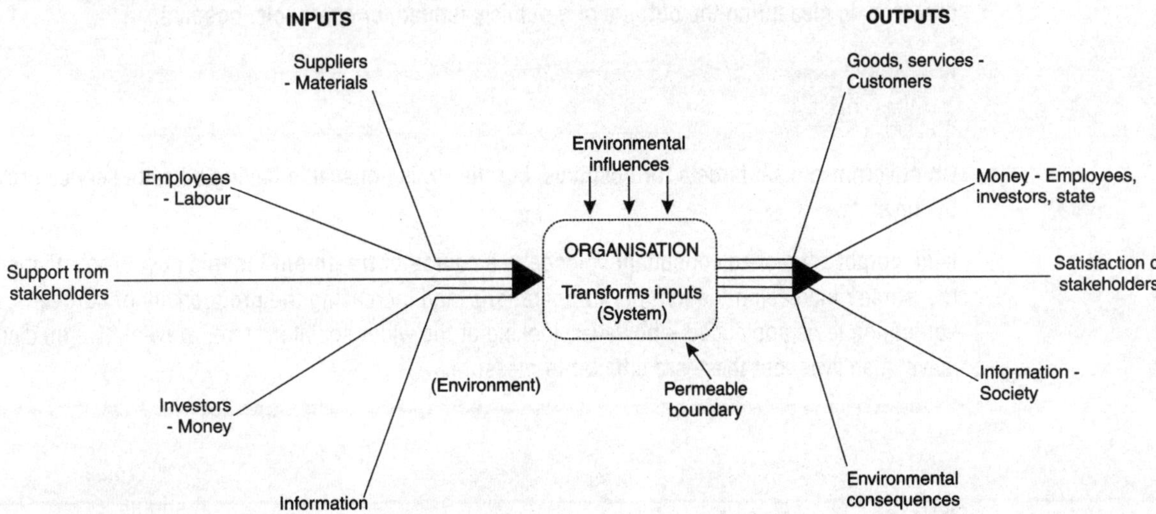

2.3.1 Inputs

Inputs **provide the system with what it needs** to be able to operate. Input may vary from matter, energy or human actions, to information.

- Matter might include, in a manufacturing operation, adhesives or rivets.
- Human input might consist of typing an instruction booklet or starting up a piece of machinery.

Inputs may be outputs from other systems, for example, the output from a transactions processing system forms the input for a management information system.

2.3.2 Processes

A process **transforms an input into an output**. Processes may involve tasks performed by humans, plant, computers, chemicals and a wide range of other actions.

Processes may consist of **assembly**, for example where electronic consumer goods are being manufactured, or **disassembly**, for example where oil is refined. Some of this is automated, and some may be done by people. The word process is used more loosely than this, too, to discuss items such as the 'process of change' or 'the transformation process'. There is **not necessarily a clear relationship** between the number of inputs to a process and the number of outputs.

2.3.3 Outputs

Outputs are the **results of the processing**. They could be said to represent the **purpose** for which the system exists. For example, a product is output at the end of a manufacturing process. In service terms, an output might be a completed medical procedure resulting in a well patient. Many outputs are used as **inputs to other systems** – either within the organisation (information flows from one department to another) or to other organisations (which may buy the output).

Some outputs may be discarded as **waste** (an input to the ecological system) or **re-input** to the system which has produced them, for example, in certain circumstances, defective products.

Question — **Which outputs?**

Learning outcome: A(iii)

A problem faced by public sector organisations is that outputs are harder to measure. Identify the problems in measuring the outputs of a publicly funded, or charitable, hospital.

Answer

UK governments set targets for hospitals, but the UK is unusual in having a health service provided largely by the state.

Is an output a 'finished consultant episode' – a **course of treatment**? Is this how productivity would be measured? Increasing the number of operations, and increasing the productivity of surgeons, may be something to be applauded – however, looking at the wider social system, preventative medicine may 'save' man lives, but these are difficult to measure.

2.4 The system boundary

Every system has a boundary that **separates it from its environment**. For example, a cost accounting department's boundary can be expressed in terms of who works in it and what work it does. This boundary will separate it from other departments, such as the financial accounts department.

System boundaries may be **natural** or artificially created (an organisation's departmental structures are artificially created).

There may be **interfaces** between various systems, both internal and external to an organisation, to allow the exchange of resources. In a commercial context, this is most likely to be a reciprocal exchange, for example money for raw materials.

Physical boundaries	Like a prison, an organisation might occupy buildings, which act as **physical** boundaries. These may need to be protected.
Legal boundaries	Organisations engage in legal contracts with suppliers and customers. From the supplier or customer viewpoint, the organisation is a legal entity in its own right. The organisation is accountable for products or services.
Social boundaries	Organisation culture may create social divisions. In recruiting, managers may recruit people like themselves.

2.5 The environment

Anything which is outside the system boundary belongs to the system's environment and not to the system itself. A system **accepts inputs** from the environment and **provides outputs** into the environment. The parts of the environment from which the system receives inputs may not be the same as those to which it delivers outputs.

The environment exerts a considerable influence on the behaviour of a system; at the same time the system can do little to **control** the behaviour of the environment.

Question

Environmental impact

Learning outcome: A(i)

The environment affects the performance of a system. Using a business organisation as an example of a system, give examples of environmental factors which might affect it.

Answer

(a) **Policies** adopted by the government or ruling political body.
(b) The **strength of the domestic currency** of the organisation's country of operation.
(c) **Social attitudes**: concern for the natural environment.
(d) The **regulatory and legislative framework** within which the company operates.
(e) The **number of competitors** in the marketplace and the strategies they adopt.
(f) The **products of competitors**; their price and quality.

3 Subsystems

FAST FORWARD

Many systems are made up of **subsystems**. In an organisation, for example, there are subsystems related to the **structure**, **technology**, **goals and values**, **management** and the **underlying social system** of the organisation.

3.1 Aspects of subsystems

A system itself may contain a number of systems, called **subsystems**. Each subsystem consists of a process whereby component parts interact to achieve an objective. Separate subsystems **interact** with each other, and **respond** to each other by means of **communication** or observation. The goals of subsystems must be consistent with the goal of the overall system.

Subsystems may be **differentiated** from each other by:

Function	Formality
Space	People
Time	Automation

3.2 Interlinked subsystems

Another point of view suggests that an organisation is a 'structured **socio-technical** system', that is, it consists of at least three subsystems.

(a) A **structure**.

(b) A **technological system** (concerning the work to be done, and the machines, tools and other facilities available to do it).

(c) A **social system** (concerning the people within the organisation, the ways they think and the ways they interact with each other).

Question

Differentiated subsystems

Learning outcome: A(i)

Using each of the above six factors by which subsystems may be differentiated, give examples of how an organisation may be structured. (For example, an organisation structured by function might have a production department, a sales department, an accounts department and a personnel department.)

Answer

(a) **Functional departments** might **include production, sales, accounts and personnel**.

(b) **Differentiation by space** might include **the geographical division** of a sales function (subsystem) into sales regions (sub-subsystems).

(c) A **production system** might be **subdivided** into three eight-hour shifts.

(d) The **hierarchy** may consist of **senior management, middle management, junior** (operational) **management** and the **workforce**.

(e) There may be a **formal management information system** and a 'grapevine'.

(f) Some systems might be **automated** (sales order processing, production planning), while others may be **'manual'** (public relations, staff appraisal).

Often, whether something is a system or a subsystem is a matter of definition, and depends on the context of the **observer**. For example, an organisation is a social system, and its 'environment' may be seen as society as a whole. Another way of looking at an organisation would be to regard it as a **subsystem** of the entire social system.

Case Study

A nuclear power station contains many technical systems, but there are underlying social systems determining what is good practice.

3.3 Information and the hierarchical subsystem: filtering

The organisation hierarchy is a type of subsystem, in that, typically, it structures people into departments, has a purpose, and processes information.

Key term

Filtering means removing 'impurities' such as excessive detail from data as it is passed up the organisation hierarchy.

Operational staff may need all the detail to do their jobs, but when they report to higher and higher subsystems the data can be progressively **summarised**. Extraneous detail is filtered out leaving only the important points.

The **problem** with this is that sometimes the 'filter' may let through unimportant information and/or remove important information, with the result that the message is **distorted** at the next level.

3.4 Coupling and decoupling

If systems or subsystems are very closely linked or **coupled** this may cause difficulties.

For example, in order to sell goods, a manufacturing company must first of all make them. If the sales and production subsystems are closely coupled, the company may be able to produce almost exactly the amount required for a given period's sales. However the system would be prone to inefficiency through a 'mishap', such as a late delivery of raw materials, a machine breakdown, or a strike, as then goods would not be available to meet sales demand.

From a traditional point of view, greater efficiency is achieved between the production and sales systems by **decoupling** them. In the example above, this would mean reducing the interaction between sales and production by creating a finished goods stock.

From a modern point of view, holding finished goods stock is expensive, and greater efficiency is achieved by adopting **quality management** philosophies to try to ensure that mishaps do not occur. If this is successful this means that a **Just-In-Time (JIT)** approach to production and purchasing can be adopted. JIT closely couples the sales and production subsystems and closely couples one organisation's purchasing function with another's supplying function.

4 Open and closed systems

FAST FORWARD

Organisations are examples of **open systems**. The open systems model helps us understand human behaviour in organisations, the relationship between people and the organisation, and the relationship between the organisation and the wider environment.

4.1 Open and closed systems

Organisations have many relationships with the environment, and we can use systems theory to explore this point. In systems theory a distinction is made between open and closed systems.

(a) A **closed system** is a system which is isolated from its environment and independent of it, so that no environmental influences affect the behaviour of the system, nor does the system exert any influence on its environment.

Shut off from its environment

Figure 1.1 Closed system

(b) Many are **semi-closed**, in that the relationship with the environment is in some degree restricted.

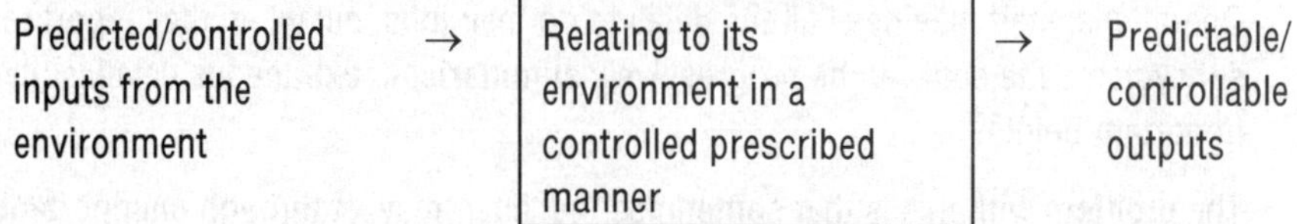

Figure 1.2 Semi-closed system

This type of system could be nicknamed 'the thermostat' and the control mechanism in this system would be self-regulating in maintaining equilibrium.

(c) An **open system** is a system interacting with its environment. It takes in influences from its environment and also influences this environment by its behaviour. An open system is a stable system which is nevertheless continually changing or evolving.

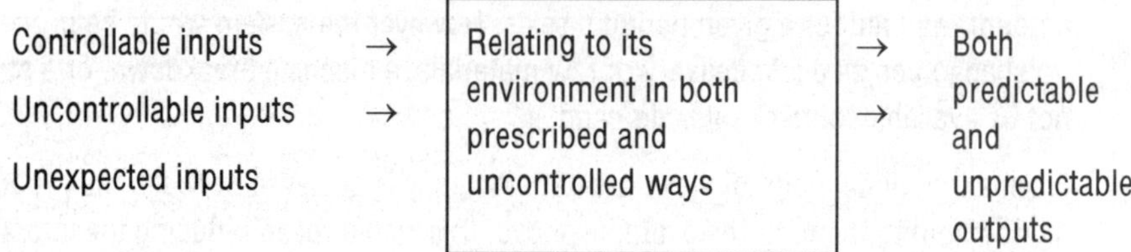

Figure 1.3 Open system

Social organisations, for example businesses and government departments, are by definition open systems. Why? All social organisations are comprised of human beings.

(a) Human beings participate in any number of social systems (eg family), of which the work organisation is only one, although it is important.

(b) In most societies, human beings are exposed to a variety of influences from the social environment, for example: advertising messages; family attitudes and pressures; government demands (eg for tax revenue).

Some business systems have some of the operational features of a **semi-closed system**. The inputs to a nuclear power station are controllable, predictable (uranium), as (we hope!) are its outputs (a steady supply of electricity).

4.1.1 The open systems approach

Stacey (2000) sums up the open systems approach to organisation like this.

'Open systems explanations of managing and organising … focus attention on:

- Behaviour of people within a subsystem or system.
- Nature of the boundary around a subsystem or system.
- Nature of the relationships across the boundaries between subsystems and systems.
- Requirements of managing the boundary.

The open systems concept provides a tool for understanding the relationship between:

- The technical and the social aspects of an organisation.
- The parts and the whole organisation (eg the individual and the group, the individual and the organisation).
- The whole organisation and the environment.

It is obvious that a fundamental aspect of this approach is the way that human interaction affects the system and its subsystems. A further important relationship is between the human and non-human or technical and psychosocial elements. The interconnection between systems can produce **destabilising feedback effects**.

Question

Open social systems

Learning outcome: A(i)

Relationships marketing is the term used to describe a process by which firms build long term relationships with customers, hoping to sell them products over a life. What does this say about system boundaries?

Answer

A hard one here – in many models, sales are discussed solely in terms of transactions, number of products sold and so on. But it is harder to measure the quality of a business relationship, as this has a future value, or the value of a brand. The openness of the organisation system means that participants in it do have another life, influence and value system outside the organisation. Building up a relationship – like loyalty – or requiring loyalty from employees – suggests that organisational boundaries are permeable. If the reputation of the organisation is something that can be valued, then controls need to exist to safeguard it.

4.2 Adapting to the environment

Social systems have to adapt to survive. Businesses, in particular, have to adapt to changes in the legal, political, economic, social and competitive environment.

If a system does not alter its own performance, it risks extinction. **Adaptive systems**, which can **learn with time**, are therefore more likely to survive. A system adapts by acquiring information about its environment and responding **appropriately**.

As the environment changes, a system may **react in one of two ways**.

(a) It may respond to external changes by making adjustments to its own operations. These changes are **short-term**, functional adaptations.

(b) It may also adopt a **long-term** approach, making structural alterations.

These are similar to the difference between changing performance and changing the plan.

4.3 Deterministic, probabilistic and self-organising systems

The degree of adaptation varies from system to system.

4.3.1 Deterministic system

A **deterministic system** is one in which various states or activities follow on from each other in a completely predictable way, ie A will happen, then B, then C. A **fully-automated production process** is a typical example.

A computer program is another.

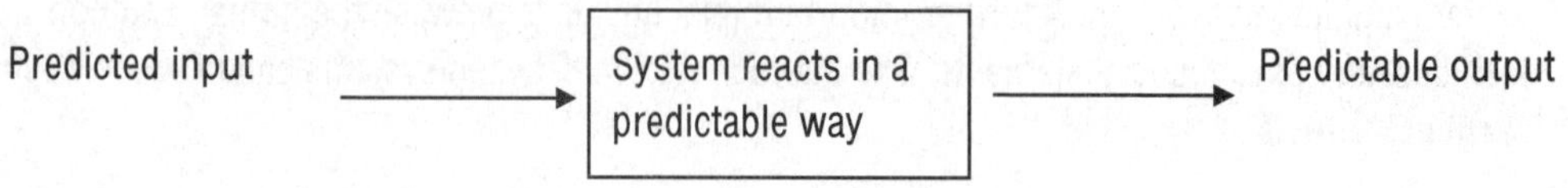

Predicted input ⟶ [System reacts in a predictable way] ⟶ Predictable output

Figure 1.4 Deterministic system

4.3.2 Probabilistic or stochastic system

A probabilistic or stochastic system is one in which, although some states or activities can be predicted with certainty, others will occur with varying degrees of **probability**. In business, many systems can be regarded as stochastic systems.

A purchasing department might assess a supplier's delivery times as 75% likely to arrive on schedule, 20% likely to be one week late and 5% likely to be two weeks late. The purchasing system might therefore act to keep some materials in inventory to minimise the risk of stock outs.

4.3.3 Self-organising system

A **self-organising system** is one which adapts and reacts to a stimulus. The way in which it adapts is uncertain and the same input (stimulus) to the system will not always produce the same output (response).

A bank which pays a rate of interest to depositors depending on the amount of money in the deposit account. Interest calculations (the output of the system is the calculated interest) will vary as the money in each depositor's account goes up or down.

The three classifications are not mutually exclusive, and a system may contain elements of all three types.

4.3.4 Homeostasis

A system might keep an unchanging state, or it might change. A **homeostatic system** is one which remains static, but in order to do so, has to react to its own dynamic elements and also to a dynamic environment. It must make internal adjustments so as to remain the same. A 'dynamic' open system is one which transforms inputs from the environment so as to be continually changing (growing or shrinking).

For a business, homeostasis would not mean keeping an absolutely steady state, but would mean that the business has a 'dynamic or moving equilibrium', so that it is continually adjusting (eg to changes in customer demand or raw material supply), without necessarily growing in size or changing radically in character.

4.4 Requisite variety

Key term

The **law of requisite variety** states that the variety **within a system** must be at least as great as the **environmental variety** against which it is attempting to regulate itself.

In other words, if there is **variety** in the environmental influences in the system, then the **system itself must be suitably varied and variable** to adapt itself successfully to its environment. If a system does not have the requisite amount of variety, it will be **unable to adapt to change** and will eventually die or be replaced.

The law of requisite variety applies to self-regulating systems in general, but one application of the law relates to control systems. A control system (which is a sub-system of a larger system) must be sufficiently flexible to be able to deal with the variety that occurs naturally in the system that it is attempting to control.

Case Study

A company making heavy equipment suddenly found its raw materials and in-process inventory climbing, but, at the same time, it was experiencing reduced sales and reduced production. The system was out of control.

The cause was traced to the materials analysts who made the detailed inventory decisions. They had been furnished with decision rules for ordering, cancelling, etc, under normal conditions, but they had no rules governing how to handle the inventory when production was decreasing and production lots were being cancelled.

In other words, the system did not provide the requisite variety of control responses. In this case, the urgency of remedy did not allow new rules to be formulated and validated. Instead, each materials analyst was treated as a self-organising system, given a target inventory, and told to achieve it. With the analysts given the freedom to generate control responses, the inventory was reduced in a few months.

Question

Requisite variety

Learning outcome: A(iii)

How might you introduce the requisite variety into a control system?

Answer

(a) **Allowing a controller some discretion**

The controller judges what control action is needed. In a business system, managers should not be instructed that a problem must be handled in a particular way, especially when the problem involves labour relations, disciplinary procedures, motivating the workforce or any other such 'behavioural' matters. The response of individuals to control action by managers will be variable because people are different, and even one person's moods change from day to day. The control system must be flexible enough to use different methods to achieve the same ends.

(b) **Introducing tolerance limits**

When actual results differ from planned results, control action should not be instigated automatically in every instance. Control action should only be applied when the variance becomes excessive and exceeds allowable tolerance limits. Tolerance limits recognise that plans are based on an 'average' or 'norm' of what is expected to happen, and some variation around this average will be due to 'natural' causes which there should be no reason to get alarmed about.

5 Control systems and cybernetics

FAST FORWARD

A **cybernetic control system** is one whose behaviour is coupled to feedback from its own performance. Most control systems in organisations fit this model.

The most common model of a control system is, in effect, the cybernetic model. We can build this up from basic discussions about controls having mentioned that many systems have a target or objective that they are designed to reach.

A **cybernetic control system describes the process of control within a system**. A general cybernetic control model has **five stages**.

- Identification of system objectives
- Measuring achievements/outputs of the system
- Comparing achievements with objectives
- Identifying what corrective action might be necessary
- Implementing corrective action

5.1 What does a control system contain?

There are four basic concepts in talking about control

Plan, target, standard, objective	What the system is designed to achieve, eg budgeted revenues? Objectives for the process being controlled must exist, for without an aim or purpose control has no meaning
Sensor	Detects the actual system behaviour, and gathers information about it –sales force and output from sales order processing system The **output of** the process must be **measurable** in terms of the dimensions defined by the objectives.
Comparator	Compares actual system behaviour with the plan above, eg management accounts with variances. A **predictive model** of the process being controlled is required so that causes for the non-attainment of objectives can be determined and proposed corrective actions evaluated
Effector	Enacts control action to change the actual system behaviour, eg the instructions of a manager There must be a **capability of taking action** so that deviations of attainment from objectives can be reduced

The above must be in place if control is being exercised cybernetically, but we shall see later how this causes difficulties and how other means of ensuring people do what they ought to do are bought into play.

This concept of control involves more than just measuring results and taking corrective action. Control in the broad sense also embraces the formulation of objectives - deciding what are the 'right things' that need to be done - as well as monitoring their attainment by way of feedback

5.2 Controlling performance without a control system: open loop systems

The control action is introduced from the environment, and it is not generated by the system itself, so it is not strictly a control system as such.

Simple example	You are watching a pan of boiling water. It is boiling dry. You intervene to turn off the heat
Complex example	A company is not doing very well. It is acquired by another company, whose management makes lots of changes and improves the performance

This is what is called an open loop system: if control is exercised, it operates independently. Control is not provided by the system itself.

5.3 Closed loop systems and feedback

Part of the output is fed back to it. This is called feedback. **Feedback** is part of the output generated by a system, but is used to control the behaviour of the system. (We shall discuss the types of feedback later.)

5.3.1 Introducing single loop control to a system

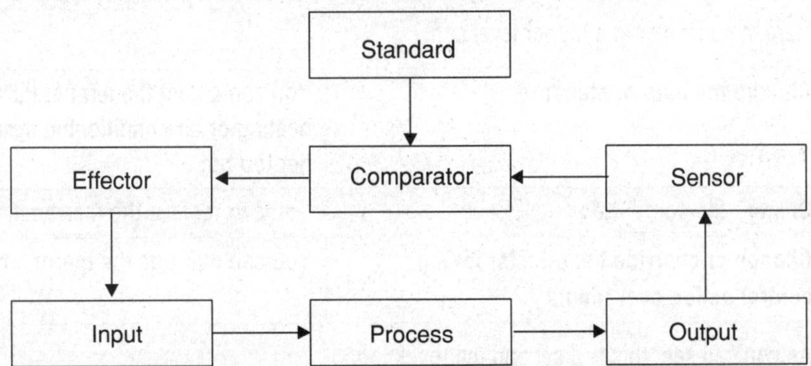

In this example, there is one loop of control. The actual output is compared to the standard or plan, and the effector controls the input to the system.

Simple example: a kettle is switched off by a thermostat once the water has boiled; no external intervention is needed. For a business example, see the case study below.

Case Study

Booking airline tickets for low-cost airlines

An airline's system keep records of seats booked. As the plane fills up, the airline maximises revenue by increasing the price of the remaining, and scarcer seats, so that those who book late pay more. The output of the system – filled seats – automatically adjusts one of the inputs, the price of the remaining tickets.

Not all airlines have priced seats in this way. Some airlines would charge the maximum possible price early on, only to offer discounts to 'bucket' shops to fill up seats near to take off. This is a fundamentally different approach to pricing.

5.3.2 The need for double loop feedback

Notice that the control loop is a single loop control system; control is exercised once and there is no control over the plan. Sometimes the plan or standard is at fault, and so feedback has to be exercised twice.

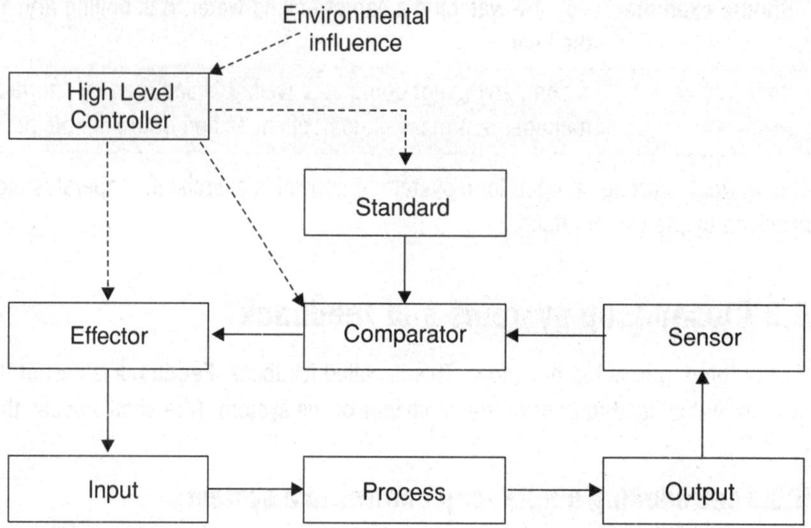

Here, a controller at a higher level can:

Change the plan or standard	You can adjust the temperature control on a central heating or air conditioning system so that it does not get too hot.
Change the comparator	You can replace the thermostat
Change or override the effector taking control action over inputs	You can override the thermostat

As you can see, this is a second feedback loop.

6 Feedback and control systems

FAST FORWARD

Feedback occurs at several levels: single loop, in which **performance is changed**, and double loop in which **the plan itself is adjusted**.

Because feedback occurs after the event, many organisations use **feedforward control**, eg through variance analysis and budgeting systems

6.1 Feedback

Feedback is **information about actual achievements**. In a business organisation, it is information about actual results, produced from within the organisation (for example management accounting control reports) with the purpose of helping with control decisions.

Key term

Feedback control is 'The measurement of differences between planned outputs and actual outputs achieved, and the modification of subsequent action and/or plans to achieve future required results'.

A feature of **feedback** is that it is information that is gathered by measuring the outputs of the system itself. It has an **'internal' source**, as distinct from 'environmental' information, which comes from outside the system. For **some control systems**, notably for control by senior management at a strategic planning level, **control information** will be **gathered** from both **environmental sources and internal sources**. For example, a company might be unable to judge the success or failure of its activities without putting them into the context of the national economy (is it booming? is it in recession? how high is the rate of inflation?) and its markets (how well are competitors doing? is the number of potential customers rising or falling?)

Some form of **internally generated feedback** is **essential** if there is to be any **effective control within an organisation**, and the most common types of control system in businesses, such as **budgetary control, inventory control and production control systems,** are all based on **feedback cycles**.

6.2 Negative feedback

Key term

Negative feedback is information which indicates that the system is deviating from its planned or prescribed course, and that some re-adjustment is necessary to bring it back on to course. This feedback is called 'negative' because control action would seek to reverse the direction or movement of the system back towards its planned course.

Negative feedback gives rise to attempts to change the direction of the actual movement of the system to **bring it back into line with the plan**.

Thus, if the budgeted sales for June and July were £100,000 in each month, whereas the report of actual sales in June showed that only £90,000 had been reached, this negative feedback would indicate that control action was necessary to raise sales in July to £110,000 in order to get back on to the planned course.

6.3 Positive feedback

Key term

Positive feedback results in control action which causes actual results to maintain (or increase) their path of deviation from planned results. This contrasts with negative feedback, which attempts to reverse the deviation and bring actual results back on to the prescribed course.

Suppose, for example, that a company budgets to produce and sell 100 units of product each month, maintaining an average inventory level of 40 units. Now if actual sales exceed the budget, and show signs of sustained growth, it will obviously be in the company's interests to produce and sell as much as possible (provided additional output earns extra contribution to profit).

(a) Feedback in the first month might show that **sales** are **above budget**, selling costs are a little higher than budget and that inventory has been run down to meet demand.

(b) Action should attempt to **increase sales** (in other words, to promote the deviation of actual results from the plan) even if this requires extra selling costs for advertising or sales promotion, maintaining the 'adverse' deviation of actual costs from budget.

Additional production volumes would be required, although initially some extra sales might be made out of remaining inventory (resulting in further deviations from the production and finished goods inventory budgets).

Positive feedback has the effect of following the current course, and doing more of the same. It is not necessarily a 'good thing'.

Enron misreported its results, and the share price rose. Shareholders wanted even more.

6.4 Feedforward control and planning

Key term

Feedforward control is 'The forecasting of differences between actual and planned outcomes, and the implementation of action, before the event, to avoid such differences'.

(CIMA *Official Terminology)*

Deviations in the system are **anticipated**, so that 'corrective action' can be taken in advance of them actually happening. (With feedback control, in contrast, actual errors have happened before they are reported and corrective action is taken.)

An example of feedforward control is a **cash budget**, prepared regularly. Future cash flows and cash balances are checked to make sure that the organisation will have available the cash resources that it needs, without overstepping its borrowing facility limits.

More generally, **feedforward control** is the **fulfilment of Emmanuel et al's first condition for control** - putting the objectives in place - or, in conventional terms, **'planning'**. Thus control encompasses 'both the activity of planning and of ensuring conformity to plan including, if necessary, the generation of new plans.'

7 Problems with cybernetic control systems

FAST FORWARD

Critics of cybernetic control models suggest that the amplifying effects of **positive feedback**, encouraging an organisation to go further along its course, are ignored. Furthermore, a cybernetic model depends on predictability, and organisations and people, cannot always be relied on to act **predictably**.

The diagram below marries the overall measures of control with the discussion.

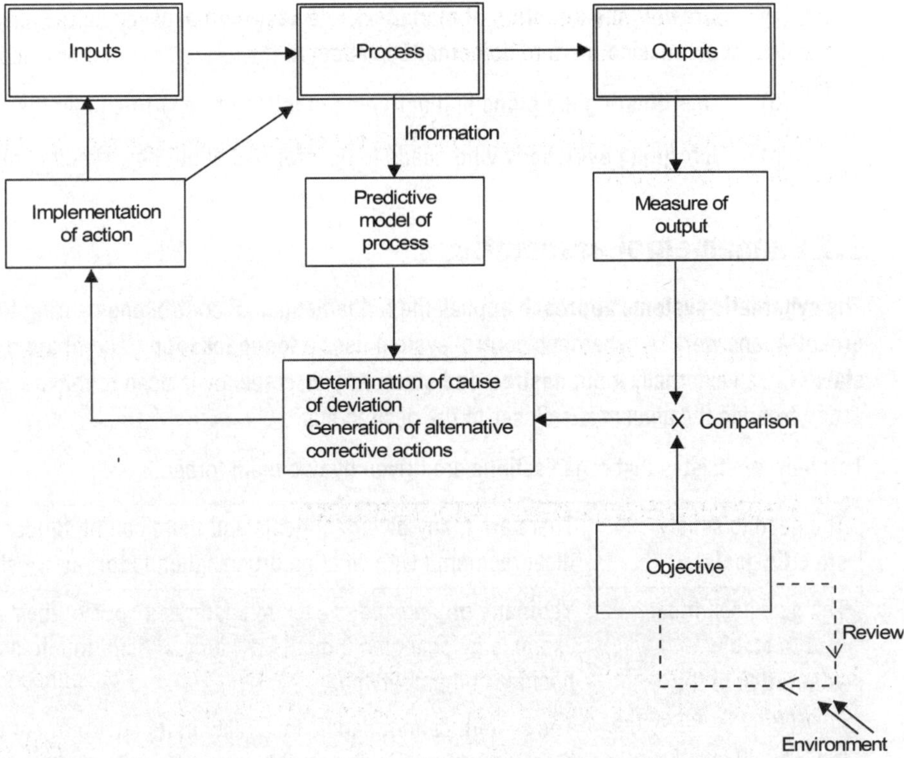

7.1 Practical problems with the predictive model

It is **not generally possible in practice for an organisation to construct a satisfactory predictive model of the process being controlled** for two reasons.

(a) Because an **organisation is an open system** which is connected to and interacts with its environment. That environment is the world at large and it is chiefly characterised by **change.** Attempts have to be made to forecast what will happen in the future, but in most situations such attempts are beset with **uncertainty**: there are too many variables involved and too few of them are under the direct control of the organisation.

(b) Because **organisations are made up of individuals**, who are themselves 'sub-systems', and who have the capacity to control themselves independently of the organisation. People **cannot be relied upon to react predictably** in response to efforts to direct their behaviour towards a particular end.

There are a number of other **problems to overcome** in applying theory to practice.

(a) **Preparing a standard or plan** in the first place, which is reliable and acceptable to the managers who will be responsible for the achievement of the standard or plan.

(b) **Measuring actual results** with **sufficient accuracy**.

(c) **Measuring actual results** with **suitable feedback periods**. The reporting cycle time must be kept sufficiently short to give managers a chance to take prompt control action when serious deviations from plan occur.

(d) **Providing non-accounting** as well as **accounting information** to help with the assessment of plans and results.

(e) **Identifying the causes of variations** between actual results and the standard or plan, and distinguishing controllable from uncontrollable causes.

(f) **Drawing the attention of managers** to a **deviation** between actual results and plan, and persuading them to do something about it.

(g) **Coordinating the plans** and **activities** of different departments in the organisation.

(h) **Informing everybody** who needs to be informed about how results are going.

7.2 Fundamental assumptions

The **cybernetic systems approach** applies the fundamentals of control engineering to explain how organisations work. A cybernetic control system uses a **feedback loop** to compare the system's **actual state** with an externally input **desired end state**. Any discrepancy is used to initiate **control action**, that is, action to bring the actual state closer to the desired state.

This view postulates that organisations are driven by two main forces.

The need to satisfy **specific goals**	There are many divergent goals and there can be fundamental disagreements with what an organisation is for, as we shall discover shortly
The goal itself must lead to **stable adaptation** to the environment, hence the dampening effect of negative feedback	Yet many organisations seek to shape and control their environment, for example by changing industry dynamics. Also, much feedback can be positive and amplifying. The system cannot handle instability in its environment that extends beyond the parameters it is designed to track. Complex cybernetic systems, such as organisations, must foresee all possibilities if they are to be able to respond to them.

8 Hard and soft systems

FAST FORWARD

Soft systems methodology, used for developing information systems, also describes systems, but the approach embraces the different objectives of the participants in the system rather than just ignoring it.

In your earlier studies, you will have come across the concept of stakeholders, those people or groups with an interest in the organisation's activities. For many organisations, the principal stakeholders are diffuse. After all, for a hospital, patients are stakeholders as 'consumers' of treatments even though they do not pay for them directly. Furthermore, many stakeholders will have different expectations of the organisation or even a different outlook as to what it is.

Such insights have been captured by Peter Checkland's **soft systems methodology** (SSM). It is meant to deal with poorly defined problems or situations on the basis that a person's interpretation of a situation derives from prior experiences, and so different people interpret the same situation in different ways. Once a person has interpreted a situation he may form intentions to follow a particular course of action.

As far as systems are concerned, we can talk about a **root definition** in terms of what the system, or organisation, is for.

Clients	These are the people or groups who **benefit** or **suffer** from the system.
Actors	Actors are those who will carry out the **transformation process**.
Transformation process	This is the **conversion of input to output**.
Weltanschauung	This is the **'world view'** which underlies the assumptions behind the root definition.
Owners	These are people who could **stop** the transformation process.
Environmental constraints	These are **fixed elements** outside the system.

Eventually, a picture can be built up which shows the various elements of the system/organisation and the objectives of the people within it. (The following diagram is adapted from Avison and Fitzgerald, 1995.)

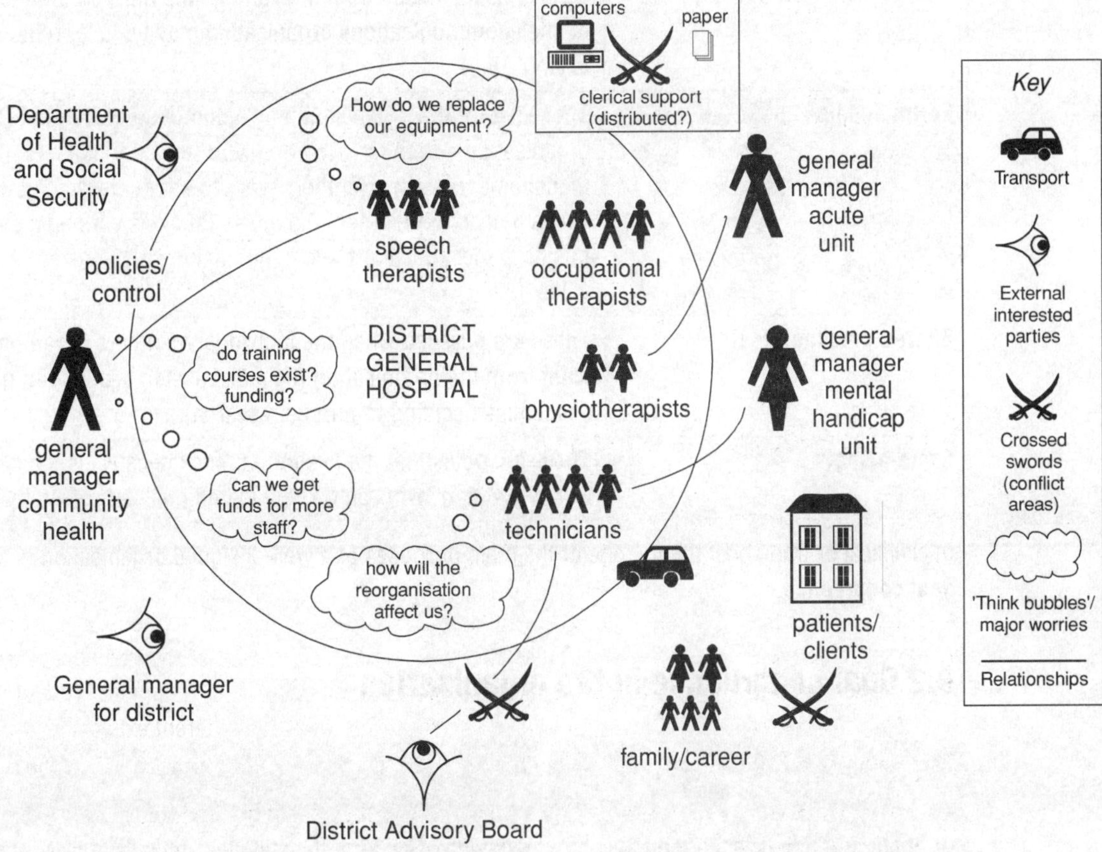

Source: adapted from Avison and Fitzgerald 1995

Soft system

Although this methodology is developed for information systems design it does help us understand **organisations** and the different concerns of **stakeholders** in the situation, and their conflicts of interest. In many **businesses**, conflicts of interest are reconciled by the fact that profit is generally the most important deciding factor, and that management hierarchies are where decisions are made: power is fairly concentrated and easy to identify.

What this shows us is that there are sometimes fundamental problems in setting objectives for organisations, especially those in the public sector. As an objective is supposed to be fundamental to any system, in that performance is measured against the achievement of the objective.

9 Problems in enforcing goal congruence

FAST FORWARD

Goal congruence is an ideal state – but organisations and people in them pursue many different types of goal, including ideological goals, formal goals, shared personal goals and goals that the system, by its very nature, tends to pursue (eg its continuation).

9.1 Types of goal

The types of goals that organisations pursue can be described as follows (based on Mintzberg).

Goals	Comment
Ideological goals	These cover **beliefs and values**, and what the organisation has defined as its 'mission'. (For example, the mission or ideological goal of a telecommunications organisation may be to 'get the world talking'.)
Formal goals	Those set for the organisation by a **dominant individual** (the organisation's founder, say) or group (the shareholders or management team). Members work to attain these goals because it is also a means to their personal goals (such as earning a salary). In a business these formal goals might include maximising shareholder value.
Shared personal goals	These are pursued when the individual members **agree on what they want** from the organisation (eg a discussion group, or a group of academics deciding to pursue research).
System goals	These are goals that the system pursues because it is a system. Survival and growth can be considered goals of a system.

In classical or traditional theory, one of the main purposes of a well-designed organisation is to ensure **goal congruence**,

9.2 Goal congruence in the organisation

Key term

Goal congruence is, according to CIMA, 'in a control system, the state which leads individuals or groups to take actions which are in their self interest and in the best interest of the entity.'

Goal congruence is not easy to achieve, simply because organisations are political institutions, there are large number of goals being pursued and, finally, people may not agree on the most important. In budgeting managers use **skill** and **cunning** to finalise their estimates. Reasons are found for **increasing estimates**, and **'padding'** is incorporated to allow for the expectation that top management will reduce budget expenditure levels by arbitrarily cutting x% from every manager's claim. The ability to estimate 'what will go' is thus regarded as a vital skill.

A budget is meant to be formulated so as to achieve the overall objectives of the organisation but organisational **objectives are very rarely clearly defined** (and one organisation is likely to have a **number of different objectives** anyway). Different managers will perceive their objectives differently, and so the **budget demands of managers** will frequently be **incompatible**.

Unfortunately, emphasis on multiple goals makes it **difficult to identify areas for action and improvement**, and it is also **difficult** for an accounting system of **budgeting to incorporate non-financial or non-monetary goals** successfully.

In any case, any attempt to formalise 'multiple goals' will be **subject to the politics and power structure** within the organisation. Some managers have greater influence than others in the bargaining structure, but all management in turn is subject to the influence of trade union or government pressure, changing technology, changing markets and other environmental pressures.

Thus although the accounting system of **budgeting** is still dominant as the means of setting (short-term) goals in an organisation, it has a severely limited capacity to do so, because it **emphasises profit to the exclusion of other goals**.

Question

Management styles

Learning outcome: A(ii)

Past studies have found that European managers are subtle, socially responsible and humane, believe that maximum profit is not the primary aim of business, and consider it better to be shrewd and cunning than simply rational.

What do you think are the consequences of these findings for organisational control in general and budgeting and standard costing in particular?

Answer

This question is intended for class discussion. There are no right answers (although some of the consequences identified by the authors are referred to later in this Study Text).

For organisations without a clear overarching objective, such as profit, fundamental issues of prioritisation might arise. The government, for example, might set overarching targets which require other bodies to find resources.

Case Study

Activists have attacked companies such as McDonald's for supersizing food and promoting a culture of obesity. Obesity brings many individual and social costs, but the number of messages to consume are relentless. Other food conglomerates, such as Unilever, have full fat rather than dietary ranges. A Marxist will say that late capitalism takes your money to make you fat, and then takes your money to make you thin.

10 Structuration theory

FAST FORWARD

Any social system has **properties of structure** – determining power and communication -and agency. Different degrees of each are appropriate at different times.

Another way of looking at control systems in organisations is to model how they work on how human beings interact with each other, the power of habit, and the power of changed circumstances. Structuration theory **suggests that a social system** (such as an organisation) **has two major properties: structures** and **agency.**

10.1 Agency

Key term

Agency describes the conscious, **intentional actions of people interacting with others**, which may or may not be in accordance with 'structures' (see below).

Although they do not have to, people often react to a situation automatically, in a programmed way, even though really they know a great deal about why they act in the way they do and could justify their actions if called upon to do so.

10.2 Structure

Key term

Structures are **codes that guide behaviour**.

A **social system has three main structures** (or 'dimensions').

10.2.1 Signification structures

Signification structures are what people use to communicate with and understand each other: they consist of codes (such as language), shared ideas and knowledge, and discursive practices such as speech and writing. 'For example, management accounting provides managers with a means of making sense of the activities of their organization and it allows them to communicate meaningfully about those activities.'

10.2.2 Legitimation structures

Legitimation structures are moral or ethical rules about what is regarded as good or important, and what is wrong, trivial or should not happen.

'Management accounting and control systems are vitally involved in the moral constitution of managers' actions and interactions. They embody norms of organisational activity and provide the moral underpinning for the signification structure. In most large complex industrial and commercial enterprises, for example, profit making is the paramount moral ideal. Management accounting systems also legitimate the rights of some participants to hold others accountable in financial terms for their actions. This is widely recognized and accepted as the responsibility centre concept.'

10.2.3 Domination structures

Domination structures are concerned with the distribution of power, which in turn depends upon allocative resources (the rights of some to be in command of physical objects and of the knowledge of how to operate them – 'resource power' and 'expert power', if you prefer) and authoritative resources (rights of command over other people).

Management accounting and control systems are deeply implicated in relations of domination. The master budget, for example, contains the detailed and all-encompassing blueprint for resource allocation for the entire organization and is a powerful lever in terms of ability to make a difference, to get things done and to dominate the organization.'

10.2.4 Structuration

Structuration is 'the process whereby social structures sometimes function to ... **reproduce the status quo**, while at other times they undergo radical change' (Macintosh). The **duality of structure** means that structures both guide people and are produced by people. In **routine situations** people do not need to think consciously about their actions or devise new social codes to conduct their affairs. **Prevailing social structures are therefore predominant**. In **crisis situations** established routines are not appropriate and **agency comes to the fore**, to bring different structures into existence (perhaps to resurrect old ones).The **dialectic of control** suggests that control is a two-way affair: superiors command subordinates but they also depend on them; subordinates control resources such as time and knowledge, but they are never completely autonomous. Because of 'agency', people can exert power by following, or not following, 'structures'.

10.3 Control theory and organisation power

Michel Foucault was a French writer who published a wide range of historical studies, mainly in the 1960s and 70s..

'Foucault is concerned with the way in which regimes of power have grown and been sustained through disciplinary mechanisms and the institution of norms for human behaviour.'

'They are juxtaposed to raise questions about the change from visible punishment to the hidden but all-embracing regimen of the prison. This latter, in turn, may illustrate what has happened more generally in society over the past 200 years. Through the close specification of methods of ordering prisons and prisoners, and through the close observation of the activities of those prisoners ... it may be seen as a microcosm of the increased control under which the person has been placed since that time.' (Puxty)

One of the accounting studies working in this tradition attempts to show how the origins of accounting reside in the exercise of social power and how **accounting is 'implicated in the creation of structures of surveillance and power that permit modern management to function at a distance from the work process itself.'**

Case Study

Call centres

Many customer service transactions are conducted in call centres, and staff are given a precise set of targets:

- The number of rings a phone makes before it is answered
- The speed of dealing with a customer's query
- Rehearsal of a 'script' or use of precise responses from software

At times, the call centre might be overwhelmed with calls. In the short term, programmed information might be given to customers as to how long their call will take to be answered.

They are in 'open plan' offices – these are supposed to nurture good communication, but are also places where everybody is observed and there is no privacy.

Question

Control and error

Learning outcome: A(iii)

Apply some of the models discussed to the example of Enron described at the beginning of this chapter

Answer

Enron is a complicated tale because the issues of control and risk permeate the whole case study.

(a) We have not explicitly mentioned **ethics** as part of a control system, although this is an aspect of cultural control.

(b) US companies have to report **quarterly according to financial reporting standards** that are very detailed. The processes of reporting were followed meticulously. Quarterly reports were issued. Lawyers signed off the legality of accounting treatments, however aggressive. Even so, the fundamental purpose of financial reporting was subverted in that a false picture was given.

(c) Enron was admired as a company that brought **radical new approaches** to its markets, replacing structure with agency at a macro level. Within the company, the 'structure' of power and communication was all powerful. Those staff members who tried to exercise 'agency' – by protesting – were excluded.

(d) The **soft systems model** is also relevant. For a time, almost every stakeholder had an interest in maintaining an artificially high reported performance. Shareholders benefited because their shares were valued highly. Those in the pension scheme wanted highly valued shares. Managers, rewarded by share based incentives, also wanted highly valued shares which they could sell. There was, arguably, goal congruence.

(e) Foucault's **correct comportment** principle is also evident – the way in which people carried on in ways they knew were false.

(f) To some extent, you find a **cybernetic control system** in operation. What such a system does not do is tell you what control action to take. Let us suppose that reported results are away from target. In most cases, control action is taken to improve performance or, at double loop level, to change the plan. Control action was taken, and this was to massage the reported figures. 'Control' of a sort was exercised over the company, but it was malign.

Chapter Roundup

- Control matters at all levels of an organisation, from its **overall governance**, to the **details of its operating practices**. The purpose and types of control at each level will differ and even the best intentioned controls can be undermined.
- Control is often discussed in the **context of systems theory**. An organisation is a type of system, and a control system is a type of system.
- Most systems have **inputs, processes and outputs** and are separated from the environment by a **boundary** that can be physical, social, legal, or all three.
- Many systems are made up of **subsystems**. In an organisation, for example, there are subsystems related to the **structure**, **technology**, **goals and values, management** and the **underlying social system** of the organisation.
- Organisations are examples of **open systems**. The open systems model helps us understand human behaviour in organisations, the relationship between people and the organisation, and the relationship between the organisation and the wider environment.
- A **cybernetic control system** is one whose behaviour is coupled to feedback from its own performance. Most control systems in organisations fit this model.
- Feedback occurs at several levels: single loop, in which **performance is changed**, and double loop in which the **plan itself is adjusted**.
- Because feedback occurs after the event, many organisations use **feedforward control**, eg through variance analysis and budgeting systems
- Critics of cybernetic control models suggest that the amplifying effects of **positive feedback**, encouraging an organisation to go further along its course, are ignored. Furthermore, a cybernetic model depends on predictability, and organisations and people, cannot always be relied on to act **predictably**.
- **Soft systems methodology**, used for developing information systems, also describes systems, but the approach embraces the different objectives of the participants in the system rather than just ignoring it.
- **Goal congruence** is an ideal state – but organisations and people in them pursue many different types of goal, including ideological goals, formal goals, shared personal goals and goals that the system, by its very nature, tends to pursue (eg its continuation).
- Any social system has **properties of structure** – determining power and communication and agency. Different degrees of each are appropriate at different times.

Quick Quiz

1 A system is......

2 What is special about a cybernetic system?

3 Organisations are closed systems.

True ☐
False ☐

4 A system with tightly coupled subsystem is more flexible than one with loosely coupled subsystems.

True ☐
False ☐

5 Positive feedback leads a system to....... its current course. Negative feedback encourages a system to.....its current course in the light of the plan.

6 How can you introduce requisite variety to a system?

7 What are the main problems in adapting cybernetic control systems to organisations?

8 What are the three main structures in social systems?

Answers to Quick Quiz

1 A set of interacting components that operate together the accomplish a purpose

2 A cybernetic system is special because the output of a system is used to control it.

3 False. Organisations are open as they depend on the environment. They still have boundaries, however (physical, legal, social)

4 False. A tightly coupled subsystem is closely related to another subsystem thereby reducing flexibility in the operation of the subsystem.

5 Positive feedback leads a system to **continue** its current course. Negative feedback encourages a system to **change** its current course in the light of the plan.

6 Allowing the controller discretion as to control action, introduce tolerance limits. You can also consider whether your measures are complex enough.

7 It is hard to develop a predictive model of the organisation, so control has to be exercised in a different way. The fundamental assumptions of rationality and non-linearity can be challenged. In many cases, there is no agreement on the purpose of the organisation.

8
- Signification structures
- Legitimation structures
- Domination structures

Now try the question below from the Exam Question Bank

Number	Level	Marks	Time
Q1	Introductory	N/a	30 mins

Controlling people

Introduction

The previous chapter discussed control from a systems perspective. This is important as it underpins many management accounting models and systems including strategic planning systems that have been identified earlier.

This chapter looks at control from the broader perspectives of the organisation – the necessity of such a view was suggested by the Enron case study in chapter 1. After all, organisations in which control is exercised are contested areas, and mean different things to many people. To provide a link between the hard systems approach described in chapter 1, and the wider issues of organisational control, we shall briefly discuss soft systems methodology.

We then discuss human resources management systems as an aspect of control, and the importance of designing organisation structure.

Topic list	Learning outcomes	Syllabus references	Ability required
1 Models of control in the organisation	A (ii)	A (1)	Evaluation
2 Locus of control: behaviour or output?	A (ii)	A (1)	Evaluation
3 Strategic human resources management as a control device	A (ii)	A (1)	Evaluation
4 Control techniques over human resources	A (ii)	A (1)	Evaluation
5 Employee reward	A (ii)	A (1)	Evaluation
6 Recruitment and selection: control implications	A (ii)	A (1)	Evaluation
7 Performance management	A (ii)	A (1)	Evaluation
8 Training and learning	A (ii)	A (1)	Evaluation
9 Managerial performance and reward	A (ii)	A (1)	Evaluation

1 Models of control in the organisation

FAST FORWARD

Because of the difficulties in strictly applying a cybernetic model to organisations, many organisations, in effect, use other types of control. Two influences are **centralisation/decentralisation** of decision-making and the **formality or informality** of the system.

Control can be exercised on market lines (market control), through bureaucracy (bureaucratic control) and via **people's views and beliefs** (cultural control).

What is best is contingent on **technology used**, the **environment**, and the **size and structure** of the organisation.

1.1 Difficulties in applying the cybernetic model

Applying the cybernetic control model in chapter 1 is not always practical for managers: measurement happens too late **after** the event. For example, it is widely known in service industries that the cost of attracting a new customer far exceeds the cost of keeping existing customers satisfied: repeat business, rather than new business, is the key to success.

The factors that lead to repeat business are often intangible, such as **staff courtesy**. How do you control these factors?

- Regular staff appraisal is an example, but that only occurs *after* the event.
- You cannot really have a feedforward control system: you cannot **predict** when a member of staff is going to be rude. You can **train** staff in stress management, so they can control their own behaviour, perhaps.

A wider concept of control is therefore needed.

Control can relate to qualitative factors as well as to quantifiable factors. There can be targets for qualitative performance (eg ethical standards of behaviour) because unless there is a standard or target, it will be impossible to establish whether or not actual achievements have been satisfactory.

1.2 Influences over control strategies

Control is something that can be gained or lost in a variety of ways. There are, perhaps, three main design choices in establishing control in an organisation: we are not simply talking about hard systems here, but the wider issues of control as an aspect of people management, as we shall discuss shortly.

Choice	Comment
Centralisation or decentralising of decision making	Is control exercised in one place? Do all decisions have to go through head office? How much autonomy do people have to make decisions down the line?
Formality or informality in control	Is control exercised via impersonal rules or procedures, or is there management discretion?
Degree of supervision	Do managers directly supervise the work or are employees allowed to get on with it?

The following have been suggested as control strategies, based on the work of Child and also Ouchi

1.3 Control through markets and the price mechanism

Market control is the use of the **price mechanism and related performance measures** internally and externally, to control organisational behaviour.

At **corporate level** (ie the judging organisation as a whole) **market control is always used**: profit and loss, cash flow and balance sheet information is published, and so the organisation's performance can be judged in comparison with other organisations, or with previous years. If investors are dissatisfied with corporate performance, they can sell their shares (and so exit from the control system) or, in co-operation with other investors, change the managers. Managers need little prompting to ensure profitability. In this case, the market mechanism is provided by the capital markets and competitors.

At **divisional level**, market control can also be used, although this is sometimes problematic. It is only relevant if there are separate divisions, which are established as **profit centres, or investment centres**.

At **operational level**, the price mechanism can be used as a means to control activities, as in the examples below.

- **Target costing** is a technique used by some Japanese companies in product development. They try and assess what would be the market price for a product, and then they design a product whose costs in the long run are lower than the target price. In other words, they reverse the normal sequence (which is to design a product and *then* price it).
- Outsourcing **and market testing**. Many organisations outsource some functions to other firms.
- To encourage efficient use of internally generated resources a **transfer pricing** mechanism is used, with the transfer price being set as the market price.

Such control systems are only effective where it is possible to price the output of a division effectively and where there is **external competition as a reference**.

1.4 Control through bureaucracy

This is the use of 'rules, policies, hierarchies of authority, documentation, and so forth' to standardise behaviour and assess performance.

Organisations regulate behaviour to greater or lesser degrees, or example health and safety or even appearance.

This features as much programmed decision-taking as possible. In other words, the amount of individual discretion is limited. For example, customers over thirty days 'Late in Payment' are *always* sent a letter, if this is set out in a procedure.

Control is based on the principles of **scientific management** - specialisation of work, simplification of work methods, and standardisation of procedures.

1.4.1 Standard operating procedures controls

Policies are general statements that provide guidelines for management decision making. Company policies might include those below.

(a) To **promote managers** from **within the organisation**, wherever possible

(b) To **encourage all recruits** to **certain jobs** within the organisation to work towards obtaining an appropriate professional qualification

(c) To be **price-competitive** in the market

Policy guidelines should allow managers to exercise their **own discretion** and **freedom of choice**, but within certain acceptable limits.

Procedures are sequences of required actions for performing certain tasks. Procedures exist at all levels of management but become more numerous, onerous and extensive lower down in an organisation's hierarchy. They ought to be efficient, and ensure standardisation.

A **rule** prescribes a specific, definite action that **must be taken** in a given situation. For example, the following are rules but not procedures:

(a) Employees in department X are **allowed 10 minutes** exactly at the end of their shift for clearing up and cleaning their workbench.

(b) Employees with **access to a telephone must not use** the telephone for **personal calls**.

Rules allow **no deviations or exceptions**, unlike policies, which are general guidelines allowing the exercise of some management discretion.

A budget is a formal statement of expected results set out in numerical terms, and summarised in money values. It is a plan for carrying out certain activities with specified resources within a given period of time, in order to achieve certain targets. Budgets are **numerical statements** and, as such, tend to ignore **qualitative aspects** of planning and achievement.

Performance appraisal systems are used to evaluate the performance of the departments, and hence their managers. These are discussed shortly.

1.5 Cultural (and clan) control

Clan control is control based on **corporate culture**, and where employees develop a strong personal identification with the values of the organisation. Clan control involves the following.

- **Shared values** and **traditions**
- It is assumed that those who are hired are **committed to the organisation** and its customers. In other words, they share the same assumptions as management and share a common purpose.
- Culture is a powerful way of showing **'appropriate'** and **'inappropriate' behaviour**.

Case Study

Sexism in the City

Culture as a risk factor

Financial dealing firms in New York and in the City of London have been sued by their women employees. These stories have hit the media, as the sums involved are so large.

Sometimes the cause has related to issues of pay equality and sex discrimination legislation. At other times, the concern has been the culture of sexism and sexual harassment. The point is that this culture is not something that is 'inevitable' or even natural. This is culture is not present in all organisations and is actively discouraged in some (eg the public sector).

Similarly, a culture of shoddy workmanship and carelessness, or lack of attention to quality, can damage a firm's reputation

Changing culture as control action

Culture change has been seen as a control action in its own right. Organisational restructuring is carried out to improve the effectiveness of the organisation. A programme of cultural change is hardest to achieve as it means changing the way people relate to each other, the underlying assumptions of working life, and so on. Even so, firms try it.

Question

Types of control

Learning profit: A (ii)

Sally Keene works for a large department store, as a manager.

- At the beginning of each year she is given a yearly plan, subdivided into twelve months. This is based on the previous year's performance and some allowance is made for anticipated economic conditions. Every three months she sends her views as to the next quarter to senior management, who give her a new plan in the light of changing conditions.
- She monitors sales revenue per square foot, and sales per employee. Employees who do not meet the necessary sales targets are at first counselled and then if performance does not improve they are dismissed. Sally is not unreasonable. She sets what she believes are realistic targets.
- She believes there is a good team spirit in the sales force, however, and that employees, whose commission is partly based on the sales revenue earned by the store as a *whole*, discourage slackers in their ranks.

What kind of control, control system or control information can you identify in the three cases above?

Answer

- This shows the operation of **double loop feedback**. The plan has to be altered.
- This is a **standard**, in other words, a measure of expected performance. Counselling is control action to improve the individual's performance. Dismissal is control action too, if the employee is replaced by someone who performs better, thus raising the performance of the department as a whole.
- This is an example of **cultural or clan control**, perhaps.

1.6 What type of control is best?

Contingency control models

As with organisation structure, there is no 'one best way' to design a control system. It can be argued that different constellations of factors suggest a predominance of one of the control models mentioned. **All organisations contain a mix of control mechanisms.**

The table below summarises some of the control models you have covered.

Contingencies	Control strategies
Routine technology Stable environment Large size Functional structure	*Mainly* bureaucratic
Priced internal outputs Competition on price Size - not relevant Product/brand structure	*Mainly* market
Non-routine technology Unstable environment Small size Matrix structure	*Mainly* clan control

It can also be added that for a control system to be effective, people should:

(a) **Understand** what is expected (ie the control system must be properly communicated); and
(b) Be **motivated** in some way to obey the control system.

2 Locus of control: behaviour or output?

FAST FORWARD

It is possible to focus control attention on **behaviour** – making sure that processes are enacted in the right way – and **output**, the results of the control.

2.1 Individuals

Control is exercised over individual employees. How much autonomy should they be given? **Empowerment** means giving responsibility and authority to employees. Managers are required to **delegate** to improve performance. Even so, a system of control is needed as those in charge have **absolute responsibility** for the performance of their subordinates. If an efficient control system is in operation, responsibility and accountability will be monitored at all levels of the management hierarchy, and the dangers of relinquishing authority and control to subordinates are significantly lessened.

2.2 Control over divisions and strategic business units

Different firms have different approaches to managing and controlling business units. Just as it is possible to have a 'poorly performing' employee, so it is possible to have a poorly performing division, and sometimes action from head office is necessary to bring about change. On other occasions, an over-mighty, over-controlling head office may inhibit the creativity and effectiveness of local management.

There are two types of control strategies related to supervision, behaviour control and output control

2.3 Behaviour control

Behaviour control deals with how the work is performed, the **precise sequencing of tasks and procedures**. Behaviour control is exercised when outcomes cannot be assessed easily, or where procedure is everything.

Behaviour control should **not** be confused with the practice of **'close supervision'** whereby a subordinate has his or her boss hanging around in the background eager to find fault, and refusing to give the subordinate the ability to set his or her own pace, although 'close supervision' *can* be practised with

behaviour control. Behaviour control can be exercised bureaucratically, with precisely detailed procedures for certain tasks.

At corporate level, control over how tasks are done and behaviour might be necessary to avoid or mitigate certain types of risk. For example:

- If a firm is sued for unfair dismissal, evidence **that disciplinary procedures** were **followed to the letter** will offer some assurance that the dismissal was fair
- Many procedures for **health and safety** are designed to minimise risk.
- Finally, if a firm wishes to take over another, or enter into a joint venture, arrangement, due **diligence procedures** must often be followed.

2.4 Output control

Output control is based on specifying **key outputs** that must be achieved. This can be applied at various levels in the organisation.

- A **specified level of sales or profitability** for a division: managers might be left to get on with the actual targets
- **Specified targets for service delivery** (eg waiting lists for hospital appointments)
- **Operational matters** such as quantity of products made, for example the number of cars per hour made in a factory (very different in different manufacturers, showing major differences in efficiency)
- **Performance targets** for individuals, for example deadlines, productivity, accuracy

Again, these can be measured easily, and it is hoped that control action can be taken to rectify them.

2.5 Choosing between them

Which is better, output or behaviour control? This depends, and two possible criteria are:

How easy it is to **measure output**? For example, a pieceworker's output is easier to measure, but it is harder to measure the output of, say, someone in the service industry who must smile all day.

How easy it is to **programme** the task to routine instructions?

We can plot these on a grid as follows.

		Task programmability	
		Low	*High*
Outcome measurability	*High*	Output	Behaviour or output
	Low	Culture/clan	Behaviour

3 Strategic human resources management as a control system

FAST FORWARD

The organisational subsystem for **human resources management** is an attempt to control the behaviour of people.

Hard HRM is tightly coupled with business strategy, and HRM plans are determined by competitive advantage.

Soft HRM places greater emphasis on developmental issues, and is loosely coupled to product/market issues.

The sections above described certain control choices for the organisation, and described how much was to do with the control of the work processes and workers. Mintzberg identified five ways of co-ordinating work.

Mutual adjustment	For example, researchers work together to control each others' output
Direct supervision	A boss or supervisor directs and monitors the work done by subordinates
Standardisation of processes	Like behaviour control, in other words, all tasks are done in the same way
Standardisation of outputs	Like output control
Standardisation of skills	Every one working has a common set of skills and knowledge that can be deployed flexibly depending on circumstances

Case Study

Surgeons are qualified and share common skills, and so one control for a hospital is to recruit people with the right qualifications. At the same time, British hospitals are subjected to a regime of targets for waiting lists, treatment times and so on, although this does not affect the individual surgeon directly. Finally, the UK has a National Institute for Clinical Excellence, which advises on best practices and cost effectiveness.

However, control is so fundamentally involved with the management of people, that the systems and techniques of human resources management are part of the organisation's control system.

The economies of the developed world are more and more focused on services, as manufacturing productivity rises. Services are different in that they are delivered by people; each service encounter between a customer and an organisation is a 'moment of truth'.

3.1 Role of HRM and strategic HRM

The syllabus refers to the 'ways in which systems are used to achieve control within the framework of the organisation.

The management of people in an organisation can be modelled in all the control theories mentioned above and in the previous chapter.

Performance appraisal and **reward systems**	Appraisals are supposed to obtain performance details (sensor), compare it to some standard (job description, behavioural standards), with a view to improving performance
Foucault's principles: enclosure, efficient body, correct comportment	These can apply to: – **design of office spaces** (many people hate open plan, not only for the noise which impedes concentration, but also for the lack of privacy) – **scientific management** for time and motion studies – **correct comportment** - dress codes, company jargon, corporate culture even
Structuration theory	HRM has to **deal with change**, requiring agents to champion or implement change. Resistance to change is often seen as individual resistance, rather than something that is embedded in systems.
Radical theory	Human resource management is a means of **seducing and controlling the labour force** to the interests of capital.

HRM is 'a **strategic and coherent approach** to the management of an organisation's most valued assets: the people working there who individually and collectively contribute to the achievement of its objectives for sustainable competitive advantage.' (Armstrong).

We can identify two distinct versions of HRM, which they characterise as 'hard' and 'soft'.

3.1.1 Hard HRM

Karen Legge defined the 'hard' model of HRM as a process emphasising 'the close integration of human resource policies with business strategy which regards employees as a resource to be managed in the same rational way as any other resource being exploited for maximum return'

The hard model of HRM may be summarised as follows.

(a) Its philosophy towards managing people is **business-oriented**: employees must be managed in such a way as to obtain value-adding performance, which will in turn give the organisation competitive advantage.

(b) Following 'a long-standing capitalist tradition in which the worker is regarded as a commodity' (Guest), it regards employees as a **resource of the organisation**, to be managed (exploited) in as rational and strategic a manner as any other economic resource.

(c) It emphasises the **interests, role** and **authority** of management 'over' those of employees.

(d) It is essentially a pluralist viewpoint, which maintains that the interests of the **owners** and managers of a business are inherently different from those of the workers: organisations are therefore political systems, within which there is competition for **scarce power** and resources. Workers must be controlled in order to ensure that they perform in the organisation's interests.

Features of hard HRM include:

(a) A **close matching** or **integration of the strategic objectives** of the HR function with the **business strategy** of the organisation. 'Hard strategic HRM' will emphasise the yield to be obtained by investing in human resources in the interests of the business (Storey)

(b) A **focus on quantitative, business-strategic objectives** and criteria for management

(c) An **emphasis on the need for performance management** and other forms of managerial control.

3.1.2 Soft HRM

Legge defined the 'soft' version of HRM as a process whereby employees are viewed as 'valued assets and as a source of competitive advantage through their commitment, adaptability and high level of skills and performance.

The **soft model of HRM** may be summarised as follows.

(a) Its philosophy towards managing people emphasises the influence of **socio-psychological factors** (relationships, attitudes, motivation, leadership, communication) on work behaviour.

(b) It views employees as **'means rather than objects'** (Guest): 'treating employees as valued assets, a source of competitive advantage through their commitment, adaptability and high quality (of skills, performance and so on)' (Storey).

(c) It focuses on **'mutuality'**, a unitarist viewpoint which assumes that the interests of management and employees can and should coincide in shared organisational goals, working as members of an integrated team. Employees are viewed as 'stakeholders' in the organisation.

The main **features of soft HRM** are:

(a) A **complementary approach** to strategic HRM in relation to the business strategies of the organisation. Brewster argues that a stakeholder perspective and environmental constraints (such as EU legislation) mean that HR strategies cannot be entirely governed by business strategy.

(b) A focus on **socio-psychological and cultural objectives** and criteria for management.

(c) An emphasis on the need to **gain the trust and commitment of employees** – not merely compliance with control mechanisms.

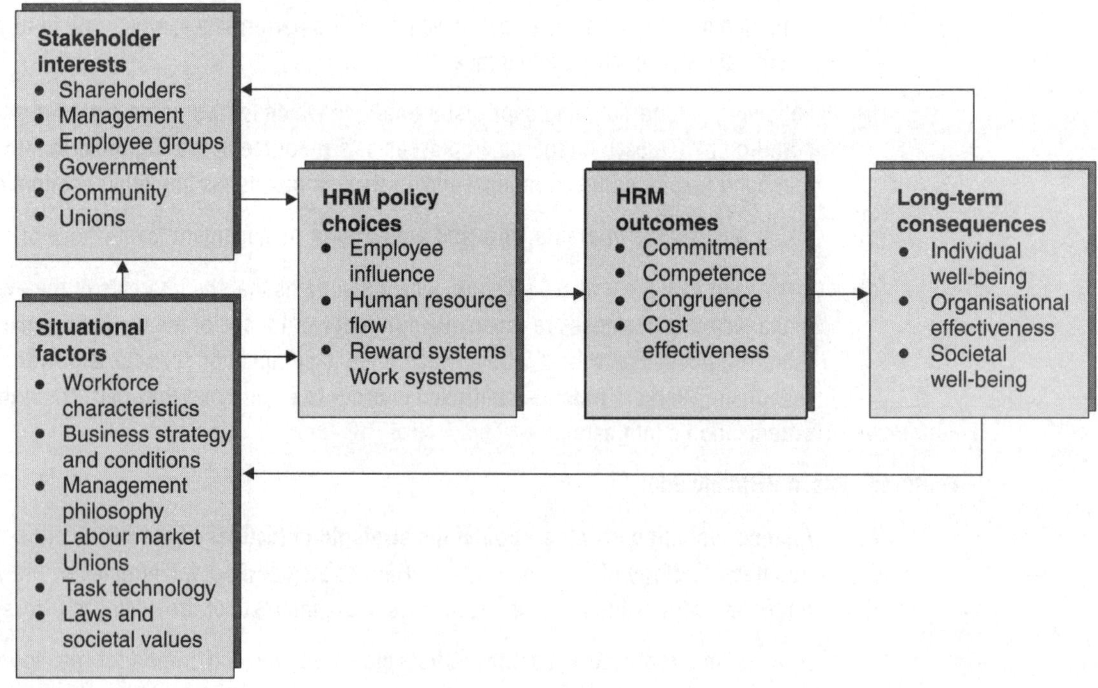

3.1.3 Hard or soft?

In practice, there are likely to be times when a hard orientation (eg in the face of the need for organisational downsizing) directly conflicts with the more developmental and paternal philosophy of the soft approach. Many organisations operate a mix of soft-hard, loose-tight systems.

One way of formalising this is to segment the labour force into a 'core' of permanent employees managed via soft HRM policies, and a 'periphery' of short-contract labour used as an exploitable commodity. (Another option is the out-sourcing of all non-core activities.).'

3.2 Compliance and commitment

The distinction between tight and loose HRM may be characterised as the difference between a system based on compliance and a system based on commitment.

Key terms

Compliance means performing according to set rules and standards, according to what you are expected and asked to do. Competence-based systems of control reflect a low level of trust and challenge: performance is expected to be no less than the set standard – but also no more, since there is little room for creative or exceptional input or effort, which may militate against tight managerial control.

Commitment has been defined as 'the relative strength of an individual's identification with and involvement in a particular organisation'.

Commitment depends on:

(a) A **strong belief** in and **acceptance** of an **organisation's goals and values**
(b) A **willingness to exert considerable effort** on behalf of the organisation
(c) A **strong desire to maintain membership** of the organisation

Commitment based systems of control reflect a high level of trust and mutuality, based on assumptions that the work relationship can offer employees opportunities to meet their needs and aspirations as well as the organisation's needs.

David Guest *(Managing Employment Relations)* set out the differences in personnel policy in a compliance-based system of control and a commitment-based system of control, as follows.

Aspects of policy	Compliance	Commitment
Psychological contract of work	'Fair day's work for a fair day's pay'	Mutual/reciprocal commitment
Behavioural references	Norms, custom and practice	Values/mission
Source of control over workers' behaviour	External (rules, instructions)	Internal (goals, values, willingness)
Employee relations	Pluralist perspective ('Us' and 'Them') Collective Low trust	Unitarist ('Us') Individual Trust

Aspects of policy	Compliance	Commitment
Organising principles/ organisational design	Formal/defined roles Top down Centralised control Hierarchy Division of labour Managerial control	Flexible roles Bottom-up Decentralised control (delegation, empowerment) Flat structures Team-work/autonomy Self control
Policy goals	Administrative/efficiency Performance to standard Minimising cost	Adaptive/effectiveness Constantly improving performance Maximising utilisation for added value

Guest also identified these contrasting dimensions as distinguishing 'traditional industrial relations' and 'HRM' approaches. These approaches to HRM are all reflected in the overall approach to control adopted by the organisation.

4 Control techniques over human resources

FAST FORWARD

HRM uses many techniques to motivate and control employees. **Employment contracts** set down the basics, but set a bare minimum. To get good performance, **motivational techniques** are used.

4.1 Contracts of employment

Employment contracts are a tool used to achieve control within an organisation. An actual **written contract stating clearly what is expected** of employer and employee (including a job description) provides a visible control tool.

As we are concerned with the use of employment contracts as a **control tool**, we will focus on the obligations the contract places on the employee.

The employee has a **fundamental duty of faithful service** to the employer. All other duties are features of this general duty. The **implied** duties of the employee include the following.

(a) **Reasonable competence** to do the job.

(b) **Obedience** to the employer's instructions unless they require him or her to do an unlawful act or to expose themselves to personal danger (not inherent in the work).

(c) **Duty to account for all money and property** received during the course of his employment.

(d) **Reasonable care and skill** in the performance of work. What is reasonable depends on the degree of skill and experience which the employee professes to have.

(e) **Personal service** - the contract of employment is a personal one and so the employee may not delegate their duties without the employer's express or implied consent.

(f) The same duty of **fidelity** to an employer to whom he or she is seconded as to a **contractual employer**.

4.1.1 Effectiveness of the employment contract as a control tool

Advantages of employment contracts as a control tool:

- A well-written contract should **spell out clearly** what is expected of an employee
- It is a **good starting point** in the employer/employee relationship
- The **boundaries of acceptable behaviour** are spelt out
- It can bring **other documentation** into the employment relationship eg ' will follow all procedures described in the Procedures Manual'

Disadvantages of employment contracts as a control tool:

- If not written well it can appear to be **dictating to employees**
- It tends to **emphasise negative consequences**
- If recourse to the contract is needed, it is likely **the relationship** has **already broken down**

4.1.2 Relevance of the employment contract as a control tool for organisational performance

The employment contract, and reference to it, has little value in **motivation** because it often too vague, and is, in part about the avoidance of risk. For example, many employment contracts:

- Do **not promote good use of the internet** but seek to inhibit inappropriate use
- **Seek to promote limitations of what an employee can do** after resigning (eg do not take trade secrets to competitors)

Furthermore, it is hard to specify, in a legal document, the value of commitment or initiative. Concentration on the employment contract offers a compliance rather than a commitment culture. You could argue that an employment contract is as much a part of the risk management systems as part of the control system.

Arguably, a more powerful influence on employee behaviour might be the **psychological contract** with the work – that encourages people to work unpaid overtime, for example.

Finally, some of the most significant scandals and control failures have as a result of poor governance at the top, in which employment contracts offer 'rewards for failure'.

4.2 Motivation

Motivation is not strictly speaking part of control theory as such, although it is an important tool for managers in driving the business.

Motivation, however, is relevant for control systems for a number of reasons.

(a) Managers **cannot control everything employees do** – it is a fantasy that employees are robots, although robots have replaced humans in some processes. Where human contact matters – particularly the case in service industries – the moment of truth is the **interaction** between the **service provider and the customer**. Such things cannot always be scripted. Or, the use Giddens' term, it is impossible to replace individual agency with structure.

(b) Motivation is **not simply a matter for employees** in the system. The managers who do the planning have to be motivated too, and their motivational characteristics may have a direct impact on the type of control action taken and the business strategy. For example, Miles and Snow's analysis of businesses into defenders, analysers, prospectors and reactors is based on the attitude of the senior management team to risk.

The words **'motives'** and **'motivation'** are commonly used in different contexts to mean:

(a) **Goals**, or **outcomes that have become desirable for a particular individual**. These are more properly **'motivating factors'** - since they give people a reason for behaving in a certain way (in pursuit of the chosen goal): thus we say that money, power or friendship are 'motives' for doing something.

(b) The **mental process** of choosing desired outcomes, deciding how to go about them, assessing whether the likelihood of success warrants the amount of effort that will be necessary, and setting in motion the required behaviours. Our motivation to do something will depend on this calculation of the relationship between needs/goals, behaviour and outcome.

(c) The **social process** by which the behaviour of an individual is influenced by others. 'Motivation' in this sense usually applies to the attempts of organisations to get workers to put in more effort by offering them certain rewards (financial and non-financial) if they do so.

4.2.1 Content theories and process theories

One way of grouping the major theories of motivation is by distinguishing between content theories and process theories.

- **Content theories** assume that human beings have an innate package of motives which they pursue; in other words, that they have a **set of needs or desired outcomes**. **Maslow's** need hierarchy theory and **Herzberg's** two-factor theory are two of the most important approaches of this type.
- **Process theories** explore the process through which outcomes become desirable and are pursued by individuals. This approach assumes that **man is able to select his goals** and **choose the paths towards them**, by a conscious or unconscious process of calculation. Most of the theories that we discuss are of this type. They take a **contingency approach**, by stressing the number of variables that influence the individual's decision in each case: there is no best way to motivate people.

4.2.2 Content: need theories

Need theories are content theories that suggest that the **desired outcome of behaviour** in individuals is the **satisfaction of innate needs**.

Maslow's hierarchy of needs

Maslow suggested that people's innate needs can be arranged in a **'hierarchy of relative pre-potency'**. This means that there are 'levels' of need, each of which is dominant until satisfied; only then does the next level of need become a motivating factor.

SELF ACTUALISATION - the need to realise one's potential by using all of one's talents.

ESTEEM - the need for self-respect and self-confidence. Respect, recognition and appreciation from others

COMPANIONSHIP - the need for group membership, friendship, affection and acceptance of one's peers.

SECURITY - the need to have a degree of safety in one's life, freedom from bodily harm or threat. This may also extend to safety of prized elements of lifestyle

PHYSIOLOGICAL - basic to everyone are the needs for food, water, shelter, rest and sex. Without fulfilment of these needs most persons are not motivated by higher needs.

The hierarchy of needs is only a **theory** - *not* an established or empirical fact - and there are various major problems associated with it. Empirical verification for the hierarchy is hard to come by. It is difficult to predict behaviour using the hierarchy: the theory is too **vague to use as a control device.** It can explain behaviour rather than predict it.

4.2.3 Expectancy theory

The expectancy theory of motivation is a **process theory**, based on the assumptions that **human beings** are purposive and rational (in other words, **aware of their goals and capable of directing their behaviour towards those goals).**

Essentially, the theory states that the strength of an individual's motivation to do something will depend on the extent to which he expects the results of his efforts, if successfully achieved, to **contribute towards** his **personal needs or goals**.

In 1964 Victor Vroom, worked out a formula by which human motivation could be assessed and measured, based on an expectancy theory of work motivation. **Vroom** suggested that the **strength of an individual's motivation** is the **product of three factors**.

(a) His **preference for a certain outcome**. Vroom called this **valence (V)**.

(b) His **assessment of whether performing an action would lead to an identifiable outcome**. Vroom calls this **instrumentality (I)**.

(c) His **expectancy (E)** that, if he tried, he **would be able to perform the action**.

Expectancy theory, sometimes called **VIE theory**, suggests that **motivation is the product of V × I × E**, where **I and E are probabilities** and **V is a subjective value**.

4.2.4 Example: the expectancy equation

A manager thinks that it is 75% probable that her division will achieve a certain profit target if she works an extra hour a day, and she is 90% sure that she will be **able** to work an extra hour a day. She will be promoted if the target is met, and on a scale of 1 to 10 she rates promotion at 7.

How strong is her motivation?

Her motivation could have a maximum value of 10 (10 × 100% × 100%). In this instance her motivation is 7 × 75% × 90% = 4.725. On days when things are going badly for the division she is unlikely to work the extra hour, given this level of motivation.

Question

Expectancy

Learning outcome: A(ii)

(a) How could this manager's organisation improve her motivation?
(b) How realistic is this question?

Answer

(a) The **profit target could be adjusted** so that the chances of achieving it are perceived to be 100%.

Some means could be found to **build the extra hour into her basic terms of employment** (for example by re-assigning less important work to others), so that it is 100% certain that she will do the work that is needed.

Promotion could be made more attractive, or another, more attractive, **reward** could be offered.

(b) How many people do you know who are quite so calculative? She would have to have cast iron assurance in her own judgment of probabilities. Other people might work because of fear, low self esteem (and the need to appear busy and stressed in a self dramatising way).

4.2.5 The usefulness of expectancy theory

If expectancy theory is valid, organisations could **motivate employees** by ensuring that:

(a) Employees believe that they possess the **necessary skills** and will be given the necessary resources to be able to do what is required of them (**expectancy**).

(b) Employees believe that they will be **rewarded** if they do what is required of them (**instrumentality**).

(c) Employees **value the rewards** they are offered (**valence**).

Expectancy theory is attractive but it does not provide all the answers for the organisation wishing to motivate its employees.

- **It does not explain why a person values some rewards and not others**. We have to return to need theories for this.
- **It assumes that people behave rationally at all times**. They do not.

Question

Universal motivator

Learning outcome: A(ii)

Ivan Robertson, *Motivation: Strategies, Theory and Practice* (1992) concludes that there is no universal motivator that can galvanise the whole of a workforce into action: 'far from being alike in capacity, some people are intrinsically and perhaps even genetically more motivated than others, and so put greater effort into anything they are called upon to do.'

Michael Dixon, in the *Financial Times*, went on to point out to Professor Robertson that the conclusion that companies have no way to turn everyone on needn't mean they have no ways of turning everyone *off*! Professor Robertson agreed that there probably were several examples of universal *de*-motivators.

How many can you think of?

Answer

Professor Robertson suggests providing **no feedback** at all, or better, **scrambling feedback** so that the links between efforts and rewards appear entirely random. **Arbitrary controls**, as exemplified by management reacting to an obviously isolated incident by clapping a permanent straitjacket on everybody were another example. You can probably think of more.

5 Employee reward

FAST FORWARD

Reward is an essential part of HRM, and the relationship between performance, motivation and reward is sometimes assumed to work on the basis that the reward system will incentivise performance towards organisational goals.

However, there are other issues involved in designing reward systems, such as **equal opportunities law**, **perceived fairness**, and **market rates**.

Bonus schemes are designed to align reward with organisational performance.

Reward systems can be designed to fulfil the dual requirements of:

(a) **Equity** – to pay rates for the job that are fair in relation to others and that accurately reflect the relative value-adding potential of the job and

(b) **Incentive** – to be able to offer extra reward for extra effort and attainment in pursuit of the organisation's goals

5.1 Job evaluation

Job evaluation is a systematic method of arriving at a wage or salary structure, so that the rate of pay for a job is felt to be **fair** in comparison with other jobs in the organisation.

The number of different inputs and environmental variables make an element of subjectivity inevitable, despite refinements aimed at minimising it.

- **Non-analytical** approaches to job evaluation make largely subjective judgements about the whole job, its difficulty, and its importance to the organisation relative to other jobs. (Ranking and classification are methods of this type.)
- **Analytical** methods of job evaluation identify the component factors or characteristics involved in the performance of each job, such as skill, responsibility, experience, mental and physical efforts required. Each component is separately analysed, evaluated and weighted.

Job evaluation is a highly political exercise, and will require openness and communication - not to mention diplomacy – throughout.

5.2 Factors influencing pay

Factor	Comment
The **market rate** – what someone could get outside	Depends on fluidity of the labour market and the competition for resources: for example, in the City of London, whole teams of brokers have left to join other banks that offered more. This can also be influenced by the degree of unionisation of the workforce: pay and benefits are arrived at after negotiation.
Payment by results	Common in small manufacturing or craft industries, for example many factory workers in some parts of the world are paid by piecework. Also applies to **commission** paid to sales people for reaching a level of sales.
The law	There are statutory minimum wages in many countries.
Internal management discretion	Some jobs – which require detailed expertise about the workings of the firm and its customers and/or processes – are hard to quantify: even so, an employee with a distinctive competence may need to be kept if such skills are rare outside.
Skills level	Pay rates may be set on the national vocational qualifications framework.
Profit based bonus schemes	Some companies operate bonus schemes, on a group or individual basis, whereby employees received bonuses based on company performance. **Advantages** **Goal congruence**: ties in employee behaviour with company endeavour and its success. **Automatic control** exercised over labour costs in any one year **Drawbacks** Individuals may find it **hard to influence corporate performance**, so it may be of little relevance. It might **discourage long term thinking**. The design of the system can be **flawed**.
Personal bonus schemes	Part of salary can be paid as bonus on achievement of certain individual performance targets. The problem is designing the targets and ensuring fairness. A personal bonus scheme can discourage teamwork.
Share incentive schemes, share options and similar schemes	Some companies offer share options or other share based payments, under certain conditions. The underlying principle is to provide a reward based on the share price, providing certain performance conditions are met, in other words to enforce **goal congruence**. The design of such schemes can be controversial – after all, a company's share price is influenced by the general investor confidence in the market, as well as individual management performance.

6 Recruitment and selection: control implications

FAST FORWARD

Recruitment and selection are inputs to the organisational system. Job and competence descriptions are needed to ensure the right people are recruited and provide benchmarks for assessing performance.

6.1 Role of recruitment and selection

Recruitment and selection have several roles in organisational control.

(a) In the cybernetic model, recruitment is one of the ways of obtaining **resource inputs**.

(b) Recruitment can be a way by which the system adapts to the environment or maintains itself in a **steady state**. It can even support requisite variety: for example, in an environment of ethnic diversity, such as London, an ethnically diverse workforce has the benefit of reflecting the community.

(c) Recruitment and selection can be **feedforward control action**, in terms of obtaining more resources to that capacity can match demand.

(d) The ability to recruit can, in fact, be a **measure of performance**. For academic institutions, the ability to recruit good staff is a statement that people want to study there.

(e) Recruitment and selection are part of the process of structuration, as people, once recruited, become **acclimatised to the new structure**. Alternatively, it can be a way of bringing a greater possibility for **agency** into the system, if a different type of person is recruited.

(f) Recruitment and selection may be necessary to ensure the **quality of the output**.

(g) Recruitment and selection are important in **maintaining cultural control** if people with the 'right' attitudes and outlook are recruited.

The process of recruitment and selection can be outlined briefly below. We will not go through this in detail, only the control aspects. Some recruitment arises out of strategic needs; in other cases, the recruitment might only be replacement.

Step 1	Plan for personnel requirements	The overall requirements of the organisation are determined by the business strategy. The organisation needs to determine the skills and competences in requires. You could argue that this is a type of feedforward control
Step 2	Identify how the skills and personnel requirements can be met	Recruitment is not the only solution to lack of staff. Alternatives might include: – Outsourcing to low-cost countries – Temporary staff – Investment in technology Abandonment of the plan
Step 3	Assess the actual/required content of jobs	A job analysis is a review of the current content of the job. This can be converted into a job specification, which describes in detail the tasks of the job. This can be based on the job analysis or, alternatively, the job can be designed in a different way.

Step 4	Person specification	The 'type of person' and the skills required are then outlined. This can be a fairly simple exercise ('We need a qualified CIMA accountant with three years post qualification experience.) In practice this can be: – Based on the skills – Based on the person Many organisations look for potential, rather than actual achievement if they want to develop staff.
Step 5	Advertisement	Internal vs external recruitment. Choice of media is important here: the internet is becoming more important.
Step 6	Selection	Candidates are chosen for the job.

Case Study

Renault is building a new 'simple' car, the Logan, in Romania. Unlike plants in the West, Renault has limited the use of automation to take advantage of Romania's low labour costs: labour and technology investment are, to a degree, substitutes for each other. Had Renault built this car in France, it would have recruited fewer workers but would have spent more money on equipment by automating more of the process. (Financial Times, 20 July 2004)

6.1.1 Selection processes

Selection is when the choice is made – obviously, a control system needs to exist to ensure the right person is selected. Again we shall not go into detail here, save to say that a variety of techniques may be used.

The important controls over recruitment and selection are as follows:

- The right candidates are recruited
- Good candidates are not passed over
- The organisation taps the right labour markets, or the most appropriate for its needs
- The selection process is timely

7 Performance management

FAST FORWARD

The performance management system is, effectively, a **monitoring and feedback system**. Employees co-operate in setting **objectives**, which are reviewed at the end of the period, to see if control action can be taken.

Performance management is that aspect of HRM that appears to reflect control systems thinking.

Key term

Armstrong (*A Handbook of Personnel Management Practice*, 1996) describes the purpose as follows.

'**Performance management** is a means of getting better results from the organisation, teams and individuals by understanding and managing performance within an agreed framework of planned goals, standards and competence requirements. It is a process for establishing shared understanding about what *is* to be achieved, and an approach to managing and developing people in a way which increases the probability that it *will* be achieved in the short and long term. It is owned and driven by line management.'

Performance management is a means of getting better results from the organisation, teams and individuals. Appraisal is part of performance management, but is not the whole story.

There is, in fact, a dual emphasis in performance management

- **Setting key accountabilities**, objectives, measures, priorities and time scales
- **Appraising performance**

7.1 Performance management activities

There are four key performance management activities.

(a) **Preparation of performance agreements** (also known as performance contracts). These set out the individual's or team's **objectives**, how performance will be measured (ie the performance measures to be used), the knowledge, skills and behaviour needed to achieve the objectives and the organisation's core values

(i) Objectives may be either:

- **Work/operational** (results to be achieved or contribution to be made to the accomplishment of team, departmental and/or organisational objectives) or
- **Developmental** (personal or learning objectives)

(ii) The following points should be borne in mind when performance measures are established.

- Measures used should be **objective and capable** of being assessed
- Appropriate data should be **readily available**
- If possible, **existing measures** should be **used or adapted**
- Measures should **relate to results** and **not to effort**
- Those results should be **within the individual's control**

(iii) Discussions between managers and individuals should ensure that individuals **fully understand** what is expected of them and that if they fulfil those expectations they will be regarded as having performed well.

(iv) The organisation's core values might cover **quality, customer service**, **equal opportunities** and so on.

(b) **Preparation of performance and development plans**. These set out performance and personal development needs.

(c) **Management of performance throughout the year**. This involves the **continuous process** of providing feedback on performance, conducting informal progress reviews and dealing with performance problems as necessary.

(d) **Provision of performance reviews**. These involve both taking a view of an individual's progress to date *and* reaching an agreement about what should be done in the future. The performance review provides the means by which:

(i) Results can be **measured** against targets
(ii) The employee can be given **feedback** on how well he is doing
(iii) **Praise** and **constructive criticism** can be given as necessary
(iv) **Views can be exchanged**
(v) An **agreement can be reached**

7.2 Appraisal

Key term

Appraisal: the systematic review and assessment of an employee's performance, potential and training needs.

We can summarise the appraisal process and see how it **appears** to be like a feedback system as follows.

Performance appraisal

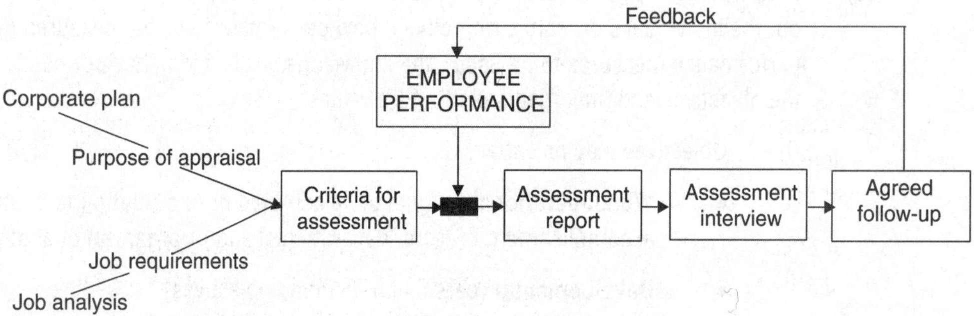

The general purpose of any appraisal system is to **improve effectiveness**. Personnel appraisal aims to ensure individuals are performing to the best of their ability, are developing their potential and that the organisation is best utilising their abilities. It may include:

(a) **Reward review**. Measuring the extent to which an employee is deserving of a bonus or pay increase as compared with his or her peers.

(b) **Performance review**, for planning and following-up training and development programmes, ie identifying training needs, validating training methods and so on.

(c) **Potential review**, as an aid to planning career development and succession, by attempting to predict the level and type of work the individual will be capable of in the future.

7.2.1 Objectives of appraisals

(a) Establishing the **key deliverables** an individual has to produce to enable the organisation to achieve its objectives.

(b) Comparing the individual's **level of performance against a standard**, as a means of quality control.

(c) Identifying the individual's **training and development needs** in the light of actual performance.

(d) Identifying areas that **require improvement.**

(e) Monitoring the organisation's **initial selection procedures** against subsequent performance.

7.2.2 A typical appraisal system

Step 1 **Identification of criteria for assessment**, perhaps based on job analysis, performance standards, person specifications and so on.

Step 2 The **preparation by the subordinate's manager of an appraisal report**. In some systems both the appraisee and appraiser prepare a report. These reports are then compared.

Step 3 An **appraisal interview**, for an exchange of views about the appraisal report, targets for improvement, solutions to problems and so on.

Step 4 **Review of the assessment by the assessor's own superior**, so that the appraisee does not feel subject to one person's prejudices. Formal appeals may be allowed, if necessary to establish the fairness of the procedure.

Step 5 The **preparation and implementation of action plans** to achieve improvements and changes agreed.

Step 6 **Follow-up** monitoring the progress of the action plan.

Most systems provide for appraisals to be recorded, and report forms of various lengths and complexity may be designed. Even so, the effectiveness of appraisal as a feedback element of the performance management control system can be questioned.

L Lockett (in *Effective Performance Management*) suggests that **appraisal barriers** can be identified. These limit the effectiveness of the appraisal system as a functioning part of the organisational control system, either through bad implementation or subversion to another agenda.

Appraisal barriers	Comment
Appraisal as confrontation	Many people dread appraisals, or use them 'as a sort of show down, a good sorting out or a clearing of the air.' (a) There is a lack of agreement on performance levels. (b) The feedback is subjective - in other words the manager is biased, allows personality differences to get in the way of actual performance etc. (c) The feedback is badly delivered. (d) Appraisals are 'based on yesterday's performance not on the whole year'. (e) Disagreement on long-term prospects.
Appraisal as judgement	The appraisal 'is seen as a one-sided process in which the manager acts as judge, jury and counsel for the prosecution'. However, the process of performance management 'needs to be jointly operated in order to retain the commitment and develop the self-awareness of the individual.'

Appraisal barriers	Comment
Appraisal as chat	The other extreme is that the appraisal is a friendly chat 'without ... purpose or outcome ... Many managers, embarrassed by the need to give feedback and set stretching targets, reduce the appraisal to a few mumbled "well dones!" and leave the interview with a briefcase of unresolved issues.'
Appraisal as bureaucracy	Appraisal is a form-filling exercise, to satisfy the personnel department. Its underlying purpose, improving individual and organisational performance, is forgotten.
Appraisal as unfinished business	Appraisal should be part of a continuing process of performance management.
Appraisal as annual event	Many targets set at annual appraisal meetings become irrelevant or out-of-date.

7.2.3 Self-appraisal

Self-appraisal occurs when individuals carry out their own self-evaluation as a major input into the appraisal process. Many schemes combine the two - manager and subordinate fill out a report and compare notes.

7.2.4 Appraisal and reward

Another issue is the extent to which the appraisal system is related to the salary and reward system. There are drawbacks to linking salary or bonuses to appraisal.

(a) The **funds available** rarely depend on an individual's performance.
(b) **Continuous improvement** should perhaps be expected, not rewarded as extra.
(c) **Comparisons between individuals** are hard to make.

7.2.5 Improving the appraisal system

The appraisal scheme should itself be **assessed** (and regularly re-assessed) according to the following general criteria for evaluating appraisal schemes.

Criteria	Comment
Relevance	• Does the system have a **useful purpose**, relevant to the needs of the organisation and the individual? • Is the purpose **clearly expressed** and widely understood by all concerned, both appraisers and appraisees? • Are the **appraisal criteria relevant** to the purposes of the system?
Fairness	• Is there **reasonable standardisation** of criteria and objectivity throughout the organisation? • Is it **reasonably objective**?

Criteria	Comment
Serious intent	• Are the managers concerned **committed to the system** - or is it just something the personnel department thrusts upon them? • Who does the **interviewing**, and are they properly trained in interviewing and assessment techniques? • Is **reasonable time and attention** given to the interviews - or is it a question of 'getting them over with'? • Is there a **genuine demonstrable link** between performance and reward or opportunity for development?
Co-operation	• Is the appraisal a **participative**, **problem-solving activity** - or a tool of management control? • Is the appraisee given **time and encouragement** to prepare for the appraisal, so that he or she can make a constructive contribution? • Does a **jointly-agreed, concrete conclusion** emerge from the process? • Are **appraisals held regularly**?
Efficiency	• Does the system seem **overly time-consuming** compared to the value of its outcome? • Is it difficult and **costly to administer**?

7.2.6 Upward appraisal

A trend adopted by companies such as BP and British Airways (and others) is **upward appraisal.** Subordinates appraise their 'superiors'. Other companies use 360 degree appraisals: the appraisee receives feedback from a number of key relationships – superiors, subordinates, important contacts in other departments.

8 Training and learning

FAST FORWARD

Training is provided to ensure the organisation has the **skills it** needs.

Training programmes can be **feedforward control**, if a skills shortage leading to defective performance is encountered, but also they function as cultural control and as part of the 'reward' system by giving people marketable skills.

Training and learning are one aspect of performance management, and hence the control system, but they are, potentially, more than that. The roles of training and development are as follows

(a) **Improve the performance** of individuals in carrying out their roles, as control action

(b) **Provide the skills and competences** that the **organisation needs** – effectively, an input to the production system

(c) **Maintain existing performance** levels (eg by keeping people up to date with new developments, for example, training in how to use simple IT applications)

(d) **Develop people** for **new roles in future**

(e) As a **form of reward**, if the training is useful and valued – skills learned in training can be portable elsewhere within the organisation or can equip people to cope outside. In a society where people believe, that there is no job security, training makes people feel more marketable. It also suggests that people invest in them.

(f) As a form of **cultural indoctrination** and team building, training programmes in big organisations can encourage a sense of team building, teach the company jargon

8.1 A training system

If training is to make a impact on performance at an individual level, let alone at a strategic level, it must be carefully designed to suit the **need for training** and the **needs** of the trainee. Training is 'the systematic development of the attitude/knowledge/skill/behaviour pattern required by an individual in order to perform adequately a given task or job.'

The application of systems theory to the design of training has gained currency in the West in recent years. A **training system**, illustrated below, uses rational methods to programme learning, from:

(a) **The identification of training needs:** by comparing the requirements of the job with an assessment of the present capacities and inclinations of the individuals available to do it; (this is called their 'pre-entry' behaviour since they have not yet entered the training system); via

(b) **The design of courses**, selection of methods and media, to

(c) **The measurement of trained performance** – the 'terminal behaviour' resulting from the training system – and its comparison against pre-determined performance targets

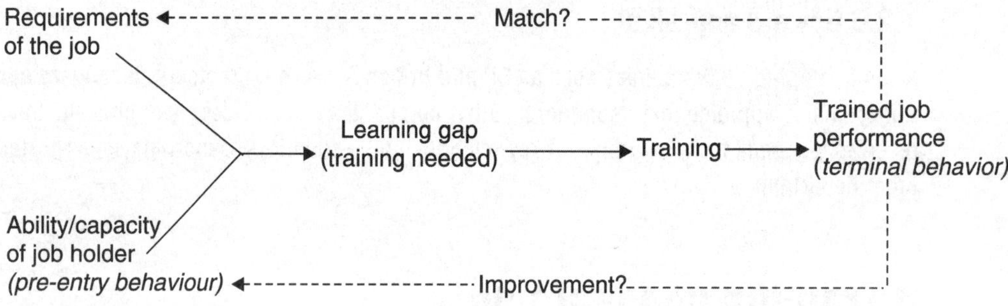

A training system

8.2 Training needs analysis

8.2.1 Whose needs and objectives?

There is no intrinsic incompatibility between a **business's** strategic goals for training, and the developmental aspirations of **individuals**. The desire for learning, skill development and self-actualisation by the individual have long been recognised (Maslow, Herzberg) as incentives to motivated performance at work, as well as offering personal satisfaction.

The training needs of individuals and groups vary enormously, according to the nature of the job and particular tasks, and the abilities and experience of the employees.

8.2.2 Training needs recognition

Some training requirements will be obvious and 'automatic'.

(a) If a **piece of legislation** is enacted which affects the organisation's operations, training in its provisions will automatically be indicated. Thus, for example, personnel staff will need to be trained as and when various EU Directives are enacted in UK law.

(b) The **introduction of new technology** similarly implies a training need: for relevant employees to learn how to use it.

(c) An organisation seeking **accreditation for its training scheme**, or seeking a British Standard or International Standard (say, for quality systems, ISO 9000), will have certain training requirements imposed on it by the approving body.

Other training requirements may emerge in response to **critical incidents**: problems or events which affect a key area of the organisation's activity and effectiveness. Some **qualitative indicators** might be taken as symptoms of a need for training: absenteeism, high labour turnover, grievance and disciplinary actions, crises, conflict, poor motivation and performance. Such factors will need to be investigated to see what the root causes are, and whether training will solve the problem.

Training needs may be defined as the gap between what people should be achieving and what they actually are achieving. In other words:

Required level of competence **minus** present level of competence = training need.

A **human resources audit** or **skills audit** may also be conducted for a more comprehensive account of the current level of competence, skill, knowledge (and so on) in the workforce.

8.3 Training objectives

Objectives should be clear, specific and related to observable, measurable targets. Ideally, there should be detailed definitions of:

(a) **Behaviour** – what the trainee should be able to do
(b) **Standard** – to what level of performance
(c) **Environment** – under what conditions

The advantage of **competency** frameworks is that they typically define competent performance in exactly this specific and quantifiable way.

Objectives are the yardsticks that will allow the trainer (and trainees) to see clearly whether and how far training has been successful. They are usually best expressed in terms of active verbs: at the end of the course the trainee should be able to describe... , or identify... or distinguish X from Y... or calculate... or assemble... and so on.

It is insufficient to define the objectives of training as 'to give trainees a grounding in... or 'to encourage trainees in a better appreciation of...': this offers no target achievement which can be objectively measured. Where possible, a **quantifiable** measure should be added: time taken to perform a task, percentage of questions answered correctly, percentage of errors acceptable, and so on.

(a) **Methods of training.** These will vary according to the training needs and location).

(b) **Training technologies.** Any of the above methods may incorporate recent innovations in training delivery, including: video, interactive video, computer-assisted learning (CAL), computer-assisted instruction (CAI) and computer-managed learning (CML)

8.4 Evaluation and validation of training

8.4.1 Validation

Key term

Validation means observing the results of a process (in this case, a training scheme) and measuring whether its objectives have been achieved

There are various ways of validating a training scheme – in effect a control device comparing trainees' requirements with the actual output..

(a) **Trainee reactions to the experience:** using feedback forms and attitude surveys to ask the trainees whether they thought the training programme was relevant to their work, and whether they found it useful.

(b) **Trainee learning:** measuring what the trainees have learned on the course, by means of a test or assessment of competence at the end.

(c) **Changes in job behaviour following training:** studying the subsequent behaviour of the trainees in their jobs, to measure how the training scheme has altered the way they do their work. This is possible, for example, where the purpose of the course was to learn a particular skill.

(d) **Impact of training on organisational goals:** seeing whether the training scheme has contributed to the overall objectives of the organisation. This is a form of monitoring reserved for senior management.

Validation is thus the measurement of terminal behaviour (trained work performance) in relation to training objectives.

8.4.2 Evaluation

Key term

Evaluation means comparing the costs of a process (in this case a training scheme) against the benefits that are being obtained.

A training programme should only go ahead in the first place if the likely benefits are expected to exceed the costs of designing and running it. The problem here is not so much in estimating the costs as in estimating the potential **benefits**.

A systematic approach to training can be illustrated as follows. You can identify the control loop ion action.

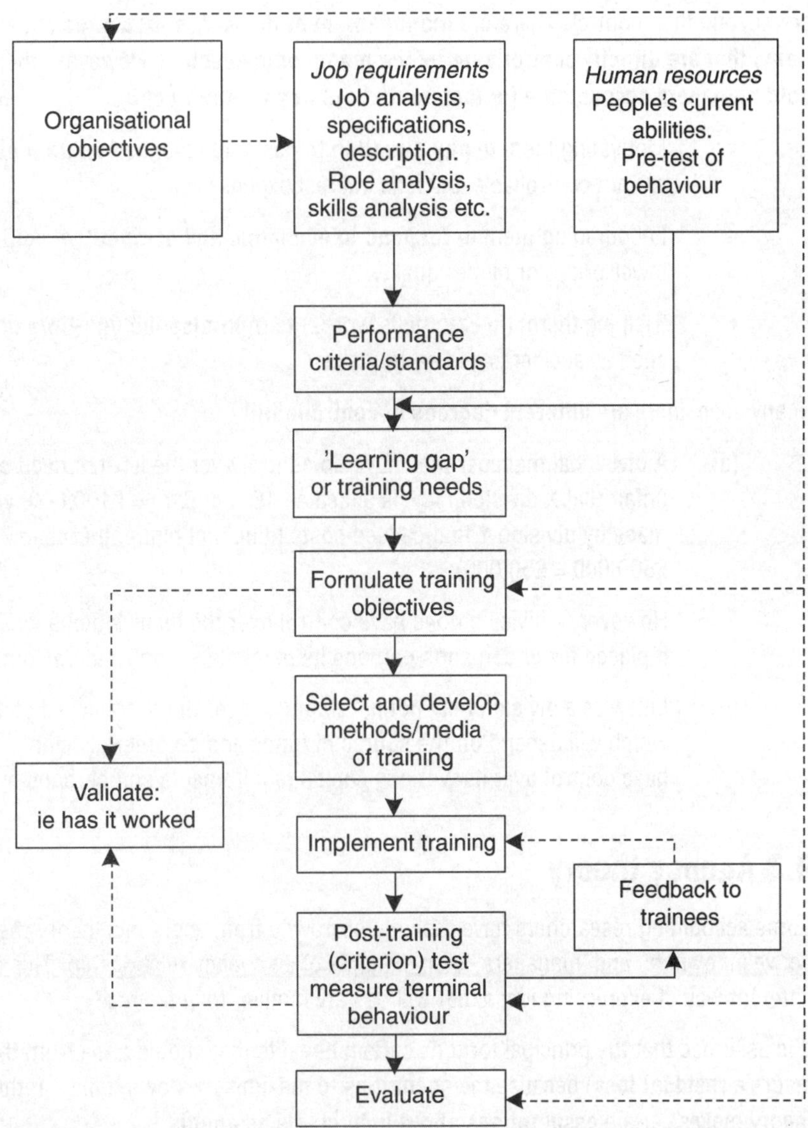

9 Managerial performance and reward

FAST FORWARD

Managers are sometimes considered to have an **agency relationship** with shareholders. Even so, there is a debate as to whether 'uncontrollable' factors over performance should be recognised.

9.1 Issues in measuring managerial performance

It is difficult to devise performance measures that relate specifically to a manager to judge his or her performance as a manager. It is possible to calculate statistics to assess the manager as an employee like any other employee (days absent, professional qualifications obtained, personability and so on), but this is not the point. As soon as the issue of **ability as a manager** arises it is necessary to **consider him in relation to his area of responsibility**. If we want to know how good a manager is at marketing the only information there is to go on is the marketing performance of his division (which may or may not be traceable to his own efforts).

9.2 Uncontrollable factors

It is generally considered to be unreasonable to assess managers' performance in relation to matters that are beyond their control. Therefore **management performance measures** should **only include those items that are directly controllable by the manager** in question. However, there may be **good reasons to hold managers accountable for factors that are beyond their control.**

- Motivating them to **pay attention** to cost and revenue **factors that are relevant** even if they are not controllable, such as interest expenses.
- Encouraging them to **respond to economic and competitive conditions** such as a rival's lower prices or higher quality.
- 'Helping them' (in Ezzamel's words) to **minimise the one-time damage** caused by events such as accidents and earthquakes.

In any case, there are **different degrees of controllability.**

(a) A divisional manager may have no control over the level of head office costs. It may seem unfair that X division, say, is allocated 10% of £1m = £100,000, when it is actually demands made by division Y that caused costs to be that high rather than £500,000 (10% × £500,000 = £50,000).

However, X division does have control over the relative demands it places on head office. If it placed fewer demands perhaps its percentage contribution could fall, say, to 5%.

(b) Likewise a division may not have control over the overall level of a group's interest charge, which will depend on the source of funds and on other division's activities. However, it may have control over its working capital requirements and perhaps over capital expenditure.

9.3 Agency theory

Some accounting researchers have recently borrowed from economic theory the idea that the relationship between 'owners' and 'managers' is an example of an agency relationship. This is really little more than a different way of expressing ideas that will be very familiar to you already.

It is assumed that the principal forgoes certain benefits that should arise from the relationship (and hence incurs a **residual loss**) because the agent tries to maximise his own 'utility' rather than the principal's. The theory makes certain **assumptions about individuals as agents**.

- They **behave rationally** in seeking to maximise their own utility.
- They **seek financial and non-financial rewards.**
- They **tend to be risk-averse** and, hence, reluctant to innovate.
- Their **individual interests** will **not always coincide** with those of their principals.
- They **prefer leisure** to hard work.
- They have **greater knowledge** about their operating performance and actions than is available to their principals.

Key issues in agency theory are **attitudes to risk** and the **observability of effort**.

(a) Conventional management accounting assumes that principals **protect agents from risk** - it only makes managers responsible for things they can control. Agency theory suggests that if principals are risk averse then they should share the risk with agents and this can increase the utility of both parties. Making a large part of an executive's potential reward subject to some profit target is a simple example of such a contract.

(b) The principal may find it difficult to **observe the agent's efforts**. Alternatively the principal may not be able to evaluate the effort because he does not possess the information on which the decision to expend that much effort was based.

9.4 Possible management performance measures

In the light of the above the following can be suggested.

(a) **Subjective measures** may be used, for example ranking performance on a scale of 1 to 5. This approach is used in the civil service. To work well it must be perceived by managers generally to be fair, and this will usually mean that the judgement is made by somebody impartial, but close enough to the work of each manager to appreciate the efforts he has made and the difficulties he faces.

(b) **The judgement of outsiders** can be regarded as a measure of managerial performance. This may be difficult to implement for many companies but the method is used.

(c) **Upward appraisal** is used by some businesses. This involves staff giving their opinions on the performance of their managers. To be effective this requires very healthy working relationships, however.

(d) **Accounting measures** can be used, but must be tailored according to what or whom is being judged.

(e) **Non-financial measures** may include market share measurements or a variety of other qualitative criteria.

Exam focus point

Your exam may discuss the validity of using **accounting measures**. In essence, this means **profitability**, whether it is calculated in terms of sales volume, or as profits or as return on investment, or residual income, or something else. You may be asked to consider this from the point of view of the manager, or of the organisation, or of both.

9.5 Performance-related rewards

The following section talks mainly about rewarding **managerial performance** but most points can be made **equally about employees** in general. Moreover, in some organisations such as the public sector, the focus might be on doctors or teachers, for example, rather than on 'managers'.

Rewarding managers for their performance is a method of control in the sense that it is assumed that attempts will be made to achieve the organisation's objectives in return for rewards. This, in turn, derives from **motivation theory,** which suggests that people have wants or desired outcomes and modify their behaviour accordingly.

9.5.1 How to link performance and rewards

A good reward system should have the following characteristics.

(a) It should **offer real incentives**, sufficiently high after tax to make extraordinary effort worthwhile.

(b) It should **relate payments to criteria over which the individual has control** (otherwise he will feel helpless to ensure his reward, and the expectancy element in motivation will be lacking).

(c) It should **make clear the basis on which payments are calculated**, and all the conditions that apply, so that individuals can make the calculation of whether the reward is worth the extra level of effort.

(d) It should be **flexible** enough to reward different levels of achievement in proportion, and with provision for regular review and adaptation to the changing needs of the organisation.

(e) It should be **cost effective** for the organisation.

(f) It should have **cut-off points** so that mediocre performance is not rewarded, and that excess bonuses are not paid to 'reward' windfall gains, and to ensure the sustainability of growth.

9.5.2 Non-explicit links

Sometimes the link between performance and reward is not made explicit, especially when performance is evaluated subjectively. This may be a useful approach 'to counteract the short-term opportunism that more explicit contracts may engender', as Emmanuel *et al* contend. The argument is somewhat questionable, however.

Question — Linking bonuses

Learning outcome: A(ii)

Suppose an organisation's objectives require a certain manager to achieve sales of at least £100,000 per month. Suggest three ways in which the manager's monthly bonus could be linked to this target.

Answer

(a) The manager could be offered a bonus of, say, 10% of salary for every, say, £10,000 of sales achieved over the basic target.

(b) The manager could be offered a fixed sum if he or she achieves the target - a £500 bonus, say.

(c) There could be a penalty of some kind if sales fall below target - the sack, say!

The question raises all sorts of other issues, of course. How difficult is the target, for example, and how easy is it for managers to manipulate results for their own ends?

9.6 Common types of scheme

There are three common types of scheme.

(a) Under a **profit-related pay scheme**, pay (or part of it) is related to results achieved (performance to defined standards in key tasks, according to plan).

- Key results can be identified and specified.
- There will be a clear model for evaluating performance and knowing when or if targets have been reached and payments earned.
- The exact conditions and amounts of awards can be made clear to the employee, to avoid uncertainty and later resentment.

(b) **Profit-sharing schemes** offer managers bonuses, perhaps in the form of shares in the company, related directly to profits. The profit formula itself is not easily calculated - profit levels being subject to accounting conventions - so care will have to be taken to publish and explain the calculations to managers if the scheme is to be effective as a motivator.

(c) **Group incentive schemes** typically offer a bonus for a group (equally, or proportionately to the earnings or status of individuals) which achieves or exceeds specified targets. Offering bonuses to a whole team may be appropriate for tasks where individual contributions cannot be isolated..

9.7 Problems with incentive schemes

9.7.1 Short-termism

There are a number of **problems associated with measures specifically designed to avoid short-termism.**

(a) The **link between current expenditure** or **savings** and **long-term effect** may not be clear.

(b) There is a danger that **over-investment for the future** may have such an **adverse impact** on **present performance** that the future envisaged is impossible to achieve.

(c) Incentive schemes for long-term achievements may **not motivate** since effort and reward are too distant in time from each other (or managers may not think that they will be around that long!).

9.7.2 Problems of measurement

Clearly the way in which measurements are taken could seriously affect the reward a manager receives. There are three main issues.

(a) It is **questionable** whether any performance measures or set of measures can provide a **comprehensive assessment** of what a single person achieves for the organisation. There will always be the old chestnut of **lack of goal congruence,** employees being committed to what is measured, rather than the objectives of the organisation.

(b) Particularly where performance has to be measured by **non-financial performance measures** (such as in the public sector), the results are formed from **subjective judgement.**

(c) It is difficult to **segregate the controllable component** of performance from the uncontrollable component.

9.7.3 Problems of motivation

Schemes will only work if **rewards** seem both **desirable and achievable.**

(a) **Money is not the only motivator** - different individuals value different types of reward. **Personal objectives** may also be important; public sector nurses or teachers may feel they are following a vocation regardless of the rewards offered.

(b) When an individual's work performance is dependent on work done by other people (and much work involves co-operation and interdependence with others), an **individual bonus scheme is not always effective**, since **individual performance can be impaired by what other people have done.**

(c) There is evidence that the **effectiveness** of incentive schemes **wears off over time**, as acceptable 'norms' of working are re-established.

(d) The **value of a reward may be affected by factors beyond the organisation's control.** For example a reward such as a company car (associated with achieving a certain status) may be so highly taxed that managers do not consider the effort of achieving the reward to be worthwhile.

9.7.4 Particular problems in the public sector

n addition to the general problems outlined above, performance-related reward schemes in the public sector have particular problems.

(a) **Timescale.** Many projects (for example, environmental programmes) can only be assessed for effectiveness in the longer term.

(b) **The political dimension.** A senior manager in the public sector may be set a goal which is highly undesirable from the point of view of opposition parties: if a change of power is imminent, might the manager later be rewarded for **not** achieving it!

Question

Mix of pay

Learning outcome: A(ii)

An incentive scheme offers a manager a basic salary of £20,000 and a bonus of up to 50% of basic salary, depending on performance. Why might this scheme create problems for the recruitment and retention of a manager for this position?

Answer

People tend not to include bonuses when considering whether to accept a job. Candidates who could earn £30,000 elsewhere will not be attracted, but this is the quality of manager required. The **bonus percentage is far too high**, especially in the medium-term: if the manager achieves earnings of £30,000 in year 1, he or she is under excessive pressure to maintain that standard of living in future years. If it is easy to achieve the 50% bonus, its motivational value is very limited.

A basic salary of, say, £27,000 and a bonus of 10% of basic would cost the company about the same amount and be more effective.

Chapter Roundup

- Because of the difficulties in strictly applying a cybernetic model to organisations, many organisations, in effect, use other types of control. Two influences are **centralisation/decentralisation** of decision-making and the **formality or informality** of the system.
- Control can be exercised on market lines (market control), through **bureaucracy** (bureaucratic control) and **via people's views and beliefs** (cultural control).
- What is best is contingent on **technology used**, the **environment**, and the **size and structure** of the organisation.
- It is possible to focus control attention on **behaviour** – making sure that processes are enacted in the right way – and **output**, the results of the control.
- The organisational subsystem for **human resources management** is an attempt to control the behaviour of people.
- **Hard HRM** is tightly coupled with business strategy, and HRM plans are determined by competitive advantage.
- **Soft HRM** places greater emphasis on developmental issues, and is loosely coupled to product/market issues.
- HRM uses many techniques to motivate and control employees. **Employment contracts** set down the basics, but set a bare minimum. To get good performance, **motivational techniques** are used.
- **Reward** is an essential part of HRM, and the relationship between performance, motivation and reward is sometimes assumed to work on the basis that the reward system will incentivise performance towards organisational goals.
- However, there are other issues involved in designing reward systems, such as **equal opportunities law**, **perceived fairness**, **market rates**.
- **Bonus schemes** are designed to align reward with organisational performance.
- **Recruitment and selection** are inputs to the organisational system. Job and competence descriptions are needed to ensure the right people are recruited and provide benchmarks for assessing performance.
- The performance management system is, effectively, a **monitoring and feedback system**. Employees co-operate in setting **objectives**, which are reviewed at the end of the period, to see if control action can be taken.
- **Training** is provided to ensure the organisation has the **skills** it needs.
- **Training programmes** can be **feedforward control**, if a skills shortage leading to defective performance is encountered, but also they function as cultural control and as part of the 'reward' system by giving people marketable skills.
- Managers are sometimes considered to have an **agency relationship with shareholders**. Even so, there is a debate as to whether 'uncontrollable' factors over performance should be recognised.

Quick Quiz

1. What factors influence the type of control used in an organisation?
2. Fill in the matrix below to show the most suitable type of control.

Outcome measurability	*High*		
	Low		
		Low	*High*
		Task programmability	

3. What is the difference between 'hard' and 'soft' HRM?
4. Why do managers need to motivate?
5. Identify two key aspects of a reward system.
6. What control 'standards' are employed in a recruitment process?
7. How does performance management differ from appraisal?
8. Define training need.

Answers to Quick Quiz

1. Centralisation/decentralisation; formality/informality/degree of supervision
2.

Outcome measurability	*High*	Output	Behaviour or output
	Low	Culture/clan	Behaviour
		Low	*High*
		Task *programmability*	

3. Hard HRM is directly concerned with the business strategy for products and markets – employees are 'resources' or 'commodities', an economic resource. 'Soft' HRM treats employees as 'assets' rather than 'costs', and puts greater emphasis on the non-economic aspects of HRM.
4. An employment contract or job description cannot specify everything. Management also has to be forward-looking. Expectancy theory suggests that rewards can be built into a control system.
5. Equity, or fairness; incentive
6. The job description and person specification are benchmarks against which recruits are judged
7. Performance management depends on shared development of objectives. This is more than appraisal which focuses on performance, although objective setting can be part of appraisal.
8. The required level of competence minus the present level of competence

Now try the question below from the Exam Question Bank

Number	Level	Marks	Time
Q2	Examination	25	45 mins

Control and the organisation

3

Introduction

In chapter 1, when we discussed soft systems, we suggested that different people involved in a system would have different views as to what an organisation is for, and what it is. We also suggested the **potential importance** of **ritual** in the way that some management processes operate, that they have psychological as much as practical value. The strength of organisation culture means that managers do share a world view, and we suggested that cultural control is an important aspect of organisational life. We also discussed the power of 'structure' in imposing ways of behaving. In this chapter we look at the importance of organisation structure in control.

Topic list	Learning outcomes	Syllabus references	Ability required
1 Images of organisations	A (i), (iii)	A (1), (4)	Evaluation
2 Components of organisations	A (i), (iii)	A (1), (4)	Evaluation
3 Hierarchy as a control mechanism	A (i), (iii)	A (1), (4)	Evaluation
4 Traditional hierarchy	A (i), (iii)	A (1), (4)	Evaluation
5 Design of hierarchies	A (i), (iii)	A (1), (4)	Evaluation
6 Divisionalisation and strategic business units	A (i), (iii)	A (1), (4)	Evaluation
7 New organisation structures and problems of control	A (i), (iii)	A (1), (4)	Evaluation
8 Organisation culture	A (i), (iii)	A (1), (4)	Evaluation

1 Images of organisations

FAST FORWARD

People can have **fundamentally different understandings** as to what an organisation is for. This can mean that the control system in the organisation can appear to mean something quite different depending on the perspective of those being controlled.

Morgan (1986) identified some useful ways of talking about the organisations we work for or interact with. The list below does not describe different types of organisation: it seems to describe ways by which we can appreciate the complexity of what organisations are and what they do.

Metaphor	Comment	
Organisations are machines	An organisation is a set of **interrelated components** whose combined, structured operation caries out a common task. Machines have replaced people, and organisations to carry out certain tasks.	This is similar, perhaps, to the cybernetic model described in chapter 1, which draws upon engineering as analogy.
Organisations are biological organisms	Biological organisms are born, grow, mature and die, and are in a series of constant interchanges with the environment. Is **organisational decline** inevitable?	Accounting controls tend to be short term in nature (comparing budget to actual over the past few months). However the type of control system might depend on the age and position of the organisation.
Organisations are human brains	This metaphor leads to three insights. • **Organisations are stocks of knowledge**. Any organisation contains expertise accumulated from experience. • **Organisations can learn**. • **Organisations are networks of information flows** rather like a telecommunications network.	In a control system, **learning** is an example of a system changing its behaviour in response to environmental stimulus. **Accounting control information** is part of the information flow around the organisation, and need to adapt to the changed circumstances of the business. Control systems also exclude other sources of knowledge.
Organisations are cultures or subcultures	Culture refers to **shared assumptions, beliefs, values and ways of behaving**. A religious organisation is the most obvious example of an organisation built around a strong set of beliefs.	Cultural control has already been mentioned in the context of human resource management, and will be discussed later.
Organisations are political systems	Organisations are arenas where **managers** compete with each other for status (empire building), and where they promote their careers. Organisations are arenas where **outsiders** compete for power over the organisation's activities.	Is management accounting really neutral or can it be **manipulated** to give an excessively favourable or partial view of the performance of an organisation or department? However, where people pursue personal goals in organisations, the control system and control in information can be a source of contested data.

Metaphor	Comment	
Organisations are psychic prisons	Living in an organisation can create a sense of **psychological dependency** on it: witness the problems that real prisoners encounter on leaving prison and its familiar, if unpleasant, routines.	People's reaction to control may be in part determined by their psychological state.
Organisations are systems of change and transformation	An organisation takes **inputs** from the environment and converts them into outputs of goods and services.	This is a widely accepted way of thinking about business, and we have already discussed this in chapter 1.
Organisations are instruments of domination	Organisations influence people's relationships with society and their expectations of it (eg by advertising) but are also designed to control people within them.	This perhaps reflects a radical perspective, that there can never be goal congruence outlined in Chapter 2. If organisations dominate society, then should organisations themselves be made accountable? Management accountants might have to produce information about social and environmental practices.

2 Components of organisation

FAST FORWARD

An organisation generally exists to **co-ordinate working activities** in some way. The **type of co-ordination employed**, and the **type of supervision** and control over the work process, influence the type of organisation it is, and its control systems.

According to Mintzberg (1979), organisations contain five main components.

- The **strategic apex** (eg board of directors) directs strategy.
- The **operating core** contains those people directly involved in the process of adding value.
- The **middle line** converts the wishes of the strategic apex into the work of the operating core. Middle managers at this level exert a pull to make autonomous decisions, for example the establishment of separate business units.
- The **technostructure** standardises the work of others, by designing procedures they must follow, and can include finance department personnel, H&M specialists, work study analysts, and all people who 'design' jobs and who design control mechanisms.
- **Support staff** provide ancillary services such as public relations or legal counsel.

These elements are linked in five ways.

Organisation hierarchy	This is the **structure of departments**, formal authority, divisions and so on. Departmental and divisional performance measurement is the main subject of the control system.
Flows of regulated activity	**Inputs are processed into outputs**. The activities in the value chain are controlled and linked in these flows. Again, controls exist over the inputs and outputs of each process.
Flows of informal communications	This may denote the real structure of communication, supplementing or bypassing the formal communication system. These **cannot be formally controlled**, but a **shared culture and understanding** can affect informal communications. Cultural control is perhaps relevant here.
Systems of work constellations	Groups of people work on distinct tasks. For example, producing a strategic plan may require people from the finance department, the marketing department and so on to co-operate.
Ad hoc decision processes	A decision process involves recognising a problem, diagnosing its causes, finding a solution and implementing it. For any one decision, these activities occur in a number of different places in the organisation.

Mintzberg suggests that there are five ideal types of organisation, each of which configures the five components above in a significantly different way.

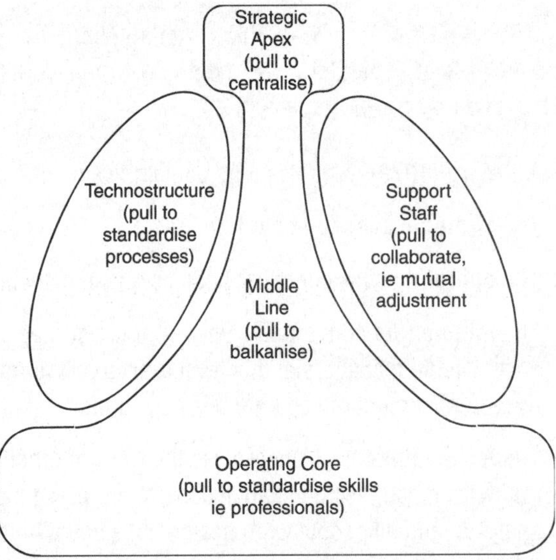

Source: Adapted from Mintzberg, H. (1979) *The Structuring of Organizations*, Englewood Cliffs: Prentice Hall.

Figure 1 Configuration

Each component of the organisation has its own dynamic, which leads to a distinct type of organisation or configuration. Their possible characteristics are outlined in the table below.

Configuration choices

Configuration	Key influence	Co-ordination mechanism	Implications for control
Simple	Strategic apex	Direct supervision	Small, young, centralised, personality-driven: may fail to enforce necessary bureaucratic and financial controls, as effort is on growing the business.
Machine bureaucracy	Techno-structure	Standardised work processes	Old, large, rule-bound, specialised, such as a tax collection office. Plenty of procedures.
Professional bureaucracy	Operating core	Standardised skills	Decentralised, emphasis on training, and skills. Controls over recruitment and performance management will be important.
Divisional form	Middle line	Standardised outputs	Divisions are quasi-autonomous, effectively run as strategic business units. The divisional form is popular in some countries (eg Korea). Divisional performance measurement and the type of strategic control are key issues for control systems.
Adhocracy	Support staff	Mutual adjustment	An example is a film production company; lots of different projects needing different people. Many do employ accountants to keep control and all projects have a budget. Realistic budgetary and project controls are important.

3 Hierarchy as a control mechanism

FAST FORWARD

Work is a series of transactions and the purpose of hierarchy is to **reduce the cost of these transactions**.

3.1 Transaction cost analysis: the need for hierarchy

What do people actually do in organisations? One point of view argues that work is a series of transactions. For example, A asks B to type up a letter. B provides this service (and others) for A in exchange for a monthly salary. In terms of what is achieved this is exactly the same as if A worked for one organisation and B worked for an independent typing bureau: A could engage in a transaction with the typing bureau to get the letter typed.

Organisation structure, it is argued, is determined by the relative cost of the alternatives: is it cheaper to

(a) Complete the transaction through a market, or

(b) Arrange it so that it takes place within a long-term contractual relationship, such as an organisation?

Transaction costs are the costs of using arm's length market exchange to carry out exchange of goods and services. The existence of significant transaction costs can explain why organisations sometimes carry out transactions internally rather than relying on market specialists.

As the **level of complexity increases**, **transaction costs** can be **reduced** by **adopting some kind of hierarchy**. For example, this will reduce the costs of collecting sufficient information to know the best places to go in the market to conduct transactions. It will also cut the costs of entering into contracts with individuals to supply their labour: if individuals are employed on a continuing basis they can be required to perform a variety of tasks as the need arises.

As the level of complexity increases still further, however, these **savings** are **counterbalanced** by the **increasing costs of keeping control** because information tends to be lost or distorted as it passes through the hierarchy.

This reduces the possibility for market control, as identified in the previous chapter, but there are cases where outsourced services can be acquired more cheaply.

Williamson then goes on to consider the impact of transaction cost economics at different levels of complexity. Williamson distinguishes between **peer groups**, **U-form** and **M-form**.

Key terms

M-form is a multidivisional organisational structure.

U-form is a unitary or centralised organisational structure.

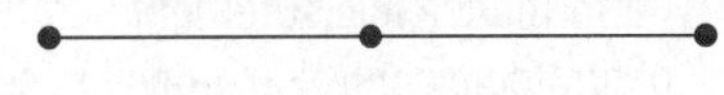

PEER GROUPS
Share expertise, information and physical assets

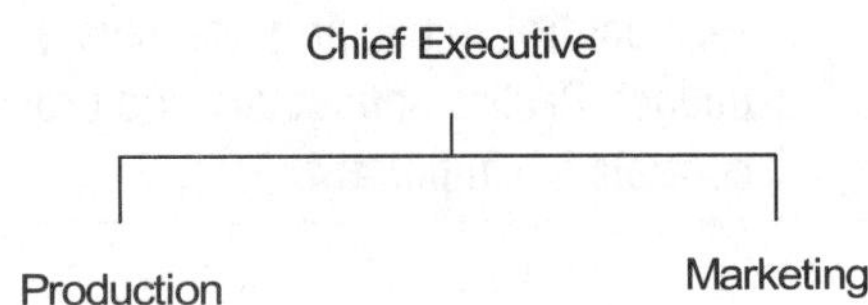

U-FORM
At least two management layers. Increasing amounts of information. Loss of information due to
(a) communication up and down hierarchy
(b) bounded rationality

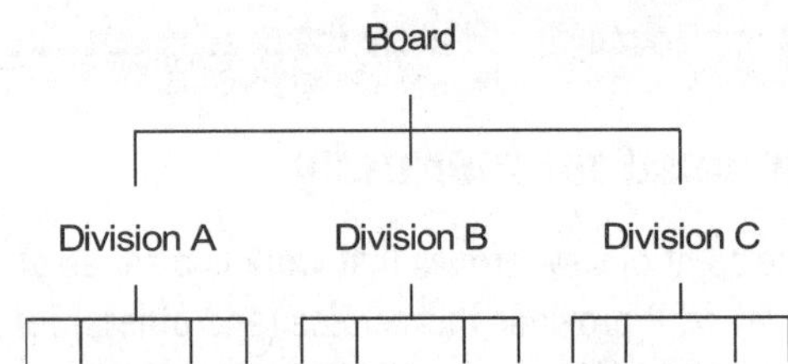

M-FORM
Day-to-day operations are carried out at divisional level. The organisation as a whole is controlled from the centre. Information loss is reduced.

What is not considered in this analysis is the changes in managers' perceptions of transaction costs. With outsourcing and 'offshoring' (outsourcing to other countries) increasingly common, it appears that the value of hierarchy in reducing transaction costs is being questioned.

4 Traditional hierarchy

FAST FORWARD

The organisation hierarchy embodies **relationships of responsibility, direction and control**. Often it is seen as a **scalar chain** of people with authority to direct the work of others. Each manager has a **span of control**, the number of people for whom he/she is directly responsible.

4.1 Scalar chain

The **scalar chain** is the hierarchy of management within an organisation Within this hierarchy there are lines of authority or **chains of command**, running from senior management vertically downwards through the organisation connecting the various levels of managers.

The chain of command not only represents the decision making hierarchy, it also provides a **defined channel for formal communication up and down the organisation**.

Decisions on chains of command must also take into account the following issues.

4.1.1 Communication effectiveness

Distortion of communications occur as **additional layers** are added to the chain of command.

4.1.2 Decision-making effectiveness

In addition to the problems of distortion, long chains of command will increase the amount of time taken for **information** to reach the **relevant decision makers**.

4.1.3 Management development and motivation

Long chains of command **distance junior managers** from thinking and decision making at the top, and limit opportunity for development into a general management role. Promotion from the bottom to the top of the chain is virtually impossible.

Staff may therefore become **frustrated** and **de-motivated**, and may leave the organisation in search of flatter organisations and greater opportunities for development and promotion.

4.2 Span of control

The **span of control** or span of management refers to the number of people directly reporting to a manager or supervisor or team leader. In other words, if a manager has five direct reports, the span of control is five.

We can describe the influences on control spans as follows.

(a) The **nature of the manager's work** load is likely to influence the span of control he or she can deal with efficiently,

(b) The **geographical dispersion** of the subordinates (particularly relevant in the case of homeworking).

(c) Whether **subordinates' work** is all of a **similar nature** (wide span possible) or diversified.

(d) The **nature of problems** that a supervisor might have to help subordinates with.

(e) The **degree of interaction** between subordinates (with close interaction, a wider span of control should be possible).

(f) The **competence and abilities** of both management and subordinates.

(g) Whether **close group cohesion** is desirable. Small groups will be more cohesive, with a better sense of team work. This would call for narrow spans of control.

(h) The **amount of help** that supervisors receive from staff functions (such as the human resources department).

4.3 Tall and flat organisations

The span of control concept has implications for the **shape** of an organisation. A **tall organisation** is one which, in relation to its size, has a large number of management levels, whereas a **flat organisation** is one which, in relation to its size, has a smaller number of hierarchical levels. A tall organisation implies a narrow span of control, and a flat organisation implies a wide span of control.

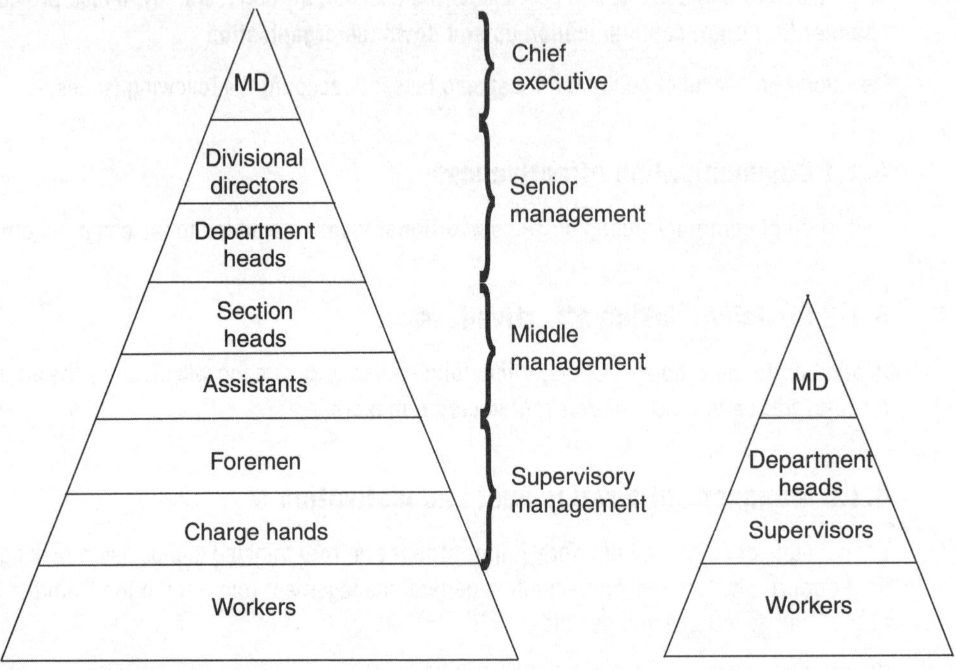

Tall and flat organisations

A tall organisation structure might be inefficient, despite the advantages of a narrow span of control and the possibility of graduated promotions. Behavioural theorists add that tall structures impose rigid supervision and control and therefore block initiative and ruin the motivation of subordinates. A wide span of control means that more authority will be delegated to subordinates. Greater discretion leads to job enrichment and motivation.

A flatter organisation structure would reduce these effects. **Flat organisations** have become more common as a result of the current fashion for **delayering and empowerment**. Moreover, some of the former information analysis and processing tasks of middle management are being replaced by information technology.

Question — Middle managers

Learning outcome: A(i)

What's good about middle managers?

Answer

(a) Middle managers **convert the grand designs** of the people at the top into real operational reality. They are a necessary co-ordinating force.

(b) Senior managers with too wide a span of control may **have too many issues** to deal with; people with a narrower range of concerns may be needed to ensure things are properly co-ordinated and executed.

(c) They keep hold of the informal 'knowledge' of the organisation, about customers, how things are done and so on.

4.4 Empowerment

Empowerment and delegation are related. **Empowerment** is the term for making workers (and particularly work teams) responsible for achieving, and even setting, work targets, with the freedom to make decisions about how they are to be achieved.

Empowerment goes hand in hand with the following developments.

(a) **Delayering** or a cut in the number of levels (and managers) in the chain of command, since responsibility previously held by middle managers is, in effect, being given to operational workers.

(b) **Flexibility**, since giving responsibility to the people closest to the products and customer encourages responsiveness - and cutting out layers of communication, decision-making and reporting speeds up the process.

(c) **New technology**, since there are more 'knowledge workers'. Such people need less supervision, being better able to identify and control the means to clearly understood ends. Better information systems also remove the mystique and power of managers as possessors of knowledge and information in the organisation.

Establishing control in an empowered culture can be achieved perhaps through:

- Some **standardisation of processes**, with clear guidelines (eg bank lending)
- **Cultural control**, so that everyone accepts the responsibilities that come with empowerment
- **Team working**

5 Design of hierarchies

FAST FORWARD

Organisation structure determines how **work is carried out**, and is the result of the **environment**, **technology** and the **organisation's** and **industry's development**.

Centralisation gives more central control at the expense of rigidity and inflexibility, perhaps reducing the long term adaptive power of the organisation.

Decentralisation reduces the benefits from standardisation: complexity imposes its own costs.

5.1 Design parameters

The overall concerns involved in designing organisational structure were described by Child (1984).

Issue	Comment
Specialisation	Should people do a 'narrow set of tasks' to benefit from specialisation; or should people be given a broad set of tasks? There are implications for motivation and job design.
Structure	'Tall' or 'flat', as discussed. Information technology reduces the purely information processing role of managers.

Issue	Comment
Departments	How should activities be grouped together?
Integration	How close should different activities or subsystems be integrated?
Control	How should work be controlled? By detailed rules and procedures? By organisation culture?

5.2 Influences on organisation structure

Organisational design or structure implies a framework or mechanism intend to do the following.

(a) To **link individuals** in an established network of relationships so that authority, responsibility and communications can be controlled, using the concept of hierarchy.

(b) To **group together** (in any appropriate way) the **tasks** required to fulfil the objectives of the organisation, and allocate them to suitable individuals or groups.

(c) To give each individual or group the **authority** required to perform the allocated functions, while **controlling behaviour and resources** in the interests of the organisation as a whole.

(d) To **co-ordinate** the objectives and activities of separate units, so that overall aims are achieved without gaps or overlaps in the flow of work required.

(e) To **facilitate the flow** of work, information and other resources required, through planning, control and other systems.

A number of variables need to be considered in the design of organisations. Essentially, it depends on the internal factors and external environment of each organisation and the design of organisational structure is a best fit between the tasks, people and environment **in the particular situation**. Here are some hypotheses about the influences on an organisation's structure.

1	The **older** the organisation, the **more formalised** its behaviour. Work is repeated, so is more easily formalised, and so is more easily measured and controlled.
2	Organisation structure reflects the age of the **industry's** foundation.
3	The **larger** the organisation, the more **elaborate** its structure. This is because there are more activities that need to be measured.
4	The **larger** the organisation, the larger the **average size of the units** within it.
5	The **larger** the organisation, the more **formalised** its behaviour (for consistency).
6	The more **sophisticated** the technology, the more **elaborate and professional** the administrative structure will be.
7	The automation of the work transforms a controlled **bureaucratic** administrative structure into an organic one. An **organic organisation** is characterised by fluid hierarchies and communications, and is the opposite of the rigid rule-bound bureaucracy. This is because procedures are incorporated into equipment routines or software. It requires specialists to manage the process, and such people tend to communicate informally.
8	The more **dynamic the environment**, the more **organic the structure** (see para 7 above).
9	The more **complex the environment**, the more **decentralised the structure**.
10	The more **diversified the markets**, the greater the propensity to split into **market based departments**.

11	Extreme environmental hostility is a force for centralisation, since central control permits rapid action.
12	Environmental disparities encourage selective decentralisation for some activities, centralisation for others.
13	The more an organisation is subject to **external control** (eg by government, holding company) the more **centralised and formalised its structure**.
14	The **power needs** of organisational members (to control others, or at least to control their own working conditions) lead to centralisation.
15	**Fashion** is a poor guide. For example, while bureaucracies are deeply unfashionable, they are often the best at doing certain kinds of work.

5.3 Departmentation

In most organisations, people are grouped into **departments**. Different patterns of departmentation are possible and the pattern selected will depend on the individual circumstances of the organisation. Some examples are given below.

Function	This is departmentation by type of work done (eg finance department, marketing department, production function).
Geographic area	Reporting relationships are organised by **geography**. In each area functional specialists report to an area boss, who ensures co-ordination.
Product/brand	A **divisional manager** for each product is responsible for marketing and production. Some divisions are effectively run as independent businesses, in which case the division's finance specialists will report to the division's head.
Customer/market segment	Reporting relationships are structured by **type of customer**.
Hybrid designs	In practice, organisations may draw on a number of these approaches. Product/brand departmentation for marketing and production, say, might be combined with a centralised R&D function.

5.4 Centralisation and decentralisation

Centralisation and decentralisation refer to the degree to which authority is delegated in an organisation – and therefore the level at which decisions are taken in the management hierarchy. There are several issues.

(a) In some businesses, authority is **centralised** and **decisions are taken at the top**. In a small business, the owner-manger may take all the decisions. However, in a hospital environment, 'life or death' decisions are taken at 'operations level'.

(b) Some businesses have **regional offices** with **decision autonomy**. In other businesses, decisions of any significance have to be referred back to head office.

(c) **Operations** might be **decentralised**, but standards might be set centrally and distributed throughout the organisation.

Arguments in favour of centralisation and decentralisation	
Pro centralisation	***Pro decentralisation/delegation***
1 Decisions are made at **one point** and so easier to co-ordinate.	1 **Avoids overburdening top managers**, in terms of workload and stress.
2 Senior managers in an organisation can take a **wider view of problems** and **consequences**.	2 **Improves motivation** of more junior managers who are given responsibility – since job challenge and entrepreneurial skills are highly valued in today's work environment.
3 Senior management can keep a **proper balance** between different departments or functions – eg by deciding on the resources to allocate to each.	3 **Greater awareness of local problems** by decision makers. Geographically dispersed organisations should often be decentralised on a regional/area basis.
4 **Quality of decisions is (theoretically) higher** due to senior managers' skills and experience.	4 **Greater speed of decision making**, and response to changing events, since no need to refer decisions upwards. This is particularly important in rapidly changing markets.
5 **Possibly cheaper**, by reducing number of managers needed and so lower costs of overheads.	5 **Helps junior managers to develop** and helps the process of transition from functional to general management.
6 **Crisis decisions are taken more quickly** at the centre, without need to refer back, get authority etc.	6 **Separate spheres of responsibility** can be identified: controls, performance measurement and accountability are better.
7 **Policies, procedures and documentation** can be standardised organisation-wide.	7 **Communication technology** allows decisions to be **made locally**, with information and input from head office if required.

Whatever system is set up, it is of paramount importance that all managers at all levels should clearly know where they fit into the organisation.

The structural trick for organisations is to balance two opposing sets of forces.

(a) The **centralising impact** of professional management, designed to produce a cohesive corporate strategy and the rational, efficient allocation of resources which will support this strategy; and

(b) The **centrifugal** effect of the forces important for fostering entrepreneurship, risk-taking and innovation.

Professional management (centralising forces)	The entrepreneurial organisation (centrifugal forces)
Focused, cohesive corporate strategy	Opportunistic, unpredictable action
Centralised information, influence	Peripheral, autonomous activity (less control)
Organise for stability (bureaucracy)	Loose structure, independent business units (flexibility)
Reward administrative ability	Reward innovative ability
Preserve *status quo*	New opportunities, change

Professional management (centralising forces)	The entrepreneurial organisation (centrifugal forces)
Rational, efficient allocation of resources	Unplannable, variable resource requirement
Management of risk	Taking of risk
Top-down decision making	Bottom-up decision making
Shared beliefs/common practices	Challenges to conventional wisdom

5.5 Centralisation and decentralisation: a false opposition

The decision to centralise or decentralise is not an either/or decision, and there are many organisations which combine both. Centralisation requires that all decisions are taken centrally, but this is not the case in many organisations.

Instead, there are a variety of approaches adopted by multinational organisations.

Centralised direction of activities	This is when head office governs everything, and all decisions must be referred back.
Dispersed centralisation	Head office functions are dispersed to different countries (eg R&D in one, finance in another). This gives the appearance of decentralisation.
Central standards and policies, local initiative	A firm might have a group policy to use Windows operating systems, for the benefits of co-ordination and standardised support services. Accounting packages tend to be uniform: HR tends to be more adapted.

5.6 Matrix and project organisation

5.6.1 Project teams

Project teams are often used where the organisation needs the contributions of specialists from different departments. A new product may need designers, engineers and marketers to work together, but they would still 'belong' to different departments.

Level in departmental hierarchy	*Department* A	B	C	D	E
1	X	(X)	X	X	(X)
2	(X)	X	X	X	X
3	X	X	(X)	X	X
4	X	X	X	(X)	X

Project team

Members of the project team (circled) would provide formal lateral lines of communication and authority, superimposed on the functional departmental structure. Leadership of the project team would probably go to one of the more senior members in the hierarchy, but this is not a requirement of the matrix structure.

5.6.2 Matrix organisation

Matrix organisation is a structure which provides for the **formalisation** of management control between different functions, whilst at the same time maintaining functional departmentation. It can be a mixture of functional, product, and territorial organisation.

A golden rule of classical management theory is **unity of command**: everyone should have only one boss. Thus, staff management can only act in an advisory capacity, leaving authority in the province of line management alone. Matrix management may possibly be thought of as a reaction against the classical form of bureaucracy by establishing a structure of dual command.

It is also possible to have a product management structure superimposed on top of a functional departmental structure in a matrix; product or brand managers may be in order to bring the product on to the market and achieve sales targets, ie:

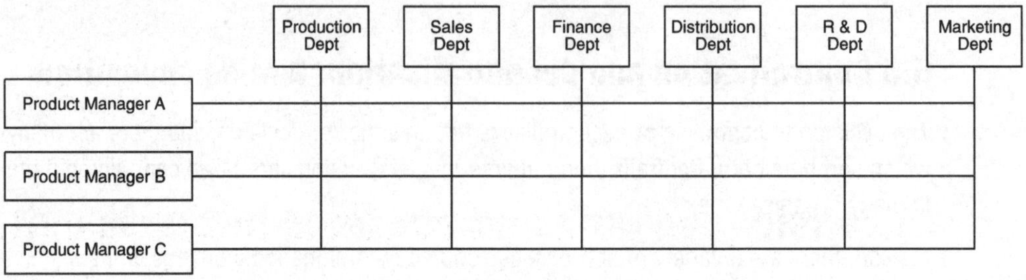

	Production Dept	Sales Dept	Finance Dept	Distribution Dept	R & D Dept	Marketing Dept
Product Manager A						
Product Manager B						
Product Manager C						

Matrix

Note. The product managers may each have their own marketing team; in which case the marketing department itself would be small or non-existent. **Matrix organisation** institutionalises this approach and takes it further.

Matrix organisation means that **subordinates have two (or more) superiors**, in the sense that they must report to both a functional manager and a project manager. However, a subordinate cannot easily take *orders* from two or more bosses. The authority of each would have to be carefully defined. Even so, good co-operation would still be necessary.

Advantages	Disadvantages
• **It is flexible**. Members of project teams adapt quickly to a new challenge or new task, and develop an attitude which is geared to accepting change. It may be short-term, as with project teams or readily amended. Flexibility should facilitate efficient operations in the face of change. • It should **improve communication** within the organisation. • Dual authority gives the **organisation multiple orientation**. For example, a functional departmentation will often be production-oriented, whereas the superimposition of product managers will provide the organisation with some market orientation. • It provides a **structure for allocating responsibility** to managers for end-results, rather than merely fulfilling processes. • It provides for **inter-disciplinary co-operation** and a mixing of skills and expertise.	• **Dual or triple authority** threatens a conflict between functional managers, product/project managers and nation/country managers. • **One individual with two or more bosses** is **more likely** to **suffer role stress** at work. • It is **complex and thus more costly** – eg product managers are additional jobs which would not be required in a simple structure of functional departmentation. There may be other ways of improving communication or obtaining the benefits than a complex structure.

Setting up a matrix organisation often implies the existence of a **project-based culture**. It is therefore worthwhile to spend a paragraph explaining the differences between a **project culture** and an **operations environment** in which most activities are part of a regular routine.

(a) The **operations** environment is (relatively) stable, whereas the project environment is flexible, because all projects are unique.

(b) Operations, through **habitual incremental improvement** or the learning/experience curve, become efficient more or less automatically over time, whereas projects, having no precedent, can be measured against genuine value-added effectiveness.

(c) In an operations environment, people fulfil roles defined by precedent, and so can lose sight of their objectives; project teams must be goal-orientated.

(d) All projects carry the risk of failure because they are breaking new boundaries; in operations, previous experience means that the level of risk is much reduced. In essence, therefore, projects are risk management; operations are *status quo* management.

6 Divisionalisation and strategic business units

FAST FORWARD

Divisionalisation is an approach where some of the activities of the organisation are run autonomously from other activities. These can relate to particular **products and markets**. It means the head office does not manage everything and that the divisions are accountable for their performance.

6.1 Divisionalisation

The m-form, or **divisionalised** form has been adopted to reduce the level of complexity in large organisations. Responsibility is devolved to divisions which have a clear business focus, but which, according to Mintzberg, take on a bureaucratic type aspect.

The classic model is a conglomerate with a number of strategic business units, each occupying a different niche in the industry and market, or working in different markets.

Strategic business units are run as separate businesses, with local autonomy.

A division can be constructed on the bases below.

Geography	Not all multinational firms operate as genuinely global or boundaryless companies. Instead, they have regional or national operating units. The challenge is to avoid duplication of effort and to enable both sides to learn from each other.
Product-market	Big car manufacturers have divisions for cars and trucks
Customer	For example, divisions for business customers and for personal customers
Technology	Different divisions may use different information systems

Divisionalisation is a solution to the problem of too much complexity, by driving down responsibility to a lower level.

Mintzberg argues that the **divisional form emerges when the 'middle line' exerts a pull to 'balkanise'** - in other words to split into small self-managed units. Mintzberg identifies a number of problems in divisionalisation.

(a) Divisions are **not usually exposed to capital markets**: they are funded by the holding company. Divisions are therefore not directly answerable to those who ultimately reward performance.

(b) Central management tends to **usurp divisional profit** through management charges and so on.

(c) Divisions **may not be completely independent**: is it fair to measure and compare a division's performance in terms of, say, profit, if the division is forced to pay a centrally imposed transfer price?

(d) Divisionalisation assumes that head office can allocate resources better than the market.

(e) It can make the **investment hard to value**.

(f) Where divisions are not interdependent there are **problems in transfer pricing**.

6.2 Implications of divisionalisation

Setting up a separately managed unit (**federal decentralisation**) alters the way in which its activities are controlled.

When federal decentralisation of authority occurs, **head office managers** will cease to be involved in many of the routine planning and control activities of the organisation. Their function will become one of **strategic development, co-ordination and control**. As a consequence, they will receive planning and control information in much less detail than before and they will provide much less specific planning and control information to the managers of the separate 'divisions' or business units.

Managers of decentralised units will be the focal point for much of the **routine planning and control information**.

(a) They will receive strategic planning or overall budget guidelines from head office, but will formulate **detailed plans** themselves, and inform head office management by presenting budgets.

(b) Routine **control data** will be reported to unit managers rather than head office.

(c) Most **planning and control decisions at an operational level** will be taken by unit managers without reporting them to head office.

6.3 Problems of divisionalisation

(a) For **central management**, there will be a **reduction in the amount of information** that they receive about each unit's operations. Reports to them from unit managers will be selected and edited. With this information, central management must try to apply overall strategic planning and control measures. There could be some danger that head office managers will **lose touch** with what is happening at an operational level.

(b) For unit managers, information about their own unit's performance should be readily accessible, but the **flow of information about the organisation** as a whole, or about other units within the organisation, will be **restricted**. Some information will come from head office, and inter-divisional information flows might be established, but it might nevertheless be difficult for unit managers to **assess the contribution of their own unit to the organisation as a whole**.

Question — **Autonomy**

Learning outcome: A(iii)

(a) What do you understand by the term 'divisional autonomy'?

(b) What are the likely behavioural consequences of a head office continually imposing its own decisions on divisions?

Answer

(a) The term refers to the **right of a division to govern itself**, that is, the freedom to make decisions without consulting a higher authority first and without interference from a higher body.

(b) Decentralisation recognises that **those closest to a job are the best equipped to say how it should be done** and that people tend to **perform to a higher standard if they are given responsibility**. Centrally imposed decisions are likely to make managers feel that they do not really have any authority and therefore that they cannot be held responsible for performance. They will therefore make less effort to perform well.

6.3.1 Comparing units

Head office management may wish to compare units in order to rank performance or perhaps to decide where cuts should be made.

The general rule is to **compare like with like** (comparing a retail branch with a distribution centre is unlikely to provide much useful information). Even if units seem similar, however, various **factors need to be considered**.

(a) The **amount of resources** devoted to the units may differ.

(b) There may be **local differences** (use of different computer hardware or software packages).

(c) **Inputs and outputs may be difficult to define**.

(d) Comparisons will only be valid **if the figures reported are utterly reliable** but this is highly unlikely in practice.

(e) The possibility of the **manipulation of figures** must be considered.

6.3.2 Problems with transfer prices

When separate units depend on each other for output, the transfer price of goods and services between divisions is a focal issue.

(a) One profit centre manager might be **reluctant** to transfer goods and services to another division, arguing that he is **not paid enough for the work**.

(b) Alternatively, one profit centre manager might **refuse to accept more transfers** of goods from another division, arguing that it is too costly or unprofitable to take the extra transfers.

Ideally, a transfer price should be **set at a level that overcomes these problems**.

(a) The transfer price should provide an **'artificial' selling price that enables the transferring division to earn a return for its efforts**, and the **receiving division to incur a cost for benefits received**.

(b) The transfer price should be set at a level that enables **profit centre performance to be measured 'commercially'**. This means that the transfer price should be a **fair commercial price**.

(c) The transfer price, if possible, should encourage profit centre managers to **agree** on the **amount of goods and services to be transferred**, which will also be at a **level that is consistent with the aims of the organisation as a whole**, in particular the aim of maximising company profits.

When authority is decentralised in an organisation to the extent that unit managers **negotiate transfer prices** with each other, the agreed price may be finalised from **a mixture of accounting arithmetic, politics and compromise**.

Even so, **inter-departmental disputes** about transfer prices are likely to arise and these may need the **intervention or mediation of head office** to settle the problem. Head office management may then impose a price which maximises the profit of the company as a whole. The more head office has to impose its own decisions on separately managed units, the less decentralisation of authority there will be and the less effective the system of accounting will be for motivating divisional managers.

Question

Divisionalisation

Learning outcome: A(iii)

Company Y began manufacturing a single project. As the company grew, it adopted a typical functional structure. More recently, as a result of both internal development and a series of acquisitions, it has become a multi-product company serving diverse markets.

What are the limitations of Company Y's functional structure, given its recent development into a multi-product company? What type of organisation structure might be more appropriate?

Answer

Problems of functional structure

A functional structure organises staff and work by professional speciality, all the accountants working for the finance director and all the sales people working for the sales director, for example. This is a logical approach and suitable for a small- to medium-sized company, since it enhances work standards by expert planning and supervision.

However, it tends to **preclude a multidisciplinary approach** to the management of complex projects; it can lead to poor interfunctional co-operation in simple matters; and it can even be a major cause of conflict within the organisation. A further problem is that it complicates the allocation of costs, hampering the identification of profitable and unprofitable products.

These problems are likely to be **particularly relevant** to the **situation Company Y** finds itself in.

Company Y's situation

The directors of Company Y may find that the **product/brand division** is more appropriate for its needs. The company would be organised into a number of divisions, each with responsibility for a coherent group of products and markets.

Advantages of divisionalisation

The overall aim would be to achieve **specialised expertise** and **economy of effort**. Each division would resemble a complete business, with its own management and functional specialists, and significant responsibility for its operations and financial success. Some element of central service may be retained: purchasing is often controlled centrally in order to achieve bulk buying economies, for example.

From the strategic point of view, such an organisation has several other advantages. It **enables costs** and **revenues to be analysed easily**. The overall business can, in fact, be treated as a portfolio of assets, with resources being directed to the ones with the best prospects.

The management of each division can keep a **very close eye on its own markets** and respond rapidly to problems and opportunities. The autonomy given to the people at the top of each division can be highly motivating.

An important HRM consideration is the **expanded opportunity** for practical experience at the strategic level within a division. Being in charge of a division is excellent training for a manager with high potential.

Problems with divisionalisation

There are several problems with the idea of divisionalisation that may be relevant here.

First, it may be **difficult**, if not impossible, to **identify clearly discrete product/market** areas suitable for exploitation by independent divisions. There are likely to be loose ends that have to be disposed of or swept up in a poor fit.

Also, as Company Y has grown partly by acquisition, there may be **major dislocation of premises** and staff if it seems necessary to form divisions from elements of more than one original company. There is clear potential for internal conflict here.

Divisions will **require able managers**, initially to set them up and later to run them. It may be that Company Y has plenty of such people, but, equally, it may not. Even the managers it thinks it can rely on may respond poorly to their isolation and responsibility.

The control of divisionalised companies raises two important problem areas. First, each division must have its own **functionally organised bureaucracy**, both to operate its own internal controls and to prepare the control reports the corporate headquarters will require. This can represent a significant duplication and reduplication of effort. Second, there will be a tendency towards short-termism in the divisions unless those control reports give due weight to the long-term view.

A final point is that the **divisions will be in competition for scarce resources**, including promotion for their heads. This can lead to undesirable political activity such as lobbying and a general lack of co-operation between divisions.

7 New organisation structures and problems of control

FAST FORWARD

Attacks on hierarchy, have developed out of **technology** and a **changed perception** of the relative cost of hierarchy compared to market and process mechanisms. Horizontal organisations require that control is exercised over the process as a whole. Similarly, there is a growth in business networks and outsourcing relationships.

Organisation structures are responding to the problems of control, as follows.

Outsourcing	Third party firms take over some functions they can perform more effectively than the firm outsourcing the work.
Growth of knowledge work	'Today's economy runs on knowledge and most companies work assiduously to capitalise on that fact. They use cross-functional teams, customer- or product-focused business units, and workgroups.' (Wenger and Snyder, 2000).
Delayering	A reduction in the number of levels in the management hierarchy.
Communications technology	Organisational life has been revolutionised by email and network technology.
Core/periphery	Some firms have been changing the structure of their workforces for the sake of greater flexibility, eg a core of full-time permanent staff and periphery part-timers and temporary or contract workers.

Earlier, it was mentioned that hierarchies developed to minimise transactions costs. In recent years increasing technological sophistication and the growth of IT, has meant that the value of hierarchy is, inevitably, questioned. Empowerment, discussed earlier, is only one aspect of this process.

7.1 Business process re-engineering and the horizontal organisation

7.1.1 BPR Business Process Re-engineering (BPR)

Key term

Business Process Re-engineering (BPR) means re-organising the activities of an organisation in response to the demands of the modern business environment.

There are three common themes.

(a) The **need to make radical changes to the entire organisation**. Changing conditions 'impact all functions of the company and lead to a radically different way of doing business, sweeping away the previous methods.'

(b) The **need to change functional hierarchies**: 'existing hierarchies have evolved into functional departments that encourage functional excellence but which do not work well together in meeting customers' requirements; in particular, they incur excess cost, are too slow and create quality problems by creating inter-departmental interfaces.'

(c) The **need to address the problem of fragmented staff roles**: 'roles have become specialised with the result that staff are only responsible for a small part of an overall task. This can result in loss of accountability for a finished task, de-skilling of work and the need for highly complex scheduling systems.'

Properly implemented BPR may help an organisation to **reduce costs, improve customer services, cut down on the complexity of the business and improve internal communication**. At best it may bring about **new insights into the objectives of the organisation and how best to achieve them**.

At worst, BPR is simply a **synonym for squeezing costs** (usually through redundancies). Some organisations have taken it too far and become so 'lean' that they cannot respond when demand begins to rise. This is possibly because the spirit of BPR is not understood in the first place and also because senior management lose enthusiasm after the first wave of BPR has achieved short-term results.

7.1.2 The horizontal organisation

Based on business process reengineering, the horizontal organisation is a technique which breaks down 'vertical' departmental boundaries, and claims to eliminate the hierarchies of command and control. Instead management is based on processes.

Characteristic	Comment
Structure	Organisation structure is based on cross-functional processes rather than tasks or geography.
Team	Teams, not individuals, are the basis of this approach.
Ownership	A process owner is responsible for the whole process.
Customers	Customers drive the process: the process owner puts customer-performance first.

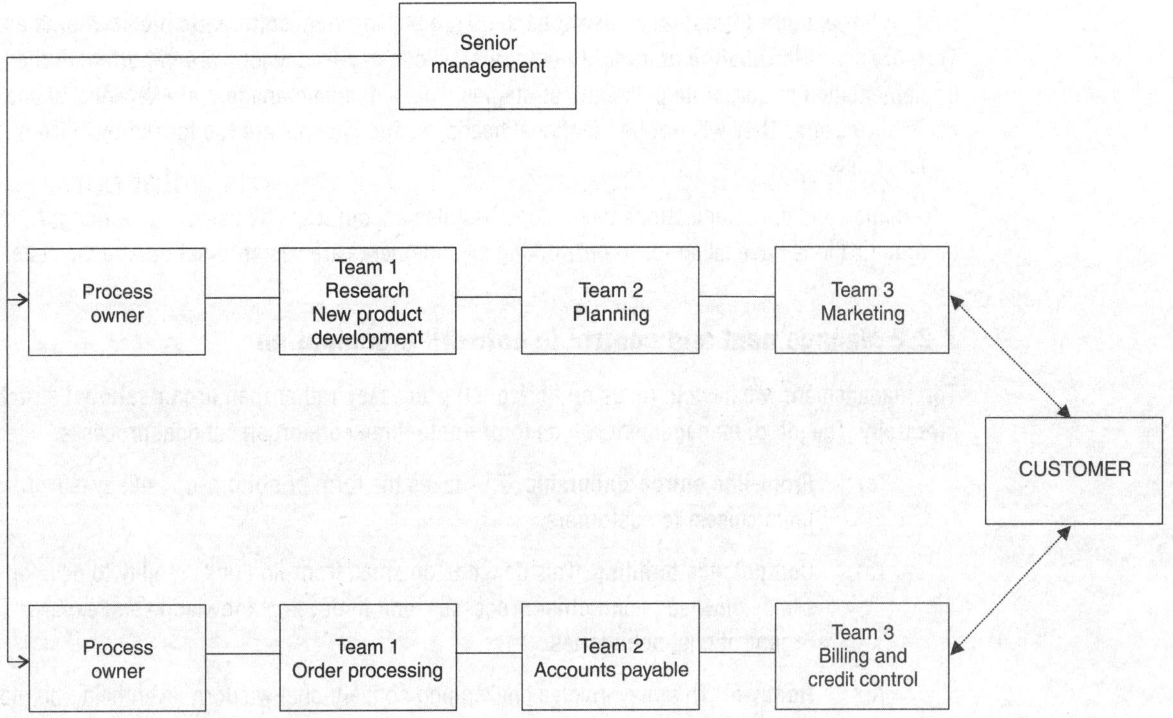

Horizontal structure

The process does focus the organisation on the customer. However, the customer may be at the receiving end of several **'core' processes**.

The basic problem remains as to the locus of control. Arguably, the process owner should be the person or group that controls the process. Where, however, a matrix structure in the place, the responsibility for taking control action is not always clear.

7.2 Internal networks, the management process and the management role

7.2.1 Networks and co-ordination

Some trends in organisational structure are listed below: all of them remove the activities of the organisation from hierarchical control.

These trends possibly reach their extreme form in the **adhocracy**. This gives us a very good backdrop for the role of networks and networking. The **adhocracy** (Mintzberg, 1979, p. 431) is a fluid organisation requiring many forms of co-ordination.

(a) Specialists are **deployed in market-based project teams** which group together and disperse as and when a project arises and ends. Co-ordination is informal. The adhocracy relies on the expertise of its members. (The mix of skills is important. For example, a film is made by a director, actors, camera people, set designers etc.) Managers do not plan or supervise, but co-ordinate.

(b) In this case, **networks of contacts** are vital for the **effective conduct of organisational decision making and activity**. People and skills, from within and external to the organisation, are important and need to be contacted and brought into project teams. Such networks of contacts and skills might span the boundaries of the organisation. Networking is necessary to draw people into temporary or semi-permanent work arrangements for planning, decision making and the production process. Where expertise or information is an important commodity, then networking is a means of obtaining such information.

Even in **large**, **more formal**, **organisations** there are still informal **communication patterns and networks**. They **ensure co-ordination of middle managers**, whose day-to-day jobs are important in the implementation of corporate plans and strategies. These middle managers are key tactical and operational decision-makers. They will not be functional heads, as such people are too far removed from the decisions under review.

Information and communications technology has also encouraged the use of networking. As the costs of communications have fallen, such networking arrangements are easier to set up and facilitate.

7.2.2 Management and control in network organisation

Top management will have to focus on **horizontal processes** rather than **organisational structure and hierarchy**. The job of management will be to promote three core organisational processes.

(a) **Front-line entrepreneurship**. This takes the form of bottom-up initiatives from operating units closest to customers.

(b) **Competence building**. This depends on small front-line units' ability to develop scarce skills, knowledge and other processes, and to develop knowledge and expertise across organisational boundaries.

(c) **Renewal**. This may involve challenging conventional wisdom, even being disruptive in certain cases.

Systems of planning and control enabled companies to grow and helped managers deal with sprawling enterprises. However, the systems that allowed managers to control employees also inhibited creativity and initiative.

The **direct personal contact** that top-level managers maintain with others not only keeps those at the top appraised of the real issues and challenges their businesses face but also gives them the opportunity to shape front-line managers' responses to those issues. Systems, no matter how sophisticated, can never replace the richness of **close personal communication** and contact between top-level and front-line managers. We shall look at this again when we consider in Part C how managers obtain information in order to review control and risk management in their organisation.

7.3 External networks and alliances

7.3.1 External networks

In many industries, collaborative ventures and strategic alliances are becoming increasingly common. Whilst some strategic alliances are relatively clear cut, other forms of networking activity and organisational relationships require new forms of dealing with the end-customer.

Here is an example of the relative complexities of networks.

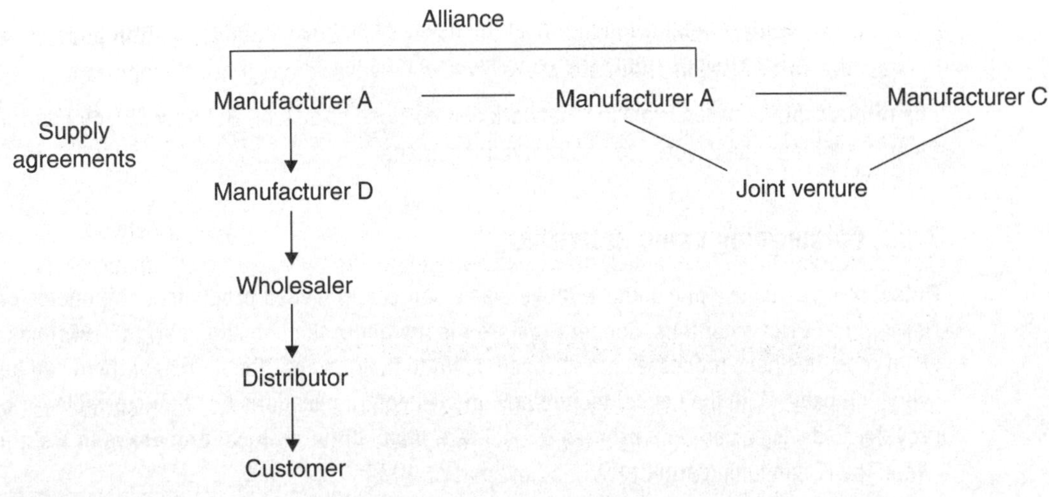

Network

As we can see, there are many types of organisational forms that can be developed. Networks display **horizontal** (eg joint ventures) and **vertical** (supply chain) linkages.

There is no broadly accepted typology However it is possible to model types of network on the axes of environmental volatility or turbulence and the type of network **relationship**.

(a) **Volatility** or **environmental turbulence** relates to the degree and speed of change in the external environment to which the organisation is exposed.

(b) The type of network relationship can range from the **collaborative** to mainly **transactional**. A **collaborative** network involves a great deal of co-operation, which may be enshrined in joint venture agreements. In a **transactional relationship**, there is no commitment to the long term.

		Environmental turbulence	
		Low	*High*
Relationship	*Collaborative*	Virtual network	Flexible
	Transactional	Value-added	Hollow

Types of network

1. A **hollow network** combines high environmental volatility with a transactional-based approach. The organisation draws heavily on other organisations to satisfy customer needs. Such organisations can be quite small, but have a large number of contacts. For example, in the publishing industry, there are print brokers who will deal with a variety of printing needs by accessing a network of subcontractors.

2. **Flexible network**. This is a collaborative network existing in conditions of high environmental turbulence. The links between organisations are of a long-term nature, but are on specific projects. For example, pharmaceuticals companies aim to build up alliances with biotechnology firms (as their competence bases are different).

3. **Value-added network**. This is typical of many Japanese firms. In this case, certain specific value added items are outsourced to specialists. This is typical of outsourcing arrangements. There is nothing particularly new in this, in principle. Publishers have subcontracted printing to specialist printing firms for many years. The outsourcer is performing a standard service.

4. **Virtual network**. Environmental volatility is low but the organisation wants to build collaborative relationships with other organisations. A firm wishes to use the network to

achieve 'adaptability to meet the needs of segmented markets through long-term partnerships rather than internal investment'.

The **relationship** between firms in a network can be close or distant. But how do you control a network? Clearly, a lot must be devoted to contract management.

7.3.2 Outsourcing value activities

Outsourcing is the use of external suppliers as a source of finished products, components or services. Research by PricewaterhouseCoopers (before the merger of the consulting arm to IBM) has found that when most business processes are stripped down to their basics, about 70% of them can be found in every company. With the help of technology and telecommunications it is now possible for one service provider to devise a common process to deal with **many different local processes in a single location**. (Note: the IT consulting arm of PWC is now part of IBM.)

As governments have found, outsourcing has to be managed carefully. Arguably the outsourcer is relying on the management of the company contracted to do the work to control matters properly. Because of the contractual nature of the relationship, a careful specification of the rights and duties of both parties, and a specification of key results to be achieved is needed. This can add an extra layer of bureaucracy.

We shall examine outsourcing in the context of internal audit and IT functions later in this text.

Case Study

The maintenance of the infrastructure of the London Underground is subcontracted for a 30 year period to three private sector companies. Newspapers reports described a complicated mathematical formula to determine the precise level of platform cleanliness needed to avoid a fine.

8 Organisation culture

FAST FORWARD

Culture is the **shared pattern** of **behaving and thinking**. As part of a control system, it identifies what is 'unacceptable' behaviour, and shows common responses. It is therefore a source of control. As it involves shared attitudes, it is also manifested in different attitudes to risk.

8.1 What is culture?

Key term

Culture is the sum total of the beliefs, knowledge, attitudes of mind and customs to which people are exposed. It is the 'the pattern of basic assumptions that a given group has invented, discovered, or developed, in learning to cope with its problems of external adaptation and internal integration, and that have worked well enough to be considered valid and, therefore, to be taught to new members as the correct way to perceive, think and feel in relation to these problems.'

Different writers have identified different types of culture, based on particular aspects of organisation and management. Again, all have relevance for control in the organisation.

8.2 Handy: power, role, task and person cultures

Charles Handy discusses four cultures and their related structures. Handy recognises that while an organisation might reflect a single culture, it may also have elements of different cultures appropriate to the structure and circumstances of different units in the organisation.

8.2.1 The power culture

Found mainly in **smaller organisations**, this is where power and influence stem from a **central source**, through whom all communication, decisions and control are channelled. The organisation, since it is **not rigidly structured**, is capable of adapting quickly to meet change; however, the success in adapting will depend on the luck or judgement of the key individuals who make the decisions. **Political competition** for a share of power is rife, and emotional behaviour is encouraged by the **personality cult surrounding the leader**.

8.2.2 The role culture or bureaucracy

Such organisations have a **formal structure** and operate by well-established **rules and procedures**. **Job descriptions** establish definite tasks for each person's job and **procedures** are established for many work routines, for communication between individuals and departments, and for the settlement of disputes and appeals. Individuals are required to perform their job to the full but not to overstep the boundaries of their authority. A wide variety of different personalities are capable of doing the same job and so job structure and formal relationships tend to be more important than individual personalities.

8.2.3 The task culture

This is reflected in a **matrix organisation**, in **project teams** and **task forces**. The principal concern in a task culture is to **get the job done**; therefore the individuals who are important are the experts with the ability to accomplish a particular aspect of the task. Such organisations are flexible and constantly changing as tasks are accomplished and new needs arise. Innovation and creativity are highly prized. **Job satisfaction** tends to be high owing to the degree of individual participation, communication and group identity.

8.2.4 The person culture

This is an organisation whose purpose is to **serve the interests** of individuals within it. Organisations designed on these lines are rare, but some individuals may use any organisation to suit their own purposes; to gain experience, further their careers or express themselves.

The descriptions above interrelate four different strands.

- The individual
- The type of the work the organisation does
- The culture of the organisation
- The environment

Organisational effectiveness depends on an appropriate fit of all four strands.

8.3 Culture, strategy and attitudes to risk

Miles and Snow analyse three strategic cultures and provide some further useful terminology.

Culture	Detail
Defenders	Firms with this culture like low risks, secure markets, and tried and trusted solutions. These companies have cultures whose stories and rituals reflect historical continuity and consensus. Decision taking is relatively formalised. (There is a stress on 'doing things right', that is, efficiency.)
Prospectors	Organisations where the dominant beliefs are more to do with results (doing the right things, that is, effectiveness). Prospectors take risks. They are decentralised. Plans are broad but not detailed. They have short lines of communication.
Analysers	Try to balance risk and profits. They use a core of stable products and markets as a source of earnings to move into innovative prospector areas. Analysers follow change, but do not initiate it.
Reactors	Do not have viable strategies.

Deal and Kennedy (*Corporate Cultures*) consider cultures to be a **function of the willingness of employees to take risks, and how quickly they get feedback on whether they got it right or wrong**.

8.4 Culture and the environment

Denison maps the strategic orientation of organisation culture on a grid, to assess the **relationship of culture with the environment**. There are two dimensions.

(a) **How orientated** is the firm to the environment rather than to its internal workings?
(b) To what extent does the environment **offer stability or change**?

Cultural types are recommended as follows.

		Orientation	
		Internal	**External**
Environmental responses required	**Stability**	**Consistency**	**Mission**
	Change/flexibility	**Involvement**	**Adaptability**

A brief description of each type of culture is now provided.

Type of culture	Description
Consistency culture	This exists in a stable environment, and its structure is well integrated. Management are preoccupied with efficiency. Such cultures are characterised by formal ways of behaviour. Predictability and reliability are valued. This has some features in common with the role culture.
Mission culture	The environment is relatively stable, but the organisation is orientated towards its key elements (eg 'customers'). A mission culture, whereby members' work activities are given meaning and value, is appropriate (eg, hospitals).
Involvement culture	This is similar to clan control identified in the previous chapter. The basic premise behind it is that the satisfaction of employees' needs is necessary for them to provide optimum performance. An example might be an orchestra, whose performance depends on each individual. Involvement and participation create a greater sense of commitment and hence performance.
Adaptability culture	The company's strategic focus is on the external environment, which is in a state of change. Corporate values encourage inquisitiveness and interest in the external environment. Fashion companies are an example: ideas come from a variety of sources. Customer needs are fickle and change rapidly.

8.5 Cultural control

This means **applying control** (through firm central direction, and shared values and beliefs) but also **allowing maximum individual autonomy and even competition between individuals or groups within the organisation**. Peters and Waterman call this **loose-tight management**. Culture, peer pressure, a focus on action, customer-orientation and so on are 'non-aversive' ways of exercising control over employees. In other words, the control system used is cultural control.

The implication of this for work behaviour affects the way in which individuals can be motivated and managed. As Peters and Waterman argue, a strong **'central faith'** (a mission) which binds the organisation together as a whole, should be **combined with a strong emphasis on individual self-expression, contribution and success**: individuals should be given at least the **'illusion of (personal) control'** over their destinies, while still being given a **sense of belonging and a secure, perceived meaningful framework in which to act**.

Chapter Roundup

- People can have **fundamentally different understandings** as to what an organisation is for. This can mean that the control system in the organisation can appear to mean something quite different depending on the perspective of those being controlled.
- An organisation generally exists to **co-ordinate working activities** in some way. The **type of co-ordination employed**, and the **type of supervision** and control over the work process, influence the type of organisation it is, and its control systems.
- **Work** is a series of transactions and the purpose of hierarchy is to **reduce the cost of these transactions**.
- The organisation hierarchy embodies relationships of **responsibility, direction and control**. Often it is seen as a **scalar chain** of people with authority to direct the work of others. Each manager has a **span of control**, the number of people for whom he/she is directly responsible.
- Organisation structure determines how work is carried out, and is the result of the **environment**, **technology** and the **organisation's and industry's development**.
- **Centralisation** gives more central control at the expense of rigidity and inflexibility, perhaps reducing the long term adaptive power of the organisation.
- **Decentralisation** reduces the benefits from standardisation: complexity imposes its own costs.
- **Divisionalisation** is an approach where some of the activities of the organisation are run autonomously from other activities. These can relate to particular **products and markets**. It means the head office does not manage everything and that the divisions are accountable for their performance.
- Attacks on hierarchy have developed out of **technology** and a **changed perception** of the relative cost of hierarchy compared to market and process mechanisms. Horizontal organisations require that control is exercised over the process as a whole. Similarly, there is a growth in business networks and outsourcing relationships.
- **Culture** is the shared pattern of **behaving and thinking**. As part of a control system, it identifies what is 'unacceptable' behaviour, and shows common responses. It is therefore a source of control. As it involves shared attitudes, it is also manifested in different attitudes to risk.

Quick Quiz

1 What is useful when discussing control in considering organisations as 'psychic prisons' (in Morgan's categorisation)?

2 What type of control is exercised by the technostructure and the strategic apex respectively?

3 What issues might be taken into account when designing a 'chain of command'.

4 What is the purpose of management in an empowered culture? Are there any issues for control?

5 According to Mintzberg, divisionalisation results from a split into self-managed units. What are the main problems for control at the centre?

6 In a horizontal organisation, organisational structure is based around .... as opposed to tasks or geography. Control is likely to be exercised, if at all, by a ....

7 How can senior managers keep in touch in a delayered organisation?

8 What are the main issue in managing networks?

Answers to Quick Quiz

1 People's reaction to their control might depend on their personal psychology. Some hate control, others might welcome it as a source of personal security.

2 The technostructure standardises work. The strategic apex is more likely to be interested in outputs, for example a target level of profits achieved from a division.

3
- Communication effectiveness
- Decision making effectiveness
- Management development and motivation.

4 To create the right environment for customer service, and to act as facilitators rather than directors. It implies a limitation to the type of control action that managers can take.

5 The main control problems are that head office at the top may be less aware of what is going on, and the flow of information may be filtered on the way up. Divisions are not directly exposed to capital markets.

6 Cross-functional processes. Process owner

7 Personal communication

8 Networks ultimately depend on good relationships underpinned by robust contracts. Goal congruence helps too.

Now try the question below from the Exam Question Bank

Number	Level	Marks	Time
Q3	Examination	25	45 mins

4

Management accounting control systems

Introduction

The previous chapters covered control systems generally, and recognised that the wider context of control involves people management and organisation structure. In this chapter we narrow the focus to control systems and management accounting. The purpose of management accounting in control and some of the motivational implications are explored. We also discuss the influences on management accounting data.

Topic list	Learning outcomes	Syllabus references	Ability required
1 Management accounting and control	A (iv)	A (3)	Evaluation
2 Contingency theory	A (iv)	A (3)	Evaluation
3 Strategy and management control	A (iv)	A (3)	Evaluation
4 Limitations of contingency theory	A (iv)	A (3)	Evaluation
5 Design of management accounting systems	A (iv)	A (3), (5), (6)	Evaluation
6 Management accounting and organisational culture	A (iv)	A (3)	Evaluation
7 Organisation structure and budget centre selection	A (iv)	A (3), (5)	Evaluation
8 Participation in budgeting	A (iv)	A (3), (5)	Evaluation
9 Evaluating the accounting function	A (iv)	A (3), (5), (6)	Evaluation

1 Management accounting and control

FAST FORWARD

Management accounting developed from cost accounting, for **scorekeeping**, **directing management attention** and **problem solving**. It has since branched out into behavioural aspects.

1.1 The development of management accounting

A classic study in the 1950s by **Simon *et al*** was typical of the general agreement at that time that the **management process was one of decision making, planning and control.** Simon identified **three attributes** of what could by now be called **management accounting information** as follows.

- It should be useful for **scorekeeping** - seeing how well the organisation is doing overall.
- It should be **attention-directing** - indicating problem areas that need to be investigated.
- It should be useful for **problem-solving** - providing a means of evaluating alternative responses to the situations in which the organisation finds itself.

Robert Anthony made what could be the most important contribution in his 1965 book *Planning and Control Systems*. He suggested that there are **three levels or tiers within an organisation's decision-making hierarchy.**

Key terms

Strategic planning is 'the process of deciding on objectives of the organisation, on changes in these objectives, on the resources used to attain these objectives, and on the policies that are to govern the acquisition, use and disposition of these resources'.

Management control is 'the process by which managers assure that resources are obtained and used effectively and efficiently in the accomplishment of the organisation's objectives'.

Operational control is 'the process of assuring that specific tasks are carried out effectively and efficiently'.

Management control is sometimes called **tactics** or **tactical planning**. Operational control is sometimes called **operational planning**.

1.2 Behavioural aspects

Research into the behavioural aspects of budgeting did not begin in earnest until the late 1960s. Particularly influential was the work of Anthony **Hopwood**, who carried out empirical studies of the interaction between people and budgets.

Hopwood identified three distinct styles of evaluating managers, which we discuss later in this chapter. Hopwood favours the profit-conscious style. He recognises that:

> 'the precise balance of costs and benefits associated with these three styles might well be different for the control of a stable technologically simple situation ... than for an uncertain and highly complex situation'.

This is another way of saying '**it all depends'**, 'there is no **'one best way'**.

Moreover, since these developments the scope of management accounting has extended into more general concerns of performance measurement, strategic management accounting and organisational performance.

2 Contingency theory

FAST FORWARD

Management accounting in an organisation is influenced by the **environment**, **organisation structure**, the **size of the organisation**, the **technology** it uses and the **culture of the organisation**. **Uncertainty** is the major factor in the environment.

Key term

Contingency theory is the 'hypothesis that there can be no universally applicable best practice in the design of organisational units or of control systems such as management accounting systems. The efficient design and functioning of systems is dependent on an awareness by the system designer of the specific environmental factors which influence their operation, such as organisational structure, technology base and market situation'.

(CIMA *Official Terminology)*

The major factors that have been identified are classified by Emmanuel *et al* as follows.

(a) **The environment**

- Its degree of predictability
- The degree of competition faced
- The number of different product markets faced
- The degree of hostility exhibited by competing organisations

(b) **Organisational structure**

- Size
- Interdependence of parts
- Degree of decentralisation
- Availability of resources

(c) **Technology**

- The nature of the production process
- The routineness/complexity of the production process
- How well the relationship between ends and means is understood
- The amount of variety in each task that has to be performed

The following example is a highly simplistic application of the theory but it may help you to grasp ideas that are generally presented in a highly abstract way by accounting academics.

2.1 Example: contingency theory and management accounting systems

Stable makes three different products, X, Y and Z. It has never had any competitors. Every month the managing director receives a report from the management accountant in the following form (the numbers are for illustration only).

	£
Sales	10,000
Production costs	5,000
Gross profit	5,000
Administrative costs	1,000
Net profit	4,000

A few months ago **another company**, Turbulence & Co, **entered the market** for products X and Y, **undercutting the prices** charged by Stable. Turbulence has now started to **win some of Stable's customers.**

The managing director asks the management accountant for **information about the profitability of its own versions of products X and Y**. Sales information is easy to reanalyse, but to analyse production information in this way requires a **new system of coding** to be introduced. Eventually the management accountant comes up with the following report.

	X	*Y*	*Z*	*Total*
	£	£	£	£
Sales	3,000	3,000	4,000	10,000
Production costs	500	500	4,000	5,000
Gross profit	2,500	2,500	-	5,000
Administrative costs				1,000
Net profit				4,000

As a result of receiving this information the MD **drops the price** of Stable's products X and Y. He **divides the production function into two divisions**, one of which will concentrate exclusively upon reducing the costs of product Z while maintaining quality.

The **management accountant** is asked to **work closely** with the division Z **production manager** in designing a system that will help to monitor and control costs. He is also to work closely with the **marketing managers** of products X and Y so that the organisation can respond rapidly to any further competitive pressures. **Reports** are to be made **weekly** and are to include as **much information** as can be determined about Turbulence's financial performance, pricing, marketing penetration and so on.

This example may be **explained in terms of contingency theory** as follows.

(a) **Originally the design of the accounting system** is determined by the facts that Stable faces a **highly predictable environment**, and that it is a **highly centralised organisation**.

(b) The **design of the new system** is the **result of a new set of contingent variables**: the entry of Turbulence into two of Stable's markets requires the system to adopt a product-based reporting structure with more externally-derived information in the case of products X and Y and more detailed analysis of internal information in the case of product Z. This is matched by a change in the structure of the organisation as a whole.

To recap, **contingency theorists' aim is to identify specific features of an organisation's context that affect the design of particular features of that organisation's accounting system.**

2.2 Contingent variables

In the 1990 edition of Emmanuel *et al's* book there is a review of the major studies in the contingency theory tradition up until that time. These are classified under the headings 'environment' and technology' (as before), with 'organisation' being sub-divided into 'size', 'strategy' and 'culture'. In the remainder of this section we give a summary of the main points made in this discussion.

None of the points made should be regarded as universal truths: they are simply **observations made by different researchers in the light of investigations into particular cases.**

Exam focus point

That said, however, it is certainly worth spending some time reading through the lists of points. Once you have glanced through a few examination questions asking you to suggest an appropriate control system for a particular scenario you will be very glad to have a head full of ideas such as the following. In the exam, stating the obvious is sometimes very hard to do.

2.3 Environment

As you might expect if you look back at the previous chapter (and as is entirely reasonable), Emmanuel *et al* identify **uncertainty as the major factor in the environment affecting the design of accounting control systems.**

- The **sophistication** of an accounting system is influenced by the intensity of **competition** faced.
- Organisations use accounting information in different ways depending upon the **type of competition faced** (for example competition on price as opposed to product rivalry).
- **Budget information is evaluated** by senior managers **rigidly in 'tough' environments**, but **more flexibly** in **'liberal' environments.**
- The **more dynamic** the environment (that is the more rapidly it changes), the **more frequently accounting control reports** will be required.
- The **larger the number of product markets** an organisation is in, the **more decentralised its control system** will be, with quasi-independent responsibility centres.
- The more **severe** the **competition**, the **more sophisticated the accounting information system** will be, for example incorporating non-financial information.
- The design of an organisation's accounting system will be affected by its environment. An organisation's **environment** will be somewhere **between** the **two extremes simple/complex** and somewhere between the **two extremes static/dynamic.**
- The **more complex the structure** of an organisation the **more accounting control 'tools'** it will have.
- **'Turbulence'** or discontinuity in an organisation's environment often requires the **replacement of control tools** which have been rendered obsolete by new ones.
- Control systems are not determined by organisation structure: **both structure and control systems are dependent on the environment**. In an **uncertain environment** more use will be made of **external, non-financial and projected information.**
- In conditions of **uncertainty, subjective methods of performance evaluation** are more effective.
- Accounting systems are **affected by** the extent to which the organisation is **manipulated by other organisations** such as competitors, suppliers, customers or government bodies.

2.4 Technology

- The nature of the **production process** (for example jobbing on the one hand or mass production on the other) determines the **amount of cost allocation** rather than **cost apportionment** that can be done.
- The **complexity of the 'task'** that an organisation performs **affects the financial control structure**. It does so via organisation structure however. (For example, a railway operator's 'task' of getting people from A to B involves keeping them fed via a catering division that is accounted for differently to the transport division.)

- The **amount of data** produced, **what** that data is **about** and **how it is used** closely **correlates** with the **number of things that go wrong in a production process and the procedures used to investigate the problems**. (This correlation exists but the research does not consider whether there is an optimum correlation between data availability and use and problem solving.)
- The **more automated** a production process is, the **more 'formality'** there will be in the use of budget systems.
- The **less predictable** the production process is, the more likely production managers are to create **budgetary slack**. (The evidence for this is weak, however, as the proponent of the view (Merchant) admits.)
- The structure and processes of (and so, presumably, the method of accounting for) **operational units** tend to be related to **technological variables** while the structure and processes of **managerial/planning units** tend to be related to **environmental variables**.

2.5 Size

- As an organisation grows it will initially organise on a **functional basis**. If it diversifies into different products or markets it will re-organise into **semi-autonomous divisions**. The **same accounting system** that is used to measure overall performance can then be **applied en bloc to each individual division**.
- In larger organisations the greater degree of **decentralisation** seems to lead to greater **participation** in budgeting.
- In **large organisations a bureaucratic** approach to budgeting produces the best performance; in **small organisations** a more **'personal' approach** gives better results. (Note that this finding was reported in 1981 when bureaucracies were less unfashionable: few modern commentators associate bureaucracy with efficiency.)
- Organisations may grow by acquisition: when this occurs, differences in the accounting system used by the **acquired company** disappear, and it **conforms to the practices used by the acquiring company.**

2.6 Culture

- Control systems which are inconsistent with an organisation's value system or with the language or symbols that help to make up its culture are likely to create **resistance**: typically people would develop informal ways to get round controls that were regarded as intrusive.
- New control systems that **threaten to alter existing power relationships** may be **thwarted** by those affected.
- Control processes will be most **effective** if they operate by generating a corporate culture that is **supportive** of organisational aims, objectives and methods of working, and which is **consistent** with the demands of the environment in which the organisation operates.

Caveat

Remember that the above points are simply observations made by different researchers in the light of investigations into particular cases. They are not universal truths.

3 Strategy and management control

FAST FORWARD

Business strategy also **influences management accounting**, the extent of management accounting data, and management supervision.

Top managers control strategy in different ways, via **mission**, **limits**, **diagnostic systems**, and **interactive control systems**. In a divisionalised organisation, the style of head office control can be strategic planning (high involvement), financial control (financial profit targets) or strategic control (autonomy for local business units).

3.1 Strategy

Key term

'A **strategy** is a plan for interacting with the competitive environment to achieve organisation goals.'

3.2 Management control systems and competitive advantage

Robert Simons conducted a study that examined the **effects of strategy on management control systems and vice versa**. Management control systems, he says, are 'the formalised procedures and systems that use information to maintain or alter patterns in organisational activity ... [including] procedures for such things as planning, budgeting, environmental scanning, competitor analysis, performance reporting and evaluation, resource allocation and employee rewards.' **Management control** is therefore **concerned as much with the formation of strategy as with its implementation**.

Simons looked at two companies competing in the same industry. One followed a 'cost leadership' strategy, the other a 'differentiation' strategy (review Business Strategy for details). He found that there were significant differences in the way that the two companies used basically similar control systems.

Top management control systems	Cost leadership strategy	Differentiation strategy
Strategic planning review	**Sporadic**. Last update 2 years ago. Does not motivate a lot of discussion in the company.	**Intensive annual process**. Business managers **prepare strategic plans** for debate by top management committee.
Financial goals	**Set by top management** and communicated down through organisation.	**Established by each business unit** and **rolled up** after a series of review and challenge meetings.
Budget preparation and review	**Budgets prepared to meet financial goals**. Budgets coordinated by Finance Dept and presented to top management when assured that goals will be met.	Market segment **prepares budgets with focus on strategy** and tactics. Intensive debate at presentations to top management committee.
Budget revisions and updates	**Not revised** during budget year	Business units **rebudget from lowest** expense three times during year with action plans to deal with changes.

Top management control systems	Cost leadership strategy	Differentiation strategy
Program reviews	**Intensive monitoring of product** and **process-related programs**. Programs cut across organisational boundaries and affect all layers of company.	**Programs limited to R&D** which is delegated to local operating companies.
Evaluation and reward	**Percentage of bonus** based on contribution to generating profit in excess of plan based on personal goals (usually quantified).	Bonus based on **subjective evaluation of effort**, MBO system used throughout organisation.

Simons explains these differences in terms of how and why top managers choose to monitor certain management control systems personally. He identifies **four factors** that have a bearing on this.

Factor	Detail
Limited attention	'Managers have **neither the time nor the capacity to process all the information** available to them.'
Strategic uncertainties	These are **'uncertainties** that top managers believe they must monitor personally to ensure that the goals of the firm are achieved'. Which uncertainties are chosen is strongly dependent on the strategy of the firm.
Interactive management control	This is **actively monitoring and intervening** in the activities of subordinates using planning and control procedures, as opposed to programmed controls which rely on staff specialists. Top managers make a management control system interactive if it collects information about strategic uncertainties.
Organisational learning	This is how the **organisation adjusts** to fit its environment. Because management control is made 'interactive' in the area of strategic uncertainties the ensuing review and discussion of the control process gives rise to new ideas and new strategies.

The argument, in summary is that management control plays a key role in the process of 'interacting with the competitive environment to achieve organisation goals.'

3.3 Types of control system

Simons identified **four types of control system** used by top managers.

Type of control system	Detail
Beliefs systems	**Determine purpose** from such [documents] as mission statements or statements of purpose, and guide or limit the search for opportunities.
Boundary systems	**Define limits.** These vary from codes of conduct to operational guidelines, but include strategic planning systems and capital expenditure authorisation systems which define the limits of areas in which the search for opportunities can be conducted.
Diagnostic control systems	**Monitor operations** against preset standards of performance - typically budgeting systems and operating statements.

Type of control system	Detail
Interactive control systems	**Typically profit-planning systems**, project and brand management systems, budget formulation and planning - focusing on forecast information and possible opportunities.

Simons also distinguishes **internal control systems** as essential to **ensure the integrity and reliability of all other systems** - but not used by managers to control strategy.

3.4 Strategies and styles

Goold and Campbell conducted a study of a large number of high profile diversified companies to examine **how different companies cope with the problem of managing diversity**. They discovered three main philosophies and three corresponding styles of strategic management.

Philosophy	Example	Style of management
Core businesses	Cadbury's. 'The company commits itself to a few industries and sets out to win big in those industries.'	Strategic planning style
Manageable businesses	'The emphasis is on selecting businesses for the portfolio which can be effectively managed using short-term financial controls...' The businesses have few linkages with each other, should be in relatively stable competitive environments and should not involve large or long-term investment decisions.	Financial control style
Diverse businesses	Samsung, perhaps. 'The centre seeks to build a portfolio that spreads risk across industries and geographic areas as well as ensuring that the portfolio is balanced in terms of growth, profitability and cash flow.'	Strategic control style

Goold and Campbell describe the features of the different styles of central management as follows.

Style of central management	Features
Strategic planning	Entails the centre **participating in** and **influencing the strategies** of the **core businesses**. The centre establishes a planning process and contributes to strategic thinking. Rather less emphasis is placed on financial controls and performance targets are set flexibly and reviewed within the context of long-term progress.
Financial control	As the name suggests, **focuses on annual profit targets**. There are no long-term planning documents and no strategy documents. The role of the centre is limited to approving budgets and monitoring performance.
Strategic control	Concerned with the plans of its business units but believes in **autonomy for business unit managers**. Plans are therefore made locally but reviewed in a formal planning process to upgrade the quality of the thinking. The centre does not advocate strategies or interfere with major decisions but maintains control through financial targets and strategic objectives.

Since they conducted their original work Goold and Campbell have periodically reviewed the companies they visited. Several found it necessary to **change their style in response to factors** such as the **recession** in the late 80s and early 90s.

4 The limitations of contingency theory

FAST FORWARD

It is not clear exactly how **contingent factors** affect the management accounting systems, and furthermore the contingency approach underestimates the power of management – as change agents – to impose their own systems and views.

(a) It is by **no means clear how the various contingent variables** proposed **affect the management accounting system**. In several of the observations listed in Section 2, for example, it seems that it is the organisation structure that adapts to its environment and the management accounting system simply reflects the organisation structure.

(b) Contingency theory **plays down the importance of power**, both the **power of the strategically-placed managers and the power of the organisation itself**. An example of the latter would be the acquiring company in a take-over imposing its own accounting system on its new subsidiary.

(c) For **financial accounting** purposes accountants are expected to accept the idea of 'best practice' and to follow the rules and regulations of accounting standards and company law. Although financial accounting does not go quite so far as to insist upon one best way, it does not allow many alternatives for external reporting purposes. This is quite at **odds with the contingency approach.**

(d) The theory tend to **ignore the influence of aspects of an organisation's context which are more difficult to quantify**. It fails to recognise the impact of the people within an organisation, of management structure, managerial style and, particularly, organisational culture - those factors that make an organisation unique.

4.1 Conclusion: vive la différence

In spite of the many reservations, it is evidently true that there is not 'one best way' of designing an organisation or its accounting system: otherwise all successful organisations (and their accounting systems) would be identical. Even if this is the only real insight that contingency theory has to offer it is a very valuable one.

Question — **Contingent power**

Learning outcome: A(iv)

Is it fair to say that if a management accounting system does not fit its environment it will inevitably change?

Answer

(a) It may not change, for example, if the management accountant operating the system is powerful enough in the organisation to prevent it from changing.

(b) Going back to chapter 1, this could reflect the power of structure over agency.

(c) It may be the case that the 'fit' between the management accounting system and the environment is not particularly important, if management control is exercised in other ways.

5 Design of management accounting systems

FAST FORWARD

A management accounting system comprises **people**, **accounting knowledge**, **records**, **processes**, **mathematical techniques**, and **reports**: inputs, processes and outputs. It is used for strategic decision making, performance measurement, operational control and costing.

5.1 What is a management accounting system (MAS)?

Textbooks at this level generally do not ask such basic questions as this, but if you are given a blank sheet and asked to select an appropriate management accounting system for a specific purpose it is helpful to have some concrete ideas. Let us **define a MAS by means of its more tangible components.**

(a) Some **people** with accounting knowledge

(b) The **equipment** they use

(c) Paper or computer **records of financial transactions**

(d) **Codes** or **titles** describing the purpose of the financial transaction ('Rent') and who it was incurred on behalf of ('Factory A')

(e) **Records of the usage of resources** other than money, such as time, physical materials, energy and so forth

(f) A large variety of simple and complex **mathematical techniques** for arranging and analysing (c) in terms of (d) and (e). Examples include:

(i)	Double-entry analysis	(vi)	Adding up and subtracting lists of numbers
(ii)	Percentages and ratios	(vii)	Linear programming
(iii)	Tabulation of figures	(viii)	Methods of allocating costs
(iv)	Budgets	(ix)	Risk analysis (probabilities etc)
(v)	DCF calculations	(x)	Relevant costing

and so on.

(g) **Report**s that are produced by the people in (a), using (b) to (f). Also, prescribed formats for reports, at least in larger, more bureaucratic organisations

(h) Some **more people**, to whom the reports are given

This is a **system because it has inputs** (items (a) to (e)), **processes** (item (f)) and **outputs** (item (g)). The list is not meant to be comprehensive.

5.2 Designing a management accounting system

The following factors should be considered when designing a management accounting system.

Factor	Detail
Output required	The management accountant must **identify the information needs of managers**. If a particular manager finds pie-charts most useful the system should be able to produce them. If another manager needs to know what time of day machinery failures occur, this information should be available. Levels of detail and accuracy of output must be determined in each case.
Response required	A further, vitally important issue is how managers are **likely to behave**, depending on what factors or figures are stressed in the information they are given.
When the output is required	If **information is needed** within the hour the system should be **capable of producing it at this speed**. If it is only ever needed once a year, at the year end, the system should be designed to produce it on time, no matter how long it takes to produce.
Sources of input information	The production manager may require a **report detailing** the **precise operations of his machines**, second by second. However, the management accounting system could only acquire this information if suitable production technology had been installed.
Processing involved	This is **generally a cost/benefit calculation**: some of the information that could be provided would cost more to produce than the benefit obtained from having it.

Designing a management accounting system effectively means devising ways to provide accounting information for managers to use. Managers need information that financial accounting systems and cost accounting systems on their own do not provide.

(a) They need **more detailed** information, to help them to run the business.

(b) They also need **forward-looking** information, for planning.

(c) They will want data to be **analysed differently**, to suit their specific requirements for information.

Question — Good management accounting information

Learning outcome: A(iv)

What are the features of good management accounting information?

Answer

All good information should have the following features.

(a) It should be **relevant** to the user's needs.
(b) It should be **accurate** within the user's needs.
(c) It should inspire the user's **confidence.**
(d) It should be **timely.**
(e) It should be **appropriately communicated.**
(f) It should be **cost-effective.**

We may further identify features that pertain particularly to management accounting information.

(a) It is generally **forward-looking**.
(b) It can be **financial or non-financial, quantitative or qualitative.**
(c) It should be **free from bias.**
(d) It is often **comparative**.

Management accounting information is **used by managers for a variety of purposes.**

(a) To **make decisions**. Managers are faced with several types of decision.

- **Strategic decisions** (which relate to the longer term objectives of a business) require information which tends to relate to the organisation as a whole, is in summary form and is derived from both internal and external sources.
- **Tactical and operational decisions** (which relate to the short or medium term and to a department, product or division rather than the organisation as a whole) require information which is more detailed and more restricted in its sources.

(b) To **plan** for the future. Managers have to plan and they need information to do this, much of it management accounting information.

(c) To **monitor the performance** of the business. Managers need to know what they **want the business to achieve** (targets or standards) and what the business is **actually achieving**. By comparing the actual achievements with targeted performance, management can decide whether control action is needed.

(d) To **measure profits** and put a **value to inventory**.

5.3 Strategic planning, management control and operational control

Another way of looking at the information that a MAS may be required to produce is to consider the question under Anthony's three headings, strategic planning, management control and operational control.

5.3.1 Strategic planning information

Strategic plans include such matters as the selection of products and markets, the required levels of company profitability and the purchase and disposal of subsidiary companies or major fixed assets.

Strategic planning information is generally **external data** about competitors, customers, suppliers, new technology, the state of markets and the economy, government legislation, political unrest and so on.

Such information includes overall profitability, the profitability of different segments of the business, future market prospects, the availability and cost of raising new funds, total manning levels and capital equipment needs. Much of this information must come from **environmental sources,** although internally generated information will always be used. Strategic information is prepared on an **ad hoc basis**. It also tends to be more **approximate** and **imprecise** than management control information.

5.3.2 Management control information

The information required for management control **embraces the entire organisation** and **provides a comparison between actual results and the plan**. The information is often **quantitative** (labour hours, quantities of materials consumed, volumes of sales and production) and is commonly **expressed in money terms.**

Such information includes productivity measurements, budgetary control or variance analysis reports, cash flow forecasts, profit results within a particular department of the organisation, labour turnover statistics within a department and so on. A large proportion of this information will be **generated from within the organisation** and it will often have an **accounting emphasis**. Tactical information is usually **prepared regularly**, perhaps weekly, or monthly.

5.3.3 Operational control information

Operational information is information which is **needed for the conduct of day-to-day implementation of plans**. It will include much **'transaction data'** such as data about customer orders, purchase orders, cash receipts and payments. Operating information must usually be **consolidated into totals in management reports** before it can be used to prepare management control information.

The amount of **detail** provided in information is likely to vary with the purpose for which it is needed, and operational information is likely to go into much more detail than management control information, which in turn will be more detailed than strategic information. Operational information, although quantitative, is more often **expressed in terms of units, hours, quantities of material and so on.**

6 Management accounting and organisational culture

FAST FORWARD

Culture determines the **context** of management accounting information and what it is used for.

The relevance of organisational culture to management accounting can be explained in simple terms as follows. The business of management accounting is to provide managers with information to help them run the business. **If the management accountant is not sensitive to the culture of his organisation he will not understand how it is run and will not know what sort of information to provide.**

An important influences on Western corporate cultures in recent years has been ideas ' such as **Just-in-Time** and **Total Quality Management,** which have a direct impact on business areas that have long been the preserve of accountants - purchasing and inventory control, quality costs, waste and scrap and so on. The **teamworking** approach is a radical change from the individualistic culture of the West, and this has further implications for performance measurement and reporting.

7 Organisational structure and budget centre selection

FAST FORWARD

Organisation structure determines **budget centres**. If managers are to be held accountable for expenditure they have to be able to **control it**.

The **behavioural implications vary** depending on participation, the use of budgets (as plans or pressure devices), and the style of management (budget-constrained, profit-conscious, non-accounting).

7.1 Why have budget centres?

Consider the following budget.

	£
Sales	X
Costs	(X)
Profit	X

A budget in this form is of value as an **overall objective** for an organisation. It is probably all that is required if the organisation **comprises one person** buying and selling a single item.

Suppose the budget and actual figures are as follows, however.

	Budget	*Actual*
	£'000	£'000
Sales	10,000	5,000
Costs	5,000	(10,000)
Profit/(Loss)	5,000	(5,000)

Suppose also that the organisation employs 200 people, manufacturing and selling ten different products in four different countries. Its activities are clearly wildly out of control, and the control model in use (the budget above) is inadequate because it **provides no useful information** that can help to **identify the causes for non-attainment of objectives.**

Key term

A **budget centre** is 'A section of an entity for which control may be exercised and budgets prepared'.
(CIMA *Official Terminology)*

The illustration above indicates one of the reasons why an entity might wish to **prepare separate budgets for separate sections:** to analyse the performance of the organisation in a way that enables the **identification of those activities that are not being performed as expected.** (The other main reason is for motivational purposes: this is dealt with in the next chapter.)

7.2 Budget centres and organisation structure

The selection of budget centres will be influenced by issues such as size, task, staff, environment, age and culture. A large organisation engaged in heavy engineering using large numbers of low-skilled workers in a stable environment with an autocratic management is certain to have a different set of budget centres to a small service business like a firm of management consultants.

Possible **bases** for budget centres are **different activities** or **functions**, different **products**, different **geographical areas**, different **customers** and so on. Budget centres may overlap in the case of a matrix organisation.

7.3 Budget centres and measurement

Having decided what parts of the organisation will be budget centres the next problem is to decide **what will be the focus of their budgets** - effectively whether they will be measured in terms of costs, revenues, profits or by return on investment.

The performance of cost centres, for example, might be measured in terms of total actual costs, total budgeted costs and total cost variances sub-analysed perhaps into efficiency, usage and expenditure variances. In addition, the information might be analysed in terms of ratios, such as cost per unit produced (budget and actual), selling costs per £ of sales (budget and actual) and transport costs per tonne/kilometre (budget and actual).

The **general principle**, as you will no doubt remember, is that **managers should be held responsible only for those costs and revenues that they can control.**

Question

Budget centres

Learning outcome: A(iv)

PS has three production departments. Output from department A is further processed in department B. Department B's output can either be transferred to department C for finishing, or sold on the open market as a raw material.

How can PS design its accounting system so as to ensure that correct decisions are made on the question of whether to process department B's output further or sell it on the open market?

Answer

Department A will be a **cost** centre. Departments B and C will be **profit** centres. The product should only be processed in department C if the overall net revenue earned thereby is greater than the overall net revenue that can be earned once the output has been processed by department B. The 'price' at which the product is transferred from B to C can be set at a level that encourages the optimal behaviour for PS as a whole.

A **hierarchy** of investment centres, profit centres and cost centres might need to be selected. A decision will have to be taken about **how far down** the management hierarchy this 'tree' of responsibility centres should extend.

Having **budget centres down to a low level in the management hierarchy** has a number of **advantages**.

- **Motivation and encouragement** of junior managers.
- **An awareness of management's authority** and responsibility is reinforced by a reporting system based on budget centres.
- **Perhaps, better budgeting** because of the better knowledge of detail that management will possess at budget centres lower down in the hierarchy of the organisation.

Establishing budget centres down to a low level in the management hierarchy also has **disadvantages**.

- **Greater decentralisation**, when head office might wish to retain greater control itself.
- The danger that junior managers will seek to **improve their own budget centre's** performance regardless of the consequences for other budget centres (sub-optimality in decision making).
- The **greater administrative problems** of having a reporting system with greater numbers of budget centres.
- The **greater opportunities for building slack** into the organisation's budgets.

Question

Who is responsible?

Learning outcome: A(iv)

What problems might arise when determining responsibility for the following costs?

(a) Maintenance of sales reps cars
(b) Induction of secretarial staff
(c) Insurance of office buildings
(d) Corporation tax
(e) Reworking defective items
(f) External audit fees

Answer

Think about why the cost is incurred; whether it is controllable and if so who by; who would be responsible in different organisation structures and different types of organisation.

(The types of cost chosen are a fairly random selection: you can probably think of many other potentially problematic costs and revenues.)

7.4 Budget centre selection as a means of control

As Emmanuel *et al* point out, although 'it may appear that the structure of organizational responsibilities determines the form of the budgetary control system' nevertheless 'Organisations may adapt their responsibility structure so as to attempt to gain the advantages of profit or investment centre control'.

7.4.1 Example: controlling service provision

In some organisations, service or support departments might be established as profit centres, earning most or all of their revenue from internal services which are charged for at a transfer price rate. Thus a data processing department might be made into a profit centre, which then charges user departments for the mainframe computer services it provides and for the systems analysis, design and programming work it carries out for new computer project developments.

Two **advantages** of a control system such as this are as follows.

(a) The **manager** of the centre will be encouraged to **think about the volume of services his or her centre provides.** More activity would generally result in more revenue and more profits, and so higher activity levels might be encouraged.

(b) The **manager** would be encouraged to **look at the value of the services the centre is providing, and their cost**. Services should not cost more to provide than they are worth to the beneficiary. In a profit centre system, a profit centre would make a loss if it spent too much providing services that are not worth having, and so whose cost exceeds their transfer price.

Kaplan *(Advanced Management Accounting)* argues that **not charging production departments** according to the use they make of service departments may have several **negative consequences** in terms of controlling the organisation as a whole.

(a) **More of the service will be demanded by user departments than is economically reasonable to supply.** Users will continue to ask for service department work up to the point where the **marginal benefit** is zero, ignoring the marginal **costs** of work in the service department.

(b) It will be **difficult to establish whether the service department is operating efficiently**.

(c) There will be no indication as to whether the firm should continue to **supply the service internally**, or whether it might be less costly to obtain the service from an **external supplier or contractor**.

(d) There is no easy way to determine the **quality** of service that the department should provide. Unless user departments are aware of the cost to them of service department work, there would be 'little opportunity for a user department to communicate its preferences on the price-versus-quality dimension'.

In addition Kaplan argued that **charging user departments** for the output of service departments would **help in planning the allocation of resources when service department resources are in scarce supply**.

7.5 Behavioural implications

7.5.1 Human behaviour and budgetary planning and control

Interest in the human behavioural factors at work in budgetary planning and control the topic was stimulated by an article written in the 1950s by Chris **Argyris**. Argyris identified **four issues**.

Issues	Comment
Pressure device	The budget is seen as a pressure device, used by management to force 'lazy' employees to work harder. The intention of such pressure is to improve performance, but the unfavourable reactions of subordinates against it 'seems to be at the core of the budget problem'.
Budget men want to see failure	The accounting department is usually responsible for recording actual achievement and comparing this against the budget. Accountants are therefore 'budget men'. Their success is finding significant adverse variances, and identifying the managers responsible. **The success of a 'budget man' is the failure of another manager** and this failure causes loss of interest and declining performance. The accountant, on the other hand, fearful of having his budget criticised by factory management, obscures his budget and variance reporting, and deliberately makes it difficult to understand.
Targets and goal congruence	The budget usually sets targets for each department. Achieving the target becomes of paramount importance, regardless of the effect this may have on other departments and the overall company performance. This is the problem of goal congruence.
Management style	Budgets are used by managers to express their character and patterns of leadership on subordinates. Subordinates, resentful of their leader's style, blame the budget rather than the leader.

7.5.2 Management styles

The final point is developed by **Hopwood,** who identifies three distinct supervisory styles.

Supervisory style	Hopwood says...
Budget-constrained	'The manager's performance is primarily evaluated upon the basis of his ability to **continually meet the budget** on a short-term basis.'
Profit-conscious	'The manager's performance is evaluated on the basis of his ability to **increase the general effectiveness** of his unit's operations in relation to the long-term purposes of the organisation.'
Non-accounting	'The budgetary information plays a **relatively unimportant** part in the superior's evaluation of the manager's performance.'

Question

Style of evaluation

Learning outcome: A(iv)

Hopwood summarised the effects of the three styles of evaluation in a table with the following headings and categories.

	Style of evaluation		
	Non-accounting	*Profit-conscious*	*Budget-constrained*
Involvement with costs			
Job-related tension			
Manipulation of accounting reports			

(a) Which style or styles led to extensive manipulation of accounting reports?
(b) Which style or styles created a medium level of job-related tension?
(c) Which style or styles encouraged managers to be greatly concerned about costs?

Answer

(a) Budget-constrained
(b) Non-accounting and profit-conscious
(c) Profit-conscious and budget-constrained

Question

Power

Learning outcome: A(iv)

What is the relevance of **power** to the foregoing discussion of management styles and contexts?

Answer

Some suggestions are as follows.

(a) The extent to which an accountant can get managers to take budgets seriously will depend upon the **'expert power'** that he or she is perceived to have, both in accounting matters and operational matters.

(b) Otley's research indicates the importance of **position power** and **resource power** to styles of evaluation and their effects.

These are not the only possible answers. The point of exercises like this is to encourage you to think about what you are studying currently in the context of what you have read in this Study Text already.

8 Participation in budgeting

FAST FORWARD

Participation is sometimes seen as the way to **better budgeting** and **motivation**. However the effectiveness depends on management commitment and expertise, and there is always the temptation to introduce budgetary slack.

8.1 Potential benefits of participation

The idea that when individuals (employees or managers) **participate** in decision making, they will be **more satisfied** with their job and colleagues and they will be more productive derives from **'human relations' thinking** about organisational behaviour, and is also broadly in line with the **goal theory of motivation** and, as Macintosh (1994) points out, fits well with the currently fashionable ideas of **employee empowerment.**

As well as improving motivation, **Hofstede** thought that participation by managers would give budgets more legitimacy and make them more realistic.

However, several writers, have stressed that the **effectiveness of participation depends upon the nature of the task being undertaken.**

Others have drawn attention to the **importance of organisation structure.** It has been found that where an organisation is **decentralised** managers perceive themselves to be **participating** more in the budgeting process and to be more satisfied with it than managers in centralised organisations. In **centralised** organisations a **lack of participation** is felt to be the more effective approach, indeed an authoritarian approach may be welcomed by employees.

Still others have focused on the impact of **individual personality traits**. A participative approach has been found to be more effective when it involves people who feel that they have control over their destiny than with those who believe that their fortunes are dictated by 'luck'.

8.2 Problems with participation

8.2.1 Lack of commitment

There are several reasons why managers **may not be committed** to producing a good budget.

- Managers who **dislike financial figures** will tend to minimise the amount of time they spend budgeting.
- Some managers may **dislike the formality** of a budget plan and wish to have more flexibility.
- Some may consider themselves to be **too busy** to 'waste' time on budgeting.
- **Job dissatisfaction** or an **imminent job change** will decrease the effectiveness of participation.

8.2.2 Lack of expertise

Particularly if they have **not received adequate training,** managers may not know how to produce a budget to reflect the business strategy of the company. Ideas may be based solely on past results **without considering alternative options**. In addition managers may not **understand how to co-ordinate** their plans with those of other budget centres.

8.2.3 Budget slack

Key term

Budget slack is 'The intentional overestimation of expenses and/or underestimation of revenue in the budgeting process'. (CIMA *Official Terminology)*

Participation in budgeting allows managers scope for overestimating costs (or underestimating income) in budgets, of introducing slack. There are several **reasons why** managers may do this.

- Managers will **'look good'** if actual costs are less than budgeted costs and their bonuses may even depend on it. And of course, they would not wish to be blamed for overspending.
- They may believe that budget padding is necessary so as to **cover unforeseen events** or they may fear that some expense has been forgotten in the budget.
- A **bigger budget** may be perceived as **indicating greater importance**.

Before the **management accountant** can make any judgement on slack, he needs to **understand the demands made on, and areas of responsibility of, managers. Past data** (adjusted for inflation, changes in work practices and so on) can be **reviewed** to assess whether he current budget is realistic. Budget slack can then be **monitored** by comparing new projections with previous actual figures and with independent data, such as forecasts by similar divisions, external economic data and market information.

Senior management can attempt to minimise slack by using a **range of performance measures** for assessment purposes (not just the achievement of budget targets) or by imposing **pressure** on the budget holder by, for example, not allowing for any inflationary increase in the following year's budget.

Particular **tricks** that can be used to **hide the slack** include the following.

- **Treating fixed costs as variable**
- **Budgeting fully** for items such as training when there is no **intention of utilising the allowance** (and later transferring the surplus to another expenditure category)
- **Unnecessarily increasing current period actual spending** to ensure a higher allowance next period

Recent studies have shown that a **balanced scorecard approach minimises opportunities for padding**.

Question — **Budgetary slack**

Learning outcome: A(iv)

Can you think of any reasons why some level of budget slack should be accepted?

Answer

- To **take account of forecasting errors** so that budget targets are still achievable
- To ensure that quoted companies **achieve profit forecasts** and hence maintain share prices
- To allow public sector organisations **sufficient resources** at the outset of the budget period to provide services
- To **motivate budget holders**
- To **encourage innovation** (as tight financial targets are constraining)

8.2.4 Unachievable budgets

There are a variety of circumstances in which **managers may set themselves** extremely high or even unachievable budgets, including the following.

(a) When the manager in question is trying to **impress** his or her seniors, with a view to obtaining promotion or some other reward. Such a manager may in any case be a high achiever and believe that his or her department will put more effort into achieving difficult targets than it would into less demanding but more realistic ones. In this case, even if actual results fall short of the levels set the department will have performed very well.

(b) The manager in question may be **under pressure** from above to do better than in previous years or even to justify the very existence of his or her department. In other words the manager is **trying to avoid failure rather than to achieve success.** In this case the manager may find it difficult to motivate staff to achieve results that, by comparison with previous periods, are quite unrealistic.

(c) The budget may be based on a **mistaken assessment** of his or her department's prospects in the coming period or in **ignorance** of external developments that will make high projections unrealistic.

8.2.5 Undermining the implementation

Problems can also arise when a **budget is implemented.**

(a) Managers might put in **only just enough effort** to achieve budget targets, without trying to beat targets.

(b) A formal budget might **encourage rigidity and discourage flexibility** in operational decision making.

(c) **Short-term planning** in a budget can **draw attention away from the longer term consequences of decisions.**

(d) Managers might tolerate **slapdash and inaccurate methods of recording**, classifying and codifying actual costs.

(e) **Co-operation and communication** between managers might be **minimal**.

(f) Managers will often try to make sure that they **spend up to their full budget allowance**, and do not overspend, so that they will not be accused of having asked for too much spending allowance in the first place.

8.2.6 Budgets as targets

As targets, budgets can motivate managers to achieve a high level of performance. But **how difficult** should targets be? And how might people react to targets of differing degrees of difficulty in achievement?

(a) There is likely to be a **demotivating** effect where an **ideal** standard of performance is set, because **adverse efficiency variances** will always be reported.

(b) A **low standard** of efficiency is also demotivating, because there is **no sense of achievement** in attaining the required standards: targets will be achieved easily, and there will be no impetus for employees to try harder to do better than this.

(c) A budgeted level of attainment could be **'normal'**: that is, the same as the level that has been achieved in the past. Arguably, this level will be **too low**. It might **encourage budget slack** ('normal' levels which are not challenging but easy to achieve, although they must not be 'beaten', because targets would then be made harder to achieve next year).

Employees often know what is a reasonable level of performance to which to aspire. However, some care may be needed in applying these aspirations. Hopwood stated that 'while **budgets** which are best **for motivational purposes** need to be stated in terms of **aspirations** rather than expectations, the **budgets** which are so necessary for **planning and decision purposes** need to be stated in terms of the best available estimate of **expected** actual performance.'

Question — **Budget comparisons**

Learning outcome: A(iv)

What is a possible solution to reconciling targets and forecasts?

Answer

The solution normally suggested is to have two budgets:

(a) a budget for planning and decision making based on reasonable **expectations**; and

(b) an **'aspirations budget'**, for motivational purposes, with more difficult targets of performance (ie targets of an intermediate level of difficulty).

How satisfactory do you think this proposal is?

8.3 Motivational implications of standards

Senior management might **pick a particular costing method** simply because it **focuses management attention on a particular area where it was felt that improvements could be made.**

For instance, a product may have a standard cost with overheads apportioned on the basis of **labour hours** one year, because it was felt that economies could be made in this area, but on a **material cost** basis the next year, because the cost or usage of material was felt to be capable of improvement.

This may seem a valid approach in principle, but **problems** may arise if instead of, or in addition to, devoting more attention to the problem area, **managers take other decisions based on the revised cost.** Some of these decisions may not be truly in the interests of the business.

- Promotional expenditure might be shifted to products that apparently earn the greatest contribution, but only because of the particular costing method adopted.
- Decisions may be made about whether to outsource an activity or do it in-house.
- Design and quality may be changed for the worse to keep costs down.
- Human labour may be replaced with technology, increasing fixed costs and overheads and decreasing flexibility.
- Non-financial factors may be ignored.

The point is that an attempt to influence one aspect of managerial behaviour may have undesirable side-effects, especially if managerial performance is measured by reference to factors that go beyond that one aspect, such as overall profitability.

9 Evaluating the accounting function

FAST FORWARD

Accounting data is an **important part of the organisation's information system**, although other data, as in the balanced scorecard, is also needed for successful strategic direction. The quality of management accounting data, and the detail it contains, depends on its overall usefulness to internal customers (as die from legal and regulatory requirements).

9.1 The accounts department and the balanced scorecard

The accounts department is part of the technostructure, in Mintzberg's terms. It standardises the work of some other departments by laying down procedures and also by providing the 'language' in which business is conducted. Accounting information is therefore relatively privileged.

Even so, it is difficult to argue that accounting data adds value for the customer, as such, other than in the incidentals (eg attractive credit terms as part of the marketing mix, or efficient sales order processing). Provision of some accounting data is a legal requirement. Otherwise it needs to add value to managers, as they monitor the performance of the business.

The balanced scorecard focuses on **four different perspectives**, as follows.

Perspective	Question	Explanation
Customer	What do **existing and new customers** value from us?	**Gives rise to targets** that matter to customers: cost, quality, delivery, inspection, handling and so on.
Internal	**What processes** must we excel at to achieve our financial and customer objectives?	Aims to improve internal processes and decision making.
Innovation and learning	Can we **continue to improve** and create future value?	**Considers the business's capacity** to maintain its competitive position through the acquisition of new skills and the development of new products.
Financial	How do we **create value** for our shareholders?	**Covers traditional measures** such as growth, profitability and shareholder value but set through talking to the shareholder or shareholders direct.

Performance targets are set once the key areas for improvement have been identified, and the balanced scorecard is the **main monthly report**.

The scorecard is **'balanced'** in the sense that managers are required to **think in terms of all four perspectives**, to **prevent improvements being made in one area at the expense of** another.

- It looks at both **internal and external matters** concerning the organisation.
- It is **related to the key elements of a company's strategy**.
- **Financial and non-financial measures** are linked together.

As with all techniques, problems can arise when it is applied.

Problem	Explanation
Conflicting measures	Some **measures in the scorecard** such as **research funding** and cost reduction may naturally conflict. It is often difficult to determine the balance which will achieve the best results.
Selecting measures	Not only do appropriate measures have to be devised but the **number of measures** used must be **agreed**. Care must be taken that the impact of the results is not lost in a sea of information.
Expertise	Measurement is only useful if it **initiates appropriate action**. Non-financial managers may have difficulty with the usual profit measures. With more measures to consider this problem will be compounded.
Interpretation	Even a financially-trained manager may have difficulty in putting the figures into an **overall perspective.**

The point, though, is that management accounting information is one of a variety of measures to assist the strategic management of the business. As importantly, though, management accounting data relies on the integrity of operational control.

The principles of control theory still apply, so that a **system of performance evaluation for support departments needs the following**.

- A **budget, standard or target** for the department to work towards
- A **system of measuring actual performance and comparing it against the budget, standard or target**
- A **system for deciding when control action ought to be considered**

9.2 Example: measuring the accounts department

You could be asked to explain how the performance of the finance function, or a part of it such as purchasing, can be measured. Here is a suggested approach.

Step 1 **Define the boundaries** of the function or department. Does it include computing services, for example, or stock control or treasury management?

Step 2 **Define formal objectives** for the function as a whole, and then for each main section, for supervisory and managerial staff and for the operation of systems (for example payroll).

Step 3 **Ascertain what activities** each section does (or should do) to achieve its objectives.

Step 4 **Identify appropriate measures**, on the basis of the objectives and activities identified.

Step 5 **Select suitable bases of comparison**. Possibilities are time, budgets, standards or targets, intra-group comparison, or intra-organisational comparison.

Benchmarking of finance function activities may be useful (*Management Accounting*, February 1995), perhaps against other service departments such as customer service, or perhaps against finance functions in other organisations.

9.2.1 Internal customers

Market forces can be a useful way of compelling departments or functions in an organisation to reappraise their performance, and their relationship to each other. Accounts - like any other unit - may **focus on its activity for its own sake**, as if it had no objective, no purpose outside the department. It may take for granted its relationship to other units, having a 'take it or leave it' attitude to the service it provides, being **complacent** about quality because it appears to have an effective monopoly on that service or task ('if we don't do it - it doesn't get done').

The **internal customers** of the accounting function include the following.

- **Line management**, who need accounting information to help them do their jobs
- **Senior management and shareholders**, who need information to assess how well jobs are being done
- **Employees**, who also need information to do their jobs, and who are almost equivalent to external customers for some accounting services like payroll

9.2.2 Defining objective of the accounting function

This may involve **discussions with the function's customers.** The **overall objective** is the **provision of a quality service** but it will be possible to break down this objective into **a number of sub-objectives**.

Sub-objective	Detail
The provision of good information	This requires supplying information that is **relevant** to the needs of the users (which involves identifying the user, getting the purpose right and getting the volume right), that is **accurate** within their needs (in the sense of correct, although an approximate or average figure is often suitable), that **inspires their confidence** (so it should not be out-of-date, badly presented or taken from an unreliable source), that is **timely** (it must be in the right place by the right time) and that is **appropriately communicated** (since it will lose its value if it is not clearly communicated to the user in a suitable format and through a suitable medium).
The provision of a value-for-money service	User departments are likely to be charged in some way for the management accounting service and are therefore likely to require that the **charge incurred is reflected in the level of service and the quality of information provided.**
The availability of informed personnel	Users will require management accounting staff to be available to **answer queries and resolve problems** as and when required.
Flexibility	The management accounting function should be flexible **in its response to user requests** for information and reports.

9.2.3 Ascertaining activities

Once the objectives have been defined, the activities that the function should carry out to achieve its objectives must be ascertained. The function must be sufficiently organised and staffed, for example, to ensure that reports are received on time and that queries can be answered promptly.

9.2.4 Identifying measures

Appropriate measures can then be established on the basis of the objectives and activities identified. There should **not be too many measures or too few**, but just enough to provide **relevant indicators**, on a **timely** basis and in a **readily understood form**. The **'pyramid' approach** should be considered, whereby successively more detailed information is provided for successively junior levels of staff.

Suitable **specific performance measures** might be as follows.

(a) **Relating to the provision of good information**, such as number of complaints from users about accuracy/timeliness and so on of reports and information

(b) **Relating to value for money**, such as cost of similar service provided by specialist contractor or cost of service provided by function in similar organisation (via benchmarking)

(c) **Relating to the availability of informed persons**, such as proportion of the time the staff mix and numbers are within required limits or proportion of telephone calls answered within, say, eight rings

(d) **Relating to flexibility**, such as number of ad-hoc reports/requests for information issued within pre-set time limit

(e) Given the continuing importance of the views of the function's customers, any **ratings provided from user satisfaction surveys** would provide extremely useful measures of performance.

9.3 Quality and accounting data

Key term

The **cost of quality** is 'The difference between the actual cost of producing, selling and supporting products or services and the equivalent costs if there were no failures during production or usage'.

(CIMA *Official Terminology*)

In other words it is the costs incurred by an organisation because the quality of its products or services is not perfect.

The *Official Terminology* goes on to split the cost of quality into the **cost of conformance** and the **cost of non-conformance**.

Key terms

The **cost of conformance** is 'The cost of achieving specified quality standards' whereas the **cost of non-conformance** is 'The cost of failure to deliver the required standard of quality'.

(CIMA *Official Terminology*)

The **cost of conformance** is further analysed into the **cost of prevention and the cost of appraisal** while the **cost of non-conformance** is analysed into **the cost of internal failure and the cost of external failure.**

Key terms

Prevention cost is 'The costs incurred prior to or during production in order to prevent substandard or defective products or services from being produced'.

Appraisal cost is 'The costs incurred in order to ensure that outputs produced meet required quality standards'.

Internal failure cost is 'The costs arising from inadequate quality which are identified before the transfer of ownership from supplier to purchaser'.

External failure cost is 'The cost arising from inadequate quality discovered after the transfer of ownership from supplier to purchaser'. (CIMA *Official Terminology*)

Question

Quality of accounting data

Learning outcome: A(iv)

Think of examples of quality costs in each category for a manufacturing environment and a management accounting section.

Answer

Examples of each category appropriate to management accounting

(a) Prevention cost

- (i) Cost of staff training programmes
- (ii) Cost of introducing computers to perform tasks previously performed manually

(b) Appraisal cost

- (i) Cost of batch input controls to check the validity of processed data
- (ii) Cost of performing computer audits to confirm the reliability of computer software

(c) Internal failure cost

- (i) Cost of reprocessing data input to the system incorrectly
- (ii) Cost of reproducing incorrect reports

(d) External failure cost

- (i) Cost to other functions in the organisation of incorrect decisions made on the basis of inaccurate or untimely information provided by the management accounting function (such as quoting uneconomical prices for jobs on the basis of incorrect information about labour, material and overhead)
- (ii) Cost of dealing with external audit queries

Given the increasing importance of quality as a tool for competitive advantage, quality-based performance measures are extremely useful.

Chapter Roundup

- Management accounting developed from cost accounting, for **scorekeeping**, **directing management attention** and **problem solving**. It has since branched out into behavioural aspects.
- Management accounting in an organisation is influenced by the **environment**, **organisation structure**, the **size of the organisation**, the **technology** it uses and the **culture** of the **organisation. Uncertainty** is the major factor in the environment.
- Business strategy also influences management accounting, the extent of management accounting data., and management supervision.
- Top managers control strategy in different ways, via **mission, limits, diagnostic systems,** and **interactive control systems**. In a divisionalised organisation, the style of head office control can be strategic planning (high involvement), financial control (financial profit targets) or strategic control (autonomy for local business units).
- It is not clear exactly how **contingent factors** affect the management accounting systems, and furthermore the contingency approach underestimates the power of management – as change agents – to impose their own systems and views.
- A management accounting system comprises **people**, **accounting knowledge**, **records**, **processes**, **mathematical techniques**, and **reports**: inputs, processes and outputs. It is used for strategic decision making, performance measurement, operational control and costing.
- **Culture** determines the **context** of management accounting information and what it is used for.
- Organisation structure determines **budget centres**. If managers are to be held accountable for expenditure they have to be able to **control** it.
- The **behavioural implications vary** depending on participation, the use of budgets (as plans or pressure devices), and the style of management (budget-constrained, profit-conscious, non-accounting).
- **Participation** is sometimes seen as the way to **better budgeting** and **motivation**. However the effectiveness depends on management commitment and expertise, and there is always the temptation to introduce budgetary slack.
- **Accounting data** is an **important part of the organisation's information system**, although other data, as in the balanced scorecard, is also needed for successful strategic direction. The quality of management accounting data, and the detail it contains, depends on its overall usefulness to internal customers (as die from legal and regulatory requirements).

Quick Quiz

1. What are the main uses of a management accounting control system?
2. What contingent factors shape the management accounting system?
3. What three types of strategic management control might be employed in a divisionalised business?
4. The general principle is that managers should be held........only for those costs they can........
5. Why should user departments be charged for services?
6. Where a manager's performance is primarily evaluated on the basis of his or her ability to continually meet the budget on a short term basis this is known as........What other styles are there?
7. What is the cost of non-conformance?
8. What main steps are involved in measuring the performance of the accounts department?

Answers to Quick Quiz

1.
   - Score keeping
   - Attention-directing
   - Problem-solving
2.
   - Environment
   - Organisational structure
   - Technology
   - Size
   - Culture
   - Strategy
3.
   - Strategic planning
   - Financial control
   - Strategic control
4. Managers should only be held **responsible** for those costs they can **control**.
5. User departments should be charged for services to encourage them to work efficiently and to establish that the service department is itself operating efficiently.
6. Budget constrained. Other approaches are profit-conscious and non-accounting.
7. The cost of failure to deliver the required standard of excellence.
8.
   (a) Define boundaries
   (b) Define formal objectives
   (c) Ascertain activities each section does
   (d) Identify appropriate measures
   (e) Select suitable basis of comparison

Now try the question below from the Exam Question Bank

Number	Level	Marks	Time
Q4	Examination	25	45 mins

Part B
Risk and internal control

Risks and risk management

Introduction

This chapter introduces themes that will be developed not only in Part B, but throughout the rest of this text. We start by considering a number of the most significant risks organisations face, and we shall look at these in more detail later in this text.

Given the risks organisations face it is vital that they adopt a coherent framework for dealing with risks. COSO's **enterprise risk management** framework, which we discuss in Section 2, is a popular framework that has been evolving over the last few years.

In Section 3 we deal with how organisations **identify and analyse risk.** One important aspect of this process is to try to quantify risk exposure, and we shall examine risk quantification in more detail in Chapter 6.

The last section of this chapter deals with how organisations can **manage risks**. They can take certain steps to deal with all risks including appointing specialists to deal with the risks. However organisations have also to consider how to deal with each significant risk, and we shall look at the choices that they have.

Topic list	Learning outcomes	Syllabus references	Ability required
1 Types of risk faced by organisations	B(i)	B(1), (2)	Evaluation
2 Enterprise risk management	B(iii), (iv)	B(9)	Evaluation
3 Risk analysis and assessment	B(ii)	B(3)	Evaluation
4 Risk management	B(iii), (iv)	B(7), (9)	Evaluation

1 Types of risk faced by organisations

FAST FORWARD

Risks can be classified according to **who** they affect, whether their outcomes will be **beneficial** or **adverse**, and the **area** of an organisation's **affairs affected**.

Key term

Risk is a condition in which there exists a quantifiable dispersion in the possible outcomes from any activity. *(OT 2000)*

Question — Risks

Learning outcome: B(i)

What sort of risks might an organisation face?

Answer

Make your own list, specific to the organisations that you are familiar with. Here is a list extracted from an article by Tom Jones 'Risk Management' (*Administrator*, April 1993).

- Fire, flood, storm, impact, explosion, subsidence and other hazards
- Accidents and the use of faulty products
- Error: loss through damage or malfunction caused by mistaken operation of equipment or wrong operation of an industrial programme
- Theft and fraud
- Breaking social or environmental regulations
- Political risks (the appropriation of foreign assets by local governments, or of barriers to the repatriation of overseas profit)
- Computers: fraud, viruses, and espionage
- Product tamper
- Malicious damage '

1.1 Types of risk

A risk is a potential source of loss. There are various types of risk that exist in business and in life generally.

(a) **Fundamental risks** are those that affect society in general, or broad groups of people, and are beyond the control of any one individual. For example there is the risk of atmospheric pollution which can affect the health of a whole community but which may be quite beyond the power of an individual within it to control.

(b) **Particular risks** are risks over which an individual may have some measure of control. For example there is a risk attaching to smoking and we can control that risk by refraining from smoking.

(c) **Speculative risks** are those from which either good or harm may result. A business venture, for example, presents a speculative risk because either a profit or loss can result.

(d) **Pure risks** are those whose only possible outcome is harmful. The risk of damage to property by fire is a pure risk because no gain can result from it.

1.2 The role of risk in an organisation

All organisations will face risk. Only by the taking of some degree of risk can potentially profitable opportunities be exploited. However, all risks must be recognised, most managed to some extent, and some should be sought to be eliminated as being outside the scope of the remit of the management of a business run for, in general, risk-averse shareholders.

For example, a business in a high-tech industry, such as computing, which evolves rapidly within ever-changing markets and technologies, has to accept high risks in their research and development activities; but should they also be speculating on interest and exchange rates within their treasury activities?

Insurance premiums and transaction costs incurred in the reduction or elimination of risk can be expensive, and, as always, the costs must be balanced against the expected benefits.

Some of the benefits to be derived from the management of risk, possibly at the expense of profits are:

- **Predictability** of **cash flows**
- **Limitation of the impact** of potentially **bankrupting events**
- **Increased confidence** of its shareholders and other investors

There are many different types of risks faced by commercial organisations, particularly those with international activities. They may be categorised under the following headings.

- General business risk
- Financial risk
- Legal and political risk
- Information and technology risk
- Operational risk

The nature of these risks is discussed briefly below. In this and the next few chapters we shall go on to look at the most significant areas and management techniques in greater depth.

1.3 General business risk

Key term

Business risk is **the potential volatility of profits caused by the nature and type of the business operations involved.**

The most significant business risks are focused on the **strategy** the business adopts including concentration of resources, mergers and acquisitions and exit strategies. Planning and benchmarking procedures are also important. Organisations also need to guard against the risks that **business processes and operations** are **not aligned** to strategic goals.

Relations with stakeholders will also have a significant impact upon business risks because of the consequences of non-cooperation, for example investors not contributing new funds, suppliers not delivering on time, employees disrupting production and ultimately of course customers not buying goods and services. Organisations must be aware of the key factors that may lead to problems in relations with stakeholders.

- **Investors** will be concerned with financial returns, accuracy and timeliness of information and quality of leadership
- Relations with **suppliers** and **employees** will be influenced by the terms and conditions. With employees, the organisation also needs to consider whether they have the appropriate knowledge and attitudes
- Customers obviously be influenced by the **level** of **customer service,** also product safety issues and perhaps whether the organisation is 'ethical' in matters such as marketing practice

Other factors contributing to business risk will include:

- The types of industries/markets within which the business operated
- The state of the economy
- The actions of competitors and the possibility of substitutes
- The stage in a product's life cycle, higher risks in the introductory and declining stages
- The dependence upon inputs with fluctuating prices, eg wheat, oil etc
- The level of operating gearing – the proportion of fixed costs in total costs
- The flexibility of production processes to adapt to different specifications or products
- The organisation's research and development capacity and ability to innovate

There may be little management can do about some of these risks, they are inherent in business activity. However, strategies discussed later in this chapter such as **diversification** can contribute substantially to the reduction of many business risks.

1.4 Financial risks

You may have come across financial risks in your earlier studies and we shall examine many of them in detail in Chapters 17 to 20. The ultimate financial risk is that the organisation will not be able to continue to function as a going concern.

Financial risks include the risks relating to the **structure of finance** the organisation has, in particular the risks relating to the mix of equity and debt capital, also whether the organisation has an insufficient long-term capital base for the amount of trading it is doing (overtrading). Finance structure risk is covered in detail in Chapter 8 of BPP's *Management Accounting Financial Strategy* text.

Organisations also must consider the risks of **fraud and misuse** of financial resources, covered in Chapter 15.

Other shorter-term financial risks include:

- **Credit risk** – the possibility of payment default by the customer
- **Liquidity risk** – the risk of being unable to finance the credit
- **Cash management risk** - risks relating to the security of cash, also the risks of security of cash

Longer-term risks include currency and interest rate risks.

1.4.1 Currency risk

Key term

Currency risk is the possibility of loss or gain due to future changes in exchange rates. *(OT 2000)*

When a firm trades with an overseas supplier or customer, and the invoice is in the overseas currency, it will expose itself to exchange rate or currency risk. Movement in the foreign exchange rates will create risk in the settlement of the debt – ie the final amount payable/receivable in the home currency will be uncertain at the time of entering into the transaction. Investment in a foreign country or borrowing in a foreign currency will also carry this risk.

There are three types of currency risk.

(a) **Transaction risk** – arising from exchange rate movements between the time of entering into an international trading transaction and the time of cash settlement.

(b) **Translation risk** - the changes in balance sheet values of foreign assets and liabilities arising from retranslation at different prevailing exchange rates at the end of each year.

(c) **Economic risk** – the effect of exchange rate movements on the international competitiveness of the organisation, eg in terms of relative prices of imports/exports, the cost of foreign labour etc.

Of these three, transaction risk has the greatest immediate impact on day to day cash flows of an organisation, and there are many ways of reducing or eliminating this risk, for example by the use of **hedging** techniques. These and other currency risk management strategies are discussed in detail in Chapters 18 and 19.

1.4.2 Interest rate risk

As with foreign exchange rates, future interest rates cannot be easily predicted. If a firm has a significant amount of variable (floating) rate debt, interest rate movements will give rise to uncertainty about the cost of servicing this debt. Conversely, if a company uses a lot of fixed rate debt, it will lose out if interest rates begin to fall.

There are many arrangements and financial products that a firm's treasury department can use to reduce its exposure to interest rate risk for example, involving **hedging** techniques similar to those used for the management of currency risk. The topic of interest rate risk is covered in greater depth in Chapter 20.

1.4.3 Financial records and reporting risks

Financial risks can also be said to include **misstatement risks** relating to published financial information. This in turn may arise from **breakdown in the accounting systems**, **unrecorded liabilities** and **unreliable accounting records**.

1.5 Legal and political risks

Breaches of legislation, regulations or codes of conduct can have very serious consequences for organisations. Risks include financial or other penalties (including ultimately closedown), having to spend money and resources in fighting litigation and loss of reputation.

Governance codes are a particularly important example of best practice, and organisations must consider the risks of breaching provisions relating to integrity and objectivity, and also control over the organisation. We shall look at corporate governance in detail in Chapter 8.

Political risk is the risk that political action will affect the position and value of a company. It is connected with **country risk**, the risk associated with undertaking transactions with, or holding assets in, a particular country.

We shall examine these risks further in Chapter 17.

1.6 Information and technology risks

Risks relating to information and technology systems are covered in detail in Part E of this text, in particular in Chapter 24. They include taking decisions based on inadequate information and the threats of losing information.

Important technology risks relate to the **accuracy and continuing operation** of information systems. Organisations will be particularly concerned with the risk of unauthorised access and consequent disruption to computer systems.

In addition, as technology evolves and develops, organisations will be at risk from using out of date equipment and marketing methods, which may leave them at a **competitive disadvantage**. Products in a high-tech industry have a very short life-cycle, and an organisation must recognise and plan for continual replacement and upgrading of products if it is not to lose market share.

1.7 Operational risks

1.7.1 Property risks

Property risks are the risks from **damage**, **destruction** or **taking of property.** Perils to property include fire, windstorms, water leakage and vandalism.

If the organisation suffers damage, it may be liable for repairs or ultimately the builing of an entirely new property. There may also be a risk of **loss of rent**. If a building is accidentally damaged or destroyed, and the tenant is not responsible for the payment of rent during the period the property cannot be occupied, the landlord will lose the rent.

If there is damage to the property, the organisation could suffer from having to **suspend or reduce** its **operations**.

1.7.2 Trading risks

Both domestic and international traders will face trading risks, although those faced by the latter will generally be greater due to the increased distances and times involved. The types of trading risk include:

(a) **Physical risk**

Physical risk is the risk of goods being lost or stolen in transit, or the documents accompanying the goods going astray.

(b) **Trade risk**

Trade risk is the risk of the customer refusing to accept the goods on delivery (due to sub-standard/inappropriate goods), or the cancellation of the order in transit

(c) **Liquidity risk**

Liquidity risk is the inability to finance the credit

1.8 Fraud risk

All businesses run the risk of loss through the fraudulent activities of employees including management. This is perhaps one of the risk areas over which the company can exert the greatest control, through a coherent corporate strategy set out in a **fraud policy statement** and the setting up of strict **internal controls**. This is covered in Chapter 15.

2 Enterprise risk management

FAST FORWARD

Enterprise risk management provides a coherent framework for organisations to deal with risk, based on the following components:

- Internal environment
- Objective setting
- Event identification
- Risk assessment
- Risk response
- Control activities
- Information and communication
- Monitoring

2.1 Nature of enterprise risk management

Key term

Enterprise risk management is a process, effected by an entity's board of directors, management and other personnel, applied in strategy setting and across the enterprise, designed to identify potential events that may affect the entity and manage risks to be within its risk appetite, to provide reasonable assurance regarding the achievement of entity objectives. **COSO**

The Committee of Sponsoring Organisations of the Treadway Commission (COSO) goes on to expand its definition. It states that enterprise risk management has the following characteristics.

(a) It is a **process**, a means to an end, that should ideally be intertwined with existing operations and exist for fundamental business reasons.

(b) It is operated by **people at every level** of the organisation and is not just paperwork. It provides a mechanism helping people to understand risk, their responsibilities and levels of authority.

(c) It applied in **strategy setting,** with management considering the risks in alternative strategies

(d) It is applied **across the enterprise.** This means it takes into account activities at all levels of the organisation from enterprise-level activities such as strategic planning and resource allocation, to business unit activities and business processes. It includes taking an entity level portfolio view of risk. Each unit manager assesses the risk for his unit. Senior management ultimately consider these unit risks and also **interrelated risks.** Ultimately they will assess whether the overall risk portfolio is consistent with the organisation's risk appetite.

(e) It is designed to **identify events** potentially affecting the entity and manage risk within its **risk appetite,** the amount of risk it is prepared to accept in pursuit of value. The risk appetite should be aligned with the desired return from a strategy.

(f) It provides **reasonable assurance** to an entity's management and board. Assurance can at best be reasonable since risk relates to the uncertain future

(g) It is geared to the **achievement of objectives** in a number of categories, including **supporting** the **organisation's mission**, making **effective and efficient use** of the **organisation's resources**, ensuring **reporting is reliable**, and **complying** with **applicable laws and regulations.**

Because these characteristics are broadly defined, they can be applied across different types of organisations, industries and sectors. Whatever the organisation, the framework focuses on **achievement of objectives.**

Case Study

Different commentators have developed guidance on enterprise risk management in different ways. Arthur Andersen, as was, have argued that enterprise risk management must begin with the following actions:

- Establishing an oversight structure
- Defining a common language and framework
- Targeting risks and processes
- Establishing goals, objectives and a uniform process
- Assessing risk management capability

Ernst and Young identified six components of risk management:

- Risk strategy
- Risk management processes
- Appropriate culture and capability
- Risk management functions
- Enabling technologies
- Governance

2.2 Framework of enterprise risk management

The COSO framework consists of eight interrelated components:

They are covered in this text as follows:

- **Internal environment** or control environment – see Chapter 9
- **Objective setting** – covered in this section below
- **Event identification** – see Section 3 of this chapter
- **Risk assessment** – see Section 3 of this chapter
- **Risk response** – see Section 4 of this chapter
- **Control activities** or procedures – see Chapter 9
- **Information and communication** – see Chapter 7
- **Monitoring** – see Chapter 12

2.2.1 Objective setting

You will have discussed objective setting in a number of other papers. Enterprise risk management emphasises the importance of **setting strategic objectives** at entity and activity levels and **identifying critical success factors,** which feed into operations, reporting and compliance objectives.

2.3 Benefits of enterprise risk management

COSO highlights a number of advantages of adopting the process of enterprise risk management.

Alignment of risk appetite and strategy	The framework demonstrates to managers the need to consider risk toleration, then set objectives aligned with the strategy and develop mechanisms to manage the accompanying risks.
Link growth, risk and return	Risk is part of value creation, and organisations will seek a given level of return for the level of risk tolerated.
Choose best risk response	Enterprise risk management helps the organisation select whether to reduce, eliminate or transfer risk.
Minimise surprises and losses	By identifying potential loss-inducing events, the organisation can reduce the occurrence of unexpected problems.
Identify and manage risks across the organisation	As indicated above, the framework mean that managers can understand and aggregate connected risks.
Provide responses to multiple risks	For example risks associated with purchasing, over and under supply, prices and dubious supply sources might be reduced by an inventory control system that is integrated with suppliers.
Seize opportunities	By considering events as well as risks, managers can identify opportunities as well as losses.
Rationalise capital	Enterprise risk management allows management to allocate capital better and make a sounder assessment of capital needs.

3 Risk analysis and assessment

FAST FORWARD

Risk analysis involves **identifying, assessing, profiling, quantifying** and **consolidating risks.**

3.1 Analysis framework

A commonly used framework for analysing risk is made up of five stages:

- Identification
- Assessment
- Profiling
- Quantification
- Consolidation

3.2 Risk identification

No-one can manage a risk without first being aware that it exists. Some knowledge of perils, what items they can affect and how, is helpful to improve awareness of whether **familiar risks** (potential sources and causes of loss) are present, and the extent to which they could harm a particular person or organisation. The risk manager should also keep an eye open for **unfamiliar risks** which may be present.

Risk identification is a **continuous process**, so that new risks and changes affecting existing risks may be identified quickly and dealt with appropriately, before they can cause unacceptable losses.

Means of identifying risks (potential sources of loss) include:

(a) **Physical inspection**, which will show up risks such as poor housekeeping (for example rubbish left on floors, for people to slip on and to sustain fires)

(b) **Enquiries**, from which the frequency and extent of product quality controls and checks on new employees' references, for example, can be ascertained

(c) **Checking** a copy of every letter and memo issued in the organisation for early indications of major changes and new projects

(d) **Brainstorming** with representatives of different departments.

3.2.1 Event identification

A key aspect of risk identification, emphasised by the Committee of Sponsoring Organisations of the Treadaway Commission's report *Enterprise Risk Management Framework* is identification of events that could impact upon implementation of strategy or achievement of objectives.

Events analysis includes identification of:

(a) **External events** such as economic changes, political developments or technological advances

(b) **Internal events** such as equipment problems, human error or difficulties with products

(c) **Leading event indicators**. By monitoring data correlated to events, organisations identify the existence of conditions that could give rise to an event, for example customers also have balances outstanding beyond a certain length of time being very likely to default on those balances

(d) **Trends and root causes**. Once these have been identified, management may find that assessment and treatment of causes is a more effective solution than acting on individual events once they occur

(e) **Escalation triggers**, certain events happening or levels being reached that require immediate action

(f) **Event interdependencies**, identifying how one event can trigger another and how events can occur concurrently. For example a decision to defer investment in an improved distribution system might mean that downtime increases and operating costs go up

Once events have been identified, they can be **classified** horizontally across the whole organisation and vertically within operating units. By doing this management can gain a better understanding of the interrelationships between events, gaining enhanced information as a basis for risk assessment.

3.3 Risk assessment

It is not always simple to forecast the financial effect of a possible disaster, as it is not until *after* a loss that extra expenses, inconveniences and loss of time can be recognised. Even then it can be difficult to identify all of them. If your car is stolen, for example, and found converted to a heap of scrap metal, in addition to the cost of replacing it you can expect to pay for some quite **unexpected items**:

(a) Fares home, and to and from work until you have a replacement

(b) Telephone calls to the police, your family, your employer, and others affected

(c) Movement and disposal of the wrecked car

(d) Increased grocery bills from having to use corner shops instead of a distant supermarket

(e) Notification of DVLC that you are no longer the owner

(f) Work you must turn down because you have no car

(g) Hire purchase charges on the new car because you have insufficient funds to buy one, when all this happens

(h) Your time (which is difficult to value)

Organisations will probably keep more detailed records of their activities and the unit costs involved, but it is unlikely that any organisation can predict the full cost of every loss that might befall it with certainty.

3.3.1 Sources of information

Organisation charts will be needed if a manager is taken ill, for example to calculate which personnel will have extra work in his and other departments, how much will need be paid in overtime rates and whether additional expertise may have to be brought in temporarily. The personnel department may be asked for lists of employees with appropriate skills and experience who are prepared to help out.

Production flow charts must be used to discover the extent to which a factory's production will be affected by one machine breaking down, and whether alternative machines can be obtained or constructed, or alternative processes used.

Supplies flow charts and forecasts will help to assess how long a factory can maintain some or all of its production if a particular supplier suffers a major fire, or bankruptcy, and whether there are alternative suppliers.

Details of **major customers** can be monitored to identify those whose bankruptcy could damage the organisation.

Published accounts, internal accounts and budgets are a fertile source of information. The more carefully costs are allocated to each department, the easier it should be to calculate additional costs which would be incurred in a given emergency, which budgets will be affected and how quickly necessary funds can be made available.

Detailed **plans of site and buildings** will show potential bottlenecks in fire escape routes, obstructions which might make difficulties for fire engines and problems of access which could occur for both the site and its neighbours from fire, explosion, or escaping gas.

Physical inspection should be carried out regularly. Potential backup storage space and other possible emergency measures may be spotted, which may not appear in records.

3.4 Risk profiling

This stage involves using the results of a risk assessment to group risks into risk families. One way of doing this is a likelihood/consequences matrix.

	Consequences	
Likelihood	*Low*	*High*
High	Loss of lower-level staff	Loss of senior or specialist staff Loss of sales to competitor Loss of sales due to macroeconomic factors
Low	Loss of suppliers	Loss of key customers Failure of computer systems

This profile can then be used to set priorities for risk mitigation

3.5 Risk quantification

Risks that require more analysis can be quantified, where **possible results or losses** and **probabilities** are **calculated** and **distributions** or **confidence limits** added on. From this exercise is derived the following key data.

- **Average or expected result or loss**
- **Frequency of losses**
- **Chances of losses**
- **Largest predictable loss**

to which the organisation could be exposed by a particular risk. The risk manager must also be able to estimate the effects of each possible cause of loss, as some of the effects that he needs to consider may not be insured against.

We shall look further at how an organisation can measure expected results and worse possible results in the next chapter.

The likely **frequency** of losses from any particular cause can be predicted with some degree of confidence, from studying available records. This confidence margin can be improved by including the likely effects of **changed circumstances** in the calculation, once they are identified and quantified. Risk managers must therefore be aware of the possibility of the **increase of an existing risk**, or the **introduction** of a **new risk**, affecting the probability and/or possible frequency of losses from another cause.

Ultimately the risk manager will need to know the **frequency** or **magnitude** of **losses** that could place the organisation in serious difficulties.

3.6 Risk consolidation

Risk that has been analysed and quantified at the divisional or subsidiary level needs to be aggregated to the corporate level. This aggregation will be required as part of the overall review of risk that the board needs to undertake which we shall look at in more detail in later chapters.

4 Risk management

FAST FORWARD

General steps organisations can take to manage risks include issuing a **risk policy statement**, appointing a **risk manager** or **risk specialists** and **communicating risks** to staff and shareholders.

Having analysed its risks, the organisation then has to decide what to do about them. There are certain general steps that can be taken.

4.1 Risk policy statement

Organisations ought to have a statement of risk policy and strategy that is distributed to all managers and staff and covers the following areas:

- Definitions of risk and risk management
- Objectives of risk policy
- Regulatory requirements
- Benefits of risk management
- How risk management is linked into strategic decision-making and performance
- What areas of risk management (risk avoidance, risk reduction) are particularly important
- Risk classification
- Roles of board, managers, staff and audit and risk committees
- Internal control framework and important controls
- Other tools and techniques
- Assurance reporting
- Role of training
- How to obtain help

4.2 Risk personnel

4.2.1 Risk manager

A risk manager's job is **handling the risks** (that is, perils, such as the possibility of the death of a breadwinner, or of destruction of property) likely to harm a person or organisation, in the most appropriate manner. Whether a specialist is employed depends on the **amount of work involved**, and the time and expertise that the person, or the organisation's officers, have available for it.

Large companies, or groups of companies, have a person or section to deal with risks full time. In many organisations, however, detailed risk management functions are **divided** among those officers whose jobs are related to them. The office manager may deal with fire precautions, and the managing director with buying insurances, for example, and each may call in experts to assist with these functions; while the transport manager may manage the motoring risks by himself.

In much smaller organisations, all such jobs are naturally dealt with by the executive manager, who may well have an outside expert such as an insurer's inspector or broker's account handler to do much of the technical planning.

4.2.2 Risk specialists

Most individuals have little time for looking after their personal safety and security, still less for searching the market for the most suitable insurances; they frequently employ agents to help manage some of their risks.

A **specialist** advising on management of personal risks can work only as well as the client allows. A good specialist will ask for information and for co-operation with the expert surveys that enable him to provide a proper service; he will ensure that the client understands what safety measures are required and he will see that they are put into practice.

4.3 Risk register

Organisations should have formal methods of collecting together information on risk and response. A risk register listing each significant risk and the management action taken is often used.

4.4 Communication of risk

Communicating to shareholders and other stakeholders particularly those risks that cannot be avoided is an important aspect of risk management. Of course the stock market may react badly to this news. If risks are to be successfully communicated, the messages need to be consistent and the organisation has to be trusted by the recipients.

4.5 Dealing with risk

FAST FORWARD

Methods for dealing with risk include **risk avoidance, risk reduction, risk retention, self-insurance** and **risk transfer**.

In the rest of the section we shall consider the various ways in which organisations can try to mitigate risks or indeed whether it will be worthwhile for them to accept risks.

4.6 Avoidance of risk

Organisations will often consider whether risk can be avoided and if so whether avoidance is desirable. That is, will the possible savings from losses avoided be greater than the advantages that can be gained by not taking any measures, and running the risk?

An extreme form of business risk avoidance is termination of operations, for example operations in politically volatile countries where the risks of loss (including loss of life) are considered to be too great or the costs of security are considered to be too high.

Case Study

In 1976 M&M Mars reacted to adverse publicity about the carcinogenic effects of red dye Number 2 by removing red M&Ms from the market. Although red M&Ms were not actually made with red dye number 2, the public perceived that they **were,** and thus management felt compelled to counter the risk to the company's reputation by removing the product from sale.

The scare subsequently disappeared, and red M&Ms were re-introduced in the late 1980s.

4.7 Reduction of risk

Often risks can be avoided in part, or reduced, but not avoided altogether. This is true of many business risks, where the risks of launching a new product can be reduced by market research, advertising and so on.

Other risk reduction measures include contingency planning and loss control.

4.7.1 Contingency planning

Contingency planning involves identifying the **post-loss needs** of the business, **drawing up plans** in advance and **reviewing them regularly** to take account of changes in the business. The process has three basic constituents.

Information	How, for example, do you turn off the sprinklers once the fire is extinguished? All the information that will need to be available during and after the event should be gathered in advance. This will include names and addresses of staff, details of suppliers of machinery, waste disposal firms and so on. The information should be kept up to date and it should be circulated so that it will be readily available to anyone who might need it.
Responsibilities	The plan should lay down what is to be done by whom. Duties should be delegated as appropriate; deputies should be nominated to take account of holidays and sickness. Those who hold responsibilities should be aware of what they are, how they have changed, who will help them and so on.
Practice	Unless the plan has been tested there is no guarantee that it will work. A full-scale test may not always be possible; simulations, however, should be as realistic as possible and should be taken seriously by all involved. The results of any testing should be monitored so that amendments can be made to the plan as necessary.

4.7.2 Loss control

Control of losses also requires careful advance planning. There are two main aspects to good loss control, the physical and the psychological.

(a) There are **many physical devices** that can be installed to minimise losses when harmful events actually occur. Sprinklers, fire extinguishers, escape stairways, burglar alarms and machine guards are obvious examples.

It is **not enough** however to **install such devices**. They will need to be **inspected** and **maintained** regularly, and back-up measures will be needed for times when they are inoperational. Their adequacy and appropriateness in the light of changes to the business also needs to be kept under constant review.

(b) The key psychological factors are **awareness** and **commitment**. Every person in the business should be made aware that losses are possible and that they can be controlled. Commitment to loss control can be achieved by making individual managers accountable for the losses under their control. Staff should be encouraged to draw attention to any aspects of their job which makes losses possible.

We shall talk more about how controls and control systems can be used to reduce risk in later chapters.

4.8 Retaining risks

Risk retention is where the organisation bears the risk itself, and if an unfavourable outcome occurs, it will suffer the full loss. Risk retention is inevitable to some extent. However good the organisation's risk identification and assessment processes are, there will always be some unexpected risk. Other reasons for risk retention are that the risk is considered to be **insignificant** or the cost of avoiding the risk is considered to be too great set against the potential loss that could be incurred.

The decision of whether to retain or transfer risks depends first on whether there is anyone to transfer a risk to. The answer is more likely to be 'no' for an individual than for an organisation, because:

(a) Individuals have **more small risks** than do organisations and the administrative costs of transferring and carrying them can make the exercise impracticable for the insurer.

(b) The individual has **smaller resources** to find a carrier.

In the last resort organisations usually have customers to pass their risks or losses to, up to a point, and individuals do not.

4.9 Self-insurance

An option sometimes associated with retaining risks is **self-insurance**. In contrast to non-insurance, which is effectively gritting one's teeth and hoping for the best, self-insurance is putting aside funds of whatever size, in a lump or at intervals, in a reserve dedicated to defraying the expenses involved should a particular sort of loss happen.

A **more sophisticated method of self-insurance** is setting up a **captive**.

4.10 Captive insurance

Key term

A **captive**, or **captive insurer**, is an insurance company wholly owned by a commercial organisation, and usually dedicated solely to the underwriting of its parent company's risks. Its primary purpose, therefore, is to be a vehicle for transfer of the parent company's risks.

An organisation with a risk that it cannot carry, which cannot find one or more insurers to take the bulk of that risk from it, may form a **captive insurer** to carry that risk. The captive insurer has all the parent's experience of the horrible risk to call on, so its premiums will not be unnecessarily large, and its policy terms will be reasonable.

Captives are sometimes formed because the parent organisation hopes to exchange a regular large expense on premiums for a profit centre. In addition:

(a) **Premiums** remitted to the captive (tax deductible as business expenses) can be **invested** by the captive to earn dividends etc.

(b) The captive's **underwriting**, even if restricted to the parent's risks, can be **profitable**.

(c) As premiums and claims are paid back and forth between countries, **payments** can be **timed** to some extent so that profits can be made in currency exchange.

(d) A foreign captive may be able to work on a **smaller initial investment**, and with lower taxes on its profits, than a local insurer. (This may be reflected in the size of premiums it quotes.)

(e) If the company trades in several different countries with local regulations, it often becomes apparent that the buying power associated with a large group is **not reflected** in **premiums obtainable** in individual countries. Furthermore the local policy conditions will often fall short of the cover required by the group that may well then have to take out a further policy to cover the 'difference in conditions'. A captive is one way to solve this problem.

In other cases, companies subject to large risks, but wishing to retain a sizeable slice of that risk (a large excess, or deductible) are **unable** to **find insurers** in the market who would allow such a large 'excess'. If they did, those insurers are reluctant to allow a sufficiently large discount on the premium. The dissatisfied companies can form captive insurers to write business on terms more acceptable to their parents.

4.10.1 Advantages of using a captive

(a) Using a captive insurance company should have the dual advantages of **minimising costs** and **ensuring conformity of cover**. This is particularly useful in sensitive, and therefore potentially expensive, areas of risk such as environmental pollution, product liability and professional indemnity.

(b) Premiums will purely reflect the group's **own claims experience** rather than the industry as a whole that may be tainted by more reckless operators.

(c) Costs and **administration** are more easily **controlled** with smaller overheads than a large insurance company and the commercial profit element removed, though the captive should not make losses. There is also a direct management link between the insurance of the business and its operations with a powerful incentive for effective risks and claims management.

(d) The captive can link into the **re-insurance market**. This enables a significant part of the risk to be 'laid off' with re-insurers at comparatively low rates.

However a captive is unlikely to absorb all of its parent's insurances. Indeed, some established insurers and insurance brokers provide an advisory service, investigating and reporting for companies on whether a captive would be a viable project for them, and the best way for them to establish one.

4.10.2 Problems with using a captive

If a captive is set up, there will be a loss of the **expertise** that was previously obtained from using a professional insurance company. Choice of staff and professional advisers will be critical.

The captive may also be vulnerable if it faces a **large claim** in its early years before sufficient premiums have been built up. The company would have to bear the losses itself. It is therefore normal practice for a captive to cover only a set proportion of the risk until premiums have been built up.

Captives are not always owned by a single organisation or company. It is becoming increasingly common in some countries to find groups of companies forming joint captives.

The principal reason for joint captives seems to be that the initial outlays required are too large, and the projected premium available too small, for a company to support a captive alone. These captives have the following other advantages.

(a) The **risks** they write can be **smaller** (if they belong to small businesses) and will be more numerous than if they had a single parent.

(b) The **claims** they pay will generally be **smaller** and less likely to exhaust their funds.

(c) There is likely to be a **larger number of risks** insured which do not produce claims in any one year.

(d) Where the individual premiums are worth hundreds of pounds, increased numbers of risks do **not involve incurring** an **unacceptably large ratio** of administrative expenses to premium.

4.10.3 Location of captives

There are about twenty countries where captives are registered. The attraction of a foreign location can be low rates of local company taxation. These may not remain constant, but small countries attracting large volumes of such business are unlikely to increase their taxation to unattractive levels.

A second, but very important, consideration is the **political stability** of the country considered: the risk of a new regime nationalising the business, or imposing restrictive exchange control, must be small.

Setting up a captive abroad is easier initially if:

(a) **Local laws facilitate** setting up a firm.

(b) **Local officials** are **helpful** and know what is involved.

(c) The **local facilities**, from communications and electricity supplies to office personnel available, are at least **adequate**.

4.11 Transfer of risk

Alternatively, risks can be transferred - to suppliers, customers or insurers. Risk transfer can even be to the state.

Decisions should not be made without careful checking to ensure that as many influencing factors as possible have been included in the assessment. A decision not to rectify the design of a product, because rectification could be as expensive as paying any claims from disgruntled customers, is in fact a decision to transfer the risk to the customers without their knowledge: it may not take into account the possibility of courts' awarding exemplary damages to someone injured by the product, to discourage people from taking similar decisions in the future.

4.11.1 Hold harmless agreements

Indemnity or **hold harmless agreements** can be useful. They:

- **Reduce the price of goods** for a party who takes on extra responsibility
- **Preserve good trading relations** by avoiding arguments
- **Preserve good public relations** if efficiently and sympathetically operated

Well-known examples of hold harmless agreements, where legal liability falls on one party but claims are dealt with and paid by another, are construction contracts involving builders, civil engineers, or electrical or mechanical engineers. Standard forms of contract are published, providing for agreed distribution of liability for injury, loss and damage under various headings, as well as (usually) for insurance of particular items and liabilities by one party, frequently in both their names.

4.11.2 Limitation of liability

Some contracts, in which one party accepts strict liability up to a set limit, or liability which is wider than the law would normally impose, follow very ancient customs. Examples are contracts for carriage of passengers or goods by air or sea.

4.11.3 Legal and other restrictions on transferring risks

The first restriction is that a supplier or customer may **refuse** to enter a contract unless your organisation agrees to take a particular risk. This depends on the trading relationship between the firms concerned, and not a little on economics: how many suppliers could supply the item or service in question, for example, and how great is your need for the item?

4.12 Risk sharing

Risks can be partly held and partly transferred to someone else. An example is an insurance policy, where the insurer pays any losses incurred by the policyholder above a set amount.

Risk-sharing arrangements can be very significant in business strategy. For example in a **joint venture** arrangement each participant's risk can be limited to what it is prepared to bear.

4.13 Risk pooling and diversification

Risk pooling and diversification involves using portfolio theory to manage risks. You may well remember that portfolio theory is an important part of an organisation's financial strategy, but its principles can be applied to non-financial risks as well.

Risk pooling or diversification involves creating a **portfolio of different risks** based on a number of events, which, if some turn out well others will turn out badly, and the average outcome will be neutral. What an organisation has to do is to avoid having all its risks **positively correlated** which means that everything will turn out **extremely well** or **extremely badly.**

4.14 Risk hedging

Hedging means taking an action that will **offset** an **exposure to a risk** by incurring a **new risk** in the **opposite direction.** Hedging is perhaps important in the area of currency or interest rate risk management, and we shall discuss in detail various hedging instruments such as forward agreements, futures and options in Part D of this text. What these have in common generally speaking is that the organisation makes a commitment, possibly to undertake a contract in the future at a set price, to offset the risk of a transaction that will take place in the future, the value of which is currently uncertain.

Chapter roundup

- Risks can be classified according to **who** they affect, whether their outcomes will be **beneficial** or **adverse**, and the **area** of an organisation's **affairs** affected.
- **Enterprise risk management** provides a coherent framework for organisations to deal with risk, based on the following components:
  - Internal environment
  - Objective setting
  - Event identification
  - Risk assessment
  - Risk response
  - Control activities
  - Information and communication
  - Monitoring
- **Risk analysis** involves **identifying, assessing, profiling, quantifying** and **consolidating risks**.
- General steps organisations can take to manage risks include issuing a **risk policy statement**, appointing a **risk manager** or **risk specialists** and **communicating risks** to staff and shareholders.
- Methods for dealing with risk include **risk avoidance**, **risk reduction**, **risk retention**, **self-insurance** and **risk transfer.**

Quick quiz

1 What is the difference between pure risks and speculative risks?

2 What are the major property risks that organisations face?

3 What according to COSO are the key characteristics of enterprise risk management?

4 What does events analysis aim to identify?

5 What key indicators should risk quantification provide?

6 What are the main elements that should be covered by a risk policy statement?

7 What is a captive insurer?

8 Fill in the blank.

------ is taking an action that will offset an exposure to a risk by incurring a new risk in the opposite direction.

Answers to quick quiz

1 Pure risks just relate to harmful outcomes whereas speculative risks relate to positive as well as harmful outcomes.

2 Damage, destruction or taking of property

3
- Process
- Operated by people at every level
- Applied in strategy setting
- Applied across the organisation
- Identifies significant events
- Provides reasonable assurance
- Geared to the achievement of objectives

4
- External events
- Internal events
- Leading event indicators
- Trends and root causes

5
- Average or expected result
- The frequency of losses
- The chances of loss
- The largest predictable loss

6
- Definitions of risk and risk management
- Objectives of risk policy
- Regulatory requirements
- Benefits of risk management
- How risk management is linked into strategic decision-making and performance
- What areas of risk management (risk avoidance, risk reduction) are particularly important
- Risk classification
- Roles of board, managers, staff and audit and risk committees
- Internal control framework and important controls
- Other tools and techniques
- Assurance reporting
- Role of training
- How to obtain help

7 An insurer whose main purpose is to underwrite its owner's risks

8 **Risk hedging** is taking an action that will offset an exposure to a risk by incurring a new risk in the opposite direction.

Now try the question below from the Exam Question Bank

Number	Level	Marks	Time
Q5	Introductory	N/a	35 mins

6

Risk measurement

Introduction

Having looked at the risks organisations may face in the last chapter, in this chapter we examine the ways in which risks can be measured. We start by describing a methodology for assessing risk, and then look at the ways in which risk can be calculated.

You may be asked to calculate risk using fairly straightforward calculations and we give examples of these in Section 1. In Sections 2 to 6 we concentrate on specific statistical techniques that give an indication of risk and also perhaps the most likely outcome.

In the last section of this chapter we deal with the process of building up more complex scenarios to model risk, and how organisations use the results of the scenarios they have developed.

Topic list	Learning outcomes	Syllabus references	Ability required
1 Risk quantification	B(ii)	B(3)	Comprehension
2 Sensitivity analysis	B(ii)	B(3)	Comprehension
3 Expected values and probability models	B(ii)	B(3)	Comprehension
4 Decision trees and matrices	B(ii)	B(3)	Comprehension
5 Simulation models	B(ii)	B(3)	Comprehension
6 Using the results of statistical analysis	B(ii)	B(3)	Comprehension
7 Scenarios	B(ii)	B(3)	Comprehension

1 Risk quantification

FAST FORWARD

Sometimes the **potential loss** may be a **single definite figure**. How this figure is calculated will depend on the asset or benefit to which the loss relates.

1.1 Quantification of losses

Often quantification of losses will not involve statistical techniques, but a simple single estimate of what would be lost if adverse events or circumstances occur. For example if an accountancy firm had a client that generated a fixed fee each year, the loss would be the **contribution** (**fees lost** less **labour and other variable costs saved**).

1.2 Exposure of physical assets

Exposures with physical assets may include:

- **Total value of the assets**, for example the value of items stolen from a safe
- **Costs of repair**, if for example an accident occurs
- **Change of value of an asset,** for example property depreciating in value because of a new airport development nearby
- **Decrease in revenues**, for example loss of rent through a rental property being unlettable for a period
- **Costs of unused capacity**, costs incurred by spare capacity that is taken as a precaution but does not end up being used

Managers need to be aware of indirect risks as well as direct risks. For example if assets are damaged, the direct costs are the costs of repairing the asset, whilst the indirect costs might be the costs of interruption of operations, the **loss of contribution** and the **extra expenses** incurred to keep the organisation operating.

1.3 Exposure of financial assets

We shall examine in detail the risks of financial assets in Part D of this text. For now it is worth noting that whilst the risk of trading shares and most forms of debt might be that their values fall to zero, this is not necessarily true of futures and options, where the loss depends on margin requirements. In addition anyone who is exposed to loss as a **result of price rises** is in theory exposed to the risk of **infinite loss**, since prices could rise indefinitely.

1.4 Exposure of human assets

1.4.1 Death or serious injury

The most severe risk to employees is the risk of death or serious injury. The loss to the employee's family, for which the organisation may be liable, could be the **future value** of their **expected income stream**, mitigated by any benefits available but enhanced by other losses that arise as a result of death, for example loss of married person's tax allowance. Alternatively it could be measured by the expenditure required to fulfil the **needs** of the deceased's dependent family. For less serious injuries, the costs of medical care may be the relevant figure.

1.4.2 Key persons

Certain individuals may make a significant contribution to the office because of their knowledge, skills or business contacts. One measure of this loss will be the present value of the individual's contribution (attributable earnings less remuneration). Indirect costs may include the effect on other staff of the loss of the key person (decreased productivity or indeed the costs of their own departure)

1.4.3 Business discontinuation losses

If a director, partner or senior employee dies or departs, there may be costs of having to cope with the disruption, including even the costs of dissolution if local law requires termination of a partnership on the departure of a single partner.

2 Sensitivity analysis

FAST FORWARD

Sensitivity analysis assesses how responsive the project's NPV is to changes in the variables used to calculate that NPV. One particular approach to sensitivity analysis, the **certainty - equivalent approach**, involves the conversion of the expected cash flows of the project to riskless equivalent amounts.

2.1 Sensitivity analysis and NPV

Key term

Sensitivity analysis is one method of analysing the risk surrounding a capital expenditure project and enables an assessment to be made of how responsive the project's NPV is to changes in the variables that are used to calculate that NPV.

The NPV could depend on a number of uncertain independent variables.

- Selling price
- Sales volume
- Cost of capital
- Initial cost
- Operating costs
- Benefits

The basic approach of sensitivity analysis is to **calculate the project's NPV** under **alternative assumptions** to determine how sensitive it is to changing conditions. An indication is thus provided of those variables to which the NPV is most sensitive (**critical variables**) and the **extent** to which those variables **may change** before the investment results in a negative NPV.

Sensitivity analysis therefore provides an indication of why a project might fail. Management should review critical variables to assess whether or not there is a strong possibility of events occurring which will lead to a negative NPV. Management should also pay particular attention to controlling those variables to which the NPV is particularly sensitive, once the decision has been taken to accept the investment.

2.2 Example: sensitivity analysis

Kenney is considering a project with the following cash flows.

Year	Initial investment	Variable costs	Cash inflows	Net cash flows
	£'000	£'000	£'000	£'000
0	7,000			
1		(2,000)	6,500	4,500
2		(2,000)	6,500	4,500

(650,000 units at £10 per unit)

Required

Measure the sensitivity of the project to changes in variables.

Solution

The PVs of the cash flow are as follows.

Year	Discount factor 8%	PV of initial investment £'000	PV of variable costs £'000	PV of cash inflows £'000	PV of net cash flow £'000
0	1.000	(7,000)			(7,000)
1	0.926		(1,852)	6,019	4,167
2	0.857		(1,714)	5,571	3,857
		(7,000)	(3,566)	11,590	1,024

The project has a positive NPV and would appear to be worthwhile. The changes in cash flows which would need to occur for the project to breakeven (and hence be on the point of being unacceptable) are as follows.

(a) **Initial investment.** The initial investment can rise by £1,024,000 before the investment breaks even. The initial investment may therefore increase by 1,024/7,000 = 15%.

(b) **Sales volume.** The present value of the cash inflows less the present value of the variable costs will have to fall to £7,000,000 for the NPV to be zero.

We need to find the net cash flows in actual values. As the cash flows are equal each year, cumulative discount tables can be used.

(i) The discount factor for 8% and year 2 is 1.783.

(ii) If the discount factor is divided into the required present value of £7,000,000 we get an annual cash flow of £3,925,968.

(iii) Given that the most likely net cash flow is £4,500,000, the net cash flow may decline by approximately £574,032 (4,500,000 – 3,925,968) each year before the NPV becomes zero.

(iv) Total sales revenue may therefore decline by £831,930 (assuming net cash flow is 69% (4,500/6,500) of sales) (therefore sales = 574,032 × 6,500/4,500). At a selling price of £10 per unit this represents 83,193 units.

(v) Alternatively we may state that sales volume may decline by 13% before the NPV becomes negative.

(c) **Selling price.** When sales volume is 650,000 units per annum, total sales revenue can fall to £5,925,968 (£(6,500,000 – 574,032) per annum before the NPV becomes negative. This represents a selling price of £9.12 per unit, which represents a 8.8% reduction in the selling price.

(d) **Variable costs.** The total variable cost can increase by £574,032, or £0.88 per unit. This represents an increase of 28.6%.

(e) **Cost of capital.** We need to calculate the IRR of the project. Let us try discount rates of 15% and 20%.

Year	*Net cash flow*	*Discount factor*	*PV*	*Discount factor*	*PV*
	£'000	15%	£'000	20%	£'000
0	(7,000)	0.870	(6,090)	0.833	(5,831)
1	4,500	0.756	3,402	0.694	3,123
2	4,500	0.658	2,961	0.579	2,606
		NPV =	273	NPV =	(102)

$$IRR = 0.15 + \left[\frac{273}{273+102} \times (0.20-0.15)\right] = 18.64\%$$

The cost of capital can therefore increase by 133% before the NPV becomes negative.

The elements to which the NPV appears to be most sensitive are the selling price followed by the sales volume. Management should thus pay particular attention to these factors so that they can be carefully monitored.

2.3 Weaknesses of this approach to sensitivity analysis

These are as follows.

(a) The method requires that **changes** in each key variable are **isolated.** However management is more interested in the combination of the effects of changes in two or more key variables.

(b) Looking at factors in isolation is unrealistic since they are often **interdependent**.

(c) Sensitivity analysis does not examine the **probability** that any particular variation in costs or revenues might occur.

(d) **Critical factors** may be those over which managers have no control.

(e) In itself it does not provide a decision rule. Parameters defining **acceptability** must be laid down by managers.

Question — Sensitivity analysis

Learning outcome: B(ii)

Nevers Ure has a cost of capital of 8% and is considering a project with the following 'most-likely' cash flows.

Year	*Purchase of plant*	*Running costs*	*Savings*
	£	£	£
0	(7,000)		
1		2,000	6,000
2		2,500	7,000

Required

Measure the sensitivity (in percentages) of the project to changes in the levels of expected costs and savings.

Answer

The PVs of the cash flows are as follows.

Year	Discount factor 8%	PV of plant cost £	PV of running costs £	PV of savings £	PV of net cash flow £
0	1.000	(7,000)			(7,000)
1	0.926		(1,852)	5,556	3,704
2	0.857		(2,143)	5,999	3,856
		(7,000)	(3,995)	11,555	560

The project has a positive NPV and would appear to be worthwhile. The changes in cash flows which would need to occur for the project to break even (NPV = 0) are as follows.

(a) Plant costs would need to increase by a PV of £560, that is by (560/7,000) × 100% = 8%

(b) Running costs would need to increase by a PV of £560, that is by (560/3,995) × 100% = 14%

(c) Savings would need to fall by a PV of £560, that is by (560/11,555) × 100% = 4.8%

2.4 The certainty-equivalent approach

Another method is the **certainty-equivalent approach**. By this method, the expected cash flows of the project are converted to riskless equivalent amounts. The greater the risk of an expected cash flow, the smaller the 'certainty-equivalent' value (for receipts) or the larger the certainty equivalent value (for payments).

2.5 Example: certainty-equivalent approach

Dark Ages, whose cost of capital is 10%, is considering a project with the following expected cash flows.

Year	Cash flow £	Discount factor 10%	Present value £
0	(9,000)	1.000	(9,000)
1	7,000	0.909	6,363
2	5,000	0.826	4,130
3	5,000	0.751	3,755
		NPV	+5,248

The project seems to be clearly worthwhile. However, because of the uncertainty about the future cash receipts, the management decides to reduce them to 'certainty-equivalents' by taking only 70%, 60% and 50% of the years 1, 2 and 3 cash flows respectively. (Note that this method of risk adjustment allows for different risk factors in each year of the project.)

On the basis of the information set out above, assess whether the project is worthwhile.

Solution

The risk-adjusted NPV of the project is as follows.

Year	Cash flow £	PV factor	PV £
0	(9,000)	1.000	(9,000)
1	4,900	0.909	4,454
2	3,000	0.826	2,478
3	2,500	0.751	1,878
		NPV =	– 190

The project is too risky and should be rejected.

The disadvantage of the 'certainty-equivalent' approach is that the amount of the adjustment to each cash flow is decided **subjectively**.

3 Expected values and probability analysis

FAST FORWARD

Bayes' strategy is that if a manager is faced with a number of alternative decisions, each with a range of possible outcomes, the optimum decision will be the one that gives the highest expected value (of profit/contribution).

3.1 Expected values

Where probabilities are assigned to different outcomes, it is common to evaluate the worth of a decision as the expected value, or weighted average, of these outcomes.

Key term

Expected value is 'The financial forecast of the outcome of a course of action multiplied by the probability of achieving that outcome. The probability is expressed as a value ranging from 0 to 1.'

(CIMA *Official Terminology*)

If a decision maker is faced with a number of alternative decisions, each with a range of possible outcomes, the **optimum decision** will therefore be the **one which gives the highest expected value**.

Key term

The choice of the option with the highest EV is known as **Bayes' strategy**.

3.2 Example: Bayes' strategy

Suppose a manager has to choose between mutually exclusive options A and B, and the probable outcomes of each option are as follows.

Option A		*Option B*	
Probability	*Profit*	*Probability*	*Profit*
	£		£
0.8	5,000	0.1	(2,000)
0.2	6,000	0.2	5,000
		0.6	7,000
		0.1	8,000

The expected value (EV) of profit of each option would be measured as follows

Probability		*Option A Profit*		*EV of Profit*	*Probability*		*Option B Profit*		*EV of Profit*
		£		£			£		£
0.8	×	5,000	=	4,000	0.1	×	(2,000)	=	(200)
0.2	×	6,000	=	1,200	0.2	×	5,000	=	1,000
		EV	=	5,200	0.6	×	7,000	=	4,200
					0.1	×	8,000	=	800
							EV	=	5,800

Formula to learn

The **expected value** of an opportunity is equal to the sum of the probabilities of an outcome occurring multiplied by the return expected if it does occur:

$$EV = \Sigma px$$

where p is the probability of an outcome occurring and x is the value (profit or cost) of that outcome.

In this example, since it offers a higher EV of expected profit, option B would be selected in preference to A, unless further risk analysis is carried out.

Question — EV calculations

Learning outcome: B(ii)

A manager has to choose between mutually exclusive options A, B, C and D and the probable outcomes of each option are as follows.

Option A		*Option B*		*Option C*		*Option D*	
Probability	*Cost*	*Probability*	*Cost*	*Probability*	*Cost*	*Probability*	*Cost*
	£		£		£		£
0.1	30,000	0.5	21,000	0.29	15,000	0.03	14,000
0.1	60,000	0.5	20,000	0.54	20,000	0.30	17,000
0.1	80,000			0.17	30,000	0.35	21,000
0.7	5,500					0.32	24,000

All options will produce an income of £30,000.

Which option should be chosen?

A Option A
B Option B
C Option C
D Option D
E There is no difference between the options.

Answer

The correct answer is C.

A: EV of cost = £20,850
EV of profit = £9,150

B: EV of cost = £20,500
EV of profit = £9,500

C: EV of cost = £20,250
EV of profit = £9,750

D: EV of cost = £20,550
EV of profit = £9,450

C has the highest EV of profit.

3.3 Limitations of expected values

Referring back to the example above, the preference for B over A on the basis of expected value is marred by the fact that A's **worst possible outcome is a profit of £5,000**, whereas **B might incur a loss of £2,000** (although there is a 70% chance that profits would be £7,000 or more, which would be more than the best profits from option A).

Since the **decision must be made once only** between A and B, the expected value of profit (which is merely a weighted average of all possible outcomes) has severe limitations as a decision rule by which to judge preference as it ignores the range of outcomes and their probabilities.

Expected values are more **valuable** as a guide to decision making where they refer to **outcomes which will occur many times over**.

- The probability that so many customers per day will buy a tin of peaches
- The probability that a call centre will receive so many phone calls per hour

Exam focus point

The pilot paper contained a relatively straightforward multiple choice question which required the calculation of an expected value. A Section A question on the topic in May 2003 was also not difficult.

3.4 EVs and risk analysis

Where some analysis of risk is required when probabilities have been assigned to various outcomes, an elementary, but extremely useful, form of risk analysis is the worst possible/most likely/best possible technique.

3.5 Example: risk analysis

Skiver has budgeted the following results for the coming year.

Sales	*Probability*	*EV of Sales*
Units		Units
30,000	0.3	9,000
40,000	0.4	16,000
50,000	0.3	15,000
		40,000

The budgeted sales price is £10 per unit, and the expected cost of materials is as follows.

Cost per unit of output	*Probability*	*EV*
£		£
4	0.2	0.8
6	0.6	3.6
8	0.2	1.6
		6.0

Materials are the only variable cost. All other costs are fixed and are budgeted at £100,000.

The **expected value of profit** is £60,000.

	£
Sales (EV 40,000 units) at £10 each	400,000
Variable costs (40,000 × £6)	240,000
Contribution	160,000
Fixed costs	100,000
Profit	60,000

The worst possible outcome would be sales of 30,000 units and material costs of £8 per unit.

If sales are only 30,000 units, the total contribution would be:

(a) £180,000 at a material cost of £4 (contribution £6 per unit);
(b) £120,000 at a material cost of £6 (contribution £4 per unit);
(c) £60,000 at a material cost of £8 (contribution £2 per unit).

Since there is a 20% chance that materials will cost £8, there is a **20% chance of making a loss,** given fixed costs of £100,000. This applies only if **sales are 30,000 units**.

If materials cost £8 per unit, there would be a **loss** at sales volumes of both 30,000 and 40,000 units. The **chance** that one or other of these events will occur is **14%,** as calculated below.

Sales	*Probability*	*Material cost*	*Probability*	*Joint* probabilities
30,000 units	0.3	£8	0.2	0.06
40,000 units	0.4	£8	0.2	0.08
		Combined probabilities		0.14

However there is also a chance that sales will be 50,000 units and material will cost £4, so that contribution would be £300,000 in total and profits £200,000. This is the **best possible outcome** and it has a $0.3 \times 0.2 = 0.06$ or 6% probability of occurring.

3.6 EVs and more complex risk analysis

As we have seen, EVs can be used to compare two or more mutually exclusive alternatives: the alternative with the most favourable EV of profit or cost would normally be preferred. However, **alternatives can also be compared** by looking at the **spread of possible outcomes**, and the **probabilities** that they will occur. The technique of drawing up **cumulative probability tables** might be helpful, as the following example shows.

3.7 Example: mutually exclusive options and cumulative probability

QRS is reviewing the price that it charges for a major product line. Over the past three years the product has had sales averaging 48,000 units per year at a standard selling price of £5.25. Costs have been rising steadily over the past year and the company is considering raising this price to £5.75 or £6.25. The sales manager has produced the following schedule to assist with the decision.

Price	£5.75	£6.25
Estimates of demand		
Pessimistic estimate (probability 0.25)	35,000	10,000
Most likely estimate (probability 0.60)	40,000	20,000
Optimistic estimate (probability 0.15)	50,000	40,000

Currently the unit cost is estimated at £5.00, analysed as follows.

	£
Direct material	2.50
Direct labour	1.00
Variable overhead	1.00
Fixed overhead	0.50
	5.00

The cost accountant considers that the most likely value for unit variable cost over the next year is £4.90 (probability 0.75) but that it could be as high as £5.20 (probability 0.15) and it might even be as low as £4.75 (probability 0.10). Total fixed costs are currently £24,000 p.a. but it is estimated that the corresponding total for the ensuing year will be £25,000 with a probability of 0.2, £27,000 with a

probability of 0.6, £30,000 with a probability of 0.2. (Demand quantities, unit costs and fixed costs can be assumed to be statistically independent.)

Required

Analyse the foregoing information in a way which you consider will assist management with the problem, give your views on the situation and advise on the new selling price. Calculate the expected level of profit that would follow from the selling price that you recommend.

Discussion and solution

In this example, there are two mutually exclusive options, a price of £5.75 and a price of £6.25. Sales demand is uncertain, but would vary with price. Unit contribution and total contribution depend on sales price and sales volume, but total fixed costs are common to both options. Clearly, it makes sense to begin looking at EVs of contribution and then to think about fixed costs and profits later.

(a) A table of probabilities can be set out for each alternative, and an EV calculated, as follows.

Price £5.75

Sales Demand	*Probability*	*Variable cost per unit*	*Probability*	*Unit cont'n*	*Total cont'n*	*Joint proba-bility**	*EV of cont'n*
Units	(a)	£	(b)	£	£'000	(a × b)	£'000
35,000	0.25	5.20	0.15	0.55	19.25	0.0375	0.722
		4.90	0.75	0.85	29.75	0.1875	5.578
		4.75	0.10	1.00	35.00	0.0250	0.875
40,000	0.60	5.20	0.15	0.55	22.00	0.0900	1.980
		4.90	0.75	0.85	34.00	0.4500	15.300
		4.75	0.10	1.00	40.00	0.0600	2.400
50,000	0.15	5.20	0.15	0.55	27.50	0.0225	0.619
		4.90	0.75	0.85	42.50	0.1125	4.781
		4.75	0.10	1.00	50.00	0.0150	0.750
					EV of Contribution		33.005

The EV of contribution at a price of £5.75 is £33,005.

* Remember to check that the joint probabilities sum to 1.

Alternative approach

An alternative method of calculating the EV of contribution is as follows.

EV of contribution = EV of sales revenue – EV of variable costs

EV of sales revenue = EV of sales units × selling price
= ((35,000 × 0.25)+ (40,000 × 0.60) + (50,000 × 0.15)) × £5.75
= 40,250 × £5.75 = £231,437.50

EV of variable costs = EV of sales units × EV of unit variable costs
= 40,250 × ((£5.20 × 0.15) + (£4.90 × 0.75) + (£4.75 × 0.10)) = 40,250 × £4.93 = £198,432.50

∴ EV of contribution = £(231,437.50 – 198,432.50) = £33,005

This method is quicker and simpler, but an extended table of probabilities will help the risk analysis when the two alternative selling prices are compared.

Price £6.25

Sales demand Units	*Probability* (a)	*Variable cost per unit* £	*Probability* (b)	*Unit cont'n* £	*Total cont'n* £000	*Joint probability* (a × b)	*EV of cont'n* £000
10,000	0.25	5.20	0.15	1.05	10.50	0.0375	0.394
		4.90	0.75	1.35	13.50	0.1875	2.531
		4.75	0.10	1.50	15.00	0.0250	0.375
20,000	0.60	5.20	0.15	1.05	21.00	0.0900	1.890
		4.90	0.75	1.35	27.00	0.4500	12.150
		4.75	0.10	1.50	30.00	0.0600	1.800
40,000	0.15	5.20	0.15	1.05	42.00	0.0225	0.945
		4.90	0.75	1.35	54.00	0.1125	6.075
		4.75	0.10	1.50	60.00	0.0150	0.900
			EV of Contribution				27.060

The EV of contribution at a price of £6.25 is £27,060.

(b) The EV of **fixed costs** is £27,200.

Fixed costs £	*Probability*	*EV* £
25,000	0.2	5,000
27,000	0.6	16,200
30,000	0.2	6,000
		27,200

(c) **Conclusion**

On the basis of EVs alone, a price of £5.75 is preferable to a price of £6.25, since it offers an EV of contribution of £33,005 and so an EV of profit of £5,805; whereas a price of £6.25 offers an EV of contribution of only £27,060 and so an EV of loss of £140.

Additional information

A comparison of cumulative probabilities would add to the information for risk analysis. The cumulative probabilities can be used to compare the **likelihood of earning a total contribution of a certain size with each selling price**.

The table below shows that no matter whether fixed costs are £25,000, £27,000 or £30,000, the **probability of at least breaking even** is much higher with a price of £5.75 than with a price of £6.25. The only reason for favouring a price of £6.25 is that there is a better **probability of earning bigger profits** (a contribution of £50,000 or more), and so although a risk-averse decision maker would choose a price of £5.75, a risk-seeking decision maker might gamble on a price of £6.25.

Probability of total contribution of at least £		*Price £5.75 Probability*		*Price £6.25 Probability*
15,000		1.0000	(1 – 0.0375 – 0.1875)	0.7750
20,000	(1 – 0.0375)	0.9625	(0.775 – 0.025)	0.7500
25,000	(0.9625 – 0.09)	0.8725	etc	0.6600
27,000		0.8725		0.6600
30,000	(0.8725 – 0.1875 – 0.0225)	0.6625		0.2100
35,000	etc	0.2125		0.1500
40,000		0.1875		0.1500
50,000		0.0150		0.1275
60,000		0.0000		0.0150

3.8 Expected values and NPVs

FAST FORWARD

A probability analysis of expected cash flows can often be estimated and used both to calculate an expected NPV and to measure risk. The **standard deviation of the NPV** can be calculated to assess risk when the construction of probability distributions is complicated.

A **probability distribution** of **'expected cash flows'** can often be estimated, and this may be used to do the following.

Step 1 Calculate an expected value of the NPV

Step 2 Measure risk, for example in the following ways.

(a) By calculating the worst possible outcome and its probability
(b) By calculating the probability that the project will fail to achieve a positive NPV
(c) By calculating the standard deviation of the NPV

3.9 Example: probability estimates of cash flows

A company is considering a project involving the outlay of £300,000 which it estimates will generate cash flows over its two year life at the probabilities shown in the following table.

Cash flows for project

Year 1

Cash flow	*Probability*
£	
100,000	0.25
200,000	0.50
300,000	0.25
	1.00

Year 2

If cash flow in Year 1 is:	*there is a probability of:*	*that the cash flow in Year 2 will be:*
£		£
100,000	0.25	Nil
	0.50	100,000
	0.25	200,000
	1.00	
200,000	0.25	100,000
	0.50	200,000
	0.25	300,000
	1.00	
300,000	0.25	200,000
	0.50	300,000
	0.25	350,000
	1.00	

The company's investment criterion for this type of project is 10% DCF.

You are required to calculate the expected value (EV) of the project's NPV and the probability that the NPV will be negative.

Solution

Step 1 Calculate expected value of the NPV.

First we need to draw up a probability distribution of the expected cash flows. We begin by calculating the present values of the cash flows.

Year	*Cash flow*	*Discount factor*	*Present value*
	£'000	10%	£'000
1	100	0.909	90.9
1	200	0.909	181.8
1	300	0.909	272.7
2	100	0.826	82.6
2	200	0.826	165.2
2	300	0.826	247.8
2	350	0.826	289.1

Year 1 PV of cash flow	*Probability*	*Year 2 PV of cash flow*	*Probability*	*Joint probability*	*Total PV of cash inflows*	*EV of PV of cash inflows*
£'000		£'000			£'000	£'000
(a)	(b)	(c)	(d)	(b) × (d)	(a) + (c)	
90.9	0.25	0.0	0.25	0.0625	90.9	5.681
90.9	0.25	82.6	0.50	0.1250	173.5	21.688
90.9	0.25	165.2	0.25	0.0625	256.1	16.006
181.8	0.50	82.6	0.25	0.1250	264.4	33.050
181.8	0.50	165.2	0.50	0.2500	347.0	86.750
181.8	0.50	247.8	0.25	0.1250	429.6	53.700
272.7	0.25	165.2	0.25	0.0625	437.9	27.369
272.7	0.25	247.8	0.50	0.1250	520.5	65.063
272.7	0.25	289.1	0.25	0.0625	561.8	35.113
						344.420

	£
EV of PV of cash inflows	344,420
Less project cost	300,000
EV of NPV	44,420

Step 2 Measure risk.

Since the EV of the NPV is positive, the project should go ahead unless the risk is unacceptably high. The probability that the project will have a negative NPV is the probability that the total PV of cash inflows is less than £300,000. From the column headed 'Total PV of cash inflows', we can establish that this probability is 0.0625 + 0.125 + 0.0625 + 0.125 = 0.375 or 37.5%. This might be considered an unacceptably high risk.

3.10 The standard deviation of the NPV

The disadvantage of using the EV of NPV approach to assess the risk of the project is that the **construction** of the **probability distribution** can become **very complicated**. If we were considering a project over 4 years, each year having five different forecasted cash flows, there would be 625 (5^4) NPVs to calculate. To avoid all of these calculations, an indication of the risk may be obtained by calculating the **standard deviation** of the NPV.

3.11 Example: standard deviation of the net present value

Frame is considering which of two mutually exclusive projects, A or B, to undertake. There is some uncertainty about the running costs with each project, and a probability distribution of the NPV for each project has been estimated, as follows.

Project A		*Project B*	
NPV	*Probability*	*NPV*	*Probability*
£'000		£'000	
– 20	0.15	+ 5	0.2
+ 10	0.20	+ 15	0.3
+ 20	0.35	+ 20	0.4
+ 40	0.30	+ 25	0.1

You are required to decide which project should the company choose, if either.

Solution

We can begin by calculating the EV of the NPV for each project.

	Project A			*Project B*	
NPV	*Prob*	*EV*	*NPV*	*Prob*	*EV*
£'000		£'000	£'000		£'000
– 20	0.15	(3.0)	5	0.2	1.0
10	0.20	2.0	15	0.3	4.5
20	0.35	7.0	20	0.4	8.0
40	0.30	12.0	25	0.1	2.5
		18.0			16.0

Project A has a higher EV of NPV, but what about the risk of variation in the NPV above or below the EV? This can be measured by the standard deviation of the NPV.

The standard deviation of a project's NPV, s, can be calculated as:

$$s=\sqrt{\Sigma p(x-\overline{x})^2}$$

where $\overline{x}$ is the EV of the NPV.

	Project A, $\overline{x}$ = 18				*Project B*, $\overline{x}$ = 16		
x	*p*	$x-\overline{x}$	$p(x-\overline{x})^2$	*x*	*p*	$x-\overline{x}$	$p(x-\overline{x})^2$
£'000		£'000		£'000		£'000	
– 20	0.15	– 38	216.6	5	0.2	– 11	24.2
10	0.20	– 8	12.8	15	0.3	– 1	0.3
20	0.35	+ 2	1.4	20	0.4	+ 4	6.4
40	0.30	+ 22	145.2	25	0.1	+ 9	8.1
			376.0				39.0

		Project A			*Project B*
s	=	√376	s	=	√39.0
	=	19.391		=	6.245
	=	£19,391		=	£6,245

Although Project A has a higher EV of NPV, it also has a higher standard deviation of NPV, and so has greater risk associated with it. Which project should be selected? Clearly it depends on the attitude of the company's management to risk.

(a) If management are prepared to take the **risk** of a **low NPV** in the hope of a high NPV they will opt for project A.

(b) If management are **risk-averse**, they will opt for the less risky project B.

3.12 Problems with expected values

There are the following problems with using expected values in making investment decisions.

- An investment may be **one-off**, and 'expected' NPV may never actually occur.
- **Assigning probabilities** to events is highly **subjective**.
- Expected values **do not evaluate the range** of possible NPV outcomes.

4 Decision trees and matrices

FAST FORWARD

Decision tree analysis clarifies the range of alternative courses of action open and their possible outcomes.

4.1 Uses of decision trees

Exam focus point

If decision tree analysis comes up in a question, you can expect that it will involve a relatively simple decision tree.

You may have come across decision trees in your previous studies, but they can be a useful way of modelling a finite number of possible outcomes, so we shall briefly revise them here.

When appraising a project using the NPV method, it is possible that, of the many variables which affect the NPV, more than one will be **uncertain**. The value of some variables may be dependent on the values of other variables. Many outcomes may therefore be possible and some outcomes may be dependent on previous outcomes. Decision trees are useful tools for clarifying the range of alternative courses of action and their possible outcomes.

There are two stages in preparing a decision tree.

Step 1 Drawing the tree itself, to show all the choices and outcomes

Step 2 Putting in the numbers: the probabilities, outcome values and EVs

4.2 Drawing a decision tree: the basic rules

Every decision tree starts from a decision point with the decision options that are currently being considered.

(a) You should draw a **line**, or **branch**, for each option or alternative.

(b) You should **identify** the **decision point**, and any subsequent decision points in the tree, with a symbol. Here, we shall use a square shape.

It is conventional to draw decision trees from **left to right**, and so a decision tree will start as follows.

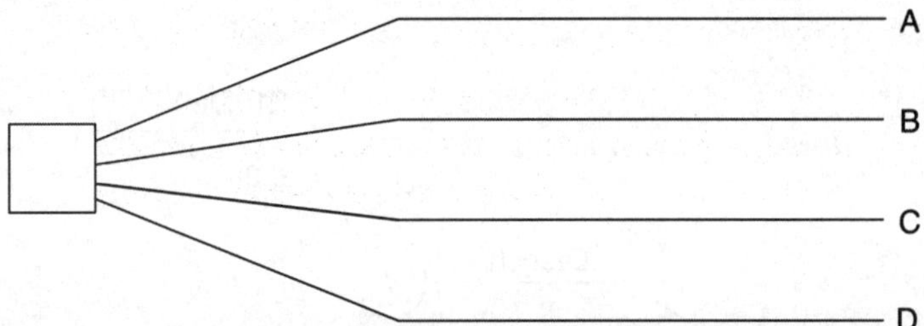

The square is the decision point, and A, B, C and D represent four alternatives from which a choice must be made.

If the outcome from any choice is certain, the branch of the decision tree for that alternative is complete.

If, on the other hand, the outcome of a particular choice is uncertain, the various possible outcomes must be shown. We show this on a decision tree by inserting an **outcome point** on the branch of the tree. Each possible outcome is then shown as a subsidiary branch, coming out from the outcome point. The **probability** of each outcome occurring should be written on to the branch of the tree which represents that outcome.

To distinguish decision points from outcome points, a circle will be used as the symbol for an outcome point.

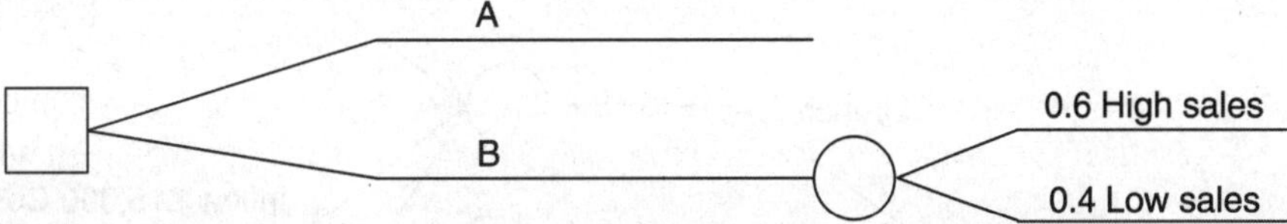

In the example above, there are two choices, A and B. The outcome if A is chosen is known with certainty, but if B is chosen, there are two possible outcomes, high returns (0.6 probability) or low returns (0.4 probability).

When several outcomes are possible, it is usually simpler to show two or more stages of outcome points on the decision tree.

4.3 Example: several possible outcomes

A company can choose to invest in project XYZ or not. If the investment goes ahead, expected cash inflows and expected costs might be as follows.

Cash inflows	*Probability*	*Costs*	*Probability*
£		£	
10,000	0.8	6,000	0.7
15,000	0.2	8,000	0.3

(a) The decision tree could be drawn as follows.

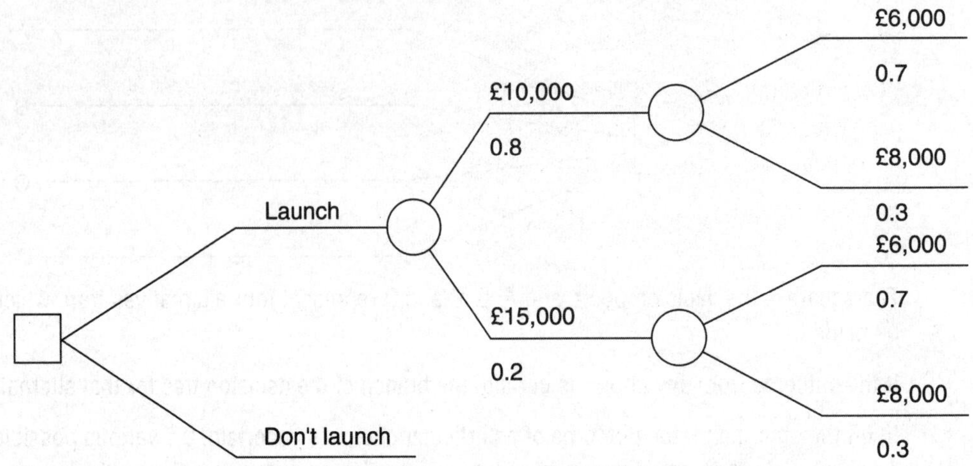

(b) The layout shown above will usually be easier to use than the alternative way of drawing the tree, which is shown below.

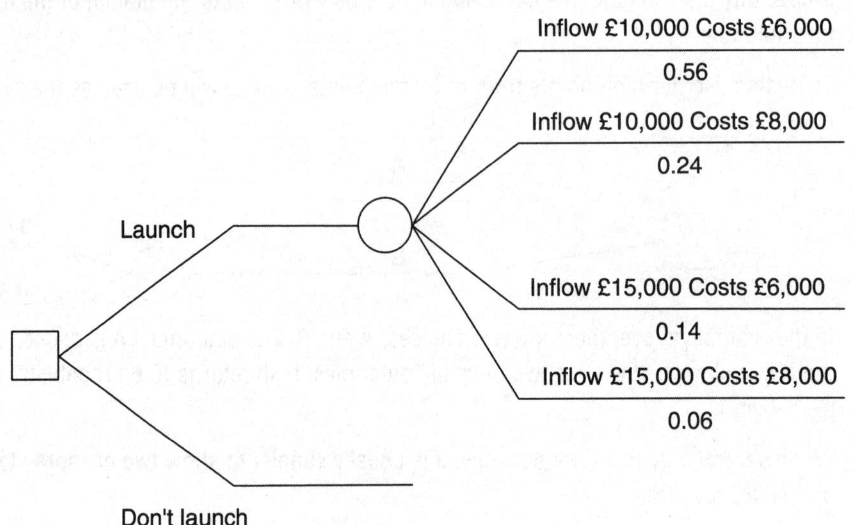

Sometimes, a decision taken now will lead to other decisions to be taken in the future. When this situation arises, the decision tree can be drawn as a two-stage tree, as follows.

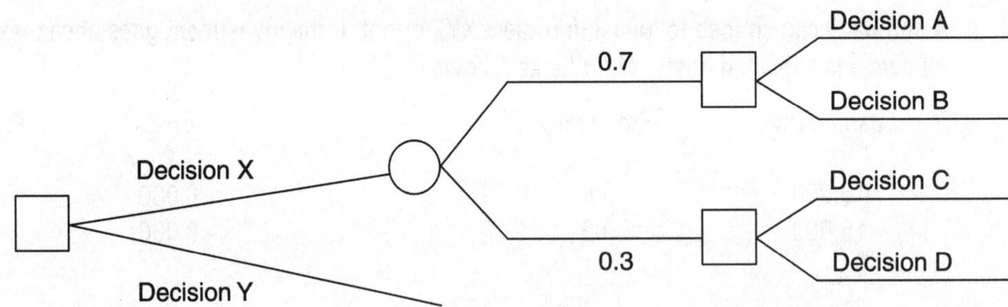

In this tree, either a choice between A and B or else a choice between C and D will be made, depending on the outcome which occurs after choosing X. The decision tree should be in **chronological order** from left to right.

4.4 Evaluating a decision with a decision tree

The basic rules are as follows.

We start on the **right hand side** of the tree and **work back** towards the left hand side and the current decision under consideration. Working from right to left, we calculate the EV of revenue, cost, contribution or profit at each outcome point on the tree.

Consider the decision tree below.

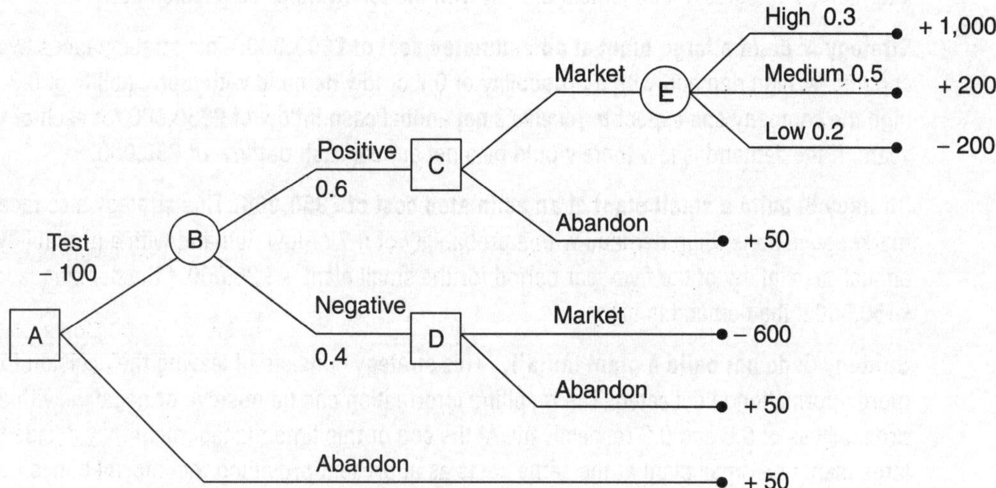

(a) At E the EV is calculated as follows.

	£'000 *x*	*Probability p*	*px*
High	1,000	0.3	300
Medium	200	0.5	100
Low	(200)	0.2	(40)
		EV	360

(b) At C, the choice is an EV of £360,000 or a value of £50,000. The choice would be £360,000 and so the EV at C is **£360,000.**

(c) At D, the choice is a value of –£600,000 or a value of £50,000. The choice would be £50,000 and so the EV at D is **£50,000**.

(d) At B the EV is calculated as follows.

EV = (0.6 × £360,000) (C) + (0.4 × £50,000) (D) = £236,000

(e) At A the choice is between an EV of £236,000 minus costs of £100,000 or a value of £50,000. The choice would be £136,000 and so the EV at A is £136,000.

To summarise:

1 At point **A, Test** (EV £136,000)

2 At point **B,** options are

(a) Test is **positive** (0.6), therefore at point **C, Market** (EV £360,000)

(b) Test is **negative** (0.4), therefore at point **D, Abandon** (EV £50,000)

Question

Decision trees

Learning outcome: B(ii)

Elsewhere is considering the production of a new consumer item with a five year product lifetime. In order to manufacture this time it would be necessary to build a new plant. After having considered several alternative strategies, management are left with the following three possibilities.

Strategy A: build a large plant at an estimated cost of £600,000. This strategy faces two types of market conditions: high demand with a probability of 0.7 or low demand with a probability of 0.3. If the demand is high the company can expect to receive a net annual cash inflow of £250,000 for each of the next five years. If the demand is low there would be a net annual cash outflow of £50,000.

Strategy B: build a small plant at an estimated cost of £350,000. This strategy also faces two types of market conditions: high demand with a probability of 0.7 or low demand with a probability of 0.3. The net annual cash inflow of the five-year period for the small plant is £25,000 if the demand is low and is £150,000 if the demand is high.

Strategy C: do not build a plant initially. This strategy consists of leaving the decision for one year whilst more information is collected. The resulting information can be positive or negative with estimated probabilities of 0.8 and 0.2 respectively. At the end of this time management may decide to build either a large plant or a small plant at the same costs as at present providing the information is positive. If the resulting information is negative, management would decide to build no plant at all. Given positive information the probabilities of high and low demand change to 0.9 and 0.1 respectively, regardless of which plant is built. The net annual cash inflows for the remaining four-year period for each type of plant are the same as those given in strategies A and B.

All costs and revenues are given in present value terms and should not be discounted.

Required

(a) Draw a decision tree to represent the alternative courses of action open to the company.

(b) Determine the expected return for each possible course of action and hence decide the best course of action for the management of Elsewhere.

Answer

(a) **Decision tree for a possible new plant**

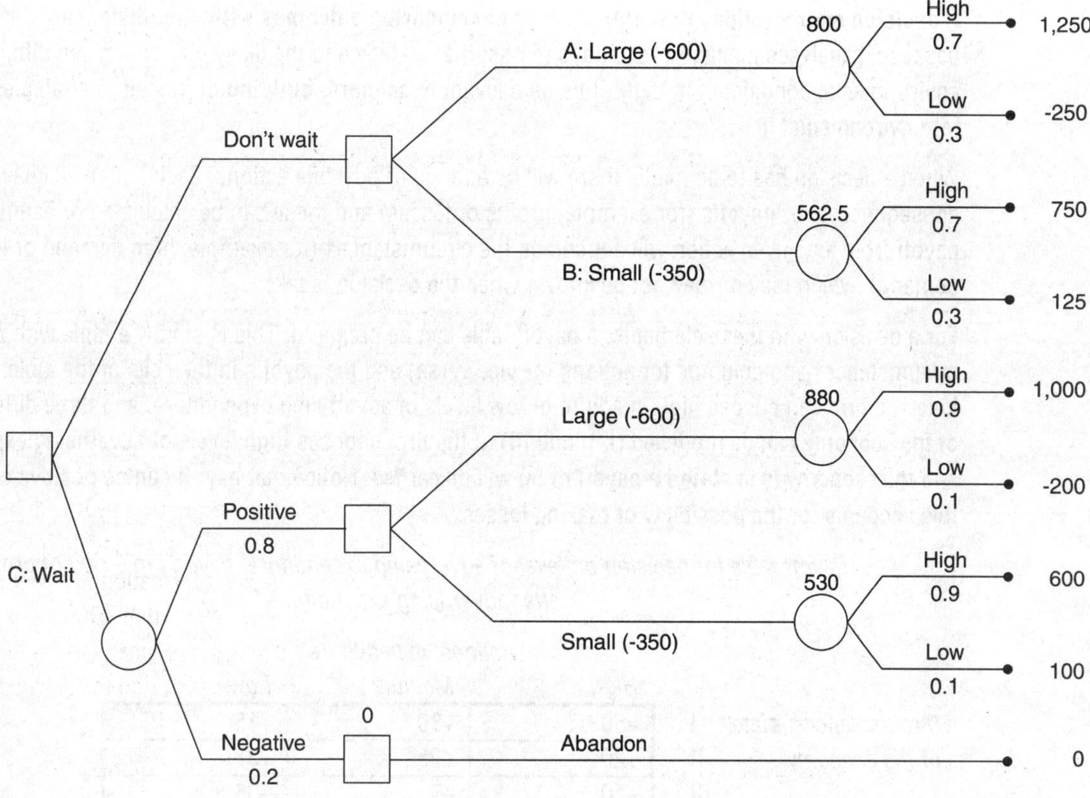

Key

□ Decision point

○ Outcome point

(b) Evaluation of the decision tree (see above) shows that the best course of action is to wait a year, and then build a large plant if positive information is received, but abandon the project if negative information is received.

Expected values (in thousands of pounds) are calculated as follows.

Large plant now (A) $(0.7 \times 5 \times 250) - (0.3 \times 5 \times 50) - 600 = 200$

Small plant now (B) $(0.7 \times 5 \times 150) + (0.3 \times 5 \times 25) - 350 = 212.5$

Large plant following positive information

$(0.9 \times 4 \times 250) - (0.1 \times 4 \times 50) - 600 = 280$

Small plant following positive information

$(0.9 \times 4 \times 150) + (0.1 \times 4 \times 25) - 350 = 200$

Positive information: higher of 280 and 200, ie 280

Waiting (C) $(0.8 \times 280) + (0.2 \times 0) = 224$

224 is higher than either 200 or 212.5, hence the recommendation to wait.

4.5 Decision matrices

FAST FORWARD

Decision matrices enable the organisation to develop a coherent approach to dealing with projects (ie to maximise potential profits or minimise losses).

A **decision matrix** (or **payoff table**) is a way of **comparing outcomes with circumstances**. It is useful because it analyses managers' attitudes to risk, the strategy and the likely outcome given different environmental conditions. It might thus be relevant to **scenario building** or indeed to strategies which aim for environmental fit.

When a decision has to be made, there will be a range of possible actions. Each action will have certain consequences, or **payoffs** (for example, profits or losses) and these can be calculated or estimated. The payoff from any given action will depend on the circumstances (for example, high demand or low demand), which may or may not be known when the decision is taken.

For a decision with these elements, a payoff table can be prepared. This is simply a table with rows for circumstances and columns for actions (or vice versa) and the payoffs in the cells of the table. In the table below, a firm can choose high, medium or low levels of advertising expenditure, and three different states of the economy can be modelled (I, II and III): if the firm chooses **high** levels of advertising expenditure and the economy is in **state I** a payoff of 50 will be earned. Notice that payoff can be positive or negative: this accounts for the possibility of making losses.

Payoff table for decision on level of advertising expenditure: payoffs in £'000 of profit after advertising expenditure

		Actions: expenditure		
		High	*Medium*	*Low*
Circumstances: state	I	+50	+30	+15
of the economy	II	+20	+25	+5
	III	–10	–5	–35

Sometimes, the circumstances we have to consider will be another person's action, for example a competitor's level of advertising expenditure. (Note that payoff tables can show costs instead of profits.)

4.5.1 Using decision matrices

Having worked out the consequences of different actions under different circumstances, we need to select a **decision rule** or criterion for making our decision. There are three decision rules; they each look at just one possible payoff for each circumstance, either the best or the worst: **maximax**, **maximin** and **minimax regret**.

(a) The **maximax** decision rule is **optimistic** about the circumstances we find ourselves in and assumes we will attain the maximum payoff available from whatever course of action we choose. It therefore directs us to the course of action offering the highest possible payout. We **maximise the maximum payoff**. In the table above, we choose the high level of expenditure since it offers the highest possible payoff.

(b) The **maximin** decision rule is **pessimistic**. It assumes that circumstances will be against us and looks at the **worst possible payoffs**. The aim is to **maximise the minimum** payoff by choosing the option with the largest minimum. In the table above, the worst outcomes for all three options are negative, but we can minimise our losses by choosing the medium spend.

4.5.2 Example: decision matrices

Here are payoff tables for two separate decisions.

Profits

		Actions		
		A	*B*	*C*
Circumstances	I	100	80	60
	II	90	120	85
	III	-20	10	40
Max profit		100	120	85

Costs

		Actions		
		D	*E*	*F*
Circumstances	IV	40	50	60
	V	70	80	25
	VI	20	30	30
Min cost		20	30	25

(i) For the first decision, action B (payoff 120) would be chosen using maximax or C using maximin (payoff 40).

(ii) For the second decision, action D would be chosen using maximax or F using maximin. As the figures relate to costs, they may be assessed by subtracting them from a notional figure for turnover, such as 100.

4.5.3 Hurwicz criterion

These decision rules have the merit of simplicity, but to consider only one payoff for each course of each action may be thought unrealistic. The *Hurwicz criterion* seeks to remedy this by taking a **weighted average** of the best and worst payoffs of each action:

$$\text{Weighted payoff} = \alpha \times \text{worst payoff} \times (1 - \alpha) \times \text{best payoff}$$

α is a number between 0 and 1, sometimes called the pessimism-optimism index. The value chosen reflects one's attitude to the risk of poor payoffs and the chance of good payoffs. The action with the highest weighted payoff is selected. However, the Hurwicz criterion ignores the perhaps more probable payoffs between the best and the worst.

4.5.4 Reject

The third decision rule, **minimax regret** considers the extent to which we might come to regret an action we had chosen.

Regret for any combination of action and circumstances	=	Payoff for **best** action in those circumstances	–	Payoff of the action **actually taken** in those circumstances

An alternative term for regret is **opportunity loss**. We may apply the rule by considering the maximum opportunity loss associated with each course of action and choosing the course which offers the smallest maximum. If we choose an action which turns out not to be the best in the actual circumstances, we have lost an opportunity to make the extra profit we could have made by choosing the best action.

5 Simulation models

FAST FORWARD

Simulation models can be used to assess those projects that may have too many outcomes to allow the use of a decision tree or those projects that have correlated cash flows.

5.1 Uses of simulation models

Simulation will overcome problems of having a very large number of possible outcomes, also the correlation of cash flows (a project which is successful in its early years is more likely to be successful in its later years).

5.2 Example: simulation model

The following probability estimates have been prepared for a proposed project.

	Year	*Probability*	£
Cost of equipment	0	1.00	(40,000)
Revenue each year	1-5	0.15	40,000
		0.40	50,000
		0.30	55,000
		0.15	60,000
Running costs each year	1-5	0.10	25,000
		0.25	30,000
		0.35	35,000
		0.30	40,000

The cost of capital is 12%. Assess how a simulation model might be used to assess the project's NPV.

Solution

A simulation model could be constructed by assigning a range of random number digits to each possible value for each of the uncertain variables. The random numbers must exactly match their respective probabilities. This is achieved by working upwards cumulatively from the lowest to the highest cash flow values and assigning numbers that will correspond to probability groupings as follows.

Revenue				*Running costs*		
£	*Prob*	*Random numbers*		£	*Prob*	*Random* numbers
40,000	0.15	00 - 14	*	25,000	0.10	00 - 09
50,000	0.40	15 - 54	**	30,000	0.25	10 - 34
55,000	0.30	55 - 84	***	40,000	0.35	35 - 69
60,000	0.15	85 - 99		40,000	0.30	70 - 99

* Probability is 0.15 (15%). Random numbers are 15% of range 00 - 99.

** Probability is 0.40 (40%). Random numbers are 40% of range 00 - 99 but starting at 15.

*** Probability is 0.30 (30%). Random numbers are 30% of range 00 - 99 but starting at 55.

For revenue, the selection of a random number in the range 00 and 14 has a probability of 0.15. This probability represents revenue of £40,000. Numbers have been assigned to cash flows so that when numbers are selected at random, the cash flows have exactly the same probability of being selected as is indicated in their respective probability distribution above.

Random numbers would be generated, for example by a computer program, and these would be used to assign values to each of the uncertain variables.

For example, if random numbers 378420015689 were generated, the values assigned to the variables would be as follows.

	Revenue		Costs	
Calculation	*Random number*	*Value*	*Random number*	*Value*
		£		£
1	37	50,000	84	40,000
2	20	50,000	01	25,000
3	56	55,000	89	40,000

A computer would calculate the NPV may times over using the values established in this way with more random numbers, and the results would be analysed to provide the following.

(a) An **expected NPV** for the project

(b) A **statistical distribution** pattern for the possible variation in the NPV above or below this average

The decision whether to go ahead with the project would then be made on the basis of **expected return** and **risk**.

6 Using the results of statistical analysis

FAST FORWARD

Managers can make various **adjustments** and **allowances** to the calculations they have carried out in order to produce outcomes whose risk levels are satisfactory.

Only if management know for certainty what is going to happen in the future can they appraise a project in the knowledge that there is no risk. However the future is uncertain by nature. There are, nevertheless, steps that management can take to reduce the riskiness of a project.

(a) A **maximum payback period** can be set to reflect the fact that risk increases the longer the time period under consideration.

(b) A **high discounting rate** can be used so that a cash flow which occurs quite some time in the future will have less effect on the decision.

(c) Projects with **low standard deviations** and **acceptable average predicted outcomes** can be selected. If a business is undertaking a range of projects, it should ensure that some are **low-risk (diversification)**.

(d) **Sensitivity analysis** can be used to determine the critical factors within the decision-making process. Management effort can then be directed to those factors which are critical to the success of a particular decision.

(e) To ensure that future events are no worse than predicted, **prudence**, **slack** and **overly pessimistic estimates** can be applied.

7 Scenarios

FAST FORWARD

Scenario building, looking at an internally consistent view of the future, is a particularly useful technique of analysing the relative impact of lots of different types of risk.

7.1 Scenario building

Key term

Scenario building is the process of identifying alternative futures, ie constructing a number of distinct possible futures permitting deductions to be made about future developments of markets, products and technology.

Scenarios are used in several situations.

7.1.1 Contingency planning

To develop contingency plans to cope with the arrival of threats or risks which, although they may arise at any time, are of indeterminable probability. For example, a chemicals company may develop a scenario of a major spillage at one of its plants and then set up emergency routines to cope with it. They cannot assess how likely the spillage is to occur in actual practice.

7.1.2 As a prediction technique

A series of alternative pictures of a future operating environment are developed which are consistent with current trends and consistent within themselves. The impact of each different scenario upon the business is assessed and specific risks highlighted. Contingency plans are drawn up to implement in the event of a given scenario coming true, or to implement now to give protection against the scenario.

7.2 Use of scenarios

How can scenarios be used to formulate competitive strategy? In other words, what are the implications of each scenario?

(a) A strategy built in response to only **one** scenario is risky, whereas one supposed to cope with them all might be expensive, and might result in contradictory measures.

(b) Approaches to choosing scenarios as a basis for decisions are as follows.

   (i) **Assume the most probable**. This would seem common sense but puts too much faith in the scenario process and guesswork. Also, a less probable scenario may be one whose **failure** to occur would have the **worst** consequences for the firm.

   (ii) **Hope for the best**. A firm designs a strategy based on the scenario most attractive to the firm. Wishful thinking is usually not the right approach.

   (iii) **Hedge**. The firm chooses the strategy that produces **satisfactory** results under **all** scenarios. Hedging, however, is not **optimal** for any scenario. The low risk is paid for by a low reward.

   (iv) **Flexibility**. The firm plays a 'wait and see' game. This means that the firm waits to follow others. It is more secure, but sacrifices first-mover advantages.

   (v) **Influence**. A firm will try to influence the future, for example by influencing demand for related products in order that its favoured scenario will be realised in events as they unfold.

Chapter Roundup

- Sometimes the **potential loss** may be a **single definite figure**. How this figure is calculated will depend on the asset or benefit to which the loss relates.
- **Sensitivity analysis** assesses how responsive the project's NPV is to changes in the variables used to calculate that NPV. One particular approach to sensitivity analysis, the **certainty - equivalent approach**, involves the conversion of the expected cash flows of the project to riskless equivalent amounts.
- **Bayes' strategy** is that if a manager is faced with a number of alternative decisions, each with a range of possible outcomes, the optimum decision will be the one that gives the highest expected value (of profit/contribution).
- A **probability analysis** of expected cash flows can often be estimated and used both to calculate an expected NPV and to measure risk. The **standard deviation of the NPV** can be calculated to assess risk when the construction of probability distributions is complicated.
- **Decision tree analysis** clarifies the range of alternative courses of action open and their possible outcomes.
- **Decision matrices** enable the organisation to develop a coherent approach to dealing with projects (ie to maximise potential profits or minimise losses).
- **Simulation models** can be used to assess those projects that may have too many outcomes to allow the use of a decision tree or those projects that have correlated cash flows.
- Managers can make various **adjustments** and **allowances** to the calculations they have carried out in order to produce outcomes whose risk levels are satisfactory.
- **Scenario building**, looking at an internally consistent view of the future, is a particularly useful technique of analysing the relative impact of lots of different types of risk.

Quick Quiz

1 Give three examples of how risk exposures on physical assets might be calculated.

2 *Fill in the blanks.*

The two key types of point on a decision tree are .... points and .... points.

3 Describe three ways in which managers can reduce risk.

4 Sensitivity analysis allows for uncertainty in project appraisal by assessing the probability of changes in the decision variables.

True ☐

False ☐

5 *Fill in the blanks.*

The .... is where expected cashflows are converted to riskless equivalent amounts.

6 Give three examples of ways that risk can be measured in probability analysis.

7 Expected values can help an accountant evaluate the range of possible Net Present Value outcomes.

True ☐

False ☐

8 In which direction should a decision tree normally be drawn?

A Top of page to bottom of page
B Bottom of page to top of page
C Left of page to right of page
D Right of page to left of page

Answers to Quick Quiz

1
- Asset values
- Costs of repair
- Change in asset value
- Decrease in revenues
- Cost of unused capacity

2 The two key types of point on a decision tree are decision points and outcome points.

3
- Set maximum payback period.
- Use high discounting rate.
- Select projects with low standard deviations and acceptable average predicted outcomes.
- Use sensitivity analysis to determine the critical factors within the decision-making process.
- Use pessimistic estimates.

4 False. Sensitivity analysis assess the **effect** of changes in variables, not the probability that these will occur.

5 Certainty equivalent approach

6
- Calculating the worst possible outcome and its probability
- Calculating the probability that the project will fail to achieve a positive NPV
- Calculating the standard deviation of the NPV

7 False

8 C Left of page to right of page

Now try the question below from the Exam Question Bank

Number	Level	Marks	Time
Q6	Examination	50	90 mins

7

Internal control systems

Introduction

In this chapter we examine the main elements of internal control systems that organisations operate. You will gather that controls must be linked to organisational objectives and the main risks that organisations face. In addition control systems do not just consist of the controls themselves but also the environment within which controls operate.

Communication is a vital element in control systems. Staff must be aware of what control systems are trying to achieve. Directors and managers must have sufficient information to be able to judge how effectively controls are operating.

It is important that the costs of controls are not excessive in relation to the benefits they bring. In the last section of this chapter we shall examine how organisations weigh up costs and benefits.

Topic list	Learning outcomes	Syllabus references	Ability required
1 Purposes of internal control systems	B(v)	B(8)	Evaluation
2 Internal control frameworks	B(v)	B(10), (11), (12)	Evaluation
3 Control environment	B(v)	B(10), (11)	Evaluation
4 Control procedures	B(v)	B(10), (11)	Evaluation
5 Internal controls and risk management	B(v)	B(10), (11)	Evaluation
6 Communication of controls	B(v)	B(12)	Evaluation
7 Information requirements of directors	B(v)	B(10), (11)	Evaluation
8 Control Self Assessment (CSA)	B(v)	B(10), (11)	Evaluation
9 Costs and benefits of internal controls	B(vi)	B(13)	Evaluation

1 Purposes of internal control systems

FAST FORWARD

Internal controls should help organisations counter risks, maintain the quality of reporting and comply with laws and regulations. They provide reasonable assurance that the organisations will fulfil their objectives.

Key term

An **internal control** is any action taken by management to enhance the likelihood that established objectives and goals will be achieved. Management plans, organises and directs the performance of sufficient actions to provide reasonable assurance that objectives and goals will be achieved. Thus, control is the result of proper planning, organising and directing by management. (*Institute of Internal Auditors*)

1.1 Direction of control systems

In order for internal controls to function properly, they have to be well-directed. Managers and staff will be more able (and willing) to implement controls successfully if it can be demonstrated to them what the objectives of the control systems are, whilst objectives provide a yardstick for the board when they come to monitor and assess how controls have been operating.

1.2 Turnbull guidelines

The UK's Turnbull report provides a helpful summary of the main purposes of an internal control system.

Turnbull comments that internal control consists of 'the **policies**, **processes**, **tasks**, **behaviours** and other aspects of a company that taken together:

- Facilitate its **effective** and **efficient operation** by enabling it to respond appropriately to significant **business**, **operational, financial, compliance** and other risks to achieving the company's objectives. This includes the **safeguarding of assets** from inappropriate use or from loss and fraud and ensuring that **liabilities** are **identified** and **managed**.
- Help ensure the **quality** of **internal** and **external reporting**. This requires the **maintenance** of **proper records and processes** that generate a flow of **timely, relevant and reliable information** from within and without the organisation.
- Help ensure **compliance with applicable laws and regulations,** and also with internal policies with respect to the conduct of business'

The Turnbull report goes on to say that a sound system of internal control reduces but does not eliminate the possibilities of **poorly-judged decisions**, **human error, deliberate circumvention of controls**, **management override of controls** and **unforeseeable circumstances.** Systems will provide reasonable (not absolute) assurance that the company will not be hindered in achieving its business objectives and in the orderly and legitimate conduct of its business, but won't provide certain protection against all possible problems.

Exam focus point

Areas particularly highlighted in your syllabus are safeguarding of shareholders' investment and company assets, facilitation of operational effectiveness and efficiency, and contribution to the reliability of reporting. These areas need to be borne in mind in any question on internal control systems, although questions will doubtless cover other aims as well

2 Internal control frameworks

FAST FORWARD

Internal control frameworks include the **control environment** within which **internal controls** operate. Other important elements are the **risk assessment and response processes,** the **sharing of information** and **monitoring** the environment and operation of the control system.

2.1 Need for control framework

Organisations need to consider the overall framework of controls since controls are unlikely to be very effective if they are developed sporadically around the organisation, and their effectiveness will be very difficult to measure by internal audit and ultimately by senior management.

2.2 Control environment and control procedures

Key term

The **internal control system** comprises the **control environment** and **control procedures**. It includes all the policies and procedures (internal controls) adopted by the directors and management of an entity to assist in achieving their objective of ensuring, as far as practicable, the orderly and efficient conduct of its business, including adherence to internal policies, the safeguarding of assets, the prevention and detection of fraud and error, the accuracy and completeness of the accounting records, and the timely preparation of reliable financial information. Internal controls may be incorporated within computerised accounting systems. However, the internal control system extends beyond those matters which relate directly to the accounting system.

Perhaps the simplest framework for internal control draws a distinction between

- **Control environment** – the overall context of control, in particular the attitude of directors and managers towards control
- **Control procedures** – the detailed controls in place

We shall examine both these elements in detail in the next two sections.

The Turnbull report on Internal Control also highlights the importance of

- **Information** and **communication processes**
- **Processes** for **monitoring** the **continuing effectiveness** of the system of internal control

2.3 The COSO framework

We saw in an earlier chapter the control framework that the Committee of Sponsoring Organisations of the Treadway Commission has developed linking objectives with risk management. All elements of this framework affect what COSO call the objectives categories:

- Strategic development
- Operations
- Reporting
- Compliance

A significant advantage of the COSO framework is that it focuses on a wide concept of internal control and is not just limited to financial control.

2.4 The COCO framework

A slightly different framework is the **criteria of control** or COCO framework developed by the Canadian Institute of Chartered Accountants (CICA)

2.4.1 Purpose

The COCO framework stresses the need for all aspects of activities to be clearly directed with a sense of purposes. This includes overall objectives, mission and strategy; management of risk and opportunities; policies; plans and performance measures. The corporate purpose should drive control activities and ensure controls achieve objectives.

2.4.2 Commitment

The framework stresses the importance of managers and staff making an active commitment to identify themselves with the organisation and its values, including ethical values, authority, responsibility and trust.

2.4.3 Capability

Managers and staff must be equipped with the resources and competence necessary to operate the control systems effectively. This includes not just knowledge and resources but also communication processes and co-ordination.

2.4.4 Action

If employees are sure of the purpose, are committed to do their best for the organisation and have the ability to deal with problems and opportunities then the actions they take are more likely to be successful.

2.4.5 Monitoring and learning

An essential part of commitment to the organisation is a commitment to its evolution. This includes

- Monitoring external environments
- Monitoring performance
- Reappraising information systems
- Challenging assumptions
- Reassessing the effectiveness of internal controls

Above all each activity should be seen as part of a **learning process** that lifts the organisation to a higher dimension.

3 Control environment

FAST FORWARD

The **control environment** is influenced by **management's attitude** towards control, the **organisational structure** and the **values** and **abilities** of employees.

3.1 Nature of control environment

Key term

The **control environment** is the overall attitude, awareness and actions of directors and management regarding internal controls and their importance in the entity. The control environment encompasses the management style, and corporate culture and values shared by all employees. It provides the background against which the various other controls are operated.

The following factors are reflected in the control environment.

- The **philosophy** and **operating style** of the directors and management
- The entity's **organisational structure** and methods of assigning authority and responsibility (including segregation of duties and supervisory controls)
- The directors' **methods of imposing control**, including the internal audit function, the functions of the board of directors and personnel policies and procedures
- The **integrity, ethical values** and **competence** of directors and staff

The Turnbull report highlighted a number of elements of a strong control environment.

- **Clear strategies** for dealing with the significant risks that have been identified
- The company's **culture**, **code of conduct, human resource policies** and **performance reward systems** supporting the business objectives and risk management and internal control systems
- Senior management demonstrating through its actions and policies commitment to **competence, integrity** and **fostering a climate of trust** within the company
- **Clear definition** of **authority, responsibility** and **accountability** so that decisions are made and actions are taken by the appropriate people
- **Communication** to employees what is expected of them and scope of their freedom to act
- People in the company having the **knowledge, skills** and **tools** to support the achievements of the organisation's objectives and to manage effectively its risks

However, a strong control environment does not, by itself, ensure the effectiveness of the overall internal control system although it will have a major influence upon it.

The control environment will have a major impact on the establishment of business objectives, the structuring of business activities, and dealing with risks.

4 Control procedures

FAST FORWARD

Controls can be classified in various ways including **administrative** and **accounting**; **prevent**, **detect** and **correct**; **discretionary** and **non-discretionary**; **voluntary** and **mandated**; **manual** and **automated**.

The mnemonic **SPAMSOAP** can be used to remember the main types of control.

Key term

Control procedures are those policies and procedures in addition to the control environment which are established to achieve the entity's specific objectives. (APB)

4.1 Classification of control procedures

You may find internal controls classified in different ways, and these are considered below. Classification of controls can be important because different classifications of control are tested in different ways.

4.1.1 Administrative controls and accounting controls

Administrative controls are concerned with achieving the objectives of the organisation and with implementing policies. The controls relate to the following aspects of control systems.

- Establishing a suitable organisation structure
- The division of managerial authority
- Reporting responsibilities
- Channels of communication

Accounting controls aim to provide accurate accounting records and to achieve accountability. They apply to the following.

- The recording of transactions
- Establishing responsibilities for records, transactions and assets

4.1.2 Prevent, detect and correct controls

Prevent controls are controls that are designed to prevent errors from happening in the first place. Examples of **prevent controls** are as follows.

- Checking invoices from suppliers against goods received notes before paying the invoices
- Regular checking of delivery notes against invoices, to ensure that all deliveries have been invoiced
- Signing of goods received notes, credit notes, overtime records and so forth, to confirm that goods have actually been received, credit notes properly issued, overtime actually authorised and worked and so on

Question **Prevent controls**

Learning outcome: B(v)

How can prevent controls be used to measure performance and efficiency?

Answer

In the above examples the system outputs could include information, say, about the time lag between delivery of goods and invoicing:

(a) As a measure of the **efficiency of the invoicing section**

(b) As an **indicator of the speed and effectiveness** of **communications** between the despatch department and the invoicing department

(c) As **relevant background information** in assessing the effectiveness of cash management

You should be able to think of plenty of other examples. Credit notes reflect customer dissatisfaction, for example: how quickly are they issued?

We shall not labour the links between this and earlier parts of this text, but you should try to recognise them for yourself.

Detect controls are controls that are designed to detect errors once they have happened. Examples of **detect controls** in an accounting system are bank reconciliations and regular checks of physical inventory against book records of inventory.

Correct controls are controls that are designed to minimise or negate the effect of errors. An example of a **correct control** would be back-up of computer input at the end of each day, or the storing of additional copies of software at a remote location.

4.1.3 Discretionary and non-discretionary controls

Discretionary controls are controls that, as their name suggests, are subject to human discretion.

Non-discretionary controls are provided automatically by the system and cannot be bypassed, ignored or overridden. For example, checking the signature on a purchase order is discretionary, whereas inputting a PIN number when using a cash dispensing machine is a non-discretionary control.

4.1.4 Voluntary and mandated controls

Voluntary controls are chosen by the organisation to support the management of the business.

Mandated controls are required by law and imposed by external authorities.

4.1.5 Manual and automated controls

Manual controls demonstrate a one-to-one relationship between the processing functions and controls, and the human functions.

Automated controls are programmed procedures designed to prevent, detect and correct errors all the way through processing.

Manual controls are often used as in conjunction with automated controls, for example when an exception report is reviewed.

4.1.6 General and application controls

These controls are used to reduce the risks associated with the computer environment. **General controls** are controls that relate to the environment in which the application system is processed. **Application controls** are controls that prevent, detect and correct errors and irregularities as transactions flow through the business system.

4.2 Types of procedure

The UK Auditing Practices Board's SAS 300 *Accounting and internal control systems and risk assessments* lists some specific control procedures.

- **Approval** and **control** of **documents**
- Controls over **computerised applications** and the information technology environment

- **Checking** the **arithmetical accuracy** of the records
- Maintaining and reviewing **control accounts** and trial balances
- **Reconciliations**
- **Comparing** the results of cash, security and stock **counts** with **accounting records**
- **Comparing internal data** with **external sources** of information
- **Limiting** direct physical **access** to assets and records

The old UK Auditing Practices Committee guideline *Internal controls* gave a useful summary that is often remembered as a mnemonic.

Segregation of duties
Physical
Authorisation and approval
Management
Supervision
Organisation
Arithmetical and accounting
Personnel

At Strategic level, you should be thinking in particular about Strategic level 'management' controls. Using the above mnemonic, we can give examples of strategic internal controls.

(a) **Segregation of duties**. For example, the chairman/Chief Executive roles should be split.

(b) **Physical**. These are measures to secure the custody of assets, eg only authorised personnel are allowed to move funds on to the money market.

(c) **Authorisation and approval**. All transactions should require authorisation or approval by an appropriate responsible person; limits for the authorisations should be specified, eg a remuneration committee is staffed by non-executive directors (NEDs) to decide directors' pay.

(d) **Management** should provide control through analysis and review of accounts, eg variance analysis, provision of internal audit services.

(e) **Supervision** of the recording and operations of day-to-day transactions. This ensures that all individuals are aware that their work will be checked, reducing the risk of falsification or errors, eg managers review exception reports.

(f) **Organisation**: identify reporting lines, levels of authority and responsibility. This ensures everyone is aware of their control (and other) responsibilities, especially in ensuring adherence to management policies, eg avoid staff reporting to more than one manager. Procedures manuals will be helpful here.

(g) **Arithmetical and accounting**: to check the correct and accurate recording and processing of transactions, eg reconciliations, trial balances.

(h) **Personnel**. Attention should be given to selection, training and qualifications of personnel, as well as personal qualities; the quality of any system is dependent upon the competence and integrity of those who carry out control operations, eg use only qualified staff as internal auditors.

5 Internal controls and risk management

FAST FORWARD

An organisation's internal controls should be designed to counter the **risks** that are relevant to the objectives it pursues.

5.1 Links between controls and risks

We have looked in earlier chapters about how organisations deal with the risks they face. In this section we examine the links between risk assessment and internal controls.

COSO points out that an organisation needs to establish **clear and coherent objectives** in order to be able to tackle risks effectively. The risks that are important are those that are **linked with achievement** of the organisation's objectives. In addition there should be control; mechanisms that identify and adjust for the risks that arise out of changes in economic, industry, regulatory and operating conditions.

Question — Responses to risk

Learning outcome: B(v)

A new employee in the marketing department has asked you about the business objective of meeting or exceeding sales targets.

Required

(a) What are the main risks associated with the business objective meet or exceed sales targets?

(b) How can management reduce the likelihood of occurrence and impact of the risk?

(c) What controls should be associated with reducing the likelihood of occurrence and impact of the risk?

Answer

This question is based on an example in the COSO guidance.

(a) One very important risk would be having insufficient knowledge of customers' needs.

(b) Managers can compile buying histories of existing customers and undertake market research into new customers.

(c) Controls might include checking progress of the development of customer histories against the timetable for those histories and taking steps to ensure that the data is accurate.

COSO also suggests that the links between risks and controls may be complex. Some controls, for example calculation of staff turnover, may indicate how successful management has been in responding to several risks, for example competitor recruiting and lack of effectiveness of staff training and development programmes. On the other hand some risks may require a significant number of internal controls to deal with them.

The Turnbull report stresses the link between the **costs of operating particular controls** with the **benefits obtained in managing the related risks.**

6 Communication with employees

FAST FORWARD

Procedures improving staff abilities and attitudes should be built into the control framework. **Communication** of control and risk management issues and strong **human resource procedures** reinforce the control systems.

6.1 Importance of human element

It is very easy to design a control system that appears good on paper but is unworkable, because it is **not geared** to the **user's practicality and usefulness.** A detailed technical manual covering information technology controls may be of little use if staff lack sufficient knowledge of information technology. Controls may not work very well if staff lack motivation or the basic skills for the job in the first place. On the other hand, if good staff are taken on, they may well develop the necessary controls as part of their day-to-day work.

6.2 Important human resource issues

The UK's Turnbull report stresses that all employees have some responsibility for internal control and need to have the necessary skills, knowledge and understanding in particular of the risks the organisation faces.

A briefing supporting the Turnbull report lists a number of human issues that management need to consider:

- Whether the **remuneration policies and working practices** encourage risk management and discourage taking unnecessary risks
- **Installing** an **attitude** of 'getting things right first time'
- Ensuring that responsibility for **fulfilling business objectives** and **managing related risk** is clear
- Creating an environment where problems are **reported** rather than unresolved
- **Co-ordinating** the activities of different parts of the organisation
- Ensuring that people in the company and in outsource providers have **sufficient knowledge, skills** and **resources** to support the achievement of the organisation's objectives and to manage risks
- Introducing a **common risk management vocabulary** across the organisation
- Adoption of **work practices** and **training** that result in **improved performance**

6.3 Improving staff awareness and attitudes

Turnbull stresses that it is important that all staff understand that risk management is an **integral, embedded part** of the **organisation's operations**. Elaborate risk management innovations may not be the best way to improve performance; it may be better to build warning mechanisms into existing information systems rather than develop separate risk reporting systems.

Turnbull suggests that it is vital to communicate policies in the following areas in particular:

- Customer relations
- Service levels for both internal and outsourced activities
- Health, safety and environmental protection
- Security of assets and business continuity
- Expenditure
- Accounting, financial and other reporting

The briefing suggests that the following steps can be taken:

- **Initial guidance** from the Chief Executive
- **Dissemination of the risk management policy** and codes of conduct, also key business objectives and internal control
- **Workshops** on risk management and internal control
- A **greater proportion of the training budget** being spent on internal control
- Involvement of staff in **identifying and responding** to change and in operating warning mechanisms
- **Clear channels of communication** for reporting breaches and other improprieties

6.4 Training staff

It is important that any training workshop is seen to have the **support of senior management** and that **participants** are **carefully selected** so that they will benefit from being at the same training event. An interactive training event, with participants identifying for themselves the most significant risks and key controls is likely to be the most valuable.

Training days can be particularly useful in emphasising to staff the importance of different types of control (preventative, detective etc) and also the need for some controls to assist staff development, but others to enforce sanctions particularly in cases of dishonesty or negligence.

One caveat is that although training is important, risks will change and employees must continue to be committed to best risk management practice. This means that managers must continue to demonstrate their own commitment to mitigating risk.

7 Information requirements of directors

FAST FORWARD

Directors need **information** from a **large variety of sources** to be able to supervise and review the operation of the internal control systems. Information sources should include normal reporting procedures, but staff should also have channels available to report problems or doubtful practices of others.

7.1 Needs of directors

We have emphasised above that board and senior manager involvement is a critical element of internal control systems and the control environment. There are various ways in which management can obtain the information they need to play the necessary active part in control systems.

7.2 Information sources

The information directors need to be able to monitor controls effectively comes from a wide variety of sources

7.2.1 The directors' own efforts

Directors will receive reports from the audit committee (the role of which is discussed further in the next chapter) and also the director nominated as compliance officer. Management by **walking about**, regular visits by the directors to operations, may yield valuable insights and should help the directors understand the context in which controls are currently operating.

7.2.2 Reports from subordinates

There should be systems in place for all staff with supervisory responsibilities to report on a regular basis to senior managers, and senior managers in turn to report regularly to directors. The COSO guidelines comment:

> 'Among the most critical communications channels is that between top management and the board of directors. Management must keep the board up-to-date on performance, developments, risk and the functioning of enterprise risk management and other relevant events or issues. The better the communications, the more effective the board will be in carrying out its oversight responsibilities, in acting as a sounding board on critical issues and in providing advice, counsel and direction. By the same token the board should communicate to management what information it needs and provide feedback and direction '

7.2.3 Lines of communication

Very importantly directors must ensure that staff have lines of communication that can be used to **address concerns**. There should be normal communication channels through which most concerns are addressed, but there should also be failsafe mechanisms for reporting or **whistleblowing**, particularly serious problems and perhaps active seeking of feedback through **staff attitude surveys.**

As well as channels existing, it is also important that staff believe that directors and managers want to know about problems and will deal with them effectively. Staff must believe that there will be **no reprisals** for **reporting relevant information.**

7.2.4 Reports from control functions

Organisational functions that have a key role to play in internal control systems must report on a regular basis to the board and senior management. One example that we shall examine further later on is the need for a close relationship between **internal audit** and the **audit committee**. The **human resources function** should also report regularly to the board about personnel practices in operational units. Poor human resource management can often be an indicator of future problems with controls, since it may create dissatisfied staff or staff who believe that laxness will be tolerated.

7.2.5 Reports on activities

The board should receive regular reports on **certain activities**. A good example is major developments in computerised systems, which we shall look at in Part E of this text. As well as board approval before the start of key stages of the development process, the board need to be informed of progress and any problems during the course of the project, so that any difficulties with potentially serious consequences can be rapidly addressed.

7.2.6 Reports on resolution of weaknesses

Similarly the board should obtain evidence to confirm that control weaknesses that have previously **been identified** have been **resolved**. When it has been agreed that action should be taken to deal with problems, this should include timescale for action and also reporting that the actions have been implemented.

7.2.7 Results of checks

The board should receive confirmation as a matter of course that necessary **checks** on the operation of the controls have been **carried out** satisfactorily and that the results have been clearly reported. This includes gaining assurance that the **right sort** of check has been **performed**. For example **random checks** may be required on high risk areas such as unauthorised access to computer systems. Sufficient **independent** evidence from external or internal audit should be obtained to reinforce the evidence supplied by operational units.

7.2.8 Exception reporting

Exception reports highlighting variances in **budgeting systems**, **performance measures**, **quality targets** and **planning systems** are an important part of the information that management receives.

7.2.9 Feedback from customers

Customer responses, particularly complaints, is important evidence for the board to consider, particularly as regards how controls ensure the **quality of output**.

7.3 Making best use of information

7.3.1 Comparison of different sources of information

The pictures gleaned from different sources must be compared and discrepancies followed up and addressed. Not only do the board need to have a true picture of what is happening but discrepancies might highlight problems with existing sources of information that need to be addressed. In particular if random or special checks identify problems that should have been picked up and reported through regular channels, then the **adequacy** of these channels needs to be considered carefully.

7.3.2 Feedback to others

Directors need to ensure that as well as their obtaining the information they need to review internal control systems, that relevant information on controls is also passed to all those within the organisation who need it directly. For example sales staff who obtain customer feedback on product shortcomings need to be aware of the channels for communicating with staff responsible for product quality and also staff responsible for product design.

7.3.3 Review procedures

As well as investigating and resolving problems with the information they receive, the board ought to undertake a **regular review** of the **information sources** they need and indeed the whole system of supervision and review to assess its adequacy and also to assess whether any layers of supervision or review can be reduced.

8 Control Self Assessment (CSA)

FAST FORWARD

Control self-assessment is the assessment by senior management of the strength of the internal control system involving risk analysis and review of the adequacy of controls.

Key term

Control Self Assessment (CSA) or **Control and Risk Self Assessment** (CRSA). is a method by which senior management can obtain a view on the adequacy of internal control throughout the organisation in a consistent format.

8.1 Elements of CSA

CSA has been adopted by managers as a means of responding to reporting requirements on internal controls. However, it has many other benefits, the main one being that it helps management to control the business. CSA is described in a CIMA document *Control Self-Assessment (CSA) - a brief introduction.*

CSA consists of four elements or procedures.

(a) **Risk analysis** is carried out, with agreement to, and documentation of the consequent control objectives.

(b) The existing controls are documented.

(c) The **adequacy** of **existing controls** is **evaluated**. This may include 'benchmarking' against known best practice. The evaluation will consider how well the controls are operating and identify an improvement plan (if required).

(d) A **reporting** and **review structure** is **set up** which covers the whole organisation.

Every organisation's CSA process will be different, according to its needs. There is no set formula: some organisations will impose controls whereas others will integrate CSA as part of a continuous improvement process.

8.2 Benefits of CSA

The CIMA document lays out what CSA can do for an organisation, in addition to offering an 'effective and structured means of compliance with the (corporate governance guidelines)'. The perceived benefits of CSA are as follows.

- Formalising management's responsibility and accountability for maintaining an adequate system of internal controls.
- Improving management's understanding of risk and control issues.
- Providing positive evidence of effective internal control.
- Highlighting areas of potential weakness.
- Providing comprehensive control documentation in a consistent format for the whole organisation.
- Assisting flexibility of control response in a high change environment.
- Supporting concepts such as Total Quality Management, empowerment and benchmarking.
- Improving the utilisation of scarce internal audit resource.

8.3 Limitations of CSA

However CSA does *not*:

(a) **Provide absolute assurance** that control requirements are being complied with (it only gives reasonable assurance)

(b) **Necessarily identify**:

  (i) **Issues** which would **not** be **identified** by a **traditional** audit (although it may)

  (ii) **One-off errors** and omissions associated with individual transactions

  (iii) **Loss of assets**

  (iv) **Fraud**

There are costs involved in implementing CSA, mainly in staff time for **setting up**. As long as the procedures are accepted organisation-wide, however, the ongoing costs should be fairly moderate. Areas identified for improvement should be evaluated on a cost-benefit basis and cost savings might be made if duplicated or redundant controls are identified. Cost-benefit analysis of internal control systems is considered further in the next section.

8.4 Managers' role in CSA

Senior managers must be seen as the instigators of CSA. However, internal audit will have a significant role to play in implementing CSA. Implementation must be **well-planned** and **supported** by senior management in order to achieve acceptance by the rest of the company and to give CSA the necessary priority. Internal audit should be viewed as a co-ordinator and facilitator.

Managers will self-certify with varying levels of certificate, going up to 'high' level, with exceptions reported up from line to senior managers. Internal audit will brief line managers, help to draw up control certificates and ensure a consistent approach is adopted across the enterprise.

Internal auditors will also act as the **post-implementation reviewers** to ensure that reporting is complete, timely and accurate. Internal audit can help management in the completion of certificates, where required, and in implementing identified improvements.

CSA is not a replacement for internal audit, but it adds value to the internal audit function. Internal audit can concentrate on strategic issues, leaving operational checks to the CSA process.

The CIMA document gives an example of a certificate of internal control, which is split into three columns.

- Control
- Evidence/mechanism (that the control is operating)
- Comments (exceptions)

9 Costs and benefits of internal controls

FAST FORWARD

Sometimes the benefits of controls will be outweighed by their costs, and organisations should compare them. However it is difficult to put a monetary value on many **benefits** and **costs** of controls, and also the potential losses if controls are not in place.

9.1 Benefits of internal control

The benefits of internal control, even well-directed ones, are not limitless. Controls can provide reasonable, not absolute, assurance that the organisation is progressing towards its objectives, safeguarding its assets and complying with laws and regulations. Internal controls cannot guarantee success as there are plenty of **environmental factors** (economic indicators, competitor actions) beyond the organisation's control.

In addition there are various inherent limitations in control systems including faulty decision-making and breakdowns occurring because of human error. The control system may also be vulnerable to **employee collusion** and **management override** of controls **undermining** the **systems** of **controls.**

9.2 Costs of internal controls

As well as realising the limitations of the benefits of controls, it is also important to realise their costs. Some costs are obvious, for example the salary of a nightwatchman to keep watch over the security premises. There are also opportunity costs through for example increased manager time being spent on review rather than dealing with customers for example.

One common complaint is that controls stifle initiative, although this is not always well-founded, particularly if the initiative involves too casual an approach to risk management.

9.3 Benefits vs Costs

The principle that the costs of controls need to be compared with benefits is reasonable. We mentioned in a previous chapter that organisations will sometimes decide to accept risks and not insure them, and similarly the internal controls may not be felt to be worth the reduction in risk that they achieve.

However the comparison of benefits and costs may be difficult in practice:

- We saw in the last chapter that it can be difficult to **estimate the potential monetary loss or gain** that could occur as a result of exposure to risk if no measures are taken to combat the risk.
- It can be difficult to assess by how much the **possible loss or gain** is affected by a control measure, particularly if the benefit of control is to reduce, but not eliminate the risk (something which will be true for many controls)
- Many benefits of controls are **non-monetary,** for example improvements in employee attitudes or the reputation of the organisation.

Chapter roundup

- **Internal controls** should help organisations counter risks, maintain the quality of reporting and comply with laws and regulations. They provide reasonable assurance that organisations will fulfil their objectives.
- Internal control frameworks include the **control environment** within which **internal controls** operate. Other important elements are the **risk assessment and response processes,** the **sharing of information** and **monitoring** the environment and operation of the control system.
- The **control environment** is influenced by **management's attitude** towards control, the **organisational structure** and the **values** and **abilities** of employees.
- Controls can be classified in various ways including **administrative** and **accounting**; **prevent, detect** and **correct**; **discretionary** and **non-discretionary; voluntary** and **mandated**; **manual** and **automated.**
- The mnemonic **SPAMSOAP** can be used to remember the main types of control.
- An organisation's internal controls should be designed to counter the **risks** that are relevant to the objectives it pursues.
- Procedures improving staff abilities and attitudes should be built into the control framework. **Communication** of control and risk management issues and strong **human resource procedures** reinforce the control systems.
- Directors need **information** from a **large variety of sources** to be able to supervise and review the operation of the internal control systems. Information sources should include normal reporting procedures, but staff should also have channels available to report problems or doubtful practices of others.
- **Control self-assessment** is the assessment by senior management of the strength of the internal control system involving risk analysis and review of the adequacy of controls.
- Sometimes the benefits of controls will be outweighed by their costs, and organisations should compare them. However it is difficult to put a monetary value on many **benefits** and **costs** of controls, and also the potential losses if controls are not in place.

Quick quiz

1 What according to Turnbull should a good system of internal control achieve?

2 What are the main components of the criteria of control framework?

3 What are the main factors that will be reflected in the organisation's control environment?

4 Match the control and control type

(a) Checking of delivery notes against invoices
(b) Back-up of computer input
(c) Bank reconciliation

(i) Prevent
(ii) Detect
(iii) Correct

5 A ------ control is required by law and imposed by external authorities.

6 List the eight types of control given in SAS 300.

7 According to the Turnbull report, in which areas do internal controls particularly need to be communicated?

8 What technique can be used by managers to obtain a consistent view on the adequacy of control procedures throughout the organisation?

Answers to quick quiz

1
- Facilitate effective and efficient operation by enabling it to respond to significant risks.
- Help ensure the quality of internal and external reporting
- Help ensure compliance with applicable laws and regulations

2
- Purpose
- Commitment
- Capability
- Action
- Monitoring and learning

3
- The philosophy and operating style of the directors and management
- The entity's organisational structure and methods of assigning authority and responsibility (including segregation of duties and supervisory controls)
- The directors' methods of imposing control, including the internal audit function, the functions of the board of directors and personnel policies and procedures
- The integrity, ethical values and competence of directors and staff

4 (a) (i)
(b) (iii)
(c) (ii)

5 A **mandated** control is required by law and imposed by external authorities.

6
- Approval and control of documents
- Controls over computerised applications and the information technology environment
- Checking the arithmetical accuracy of the records
- Maintaining and reviewing control accounts and trial balances
- Reconciliations
- Comparing the results of cash, security and stock counts with accounting records
- Comparing internal data with external sources of information
- Limiting direct physical access to assets and records

7
- Customer relations
- Service levels for both internal and outsourced activities
- Health, safety and environmental protection
- Security of assets and business continuity
- Expenditure
- Accounting, financial and other reporting

8 Control self-assessment

Now try the question below from the Exam Question Bank

Number	Level	Marks	Time
Q7	Examination	25	45 mins

Corporate governance

Introduction

Corporate governance is a key area in this syllabus, and one in which you are expected to have a good knowledge of major worldwide developments. There have been a number of reports worldwide on corporate governance and to help you get your bearings, we have set out in an appendix to this chapter the main provisions of the various reports. However the examiners have stressed that the principles of corporate governance are most important, so in the main body of the chapter we cover the main areas of corporate governance, mixing in the recommendations of various reports.

The focus of this chapter is on the role of the board, its membership, its committees and how it communicates with shareholders. Other important elements of corporate governance include risk management which we have already covered, and internal control and internal audit which we will cover in Part C.

As you might have guessed this is one of the most important chapters in this book; one of the questions on the pilot paper covered various aspects of corporate governance.

Topic list	Learning outcomes	Syllabus references	Ability required
1 Developments in corporate governance	B(vii)	B(14)	Evaluation
2 Principles of corporate governance	B(vii)	B(14)	Evaluation
3 Role of the board	B(vii)	B(14)	Evaluation
4 Board membership	B(vii)	B(14)	Evaluation
5 Directors' remuneration	B(vii)	B(14)	Evaluation
6 Internal control and audit committees	B(vii)	B(14),(15)	Evaluation
7 Relationships with shareholders and stakeholders	B(vii)	B(14)	Evaluation
8 Reporting on corporate governance	B(vii)	B(14)	Evaluation
Appendix – corporate governance reports			

1 Developments in corporate governance

FAST FORWARD

Good corporate governance involves **risk management** and **internal control, accountability** to stakeholders and other shareholders and conducting business in an **ethical and effective way.**

1.1 What is corporate governance

Key term

Corporate governance is the system by which organisations are directed and controlled.

Although mostly discussed in relation to large quoted companies, governance is an issue for all bodies corporate; commercial and not for profit.

There are a number of elements in corporate governance:

(a) The management and **reduction of risk** is fundamental in all definitions of good governance.

(b) The notion that **overall performance enhanced** by **good supervision** and **management** within **set best practice guidelines** underpins most definitions.

(c) Good governance provides a **framework** for an organisation to pursue its strategy in an **ethical and effective** way from the perspective of all stakeholder groups affected, and offers safeguards against misuse of resources, physical or intellectual.

(d) Good governance is not just about externally established codes, it also requires a willingness to **apply the spirit** as well as the letter of the law.

(e) **Accountability** is generally a major theme in all governance frameworks.

1.2 The driving forces of governance development

Corporate governance issues came to prominence in the USA during the 1970s and in the UK and Europe from late 1980s. The main, but not the only, drivers associated with the increasing demand for the development of governance were:

(a) **Increasing internationalisation and globalisation** meant that investors, and institutional investors in particular, began to invest outside their home countries. This has lead to calls for companies to operate in an acceptable fashion and to report corporate performance fairly. The King report in South Africa highlights the role of the free movement of capital, commenting that investors are promoting governance in their own self-interest.

(b) The **differential treatment of domestic and foreign investors**, both in terms of reporting and associated rights/dividends caused many investors to call for parity of treatment. While this was widely accepted in the mature economies, differential treatment does still exist in some jurisdictions.

(c) Issues concerning **financial reporting** were raised by many investors and were the focus of much debate and litigation. Shareholder confidence in many instances was eroded and, while focus solely on accounting and reporting issues is inadequate, the regulation of practices such as off-balance sheet financing has led to greater transparency and a reduction in risks faced by investors.

(d) The characteristics of individual countries may have a **significant influence** in the way corporate governance has developed. The King report emphasises the importance of qualities that are fundamental to the South African culture such as collectiveness, consensus, helpfulness, fairness, consultation and religious faith in the development of best practice.

(e) An increasing number of **high profile corporate scandals** and collapses including Polly Peck International, BCCI, and Maxwell Communications Corporation prompted the development of governance codes in the early 1990s. However the scandals since then have raised questions about further measures that may be necessary.

Case Study

In the UK the Cadbury committee was set up in May 1991 because of the lack of confidence which was perceived in financial reporting and in the ability of external auditors to provide the assurances required by the users of financial statements. The main difficulties were considered to be in the relationship between external auditors and boards of directors. In particular, the commercial pressures on both directors and auditors caused pressure to be brought to bear on auditors by the board and the auditors often capitulated.

Problems were also perceived in the ability of the board of directors to control their organisations. The lack of board accountability in many of these company collapses demonstrated the need for action.

1.3 Features of poor corporate governance

The scandals over the last 25 years have highlighted the need for guidance to tackle the various risks and problems that can arise in organisations' systems of governance.

1.3.1 Domination by a single individual

A feature of many corporate governance scandals has been boards dominated by a single senior executive with other board members merely acting as a rubber stamp. Sometimes the single individual may bypass the board to action his own interests. The report on the UK Guinness case suggested that the Chief Executive, Ernest Saunders paid himself a £3million reward without consulting the other directors.

Even if an organisation is not dominated by a single individual, there may be other weaknesses. The organisation may be run by a small group centred round the chief executive and chief financial officer, and appointments may be made by personal recommendation rather than a formal, objective process.

1.3.2 Lack of involvement of board

Boards that meet irregularly or fail to consider systematically the organisation's activities and risks are clearly weak. Sometimes the failure to carry out proper oversight is due to a **lack of information** being provided.

1.3.3 Lack of adequate control function

An obvious weakness is a **lack of internal audit.**

Another important control is **lack of adequate technical knowledge** in key roles, for example in the audit committee or in senior compliance positions. A rapid turnover of staff involved in accounting or control may suggest inadequate resourcing, and will make control more difficult because of lack of continuity.

1.3.4 Lack of supervision

Employees who are not properly supervised can create large losses for the organisation through their own incompetence, negligence or fraudulent activity. The behaviour of Nick Leeson, the employee who caused the collapse of Barings bank was not challenged because he appeared to be successful, whereas he was using unauthorised accounts to cover up his large trading losses. Leeson was able to do this because he has in charge of dealing and settlement, a systems weakness or **lack of segregation of key roles** that was featured in other financial frauds.

1.3.5 Lack of independent scrutiny

External auditors may not carry out the necessary questioning of senior management because of fears of losing the audit, and internal audit do not ask awkward questions because the chief financial officer determines their employment prospects. Often corporate collapses are followed by criticisms of external auditors, such as the Barlow Clowes affair where poorly planned and focused audit work failed to identify illegal use of client monies.

1.3.6 Lack of contact with shareholders

Often board members may have grown up with the company but lose touch with the interests and views of shareholders. One possible symptom of this is the payment of remuneration packages that do not appear to be warranted by results.

1.3.7 Emphasis on short-term profitability

Emphasis on success or getting results can lead to the **concealment of problems or errors,** or **manipulation of accounts** to **achieve desired results**.

1.3.8 Misleading accounts and information

Often misleading figures are symptomatic of other problems (or are designed to conceal other problems) but clearly poor quality accounting information is a major problem if markets are trying to make a fair assessment of the company's value. Giving out misleading information was a major issue in the UK's Equitable Life scandal where the company gave contradictory information to savers, independent advisers, media and regulators.

1.4 Risks of poor corporate governance

Clearly the ultimate risk is of the organisation **making such large losses** that **bankruptcy** becomes inevitable. The organisation may also be closed down as a result of **serious regulatory breaches,** for example misapplying investors' monies.

1.5 Reports on corporate governance

A number of reports have been produced in various countries aiming to address the risk and problems posed by poor corporate governance.

1.5.1 United Kingdom

There were three significant corporate governance reports in the United Kingdom during the 1990s. The **Cadbury and Hampel reports** covered general corporate governance issues, whilst the **Greenbury report** concentrated on remuneration of directors.

The recommendations of these three reports were merged into a **Combined Code** in 1998, with which companies listed on the London Stock Exchange are required to comply.

Since the publication of the Combined Code a number of reports in the UK have been published about specific aspects of corporate governance.

- The **Turnbull report** focused on risk management and internal control
- The **Smith report** discussed the role of internal audit
- The **Higgs report** focused on the role of the non-executive director

1.5.2 USA

Corporate scandals, particularly the Enron scandal, in the United States over the last few years have led to the Sarbanes-Oxley Act 2002 and consequent changes to the listing rules that companies quoted on Wall Street have to fulfil.

1.5.3 South Africa

South Africa's major contribution to the corporate governance debate has been the **King report**, first published in 1994 and updated in 2002 to take account of developments in South Africa and elsewhere in the world.

2 Principles of corporate governance

FAST FORWARD

Most corporate governance reports are based around the principles of **integrity**, **accountability**, **independence** and **good management** but there is disagreement on how much these principles need to be supplemented by detailed rules.

2.1 Perspectives on governance

Debates about the place of governance are founded on three differing views associated with the **ownership** and **management** of organisations.

2.1.1 Stewardship theory

Some approaches to good governance view the management of an organisation as the **stewards** of its assets, charged with their employment and deployment in ways consistent with the overall strategy of the organisation. With this approach, power is seen to be vested in the stewards, that is the executive managers.

Other interest groups take little or no part in the running of the company and receive relevant information via established reporting mechanisms; audited accounts, annual reports etc. Technically, shareholders or member/owners have the right to dismiss their stewards if they are dissatisfied by their stewardship, via a vote at an annual general meeting.

Many of the scandals in recent years have highlighted the limitations of this view. The **limitations of financial reporting** have been targeted by governance frameworks. So too has the issue of **independence** of professional service providers: auditors, management consultants, merchant banks and brokers. The argument goes that increasing the independence of advisors will raise the quality of information so that owners would be better able to exercise ultimate control over the stewards, that is the board.

This in itself falls down, however, where shareholders do **not take an active interest** in the organisation, and do not exercise their right to vote. Good governance can therefore be seen to require active participation on the part of owners; an abrogation of responsibility under a stewardship approach is not acceptable practice.

2.1.2 Agency theory

Another approach to governance is enshrined in **agency theory**. This takes the stance that, rather than acting as stewards, management will act in an **agency capacity**, seeking to service their own self-interest and looking after the performance of the company only where its goals are co-incident with their own.

This approach takes a very negative, short term/tactical stance, but is one that has found a home in some elements of the frameworks. The development of **performance related remuneration** and **incentive schemes**, such as Long Term Incentive Plans (LTIPs) and executive share option schemes, are rooted in an agency theory approach. The focus of agency theory is therefore contractual, although the regulatory elements noted above indicate the acceptance of its limitations and short-termism.

2.1.3 Stakeholder theory

The stakeholder approach takes a much more **'organic' view** of the organisation, imbuing it with a 'life' of its own, in keeping with the notion of a separate legal personage. Effectively stakeholder theory is a development of the notion of stewardship, stating that management has a **duty of care, not just to the owners** of the company in terms of maximising shareholder value, but also to the **wider community** of interest, or stakeholders.

For those directly involved in the company's day to day operation, such as the employees, the theory can be seen especially in some of the European frameworks, such as in Germany where employees are represented on the supervisory board of the company, and through specific mention in the OECD (Organisation for Economic Cooperation and Development) guidelines.

The approach also has a number of drawbacks. The most obvious is the apparently insurmountable problem of producing either a **definitive list** or a rank order of importance of stakeholders and their interests. **Culture**, too, presents a major potential drawback regarding the applicability of the theory, not only in terms of those included in the list but also in terms of the best mechanisms for addressing their needs.

2.2 Governance principles

Most corporate governance codes are based on a set of principles founded upon ideas of what corporate governance is meant to achieve. This list is based on a number of reports.

(a) To **minimise risk**, especially financial, legal and reputational risks, by requiring compliance with accepted good practice in the jurisdiction in question and ensuring appropriate systems of financial control are in place, in particular systems for monitoring risk, financial control and compliance with the law.

(b) To **ensure adherence** to and **satisfaction** of the **strategic objectives** of the organisation, thus aiding effective management.

(c) To **fulfil responsibilities to all stakeholders** and to **minimise potential conflicts of interest** between the owners, managers and wider stakeholder community, however defined and to treat each category **fairly**.

(d) To **establish clear accountability** at senior levels within an organisation.

(e) To **maintain the independence** of those who scrutinise the behaviour of the organisation and its senior executive managers. Independence is particularly important for **non-executive directors,** and **internal and external auditors.**

(f) To **provide accurate and timely reporting of trustworthy/independent financial and operational data** to both the management and owners/members of the organisation to give them a true and balanced picture of what is happening in the organisation.

(g) To **encourage more proactive involvement** of owners/members in the effective management of the organisation through recognising their responsibilities of oversight and input to decision making processes via voting or other mechanisms.

(h) To **promote integrity**, that is **straightforward dealing** and **completeness**

Case Study

Identification of the most important principles of corporate governance will often depend on the standpoint taken. In an article in *CIMA Student* in February 1996, JA Williams identified the following broad aims of corporate governance at a **political** level.

- **Creating a framework** for the **control of large, powerful companies** whose interests may not coincide with the national interest
- **Controlling multinationals** which can dominate the local economy
- Ensuring that **companies** are **answerable** to all **stakeholders**, not just to shareholders
- Ensuring that **companies** are **run according** to the **laws and standards** of the country and are not in effect 'states within states'
- **Protecting investors** who buy shares in the same way as investors are protected who buy any other financial investment product, such as insurance or a pension.

2.3 Principles vs rules

A continuing debate on corporate governance is whether the guidance should predominantly be in the form of principles, or whether there is a need for detailed laws or regulations.

The Hampel report in the UK came out very firmly in favour of a principles-based approach. The committee preferred of relaxing the regulatory burden on companies and against treating the corporate governance codes as sets of prescriptive rules, and judging companies by whether they have complied ('box-ticking'). The report stated that there may be **guidelines** which will normally be appropriate but the differing circumstances of companies meant that sometimes there are valid reasons for exceptions.

However a number of commentators criticized the Hampel report for this approach. Some critics have commented that the principles set out in the Hampel report are so broad that they are of very little use as a guide to best corporate governance practice. For example the suggestion that non-executive directors from a wide variety of backgrounds can make a contribution is seen as not strong enough to encourage companies away from recruiting directors by means of the 'old boy network'.

It has also been suggested that the Hampel comments about **box-ticking** are incorrect for two reasons. Firstly, shareholders do not apply that approach when assessing accounts. Secondly, it is far less likely that disasters will strike companies with a 100% compliance record since they are unlikely to be content with token compliance, but will have set up procedures that contribute significantly to their being governed well.

3 Role of the board

FAST FORWARD

The board should be responsible for taking major **policy** and **strategic** decisions.

Directors should have a **mix of skills** and their **performance** should be assessed regularly.

Appointments should be conducted by formal procedures administered by a **nomination committee**.

3.1 Scope of role

The King report provides a good summary of the role of the board.

> 'To define the purpose of the company and the values by which the company will perform its daily existence and to identify the stakeholders relevant to the business of the company. The board must then develop a strategy combining all three factors and ensure management implements that strategy.'

If the board is to act effectively, its role must be defined carefully. The Cadbury report suggests that the board should have a **formal schedule of matters** specifically reserved to it for decision. Some would be decisions such as **mergers and takeovers** that are **fundamental** to the business and hence should not be taken just by executive managers. Other decisions would include **acquisitions and disposals of assets of the company** or its subsidiaries that are material to the company and **investments, capital projects, bank borrowing** facilities, **loans** and their repayment, foreign currency transactions, all above a certain size (to be determined by the board).

Other tasks the board should perform include:

- Monitoring the chief executive officer
- Overseeing strategy
- Monitoring risks and control systems
- Monitoring the human capital aspects of the company in regard to succession, morale, training, remuneration etc.
- Ensuring that there is effective communication of its strategic plans, both internally and externally

3.2 Attributes of directors

In order to carry out effective scrutiny, directors need to have **relevant expertise** in industry, company, functional area and governance. The board as whole needs to contain a **mix of expertise** and show a **balance** between **executive management** and **independent non-executive directors**. The King report stresses the importance also of having a good **demographic balance.**

New and existing directors should also have **appropriate training** to develop the knowledge and skills required.

3.2.1 Nomination committee

In order to ensure that balance of the board is maintained, the board should set up a **nomination committee,** to oversee the process for board appointments and make recommendations to the board. The nomination committee needs to consider the balance between executives and independent non-executives, the skills possessed by the board, the need for continuity and the desirable **size** of the board. Recent corporate governance guidance has laid more stress on the need to attract board members from a **diversity** of backgrounds.

3.3 Possession of necessary information

As we have seen above, in many corporate scandals, the board were not given full information. The UK's Higgs report stresses that it is the responsibility both of the chairman to decide what information should be made available, and directors to satisfy themselves that they have **appropriate information** of **sufficient quality** to make sound judgements. The King report highlights the importance of the board receiving **relevant non-financial information**, going beyond assessing the financial and qualitative performance of the company, looking at **qualitative measures** that involve **broader stakeholder interests**.

3.4 Performance of board

Appraisal of the board's performance is an important control over it. The Higgs report recommends that **performance of the board** should be **assessed** once a year. **Separate appraisal** of the chairman and chief executive should also be carried out, with links to the remuneration process.

4 Board membership

FAST FORWARD

Division of responsibilities at the head of an organisation is most simply achieved by separating the roles of chairman and chief executive.

Independent non-executive directors have a key role in governance. Their number and status should mean that their views carry significant weight.

4.1 Division of responsibilities

All reports acknowledge the importance of having a division of responsibilities at the head of an organisation. The simplest way to do this is to require the roles of **chairman** and **chief executive** to be held by two different people.

This division has not been made mandatory in the UK. The Cadbury report recommended that if the posts were held by the same individual, there should be a **strong independent element** on the board with a recognized senior member. The UK's Smith report suggested that a senior independent non-executive director should be appointed who would be available to shareholders who have concerns that were not resolved through the normal channels.

4.2 Non-executive directors

Key term

Non-executive directors have no executive (managerial) responsibilities.

Non-executive directors should provide a **balancing influence**, and play a key role in **reducing conflicts of interest** between management (including executive directors) and shareholders. They should provide reassurance to shareholders, particularly institutional shareholders, that management is acting in the interests of the organisation.

4.2.1 Advantages of non-executive directors

Non-executive directors can bring a number of advantages to a board of directors.

(a) They may have **external experience and knowledge which executive directors do not possess.** The experience they bring can be in many different fields. They may be executive directors of other companies, and thus have experience of different ways of approaching corporate governance, internal controls or performance assessment. They can also bring knowledge of markets within which the company operates.

(b) Non-executive directors can provide a **wider perspective** than executive directors who may be more involved in detailed operations.

(c) Good non-executive directors are often a **comfort factor** for third parties such as investors or creditors.

(d) The English businessman Sir John Harvey-Jones has pointed out that there are **certain roles** non-executive directors are well-suited to play. These include 'father-confessor' (being a confidant for the chairman and other directors), 'oil-can' (intervening to make the board run more effectively) and acting as 'high sheriff' (if necessary taking steps to remove the chairman or chief executive).

(e) The most important advantage perhaps lies in the dual nature of the non-executive director's role. Non-executive directors are **full board members** who are expected to have the level of knowledge that full board membership implies. At the same time they are meant to provide the so-called **strong, independent element** on the board. This should imply that they have the knowledge and detachment to be able to assess fairly the remuneration of executive directors when serving on the remuneration committee, and to be able to discuss knowledgeably with auditors the affairs of the company on the audit committee.

4.2.2 Problems with non-executive directors

Nevertheless there are a number of difficulties connected with the role of non-executive director.

(a) In many organisations, non-executive directors may **lack independence**. There are in practice a number of ways in which non-executive directors can be linked to a company, as suppliers or customers for example. Even if there is no direct connection, potential non-executive directors are more likely to agree to serve if they admire the company's chairman or its way of operating.

(b) There may be a **prejudice in certain companies** against widening the recruitment of non-executive directors to include people proposed other than by the board or to include stakeholder representatives.

(c) High-calibre non-executive directors may gravitate towards the **best-run companies**, rather than companies which are more in need of input from good non-executives.

(d) Non-executive directors may have **difficulty imposing** their views upon the board. It may be easy to dismiss the views of non-executive directors as irrelevant to the company's needs. This may imply that non-executive directors need good persuasive skills to influence other directors. Moreover, if executive directors are determined to push through a controversial policy, it may prove difficult for the more disparate group of non-executive directors to oppose them effectively.

(e) Sir John Harvey-Jones has suggested that not enough emphasis is given to the role of non-executive directors in **preventing trouble**, in warning early on of potential problems. Contrawise, when trouble does arise, non-executive directors may be expected to play a major role in rescuing the situation, which they may not be able to do.

(f) Perhaps the biggest problem which non-executive directors face is the **limited time** they can devote to the role. If they are to contribute valuably, they are likely to have time-consuming other commitments. In the time they have available to act as non-executive directors, they must contribute as knowledgeable members of the full board and fulfil their legal responsibilities as directors. They must also serve on board committees. Their responsibilities mean that their time must be managed effectively, and they must be able to focus on areas where the value they add is greatest.

The limited time available to non-executive directors may also work against attempts to expand their responsibilities, either as members of the full board or particularly perhaps as members of the audit committee.

4.2.3 Number of non – executive directors

Most corporate governance reports acknowledge the importance of having a significant presence of non-executive directors on the board. The question has been whether organisations should follow the broad principles expressed in the Cadbury report:

> 'The board should include non-executive directors of sufficient character and number for their views to carry significant weight.'

or whether they should follow prescriptive guidelines. New York Stock Exchange rules now require listed companies to have a majority of non-executive directors.

4.2.4 Independence of non-executive directors

Various safeguards can be put in place to ensure that non-executive directors remain independent. Those suggested by the corporate governance reports include:

(a) Non-executive directors should have **no business**, **financial** or other **connection** with the company, apart from fees and shareholdings. Recent reports such as the UK's Higgs report have widened the scope of business connections to include anyone who has been an employee or had a material business relationship over the last few years, or served on the board for more than ten years.

(b) They should **not take part in share option schemes** and their service should not be pensionable, to maintain their independent status.

(c) **Appointments** should be for a **specified term** and reappointment should not be automatic. The board as a whole should decide on their nomination and selection.

(d) Procedures should exist whereby non-executive directors may take **independent advice**, at the company's expense if necessary.

Cadbury suggests that the role of non-executive directors should be

> 'To bring an independent judgement to bear on issues of strategy, performance, resources including key appointments and standards of conduct.

4.2.5 Multi-tier boards

Some jurisdictions take the split between executive and other directors to its furthest extent. Institutional arrangements in German companies are based on a **two-tiered board**. A **supervisory board** has workers' representatives, and perhaps shareholders' representatives including banks' representatives, in equal numbers. The board has no executive function, although it does review the company's direction and strategy and is responsible for safeguarding **stakeholders**' interests. An **executive board**, composed entirely of managers, will be responsible for the **running** of the business.

In Japan there are three different types of board of director.

- **Policy boards** - concerned with long-term strategic issues
- **Functional boards** - made up of the main senior executives with a functional role
- **Monocratic boards** - with few responsibilities and having a more symbolic role

Proposals to introduce two (or more) tier boards have been particularly criticised in the UK and USA as leading to confusion and a lack of accountablilty. This has affected the debate on enhancing the role of non-executive directors, with critics claiming that moves to increase the involvement of non-executive directors are a step on the slippery slope towards two-tier boards.

5 Directors' remuneration

FAST FORWARD

Directors' remuneration should be set by a **remuneration committee** consisting of independent non-executive directors.

Remuneration should be dependent upon **organisation** and **individual performance**.

Accounts should disclose **remuneration policy** and (in detail) the **packages of individual directors.**

5.1 Need for guidance

Directors being paid excessive salaries and bonuses has been seen as one of the major corporate abuses for a large number of years. It is thus inevitable that the corporate governance provisions have targeted it.

The **Greenbury committee** in the UK set out principles which are a good summary of what remuneration policy should involve.

- Directors' remuneration should be set by **independent members** of the board
- Any form of bonus should be related to **measurable performance** or enhanced shareholder value
- There should be **full transparency of directors' remuneration** including pension rights in the annual accounts

5.2 Remuneration committee

The remuneration committee plays the key role in establishing remuneration arrangements. In order to be effective, the committee needs both to **determine** the organisation's **general policy** on the **remuneration of executive directors** and **specific remuneration packages** for each director.

Measures to ensure that the committee is **independent** include not just requiring that the committee is staffed by non-executive directors, but also placing limits on the members' connection with the organization. Measures to ensure independence include stating that the committee should have no personal interests other than as shareholders, no conflicts of interest and no day-to-day involvement in running the business.

5.3 Establishing remuneration arrangements

However the committee must also take into account the wider picture. Packages will need to **attract, retain and motivate directors** of sufficient quality, whilst at the same time taking into account shareholders' interests as well. However assessing executive remuneration in an imperfect market for executive skills may prove problematic.

The committee needs to be mindful of the **implications** of **all aspects** of the package. Particularly sensitive areas include terms of share option schemes, the phasing of rewards, and the pension consequences of various elements of the remuneration package.

Share options can be used to align management and shareholder interests, particularly options held for a long time when value is dependent on long-term performance.

Length of service contracts can be a particular problem. If service contracts are too long, and then have to be terminated prematurely, the perception often arises that the amounts paying off directors for the remainder of the contract are essentially rewards of failure. Corporate governance guidance has indicated that service contracts greater than 12 months need to be carefully considered.

Other issues the remuneration committee have to consider include:

(a) The **differentials at management/director level** (difficult with many layers of management)

(b) The **ability of managers to leave**, taking clients and knowledge to a competitor or their own new business

(c) **Individual performance** and additional work/effort

(d) The company's **overall performance**

The problem here, particularly with (c) and (d), is that it places the non-executive directors of the remuneration committee in charge of the executive directors, that is it goes further than simply providing 'transparency' as regards executive pay.

5.4 Disclosures

In order for readers of the accounts to achieve a fair picture of remuneration arrangements, the accounts would need to disclose:

- Remuneration policy
- Arrangements for individual directors

5.4.1 Remuneration policy

Necessary disclosures would include:

- Remuneration levels
- Comparator companies
- Main components of remuneration
- Performance criteria and measurement
- Pension provision
- Contracts of service
- Compensation for loss of office

5.4.2 Arrangements for individual directors

Disclosures need to cover all aspects of packages. For each director this should include **basic salary**, **benefits-in-kind**, **bonuses** and **long-term incentives**. Details should also be given of individual entitlement to share options, and pensions entitlements earned during the year.

5.4.3 Voting on remuneration

Along with disclosure, the directors also need to consider whether members need to signify their approval of remuneration policy by voting on the **remuneration statement** and elements of the remuneration packages of individual directors, for example long-term incentive schemes.

Case Study

A 1999 survey by the UK's Department of Trade and Industry indicated that many listed companies were failing to comply with a number of the recommendations originally aired in the Greenbury report on directors' remuneration. In particular:

(a) A significant number of remuneration committees did not consist solely of independent non-executive directors; a few had executive directors as members.

(b) Disclosure about the **linkage** between **performance** and **remuneration** was insufficiently clear in most accounts.

(c) Not many companies were putting their **remuneration report** to the **vote** in the annual general meeting.

6 Internal control and audit committees

6.1 Internal control

FAST FORWARD

Boards should regularly review **risk management** and **internal control**, and carry out a wider review annually, the results of which should be disclosed in the accounts.

We shall discuss internal control in detail in the next Part of this text, but in this section we shall focus on the role of the board in maintaining internal control.

The USA's Sarbanes-Oxley regulations have forced American boards to look carefully at internal controls and in particular:

(a) **Disclose to the auditors** and **audit committee deficiencies** in the operation of internal controls

(b) In the accounts **acknowledge their responsibility** for **internal control**, and assess its effectiveness based on an evaluation within 30 days prior to the report

6.1.1 Review of internal controls

The UK's **Turnbull committee** suggested that review of internal controls should be an **integral part** of the **company's operations**; the board, or board committees, should actively consider reports on control issues from others operating internal controls. We shall look in detail at this review in Chapter 12.

6.2 Audit committee

FAST FORWARD

Audit committees of **independent non-executive directors** should liase with **external audit**, **supervise internal audit**, and **review** the **annual accounts** and **internal controls**.

Exam focus point

Audit committees are very significant as far as this section of the syllabus is concerned because of their responsibilities for supervision and overall review. In particular they should have a close interest in the work of internal audit; the Cadbury report emphasised the importance of internal audit having unrestricted access to the audit committee.

The Cadbury committee summed up the benefits that an audit committee can bring to an organisation.

Role and function of audit committee

'If they operate effectively, audit committees can bring significant benefits. In particular, they have the potential to:

(a) improve the quality of financial reporting, by reviewing the financial statements on behalf of the Board;

(b) create a climate of discipline and control which will reduce the opportunity for fraud;

(c) enable the non-executive directors to contribute an independent judgement and play a positive role;

(d) help the finance director, by providing a forum in which he can raise issues of concern, and which he can use to get things done which might otherwise be difficult;

(e) strengthen the position of the external auditor, by providing a channel of communication and forum for issues of concern;

(f) provide a framework within which the external auditor can assert his independence in the event of a dispute with management;

(g) strengthen the position of the internal audit function, by providing a greater degree of independence from management;

(h) increase public confidence in the credibility and objectivity of financial statements.'

The Cadbury committee warned, however, that the effectiveness of the audit committee may be compromised if it acts as a **'barrier'** between the external auditors and the main (executive) board, or if it allows the main board to **'abdicate its responsibilities** in the audit area' as this will weaken the board's responsibility for reviewing and approving the financial statements. The audit committee must also avoid falling under the influence of a **dominant board member** or getting in the way of exercise of the 'entrepreneurial skills' of the management.

Audit committees are now compulsory for companies trading on the New York Stock Exchange.

In order to be effective, the audit committee has to be well-staffed. The UK's Smith committee recommended that the **audit committee** should consist entirely of **independent non-executive directors** (excluding the chairman), and should include at least one member with **significant and recent financial experience**.

The main duties of the audit committee are likely to be as follows.

6.2.1 Review of financial statements and systems

The committee should review both the **quarterly** (if published) and **annual accounts**. This should involve assessment of the judgements made about the overall appearance and presentation of the accounts. The Cadbury report lists the other main features the review should cover.

- Any changes in accounting policies and practices
- Major judgmental areas such as significant estimates
- Significant adjustments resulting from the audit
- The going concern assumption
- Compliance with accounting standards
- Compliance with stock exchange and legal requirements

As well as reviewing the accounts, the committee's review should cover the financial reporting and budgetary systems. This involves considering **performance indicators** and **information systems** that allow **monitoring** of the **most significant business and financial risks**, and the progress towards financial objectives. The systems should also highlight developments that may require action (for example large variances), and communicate these to the right people.

6.2.2 Liaison with external auditors

The audit committee's tasks here will include:

(a) Being responsible for the **appointment or removal of the external auditors** as well as fixing their remuneration.

(b) Considering whether there are **any other threats to external auditor independence.** In particular the committee should consider **non-audit services** provided by the external auditors, paying particular attention to whether there may be a **conflict of interest.** The strictest legislation in this area is the Sarbanes-Oxley legislation which prohibits audit firms providing a number of services and states that they can only provide other services with the pre-approval of the audit committee.

(c) **Discussing the scope of the external audit** prior to the start of the audit. This should include consideration of whether external audit's coverage of all areas and locations of the business is fair, and how much external audit will rely on the work of internal audit.

(d) Acting as a **forum for liaison** between the external auditors, the internal auditors and the finance director.

(e) **Helping the external auditors to obtain the information** they require and in resolving any problems they may encounter.

(f) **Making themselves available** to the external auditors for consultation, with or without the presence of the company's management.

(g) Dealing with any **serious reservations** which the external auditors may express either about the accounts, the records or the quality of the company's management.

6.2.3 Review of internal audit

The review should cover the following aspects of internal audit.

- **Standards** including **objectivity**, **technical knowledge** and **professional standards**
- **Scope** including how much emphasis is given to different types of review
- **Resources**
- **Reporting arrangements**
- **Work plan**, especially review of controls and coverage of high risk areas
- **Liaison** with external auditors
- **Results**

The head of internal audit should have direct access to the audit committee.

6.2.4 Review of internal control

The audit committee should play a significant role in reviewing internal control.

(a) Committee members can use their own experience to **monitor** continually the **adequacy** of **internal control systems**, focusing particularly on the control environment, management's attitude towards controls and overall management controls.

(b) The audit committee's review should cover **legal compliance** and **ethics**, for example listing rules or environmental legislation. Committee members should check that there are systems in place to promote compliance. They should review reports on the operation of **codes of conduct** and review violations.

(c) The committee should also address the risk of **fraud**, ensuring employees are aware of risks and that there are mechanisms in place for staff to report fraud, and fraud to be investigated.

(d) Each year the committee should be responsible for **reviewing the company's statement on internal controls** prior to its approval by the board.

(e) The committee should consider the **recommendations of the auditors** in the management letter and management's response. Because the committee's role is ongoing, it can also ensure that recommendations are publicised and see that actions are taken as appropriate.

(f) The committee may play a **more active supervisory role**, for example reviewing major transactions for reasonableness.

6.2.5 Review of risk management

The audit committee can play an important part in the review of risk recommended by the Turnbull report This includes confirming that there is a **formal policy** in place for **risk management** and that the policy is backed and regularly monitored by the board. They should also **review** the **arrangements**, including training, for ensuring that managers and staff are aware of their responsibilities. They should use their own knowledge of the business to confirm that risk management is updated to **reflect current positions and strategy.**

6.2.6 Investigations

The committee will also be involved in implementing and reviewing the results of **one-off investigations**. The Cadbury report recommends that audit committees should be given specific authority to investigate matters of concern, and in doing so have access to sufficient resources, appropriate information and outside professional help.

7 Relationships with shareholders and stakeholders

FAST FORWARD

Auditors should maintain a **regular dialogue with shareholders**, particularly **institutional shareholders**. **The annual general meeting** is the most significant forum for communication.

How much organisations consider the interests of other stakeholders will depend on their **legal responsibilities** and their **view of stakeholders as partners**.

7.1 Relationships with shareholders

A key aspect of the relationship is the accountability of directors to shareholders. This can ultimately be ensured by requiring all directors to submit themselves for **regular re-election** (the corporate governance reports suggest once every three years is reasonable).

The need for regular communication with shareholders is emphasised in most reports. Particularly important is communication with **institutional shareholders** such as pension funds who may hold a significant proportion of shares. A number of the reports stress how institutional shareholders can be an important force for good corporate governance, and that they have a responsibility to use their votes wisely.

The annual general meeting is the most important formal means of communication, and the governance guidance suggests that boards should **actively encourage** shareholders to attend annual general meetings. The UK's Hampel report contained some useful recommendations on how the annual general meeting could be used to **enhance communications** with shareholders.

(a) Notice of the AGM and related papers should be **sent** to shareholders **at least 20 working days** before the meeting.

(b) Companies should consider providing a **business presentation** at the **AGM**, with a question and answer session. The chairmen of the key sub-committees (audit, remuneration) should be available to answer questions

(c) Shareholders should be able to **vote separately** on each substantially separate issue; the practice of 'bundling' unrelated proposals in a single resolution should cease.

(d) Companies should propose a resolution at the AGM relating to the **report and accounts**.

The most important document for communication with shareholders is the annual report and accounts, covered in Section 8 below.

7.2 Relationships with stakeholders

How much the board are responsible for the interests of stakeholders other than shareholders is a matter of debate. The Hampel committee claimed that although relationships with other stakeholders were important, making the directors responsible to other stakeholders would mean there was no clear yardstick for judging directors' performance.

However the OECD guidelines see a rather wider importance for stakeholders in corporate governance, concentrating on employees, creditors and the government. Creditors supply external capital to the firm and employees human capital. The guidelines comment;

> 'The competitiveness and ultimate success of a corporation is the result of teamwork that embodies contributions from a range of different resource providers, including investors, employees, creditors and suppliers.'

The OECD guidelines stress that the corporate governance framework should therefore ensure that respect is given to the **rights of stakeholders** that are protected by law. These rights include rights under labour law, business law, contract law and insolvency law.

The corporate governance framework should also permit **'performance-enhancing mechanisms** for stakeholder participation'. Examples of this are employee representation on the board of directors, employee share ownership, profit-sharing arrangements and the right of creditors to be involved in any insolvency proceedings.

The King report in South Africa also pointed out the responsibility of companies towards stakeholders, although it drew a clear distinction between **responsibility** and **accountability**, stating that if companies were accountable to everyone, they would end up being accountable to no-one.

8 Reporting on corporate governance

FAST FORWARD

Annual reports must **convey** a **fair and balanced view** of the organisation. They should state whether the organisation has complied with governance regulations and codes, and give specific disclosures about the board, internal control reviews, going concern status and relations with stakeholders.

8.1 Reporting requirements

The London Stock Exchange requires the following general disclosures:

(a) A **narrative statement** of how companies have **applied the principles** set out in the Combined Code, providing explanations which enable their shareholders to assess how the principles have been applied

(b) A **statement** as to whether or not they **complied** throughout the accounting period with the **provisions** set out in the Combined Code. Listed companies that did not comply throughout the accounting period with all the provisions must specify the provisions with which they did not comply, and give reasons for non-compliance

The corporate governance reports also suggest is that the directors should **explain** their **responsibility for preparing accounts**. They should **report that the business is a going concern**, with supporting assumptions and qualifications as necessary.

In addition further statements may be required depending on the jurisdiction such as:

(a) Information about the **board of directors**: changes in the composition of the board in the year, the identity of the chairman, chief executive and senior non-executive director and information about the independence of the non-executives, frequency of and attendance at board meetings, how the board's performance has been evaluated. The King report suggests a charter of responsibilities should be disclosed.

(b) Brief report on the **remuneration, audit and nomination committees** covering terms of reference, composition and frequency of meetings

(c) Information about **relations with auditors** including reasons for change and steps taken to ensure auditor objectivity and independence when non-audit services have been provided

(d) A statement that the directors have reviewed the **effectiveness** of **internal controls**, including risk management

(e) A statement on relations and **dialogue with shareholders**

(f) A statement that the company is a **going concern**

(g) **Sustainability reporting,** defined by the King report as including the nature and extent of social, transformation, ethical, safety, health and environmental management policies and practices.

(h) An **operating and financial review.** The UK's Accounting Standards Board summarised the purpose of such a review;

'The Operating and Financial Review (OFR) should set out the directors' analysis of the business, in order to provide to investors a historical and prospective analysis of the reporting entity 'through the eyes of management'. It should include discussion and interpretation of the performance of the business and the structure of its financing, in the context of known or reasonably expected changes in the environment in which it operates.'

Furthermore the information organisations provide cannot just be backward-looking. The King report points out investors want a forward-looking approach and to be able to assess companies against a **balanced scorecard.** Companies will need to weigh the need to keep commercially sensitive information sensitive with the expectations that investors will receive full and frank disclosures.

Question

Codes and corporate governance

Learning outcome: B(vii)

Briefly explain what is meant by corporate governance and discuss how the main measures recommended by the corporate governance codes should contribute towards better corporate governance.

Answer

Definition of corporate governance

Corporate governance can be defined broadly as the **system** by which an **organisation** is **directed and controlled.** It is concerned with systems, processes, controls, accountability and decision making at the heart of and at the highest level of an organisation. It is therefore concerned with the way in which top managers **execute their responsibilities** and authority and how they **account** for that authority to those who have entrusted them with assets and resources. In particular it is concerned with the potential abuse of power and the need for openness, integrity and accountability in corporate decision making.

Problem of lack of accountability

A key issue in corporate governance is the problem that major public companies are run by powerful executives, who do not necessarily manage the company in the best interests of its owners, the shareholders. In principle, the **shareholders appoint** a **board of directors** and an **external auditor** and need to satisfy themselves that an appropriate governance structure exists. The board of directors is responsible for running the company on **behalf of shareholders**, considering the interests of other stakeholders such as employees, and reporting to shareholders on the company's progress. The auditor provides an **independent examination** of the company's financial statements. In practice, there is widespread concern that executives run a company more for their **own benefit** than for the benefit of the shareholders, and that the role of external auditors is not a sufficient check.

Recommendations of corporate governance codes

Clearly, a company must have senior executives. The problem is how to ensure as far as possible that the actions and decisions of the executives will be for the benefit of shareholders. Measures that have been recommended by various corporate governance codes include the following.

Directors

(a) A listed company is required by the 'voluntary' Combined Code should appoint **non-executive directors**, most of whom should be **independent.** The non-executives are intended to provide a check or balance against the power of the chairman and chief executive.

(b) The posts of **chairman and chief executive** should not be held by the same person, to prevent excessive executive power being held by one individual.

(c) Non-executive directors should **make up** the **membership** of the remuneration committee of the board, and should determine the remuneration of executive directors. This is partly to prevent the executives deciding their own pay, and rewarding themselves excessively. Another purpose is to try to devise incentive schemes for executives that will motivate them to **achieve results** for the company that will also be in the best interests of the shareholders.

Risk assessment

The requirement in many codes for a risk audit should ensure that the board of directors is **aware** of the **risks** facing the company, and have **systems** in place for managing them. In theory, this should provide some protection against risk for the company's shareholders.

Dialogue with shareholders

The Combined Code encourages **greater dialogue** between a **company** and its **shareholders**. Institutional investor organisations are also encouraging greater participation by shareholders, for example in voting.

Audits

The **audit committee** of the board is seen as having a **major role** to play, in promoting dialogue between the external auditors and the board. Corporate governance should be improved if the views of the **external auditors** are given greater consideration.

Chapter roundup

- Good corporate governance involves **risk management** and **internal control, accountability** to stakeholders and other shareholders and conducting business in an **ethical and effective way.**
- Most corporate governance reports are based around the principles of **integrity**, **accountability**, **independence** and **good management** but there is disagreement on how much these principles need to be supplemented by detailed rules.
- The board should be responsible for taking major **policy** and **strategic** decisions.
- Directors should have a **mix of skills** and their **performance** should be assessed regularly.
- Appointments should be conducted by formal procedures administered by a **nomination committee**.
- **Division of responsibilities** at the head of an organisation is most simply achieved by separating the roles of chairman and chief executive.
- **Independent non-executive directors** have a key role in governance. Their number and status should mean that their views carry significant weight.
- Directors' remuneration should be set by a **remuneration committee** consisting of independent non-executive directors.
- Remuneration should be dependent upon **organisation** and **individual performance**.
- Accounts should disclose **remuneration policy** and (in detail) the **packages of individual directors.**
- Boards should regularly review **risk management** and **internal control**, and carry out a wider review annually, the results of which should be disclosed in the accounts.
- Audit committees of **independent non-executive directors** should liaise with **external audit**, **supervise internal audit**, and **review** the **annual accounts** and **internal controls.**
- Auditors should maintain a **regular dialogue with shareholders**, particularly **institutional shareholders**. **The annual general meeting** is the most significant forum for communication.
- How much organisations consider the interests of other stakeholders will depend on their **legal responsibilities** and their **view of stakeholders as partners**.
- Annual reports must **convey** a **fair and balanced view** of the organisation. They should state whether the organisation has complied with governance regulations and codes, and give specific disclosures about the board, internal control reviews, going concern status and relations with stakeholders.

Quick quiz

1 Define corporate governance.

2 Give four examples of symptoms of poor corporate governance.

3 How did the Cadbury report suggest that board's responsibilities be defined?

4 How can an organisation ensure that there is a division of responsibilities at its highest level?

5 What according to the Greenbury report were the key principles in establishing a remuneration policy?

6 Audit committees are generally staffed by executive directors.

True ☐

False ☐

7 List the main responsibilities of audit committees.

8 An ________ sets out the directors' analysis of the business, in order to provide to investors a historical and prospective analysis of the reporting entity 'through the eyes of management'.

Answers to quick quiz

1 The system by which organizations are directed and controlled.

2
- Domination by a single individual
- Lack of board involvement
- Inadequate control function
- Inadequate supervision
- Lack of independent scrutiny
- Lack of contact with shareholders
- Excessive emphasis on short-term profitability
- Misleading accounts

3 Boards should have a formal schedule of matters reserved for their decisions including decisions such as approval of **mergers and acquisitions**, major **acquisitions and disposals of assets** and **investments, capital projects, bank borrowing** facilities, major **loans** and their repayment, foreign currency transactions above a certain limit.

4
- Splitting the roles of chairman and chief executive
- Appointing a senior independent non-executive director
- Having a strong independent element on the board with a recognized leader

5
- Directors' remuneration should be set by **independent members** of the board
- Any form of bonus should be related to **measurable performance** or enhanced shareholder value
- There should be **full transparency of directors' remuneration** including pension rights in the annual accounts

6 False. They should be staffed by non-executive directors; possibly the chairman can be an executive director.

7
- Review of financial statements and systems
- Liasion with external auditors
- Review of internal audit
- Review of internal control
- Review of risk management
- Investigations

8 An **operating and financial review** sets out the directors' analysis of the business, in order to provide to investors a historical and prospective analysis of the reporting entity 'through the eyes of management'.

Now try the question below from the Exam Question Bank

Number	Level	Marks	Time
Q8	Examination	25	45 mins

APPENDIX: Corporate governance reports

1 Cadbury report

1.1 Board of directors

The report stressed the importance of the board of directors meeting on a **regular basis**, retaining full control over the company and monitoring executive management. Certain matters such as major acquisitions or disposals of assets, should be **referred** automatically to the **board**. The chairman's role in good corporate governance is crucial. There should be a **clear division of responsibilities** at the head of a company, with no one person having complete power. Generally this would mean the posts of chairman and chief executive being held by different people; if they were held by the same person there should be a **strong independent element** on the board.

1.2 Non-executive directors

The report saw non-executive directors as important figures because of the **independent judgement** they brought to bear on important issues. There should be at **least three non-executive** directors on the board, a **majority** of whom should be **independent** of management and free from any other relationship that might compromise independence. They should be formally appointed by a **nomination committee**, which should itself have a majority of non-executive directors.

1.3 Executive directors

The report contained provisions about the length of service contracts and disclosure of remuneration which were developed further in the Greenbury and Hampel reports (see below).

1.4 The audit committee

The audit committee was seen by the Cadbury committee as a key board committee. The audit committee should **liase** with **internal** and **external auditors**, and provide a forum for both to express their concerns. The committee should also **review** half yearly and annual **statements**.

1.5 Accounts

The Cadbury committee stressed the importance of the board presenting a **balanced** and **understandable assessment** of the company's position. The directors should **explain** their **responsibilities** for preparing accounts. Statements should also be made about the company's ability to continue as a **going concern**, and the effectiveness of its **internal controls**.

2 Greenbury report

2.1 The remuneration committee

The most important recommendation was that the board should set up a remuneration committee of non-executive directors to **determine** the company's **general policy** on the **remuneration** of **executive directors** and **specific remuneration packages** for each director. The non-executive directors on the committee should have no personal interests other than as shareholders, no conflicts of interest and no

day-to-day involvement in running the business. The remuneration committee chairman should be available to answer questions at the AGM.

2.2 Disclosures

The report suggested that a report on **remuneration policy** should be included or attached to the annual accounts. The report on remuneration should give details of the company's policy on the remuneration of executive directors including:

- Remuneration levels
- Comparator companies
- Main components of remuneration
- Performance criteria and measurement
- Pension provision
- Contracts of service
- Compensation for loss of office

The remuneration committee should consider whether shareholders should approve this policy at each AGM.

The remuneration report should also contain details of the **remuneration packages** of **individual directors** including basic salary, benefits-in-kind, bonuses and long-term incentives. Details should also be given of individual entitlement to share options, and pensions entitlements earned during the year.

In addition **service contracts** with notice periods **greater than one year** should be **disclosed**, and the **reasons** for longer notice periods explained. **Incentive schemes** should be **performance-related** and shareholders should be invited to approve long-term incentive schemes.

2.3 Remuneration policy

The report emphasised that the remuneration committee should consider the **wider pay scene**, and should provide packages sufficient to attract, retain and motivate directors of sufficient quality. Performance-related elements should reconcile the interests of directors and shareholders.

The remuneration committee should consider the level and form of rewards in the light of performance criteria set. Matters to be carefully considered would include the terms of share option schemes, the phasing of rewards, and the pension consequences of various elements of the remuneration package. Share options should not be issued at a discount.

2.4 Service contracts and compensation

The report generally favoured notice and contract periods of less than one year, though up to two years may be acceptable in certain circumstances. **Periods longer** than **two years** should only be set in **exceptional circumstances**, for example initial contracts necessary to attract directors from outside.

In general remuneration committees should take a tough line over dismissal for unsatisfactory performance, and also mitigation of compensation by directors. Committees should consider phasing of compensation payments over a period, and stopping them when the director starts a new job.

3 The Hampel report

3.1 Directors

The committee stressed that executive and non-executive directors should continue to have the same duties under the law. The committee stated that the roles of **chairman** and **chief executive** should generally be **separate**, but whether or not the roles of chairman and chief executive are combined, a **senior non-executive director** should be **identified. Non-executive directors** should make up **at least one third** of the **board**. The report also stressed the importance of monitoring director performance with all directors submitting themselves for **re-election at least once every three years**, and boards assessing the performance of individual directors and collective board performance.

3.2 Directors' remuneration

In common with the Cadbury and Greenbury reports, the Hampel committee saw the remuneration committee as the key mechanism for setting the pay of executive directors. Remuneration committees should develop policy on remuneration and devise reasonable remuneration packages for individual executive directors. The committee believed that boards should try to reduce directors' contract periods to **one year or less**. The accounts should include a **general statement** on **remuneration policy**, but the committee saw no need for this statement to be the subject of an AGM vote.

3.3 Shareholders and the AGM

The major recommendations of the committee were that shareholders should be able to **vote separately** on each **substantially separate issue**; and that the practice of 'bundling' unrelated proposals in a single resolution should cease. Companies should **propose** a **resolution** at the AGM relating to the **report and accounts**. Notice of the AGM and related papers should be sent to shareholders at least 20 working days before the meeting. Institutional shareholders should adopt a considered policy on voting shares which they control.

3.4 Accountability and audit

The Hampel committee stressed, as the Cadbury committee had, the importance of the **audit committee**. However, whilst the report stated that directors should report on internal control, the committee did not believe that the directors should be required to report on the effectiveness of controls. Auditors should **report privately** on internal controls to directors. Directors should maintain and review controls relating to all relevant control objectives, and not merely financial controls.

4 Stock Exchange Combined Code

4.1 Directors

4.1.1 The board

All listed companies should be led by an **effective board**. The board should meet regularly and have **certain matters** reserved for its decision. Directors should be able to obtain independent professional advice and have access to the services of the company secretary. The company secretary is **responsible for ensuring** that **board procedures** and **relevant regulations** are followed. The whole board should be responsible for removing the company secretary. Every director should use **independent judgement** when making decisions. Every director should receive appropriate **training**.

4.1.2 Chairman and Chief Executive

There are two leading management roles; running the board and running the company. A **clear division of responsibilities** should exist so that there is a balance of power, and no-one person has unfettered powers of decision. Combination of the roles of **chairman** and **chief executive** should be **justified publicly**. There should also be a **strong and independent** body of **non-executive directors** with a recognised senior member other than the chairman.

4.1.3 Board balance

The board should have a **balance** of **executive and non-executive directors** so that no individual or small group is dominant. The non-executive directors should be of sufficient calibre and number to have a significant influence and should comprise at least one third of the board. The majority of non-executive directors should be independent.

4.1.4 Supply of information

The board should be **promptly supplied** with **enough information** to enable it to carry out its duties. Information volunteered by management will sometimes need to be supplemented by information from other sources. All directors should be properly briefed.

4.1.5 Appointment of directors

There should be a **clear, formal procedure** for appointing new directors. A nomination committee should make recommendations about all new board appointments.

4.1.6 Re-election

All directors should submit themselves for **re-election regularly**, and at least once every three years.

4.2 Directors' remuneration

4.2.1 Remuneration policy

Remuneration levels should be sufficient to attract directors of **sufficient calibre** to run the company effectively, but companies should not pay more than is necessary. A proportion of remuneration should be based on **corporate and individual performance.** Comparisons witn other companies should be used with caution. When designing performance-related elements of remuneration, the remuneration committee should consider annual bonuses and different kinds of long-term incentive schemes.

4.2.2 Service contracts and compensation

Boards' ultimate objectives should be to set **notice periods at one year or less**. Directors should consider whether to include compensation commitments in the contracts of service.

4.2.3 Procedure

Companies should establish a formal and clear procedure for **developing policy** on **executive remuneration** and for fixing the remuneration package of individual directors. **Directors should not be involved** in **setting their own remuneration**. A **remuneration committee**, staffed by independent non-executive directors, should make **recommendations** about the framework of executive remuneration, and

should determine specific remuneration packages. The board should determine the remuneration of non-executive directors

4.2.4 Disclosure

The annual report should contain a **statement about remuneration policy** and **details of the remuneration of each director**. The report should give details about **all elements of the remuneration package,** share options, pension entitlements and service contracts or compensation in excess of one year. Shareholders should approve all new long-term remuneration schemes. The remuneration report need not be a standard AGM item, but the board should consider whether the report needs to be approved.

4.3 Relations with shareholders

4.3.1 Institutional shareholders

Companies should be prepared to **communicate** with **institutional shareholders**.

4.3.2 Use of the AGM

The AGM should be a **means of communication** with **private investors.** Companies should count all proxies and announce proxy votes for and against on all votes on a show of hands. Companies should propose a **separate resolution** on each substantially separate issue, and there should be a resolution covering the **board and accounts**. The chairmen of the audit, nomination and remuneration committees should be available to answer questions at the AGM. Papers should be sent to members at least 20 working days before the AGM.

4.4 Accountability and audit

4.4.1 Financial reporting

The board should present a **balanced and understandable assessment** of the **company's position and prospects** in the annual accounts and other reports such as interim reports and reports to regulators. The directors should explain their responsibility for the accounts, and the auditors should state their reporting responsibilities. The directors should also report on the going concern status of the business.

4.4.2 Internal control

A good system of control should be maintained. The directors should **review effectiveness** annually and report to shareholders that they have done so. The review should cover all controls including financial, operational and compliance controls and risk management. Companies who **lack** an **internal audit function** should regularly consider whether they need one.

4.4.3 Audit committees and auditors

There should be **formal and clear arrangements** with the **company's auditors**, and for applying the financial reporting and internal control principles. Companies should have an **audit committee** consisting of non-executive directors, the majority of whom should be independent. The audit committee should review the audit, and the independence and objectivity of the auditors. In particular the committee should keep matters under review if the auditors supply significant non-audit services.

4.5 Shareholder voting

Institutional shareholders should use their votes carefully and **disclose** how they have **voted** to their clients. They should also enter into a dialogue with companies, and should give appropriate weight to all relevant criteria when considering corporate governance arrangements.

4.6 Compliance with the Code

The Combined Code requires listed companies to include in their accounts:

(a) A narrative statement of how they **applied** the **principles** set out in the Combined Code. This should provide explanations which enable their shareholders to assess how the principles have been applied.

(b) A statement as to whether or not they **complied throughout** the **accounting period** with the provisions set out in the Combined Code. Listed companies that did not comply throughout the accounting period with all the provisions must specify the provisions with which they did not comply, and give **reasons** for **non-compliance**.

5 Sarbanes-Oxley Act 2002

5.1 Public Oversight Board

A **Public Oversight Board** will be established to register and regulate accounting firms

5.2 Auditing standards

Audit firms should **retain working papers** for several years, have **quality control standards** in place, and as part of the audit review internal control systems to ensure that they **reflect the transactions** of the client and provide **reasonable assurance** that the transactions are recorded in a manner that will **permit preparation** of the **financial statements.**

5.3 Non-audit services

Auditors are expressly prohibited from carrying out a number of services including bookkeeping, systems design and implementation, appraisal or valuation services, actuarial services, management functions and human resources, investment management, legal and expert services. **Provision of other non-audit services** is only allowed with the **prior approval** of the **audit committee**.

5.4 Partner rotation

There should be **rotation** of lead or reviewing audit partners every five years.

5.5 Auditors and audit committee

Auditors should discuss **critical accounting policies** and **possible alternative treatments** with the audit committee.

5.6 Audit committees

All members of audit committees should be **independent.** At least one member should be a financial expert. Audit committees should be responsible for the **appointment, compensation** and **oversight** of auditors. Audit committees should establish mechanisms for dealing with complaints about accounting, internal controls and audit.

5.7 Corporate responsibility

The **chief executive officer** and **chief finance officer** should certify the **appropriateness** of the **financial statements** and that those **financial statements fairly present** the **operations and financial condition** of the issuer. If the company has to prepare a restatement of accounts due to material non-compliance with standards, the **chief finance officer** and **chief executive officer** should **forfeit their bonuses.**

5.8 Off balance sheet transactions

There should be **appropriate disclosure** of **material off-balance sheet transactions** and other relationships.

5.9 Internal control reporting

Annual reports should contain **internal control reports** that state the responsibility of management for establishing and maintaining an **adequate internal control structure** and **procedures for financial reporting.** Annual reports should also contain an **assessesment** of the **effectiveness** of the **internal control structure** and **procedures** for **financial reporting**. Auditors should report on this assessment.

Companies should also report whether they have adopted a **code of conduct** for senior financial officers and the content of that code.

5.10 Whistleblowing provisions

Employees of **listed companies** and **auditors** will be granted whistleblower protection against their employers if they **disclose private employer information** to parties involved in a fraud claim.

6 The King report

6.1 The seven characteristics of good corporate governance

(a) **Discipline**, adherence to correct and proper behaviour including the underlying principles of good corporate governance

(b) **Transparency**, ease with which analysis can be made of actions, economic fundamentals, and non-financial matters. This reflects how good management is at making necessary information available

(c) **Independence**, reflecting mechanisms to minimise or avoid conflicts of interest such as composition of board, appointments to board committees and relations with auditors

(d) **Accountability,** mechanisms allowing investors to query and assess actions of board

(e) **Responsibility,** including responsibility to stakeholders. Governance should permit corrective action and penalising of mismanagement

(f) **Fairness,** balanced systems that take into account everyone having an interest in the company

(g) **Social responsibility**, in particular ethical standards, but also laying stress on being non-discriminatory and non-exploitative

6.2 Boards and directors

6.2.1 The board

A **unitary board** ensures positive interaction and diversity of views. The board must give **strategic direction**, retain **full and effective control** over the company, **monitor management, ensure** that the company **complies** with all relevant laws, regulations and codes of practice and **communicate** with shareholders and relevant stakeholders openly and promptly. The board should consider whether its **size**, **diversity** and **demographics** make it effective.

The board should consider developing a **code of conduct** that addresses conflicts of interest of directors and management.

The board should **identify key risk areas** and **key performance indicators** and **identify and monitor non-financial aspects.**

6.2.2 Board composition

The board should comprise a mix of executive and non-executive directors, particularly **independent non-executives** to protect shareholder interests. **Formal appointment procedures** including a nomination committee should be in place. **Board continuity** should be ensured by a programme of rotation of directors.

6.2.3 Chairperson and chief executive

There should be a clear **division of responsibilities**, with preferably **separation of the roles of chairperson and chief executive** and the **chairperson** being an **independent non-executive director.** The chairperson's performance should be **appraised** regularly, the chief executive's at least annually.

6.2.4 Directors

No-one individual or **block of individuals** should dominate the board's decision-taking.

Non-executive directors should have **calibre** and **credibility** and have the necessary skill and experience to assess all strategic, operational and conduct issues. They should carefully consider the **number of appointments** that they accept.

6.2.5 Remuneration

Remuneration should be sufficient to **attract, retain** and **motivate** executives of the required quality. A **remuneration policy** should be established and a remuneration committee should make **recommendations**; the **chief executive** can be **consulted** but should not fix his own remuneration. Full disclosure should be made in the accounts. **Performance-related elements** should constitute a substantial part of **executives' total remuneration packages.** Executive directors' **fixed term service contracts** should **not exceed three years.**

Fees to non-executive directors should reflect their relative contributions and should be submitted to shareholders for approval before payment.

6.2.6 Board meetings

Boards should meet at **least once a quarter. Non-executive directors** should have **access to management**. Boards should regularly review **processes** and **procedures** to ensure the **effectiveness** of the company's **system of internal controls**. The board should receive **relevant non-financial information**, going beyond assessing the financial and quantitive performance of the company, looking at **qualitative measures** that involve **broader stakeholder interests**.

6.2.7 Board committees

Boards should not shelter behind board committees, but there should be a **formal procedure** for **certain functions** of the board to be **delegated.** At a minimum boards should have **audit** and **remuneration committees.** All board committees should preferably be chaired by an independent non-executive director.

6.2.8 Company secretary

The company secretary has a pivotal role in corporate governance, in providing detailed guidance on responsibilities, inducting new directors and assisting the chairperson in determining the board plan and the administration of other issues.

6.3 Risk management

The board is responsible for the total process of **risk management** and for forming its opinion on the **effectiveness** of the process. Management is responsible for integrating the **risk management process** into the day-to-day activities of the company. **Risk strategy policies** should be **communicated** to **all employees.**

The board should make use of **generally accepted models** to assess whether **organisational objectives** are being **achieved.** The board should **at a minimum** assess the following risks:

- Physical and operational
- Human resource
- Technology
- Business continuity and disaster recovery
- Credit and markets
- Compliance

A board committee should aid the board in risk assessment. Boards should consider the need for a **whistle-blowing** process.

A comprehensive system of control should be established to **ensure risks are mitigated and objectives obtained. Risks** should be assessed on an on-going basis and control activities respond to risks, with relevant information about risks being **identified**, **captured** and **communicated**. Management should report on significant risks, system effectiveness and weaknesses found.

Boards should acknowledge their accountability for risk management and state that there is an **ongoing process** for **identifying, evaluating and managing risks** and there is an **adequate system of internal control** in place to mitigate risks.

6.4 Internal audit

Companies should have an **effective internal audit function,** with **access** to the **chief executive**, **chairman** and **audit committee.** There should be **adequate segregation of duties** if internal and external audit are carried out by the same firm.

Internal audit should **seek assurance** that **management processes** are **adequate** to **identify and monitor significant risks**, **confirm the effective operation** of **control systems**, **review processes** for **feedback** on **risk management** and **assurance,** and **confirm** that the board **receives** the **right quality of information** from the board. The internal audit plan should be founded on **risk assessment** and **linked** with the **board's assessment** of risk.

6.5 Sustainability reporting

Companies should report at least annually on the nature and extent of its **social, transformation, ethical, safety, health** and **environmental management policies** and practices. These include concerns such as workplace accidents, impact of HIV/AIDS, environmental concerns, black economic empowerment, human capital development and equal opportunities policies.

Each company should introduce a **code of ethics** and **disclose adherence** to it. There should be systems and procedures in place to reinforce it and high level individuals should oversee compliance.

6.6 Accounting and auditing

The audit committee should recommend the **appointment of external auditors** and should **encourage consultation** between external and internal auditors. The audit committee should set out principles for whether non-audit services should also be supplied by auditors.

The audit committee should consider whether the **interim report** should be reviewed by the external auditor.

The majority of members of the audit committee should be independent non-executive directors and should be **financially literate**. It should be chaired by an independent non-executive director who is not the chairperson of the board. The committee should have formal terms of reference.

6.7 Relations with shareowners

Companies should maintain a **dialogue** with **institutional shareholders.** They should explain each item of special business and consider using **polls** to approve special business.

6.8 Accounts

Boards should present a **balanced and understandable assessment** of the company's position and a **comprehensive and objective assessment** of the activities of the company. Reports must be made in the context of society demanding **greater transparency and accountability** from companies regarding their non-financial matters.

Part C

Review and audit of control systems

9

Internal audit

Introduction

Part C of this text covers the work of internal audit. In this chapter we introduce briefly the work of internal audit and give more details about what it does in later chapters.

This chapter also discusses various other issues connected with internal audit, including how the department is organised, the standards internal audit should follow, and whether it should be outsourced.

Topic list	Learning outcomes	Syllabus references	Ability required
1 The role of internal audit	C(ii)	C(1), (4)	Evaluation
2 Internal and external audit	C(ii)	C(4)	Evaluation
3 The structure of internal audit	C(ii)	C(4)	Evaluation
4 Standards for internal audit	C(ii)	C(4)	Evaluation
5 Assessing the performance of internal audit	C(ii)	C(4)	Evaluation
6 Outsourcing the internal audit function	C(ii)	C(4)	Evaluation

1 The role of internal audit

FAST FORWARD

The role of internal audit will **vary** according to the **organisation's objectives** but is likely to include **review of internal control systems, risk management, legal compliance** and **value for money.**

Key term

Internal audit is an independent appraisal activity established within an organisation as a service to it. It is a control which functions by examining and evaluating the adequacy and effectiveness of other controls. (CIMA)

Internal audit is an appraisal or monitoring activity established by management and directors for the review of the accounting and internal control systems as a service to the entity. It functions by, amongst other things, examining, evaluating and reporting to management and the directors on the adequacy and effectiveness of components of the accounting and internal control systems. (APB)

1.1 The need for internal audit

The Turnbull report in the UK stated that listed companies without an internal audit function should **annually review** the need to have one, and listed companies with an internal audit function should review annually its **scope, authority** and **resources**.

Turnbull states that the need for internal audit will depend on:

- The **scale, diversity** and **complexity** of the company's activities
- The **number of employees**
- **Cost-benefit considerations**

However in a climate where the need for risk management is stressed more, the need for internal audit will be greater. The following factors might indicate the need for an internal audit function

- **Changes** in the organisational structures, reporting processes or underlying information systems
- **Changes** in **key risks** arising from **changes in internal processes** or entry into **new markets**
- **Changes** in **key risks** arising from **changes in external factors** such as regulatory requirements
- **Problems** with **internal control systems**
- An **increased number** of **unexplained** or **unacceptable** events

Although there may be alternative means of carrying out the routine work of internal audit, those carrying out the work may be involved in operations and hence lack **objectivity**.

1.2 Objectives of internal audit

The Institute of Internal Auditors states that:

> 'The objective of internal auditing is to **assist members** of the organisation in the effective discharge of their responsibilities. To this end internal auditing furnishes them with analyses, appraisals, recommendations, counsel and information concerning the activities reviewed.'

The role of the internal auditor has expanded in recent years as internal auditors seek to monitor all aspects (not just accounting) of the business, and add value to their organisation. The work of the internal auditor is still prescribed by management, but it may cover the following broad areas.

(a) **Review of the accounting and internal control systems**. The establishment of adequate accounting and internal control systems is a responsibility of management and the directors which demands proper attention on a continuous basis. Often, internal audit is assigned specific responsibility for the following tasks.

- Reviewing the design of the systems
- Monitoring the operation of the systems by risk assessment and detailed testing
- Recommending cost effective improvements

Review will cover both financial and non-financial controls.

(b) **Examination of financial and operating information**. This may include review of the means used to identify, measure, classify and report such information and specific enquiry into individual items including detailed testing of transactions, balances and procedures.

(c) **Review of the economy, efficiency and effectiveness** of operations.

(d) **Review of compliance** with laws, regulations and other external requirements and with internal policies and directives and other requirements including appropriate authorisation of transactions.

(e) Review of the **safeguarding of assets**.

(f) **Review of the implementation of corporate objectives**. This includes review of the effectiveness of planning the relevance of standards and policies, and the operation of specific procedures such as communication of information.

(g) Identification of **significant business** and financial **risks, monitoring** the **organisation's overall risk management policy** to ensure it operates effectively, and **monitoring** the **risk management strategies** to ensure they continue to operate effectively.

(h) **Special investigations** into particular areas, for example suspected fraud.

Exam focus point

Exam questions may well cover the objectives of internal audit, and ask how internal audit can improve efficiency and profitability as well as checking the operation of internal controls.

The relative importance of these objectives will vary according to the organisation. In some organisations, internal audit will mainly be concerned with financial controls. In others its remit may be a lot wider. For example, it might review the operation of quality assurance programmes, assess how well the organisation is handling complaints and consider compliance with laws and regulations or the corporate governance codes.

1.3 CIMA guide

CIMA has recently published a guide on internal audit, *Internal audit – a guide to good practice for internal auditors and their customers.* The guide stresses the importance of the internal audit function being properly resourced and supported by the highest levels of the organisation's management.

The guide states that the following conditions are needed for internal audit to function well:

(a) the **aims** of internal audit are **agreed** by the board;

(b) internal audit **covers all areas** of controls, and not just accounting controls;

(c) internal audit has whatever **access is necessary** to people and documents;

(d) the head of internal audit has clear access to the chairman and chief executive of the organisation, as well as to the chairman of the audit committee;

(e) the head of internal audit **reports** to a **senior director**;

(f) the internal audit department is **independent** of executive management;

(g) internal audit fulfils the requirements of **auditing standards** and **best practice;**

(h) internal audit is **consulted** if there are likely to be **significant changes** in the business or control systems;

(i) internal auditors do **not** have **operational involvement** in areas outside internal audit;

(j) the results of internal audit's work are **clearly communicated**, and its recommendations acted upon by senior management;

(k) internal audit's performance is **regularly assessed**.

1.4 Terms of reference

In its report, *A Framework for Internal Control*, the CIMA lays out the suggested terms of reference for an internal audit department. These should be laid out formally in writing and approved by the board and the audit committee.

'SUGGESTED TERMS OF REFERENCE FOR INTERNAL AUDIT

Function

1 Internal Audit is an independent review function established by management to review the internal control system as a service to the organisation.

Independence

2 Internal Audit is independent of the activities which it reviews to ensure it provides the unbiased judgements essential to its proper conduct and impartial advice to management.

Scope

3 Internal Audit has unrestricted access to all activities undertaken by the organisation in order to review, appraise and report on:

(a) the adequacy and effectiveness of the systems of financial and managerial control and their operation in practice;

(b) the extent of compliance with, relevance of, and financial effect of, established policies, plans and procedures;

(c) the extent to which the assets and interests are accounted for and safeguarded from losses of all kinds arising from waste, extravagance, inefficient administration, poor value for money, fraud or other cause;

(d) the suitability, reliability and integrity of financial and other management information and the means used to identify, measure, classify and report such information;

(e) the integrity of computer systems, including systems under development, to ensure that controls over computer processing and associated clerical procedures offer adequate protection against error, fraud and loss of all kinds;

(f) the suitability of the organisation of the units internally audited for carrying out their functions;

(g) the follow up actions taken to remedy weaknesses identified by Internal Audit review.'

2 Internal and external audit

FAST FORWARD

Internal auditors are **employees** of the organisation whose work is designed to **add value** and who report to the **audit committee. External auditors** are from **accountancy firms** and their role is to **report on the financial statements to shareholders**.

Both **internal and external auditors** review controls, and **external auditors** may **place reliance** on **internal auditors' work** providing they assess its worth.

Key term

External audit is a periodic examination of the books of account and records of an entity carried out by an independent third party (the auditor), to ensure that they have been properly maintained, are accurate and comply with established concepts, principles, accounting standards, legal requirements and give a true and fair view of the financial state of the entity. (CIMA *Official Terminology*)

2.1 Differences between internal and external audit

The following table highlights the differences between internal and external audit.

	Internal audit	External audit
Reason	Internal audit is an activity designed to **add value** and improve an **organisation's operations**.	External audit is an exercise to enable auditors to **express an opinion on the financial statements**.
Reporting to	Internal audit reports to the **board of directors**, or others charged with governance, such as the audit committee.	The external auditors report to the **shareholders**, or members, of a company on the stewardship of the directors.
Relating to	Internal audit's work relates to the **operations of the organisation**.	External audit's work relates to the **financial statements**. They are concerned with the financial records that underlie these.
Relationship with the Company	Internal auditors are very often **employees of the organisation**, although sometimes the internal audit function is outsourced.	External auditors are **independent of the company and its management**. They are appointed by the shareholders.

The table shows that although some of the procedures that internal audit undertake are very similar to those undertaken by the external auditors, the whole **basis** and **reasoning** of their work is fundamentally **different**.

The **difference** in **objectives** is particularly important. Every definition of internal audit suggests that it has a much wider scope than external audit, which has the objective of considering whether the accounts give a true and fair view of the organisation's financial position.

2.2 Relationship between external and internal audit

Co-ordination between the external and internal auditors of an organisation will minimise duplication of work and encourage a wide coverage of audit issues and areas. Co-ordination should have the following features.

- Periodic meetings to plan the overall audit to ensure adequate coverage
- Periodic meetings to discuss matters of mutual interest
- Mutual access to audit programs and working papers
- Exchange of audit reports and management letters
- Common development of audit techniques, methods and terminology

2.3 Assessment by external auditors

Where the external auditors wish to rely on the work of the internal auditors, then the external auditors must assess the internal audit function, as with any part of the system of internal control. The following important criteria will be considered by the external auditors.

(a) **Organisational status**

Internal audit's specific status in the organisation and the effect this has on its ability to be objective. Ideally, the internal audit function should have a direct line of communication to the entity's main board or audit committee, and be free of any other operating responsibility. External auditors should consider any constraints or restrictions placed on internal audit.

(b) **Scope of function**

The nature and extent of the assignments which internal audit performs. External auditors should also consider whether management and the directors act on internal audit recommendations and how this is evidenced.

(c) **Technical competence**

Whether internal audit work is performed by persons having adequate technical training and proficiency as internal auditors. External auditors may, for example, review the policies for hiring and training the internal audit staff and their experience and professional qualifications, also how work is assigned, delegated and reviewed.

(d) **Due professional care**

Whether internal audit work is properly planned, supervised, reviewed and documented. The existence of adequate audit manuals, work programmes and working papers may be considered, also consultation procedures.

However, although the reliability of records and adequacy of the reporting and accounting systems are interests shared by both types of auditor:

(a) Internal audit must **not** be seen **merely** as a **service** to the external audit and internal audit work should not be so distorted in order to fit with external audit needs that its own function is lost

(b) Internal audit is **not always** a **cheaper** way of carrying out an external audit function because:

   (i) The internal role extends into many other areas

   (ii) The special position of the external auditors make them more effective and appropriate sometimes.

Question

External and internal audit

Learning outcome: C(ii)

The growing recognition by management of the benefits of good internal control, and the complexities of an adequate system of internal control have led to the development of internal auditing as a form of control over all other internal controls. The emergence of internal auditors as specialists in internal control is the result of an evolutionary process similar in many ways to the evolution of independent auditing.

Required

Explain why the internal and independent auditors' review of internal control procedures differ in purpose.

Answer

The internal auditors **review and test the system of internal control** and report to management in order to **improve the information** received by managers and to help in their task of running the company. The internal auditors will recommend changes to the system to make sure that management receive objective information that is efficiently produced. The internal auditors will also have a duty to search for and discover fraud.

The external auditors **review the system of internal control** in order to **determine the extent of the substantive work** required on the year-end accounts. The external **auditors report** to the **shareholders** rather than the managers or directors. It is usual, however, for the external auditors to issue a letter of weakness to the managers, laying out any areas of weakness and recommendations for improvement in the system of internal control. The external auditors report on the **truth and fairness** of the financial statements, not directly on the system of internal control. The auditors do not have a specific duty to detect fraud, although they should plan the audit procedures so as to detect any material misstatement in the accounts on which they give an opinion.

3 The structure of internal audit

3.1 Organisation of internal audit

FAST FORWARD

Internal audit may be organised by **speciality** or may be a single **fully integrated department**.

The distinction between **regular reviews** and **one-off consultancy projects** may also be significant for the internal audit department.

We have discussed above that internal audit can be much broader in scope than investigation of financial systems and records, and so there are several different types of internal audit.

Traditionally, internal audit departments have been organised around these three functional groups.

- Financial audit
- Information system audit
- Operational audit

Chief auditor

Financial audit manager | IS audit manager | Operational audit manager

Financial auditors | Information system auditors | Operational auditors

Some organisations have moved towards an **integrated approach**. The senior auditor may be from any of the specialities, depending on the skills most appropriate for the particular audit.

The integrated approach takes the form of either:

- Integrated audit team organisation
- Fully integrated organisation

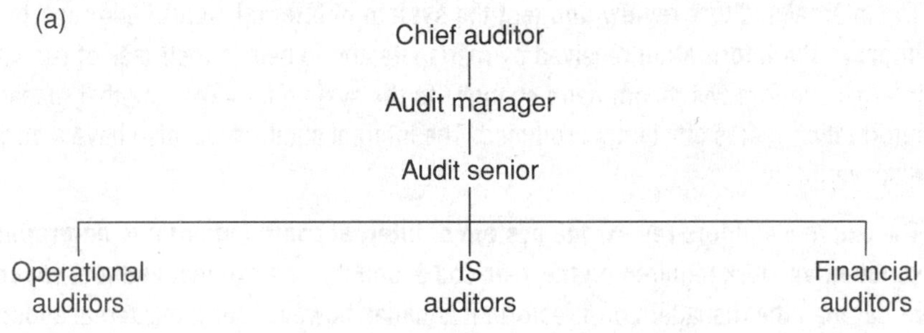

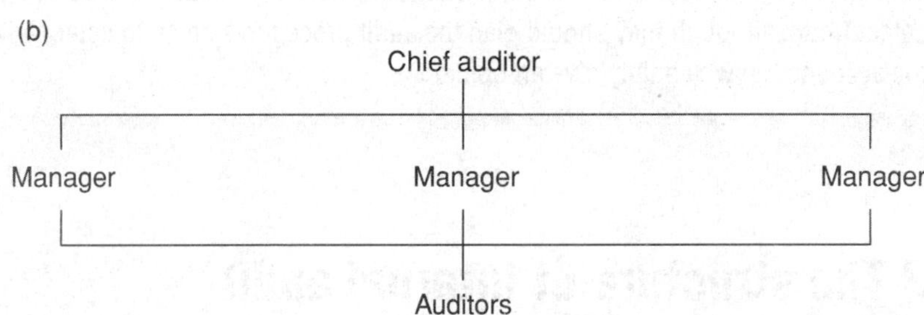

3.2 Advantages and disadvantages of a non-integrated internal audit department

3.2.1 Advantages

(a) The **management** of specific audits is performed by the manager **directly responsible** for the staff involved.

(b) **Independent scheduling** and staffing means that no co-ordination of separate efforts is required.

(c) The **chief auditor** is the focal point for exchanging information between groups.

3.2.2 Disadvantages

(a) A single business unit will receive **multiple audit reports**.

(b) There may be **overlapping** work and redundant effort during separate audits of the same unit.

(c) **Key issues** may be **overlooked** or not addressed if each team assumes an area is covered by the scope of another team.

(d) **Compensating controls** may **not** be **identified** if they reside in another department.

3.3 Advantages and disadvantages of an integrated internal audit department

3.3.1 Advantages

(a) **Audit planning** is **co-ordinated** between all audit groups and results in one audit programme with no redundancy or omission.

(b) **Cross-training** of staff occurs naturally as a result of working together.

(c) All audit procedures for an area take place at the **same time**, resulting in time efficiencies for both auditors and 'client'.

(d) **One audit report** on internal control is produced.

3.3.2 Disadvantages

(a) The **manager** of a specific audit may **not** be **fully qualified** to review and guide the work of more specialist staff.

(b) **Specialists** may **still** be **required** for certain technical audits.

3.4 Review and consultancy

Consultancy projects (one-off projects designed to address ad-hoc issues) are playing an **increasing role** in the work of **internal audit**. Taking on these projects enables internal auditors to extend their skills, and the organisation to draw on the knowledge of external auditors. However there are dangers in becoming too involved in consultancy projects.

(a) Internal audit staff may be diverted to consultancy projects, and the regular audit reviews may be **inadequately resourced**.

(b) By taking on consultancy projects, and suggesting **solutions** internal audit could be getting too involved in **operational concerns**. There is a serious potential lack of independence if internal audit has to review solutions that **internal audit** staff have provided.

(c) Management is relying on internal audit to **solve problems** instead of having operational staff and managers solve or preferably prevent them.

Certain steps therefore need to be taken in order to avoid these problems:

(a) The **terms of reference** of the internal audit department should draw a clear distinction between **regular audit services** and **consultancy work**.

(b) **Enough resources** for **regular work** should be **guaranteed**; consultancy work should be separately resourced and additional resources obtained if necessary.

(c) If managers are concerned about **improving controls**, reviewing these improvements can legitimately be included in the work of internal audit.

(d) **Regular audit reviews** and **consultancy projects** can be undertaken by different staff.

(e) If consultancy work **identifies serious control weaknesses**, these must be incorporated into **internal audit reviews** as **high risk areas**.

4 Standards for internal audit

FAST FORWARD

Internal audit standards cover **professional proficiency**, **scope of work**, **performance**, **management**, and most importantly **independence**.

4.1 IIA Standards

Whatever the scope of internal audit all staff should be aware of the standards to which they are working.

The Institute of Internal Auditors has produced a series of standards covering all areas of internal auditing. The standards comprise five general standards supported by more specific standards with accompanying guidance.

4.2 Professional proficiency

Internal audits should be performed with **proficiency** and **due professional care**. There are specific standards on the following areas.

- Appropriate staffing
- Knowledge, skills and disciplines
- Supervision
- Compliance with professional standards
- Human relations and communications
- Continuing education
- Due professional care

4.3 Scope of work

The scope of internal audit's work should include **assessment** of the **adequacy** and **effectiveness** of the internal control system and quality of performance. The assessment should include consideration of whether the organisation has met the following objectives.

- Reliability and integrity of information
- Compliance with policies, plans, procedures, laws and regulations
- Safeguarding of assets
- Economical and efficient use of resources
- Accomplishment of established objectives and goals for operations and programmes

4.4 Performance of audit work

Performance should include the following stages.

- Planning the audit
- Examining and evaluating information
- Communicating results
- Follow up of work

4.5 Management of internal audit

The chief internal auditor should manage the internal audit department properly. If the department is running well, it should have the following features.

- A statement of purpose, authority and responsibility
- Thorough planning
- Written policies and procedures
- A programme for personnel management and development
- Co-ordination with external auditors
- A quality assurance system

4.6 Independence

Internal auditors should be independent of the activities audited. This involves having **sufficient status** within the organisation and **objectivity**.

Although an internal audit department is part of an organisation, it should be **independent** of the **line management** whose sphere of authority it may audit. The department should therefore report to the board or to a special internal audit committee and not to the finance director.

The reason for this is best seen by thinking about what could happen if the internal audit department reported some kind of irregularity to a finance director without realising that the finance director was actually involved. The director would take the report and decide that it was all very interesting, but not worth pursuing. A very different line might be taken by another, independent director!

Internal auditors should also have **appropriate scope** in carrying out their responsibilities, and unrestricted access to records, assets and personnel.

Internal audit is concerned with the **appraisal** of work done by other people in the organisation, and internal auditors should not carry out any of that work themselves. Independence can be achieved by the following.

- Management should ensure staff recruited to internal audit internally **do not conduct audits** in departments in which they have worked.
- Where internal audit staff have also been involved in **designing** or **implementing new systems**, they should not **conduct post-implementation audits**.
- **Rotation of staff** over specific departmental audits should be implemented.

4.7 Authority of internal audit

To perform work effectively the internal auditors need **authority**; this may be of four types (Peabody).

- **Legitimacy**: the authority to demand sight of documents, and the resources to execute this authority
- **Position**: senior auditors should be used to dealing with sensitive issues
- **Competence**: for example computer auditing skills
- **Charismatic**: good communication and inter-personal skills

Question

Reporting to board

Learning outcome: C(ii)

Explain the reasons why internal auditors should or should not report their findings on internal control to the board of directors.

Answer

A high level of independence is achieved by the internal auditors if they report directly to the Board. However, there may be problems with this approach.

(1) The members of the Board may **not understand all the implications** of the internal audit reports when accounting or technical information is required.

(2) The Board may **not have enough time** to spend considering the reports in sufficient depth. Important recommendations might therefore remain unimplemented.

A way around these problems might be to delegate the review of internal audit reports to an **audit committee**, which would act as a kind of sub-committee to the main board. The audit committee should be made up largely of non-executive directors who have more time and more independence from the day-to-day running of the company, and who possess the necessary financial knowledge.

5 Assessing the performance of internal audit

FAST FORWARD

Formal **quality control procedures** should be used to assess the work of **internal audit** and this assessment should include the **value for money** the internal audit service provides.

5.1 Assessment criteria

The performance of internal audit can be judged by various criteria. The standards set by the Institute of Internal Auditors discussed in Section 6, can obviously be used.

The chief internal auditor will also need to be mindful of how external audit may use the work of internal audit.

5.2 Quality control and internal auditing

Whatever the criteria used to judge effectiveness, quality control procedures will be required to monitor the professional standards of internal audit. Internal audit departments should establish and monitor quality control policies and procedures designed to ensure that **all audits** are **conducted** in **accordance** with **internal standards** and should communicate those policies and procedures to their personnel in a manner designed to provide reasonable assurance that the policies and procedures are understood and implemented.

Quality control policies will vary depending on factors such as the following.

- The size and nature of the department
- Geographic dispersion
- Organisation
- Cost-benefit considerations

Policies and procedures and related documentation will therefore vary from company to company.

The Institute of Internal Auditors has suggested that a formal system of quality assurance should be implemented in the internal audit department. This should cover the department's compliance with appropriate standards, encompassing quality, independence, scope of work, performance of audit work and management of the internal audit department.

5.3 Annual review of internal audit

As mentioned above, the board or audit committee should conduct an annual review of the internal auditors' work. The reviews should include the following areas:

5.3.1 Scope of work

The review will be particularly concerned with the work done to test:

- The **adequacy** and **effectiveness** of internal control
- **Compliance with laws, regulations** and **policies**
- **Safeguarding** of assets
- **Reliability** of information
- **Value for money**
- **Attainment** of organisation's **objectives** and **goals**

It should be possible to see from the plans that internal audit submits to the audit committee that internal audit's work does forward the organisation's aims.

5.3.2 Authority

The review should cover the formal **terms of reference** and assess whether they are adequate.

It should consider whether there are senior personnel in the organisation who can ensure that the scope of internal audit's work is **sufficiently broad**, that there is **adequate consideration** of **audit reports** and **appropriate action** on audit findings and recommendations.

5.3.3 Independence

The review should consider carefully whether there are **adequate safeguards** in place to ensure the independence of internal audit, including **dismissal of the head of internal audit** being the responsibility of the board or audit committee, internal auditors not assuming operating responsibilities and internal auditors being excluded from systems, design, installation and operation work.

5.3.4 Resources

Again the review should consider the documentation provided by internal audit and confirm that resourcing plans indicate that there will be **sufficient resources** to review all areas. This should be assessed not just in terms of the hours set aside but also physical resources such as computers, and also of course the necessary knowledge, skills and disciplines.

Exam focus point

You may be asked how the effectiveness of internal audit should be assessed. Remember the assessment should reflect the objectives of internal audit; hence a range of measures is likely to be used.

5.4 Value for money

The Chartered Institute of Public finance and Accountancy (CIPFA) has highlighted the need to look at internal audit from the point of view of value for money. The review should consider the **economy, efficiency and effectiveness** (the 3E's) of internal audit.

CIPFA points out that often internal audit is mostly measured according to its **economy** and **efficiency**. This primarily involves consideration of the resources input and audit processes. Review concentrates on comparisons with budgets and targets set. This involves consideration of the following.

- Time spent (how much time is spent productively, reasons for delays)
- Costs
- Quality and scope of plan
- Abilities of staff
- Coverage of systems and departments

CIPFA however argues that less attention may be paid to the effectiveness of internal audit. The reason is assessment of effectiveness involves assessment of internal audit outputs which may not be easy to measure.

One measure of outputs is quality of internal audit reports. Criteria here may include:

(a) whether **reports** are **well-written**, and include clear opinions, detailed findings and specific recommendations for corrective action;

(b) **timeliness** of reports; the length of time between the detailed fieldwork and final reports;

(c) **reaction** from **operational departments**; feedback should be obtained as to how useful internal audit reports are perceived to be. How operational departments have responded to internal audit recommendations should also be considered.

A further measure of outputs is whether other **performance measures** have **shown** the **same results** as internal audit.

(a) In the area of financial controls, internal audit assessment of the quality of credit control procedures could be compared with the level of bad debts.

(b) Internal audit reports on efficient use of resources could be compared with how the departments reviewed have performed against budgets.

(c) Other measures with which internal audit results might be compared are internal comment, and external criticism of performance, for example press coverage.

Internal audit can also be measured by whether its **recommendations** have **resulted** in **improved performance**, for example whether reports covering improvements in the sales or marketing process have resulted in increased turnover.

6 Outsourcing the internal audit function

FAST FORWARD

Many organisations are finding it **logistically easier** or **more cost-effective** to **outsource** the internal audit function.

External auditors may be asked to provide an **internal audit function**, although this may lead to **independence** problems.

6.1 Outsourcing to external firms

It can be expensive to maintain an internal audit function staffed by an organisation's own employees. Although most corporate governance guidelines state that the directors should consider the need for internal audit annually, the directors may conclude that the cost of internal audit is too expensive. The monitoring and review required by an organisation could perhaps be done in a short amount of time and full-time employees cannot be justified.

In such circumstances, it is possible to **outsource the internal audit function**, that is, purchase the service from outside. Therefore, many of the **larger accountancy firms offer internal audit services**. This can range from a team of staff for a short term project, or a single staff member on a long term project.

It is possible that the same firm might offer one client both internal and external audit services. In such circumstances the firm and client would have to be aware of the independence issues this would raise for the external audit team.

Question — **Independence**

Learning outcome: C(ii)

Suppose the same audit firm offered both internal and external audit services to the same client.

(a) What do you think are the independence issues?

(b) Why should the issues affect the external audit team rather than the internal audit team?

Answer

(a) External auditors are employed to give an assurance to the members of a company about the stewardship of the directors and the management of that entity. They are **independent verifiers**. If the firm provides internal audit services to the entity, two issues arise:

(i) Internal auditors report to the directors so there is a **link between the firm and the directors** which is a block to independence.

(ii) The firm provides 'other services' to an external audit client, and the partners must consider whether this affects their objectivity in relation to the audit, and renders them no longer impartial

(b) The issues arise for the external audit team as independence is a key ethical issue for external auditors. As internal auditors provide a service to the directors, by whom they are employed, the issue of independence is a more tricky issue. It relates more to 'independence in the mind'. Internal auditors are not required to be 'seen to be independent' in the same way that external auditors are.

6.2 Advantages of outsourcing

Outsourcing can overcome a number of the problems mentioned above.

- Outsourcing can provide an **immediate** internal audit department. Staff do not need to be recruited, as the **service provider has good quality staff**.
- The service providers have **specialist skills** and can assess what management require them to do. As they are external to the operation, this will not cause operational problems.
- Outsourcing can lay the **basis** of a **permanent function** if that is what the client wants to do in the long-term.
- External staff can **set policies and functions**, and assist the directors in **recruiting a team** to staff a permanent internal function.
- The service contract can be for the **appropriate time scale** (a two week project, a month, etc)
- Because the **time scale is flexible**, a **team of staff** can be provided if required.
- The service provider could also provide less than a full team, but, for example, could provide one member of staff on a full-time basis for a short period, as a **secondment**.
- Internal auditors can never be **truly independent** as they are paid by the entity.
- **Certain frauds**, for example management fraud, may be **too sensitive** to be dealt with by internal audit.

6.3 Disadvantages of outsourcing

- Outsourcing internal audit appears to go **against** the spirit of the **corporate governance** reports which regards regular monitoring of key controls by internal audit as an integral part of a company's system of controls
- Using external providers may be **more expensive** because they are remunerated by fees which include a profit element rather than by salaries.
- External staff may **change frequently**. Internal auditors have continued dealings with the system, know it better and can therefore spot problems more easily.

Chapter roundup

- The role of internal audit will **vary** according to the **organisation's objectives** but is likely to include **review of internal control systems, risk management, legal compliance** and **value for money**.
- **Internal auditors** are **employees** of the organisation whose work is designed to **add value** and who report to the **audit committee. External auditors** are from **accountancy firms** and their role is to **report on the financial statements** to **shareholders**.
- Both **internal and external auditors** review controls, and **external auditors** may **place reliance** on **internal auditors' work** providing they assess its worth.
- Internal audit may be organised by **speciality** or may be a **simple fully integrated department**.
- The distinction between **regular reviews** and **one-off consultancy projects** may also be significant for the internal audit department.
- Internal audit standards cover **professional proficiency, scope of work, performance, management**, and most importantly **independence**.
- Formal **quality control procedures** should be used to assess the work of **internal audit** and this assessment should include the **value for money** the internal audit service provides.
- Many organisations are finding it **logistically easier** or **more cost-effective** to **outsource** the internal audit function.
- External auditors may be asked to provide an **internal audit function**, although this may lead to **independence** problems.

Quick quiz

1 What is internal audit?

2 What are the main elements of internal audit's review of the accounting and control systems?

3 Name three key differences between internal and external audit.

4 What matters would the external auditors consider when assessing the internal audit function?

5 Internal auditors are not required to consider fraud.

True ☐

False ☐

6 What are the most important aspects of the assessment of the professional proficiency of internal audit?

7 What criteria should be used to judge the quality of internal audit reports?

8 It is possible to buy in an internal audit service from an external organisation.

True ☐

False ☐

Answers to quick quiz

1 Internal audit is an appraisal or monitoring activity established by management and directors, for the review of the accounting and internal control systems as a service to the entity.

2
- Reviewing the design of systems
- Monitoring the operation of systems by risk assessment and detailed testing
- Recommending cost effective improvements

3 External report to members, internal to directors
External report on financial statements, internal on systems, controls and risks
External are independent of the company, internal often employed by it

4
- Organisational status
- Scope of function
- Technical competence
- Due professional care

5 False

6
- Appropriate staffing
- Knowledge, skills and disciplines
- Supervision
- Compliance with professional standards
- Human relations and communication
- Continuing education
- Due professional care

7
- Whether reports are well written
- Timeliness of reports
- Reaction from operational departments

8 True

Now try the question below from the Exam Question Bank

Number	Level	Marks	Time
Q9	Introductory	N/a	35 mins

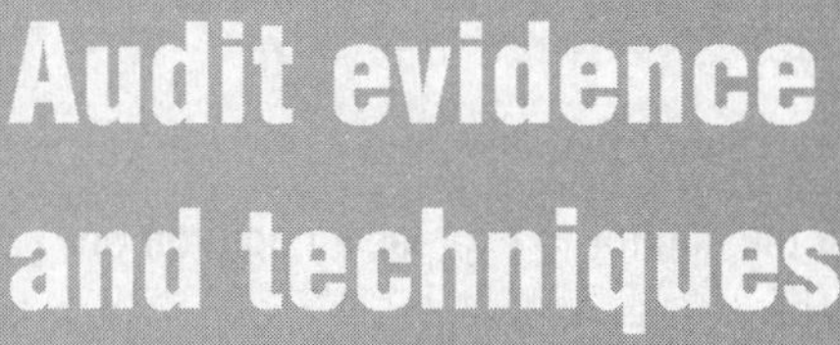

Audit evidence and techniques

10

Introduction

In this chapter we consider the ways in which auditors obtain evidence and the methods used to record audit work and accounting systems.

A lot of internal audit work will be focused on **tests of control**; whereas much of the work of external audit will be concerned with **substantiating assets, liabilities and transactions**. However the increased requirements that corporate governance guidelines have placed on external auditors and internal auditors have meant it has become more important for external auditors to take a good look at internal controls, whilst internal auditors need to be concerned with the accuracy of the accounting information (not just the annual accounts) produced by the accounting system.

A key tool in audit testing is sampling, gaining assurance that enough of an area under review has been tested to form a **reasonable basis for an opinion**, but at the same time **not testing more items than is necessary** to gain enough assurance that the test has come up with the correct result. We examine sampling in detail in Section 2.

Recording of internal audit work is very important as its results will ultimately be used as the basis for the board and audit committee's reviews of internal control. We shall look at what audit working papers should contain in Section 3 and focus on the recording of accounting and internal control systems in Section 4 as it is particularly important for internal audit to have clear records for reference.

Topic list	Learning outcomes	Syllabus references	Ability required
1 Audit evidence	C(ii),(iii)	C(2)	Evaluation
2 Audit sampling	C(ii),(iii)	C(2)	Evaluation
3 Audit documentation	C(ii), (iii)	C(2)	Evaluation
4 Recording of accounting and control systems	C(ii), (iii)	C(2)	Evaluation

1 Audit evidence

FAST FORWARD

Auditors must evaluate all types of audit evidence in terms of its **sufficiency** and **appropriateness**.

Evidence can be in the form of **tests of controls** or **substantive procedures**.

Tests of control concentrate on the **design** and **operation** of controls.

Substantive testing aims to test all the **financial statement assertions.**

The **reliability** of audit evidence is influenced by its **source** and by its **nature.**

1.1 Audit evidence and audit texts

In this section, we shall look at the audit evidence that **enables** the auditor to express an opinion on financial statements, that is, the **audit evidence** he has gathered.

Audit evidence includes all the information contained within the accounting records underlying the financial statements, and other information gathered by the auditors, such as confirmations from third parties. Auditors **do not look at all the information** that might exist. They will often select samples, as we shall see in section 2.

In order to reach a position in which they can express an opinion, the auditors need to gather evidence from various sources. There are two types of test which they will carry out.

Key terms

Test of controls are performed to obtain audit evidence about the effectiveness of the:

- Design of the accounting and internal control systems, ie whether they are suitably designed to prevent or detect and correct material misstatements; and
- Operation of the internal controls throughout the period.

Substantive procedures are tests to obtain audit evidence to detect material misstatements in the amounts. They are generally of two types:

- Analytical procedures
- Other substantive procedures such as tests of detail of transactions and balances, review of minutes of directors' meetings and enquiry.

The International Audit and Assurance Standard Board's ISA 500 *Audit evidence* requires auditors to 'obtain **sufficient appropriate** audit evidence to be able to draw **reasonable conclusions** on which to base the audit opinion'.

1.2 Sufficient appropriate audit evidence

'Sufficiency' and 'appropriateness' are interrelated and apply to both tests of controls and substantive procedures.

- **Sufficiency** is the measure of the **quantity** of audit evidence.
- **Appropriateness** is the measure of the **quality** or **reliability** of the audit evidence.

The **quantity** of audit evidence required is affected by the **level of risk** in the area being audited. It is also affected by the **quality** of evidence obtained. If the evidence is high quality, the auditor may need less than if it were poor quality. However, obtaining a high quantity of poor quality evidence will not cancel out its poor quality. The following generalisations may help in assessing the **reliability** of audit evidence.

QUALITY OF EVIDENCE	
External	Audit evidence from **external sources** is more reliable than that obtained from the entity's records.
Auditor	Evidence obtained **directly by auditors** is more reliable than that obtained indirectly or by inference
Entity	Evidence obtained from the entity's records is more reliable when related **control system operates effectively**
Written	Evidence in the form of **documents (paper or electronic)** or **written representations** are more reliable than oral representations
Originals	Original documents are more realistic than photocopies, or facsimiles

Auditors will often use information produced by the entity when obtaining audit evidence, although this will not always be a strong form of audit evidence. When doing so, the ISA requires that the auditor 'obtain audit evidence about the **accuracy and completeness** of the information'. This may be achieved by testing controls in the related area, or by other methods, for example, computer assisted audit techniques (see below).

Exam focus point

You may be asked to consider how strong certain evidence is from the auditor's viewpoint.

1.3 Financial statement assertions

Audit tests are designed to obtain evidence about the financial statement assertions. Although they are most relevant to the work of the external auditors, they have relevance to some of the work carried on by internal audit.

Key terms

Financial statement assertions are the representations of the directors that are embodied in the financial statements. By approving the financial statements, the directors are making representations about the information therein. These representations or assertions may be described in general terms in a number of ways, for example:

Completeness There are no unrecorded assets, liabilities, transactions or events, or undisclosed items

Occurrence A transaction or event took place which pertains to the entity during the relevant period

Measurement A transaction or event is recorded in the proper amount and revenue or expense is allocated to the proper period

Presentation and disclosure An item is disclosed, classified and described in accordance with the applicable reporting framework (for example, relevant legislation and applicable accounting standards)

Appropriate carrying value (valuation) An asset or liability is recorded at an appropriate carrying value

Rights and obligations An asset or liability pertains to the entity at a given date

Existence An asset or liability exists at a given date

ISA 500 states that 'the auditor should use assertions for **classes of transactions**, **account balances**, and **presentation and disclosures** in sufficient detail to form the basis for the assessment of risks of material misstatement and the design and performance of further audit procedures'. It gives examples of assertions in these areas.

Assertions used by the auditor	
Assertions about **classes of transactions** and events for the period under audit	**Occurrence**: transactions and events that have been recorded have occurred and pertain to the entity. **Completeness**: all transactions and events that should have been recorded have been recorded. **Accuracy**: amounts and other data relating to recorded transactions and events have been recorded appropriately. **Cutoff**: transactions and events have been recorded in the correct accounting period (see measurement, above). **Classification**: transactions and events have been recorded in the proper accounts.
Assertions about **account balances** at the period end	**Existence**: assets, liabilities and equity interests exist. **Rights and obligations**: the entity holds or controls the rights to assets, and liabilities are the obligations of the entity. **Completeness**: all assets, liabilities and equity interests that should have been recorded have been recorded. **Valuation and allocation**: assets, liabilities, and equity interests are included in the financial statements at appropriate amounts and any resulting valuation or allocation adjustments are appropriately recorded.
Assertions about **presentation and disclosure**	**Occurrence and rights and obligations**: disclosed events, transactions and other matters have occurred and pertain to the entity. **Completeness**: all disclosures that should have been included in the financial statements have been included. **Classification and understandability**: financial information is appropriately presented and described, and disclosures are clearly expressed. **Accuracy and valuation**: financial and other information are disclosed fairly and at appropriate amounts.

1.4 Audit procedures

FAST FORWARD

Audit evidence can be obtained by:

- Inspection
- Observation
- Enquiry and confirmation
- Computation
- Analytical procedure

Auditors obtain evidence by one or more of the following procedures.

PROCEDURES	
Inspection of assets	Inspection of assets that are recorded in the accounting records confirms existence, gives evidence of valuation, but does not confirm rights and obligations Confirmation that assets seen are recorded in accounting records gives evidence of completeness
Inspection of documentation	Confirmation to documentation of items recorded in accounting records confirms that an asset exists or a transaction occurred. Confirmation that items recorded in supporting documentation are recorded in accounting records tests completeness Cut-off can be verified by inspecting reverse population ie checking transactions recorded after the balance sheet date to supporting documentation to confirm that they occurred after the balance sheet date Inspection also provides evidence of valuation/measurement, rights and obligations and the nature of items (presentation and disclosure). It can also be used to compare documents (and hence test consistency of audit evidence) and confirm authorisation
Observation	Involves watching a procedure being performed (for example, post opening) Of limited use, as only confirms procedure took place when the auditor was watching
Inquiry	Seeking information from client staff or external sources Strength of evidence depends on knowledge and integrity of source of information
Recalculation	Checking arithmetic of client's records for example, adding up ledger account
Reperformance	Independently executing procedures or controls, either manually or through the use of CAATs (see below)
Analytical procedures	Evaluating and comparing financial and/or non-financial data for plausible relationships (see Chapter 11)
Confirmation	Confirmation means having the facts of one area confirmed by reference to another party or another source of evidence The more independent the additional evidence is, the more reliable the confirmation
Reconciliation	Carrying out reconciliations can confirm the accounting records balance, or that the organisation has procedures in place to confirm the consistency of accounting records
Expert opinion	Expert opinion can be used as a source of confirmation in technical areas where the auditors lack expertise to be able to confirm the explanations given to them
Research into published material and reports	Auditors can use various types of reports, for example internal reports on efficiency, reports on the feasibility of computer systems, or research into industry figures for the operation being reviewed
Receiving the service	Internal audit may be able to gain direct experience of using the services provided by other departments. This may be directly, for example use of the computer support function, or internal audit may themselves act as customers to gain evidence on functions that deal with external customers

PROCEDURES	
Mathematical models	Mathematical models can be used to check the reasonableness of certain business functions, for example use of stock control models to check the reasonableness of stock ordering policies
Questionnaires	Questionnaires can be a means of gaining evidence for comparisons, asking other functions within the organisations or external organisations detailed questions in order to be able to compare what they do with the operation under review
User satisfaction surveys	Obtaining feedback from customers who use the service/product can provide evidence into the success or otherwise of the service/product

Question

Audit evidence

Learning outcome: C (ii)

(a) Discuss the quality of the following types of audit evidence, giving two examples of each form of evidence.

(i) Evidence originated by the auditors

(ii) Evidence created by third parties

(iii) Evidence created by the management of the client

(b) Describe the general considerations which the auditors must bear in mind when evaluating audit evidence.

Answer

(a) **Quality of audit evidence**

(i) **Evidence originated by the auditors**

Evidence originated by the auditors is in general, the **most reliable** type of audit evidence because there is little risk that it can be manipulated by management.

Examples

(1) **Analytical procedures**, such as the calculation of ratios and trends in order to examine unusual variations

(2) **Physical inspection** or observation, such as attendance at physical inventory counts or inspection of a non-current asset

(3) **Re-performance** of calculations making up figures in the accounts, such as the computation of total inventory values

(ii) **Evidence created by third parties**

Third party evidence is **more reliable** than **client-produced evidence** to the extent that it is obtained from sources independent of the client. Its reliability will be reduced if it is obtained from sources which are not independent, or if there is a risk that client personnel may be able to and have reason to suppress or manipulate it. This, for instance, is an argument against having replies to circularisations sent to the client instead of the auditors.

Examples

(1) **Circularisation of trade accounts** receivable or creditors and other requests from the auditors for confirming evidence, such as requests for confirmation of bank balances.

(2) **Reports produced by experts**, such as property valuations, actuarial valuations, legal opinions. In evaluating such evidence, the auditors need to take into account the qualifications of the expert, his or her independence of the client and the terms of reference under which the work was carried out.

(3) **Documents held by the client** which were issued by third parties, such as invoices, price lists and statements. These may sometimes be manipulated by the client, to the extent that items may be suppressed or altered, and to this extent they are less reliable than confirmations received direct.

(iii) **Evidence created by management**

The auditors **cannot place the same degree of reliance** on evidence produced by client management as on that produced outside the client organization. However, it will often be necessary to place some reliance on the client's evidence. The auditors will need to obtain audit evidence that the information supplied is complete and accurate, and apply judgement in doing so, taking into account previous experience of the client's reliability and the extent to which the client's representations appear compatible with other audit findings, as well as the materiality of the item under discussion.

Examples

(1) The **company's accounting records** and **supporting schedules**. Although these are prepared by management, the auditors have a statutory right to examine such records in full: this right enhances the quality of this information.

(2) The **client's explanations** of, for instance, apparently unusual fluctuations in results. Such evidence requires interpretation by the auditors and, being oral evidence, only limited reliance can be placed upon it.

(3) Information provided to the auditors about the internal control system. The auditors need to check that this information is accurate and up-to-date, and that it does not simply describe an idealised system which is not adhered to in practice.

(b) **General considerations in evaluating audit evidence**

Audit evidence will often not be wholly conclusive. The auditors must obtain evidence which is **sufficient and appropriate** to form the basis for their audit conclusions. The evidence gathered should also be **relevant** to those conclusions, and sufficiently **reliable** ultimately to form the basis for the audit opinion. The auditors must exercise skill and judgement to ensure that evidence is correctly interpreted and that only valid inferences are drawn from it.

Certain general principles can be stated. **Written evidence** is preferable to oral evidence; **independent evidence** obtained from outside the organization is more reliable than that obtained internally; and that **evidence generated by the auditors** is more reliable than that obtained from others.

1.5 Computer assisted audit techniques

FAST FORWARD

Auditors may use a number of **computer assisted audit techniques** including:

- Audit interrogation software
- Test data

Exam focus point

Use of computers on audits is now common practice. The examiner expects you to consider the computer aspects of auditing as a matter of course. Therefore in answering questions on obtaining evidence, remember to include reference to CAATs if they seem relevant.

The overall objectives and scope of an audit do not change when an audit is conducted in a computerised environment. However, the application of auditing procedures may require auditors to consider techniques that use the computer as an audit tool. These uses of the computer for audit work are known as computer assisted audit techniques **(CAATs).**

(a) The absence of input documents or the lack of a visible audit trail may require the use of CAATs in the application of tests of control and substantive procedures.

(b) The effectiveness and efficiency of auditing procedures may be improved through the use of CAATs.

CAATs may be used in performing various auditing procedures, including the following.

- **Tests of details of transactions and balances**, for example the use of audit software to test all (or a sample) of the transactions in a computer file
- **Analytical review procedures**, for example the use of audit software to identify unusual fluctuations or items
- **Tests of computer information system controls**, for example the use of test data to test access procedures to the program libraries, or the functioning of a programmed procedure

There are two particularly common types of CAAT:

- Audit software
- Test data

1.5.1 Audit software

Audit software consists of **computer programs** used by the auditors, as part of their auditing procedures, to **process data of audit significance** from the entity's accounting system. Regardless of the source of the programs, the auditor should substantiate their validity for audit purposes prior to use. Audit software may consist of the following.

(a) **Package programs** are **generalised computer programs** designed to **perform data processing functions** which include reading computer files, selecting information, performing calculations, creating data files and printing reports in a format specified by the auditors.

(b) **Purpose-written programs** are computer programs designed to **perform audit tasks in specific circumstances**. These programs may be prepared by the auditors, by the entity or by an outside programmer engaged by the auditors. In some cases, existing entity programs may be used by the auditors in their original or in a modified state because it may be more efficient than developing independent programs.

(c) **Utility programs** are used by the entity to **perform common data processing functions**, such a sorting, creating and printing files. These programs are generally not designed for audit purposes and, therefore, may not contain such features as automatic record counts or control totals.

Examples of uses of audit software are:

- Interrogation software, which accesses the client's data files
- Comparison programs which compare versions of a program
- Interactive software for interrogation of on-line systems
- Resident code software to review transactions as they are processed

1.5.2 Test data

Test data techniques are used in conducting audit procedures by entering data (eg a sample of transactions) into an entity's computer system, and comparing the results obtained with predetermined results. Examples include:

(a) Test data used to test **specific controls** in computer programs. Examples include on-line password and data access controls.

(b) Test transactions selected from previously processed transactions or created by the auditors to test **specific processing characteristics** of an entity's computer system. Such transactions are generally processed separately from the entity's normal processing. Test data can for example be used to check the controls that prevent the processing of **invalid data** by entering data with say a non-existent customer code or worth an unreasonable amount, or a transaction which may if processed break customer credit limits.

(c) Test transactions used in an **integrated test facility**. This is where a 'dummy' unit (eg a department or employee) is established, and to which test transactions are posted during the normal processing cycle.

A significant problem with test data is that any resulting corruption of data files has to be corrected. This is difficult with modem real-time systems, which often have built-in (and highly desirable) controls to ensure that data entered **cannot** be easily removed without leaving a mark.

Other problems with **test data** are that it only tests the operation of the system at a **single point of time**, and auditors are only testing controls in the programs being run and controls which they know about. The problems involved mean that test data is being used less as a CAAT.

Question — **Invisible evidence**

Learning outcome: C(ii)

Try to think of examples of where visible evidence may be lacking in the accounting process.

Answer

(a) **Input documents** may be non-existent where sales orders are entered on-line. In addition, accounting transactions, such as discounts and interest calculations, may be generated by computer programs with no visible authorisation of individual transactions.

(b) The system may not produce a visible audit trail of **transactions processed** through the computer. Delivery notes and suppliers' invoices may be matched by a computer program. In addition, programmed control procedures, such as checking customer credit limits, may provide visible evidence only on an exception basis. In such cases, there may be no visible evidence that all transactions have been processed.

(c) **Output reports** may not be produced by the system. In addition, a printed report may only contain summary totals while supporting details are kept in computer files.

1.5.3 Using CAATs

The major steps to be undertaken by the auditors in the application of a CAAT are as follows.

- **Set the objective** of the CAAT application
- **Determine** the **content** and **accessibility** of the entity's **files**
- **Define** the **transaction types** to be tested
- **Define** the **procedures** to be performed on the data
- **Define** the **output requirements**
- **Identify** the audit and computer **personnel** who may participate in the design and application of the CAAT
- **Refine** the estimates of **costs** and **benefits**
- Ensure that the **use of the CAAT is properly controlled** and **documented**
- Arrange the **administrative activities**, including the necessary skills and computer facilities
- Execute the **CAAT application**
- **Evaluate the results**

Question

CAATS

Learning outcome: C(iii)

(a) Outline the major types of CAATs and describe the potential benefits that might be derived from using them.

(b) Explain what is meant by a 'test pack'.

(c) Briefly explain the use that the auditors could make of such a test pack when examining a sales ledger system maintained on a computer system.

(d) Briefly outline the main practical problems encountered when using a test pack.

Answer

(a) Audit techniques that involve, directly or indirectly, the use of a client's computer are referred to as Computer Assisted Audit Techniques (CAATs), of which the following are two principal categories.

  (i) **Audit software**: computer programs used for audit purposes to examine the contents of the client's computer files

  (ii) **Test data**: data used by the auditors for computer processing to test the operation of the enterprise's computer programs

The benefits of using CAATs are as follows.

  (i) By using **computer audit programs**, the auditors can **scrutinise large volumes of data** and concentrate skilled manual resources on the investigation of results, rather than on the extraction of information.

  (ii) Once the programs have been written and tested, the **costs of operation** are **relatively low**, indeed the auditors do not necessarily have to be present during its use (thought there are frequently practical advantages in the auditors attending).

(b) A '**test pack**' consists of **input data submitted by the auditors** for **processing** by the enterprise's computer based accounting system. It may be processed during a normal production run ('live') or during a special run at a point in time outside the normal cycle ('dead').

The primary use of the test pack is in **testing of application controls**. The data used in the test pack will often contain items which should appear in exception reports produced by the system. The results of the processed test pack will be compared with the expected results.

(c) The auditors could use a test pack to test the sales ledger system by including data in the pack which would normally be processed through the system, such as:

(i) Sales
(ii) Credits allowed
(iii) Cash receipts
(iv) Discounts allowed

The processing of the input would involve:

(i) **Production of sales invoices** (with correct discounts)

(ii) **Production of credit notes**

(iii) **Posting of cash received**, invoices and credit notes to individual debtor's accounts to appear on statements

(iv) **Posting all transactions** to the sales ledger control account and producing balances

The result produced would be compared with those predicted in the test pack. Errors should appear on exception reports produced by the computer, for example, a customer credit limit being breached.

(d) The practical problems involved in using a test pack are as follows.

(i) In using 'live' processing there will be problems **removing or reversing the test data**, which might corrupt master file information.

(ii) In using **'dead' processing** the auditors do not **test the system** actually used by the client.

(iii) Any auditors who wish to design a test pack must have **sufficient skill in computing**, and also a thorough knowledge of the client's system.

(iv) Any changes in the client's system will mean that the test pack will have to be **rewritten** which will be **costly** and time-**consuming.**

2 Audit sampling

FAST FORWARD

The main stages of **audit sampling** are:

- Determining **objectives** and **population**
- Determining **sample size**
- Choosing method of **sample selection**
- Analysing the **results and projecting errors**

2.1 The need for sampling

Auditors do not normally examine all the information available to them; it would be impractical to do so and using audit sampling will produce valid conclusions. ISA 530 *Audit sampling and other selective testing procedures* states that 'when designing audit procedures, the auditor should determine appropriate means for selecting items for testing so as to gather audit evidence to meet the objectives of audit tests'.

Key terms

Audit sampling involves the application of audit procedures to less than 100% of the items within an account balance or class of transactions such that all sampling units have a chance of selection. This will enable the auditor to obtain and evaluate audit evidence about some characteristic of the items selected in order to form or assist in forming a conclusion concerning the population.

Population is the entire set of data from which a sample is selected and about which an auditor wishes to draw conclusions.

The ISA points out that some testing procedures do **not** involve sampling, such as:

- **Testing 100%** of items in a population (this should be obvious)
- Testing all items with a **certain characteristic** as selection is not representative

Auditors are unlikely to test 100% of items when carrying out tests of control, but 100% testing may be appropriate for certain substantive procedures. For example if the population is made up of a small number of high value items, there is a high risk of material misstatement and other means do not provide sufficient appropriate audit evidence, 100% examination may be appropriate.

2.2 Statistical and non-statistical sampling

The ISA requires auditors to 'determine appropriate means of selecting the items for testing'. It distinguishes between **statistically-based sampling** and **non-statistical methods**.

Key terms

Statistical sampling is any approach to sampling that involves random selection of a sample, and use of probability theory to evaluate sample results, including measurement of sampling risk.

Non statistical sampling the approach to sampling where the auditor does not use statistical methods and draws a judgemental opinion about the population.

The auditor may alternatively select certain items from a population because of specific characteristics they possess. The results of items selected in this way cannot be projected onto the whole population but may be used in conjunction with other audit evidence concerning the rest of the population.

- **High value or key items.** The auditor may select high value items or items that are suspicious, unusual or prone to error.
- **All items over a certain amount**. Selecting items this way may mean a large proportion of the population can be verified by testing a few items.
- **Items to obtain information** about the client's business, the nature of transactions, or the client's accounting and control systems.
- **Items to test procedures,** to see whether particular procedures are being performed.

2.3 Design of the sample

When designing the sample, the ISA requires the auditor to 'consider the **objectives** of the test and the **attributes of the population** from which the sample will be drawn'.

Auditors must consider the specific audit objectives to be achieved and the audit procedures which are most likely to achieve them. The auditors also need to consider the nature and characteristics of the audit evidence sought, possible error conditions and the **rate of expected error**. This will help them to define **what constitutes an error** and **what population to use** for sampling.

Key terms

Error means either control deviations, when performing tests of control, or misstatements, when performing substantive procedures

Expected error is the error that the auditor expects to be present in the population.

The population from which the sample is drawn must be **appropriate and complete** for the specific audit objectives. The ISA distinguishes between situations where overstatement or understatement is being tested.

The population may be divided into sampling units in a variety of ways, eg an individual accounts receivable balance or, in monetary unit sampling, $1 of the total accounts receivable balance. Auditors must **define** the **sampling unit** in order to obtain an efficient and effective sample to achieve the particular audit objectives.

Key term

Sampling units are the individual items constituting a population.

2.4 Selection of the sample

FAST FORWARD

Sample sizes can be chosen by a variety of means including:

- Random selection
- Systematic selection
- Haphazard selection

The ISA requires that the auditor 'should select items for the sample with the expectation that all sampling units in the population have a chance of selection'. This requires that **all items** in the population to have an opportunity be selected.

There are a number of selection methods available.

(a) **Random selection** ensures that all items in the population have an equal chance of selection, eg by use of random number tables or computerised generator.

(b) **Systematic selection** involves selecting items using a constant interval between selections, the first interval having a random start. When using systematic selection auditors must ensure that the population is not structured in such a manner that the sampling interval corresponds with a particular pattern in the population.

(c) **Haphazard selection** may be an alternative to random selection provided auditors are satisfied that the sample is representative of the entire population. This method requires care to guard against making a selection which is biased, for example towards items which are easily located, as they may not be representative. It should not be used if auditors are carrying out statistical sampling.

(d) **Sequence or block selection**. Sequence sampling may be used to check whether certain items have particular characteristics. For example an auditor may use a sample of 50 consecutive cheques to check whether cheques are signed by authorised signatories rather than picking 50 single cheques throughout the year. Sequence sampling may however produce samples that are not representative of the population as a whole, particularly if errors only occurred during a certain part of the period, and hence the errors found cannot be projected onto the rest of the population.

(e) **Monetary Unit Sampling (MUS).** This is a selection method which ensures that every $1 in a population has an equal chance of being selected for testing. How MUS works is shown in the example below. The advantage of this selection method are that it is easy when computers are used, and that every material item will automatically be sampled. Disadvantages include the fact that if computers are not used, it can be time consuming to pick the sample, MUS does not cope well with errors of understatement of negative balances.

2.4.1 Example: MUS

You are auditing trade accounts payable. Total trade account payables is $500,000 and materiality is $50,000. You will select the balances containing the 50,000th $1 from the ledger below.

CREDITOR	BALANCE	CUMULATIVE TOTAL	SELECTED
A	30,000	30,000	
B	35,000	65,000	Yes
C	45,000	110,000	Yes
D	**52,000**	162,000	**Yes**
E	13,000	175,000	
F	**50,000**	225,000	**Yes**
G	23,000	248,000	
H	500	248,500	
I	42,000	290,000	Yes
J	47,000	337,000	Yes
K	**54,000**	391,000	**Yes**
L	17,000	408,000	Yes
M	**80,000**	488,000	**Yes**
N	12,000	500,000	Yes
	500,000		

Material items are shown in bold and have all been selected. The cumulative column shows you when the next 50,000th $1 has been reached.

Stratification may be appropriate. Stratification is the process of dividing a population into subpopulations, each of which is a group of sampling units, which have similar characteristics (often in monetary value). Each sampling unit can only belong to one, specifically designed stratum, thus reducing the variability within each stratum. This enables the auditors to direct audit effort towards items which, for example, contain the greatest potential monetary error. Ways of dividing items into strata include by age or by amount.

2.5 Sample size

As we shall see in the next chapter, in obtaining evidence, the auditor should use professional judgement to assess audit risk and design audit procedures to ensure this risk is reduced to an acceptably low level. In determining the sample size, the auditor should consider whether sampling risk is reduced to an acceptably low level.

Key terms

Sampling risk arises from the possibility that the auditor's conclusion, based on a sample of a certain size, may be different from the conclusion that would be reached if the entire population were subjected to the same audit procedure.

Non-sampling risk arises from factors that cause the auditor to reach an erroneous conclusion for any reason not related to the size of the sample. For example, most audit evidence is persuasive rather than conclusive, the auditor might use inappropriate procedures, or the auditor might misinterpret evidence and fail to recognise an error.

The auditors are faced with sampling risk in both tests of control and substantive procedures, as follows.

(a) **Tests of control**

   (i) **Risk of under-reliance**. The risk that, although the sample result does not support the auditor's assessment of control risk, the actual compliance rate would support such an assessment

   (ii) **Risk of over-reliance**. The risk that, although the sample result supports the auditor's assessment of control risk, the actual compliance rate would not support such an assessment

(b) **Substantive procedures**

   (i) **Risk of incorrect rejection**. The risk that, although the sample result supports the conclusion that a recorded account balance or class of transactions is materially misstated, in fact it is not materially misstated

   (ii) **Risk of incorrect acceptance**. The risk that, although the sample result supports the conclusion that a recorded account balance or class of transactions is not materially misstated, in fact it is materially misstated

The **greater** their reliance on the results of the procedure in question, the **lower** the sampling risk auditors will be willing to accept and the **larger** the sample size will be.

2.6 Tolerable error

Key term

Tolerable error is the maximum error in the population that the auditor would be willing to accept.

Tolerable error is considered during the planning stage and, for substantive procedures, is related to the auditor's judgement about materiality. We shall look at these matters in the next chapter. The smaller the tolerable error, the greater the sample size will need to be.

(a) In tests of control, the **tolerable error** is the **maximum rate of deviation** from a **prescribed control procedure** that auditors are willing to accept in the population and still conclude that the preliminary assessment of control risk is valid.

(b) In substantive procedures, the **tolerable error** is the **maximum monetary error** in an account balance or class of transactions that auditors are willing to accept so that, when the results of all audit procedures are considered, they are able to conclude, with reasonable assurance, that the financial statements are not materially misstated.

2.7 Expected error

Larger samples will be required when errors are expected than would be required if none were expected, in order to conclude that the actual error is less than the tolerable error. The size and frequency of errors is important when assessing the sample size; for the same overall error, larger fewer errors will mean a bigger sample size than for smaller more frequent errors. If the expected error rate is high then sampling may not be appropriate. When considering expected error, the auditors should consider:

- **Errors identified in previous audits**
- **Changes in the entity's procedures**
- **Evidence available from other procedures**

Most auditing firms use computer programmes to set sample sizes, based on risk assessments and materiality.

2.8 Evaluation of sample results

FAST FORWARD

- When evaluating results, auditors should:
  - **Analyse any errors** considering their amount and the reasons why they have occurred
  - **Draw conclusions** for the population as a whole

2.8.1 Analysis of errors in the sample

To begin with, the auditors must consider whether the items in question are **true errors**, as they defined them before the test, eg a misposting between customer accounts will not affect the total accounts receivable.

When the expected audit evidence regarding a specific sample item cannot be found, the auditors may be able to obtain sufficient appropriate audit evidence by performing **alternative procedures**. In such cases, the item is not treated as an error.

The **qualitative** aspects of errors should also be considered, including the **nature and cause** of the error. Auditors should also consider any possible effects the error might have on **other parts of the audit** including the general effect on the financial statements and on the auditors' assessment of the accounting and internal control systems.

Where common features are discovered in errors, the auditors may decide to **identify all items** in the population which **possess the common feature** (eg location), thereby producing a sub-population. Audit procedures could then be extended in this area.

On some occasions the auditor may decide that the errors are **anomalous errors**. To be considered anomalous, the auditors have to be certain that the errors are not representative of the population. Extra work will be required to prove that an error is anomalous.

Key term

Anomalous error means an error that arises from an isolated event that has not recurred other than on specifically identifiable occasions and is therefore not representative of errors in the population.

2.8.2 Projection of errors

The auditors should project the error results from the sample on to the relevant population. The auditors will **estimate the probable error** in the population by extrapolating the errors found in the sample.

For substantive tests, auditors will then **estimate any further error** that might not have been detected because of the imprecision of the technique (in addition to consideration of the qualitative aspects of the errors).

Auditors should also consider the effect of the projected error on other areas of the audit. The auditors should compare the projected population error (net of adjustments made by the entity in the case of substantive procedures) to the tolerable error, taking account of other relevant audit procedures.

2.8.3 Reassessing sampling risk

If the projected population error **exceeds** or is close to tolerable error, then the auditors should re-assess sampling risk. If it is unacceptable, they should consider extending auditing procedures or performing alternative procedures. However if after alternative procedures the auditors still believe the actual error rate is higher than the tolerable error rate, they should re-assess control risk if the test is a test of controls; if the test is a substantive test, they should consider whether the accounts need to be adjusted.

Question

Statistical sampling

Learning outcome: C(iii)

Present the arguments for and against the use of statistical sampling in auditing and reach a conclusion.

Answer

An inevitable characteristic of audit testing is that a sample only of transactions or items can be examined. The auditors examine a sample of items and thereby seek to obtain assurance that the whole group is acceptable.

Provided that conditions are appropriate for its use, a statistical approach to sampling is likely to have many advantages over the alternative of judgement sampling.

Conditions favouring the use of statistical sampling are:

(a) Existence of **large and homogeneous** groups of items

(b) **Low expected error** rate and clear definition of error

(c) **Reasonable ease of identifying** and obtaining access to items selected

If these conditions are present, statistical sampling is likely to have the following advantages.

(a) At the conclusion of a test the auditors are able to state a **definite level of confidence** they may have that the whole population conforms to the sample result, within a stated precision limit.

(b) **Sample size** is **objectively determined**, having regard to the degree of risk the auditors are prepared to accept for each application.

(c) It may be possible to use **smaller sample sizes**, thus saving time and money.

(d) The process of fixing **required precision and confidence levels** compels the auditors to consider and clarify their audit objectives.

(e) The **results of tests** can be expressed in **precise mathematical terms**.

(f) **Bias is eliminated**.

Statistical sampling is not without disadvantages.

(a) The technique may **be applied blindly without prior consideration** of the suitability of the statistical sampling for the audit task to be performed. This disadvantage may be overcome by establishing **soundly-based procedures** for use in the firm, **incorporating standards** on sampling in the firm's audit manual, **instituting training programmes** for audit staff and proper supervision.

(b) **Unsuspected patterns** or **bias in sample selection** may invalidate the conclusions. The **probability of these factors** arising must be carefully judged by the auditor before they decide to adopt statistical sampling.

(c) It frequently needs **back-up by further tests** within the population reviewed: large items, non-routine items, sensitive items like directors' transactions.

(d) At the conclusion of a statistical sampling-based test the auditors may **fail to appreciate** the **further action necessary** based on the results obtained. This potential disadvantage may be overcome by adequate training and supervision, and by requiring careful evaluation of all statistical sampling tests.

(e) The **selection exercise** can be **time consuming**.

(f) The **degree of tolerance** of **acceptable error** must be **predetermined**.

The disadvantages listed above can all be overcome if the technique is applied sensibly and competently.

Provided that the conditions favouring its use are present, statistical sampling is a useful technique for several auditing tasks.

(a) Tests of controls
(b) Substantive procedures
(c) Direct confirmation of accounts receivable and payable
(d) Fraud investigation using discovery sampling

Statistical techniques should be used when they are **convenient** and **of positive use** to the auditors in achieving a level of reliability in their results. If they are used selectively, in cases where their advantages are conspicuous and their disadvantages can be reduced to a minimum, they can make a **significant contribution** towards **greater quality control** on an audit. But it is hard to resist the argument that properly devised and controlled 'judgmental methods' can achieve the same high standards with fewer administrative or technical problems.

Exam focus point

In the exam, you may be asked to describe sampling in general terms or how it will be used in a specific situation.

3 Audit documentation

3.1 Working papers

FAST FORWARD

Documenting audit work performed in working papers:

- **Enables management** to **ensure all planned work** has been **completed adequately**
- **Provides details of work** done for future reference
- **Assists planning and control** of future audits
- **Encourages a methodical approach** and therefore quality

All audit work must be documented: the working papers are the tangible evidence of the work done in support of the audit opinion. ISA 230 *Documentation* states that 'auditors should document matters which are important in providing evidence that the audit was carried out in accordance with International Standards on Auditing'.

Key term

Working papers are the material the auditors prepare or obtain, and retain in connection with the performance of the audit. They may be in the form of data stored on paper, film, electronic media or other media.

3.2 Form and content of working papers

The reasons why auditors use working papers to record their work, and why it is necessary for auditors to record all their work, are as follows.

(a) Managers need **to be able to satisfy themselves that work delegated** by them has been **properly performed**. They can generally only do this by having available detailed working papers prepared by the audit staff who performed the work.

(b) **Working papers** will **provide**, for future reference, **details of audit problems** encountered, together with evidence of work performed and conclusions drawn in arriving at the audit opinion. This can be invaluable if, at some future date, the adequacy of the auditors' work is called into question.

(c) Good working papers will not only **assist** in the **control** of the **current audit**, but will also be invaluable in the **planning** and **control** of **future audits**.

(d) The preparation of working papers **encourages** the auditors to adopt a **methodical approach** to their audit work, which in turn is likely to improve the quality of that work.

The ISA requires working papers to be sufficiently **complete** and **detailed** to provide an overall understanding of the audit. Auditors cannot record everything they consider. Therefore judgement must be used as to the extent of working papers, based on the following general rule:

> 'What would be necessary to provide an experienced auditor, with no previous connection with the audit, with an understanding of the work performed and the basis of the decisions taken.'

The form and content of working papers are affected by matters such as:

- The **nature** of the **work carried out**
- The **form** of the **auditors' report**
- The **nature** and **complexity** of the entity's **business**
- The **nature** and **condition** of the **entity's accounting** and **internal control systems**
- The **needs** in the particular circumstances for direction, supervision and review of the work of members of the audit team
- The **specific methodology** and technology the auditors use

3.2.1 Examples of working papers

- Evidence of the planning process and any changes thereto
- Evidence of the auditors' understanding of the accounting and internal control systems
- Evidence of inherent and control risk assessments and any revisions
- Analyses of transactions and balances
- Analyses of significant ratios and trends
- A record of the nature, timing, extent and results of auditing procedures
- Notes of discussions
- Reports to directors or management
- A summary of the significant aspects of the audit

3.2.2 Contents of working papers

- The **name of** the **department** being audited
- The **balance sheet date**
- The **file reference** of the working paper
- The **name of** the **person** preparing the working paper
- The **date the working paper** was **prepared**
- The **subject** of the working paper
- The **name of** the **person reviewing** the working paper
- The **date** of the **review**
- The **objective** of the work done
- The **source of information**
- How any **sample was selected** and the sample size determined
- The **work done**
- A **key** to any audit ticks or symbols
- Appropriate **cross-referencing**
- The **results obtained**
- **Analysis of errors** or other significant observations
- The **conclusions drawn**
- The **key points highlighted**

Internal audit should have standard **referencing** and **filing** procedures for working papers, to facilitate their review.

3.3 Automated working papers

Automated working paper packages have been developed which can make the documenting of audit work much easier. Such programs aid preparation of working papers, lead schedules, trial balance and the financial statements themselves. These are automatically cross referenced, adjusted and balanced by the computer.

The **advantages** of automated working papers are as follows.

- The risk of errors is reduced.
- The working papers will be neater and easier to review.
- The time saved will be substantial as adjustments can be made easily to all working papers, including working papers summarising the key analytical information.
- Standard forms do not have to be carried to audit locations.
- Audit working papers can be transmitted for review via a modem, or fax facilities (if both the sending and receiving computers have fax boards and fax software).

Question — **Working papers**

Learning outcome: C(ii)

'Auditors base their judgement as to the extent of working papers upon what would be necessary to provide an experienced auditor, with no previous connection with the audit, with an understanding of the work performed and the basis of the decisions taken.'

Describe four benefits that auditors will obtain from working papers that meet the above requirement.

Answer

- The managers can be **satisfied that work delegated** by them has been **completed adequately**.
- Working papers are a **record of work performed** and **conclusions drawn** which might be necessary in the future, for example, in litigation.
- Good working papers aid the **planning and control** of future audits.
- Preparing working papers encourages auditors to adopt a **methodical approach**. This is likely to improve quality.

4 Recording of accounting and control systems

FAST FORWARD

Control systems may be recorded by:

- Narrative notes
- Flowcharts
- Questionnaires (for example ICQs and ICEQs)
- Checklists

4.1 Methods of recording

There are several techniques for recording the assessment of control systems.

4.2 Narrative notes

Narrative notes have the advantage of being **simple to record**. The purpose of the notes is to describe and explain the system, at the same time making any comments or criticisms that will help to demonstrate an intelligent understanding of the system.

For each system they can deal with the following questions.

- What **functions** are performed and by whom?
- What **documents** are used?
- Where do the **documents originate** and what is their **destination**?
- What **sequence** are retained documents **filed** in?
- What **books** are **kept** and where?

Narrative notes can be used to support flowcharts. They can explain effectively error procedures or uncomplicated alternatives to standard procedures.

4.3 Flowcharts

There are three types of flowcharting in regular use.

- Operational or systems flowcharts
- Document flowcharts
- Information flowcharts

You may already be familiar with **systems flowcharts**, as they are commonly used for documenting data processing operations.

Both document flowcharts and information flowcharts are used by internal auditors. **Document flowcharts** are more commonly used because they are relatively easy to prepare. All documents are followed through from beginning to end and all operations and controls are shown.

Information flowcharts are prepared in the reverse direction from the flow: they start with the entry in the general/nominal ledger and work back to the actual transaction. They concentrate on **significant information flows** and ignore any unimportant documents or copies of documents. They are consequently more compact than document flowcharts and are intended to highlight key controls. They are easy to understand but require skill and experience to compile.

4.4 Questionnaires

We can look at two types of questionnaire here, each with a different purpose.

- **Internal Control Questionnaires (ICQs)** are used to ask whether controls exist which meet specific control objectives.
- **Internal Control Evaluation Questionnaires (ICEQs)** are used to determine whether there are controls which prevent or detect specified errors or omissions.

4.4.1 Internal Control Questionnaires (ICQs)

The major question which internal control questionnaires are designed to answer is 'How good is the system of controls?'

Where strengths are identified, the auditors will perform work in the relevant areas. If, however, weaknesses are discovered they should then ask:

- What errors or irregularities could be made possible by these weaknesses?
- Could such errors or irregularities be material to the accounts?
- What substantive procedures will enable such errors or irregularities to be discovered and quantified?

Although there are many different forms of ICQ in practice, they all conform to the following basic principles:

(a) They comprise a list of questions designed to determine whether desirable controls are present.

(b) They are formulated so that there is one to cover each of the major transaction cycles.

Since it is the primary purpose of an ICQ to evaluate the system rather than describe it, one of the most effective ways of designing the questionnaire is to phrase the questions so that all the answers can be given as 'YES' or 'NO' and a 'NO' answer indicates a weakness in the system. An example would be:

Are purchase invoices checked to goods received notes before being passed for payment?	YES/NO/Comments

A 'NO' answer to that question clearly indicates a weakness in the company's payment procedures.

The ICQ questions below dealing with goods inward provide additional illustrations of the ICQ approach.

Goods inward

(a) Are supplies examined on arrival as to quantity and quality?

(b) Is such an examination evidenced in some way?

(c) Is the receipt of supplies recorded, perhaps by means of goods inwards notes?

(d) Are receipt records prepared by a person independent of those responsible for:

  (i) Ordering functions

  (ii) The processing and recording of invoices

(e) Are goods inwards records controlled to ensure that invoices are obtained for all goods received and to enable the liability for unbilled goods to be determined (by pre-numbering the records and accounting for all serial numbers)?

(f) (i) Are goods inward records regularly reviewed for items for which no invoices have been received?

  (ii) Are any such items investigated?

(g) Are these records reviewed by a person independent of those responsible for the receipt and control of goods?

4.4.2 Internal Control Evaluation Questionnaires (ICEQs)

In recent years many auditing firms have developed and implemented an evaluation technique more concerned with assessing whether specific errors (or frauds) are possible rather than establishing whether certain desirable controls are present.

This is achieved by reducing the control criteria for each transaction stream down to a handful of key questions (or control questions). The characteristic of these questions is that they concentrate on the significant errors or omissions that could occur at each phase of the appropriate cycle if controls are weak.

The nature of the key questions may best be understood by reference to the examples on the following pages.

Internal control evaluation questionnaire: control questions

The sales (revenue) cycle

Is there reasonable assurance that:

(a) Sales are properly authorised?
(b) Sales are made to reliable payers?
(c) All goods despatched are invoiced?
(d) All invoices are properly prepared?
(e) All invoices are recorded?
(f) Invoices are properly supported?
(g) All credits to customers' accounts are valid?
(h) Cash and cheques received are properly recorded and deposited?
(i) Slow payers will be chased and that bad and doubtful debts will be provided against?
(j) All transactions are properly accounted for?
(k) Cash sales are properly dealt with?
(l) Sundry sales are controlled?
(m) At the period end the system will neither overstate nor understate trade accounts receivable?

The purchases (expenditure) cycle

Is there reasonable assurance that:

(a) Goods or services could not be received without a liability being recorded?
(b) Receipt of goods or services is required in order to establish a liability?
(c) A liability will be recorded:
    (i) Only for authorised items
    (ii) At the proper amount?
(d) All payments are properly authorised?
(e) All credits due from suppliers are received?
(f) All transactions are properly accounted for?
(g) At the period end liabilities are neither overstated nor understated by the system?
(h) The balance at the bank is properly recorded at all times?
(i) Unauthorised cash payments could not be made and that the balance of petty cash is correctly stated at all times?

Wages and salaries

Is there reasonable assurance that:

(a) Employees are only paid for work done?
(b) Employees are paid the correct amount (gross and net)?
(c) The right employees actually receive the right amount?
(d) Accounting for payroll costs and deductions is accurate?

Inventory

Is there reasonable assurance that:

(a) Inventory is safeguarded from physical loss (eg fire, theft, deterioration)?
(b) Inventory records are accurate and up to date?
(c) The recorded inventory exists?
(d) The recorded inventory is owned by the company?
(e) The cut off is reliable?
(f) The costing system is reliable?
(g) The inventory sheets are accurately compiled?
(h) The inventory valuation is fair?

Non current tangible assets

Is there reasonable assurance that:

(a) Recorded assets actually exist and belong to the company?
(b) Capital expenditure is authorised and reported?
(c) Disposals of non current assets are authorised and reported?
(d) Depreciation is realistic?
(e) Non current assets are correctly accounted for?
(f) Income derived from non current assets is accounted for?

Investments

Is there reasonable assurance that:

(a) Recorded investments belong to the company and are safeguarded from loss?
(b) All income, rights or bonus issues are properly received and accounted for?
(c) Investment transactions are made only in accordance with company policy and are appropriately authorised and documented?
(d) The carrying values of investments are reasonably stated?

Management information and general controls

Is the nominal ledger satisfactorily controlled?
Are journal entries adequately controlled?
Does the organization structure provide a clear definition of the extent and limitation of authority?
Are the systems operated by competent employees, who are adequately supported?
If there is an internal audit function, is it adequate?
Are financial planning procedures adequate?
Are periodic internal reporting procedures adequate?

Each key control question is supported by detailed control points to be considered. For example, the detailed control points to be considered in relation to key control question (b) for the expenditure cycle (Is there reasonable assurance that receipt of goods or services is required to establish a liability?) are as follows.

(1) Is segregation of duties satisfactory?

(2) Are controls over relevant master files satisfactory?

(3) Is there a record that all goods received have been checked for:

- Weight or number?
- Quality and damage?

(4) Are all goods received taken on charge in the detailed inventory ledgers:

- By means of the goods received note?
- Or by means of purchase invoices?
- Are there, in a computerised system, sensible control totals (hash totals, money values and so on) to reconcile the inventory system input with the payables system?

(5) Are all invoices initialled to show that:

- Receipt of goods has been checked against the goods received records?
- Receipt of services has been verified by the person using it?
- Quality of goods has been checked against the inspection?

(6) In a computerised invoice approval system are there print-outs (examined by a responsible person) of:

- Cases where order, GRN and invoice are present but they are not equal ('equal' within predetermined tolerances of minor discrepancies)?
- Cases where invoices have been input but there is no corresponding GRN?

(7) Is there adequate control over direct purchases?

(8) Are receiving documents effectively cancelled (for example cross-referenced) to prevent their supporting two invoices?

Alternatively, ICEQ questions can be phrased so that the weakness which should be prevented by a key control is highlighted, such as the following.

Question	*Answer*	*Comments or explanation of 'yes' answer*
Can goods be sent to unauthorised suppliers?		

In these cases a 'yes' answer would require an explanation, rather than a 'no' answer.

4.4.3 Advantages of ICQs

(a) If drafted thoroughly, they can ensure **all controls** are **considered.**

(b) They are **quick** to **prepare.**

(c) They are **easy** to **use** and **control**.

4.4.4 Disadvantages of ICQs

(a) The client may be able to **overstate controls.**

(b) They may contain a large number of **irrelevant controls.**

(c) They may not include **unusual controls**, which are nevertheless effective in particular circumstances.

(d) They can give the impression that all controls are of **equal** weight. In many systems one NO answer (for example lack of segregation of duties) will cancel out a string of YES answers.

4.4.5 Advantages of ICEQs

(a) Because they are drafted in terms of **objectives** rather than specific controls, they are easier to apply to a variety of systems than **ICQs**.

(b) Answering ICEQs should enable auditors to **identify the key controls** which they are most likely to test during control testing.

(c) ICEQs can **highlight areas of weakness** where extensive substantive testing will be required.

4.4.6 Disadvantages of ICEQs

They can be **drafted vaguely**, hence **misunderstood** and important controls not identified.

4.5 Checklists

Checklists are used not only to record control systems but also as the basis of audit programmes. Their main advantage is ensuring that audit areas are **covered systematically**, and are most suited to **review and testing work** where the work programmes do not change much from period to period.

However checklists should be used with care:

- If they are **not edited carefully**, unnecessary tests that add little value can be completed.
- **Use of checklists** may mean the **work programme** becomes inflexible and additional tests are not carried out to reflect new risks that have been discovered.

Chapter roundup

- Auditors must evaluate all types of audit evidence in terms of its **sufficiency** and **appropriateness.**
- Evidence can be in the form of **tests of controls** or **substantive procedures**.
- **Tests of control** concentrate on the **design** and **operation** of controls.
- Substantive testing aims to test all the **financial statement assertions.**
- The **reliability** of audit evidence is influenced by its **source** and by its **nature.**
- **Audit evidence** can be obtained by:
  - Inspection
  - Observation
  - Enquiry and confirmation
  - Computation
  - Analytical procedures
- Auditors may use a number of **computer assisted audit techniques** including:
  - Audit interrogation software
  - Test data
- The main stages of **audit sampling** are:
  - Determining **objectives and population**
  - Determining **sample size**
  - Choosing method of **sample selection**
  - Analysing the **results** and **projecting errors**
- **Sample sizes** can be chosen by a variety of means including:
  - Random selection
  - Systematic selection
  - Haphazard selection
- When evaluating results, auditors should:
  - **Analyse any errors** considering their amount and the reasons why they have occurred
  - **Draw conclusions** for the population as a whole.
- Documenting audit work performed in working papers:
  - Enables management to **ensure all planned work** has been **completed adequately**
  - **Provides details of work** done for future reference
  - **Assists planning and control** of future audits
  - **Encourages a methodical approach** and therefore quality

Quick quiz

1 Define sufficiency and appropriateness of evidence in one line each.

2 Name seven financial statement assertions.

3 Fill in the **blanks**

Audit evidence from external sources is .... than that obtained from the entity's records.

Evidence obtained directly .... is more .... than that obtained by or from the entity.

4 Match the definitions to the terms

(a) Sampling risk

(b) Non-sampling risk

(i) The risk that the auditors' conclusion, based on a sample, may be different from the conclusions that would be reached if the entire population was subject to the same audit procedure.

(ii) The risk that the auditors might use inappropriate procedures or might misinterpret evidence and thus fail to recognise an error.

5 Name three methods of sample selection.

6 Name two types of audit software.

7 Which of the following is not a test of control?

A Inspection of documents

B Reperformance of control procedures

C Observation of authorisation of invoice

D Verification of value to invoice

8 What is the difference between ICQs and ICEQs?

Answers to quick quiz

1 Sufficiency is the measure of the quantity of audit evidence.
Appropriateness is the measure of the quality/reliability of audit evidence.

2 Existence, right and obligations, occurrence, completeness, valuation, measurement, presentation and disclosure.

3 More reliable
By auditors, reliable

4 (a) (i)

(b) (ii)

5 Random
Haphazard
Systematic

6 Package programs
Purpose-written programs
Utility programs

7 D Verification of value to invoices

8 **ICQs** ask whether controls exist that meet specific control objectives.
ICEQs are used to determine whether there are controls that prevent or detect specified errors or omissions.

Now try the question below from the Exam Question Bank

Number	Level	Marks	Time
Q10	Introductory	N/a	25 mins

11

Risk and analytical review

Introduction

It should be obvious from what you have studied so far that if internal audit work is to be carried out efficiently and effectively it needs to be founded on an effective **analysis of risks**. In the first half of this chapter we therefore look at common frameworks for analysing audit risk, covering the main factors that auditors will take into account.

You will have encountered **analytical procedures**, 'review of the figures to see if they make sense' in your earlier studies. Analytical procedures are an important audit tool and can help the auditors carry out risk analysis.

Topic list	Learning outcomes	Syllabus references	Ability required
1 Risk analysis	C(iii)	C(5)	Evaluation
2 Analytical review	C(iii)	C(5)	Evaluation

1 Risk analysis

FAST FORWARD

Business risk can be assessed as two components:

- **inherent risk**
- **Quality of control** (or control risk)

The internal auditors may use the technique of **risk analysis** to assist them in drawing up a strategic plan.

An acceptable level of **audit risk** can be obtained by:

- **Assessing** the degree of **inherent risk** and **control risk** in the system
- Planning enough testing so that **detection risk** is **reduced** to a **level** which keeps the overall audit risk within an acceptable level

1.1 Business risk

In Section B we looked at the different risks organisations face. Internal audit will often start their assessment by considering business risk.

Key term

Business risk is the risk inherent to the organisation in its operations. It is risks at all levels of the business.

The internal auditors, when planning their audit work, will try to concentrate on those areas and activities of the business which represent the highest **business risk**. There are many different ways of assessing business risk, but the CIMA document *A Framework for Internal Control* offers one approach. This approach would be used by internal audit or by executive management.

1.2 Assessment of business risks

An appendix to the CIMA document splits the assessment of business risks into three parts.

- Inherent risk
- Quality of control
- Risk formula

1.2.1 Inherent risk

Key term

Inherent risk is the level of risk relating to an activity irrespective of the quality of the associated control system or the effectiveness of management. Compare this to the definition of inherent risk given by the International Audit and Assurance Standards board.

The document then lists factors which might be taken into account when assessing inherent risk.

- **Relative size of the unit**, with reference to operational budget, capital employed and volume of transactions
- The **nature of the transactions**, taking account of unit values and convertibility
- **Complexity** of operations
- **Convertibility of assets**, with reference to liquidity, desirability, portability etc

- The extent of reliance on **computerised systems**
- **Sensitivity** to political exposure and adverse publicity

1.2.2 Quality of control

Key term

This concept is similar to control risk, as defined below. **Quality of control** is the assessment of the adequacy of control as currently perceived.

Quality of control takes into account the following factors.

- **Managerial effectiveness**, including the competence and integrity of managerial and supervisory personnel
- The **extent of change** since the last review, such as the following.
  - Changes to the accounting system or procedures
  - Changes in key personnel
  - High staff turnover
  - Rapid growth
  - Pressure on management to meet objectives
- **Time elapsed** since the last review.

1.2.3 Risk formula

Risks can be formally assessed by using an **index** which is applied to the areas under consideration and provides a kind of ranking as to which business activities are most at risk and therefore most in need of examination.

The CIMA document gives an example of such a risk assessment system. Each value is multiplied by its weighting and the results added together to give a total inherent risk (A to K) and total quality of control (G to J). These two figures are then multiplied together to produce the overall business risk of each activity. The higher the rating, the higher the business risk. In the CIMA example, factors are weighted to give a maximum of 10 for each inherent and control risk, giving a maximum overall business risk of 100 (10 × 10), which gives a form of indexation.

Risk assessment: factors, values and weightings

Factor		Values	Weighting
Inherent risk			
A	Size of unit: in terms of operational budget, capital employed, volume and value of output	1 - Insignificant 2 - Small 3 - Medium 4 - Large	0.5
B	Nature of output: in terms of unit value and convertibility eg transactions	1 - Minimal 2 - Low risk 3 - Medium risk 4 - High risk	0.5

Factor		Values	Weighting
Inherent risk			
C	Complexity of operation	1 - Simple to 4 - Extremely complex	0.5
D	Convertibility of assets: in terms of liquidity desirability, portability etc	1 - Minimal 2 - Low risk 3 - Medium risk 4 - High risk	0.5
E	Extent of computerisation	1 - Minimal use 2 - Moderate use 3 - Larger or complex systems 4 - Total reliance on systems	0.25
F	Sensitivity to public and political exposure	1 - Not sensitive 2 - Some sensitivity 3 - Significant 4 - High profile	0.25
Quality of control			
G	Adequacy of control (as at last review)	1 - Adequate 2 - Minor reservations 3 - Major reservations 4 - No controls (or not previously reviewed)	1.0
H	Managerial effectiveness	1 - Totally effective 2 - Minor reservations 3 - Major reservations 4 - Ineffective (or not previously reviewed)	0.5
I	Change factor (since last review)	1 - No change 2 - Minor change 3 - Moderate change 4 - Significant change	0.5
J	Elapsed time since last review	1 - Less than 1 year 2 - 1-2 years 3 - 2-3 years 4 - More than 3 years	0.5

Question — Risk assessment

Learning outcome: C(iii)

Using the risk assessment table above, work out an overall risk factor for the following two departments, showing the inherent and control risk factors.

Factor	*Dept X*	*Dept Y*
A	2	4
B	3	3
C	1	4
D	4	3
E	2	3
F	1	3
G	3	1
H	2	2
I	1	4
J	4	2

Answer

	Department X		*Department Y*	
Factor	*Index*	*Index × weighting*	*Index*	*Index × Weighting*
A	2	1.00	4	2.00
B	3	1.50	3	1.50
C	1	0.50	4	2.00
D	4	2.00	3	1.50
E	2	1.00	3	0.75
F	1	0.25	3	0.75
Total inherent risk		6.25		8.50
G	3	3.00	1	1.00
H	2	1.00	2	1.00
I	1	0.50	4	2.00
J	4	2.00	2	1.00
Total control risk		6.50		5.00

Overall business risk

Dept X = 6.25 × 6.50 = 40.625

Dept Y = 8.50 × 5.00 = 42.500

Department Y is higher risk due to its size and complexity, but Department X is not far behind due to the convertibility of its assets and recent changes it has gone through. Both departments are probably be due for examination by internal audit in the near future.

Clearly this technique is far from perfect. The factors, point ranges and weighting factors all have to be **determined judgementally by** the internal auditors and so does the marking index awarded. Nevertheless, many internal audit departments do use risk indexation, on the grounds that any attempt at evaluating risk is better than no attempt, and at least it provides a basis for directing audit resources towards what appear to be the areas of highest risk.

1.3 Business risk – an alternative view

You may encounter various other ways of defining and discussing business risk. One such is discussed below.

Key term

Business risk is the threat that an event or action will adversely affect an organisation's ability to achieve its business objectives and execute its strategies effectively. It is the potential for events, actions or inactions to result in the failure of a business to meet its key business objectives, or its failure to define objectives that are responsive to key stakeholders.

Different types of business risks (financial, operational and compliance) will be considered. An important distinction in an analysis of business risk is likely to be between **environment risks** (those that affect the external environment), and **process risks** (which affect a company's internal activities).

An audit of financial information based on business risks would then consider how the business risks might affect the **processing of data**, how it might cause **inaccuracy and incompleteness** of **processing** or affect its timeliness. In turn **how data** is processed will **affect** the **preparation** of, and **disclosures** in, the financial statements.

Having considered the possible consequences of business risks, the introduction of business processes to manage those risks and a sound control environment can then be considered.

1.4 IAASB definitions of risk

Key terms

Audit risk is the risk that auditors give an inappropriate opinion on the financial statements. Audit risk has three components; inherent risk, control risk and detection risk.

Inherent risk is the susceptibility of an account balance or class of transactions to misstatement that could be material individually or when aggregated with misstatements in other balances or classes, assuming there are no related internal controls.

Control risk is the risk that a misstatement would not be prevented, or detected and corrected by the accounting and internal control systems.

Detection risk is the risk that the auditors' procedures will not detect a misstatement that exists in an account balance or class of transactions that could be material, either individually or when aggregated with misstatements in other balances or classes.

The International Audit and Assurance Standards Board (IAASB) defines audit risk (the equivalent for the external auditor to business risk for the internal auditor) as a combination of *three* types of risk. Inherent risk and control risk are equivalent to the CIMA inherent risk and quality of control discussed above. Detection risk is more relevant to external auditors as it is related to substantive procedures on final account balances.

Exam focus point

In the exam you are likely to have to assess the importance of audit risks in a real-life situation.

Audit risk

Learning outcome: C(iii)

You are a newly appointed senior internal auditor at Hippo. It manufactures bathroom fittings and fixtures, which it sells to a range of wholesalers, on credit.

You have recently been sent the following extract from the draft balance sheet by the finance director.

	Budget		*Actual*	
	$'000s	$'000s	$'000s	$'000s
Non-current assets		453		367
Current assets				
Trade accounts receivable	1,134		976	
Bank	-		54	
Current liabilities				
Trade accounts payable	967		944	
Bank overdraft	9		-	

During the course of conversation with the finance director, you establish that a major new customer the company had included in its budget went bankrupt during the year.

Required

Identify any potential risks for the audit of Hippo and explain why you believe they are risks.

Answer

Potential risks relevant to the audit of Hippo

(a) **Credit sales**. Hippo makes sales on credit. This increases the risk that Hippo's sales will not be converted into cash. Trade accounts receivable is likely to be a risky area and the auditors will have to consider what the best evidence that customers are going to pay is likely to be.

(b) **Related industry**. Hippo manufactures bathroom fixtures and fittings. These are sold to wholesalers, but it is possible that Hippo's ultimate market is the building industry. This is a notoriously volatile industry, and Hippo may find that their results fluctuate too, as demand rises and falls. This suspicion is added to by the bankruptcy of the wholesaler in the year. The auditors must be sure that accounts which present Hippo as a viable company are in fact correct.

(c) **Controls**. The fact that a major new customer went bankrupt suggests that Hippo did not undertake a very thorough credit check on that customer before agreeing to supply them. This implies that the controls at Hippo may not be very strong.

(d) **Variance**. The actual results are different from budget. This may be explained by the fact that the major customer went bankrupt, or it may reveal that there are other errors and problems in the reported results, or in the original budget.

(e) **Receivables**. There is a risk that the result reported contains a balance due from the bankrupt wholesaler, which is likely to be irrecoverable.

2 Analytical review

FAST FORWARD

Analytical procedures should be used as a means of **understanding the business** and **identifying risk**.

When using analytical procedures, auditors should consider the information available, assessing its **availability, relevance** and **comparability**.

Auditors must investigate **significant fluctuations** and **unexpected relationships**.

2.1 Analytical review and analytical procedures

Analytical review is an exercise that can be carried out either during or at the end of substantive procedures in a systems audit. It is regarded as being a form of substantive testing as well as a final review procedure.

The term 'analytical review' refers to a review of the financial accounts that have been prepared, to decide whether they appear to make sense and are **coherent** and **consistent**.

Key terms

Analytical review is the examination of ratios, trends and changes in balances from one period to the next, to obtain a broad understanding of the financial position and results of operations; and to identify any items requiring further investigation. (CIMA *Official Terminology*)

2.2 Nature and purpose of analytical procedures

ISA 520 *Analytical procedures* states that analytical procedures include:

(a) The consideration of comparisons with:

  (i) **Similar information** for prior periods

  (ii) **Anticipated results** of the entity, from budgets or forecasts

  (iii) **Predictions** prepared by the auditors

  (iv) **Industry information**, such as a comparison of the client's ratio of sales to trade accounts receivable with industry averages, or with the ratios relating to other entities of comparable size in the same industry.

(b) Those between **elements of financial information** that are expected to **conform to a predicted pattern** based on the **entity's experience**, such as the relationship of gross profit to sales.

(c) Those between **financial information** and **relevant non-financial information**, such as the relationship of payroll costs to number of employees.

A variety of methods can be used to perform the procedures discussed above, ranging from **simple comparisons** to **complex analysis** using statistics, on an organisation level, branch level or individual account level. The choice of procedures is a matter for the auditors' professional judgement.

2.3 Sources of information

Possible sources of information for analytical review include:

- Interim financial information
- Budgets
- Management accounts
- Non-financial information
- Bank and cash records
- Sales tax returns
- Board minutes
- Discussions or correspondence with the client at the year-end

Auditors may also use specific industry information or general knowledge of current industry conditions to assess performance.

As well as helping to determine the **nature, timing and extent** of **other audit procedures,** such analytical procedures may also indicate **aspects of the business** and **risks** of which the auditors were previously unaware. Auditors are looking to see if developments in the business have had the expected effects. They will be particularly interested in changes in audit areas where problems have occurred in the past.

2.4 Using analytical procedures

ISA 520 lists a number of factors that the auditors should consider when using analytical procedures.

Factors to consider	Example
The **objectives** of the analytical procedures and the extent to which their results are reliable	Analytical procedures may be a good indicator of whether a population is complete
The degree to which information can be **analysed**	Analytical procedures may be more effective when applied to financial information on individual sections of an operation
The **availability of information**	Financial: budgets or forecasts Non-financial: eg the number of units produced or sold
The **reliability** of the information available	Whether budgets are prepared with sufficient care
The **relevance of the information** available	Whether budgets are established as results to be expected rather than as goals to be achieved
The **source of the information available**	Independent sources are generally more reliable than internal sources
The **comparability of the information** available	Broad industry data may need to be supplemented to be comparable with that of an entity that produces and sells specialised products
The **knowledge gained during previous audits**	The effectiveness of the accounting and internal control systems The types of problems giving rise to accounting adjustments in prior periods

Auditors will also consider the **plausibility** and **predictability** of the relationships being tested. Some relationships are strong, for example between selling expenses and sales in business where the sales force is mainly paid by commission.

ISA 520 identifies other factors that should be considered when determining the reliance that the auditors should place on the results of analytical procedures.

Reliability factors	Example
Materiality of the items involved	When inventory balances are material, auditors do not solely rely on analytical procedures
Other audit procedures directed towards the same financial statements assertions	Other procedures auditors undertake in reviewing the collectability of accounts receivable, such as the review of subsequent cash receipts, may confirm or dispel questions arising from the application of analytical procedures to an aged profile of customers' accounts
The **accuracy** with which the expected results of analytical procedures can be predicted	Auditors normally expect greater consistency in comparing the relationship of gross profit to sales from one period to another than in comparing discretionary expenses, such as research or advertising
The **frequency** with which a relationship is observed	A pattern repeated monthly as opposed to annually
Assessment of **inherent** and **control risks**	If internal controls over sales order processing is weak, and control risk is high, auditors may rely more on tests of individual transactions or balances than analytical procedures

Auditors will need to consider testing the controls, if any, over the **preparation** of **information** used in applying analytical procedures. When such controls are effective, the auditors will have greater confidence in the reliability of the information, and therefore in the results of analytical procedures.

The **controls** over **non-financial information** can often be tested in conjunction with tests of **accounting-related controls**. For example, in establishing controls over the processing of sales invoices, a business may include controls over unit sales recording. In these circumstances the auditors could test the controls over the recording of unit sales in conjunction with tests of the controls over the processing of sales invoices.

Reliance on the results of analytical procedures depends on the auditors' assessment of the **risk** that the procedures may identify relationships (between data) as expected, whereas problems exist (ie the relationships, in fact, do not exist).

2.5 Investigating significant fluctuations or unexpected relationships

The ISA says 'when analytical procedures identify significant fluctuations or relationships that are inconsistent with other relevant information or that deviate from predicted patterns, the auditor should investigate and obtain adequate explanations and appropriate corroborative evidence'. Investigations will start with **enquiries** of management and then corroboration of management's responses:

(a) By **comparing** them with the auditors' knowledge of the entity's business and with other evidence obtained during the course of the audit

(b) If the analytical procedures are being carried out as substantive procedures, by **undertaking additional audit procedures** where appropriate to confirm the explanations received

If explanations cannot be given by management, or if they are insufficient, the auditors must determine which further audit procedures to undertake to explain the fluctuation or relationship.

2.6 Ratio analysis

Ratio analysis is the **analysis** of the **relationships** between **items of financial data**, or between financial and non-financial data such as labour cost per employee.

Important ratios that could be examined include the following.

(a) **Gross profit margins**

The ratios of profit to sales. For example, if a company makes a profit of £20,000 on sales of £100,000 its profit percentage or profit margin is 20%. This also means that its costs are 80% of sales. If the profit margin changed from one accounting period to the next, then the internal auditors would be concerned that the relationship between sales and profit had either changed unexpectedly, or was mis-stated in the financial statements. For instance, if the margin dropped from 20% to 10%, they would be worried that:

(i) Costs were out of control (because they are now 90% of sales)
(ii) Sales prices were too low (because profit as a proportion of sales has dropped)
(iii) That some figures in the accounts were wrong, throwing the profit margin ratio out.

(b) **Return on capital employed**

The rates of profit to capital employed. For example, suppose a company made a profit of £15,000 and its capital employed was £150,000, so that its ROCE is 10% for that accounting period. Not only could that 10% be compared with ROCEs from earlier years, but it could also be compared with the typical ROCE of other similar companies. If their ROCEs were in the region of 15%-20%, then again the internal auditors would be worried either that something in the company was going wrong (for example asset turnover too low or prices too low), or that some figures in the financial statements were wrong.

(c) **Current ratio**

The ratio of current assets to current liabilities. This is one measure of the liquidity of a firm. If the internal auditors calculated the current ratio and it was 1.1:1 whereas in previous years it had always been 1.3:1 or better, then they would be concerned that:

(i) The company was heading for a problem period and might not be able to pay its bills

(ii) That, buried somewhere in the financial statements, there were some misleading or inaccurate figures.

Other ratios which could be used in exactly the same way, to see whether anything might be wrong within the company or in the financial statements, are as follows.

- Receivables ratio (average collection period)
- Inventory turnover ratio (inventory divided into cost of sales)
- Payables ratio (purchases divided into trade creditors)
- Quick (acid test) ratio (liquid assets to current liabilities)
- Gearing ratio (debt capital to equity capital)
- Working capital/sales ratio
- Interest cover (interest payable divided into profit before interest and tax)
- Non-current assets to long term liabilities

The following factors should be considered when deciding how much use to make of ratio analysis.

(a) Ratios mean very little when **used in isolation**. Ratios should be calculated for previous periods and for comparable companies. This may involve a certain amount of initial research, but subsequently it is just a matter of adding new statistics to the existing information on file each year.

(b) Ratios should be calculated on a **consistent basis**. Changing the calculation (for example by using average debtors to calculate debtor turnover when in previous years closing debtors were used) may mean comparisons cannot be made over time.

(c) There should be a **correlation** between the items involved. For example, sales commission will obviously vary directly with sales, whereas most administration costs will not.

(d) In general the more **detailed** the ratio analysis is, the better. For example, ratio analysis should be applied to individual outlets in a retail chain, because in the aggregated figures the trends and fluctuations of some outlets may be masked by those of others.

(e) Some ratios may be distorted by **single or unusual items**. For example, if a business has one very large customer, the debtors turnover ratio may be significantly affected by which side of the year-end the customer pays.

2.7 Trend and relationship analysis

Trend analysis is the analysis of changes in a given item over time. It can take various forms.

- Period by period comparisons
- Weighted/moving averages
- Regression analysis

Consideration of the **inter-relationship of elements of the accounts** which might be expected to conform to a predictable pattern is an important example of trend analysis.

For example, creditors and purchases: if a company's purchases increase by 50% from one year to the next, then it is reasonable to expect that its creditors figure will also increase by something in the region of 50%. If creditors only increase by, say, 10%, then it is possible that the company is being too quick to part with its cash. Alternatively, if creditors have gone up by 80%, then this might indicate a cash flow problem within the company, in that it seems to be finding it more difficult to pay for its purchases. A third possibility is that one of the figures for creditors or purchases has been incorrectly stated, and management might require the internal auditors to investigate.

Other examples of elements of the accounts with similar inter-relationships are the following.

- Inventory and cost of sales
- Non-current assets and depreciation, repairs and maintenance expense
- Intangible assets and amortisation
- Loans and interest expense
- Investments and investment income
- Receivables and bad debt expense
- Receivables and income

The following should be borne in mind when carrying out trend analysis.

(a) Trend analysis should involve **looking** at 'the **figures behind the figures**' as well as the actual items. Thus for sales, not only will the figures for total sales be considered but also changes in products, customers, levels of returns.

(b) The reviewer should also be looking for **how factors likely to cause** a **change** have **impacted** on **trends**. Any price changes or changes in production methods may impact upon the costs of direct labour and materials, and also the stock valuation. Mismatching production and sales may also indicate surplus stock, and hence a possible stock provision.

(c) Trend analysis may include **taking trends over a number of periods**, but also **trends within a period**. The auditor would wish to investigate unusual fluctuations in the monthly or weekly payroll, pay-over of pension contributions to pension schemes (undue delay here is now illegal), and so on.

Other areas that might be investigated as part of the analytical procedures include the following.

- **Examine changes** in **products, customers and levels** of **returns**
- **Assess** the effect of **price and mix changes** on the cost of sales
- **Consider** the effect of **inflation, industrial disputes, changes in production methods** and **changes in activity** on the charge for wages
- **Obtain explanations** for all **major variances** analysed using a standard costing system. Particular attention should be paid to those relating to the over or under absorption of overheads since these may, inter alia, affect inventory valuations
- **Compare trends in production and sales** and assess the effect on any provisions for obsolete inventories
- **Ensure** that **changes in the percentage labour or overhead content** of production costs are also reflected in the inventory valuation.
- **Review other expenditure**, comparing:
  - Rent with annual rent per rental agreement
  - Rates with previous year and known rates increases
  - Interest payable on loans with outstanding balance and interest rate per loan agreement
  - Hire or leasing charges with annual rate per agreements
  - Vehicle running expenses to vehicles
  - Other items related to activity level with general price increase and change in relevant level of activity (for example telephone expenditure will increase disproportionately if export or import business increases)
  - Other items not related to activity level with general price increases (or specific increases if known)
- **Review** income statement for **items** which may have been **omitted** (eg scrap sales, training levy, special contributions to pension fund, provisions for dilapidation etc).
- **Ensure expected variations** arising from the following have occurred:
  - Industry or local trends
  - Known disturbances of the trading pattern (for example strikes, depot closures, failure of suppliers)

2.8 Reasonableness tests

The aim of reasonableness tests is to develop a prediction for an item based on relationships with other financial and non-financial data. Examples of reasonableness tests include the following.

(a) **Comparison with similar firms**

These involve comparing the company's financial information with similar information produced by other companies within the same industry.

(b) **Comparison with budgets**

Explanations should be obtained for all major variances analysed using a standard costing system. Variances that relate to over or under absorption of overheads are particularly important, since these may affect stock valuations.

(c) **Comparison with other financial information**

The following are examples of tests on profit and loss expenditure.

- Rent with annual rent per rental agreement
- Rates with previous year and known rates increases
- Interest payable on loans with outstanding balance and interest rate
- Hire or leasing charges with agreed annual rate

(d) **Comparison with non-financial information**

Examples include the following.

- Rent with space occupied
- Wages and salaries with employee numbers
- Cost of sales with production volumes
- Motor expenses with delivery miles

(e) **Credibility checks**

In a small organisation for example it may be quite easy to relate the annual salaries bill to the total of individual pay cheques.

(f) **General business review**

Auditors should seek to enhance their knowledge of the organisation by **review** of **board minutes**, **talking** with employees at all levels, and keep an eye on **industry or local trends**, including known disturbances of the trading pattern (for example strikes, depot closures, failure of suppliers). By doing so, the auditors may become aware of something which should have affected the figures in the accounts, but does not appear to have done so.

2.9 The stages of analytical review

If analytical review is to be carried out effectively, the following stages will be involved:

2.9.1 Setting up

Setting up the process should involve consideration of:

(a) The **objectives** (whether analytical review is being used to aid planning or to substantiate certain figures). The auditor would also need to consider the extent of the reliance being placed on the results

(b) The **reliability of the data** being used

(c) The **relevance of the data**- for example if actual figures are to be compared with budgeted figures, the auditor will need to consider whether the budgets were designed to be a realistic target

(d) The **relationships** being tested. Profit and loss account figures tend to be more predictable as they are taken over time

(e) The **likely results**, and the **major factors likely to influence** those **results**. This should include an understanding of fixed and variable costs; if for example, sales turnover increases by 10% compared with the previous year, the likely increase in the cost of sales and the gross profit margin ought to be predicted with reasonable certainty

(f) The **level of fluctuation** from the likely results that would be regarded as significant. This will include consideration of the implications of any variations

2.9.2 Performance

Analytical review should be carried out by someone with an **in-depth knowledge** of the **organisation**, its history and industry within which it operates so the work can be put into context. A proper review requires a considerable amount of skill and judgement, and therefore must be performed by suitably experienced staff.

2.9.3 Analysis of results

Assessment will be needed of whether the results have **varied significantly** from what was expected.

2.9.4 Investigation of results

If significant fluctuations have been identified, they will need to be **explained**. Some variations may be confirmed by evidence or information that is already available. Other fluctuations may only be able to be verified by further analytical review or other audit work.

2.9.5 Drawing conclusions

The reviewer will need to consider how **reliable the results are**, and also what **further work** will be **required**. If for example analytical review has been carried out at the planning stage, results that deviate from expectations may highlight branches or audit areas requiring significant audit effort.

2.10 Analytical review during the audit

Analytical review can be used at various stages of the audit.

2.10.1 Planning stage

Analytical review is particularly important at the planning stage of internal audit. It can be used in conjunction with risk analysis to **focus on areas** or outlets that look **unusual**. For example, in a retail business internal auditors might analyse sale per square foot of all of 500 branches of a major retail chain and then concentrate on branches which have unexpected results.

2.10.2 Substantive testing

Analytical review can be used, particularly by external auditors, as a substantive test. If it is to be so used, the data analysed must be **reliable** and **sufficiently detailed**, and the relationships being tested should be plausible and predictable.

2.10.3 Final review

Analytical review is used by internal and external auditors to review financial accounts or other period-end financial information. The purpose of using analytical review at this stage is to see whether the **figures are consistent** with the auditors' **knowledge of the business**. The auditor is attempting to see that all the evidence obtained during the audit together with the final figures makes sense when viewed together.

Exam focus point

In the exam you may be given a set of figures and:

(a) Asked to calculate changes, key ratios etc and hence identify significant areas of the accounts or risks

(b) Asked what audit work will be required on these significant areas

When analysing figures, make sure that the points that you make are consistent with each other.

Mention of analytical procedures will very often be worth a couple of marks in any question on detailed audit testing. However you will not get any marks just for saying 'perform analytical procedures'; you will need to give details of the procedures that should be performed.

Question — Analytical review

Learning outcome C(iii)

You are reviewing the financial statements of Eastwood Manufacturing for the year ended 31 October 20X6. The company's main activity is the manufacture of electrically powered garden tools, including lawn mowers, cultivators and chain saws. During the year under review the company started to export some of its products to Africa; previously almost all of its sales were to the home market. The summarised accounts for the year ended 31 October 20X6 (with comparatives) are as follows.

BALANCE SHEETS AS AT 31 OCTOBER

	20X6	*20X5*
	$'000	$'000
Tangible non-current assets	4,756	4,883
Current assets		
Inventory	6,350	4,573
Payables	4,855	3,011
	11,205	7,584
Current liabilities		
Bank overdraft	2,894	1,592
Payables	2,586	2,140
Income tax	145	45
Proposed dividend	247	31
	5,872	3,808
Net current assets	5,333	3,776
Total assets less current liabilities	10,089	8,659
Long term loan	1,500	500
	8,589	8,159
Capital and reserves		
$1 ordinary shares	3,133	3,133
Revaluation reserve	1,312	1,312
Accumulated profits	4,144	3,714
	8,589	8,159

INCOME STATEMENT FOR THE YEAR ENDED 31 OCTOBER

		20X6	*20X5*
		$'000	$'000
Revenue:	home	14,470	13,923
	export	3,789	237
		18,259	14,160
Cost of sales		14,475	12,025
Gross profit		3,784	2,135
Distribution expenses		1,318	1,118
Administrative expenses		1,136	1,064
Profit from operations		1,330	(47)
Finance cost		452	308
Profit/(loss) before taxation		878	(355)
Income tax expense		201	47
Profit/(loss) after taxation		677	(402)
Dividends		247	31
Accumulated profit/(loss) for the year		430	(433)

Required

State the areas which would require special attention during an audit, supporting your observations with analytical review and ratio analysis where necessary.

Answer

(a) Income statement

(i) The **gross profit ratio** has **moved from 15.1%** in 20X5 to **20.7%** in the current year. This is a significant increase and the auditors would need to be satisfied that it was reasonable and not the result of errors in arriving at the figures in the trading account for either year. It could be acceptable given the increase in revenues which has taken place in the current year and the fact that last year the company was making losses and so may have been forced to reduce margins in order to generate some contribution.

The **level of gross profit** currently being achieved should be **considered** in the light of the **rates achieved** in earlier profitable years and the margins achieved by similar sized companies within the same industry. Another possible reason for the increase might be the higher margins achievable in the expanded export side of the company's activities.

(ii) The fact that **distribution expenses** as a percentage of turnover have gone down from 7.9% in 20X5 to 7.2% in the current year will require some investigation. Given the increased level of revenue and the higher level of export revenues, one might have anticipated an increase in this expense. However, one should also consider the element of fixed costs included in this expense as this would account for the expense remaining fairly high even where the level of turnover, as in 20X5, has decreased.

(iii) In a similar way, it would be necessary to look at the **detailed make-up of administrative expenses** which, although they have increased in absolute terms, have also gone down as a percentage of sales, from 7.5% in 20X5 to 6.2% in the current year.

(iv) The **overall finance cost** has increased in the **current year** which is to be expected given the higher level of borrowing revealed by the latest balance sheet. However, the auditors should check to ensure that the profit and loss figure does include all accrued costs as, depending on the timing of the increased borrowing, the current year's charge looks a little low in the light of the amount outstanding at the year end. The 20X5 charge against profits represented 14.7% of the year end liability, whereas the 20X6 charge is only 10.3% of the balance sheet liability.

(v) So far as the taxation charge is concerned, the most surprising thing is the fact that there was a charge last year when the **company made a loss**. It would be necessary to check the figures used in the profit and loss account for computations etc and ensure that they are in fact the correct ones.

(b) **Balance sheet**

(i) The net book value of tangible non-current assets has **decreased in comparison** with last year which could be understandable if last year the company's assets were being under utilised. However, if the company is to sustain its improved results, the auditors will need to consider whether or not the company will be able to finance any significant additions to non-current assets required in the coming year.

(ii) There must be some concern that, despite the company's increased revenues in the current year, **inventory turnover** has **dropped** from 2.6 times (not itself very high) in 20X5 to 2.2 times in the current year. The need for **provisions against slow-moving** and **possibly obsolete inventory** should be considered in the light of the auditors' detailed work on inventory values. The auditors must also check that there has been no change in the basis of valuing inventory and consider the possibility that the improvement in gross profit has in part been achieved through an over valuation of closing inventory.

(iii) The average number of days sales in receivables has increased from 77 in 20X5 to 97 in the current year. Notwithstanding the fact that one might anticipate some delay in remittances being received from African customers, this upward movement must be a cause of some concern in relation to the company's overall **liquidity position**. The auditors would need to assess the implications of this in the light of the **detailed audit work** carried out in relation to trade receivables.

(iv) The **bank overdraft** has increased dramatically and the auditors must consider carefully the **security** which the company has been able to provide and how close to the limit the company has been during the year as well as considering the year end position. Given the company's increased dependence on short-term finance, combined with the large increase in long-term borrowing, it would be necessary to review carefully any cash flow forecasts available in order to assess whether or not the company may properly be regarded as a going concern as at the balance sheet date.

(v) The **period of credit being taken from suppliers** appears to have remained fairly constant which is a little surprising given the company's level of borrowings and the auditors should ensure that year end payables are not understated.

(vi) The **income tax** and **dividend figures** appear to be reasonable and consistent with the income statement.

Chapter roundup

- Business risk can be assessed as two components:
  - **Inherent risk**
  - **Quality of control** (or control risk)
- The internal auditors may use the technique of **risk analysis** to assist them in drawing up a strategic plan.
- An acceptable level of **audit risk** can be obtained by:
  - **Assessing** the degree of **inherent risk** and **control risk** in the system
  - Planning enough testing so that **detection risk** is **reduced** to a **level** which keeps the overall audit risk within an acceptable level
- Analytical procedures should be used as a means of **understanding the business** and **identifying risk**.
- When using analytical procedures, auditors should consider the information available, assessing its **availability, relevance** and **comparability**.
- Auditors must investigate **significant fluctuations** and **unexpected relationships**.

Quick quiz

1. __________ ________ is the level of risk relating to an activity irrespective of the quality of the associated control system or the effectiveness of management.
2. What factors should be taken into account when considering the quality of control ?
3. What is detection risk?
4. What is the distinction between business risk due to environment risks and business risks due to process risks?
5. Name four sources of analytical information
6. Identify the significant relationships in the list of items below

(a)	payables	(b)	interest	(c)	purchases	(d)	sales
(e)	amortisation	(f)	loans	(g)	receivables	(h)	intangibles

7. What considerations should be taken into account when using ratio analysis?
8. Give three examples of reasonableness tests.

Answers to quick quiz

1 **Inherent risk** is the level of risk relating to an activity irrespective of the quality of the associated control system or the effectiveness of management.

2
- Managerial effectiveness
- Extent of change since last review
- Time elapsed since last review

3 The risk that auditors' procedures will not detect a misstatement that exists in an account balance or class of transactions that could be material, either individually or when aggregated with misstatements in other balances or classes.

4 Business risks due to environment risks are risks that affect the external situation, whereas business risks due to process risks are risks that affect an organisation's internal activities.

5
- Interim financial information
- Budgets
- Management accounts
- Non-financial information
- Bank and cash records
- Sales tax returns
- Board minutes
- Discussions or correspondence with the client at the year-end

6 (a) (c)

(b) (f)

(d) (g)

(e) (h)

7
- Ratios should be used for comparison
- Ratios should be calculated on a consistent basis
- There should be a correlation between the items involved
- The more detailed the ratio analysis is, the better
- Some ratios may be distorted by large or unusual items

8
- Comparison with similar firms
- Comparison with budgets
- Comparison with other financial information
- Comparison with non-financial information
- Credibility review
- General business review

Now try the question below from the Exam Question Bank

Number	Level	Marks	Time
Q11	Examination	25	45 mins

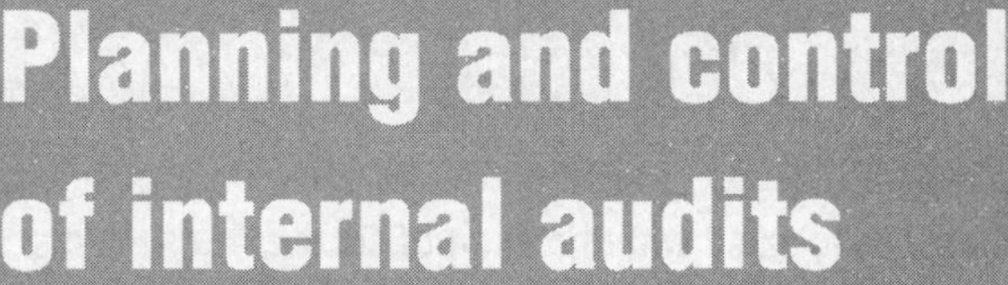

Planning and control of internal audits

Introduction

Most internal audits focus on the control systems. We therefore start this chapter by discussing the key features of a systems audit.

This chapter then goes on to consider the necessity of planning and general planning matters. Each of the levels of planning is vital to a well-directed internal audit function; it is important to focus on long-term **strategic aims**, and **select the right areas** to concentrate on, as well as carrying out the right tests within each area.

The **control** and **recording** of audits is as important as proper planning; audit results cannot be relied on unless the procedures and evidence to which they relate have been clearly documented. Internal audits must also be controlled to ensure they remain focused upon their objectives.

Topic list	Learning outcomes	Syllabus references	Ability required
1 Types of audit and the chronology of an audit	C(ii)	C(5)	Evaluation
2 Planning of internal audit work	C(ii),(iii),(iv)	C(2)	Evaluation
3 Control and management of internal audits	C(ii),(iii),(iv)	C(5)	Evaluation
4 Reporting the results of internal audits	C(ii),(iii),(iv)	C(5)	Evaluation
5 Management review of internal controls	C(ii),(vi)	C(1),(6)	Comprehension

1 Types of audit and the chronology of an audit

FAST FORWARD

Key stages of an audit are planning, ascertaining and **confirming** the **controls and systems, carrying out audit tests** and **reporting to management**.

1.1 Systems audit

Key term

Systems audit is the audit of the internal controls within a system. (CIMA *Official Terminology*)

This is the type of audit most commonly associated with the job of auditing. As its name implies, it is the **audit of any system**, although the term is commonly associated with the audit of accounting systems, such as cash and cheques, sales and receivables, non-current asset records and so on.

A systems audit tests and evaluates the internal controls within the system, to determine the following.

(a) How **good** are the **internal controls**?

(b) What **weaknesses** might there be in the **system** of **internal controls**?

(c) What **reliance** can **management place** on the internal controls that:

  (i) the **resources** of the organisation are being **managed effectively**; and
  (ii) the **information** being **provided** by the system is **accurate**.

The auditors must therefore investigate the nature of the control procedures within a system, and how well these procedures operate in practice. The objectives the audits will focus on include:

- **Suitable** and **accurate management information**
- **Compliance** with **procedures**, **laws** and **regulations**
- **Safeguarding assets**
- **Securing economies** and **efficiencies**
- **Accomplishing objectives**

The diagram overleaf shows the main stages of a systems audit. We will now look at the various stages identified in the diagram.

1.2 Stage 1

The first stage in any audit should be to determine its **scope** and the auditors' **general approach**. The scope of the audit will be determined by management and by the Chief Internal Auditor.

Auditors normally prepare an **audit planning memorandum** to be placed on the audit file. The purpose of this memorandum is to provide a record of the major areas to which the auditors attach special significance and to highlight any particular difficulties or points of concern peculiar to the subject of the audit.

The detailed audit planning which arises from the determination of the scope of work is normally contained in an **audit programme**, which details the extent of testing, the types of tests to be carried out, and so on.

1.3 Stages 2 - 4

The objectives of these stages are as follows.

(a) **Stage 2**

To **confirm** the **flow** of **documents** and extent of controls in existence. This is very much a fact-finding exercise, achieved by discussing the accounting system and document flow with all the relevant departments, including typically, sales, purchases, cash, stock and accounts personnel. It is good practice to make a rough record of the system during this fact finding stage, which will be converted to a formal record at Stage 3 below.

(b) **Stage 3**

To prepare a **comprehensive record** to facilitate evaluation of the systems or validate the existing records. The system may be recorded using the following methods.

- Charts, for example organisation charts and records of the books of account
- Narrative notes
- Internal control questionnaires (ICQs)
- Flowcharts

(c) **Stage 4**

To confirm that the system recorded is the same as that in operation. After completion of the preparation (or update) of the systems records the auditors will confirm their understanding of the system by performing **walk-through tests**. For accounting systems this will involve tracing literally a handful of transactions of each type through the system. This procedure will establish that there is no reason to suppose that the system does not operate in the manner ascertained and recorded. The need for this check arises as staff under audit will occasionally tell the auditors what they should be doing (the established procedures) rather than what is actually being done in practice.

1.4 Stage 5

The purpose of evaluating the systems is to **gauge** their **reliability** and formulate a basis for testing their effectiveness in practice. Following the evaluation, the auditors will be able to **recommend improvements** to the system and determine the extent of the further tests to be carried out at Stages 7 and 9/10 below.

1.5 Stage 6

It is normal to **submit a report** to **management** suggesting improvements to internal controls both at this stage and after evaluating the systems and carrying out tests of controls, (at Stage 8). Where internal controls are so weak that they can provide no audit evidence, then a full transactions audit may be necessary.

1.6 Stage 7

Key term

Tests of control are tests to obtain audit evidence about the effective operation of the accounting and internal control systems, that is, that properly designed controls identified in the preliminary assessment of control risk exist in fact and have operated effectively throughout the relevant period.

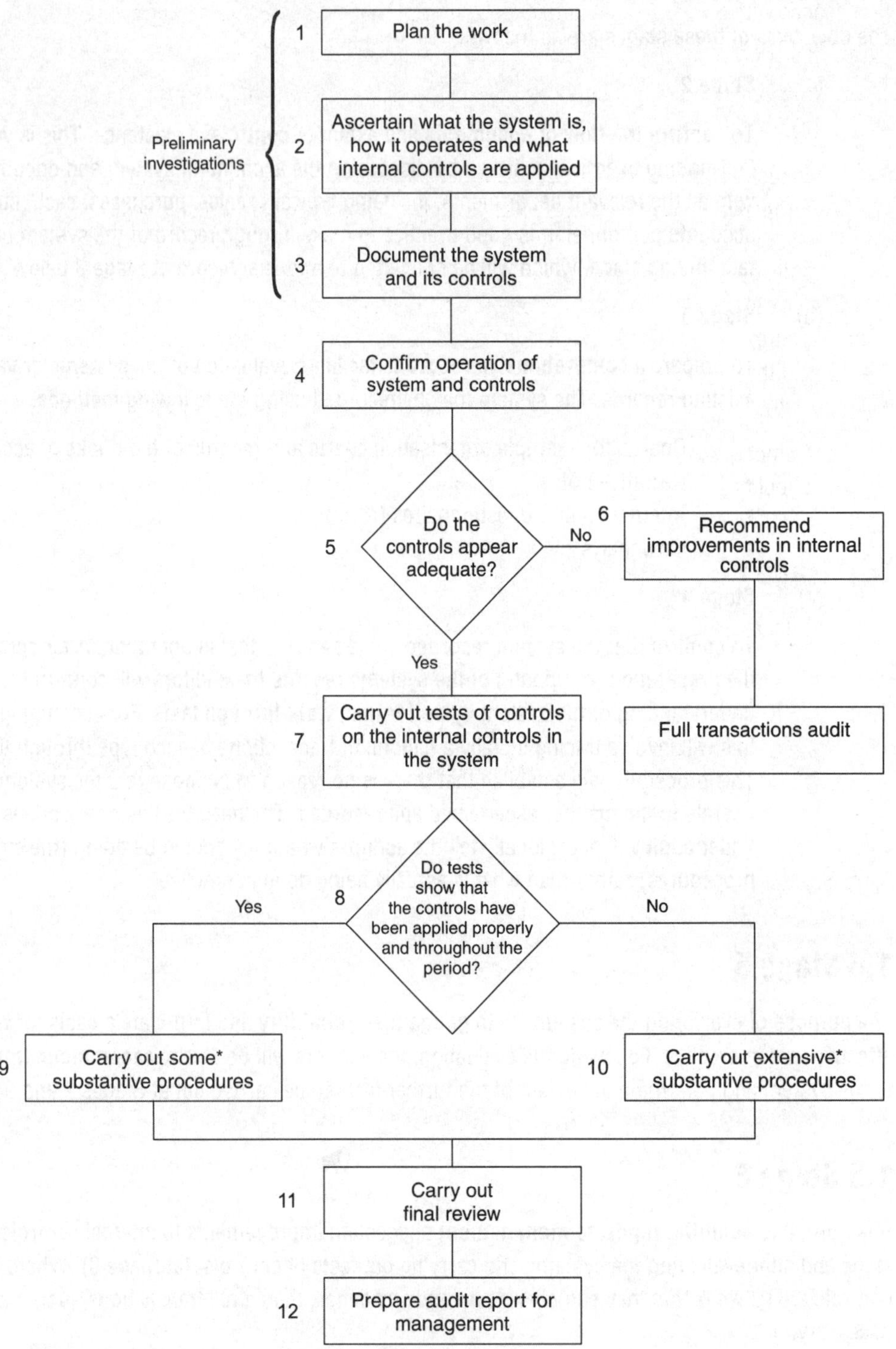

* The extent of substantive procedures will depend on:

(a) how much reliance the auditor can place on the internal controls that exist, even if they work properly;

(b) the frequency with which internal controls appear to have malfunctioned;

(c) whether other internal controls exist that act as a 'double check' to prevent errors in the financial records so that even if one has malfunctioned, there should be no adverse consequences.

Given effective controls, the objective is to select and **perform** tests or **controls** designed to establish compliance with the system, ie to test the controls. These are like walk-through checks in so far as they are concerned with the workings of the system. They differ in that they:

(a) are concerned only with those areas subject to effective control;
(b) cover a representative sample of transactions throughout the period.

When conducting **tests of controls**, the internal auditors are looking at the controls to see if they are working properly. This is *not* the same as looking at the transactions themselves.

For example, one of the internal controls might be that a clerk checks the addition on an invoice and initials a box to say that he has done so. If he fails to perform this arithmetic check, then there has been a control failure, regardless of whether the invoice had, in fact, been added up correctly or incorrectly. Similarly, if the clerk puts on his initials, indicating that the claim did add up, but the internal auditors subsequently discover that it was added incorrectly, then there has again been a control failure.

One of the most important points underlying modern auditing is that, if the controls are strong, the records should be reliable and consequently the amount of detailed testing can be reduced.

1.7 Stage 8

The conclusion drawn from the results of a test of controls may be either:

(a) That the **controls** are **effective**. This will impact on the work of external audits, as they will only need to carry out restricted substantive procedures.

(b) That the **controls** are **ineffective** in practice although they had appeared strong on paper. In this case the external auditors will need to carry out more extensive substantive procedures.

1.8 Stages 9 and 10

Key term

Substantive procedures are tests to obtain audit evidence to detect material misstatements in the financial statements. They are generally of two types:

(a) analytical procedures; and

(b) other substantive procedures, such as tests of details of transactions and balances, review of minutes of directors' meetings and enquiry. (APB)

External auditors are primarily responsible for carrying out substantive tests on the financial statements, although internal auditors may provide limited assistance. Internal auditors may also carry out their own work substantiating the figures in the management accounting records, for example reviewing the comparisons of actual with budgeted performance and confirming the figures for actual performance.

The procedures are designed for two purposes:

(a) to **support** the **figures** in the accounts and the assertions which support them; and
(b) where **errors exist**, to **assess their effect** in monetary terms.

1.9 Stages 11 and 12

(a) **Stage 11**

The aim of the **overall review** (including analytical procedures) is to determine the **overall reliability** of the accounts by making a critical analysis of content and presentation. Again this is predominantly a feature of the substantive audit.

(b) **Stage 12**

The **report to management** is the **end product** of the audit. Its purpose is to make further suggestions for improvements in the systems and to place on record specific points in connection with the audit and accounts, as well as producing an overall conclusion on the audit work.

2 Planning of internal audit work

FAST FORWARD

An internal audit department should plan its work carefully through the preparation of strategic, tactical and operational plans.

- The **strategic plan** is a rolling, long-term plan which, using various criteria, identifies areas for future investigation and specifies which types of audit are required.
- The **tactical plan** timetables audits for about a year in advance, allocates resources to each audit and spells out their objectives.
- The **operational plan** specifies exactly what work is to be carried out on an individual audit, and may utilise checklists in the form of audit programmes.

2.1 Aims of audit planning

As with any other activity or enterprise, an internal audit department must plan its work carefully if it is to achieve the audit objectives efficiently and effectively. The aim of audit planning is:

(a) **Decide priorities** for audit work
(b) **Establish objectives** (and apply control measures to ensure that objectives are achieved)
(c) Ensure that audit resources are used efficiently, effectively and cost-effectively

2.2 Benefits of audit planning

Every audit section must operate under some sort of plan. The chief internal auditor must plan his staff's workload and ensure that the varying abilities of his staff are put to the best use. Audit planning serves several needs and produces a range of benefits.

For the Chief Internal Auditor, the benefits will be as follows.

(a) Planning makes it necessary to examine and **critically assess** all **audit activity**. Ascertaining the various objectives of the audit function and specifying the steps necessary to achieve them involves seeking to use the scarce resources of audit staff to maximum effect.

(b) An audit plan **motivates** and **encourages personal commitment** by providing predetermined targets for both senior and junior staff. It should also help guide the production and control of a recruitment and training programme.

(c) The plan will assist the chief auditor to **exercise control** by providing a series of targets against which he can measure actual performance.

(d) The plan provides the chief auditor with a means of **conveying the objectives** of the audit section and evidence of results achieved, to the finance director, other directors and to the external auditor.

(e) An audit plan shows the **planned work**. It can also be used to reveal those areas of work which it will not be possible to cover during the period of the plan.

(f) The existence of an audit plan will demonstrate that the audit section has **deadlines** to meet and **targets** to achieve. It may help to avoid the use of auditors on non-audit duties.

(g) In submitting a plan to the finance director and to the board of directors, the chief internal auditor is **involving senior management** in considering and approving a work plan for his section. In some organisations an audit committee may oversee the work of the audit section.

Generally speaking, planning can be divided into three parts.

- Strategic
- Tactical
- Operational

2.3 Strategic audit planning

The strategic plan sets out audit objectives in broad terms, including areas to be covered, frequency of coverage and rough estimate of resource requirements.

Usually, the strategic plan covers a period of two to five years. It must be regularly reviewed and adjusted in the light of any changes of audit requirements or any information arising out of audit work.

The starting point for any strategic audit plan is a general awareness of the environment in which the internal audit department, and indeed the organisation as a whole, operates. The internal auditors need to be familiar with the following.

(a) The **historical background** of the organisation, and the **characteristics** of the organisation's operations. This will mean the present activities and performance of the company can be put into context.

(b) The **structure** of the **organisation**. This will include:

  (i) The **organisation chart**, showing the names, responsibilities and authority limits of the officials

  (ii) The **location** of the main operating and accounting centres, and any other centres where company assets are held

(c) **How** the organisation **operates**. This will include:

  (i) The flow of documentation including budgets and reports
  (ii) The books of account and ancillary records

Such basic information should be held in **permanent files** within the internal audit department, and it only needs to be reviewed annually or updated whenever any significant changes occur.

2.3.1 Selecting areas for investigation

The internal auditors then have to consider what areas need to be investigated. Sometimes management will instruct them to look into a certain topic, but for the most part, the internal auditors need some yardstick which they can use to determine whether some segment of the company is important enough to merit investigation. By segment of the company we mean, for example, a specific function or business process, or a transactions flow, or even the work of a physical department located somewhere in the building.

Suppose the internal auditors are considering whether the work of a section which authorises invoices for payment is worth investigation. The criteria which they should bear in mind while making this judgement are as follows.

(a) **Financial**

The volume and size of income and expenditure transactions, or the value of assets (see also Section 5 on materiality)

(b) **Internal control**

The existence or otherwise of controls which cover areas identified in (a) above

(c) **Probity**

Whether there is any evidence of past inaccuracies or fraud

(d) **Business goals**

Whether the organisation has laid down explicit objectives and policies against which its achievements can be measured

(e) **Business effects**

Whether the business generates any consequences, internal or external, which need to be investigated

(f) **Value for money**

Whether there is likely to be any waste which can be eliminated

(g) **Special investigations**: whether management has requested the internal audit department to undertake any specific tasks

Management should be asked to **approve objectives** set by the strategic audit plan, if only because it keeps senior managers aware of the importance of internal audit in the internal control system and lets them know what reports are to be expected; and it also gives management a chance to contribute towards the strategic plan.

One of the problems with setting a strategic audit plan, or almost any plan for that matter, is that it is often difficult to know just which **areas** are **important** enough to merit investigation or routine checking, and which are not.

Such an approach means that the internal auditors are forced to rely heavily on their own, or management's **judgement**. Inevitably this turns the setting of a strategic plan into rather a subjective exercise.

2.4 Tactical audit planning

Once the internal auditors have set out their strategic plan, and agreed it with management, it is necessary to prepare a **tactical plan**.

In many ways a tactical audit plan is the easiest type of audit plan to draw up. Basically, it takes the **areas of work** laid down in the strategic plan and matches them to audit resources and timetables. It covers a period of about six months to a year, and will include the following features.

- **Programme** of internal audits to be carried out
- Detailed definition of the **objectives** of each audit
- Detailed **allocation** of audit **resources**

A tactical plan must not be too rigid and should ideally include a **contingency allowance**, to take account of such factors as staff movements and unexpected requests from management for special investigations. In other words, the plan should include some unallocated 'spare' time which can be used up on any unexpected activities.

The tactical plan should be fairly straightforward to prepare, because areas for investigation have already been identified in the strategic plan, and detailed planning of individual audits does not come at this stage.

2.5 Operational audit planning

An operational internal audit plan will be drawn up for each **individual audit**. It is based on the **objectives** as broadly indicated in the strategic plan, on resource and timetabling considerations within the tactical plan, on results of previous audits, and any other relevant data. When completed, it should show:

(a) **Detailed audit objectives**
(b) The **extent of coverage** and areas to be given emphasis
(c) **Target dates** for individual stages of the audit
(d) **Names of auditors** responsible for or involved in the completion of the audit

The areas where particular emphasis will be placed include areas where:

- There are **known weaknesses** in **internal control**
- Analytical review has identified **problems or unusual features**
- **Risks** have otherwise been identified
- **Material areas**

2.6 Materiality

FAST FORWARD

Materiality is a concept fundamental to internal audit. It needs to be considered at all stages of an audit, not only in terms of amount but also by using non-quantifiable criteria.

There are no laid down standards or guidelines, but materiality is usually set as a **percentage of profit**, **turnover** or **total assets**.

Key term

Materiality is 'an expression of the relative significance or importance of a particular matter in the context of financial statements as a whole. A matter is material if its omission or misstatement would reasonably influence the decisions of an addressee of the auditors' report. Materiality may also be considered in the context of any individual primary statement within the financial statements or of individual items included in them. Materiality is not capable of general mathematical definition as it has both qualitative and quantitative aspects.'

2.6.1 Forms of materiality

Auditors should consider materiality and its **relationship** with **audit risk** when conducting an audit. Assessing the materiality of an item is essentially an attempt to decide what is **important** and what is not in the context of the area being examined. An item will be material if it involves a big cost or expense, or a large amount of income. Deciding what is material is not however a decision which is made solely on the basis of the size or amount of the item in question.

There are three **forms** of materiality in internal audit.

(a) **Materiality by value**

An error of a sufficient value or amount to be judged material by its size.

(b) **Materiality by nature**

Non-quantitative criteria by which an error or irregularity may be judged material regardless of its size. For example, an internal auditor may be looking at a cheque drawn by a director for £50. The amount is hardly likely to be material, but if the auditor suspects that the £50 should never have been cashed in the first place, then the transaction becomes very material indeed because of its sensitive nature. Weak internal controls, or internal control failures in the petty cash procedures, might also be a highly sensitive and so 'material' matter.

(c) **Materiality by form of disclosure**

It depends who an audit report is being prepared for, and why. For one manager, it might be sufficient to report information in aggregated totals, whereas for another manager, data should be desegregated and analysed in much greater detail.

2.6.2 Materiality at the planning stage

Materiality considerations during **audit planning** are extremely important. The assessment of materiality at this stage should be based on the most recent and reliable financial information and will help to determine an effective and efficient audit approach. Materiality assessment will help the auditors to decide:

(a) **What items** to **examine**
(b) Whether to use **sampling techniques**

and other such matters.

The resulting combination of audit procedures should help to reduce audit risk to an appropriately low level.

To set the materiality level the auditors need to decide the level of errors which would distort the view given by the accounts. Because many users of accounts are primarily interested in the **profitability** of the organisation, the level is often expressed as a proportion of its profits (typically 5% of profit before tax).

Some argue, however, that it is better to think of materiality in terms of the **size** of the **organisation** and hence recognise that, if the company remains a fairly constant size, the materiality level should not change; similarly if the business is growing, the level of materiality will increase from year to year. The size of a company can be measured in terms of turnover and total assets before deducting any liabilities (sometimes referred to in legislation as 'the balance sheet total') both of which tend not to be subject to the fluctuations which may affect profit.

Auditors will often calculate a range of values, such as those shown below, and then take an average or weighted average of all the figures produced as the materiality level.

Value	%
Profit before tax	5
Gross profit	½ - 1
Turnover	½ - 1
Total assets	1 - 2
Net assets	2 - 5
Profit after tax	5 - 10

The effect of **planning materiality** on the audit process is shown in the diagram below.

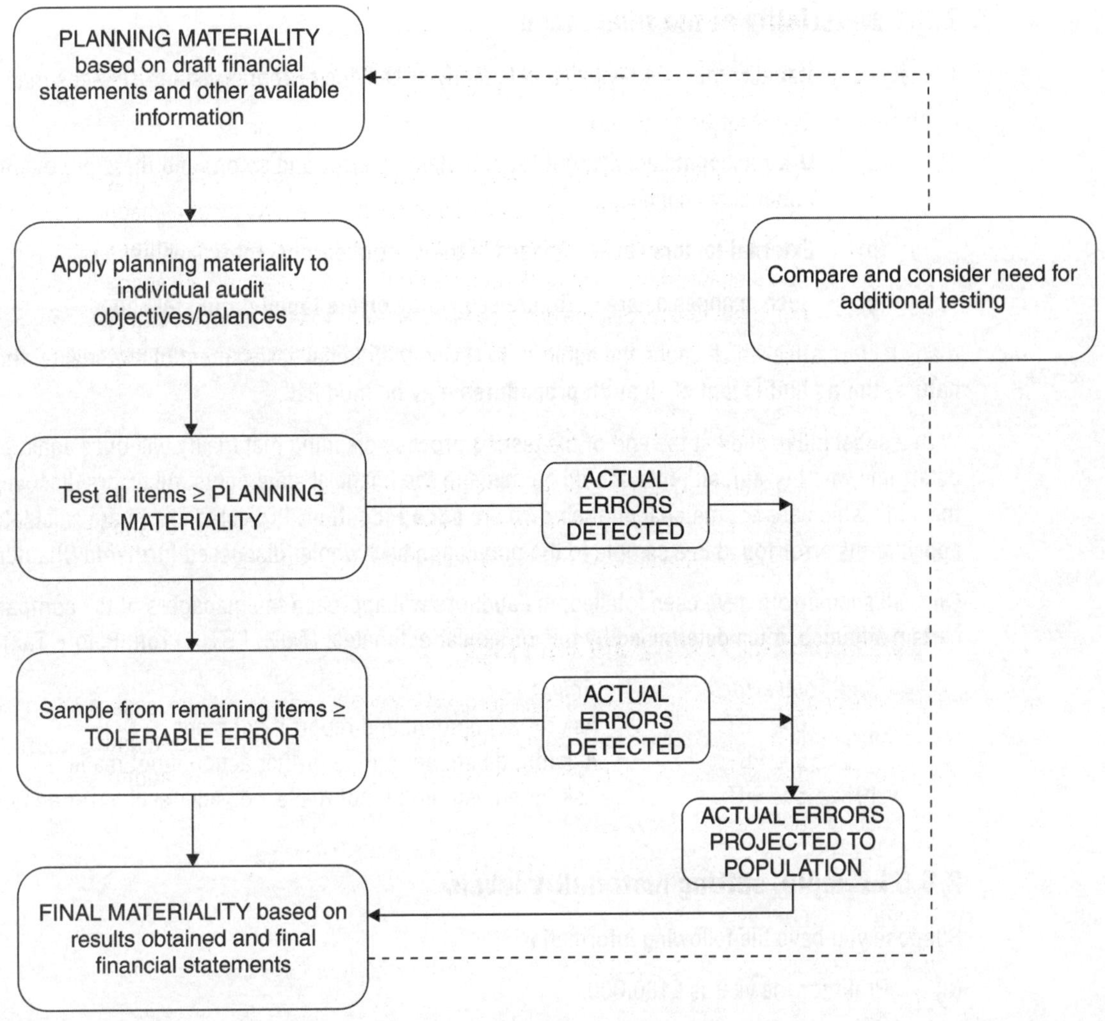

2.6.3 Tolerable error

Key term

Tolerable error is the maximum error in the population that the auditors are willing to accept and still conclude that the audit objective has been achieved.

Tolerable error may be set at planning materiality, but it is usually reduced to, say 75% or even 50% of planning materiality by taking account of sampling risk (see Chapter 22). The tolerable error is used to determine sample size.

Materiality levels should be set for individual audits as a whole and for separate parts of an individual audit.

A good example is an audit of the travel claims and payments system. Suppose that the total travel claim payments made in the year is not material to the accounts of the company (as is often the case). In other words, as far as the strategic plan is concerned, travel claim payments are not material.

But now suppose the internal audit department decides to audit travel claim payments anyway, perhaps because a fraud had been discovered there recently. What level of materiality should the auditors set? It is obviously pointless to use the level of materiality based on the accounts of the company (the strategic materiality) because it is known in advance that the total of travel payments is not material, never mind any inaccuracies discovered during the audit. Clearly some lower level of materiality (operational materiality) would have to be set for this particular area.

2.6.4 Materiality at the final stage

The level of materiality must be reviewed constantly as the audit progresses and changes may be required because:

(a) **Draft accounts** are **altered** (due to material error and so on) and therefore overall materiality changes

(b) **External factors** cause changes in the control or inherent risk estimates

(c) Such changes as are in (b) are caused by **errors found** during testing

If any factors arise which cause the auditors to revise their initial assessment of materiality, then the **nature**, **timing** and **extent** of all **audit procedures** may be modified.

With a substantive audit at the end of the testing process planning materiality will once again be used to determine whether **adjustments** should be made to the financial statements. All errors discovered during the audit which are not material on their own are **added together**. Projected errors are calculated by applying the error found in a sample to the population as a whole (discussed further in Chapter 22).

Once all such errors have been totalled, the auditors will approach the managers of the company with certain attitudes, often determined by this or similar estimates. (*Note.* PBT = Profit Before Tax).

Total error	*Action*
≥ 10% PBT	Ask for adjustment and report if not made.
≤ 5% PBT	Ask for adjustment but no further action if not made.
10% ≥ 5% PBT	Ask for adjustment; if not made, consider each error and combination.

2.6.5 Example: setting materiality levels

Suppose you have the following information.

(a) Profit for the year is £180,000.

(b) Turnover was £775,000.

(c) Total assets were £1,200,000.

(d) Travel and subsistence expenditure during the year amounted to £4,000.

(e) An extrapolation of the errors found during an audit of purchases indicated that purchases could be mis-stated in the financial accounts by as much as £9,500.

(f) Similar tests on travel and subsistence expenditure indicate that the annual charge of £4,000 could be over-stated by as much as £800.

Required

Set a level of materiality and comment on the errors found in the light of this materiality level.

Solution

A level for materiality could therefore be set at any one of the following levels.

(a) 5% of profit = £180,000 × 0.05 = £9,000.
(b) 0.75% of turnover = £775,000 × 0.0075 = £5,800 approx.
(c) 1% of total assets = £1,200,000 × 0.01 = £12,000.

Depending on which of these figures is used, the estimated £9,500 error on purchases could be viewed in three different ways.

(a) If materiality is £9,000, then strictly speaking the £9,500 is a material error. However, the sensible auditors realise that the level of materiality is set somewhat arbitrarily, so they are more likely to

say that there is a probable material error in the purchases figure and recommend to management that more time should be spent auditing the make-up of the purchases figure.

(b) If materiality is £5,800, then the £9,500 is a clear indication that there is a material error in the financial statements. The purchases figure should be altered, and management should be advised that time should be spent to find out what is going wrong.

(c) If materiality is £12,000, then the £9,500 does not represent a material error, and the audit report would say that the audit of purchases had proved satisfactory.

There are other methods of quantifying materiality for individual items within the profit and loss account or the balance sheet.

(a) For some items, *any* error would be material, because **exact values** should be obtainable. These include issued share capital, loan stock and dividends.

(b) Some errors in asset values might be considered material if their value exceeds a **certain proportion** of the total value of the assets, for example an error of more than 2% in stocks or debtors.

The point to bear in mind is that rules on setting a level for materiality are by no means fixed; an internal auditor will have to rely on **judgement** more often than on some set of figures in a textbook table.

3 Control and management of internal audits

FAST FORWARD

Audit work should be **controlled** and **recorded**. The recording of audit work assists with control. The chief internal auditor should ensure that quality control standards are maintained within his department.

Direction, **supervision** and **review** are key stages in the management of internal audit work.

3.1 Control of internal audits

The main features of control will be the **management** and **supervision** of the **internal audit staff** and the **review** of their work.

3.2 Management of internal audits

Any work delegated to assistants should be directed, supervised and reviewed in a manner which provides reasonable assurance that such work is performed competently.

3.2.1 Direction of internal audits

Direction of assistants will involve:

(a) Informing assistants of their **responsibilities** and the objectives of the procedures they are to perform

(b) Informing assistants of matters such as:

(i) The **nature** of the entity's **business**

(ii) Possible accounting or auditing **problems**, which may affect the procedures they are carrying out.

Directions are communicated orally, both informally and at briefing meetings and via audit manuals, checklists and of course the audit programme and overall audit plan.

3.2.2 Supervision of internal audits

Supervision is closely related to both direction and review and may involve elements of both. Personnel with supervisory duties will perform the following functions during an audit:

(a) **Monitor** the **progress** of the audit to consider whether:

 (i) Assistants have the **necessary skills** and competence to carry out their assigned tasks

 (ii) Assistants **understand** the **audit directions**

 (iii) The **work** is being **carried out** in accordance with the **overall audit plan** and the audit programme

(b) Become informed of and **address significant questions** raised during the audit, by assessing their significance and modifying the overall audit plan and the audit programme as appropriate

(c) **Resolve** any **differences** of **professional judgement** between personnel and consider the level of consultation that is appropriate

3.2.3 Review of internal audits

Work performed by each assistant should be **reviewed** by personnel of appropriate experience to consider whether:

(a) The **work** has been **performed** in **accordance** with **the audit programme**

(b) The **work** performed and the results obtained have been **adequately documented**

(c) Any **significant matters** have been **resolved** or are reflected in audit conclusions

(d) The **objectives** of the **audit procedures** have been **achieved**

(e) The **conclusions expressed** are **consistent** with the **results** of the **work performed** and support the audit opinion

The following should be reviewed on a timely basis:

(a) The overall **audit plan** and the **audit programme**

(b) The **assessments** of inherent and control **risks**, including the results of tests of control and the modifications, if any, made to the overall audit plan and the audit programme as a result thereof

(c) The **documentation** obtained from **audit procedures** and the conclusions drawn therefrom including the results of consultations

(d) The proposed **internal audit report** (and the financial statements where appropriate)

The Institute of Internal Auditors report *Systems Auditability and Control* suggests that **'quality assurance'** should take place at both senior/supervisor level and at the level of the Chief Internal Auditor.

4 Reporting the results of internal audit

FAST FORWARD

Reports on the results of internal audits should highlight the **risks** identified, the **weaknesses** found in controls, the **consequences** of the problems found and **recommendations** for improvements.

4.1 Objectives of reporting

4.1.1 Recommendations for change

The most important element of internal audit reporting is to **promote change** in the form of either **new or improved controls**. Descriptions of failings should promote change by emphasising the problems that need to be overcome and advising management on the steps needed to improve risk management strategies.

4.1.2 Assisting management identification of risk and control issues

We shall consider the review managers carry out of risk and control issues in Section 5. The auditors' report can emphasise the **importance of control issues** at times when other issues are being driven forward, for example new initiatives. Auditors can also help managers assess the effect of unmitigated risk. If auditors find that the internal control system is sound, then resources can be directed towards other areas.

4.1.3 Ensuring action takes place

Auditors should aim to have their **recommendations agreed by operational managers** and staff, as this should enhance the chances of their being actioned.

4.2 Forms of report

There are **no formal requirements** for such reports as there are for the statutory audit. The statutory audit report is a highly stylised document that is substantially the same for any audit.

There is however a **generally accepted format** for reports in business, which is laid out below. This format makes reports useful to readers as it highlights the conclusions drawn and gives easy reference to the user.

Standard report format
TERMS OF REFERENCE
EXECUTIVE SUMMARY – summarising conclusions drawn from assignment
BODY OF THE REPORT
APPENDICES FOR ANY ADDITIONAL INFORMATION

The report is likely also to be **dated**, **designated** as to whether it is draft or final and have a **'distribution list'** of directors and management who should read it attached.

4.2.1 Contents of the report

The **executive summary** of an internal audit report should give the following information.

- **Background** to the assignment
- **Objectives** of the assignment
- **Major outcomes** of the work
- Key **action points**
- **Summary of the work** left to do

The **main body** of the report will contain the detail; for example the audit tests carried out and their findings, full lists of action points, including details of who has responsibility for carrying them out, the future time-scale and costs.

4.2.2 Format of observations and recommendations

One clear way of presenting observations and findings in individual areas is as follows:

- **Business objective** that the manager is aiming to achieve
- **Operational standard**
- The **risks** of current practice
- **Control weaknesses** or lack of application of controls
- The **causes** of the weaknesses
- The **effect** of the weaknesses
- **Recommendations** to solve the weaknesses

The results of individual areas can be summarised in the main report:

- The **existing culture of control**, drawing attention to whether there is a lack of appreciation of the need for controls or good controls but a lack of ability to ensure compliance
- Overall opinion on **managers' willingness** to address risks and improve
- Implications of **outstanding risks**
- Results of **control evaluations**
- The **causes of basic problems**, including links between the problems in various areas

When drafting recommendations internal audit needs to consider:

- The **available options**, although the auditors' preferred solution needs to be emphasised
- The **removal of obstacles to control**. It may be most important to remove general obstacles such as poor communication or lack of management willingness to enforce controls before making specific recommendations to improve controls
- **Resource issues**, how much will recommendations actually cost and also the costs of poor control

Recommendations should be linked in with the **terms of reference**, the **audit performed** and the **results**.

5 Management review of internal controls

FAST FORWARD

Consideration of the results of internal audit work should form part of **board review of internal controls** and **risk management**.

5.1 Audit and board review

We mentioned in Section B the importance of manager review of internal controls and the results of internal audit work obviously play a major part in this review. In the last section of this chapter we shall look in more detail at management's review of internal controls since it is effectively the last stage of the audit process.

5.2 Review of internal controls

The UK's **Turnbull committee**. suggested that review of internal controls should be an **integral part** of the **company's operations**; the board, or board committees, should actively consider reports on control issues from others operating internal controls.

In particular the board should consider:

(a) The identification, evaluation and management of all **key risks** affecting the organisation

(b) The **effectiveness of internal control**; again that does not just mean financial controls but also operational, compliance and risk management controls

(c) The **action taken** if any **weaknesses** are found

The report recommends that when assessing the **effectiveness of internal control**, boards should consider the following:

(a) The **nature** and **extent** of the **risks** which face the company and which it regards as **acceptable** for the company to bear within its particular business

(b) The **threat** of such **risks becoming** a **reality**

(c) If that happened, the company's ability to **reduce** the **incidence** and **impact** on the business

(d) The **costs and benefits** related to operating relevant controls

In order to be able to carry out an effective review, boards should regularly receive and review reports and information on internal control, concentrating on:

(a) What the **risks** are and how they have been **identified**, **evaluated** and **managed**

(b) The **effectiveness** of the internal control system in the management of risk, in particular how any weaknesses have been dealt with

(c) Whether **actions** are being taken to **reduce** the risks found

(d) Whether the results indicate that **internal control** should be **monitored more extensively**

Question **Internal control review**

Learning outcome: C(i)

What sort of information would help the board carry out an effective review?

Answer

The UK's Institute of Internal Auditors suggests that the board needs to consider the following information in order to carry out an effective review.

- The organisation's **Code of Business Conduct**
- Confirmation that line managers are **clear as to their objectives**
- The overall results of a **control self assessment** process by line management or staff
- **Letters of representation** ('comfort letters') on internal control from line management
- A **report** from the board on the **key procedures** which are designed to provide effective internal control
- **Reports from internal audit** on audits performed

- The audit committee's **assessment** of the **effectiveness of internal audit**
- Reports on **special reviews** commissioned by the audit committee from internal audit or others
- Internal audit's **overall summary opinion on internal control**
- The **external auditors' report on weaknesses** in the accounting and internal control systems and other matters, including errors, identified during the audit
- **Intelligence** gathered by board members during the year
- A **report on avoidable losses** by the finance director
- A **report on any material developments** since the balance sheet date and the present
- The board's proposed wording of **the internal control report** for publication

5.3 Annual review of controls

In addition, when directors are considering annually the disclosures they are required to make about internal controls, they should conduct an **annual review** of internal control. This should be wider-ranging than the regular review; in particular it should cover:

(a) The **changes** since the last **assessment** in **risks** faced, and the company's **ability** to **respond** to **changes** in its business environment

(b) The **scope** and **quality** of management's monitoring of risk and internal control, and of the work of internal audit, or consideration of the need for an internal audit function if the company does not have one

(c) The **extent** and **frequency** of reports to the board

(d) **Significant controls**, **failings** and **weaknesses** which have or might have material impacts upon the accounts

(e) The **effectiveness** of the **public reporting** processes

5.4 Reporting on risk management

Per the Turnbull report the board should disclose as a minimum in the accounts, the existence of a **process** for **managing risks**, how the board had **reviewed** the **effectiveness** of the process and that the **process accords** with the **Turnbull guidance**. The board should also include:

(a) An **acknowledgement** that they are responsible for the company's system of internal financial control and reviewing its effectiveness

(b) An **explanation** that such a system is designed to **manage** rather than eliminate the risk of **failure** to **achieve business objectives**, and can only provide **reasonable** and not absolute **assurance** against material misstatement or **loss**

(c) A **summary** of the process that the **directors** (or a board committee) have **used to review the effectiveness** of the system of internal financial control and consider the need for an internal audit function if the company does not have one. There should also be disclosure of the process the board has used to deal with **material internal control aspects** of **any significant problems** disclosed in the annual accounts

(d) **Information** about those **weaknesses** in internal financial control that have resulted in material losses, contingencies or uncertainties which require disclosure in the financial statements or the auditor's report on the financial statements.

5.5 Significance of Turnbull recommendations

The system recommended by the Turnbull report is notable because of the following.

(a) It is **forward looking**.

(b) It is **open**, requiring appropriate disclosures to all stakeholders in the company about the risks being taken.

(c) It does **not seek** to **eliminate risk**. It is constructive in its approach to opportunity management, as well as concerned with 'disaster prevention'. To succeed companies are not required to take fewer risks than others but they do need a good understanding of what risks they can handle.

(d) It **unifies all business units** of a company into an integrated risk review, so that the same 'language' of risk (risk terminology) is applied throughout the company.

(e) It is **strategic**, and driven by business objectives, particularly the need for the company to adapt to its changing business environment.

(f) It should be **re-evaluated on a regular basis**.

(g) It should be **durable**, evolving as the business and its environment changes.

(h) In order to create shareholder value, a company needs to **manage the risks** it faces and communicate to the capital markets how it is carrying out this task.

Chapter Roundup

- **Key stages of an audit are planning, ascertaining** and **confirming** the **controls and systems, carrying out audit tests** and **reporting to management.**
- An internal audit department should plan its work carefully through the preparation of strategic, tactical and operational plans.
  - The **strategic plan** is a rolling, long-term plan which, using various criteria, identifies areas for future investigation and specifies which types of audit are required.
  - The **tactical plan** timetables audits for about a year in advance, allocates resources to each audit and spells out their objectives.
  - The **operational plan** specifies exactly what work is to be carried out on an individual audit, and may utilise checklists in the form of audit programmes.
- **Materiality** is a concept fundamental to internal audit. It needs to be considered at all stages of an audit, not only in terms of amount but also by using non-quantifiable criteria.
- There are no laid down standards or guidelines, but materiality is usually set as a **percentage** of **profit**, **turnover** or **total assets**.
- Audit work should be **controlled** and **recorded**. The recording of audit work assists with control. The chief internal auditor should ensure that quality control standards are maintained within his department.
- **Direction**, **supervision** and **review** are key stages in the management of internal audit work.
- Reports on the results of internal audits should highlight the **risks** identified, the **weaknesses** found in controls, the **consequences** of the problems found and **recommendations** for improvements.
- Consideration of the results of internal audit work should form part of **board review of internal controls** and **risk management**.

Quick Quiz

1 Why should auditors carry out walkthrough tests?

2 What criteria should the internal auditors bear in mind when deciding which areas should be covered in a strategic audit plan?

3 What is contained in a tactical audit plan?

4 What are the three forms of materiality?

5 What are the key tasks that staff with supervisory responsibilities should perform during an audit?

6 What are the main things that a review of audit work should cover?

7 When reporting on internal controls, auditors should place most emphasis on the risks of specific controls not working.

True ☐

False ☐

8 According to the Turnbull report, what should be the main elements in an annual review of audit work by the board?

Answers to Quick Quiz

1 To confirm that the systems that have been recorded are the same as those actually in operation.

2
- Financial
- Internal control
- Probity
- Business goals
- Business effects
- Value for money
- Special investigations

3
- Programme of internal audits to be carried out
- Definition of the objectives of each audit
- Allocation of audit resources

4
- Value
- Nature
- Form of disclosure

5
- Monitoring the progress of an audit
- Becoming informed of and addressing significant questions raised during the audit
- Resolving any differences of professional judgement

6
- The work has been performed in accordance with the audit programme
- The work performed and results obtained have been adequately documented
- Significant matters have been resolved or are reflected in audit conclusions
- Objectives of audit procedures have been achieved
- Conclusions expressed are consistent with results of work performed and support the audit opinion

7 False. Not necessarily. Auditors may wish to emphasise above all pervasive factors that undermine the whole system of controls, for example failure by management to realise the importance of controls. Until these are addressed, there may be little point in recommending improvements in individual controls.

8
- The changes since the last assessment in risks faced, and the company's ability to respond to changes
- The scope and quality of management's monitoring of risk and internal control, and of the work of internal audit
- The extent and frequency of reports to the board
- Significant controls, failings and weaknesses which have or might have material impacts upon the accounts
- The effectiveness of the public reporting processes

Now try the question below from the Exam Question Bank

Number	Level	Marks	Time
Q12	Introductory	N/a	35 mins

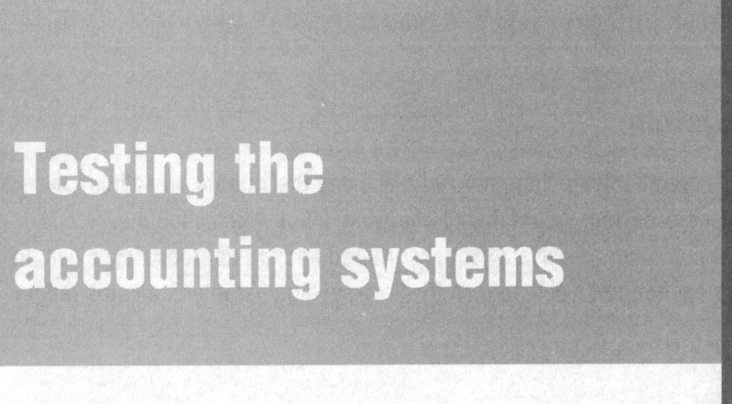

Testing the accounting systems

Introduction

We have mentioned tests of controls in previous chapters and have considered methods of sample selection and evaluation. In this chapter we will look at **how tests of controls** might be **applied in practice**. We will examine each major component of an average accounting system.

For each of the components we shall look at the risks and the aims of the control system. We give examples of common controls. We shall then go on to look at a 'standard' programme of tests of controls.

The way to approach questions is not to learn list after list of controls, but

(a) **Identify** the **risks** in the situation described

(b) Think how the business will aim to combat those risks and what controls it can use to **prevent** problems or **identify** problems and minimise their effects.

(c) Think how the internal auditors can **confirm** that these controls are operating effectively.

Topic list	Learning outcomes	Syllabus references	Ability required
1 The sales system	C(ii),(iii)	C(1)	Evaluation
2 The purchases and expenses system	C(ii),(iii)	C(1)	Evaluation
3 The wages system	C(ii),(iii)	C(1)	Evaluation
4 The cash system	C(ii),(iii)	C(1)	Evaluation
5 The inventory system	C(ii),(iii)	C(1)	Evaluation
6 Revenue and capital expenditure	C(ii),(iii)	C(1)	Evaluation

1 The sales system

FAST FORWARD

- Tests of controls of the **sales system** will be based around:
  - **Selling** (authorisation)
  - **Goods outwards** (custody)
  - **Accounting** (recording)

1.1 Features of sales system

For **sales**, businesses want to give credit only to customers who will **pay their debts**. In addition there are various stages of the selling process-**ordering**, **dispatch and charging**, all of which should be **documented** and **matched** so that customers receive what they ordered and are appropriately billed. In order to keep track of who owes what and to be able to identify slow-paying customers, a **sales ledger** should be maintained.

1.2 Risks

- **Failure** to **identify poor credit risk**
- Customers being allowed **credits** that are **not bona fide**
- **Goods being supplied** to a **poor credit risk**
- Customers being **invoiced** for the **wrong amounts**
- **Failure to record sales** completely in accounting records

1.3 Aims of controls

1.3.1 Ordering and granting of credit

- **Goods** and **services** are **only supplied** to **customers** with **good credit ratings**
- **Customers** are encouraged to **pay promptly**
- **Orders** are **recorded correctly**
- **Orders** are **fulfilled**

1.3.2 Dispatch and invoicing

- All **dispatches** of goods are **recorded**
- All **goods and services** sold are **correctly invoiced**
- All **invoices** raised **relate to goods and services supplied** by the business
- Credit notes are only given for **valid reasons**

1.3.3 Recording, accounting and credit control

- All sales that have been **invoiced** are **recorded** in the general and sales ledgers
- All **credit notes** that have been **issued** are **recorded** in the general and sales ledgers
- All **entries** in the sales ledger are **made** to the **correct** sales ledger **accounts**
- **Cut-off** is applied correctly to the sales ledger
- Potentially **doubtful debts** are **identified**

1.4 Controls

1.4.1 Controls: ordering and credit approval process

- **Segregation** of duties; credit control, invoicing and inventory dispatch
- **Authorisation** of **credit terms** to customers
  - References/credit checks obtained
  - Authorisation by senior staff
  - Regular review
- **Authorisation** for changes in **other customer data**
- Checks on customer files to ensure **orders** only **accepted** from **customers** who have no credit problems
- **Sequential numbering** of blank pre-printed order documents
- **Up-to-date price lists** used to quote prices to customers
- **Matching** of **customer orders** with production orders and dispatch notes and querying of orders not matched
- **Customer queries** are dealt with promptly

1.4.2 Controls: dispatches and invoice preparation

- **Authorisation** of **dispatch** of **goods**
  - Dispatch only on sales order
  - Dispatch only to authorised customers
  - Special authorisation of dispatches of goods free of charge or on special terms
- **Examination** of **goods outwards** as to quantity, quality and condition
- **Recording** of **goods outwards**
- **Agreement** of **goods outwards records to customer orders, dispatch notes** and **invoices**
- **Prenumbering** of dispatch notes and delivery notes and regular checks on sequence
- **Condition** of **returns checked**
- Recording of goods returned on **goods returned notes**
- **Signature** of **delivery notes** by customers
- Preparation of invoices and credit notes
  - **Authorisation** of **selling prices**/use of **price lists**
  - **Authorisation** of **credit notes**
  - **Checks on prices, quantities, extensions** and totals on invoices and credit notes
  - **Sequential numbering** of blank invoices/credit notes and regular sequence checks
- **Inventory records updated**
- **Matching** of sales **invoices** with **dispatch** and **delivery** notes and sales orders
- **Regular review** for **dispatch notes** not matched by invoices

1.4.3 Controls: accounting, recording and credit problems

- **Segregation of duties**: recording sales, maintaining customer accounts and preparing statements
- **Recording** of **sales invoices** sequence and **control** over **spoilt invoices**
- **Matching** of **cash receipts** with **invoices**
- **Retention** of **customer remittance advices**
- **Separate recording** of **sales returns, price adjustments** etc
- **Cut-off procedures** to ensure goods dispatched and not invoiced (or vice versa) are properly dealt with the correct period
- Regular **preparation** of **trade accounts receivable statements**
- **Checking** of **trade accounts receivable statements**
- **Safeguarding** of **trade accounts receivable statements** so that they cannot be altered before dispatch
- **Review** and **follow-up** of **overdue accounts**
- **Authorisation** of **writing off** of **bad debts**
- **Reconciliation** of **sales ledger control account**
- Analytical review of sales ledger and profit margins

1.5 Tests of controls

1.5.1 Tests of control: ordering and granting of credit

- **Check** that **references** are being **obtained** for **all new customers**
- **Check** that all **new accounts** on the sales ledger have been **authorised** by senior staff
- **Check** that **orders** are only **accepted** from customers who are **within** their **credit terms** and **credit limits**
- **Check** that **customer orders** are being **matched** with **production orders** and **dispatch notes**

1.5.2 Tests of control: dispatches and invoices

- **Verify details** of **trade sales** or goods dispatched notes with **sales invoices checking quantities, prices**, **discounts**, **correct analysis** and **posting to sales ledger**
- **Verify details** of trade sales with **entries in inventory records**
- **Verify non-routine** sales (scrap, non current assets etc) with **appropriate supporting evidence** and **approval** by authorised officials
- Verify **credit notes** with **correspondence** or other supporting evidence, **approval** by authorised officials and entries in inventory and sales accounting records
- **Test numerical sequence** of **dispatch notes** and **enquire** into **missing numbers**
- **Test numerical sequence** of **invoices** and **credit notes**, **enquire** into **missing numbers** and **inspect copies** of those cancelled
- **Test numerical sequence** of **order forms** and enquire into missing numbers
- **Check** that **dispatches** of **goods free of charge** or on **special terms** have been **authorised** by management

1.5.3 Tests of control: recording of and accounting for sales

Sales day book

- **Check entries** with **invoices** and **credit notes** respectively
- **Check additions** and **cross casts**
- **Check postings** to **sales ledger control account**
- **Check postings** to **sales ledger**

Sales ledger

- **Check entries** in a **sample of accounts** to sales day book
- **Check additions** and **balances** carried down
- **Note** and **enquire** into **contra entries**
- **Check** that **control accounts** have been **regularly reconciled** to total of sales ledger balances
- **Scrutinise accounts** to see if credit limits have been observed
- **Check** that **trade accounts receivable statements** are **prepared** and **sent out regularly**
- **Check** that **overdue accounts** have been **followed up**
- **Check** that **all bad debts written off** have been **authorised** by management

Exam focus point

In the exam you may be asked:

(a) What controls are appropriate for a specific situation?
(b) What are the major weaknesses in the system given in the question?
(c) What are the consequences of the failure or non-existence of controls?
(d) What tests would auditors use on the controls given in the question?

If you are asked about appropriate controls or weaknesses, remember the objectives for the accounting area and the main risks involved. Controls should be in place to fulfil the objectives given, weaknesses will mean that the objectives are not fulfilled. You should also consider the documentation and staff involved in each area.

You should give enough detail about the controls you suggest to enable a non-accountant to implement the controls.

You should use a similar thought process when deciding how to test the controls. Think of the objectives of the system; assess how the controls given fulfil those objectives; and set out tests which demonstrate whether the controls are working. Remember that different types of test can be used to test different controls. Inspection for example can be used to test whether different documents are being compared or documents are being properly authorised. Computation can be used to check invoices have been properly completed or reconciliations correctly made.

Question

Complete recording

Learning outcome: C(iii)

What tests of control can give auditors assurance that the company's system of control ensures that sales are completely recorded?

Answer

Tests of control over completeness of recording of sales include:

(a) **Sequence tests** on sales orders, dispatch notes, invoices and credit notes to ensure that there are no missing numbers or two documents with the same number

(b) **Comparisons** of **dispatch notes** with **order and invoices**, checking documents are cross-referenced to each other

(c) **Checking posting** of **sales day book** to **sales ledger control account** and **sales ledger**

(d) **Checking control account reconciliations** have been carried out and have been reviewed by senior staff

(e) **Controls over computerised input** including:

(i) Control totals
(ii) Checking of output to source documents
(iii) Procedure over resubmisson of rejected inputs

Question

Weaknesses and tests of controls

Learning outcome: C(iii)

You are the auditor of Arcidiacono Stationery, and you have been asked to suggest how audit work should be carried out on the sales system.

Arcidiacono Stationery sells stationery to shops. Most sales are to small customers who do not have a sales ledger account. They can collect their purchases and pay by cash. For cash sales:

(a) The customer orders the stationery from the sales department, which raises a pre-numbered multi-copy order form.

(b) The dispatch department make up the order and give it to the customer with a copy of the order form.

(c) The customer gives the order form to the cashier who prepares a hand-written sales invoice.

(d) The customer pays the cashier for the goods by cheque or in cash.

(e) The cashier records and banks the cash.

Required

(a) State the weaknesses in the cash sales system.
(b) Describe the systems based tests you would carry out to check the controls over the system.

Answer

(a) **Weaknesses in the cash system**

(i) The physical location of the dispatch department and the cashier are not mentioned here, but there is a risk of the customer **taking the goods without paying**. The customer should pay the cashier on the advice note and return for the goods, which should only be released on sight of the paid invoice.

(ii) There is a failure in segregation of duties in allowing the cashier to both complete the sales invoice and receive the cash as he could **perpetrate a fraud** by replacing the original invoice with one of lower value and keeping the difference.

(iii) **No-one checks the invoices** to make sure that the cashier has completed them correctly, for example by using the correct prices and performing calculations correctly.

(iv) The **completeness** of the **sequence of sales invoices** cannot be **checked** unless they are pre-numbered sequentially and the presence of all the invoices is checked by another person. The order forms should also be pre-numbered sequentially.

(v) There is also no check that the **cashier banks all cash received**, ie this is a further failure of segregation of duties.

If the sales department prepared and posted the invoices and also posted the cash for cash sales to a sundry sales account, this would solve some of the internal control problems mentioned above. In addition, the sales department could run a weekly check on the account to look for invoices for which no cash had been received. These could then be investigated.

All of these weaknesses, and possible remedies, should be reported to management.

(b) **Tests**

(i) **Select a sample of order forms** issued to customers during the year. **Trace the related sales invoice** and **check that the details correlate** (date, unit amounts etc). The customer should have signed for the goods and this copy should be retained by the dispatch department.

(ii) For the sales invoices discovered in the above test, check that the **correct order form number** is recorded on the invoice, that the **prices used are correct** (by reference to the prevailing price list) and that the **castings and cross-castings** (ie arithmetic) are correct.

(iii) Trace the **value** of the **sales invoices** to the **cash book** and from the cash book that the **total receipts** for the day have been banked and appear promptly on the bank statement.

(iv) Check that the sales invoices have been **correctly posted** to a cash or sundry sales account. For any sales invoices missing from this account (assuming they are sequentially numbered). **Trace the cancelled invoice** and check that the cancelled invoice was initialled by the customer and replaced by the next invoice in sequence.

(v) Because of the weaknesses in the system carry out the following sequence checks on large blocks of order forms/invoices, eg four blocks of 100 order forms/invoices.

(1) **Check all order forms** present; investigate those missing.
(2) **Check sales invoices** raised for all order forms.
(3) **Check all sales invoices in a sequence** have been **used**; investigate any missing.
(4) **Cash for each sales invoice** has been **entered into** the cash book.

Using the results of the above tests I would decide whether the system for cash sales has operated without material fraud or error. If I am not satisfied that it has then I will consider qualifying my audit report on the grounds of limitation of scope.

2 The purchases and expenses system

FAST FORWARD

Purchases systems tests will be based around:

- **Buying** (authorisation)
- **Goods** inwards (custody)
- **Accounting** (recording)

2.1 Features of purchases and expenses system

Businesses should ensure that only **properly authorised purchases** which are necessary for the business are made. Again all stages of the purchase process, ordering, receiving goods and being charged for them should be **documented and matched** so that the business gets what it ordered and only pays for what it ordered and received. Businesses also need to keep track of what they owe to each supplier by maintaining a purchase ledger.

2.2 Risks

- Payments being made **without being properly authorised**
- Payments being made for goods and services that are **not received** or are **wrongly valued**
- Goods and services being received **without liabilities being recorded** in the accounting records
- Suppliers' accounts being **improperly debited** and **credited**
- Goods being returned to suppliers or credit being **claimed** and **not being recorded**

2.3 Aims of controls

2.3.1 Ordering

- All **orders for goods and services** are properly **authorised**, and are for **goods and services** that are actually **received** and are for the company
- Orders are only made to **authorised suppliers**
- Orders are made at **competitive prices**

2.3.2 Receipt and invoices

- All goods and services received are used for the **organisation's purposes**, and not private purposes
- Goods and services are **only accepted if** they have been **ordered**, and the **order** has been **authorised**
- All **goods** and **services received** are accurately **recorded**
- **Liabilities** are **recognised** for all **goods and services** that have been **received**
- All **credits** to which business is due are **claimed** and **received**
- **Receipt** of **goods** and **services** is **necessary** to establish a **liability to be recorded**

2.3.3 Accounting

- All **expenditure** is for goods that are **received**
- **All expenditure** is **authorised**
- All **expenditure** that is made is **recorded** correctly in the general and purchase ledger
- All **credit notes** that are received are **recorded** in the general and purchase ledger
- All **entries** in the **purchase ledger** are **made** to the **correct purchase ledger accounts**
- **Cut-off** is **applied correctly** to the purchase ledger

2.4 Controls

2.4.1 Controls: ordering

- **Segregation** of duties; requisition and ordering
- **Central policy** for choice of suppliers
- Evidence required of **requirements** for purchase before purchase authorised (re-order quantities and re-order levels)
- **Order forms** prepared only when a **pre-numbered purchase requisition** has been **received**
- **Authorisation** of order forms
- **Prenumbered order forms**
- **Safeguarding** of **blank order forms**
- **Review** for **orders not received** or invoiced
- **Monitoring** of **supplier terms** and taking advantage of favourable conditions (bulk order, discount)

2.4.2 Controls: goods and invoices received

- **Examination** of goods inwards
  - Quality
  - Quantity
  - Condition
- **Recording arrival** and **acceptance** of goods (prenumbered goods received notes)
- **Comparison** of **goods received notes** with **purchase orders**
- **Referencing** of supplier invoices; numerical sequence and supplier reference
- **Checking** of **suppliers' invoices**
  - Prices, quantities, accuracy of calculation
  - Comparison with order and goods received note
- **Recording return of goods** (pre-numbered goods returned notes)
- Procedures for **obtaining credit notes** from suppliers

2.4.3 Controls: accounting for purchases

- **Segregation** of **duties**: accounting and checking functions
- Prompt **recording of purchases** and **purchase returns** in day books and ledgers
- **Regular maintenance** of **purchase ledger**
- **Comparison** of **supplier statements** with **purchase ledger balances**
- **Authorisation of payments**
  - Authority limits

- Confirmation that goods have been received, accord with purchase order, and are properly priced and invoiced

- **Review** of **allocation** of expenditure
- **Reconciliation** of **purchase ledger** control account to total of purchase ledger balances
- **Cut-off** accrual of goods received notes not matched by purchases at year-end

2.5 Tests of controls

A most important test of controls is for auditors to check that all **invoices** are **supported** by authorised **purchase invoices** and **purchase orders**. The officials who approve the invoices should be operating within laid-down **authority limits**.

2.5.1 Tests of control: receipts of goods and invoices

- Check invoices for goods, raw materials are:
  - **Supported** by **goods received notes** and **inspection notes**
  - **entered** in **inventory records**
  - **priced correctly** by checking to **quotations**, **price lists** to see the price is in order
  - **properly referenced** with a number and supplier code
  - **correctly coded** by type of expenditure

  Trace entry in **record of goods returned** etc and see credit note duly received from the supplier, for invoices not passed due to defects or discrepancy

- For invoices of all types:
  - **Check calculations** and **additions**
  - **Check entries in purchase day book** and verify that they are correctly **analysed**
  - **Check posting** to **purchase ledger**
- For credit notes:
  - **Verify the correctness** of credit received with correspondence
  - **Check entries** in **inventory records** and in **purchase records**
- **Check** for **returns** that **credit notes** are duly **received** from the suppliers
- **Test numerical sequence** and enquire into missing numbers of:
  - Purchase requisitions
  - Purchase orders
  - Goods received notes
  - Goods returned notes
  - Suppliers' invoices
- **Obtain explanations** for **items** which have been **outstanding** for a long time:
  - Unmatched purchase requisitions
  - Purchase orders
  - Goods received notes (if invoices not received)
  - Unprocessed invoices

2.5.2 Tests of control: recording of purchases

- Verify that invoices and credit notes recorded in the purchase day book are:
  - **Initialled** for prices, calculations and extensions
  - **Cross-referenced** to purchase orders, goods received notes etc
  - **Authorised** for payment
- **Check additions**
- **Check postings** to general ledger accounts and control account
- **Check postings** of entries to purchase ledger

2.5.3 Purchase ledger

- For a sample of accounts recorded in the purchase ledger
  - **Test check entries** back into books of prime entry
  - **Test check additions** and **balances** forward
  - **Note** and **enquire** into all contra entries
- **Confirm control account balancing** has been regularly carried out during the year
- **Examine control account** for unusual entries

3 The wages system

FAST FORWARD

Key controls over **wages** cover:

- **Documentation** and **authorisation** of staff changes
- **Calculation** of wages and salaries
- **Payment** of wages
- **Authorisation** of **deductions**

3.1 Features of wages system

For **wages and salaries** businesses are trying to ensure that they only pay for **hours worked** and that they pay the **right staff** the **right amount**. Controls should also be in place to ensure **tax liabilities** are calculated correctly otherwise penalties may be imposed by the tax authorities.

3.2 Risks

- Payroll **including invalid entries**
- **Payments being made to individuals** which differ from the names or amounts shown on the payroll
- Failure to account for **statutory tax deductions** correctly

3.3 Aims of control

3.3.1 Setting of wages and salaries

- **Employees** are **only paid** for **work** that they have **done**
- **Gross pay** has been **calculated correctly** and **authorised**

3.3.2 Recording of wages and salaries

- **Gross** and **net pay** and **deductions** are **accurately recorded** on the payroll
- **Wages and salaries paid** are **recorded correctly** in the **bank** and **cash records**
- **Wages and salaries** are **correctly recorded** in the **general ledger**

3.3.3 Payment of wages and salaries

- The **correct employees** are **paid**

Deductions

- All **deductions** have been **calculated correctly** and are **authorised**
- The **correct amounts** are **paid** to the **taxation authorities**

While in practice separate arrangements are generally made for dealing with wages and salaries, the considerations involved are broadly similar and for convenience the two aspects are here treated together.

3.4 Controls

3.4.1 Controls: general arrangements

Responsibility for the preparation of pay sheets should be delegated to a suitable person, and adequate staff appointed to assist him. The extent to which the staff responsible for preparing wages and salaries may perform other duties should be clearly defined. In this connection full advantage should be taken where possible of the division of duties, and checks available where automatic wage-accounting systems are in use.

3.4.2 Controls: Setting of wages and salaries

- **Staffing** and **segregation of duties**
- **Maintenance of personnel records** and regular checking of wages and salaries to details in personnel records
- **Authorisation**
  - Engagement and discharge of employees
  - Changes in pay rates
  - Overtime
  - Non-statutory deductions (for example pension contributions)
  - Advances of pay
- **Recording** of **changes** in **personnel** and **pay rates**
- **Recording** of hours worked by **timesheets**, **clocking** in and out arrangements
- **Review** of hours worked
- **Recording** of **advances** of **pay**
- **Holiday pay** arrangements
- **Answering queries**
- **Review** of **wages** against **budget**

3.4.3 Controls: payment of cash wages

- **Segregation of duties**

  - Cash sheet preparation
  - Filling of pay packets
  - Distribution of wages

- **Authorisation** of **wage cheque** cashed

- **Custody** of cash

  - Encashment of cheque
  - Security of pay packets
  - Security of transit
  - Security and prompt banking of unclaimed wages

- **Verification of identity**
- **Recording** of **distribution**

3.4.4 Controls: payment of salaries

- **Preparation** and **authorisation** of cheques and bank transfer lists
- Comparison of **cheques** and **bank transfer list** with **payroll**
- **Maintenance** and **reconciliation** of wages and salaries bank account

3.4.5 Controls: wages and salaries

- **Bases** for **compilation** of payroll
- **Preparation**, **checking** and **approval** of payroll
- Dealing with **non-routine matters**

3.4.6 Controls: deductions from pay

- **Maintenance** of **separate employees' records**, with which pay lists may be compared as necessary

- **Reconciliation** of **total pay** and **deductions** between one pay day and the next

- **Surprise cash counts**

- **Comparison** of actual pay totals with **budget estimates** or standard costs and the investigation of variances

- **Agreement** of **gross earnings** and **total tax deducted** with taxation returns

Appropriate arrangements should be made for dealing with statutory and other authorised deductions from pay, such as taxation, pension fund contributions, and savings held in trust. A primary consideration is the establishment of adequate controls over the **records** and authorising **deductions**.

3.5 Tests of controls

3.5.1 Tests of controls: Setting of wages and salaries

Auditors should check that the **wages** and **salary summary** is approved for payment. They should confirm that procedures are operating for **authorising changes** in **rates of pay**, overtime, and holiday pay.

A particular concern will be joiners and leavers. Auditors will need to obtain evidence that staff only start being paid when they join the company, and are removed from the payroll when they leave the company. They should check that the **engagement** of **new employees** and **discharges** have been **confirmed in writing**.

Auditors will also wish to check calculations of wages and salaries. This test should be designed to check that the client is carrying out **checks** on **calculations** and also to provide substantive assurance that **wages** and **salaries** are being **calculated correctly**.

For wages, this will involve checking **calculation** of **gross pay** with:

- Authorised rates of pay
- Production records. See that production bonuses have been authorised and properly calculated
- Clock cards, time sheets or other evidence of hours worked. Verify that overtime has been authorised

For salaries, auditors should **verify that gross salaries and bonuses are in accordance with personnel records, letters of engagement** etc and that increases in pay have been properly authorised.

3.5.2 Tests of control: Payment of wages and salaries

If wages are paid in cash

- **Arrange to attend** the **pay-out** of wages to confirm that the official procedures are being followed
- Before the wages are paid **compare payroll** with **wage packets** to ensure all employees have a wage packet
- **Examine receipts** given by employees; **check unclaimed wages** are recorded in unclaimed wages book
- **Check** that **no employee receives more than one wage packet**
- **Check entries** in the **unclaimed wages book** with the entries on the payroll
- **Check that unclaimed wages** are **banked regularly**
- **Check** that unclaimed wages books shows **reasons** why wages are unclaimed
- **Check pattern** of **unclaimed wages** in unclaimed wages book; variations may indicate failure to record

Holiday pay

- **Verify** a sample of **payments** with the **underlying records** and **check** the **calculation** of the amounts paid

For salaries, auditors should check that comparisons are being made between payment records and they should themselves **examine paid cheques** or a **certified copy** of the **bank list** for employees paid by cheque of banks transfer.

3.5.3 Tests of control: Recording of wages and salaries

A key control auditors will be concerned with will be the reconciliation of wages and salaries. For wages, there should have been reconciliations with:

- The **previous week's payroll**
- **Clock cards/time sheets/job cards**
- **Costing analyses, production budgets**

The total of **salaries** should be **reconciled** with the **previous week/month** or the **standard payroll**.

In addition auditors should confirm that important calculations have been checked by the clients and re-perform those calculations.

These include checking for wages for a number of weeks:

- **Additions** of **payroll sheets**
- **Totals** of **wages sheets** selected to summary
- **Additions** and **cross-casts** of summary
- **Postings** of **summary** to **general ledger** (including control accounts)
- **Casts** of **net cash column** to cash book

For salaries they include checking for a number of weeks/months:

- **Additions of payroll sheets**
- **Totals of salaries sheets** to **summary**
- **Additions** and **cross-casts** of **summary**
- **Postings** of **summary** to **general ledger** (including control accounts)
- **Total** of **net pay column** to cash book

3.5.4 Tests of control: deductions

Auditors should **check** the **calculations** of **taxation** and **non-statutory deductions**.

- **Scrutinise** the **control accounts** maintained to see **appropriate deductions** have been **made**
- **Check** that the **payments** to the **taxation** bodies are **correct**

They should check other deductions to appropriate records. For voluntary deductions, they should see the authority completed by the relevant employees.

Question

Control objective and tests

Learning outcomes: C(iii),(iv)

The following questions have been selected from an internal control questionnaire for wages and salaries.

Internal control questionnaire - wages and salaries

		Yes	*No*
1	Does an appropriate official authorise rates of pay?		
2	Are written notices required for employing and terminating employment?		
3	Are formal records such as time cards used for time keeping?		
4	Does anyone verify rates of pay, overtime hours and computations of gross pay before the wage payments are made?		
5	Does the accounting system ensure the proper recording of payroll costs in the financial records?		

Required

(a) Describe the internal control objective being fulfilled if the controls set out in the above questions are in effect.

(b) Describe the audit tests which would test the effectiveness of each control and help determine any potential material error.

(c) Identify the potential consequences for the company if the above controls were not in place.

You may answer in columnar form under the headings:

ICQ question *Internal control objective* *Audit tests* *Consequences*

Answer

	ICQ question	Internal control objective	Audit tests	Consequences
1	Does an appropriate official authorise rates of pay?	Employees are paid amounts authorised	Test rates of pay from payroll to schedule of authorised pay rates (personnel files, board minutes etc)	Incorrect rates of pay could lead to over/under statement of profit
2	Are written notices required for employing and terminating employment?	All employees paid through payroll exist	Check a sample of employees from payroll files for authorisation of employment or termination Check details for cheque or credit transfer salary payments to personnel files	Payroll may include fictitious employees
3	Are formal records such as time cards used for time keeping?	Employees are only paid for work done	Review time records to ensure they are properly completed and controlled Observe procedures for time recording	Overstatement of payroll costs. Employees over/under paid
			Check time records where absences are recorded to payroll to ensure they have been accounted for Review the wages account and investigate any large or unusual amounts	
4	Does anyone verify rates of pay, overtime hours and computation of gross pay before wage payments are made?	Employees are paid the correct amount	Examine payroll for evidence of verification Recompute gross pay (including overtime) Check wage rates to authorised schedule	Misstatement of payroll costs
5	Does the accounting system ensure the proper recording of payroll costs in the financial records?	Payroll costs are properly recorded	Check posting of payroll costs to the nominal ledger	Misstatement of payroll costs

4 The cash system

FAST FORWARD

Key controls over **receipts** include:

- Proper **post-opening** arrangements
- **Prompt recording**
- **Prompt banking**
- **Reconciliation** of records of cash received and banked

Key controls over **payments** include:

- **Restriction of access** to cash and cheques
- Procedures for **preparation and authorisation** of payments

A further important control is **regular independent bank reconciliations**

4.1 Features of cash system

Controls over **cash and bank balances** cannot be seen in complete isolation from controls over the sales, purchases and wages cycle. In this chapter we concentrate on controls over, and testing of, the safe **custody and prompt recording** of cash. Bear in mind also when you work through the section on bank and cash that controlling cheque receipts and payments is significantly easier than controlling cash receipts and payments.

4.2 Risks

- **Misappropriation** of cash receipts
- **Failure to record** cash receipts and payments
- Payments being made **without authorisation or supporting documentation**

4.3 Aims of controls

- **All monies received** are **recorded**
- **All monies received** are **banked**
- **Cash and cheques** are **safeguarded** against loss or theft
- **All payments** are **authorised, made** to the **correct payees** and **recorded**
- **Payments** are **not made twice** for the same liability

Controls over the **completeness** of **recording** of cash receipts are particularly important. If these controls are inadequate, there may be insufficient audit evidence available when the auditor carries out substantive procedures.

Segregation of duties is also important. The person responsible for receiving and recording cash when it arrives in the post should not be the same as the person responsible for banking it. Ideally the cash book should be written up by a further staff member, and a fourth staff member should reconcile the various records of amounts received.

4.4 Controls

4.4.1 Controls: Cash at bank and in hand - receipts

Segregation of duties between the various functions listed below is particularly important.

Recording of receipts by post

- **Safeguards** to **prevent interception of mail** between receipt and opening
- Appointment of **responsible person** to supervise mail
- **Protection** of **cash and cheques** (restrictive crossing)
- **Amounts received listed** when post opened
- **Post stamped** with date of receipt

Recording of cash sales and collections

- **Restrictions** on **receipt of cash** (by cashiers only, or by salesmen etc)
- **Evidencing** of receipt of cash
  - Serially numbered receipt forms
  - Cash registers incorporating sealed till rolls
- **Clearance** of cash offices and registers
- **Agreement of cash collections with till rolls**
- **Agreement of cash collections with bankings** and cash and sales **records**
- **Investigation** of cash shortages and surpluses

General controls over recording

- Prompt **maintenance of records** (cash book, ledger accounts)
- **Limitation** of **duties** of receiving cashiers
- **Holiday arrangements**
- **Giving** and **recording** of **receipts**
  - Retained copies
  - Serially numbered receipts books
  - Custody of receipt books
  - Comparisons with cash records and bank paying in slips

Banking

- **Daily bankings**
- **Make-up** and **comparison** of **paying-in slips** checked against initial receipt records and cash book
- **Banking** of receipts **intact**/control of disbursements

Safeguarding of cash and bank accounts

- **Restrictions** on **opening new bank accounts**
- **Limitations** on **cash floats** held
- **Restrictions** on **payments** out of **cash received**
- **Restrictions** on **access** to cash registers and offices
- **Independent checks** on cash floats
- **Surprise cash counts**
- **Custody** of **cash** outside **office hours**

- **Custody** over **supply** and issue of cheques
- **Preparation** of **cheques** restricted
- **Safeguards** over **mechanically signed cheques**/cheques carrying printed signatures
- **Restrictions** on issue of **blank** or **bearer** cheques
- **Safeguarding** of **IOUs**, cash in transit
- **Insurance arrangements**
- **Control of funds** held in trust for employees
- **Bank reconciliations**

4.4.2 Controls: Cash at bank and in hand – payments

The arrangements for controlling payments will depend to a great extent on the nature of business transacted, the volume of payments involved and the size of the company.

4.4.3 Controls: Cheque and cash payments generally

The cashier should generally not be concerned with keeping or writing-up books of account other than those recording disbursements nor should he have access to, or be responsible for the custody of, securities, title deeds or negotiable instruments belonging to the company.

The person responsible for preparing cheques or traders' credit lists should not himself be a cheque signatory. Cheque signatories in turn should not be responsible for recording payments.

Cheque payments

- **Cheque requisitions**
  - Appropriate supporting documentation
  - Approval by appropriate staff
  - Presentation to cheque signatories
  - Cancellation (crossing/recording cheque number on requisition)
- **Authority** to sign cheques
  - Signatories should not also approve cheque requisitions
  - Limitations on authority to specific amounts
  - Number of signatories
  - Prohibitions over signing of blank cheques
- **Prompt dispatch** of signed **cheques**
- **Obtaining** of paid **cheques** from **banks**
- Payments **recorded promptly** in **cash book** and **general** and **purchase ledger**

Cash payments

- **Authorisation** of **expenditure**
- **Cancellation** of **vouchers** to ensure cannot be paid
- **Limits** on **disbursements**
- **Rules** on **cash advances** to employees, IOUs and cheque cashing

4.5 Tests of controls

4.5.1 Tests of control: Receipts received by post

- **Observe procedures** for **post opening** are being followed
- **Observe** that **cheques** received by post are immediately **crossed** in the company's favour of the company
- For items entered in the rough cash book (or other record of cash, cheques etc received by post), **trace entries** to:
  - **Cash book** – **Paying-in book** – **Counterfoil** or carbon copy receipts
- **Verify amounts entered** as **received** with remittance advices or other supporting evidence

4.5.2 Tests of control: Cash sales, branch takings

- For a sample of cash sales summaries/branch summaries from different locations:
  - **Verify with till rolls** or copy cash sale notes
  - **Check to paying-in slip** date-stamped and initialled by the bank
  - **Verify that takings** are banked intact daily
  - **Vouch expenditure** out of takings

4.5.3 Tests of control: collections

- For a sample of items from the original collection records:
  - **Trace amounts** to **cash book** via collectors' cash sheets or other collection records
  - **Check entries** on **cash sheets** or collection records with collectors' receipt books
  - **Verify** that **goods delivered** to travellers/salesmen have been regularly **reconciled** with sales and inventories in hand
  - **Check numerical sequence** of collection records

4.5.4 Tests of control: receipts cash book

- For cash receipts for several days throughout the period:
  - **Check to entries in rough cash book**, receipts, branch returns or other records
  - **Check to paying-in slips** obtained direct from the bank, observing that there is no delay in banking monies received
  - **Check additions** of **paying-in slips**
  - **Check additions** of **cash book**
  - **Check postings** to the **sales ledger**
  - **Check postings** to the **general ledger**, including control accounts
- **Scrutinise the cash book** and **investigate items** of a **special** or **unusual nature**.

4.5.5 Tests of control: payments cash book(authorisation)

- For a sample of payments:
  - **Compare** with paid cheques to ensure payee agrees

  - **Note** that **cheques** are **signed** by the **persons authorised** tc do so within their authority limits
  - **Check** to **suppliers' invoices** for goods and services. Verify that supporting documents are signed as having been **checked** and **passed for payment** and have been stamped 'paid'
  - **Check** to **suppliers' statements**
  - **Check** to **other documentary evidence**, as appropriate (agreements, authorised expense vouchers, wages/salaries records, petty cash books etc)

4.5.6 Tests of control: payments cash book(recording)

- For a sample of weeks:
  - **Check the sequence of cheque numbers** and enquire into missing numbers
  - **Trace transfers** to other bank accounts, petty cash books or other records, as appropriate
  - **Check additions**, including extensions, and balances forward at the beginning and end of the months covering the periods chosen
  - **Check postings** to the **purchase ledger**
  - **Check postings** to the **general ledger**, including the control accounts

When checking that bank and cash are **secured**, auditors should consider the security arrangements over blank cheques. Bank reconciliations are also a very important control and auditors should carry out the following tests on these.

- For a period which includes a reconciliation date **reperform reconciliation** (see Chapter 15)
- **Verify** that **reconciliations have been prepared** at **regular intervals** throughout the year
- **Scrutinise reconciliations for unusual items**

4.5.7 Tests of control: petty cash

- For a sample of payments:
  - **Check** to supporting vouchers
  - **Check** whether they are properly **approved**
  - **See** that **vouchers** have been **marked and initialled** by the cashier to prevent their re-use
- For a sample of weeks:
  - **Trace amounts** received to **cash books**
  - **Check additions** and **balances carried** forward
  - **Check postings** to the **nominal ledger**

Exam focus point

Questions about the sales or purchases systems may also require consideration of controls over receipts or payments.

5 The inventory system

FAST FORWARD

Inventory controls are designed to ensure safe custody. These include:

– **Restriction of access** to inventory
– **Documentation** and **authorisation** of movements

Other important controls over inventory include regular **independent inventory counting** and **review of inventory condition**.

5.1 Features of inventory system

For **inventory**, there should be **proper security arrangements** and **prompt recording**. You should note however the other aspects of control of inventory, particularly reviews of the condition of inventory, and inventory holding policies designed to ensure that the business is not holding too much or too little inventory. These controls interest auditors since they may impact upon how inventory is valued.

5.2 Risks

Important risks include the following:

- **Misappropriation of inventory**
- **Failure** to record **inventory movements**
- **Deterioration in condition** and **value of inventory** due to age, obsolescence, or poor inventory holding conditions

5.3 Aims of controls

5.3.1 Recording

- All **inventory movements** are **authorised** and **recorded**
- **Inventory records** only **include items** that **belong** to the organisation
- **Inventory records include inventory** that **exists** and is **held** by the organisation
- **Inventory quantities** have been **recorded correctly**
- **Cut-off procedures** are **properly applied** to inventory

5.3.2 Protection of inventory

- **Inventory** is **safeguarded** against loss, pilferage or damage

5.3.3 Valuation of inventory

- The **costing system values inventory correctly**
- **Allowance** is **made** for **slow-moving**, **obsolete** or **damaged inventory**

5.3.4 Inventory-holding

- **Levels** of **inventory held** are **reasonable**

5.4 Controls

5.4.1 Control: Recording of inventory

- **Segregation** of duties; custody and recording of inventories
- **Reception, checking** and **recording** of goods inwards
- **Inventory issues supported** by **appropriate documentation**
- **Maintenance** of **inventory records**
  - Inventory ledgers
  - Bin cards
  - Transfer records

5.4.2 Control: Protection of inventory

- **Precautions** against **theft, misuse** and **deterioration**
  - Restriction of access to stores
  - Controls on stores environment (right temperature, precautions against damp etc).
- **Security** over **inventory** held by third parties, and third party inventory held by entity
- **Inventory-taking**
  - Regular inventory counts
  - Fair coverage so that all inventory is counted at least once a year
  - Counts by independent persons
  - Recording
  - Cut-off for goods in transit and time differences
  - Reconciliation of inventory count to book records and control accounts

5.4.3 Control: Valuation of inventory

- **Computation** of **inventory valuation**
  - Accords with IAS 2
  - Checking of calculations
- **Review** of **condition** of inventory
  - Treatment of slow-moving, damaged and obsolete inventory
  - Authorisation of write-offs
- **Accounting** for **scrap** and **waste**

5.4.4 Control: Inventory holding

- **Control** of **inventory levels**
  - Maximum inventory limits
  - Minimum inventory limits
  - Re-order quantities and levels
- Arrangements for dealing with **returnable containers**

5.5 Tests of controls

Most of the testing relating to inventory has been covered in the purchase and sales testing. Auditors will primarily be concerned at this stage with ensuring that the business keeps track of inventory. To confirm this, checks must be made on how inventory **movements** are **recorded** and how **inventory** is **secured**.

- **Select** a sample of **inventory movements records** and **agree** to **goods received** and **goods dispatched notes**
- **Confirm** that **movements** have been **authorised** as **appropriate**
- **Select** a sample of **goods received** and **goods dispatched** notes and agree to **inventory movement records**
- **Check sequence** of inventory records

Other tests that auditors are likely to perform include:

- **Test** check **inventory counts** carried out from time to time (eg monthly) during the period and confirm:
  - **All discrepancies** between **book** and **actual** figures have been fully investigated
  - **All discrepancies** have been **signed off** by a senior manager
  - **Obsolete, damaged or slow-moving goods** have been **marked accordingly** and written down to net realisable value
- **Observe security arrangements for inventories**
- **Consider environment** in which inventories are held

Auditors will carry out extensive tests on the **valuation** of inventory at the substantive testing stage.

Question — Cash control weakness

Learning outcome: C(iii)

Jonathan is the sole shareholder of Furry Lion Stores, a company which owns five stores in the west of England. The stores mainly stock food and groceries, and four of the stores have an off-licence as well.

Each store is run by a full-time manager and three or four part-time assistants. Jonathan spends on average ½ a day a week at each store, and spends the rest of his time at home, dealing with his other business interests.

All sales are for cash and are recorded on till rolls which the manager retains. Shop manager wages are paid monthly by cheque by Jonathan. Wages of shop assistants are paid in cash out of the takings.

Most purchases are made from local wholesalers and are paid for in cash out of the takings. Large purchases (over $250) must be made by cheques signed by the shop manager and countersigned by Jonathan.

Shop managers bank surplus cash once a week, apart from a float in the till.

All accounting records including the cash book, wages and sales tax records are maintained by the manager. Jonathan reviews the weekly bank statements when he visits the shops. He also has a look at inventories to see if inventory levels appear to be about right. All invoices are also kept in a drawer by a manager and marked with a cash book reference, and where appropriate a cheque number when paid.

Required

Discuss the weaknesses in the control systems of Furry Lion Stores, and how the weaknesses can be remedied.

Answer

Weaknesses in the system, and their remedies are as follows.

Inventory

The shops do not appear to have any inventory movement records. Jonathan has also only a very approximate indication of **inventory levels**. Hence it will be difficult to detect whether **inventory levels** are too **high**, or too low with a risk of running out of inventory. Theft of inventory would also be difficult to detect. The company should therefore introduce inventory movement records, detailing values and volumes.

In addition regular inventory counts should be made either by Jonathan or by staff from another shop. Discrepancies between the inventory records and the actual inventory counted should be investigated.

Cash controls

Too much cash appears to be held on site. In addition the fact that most payments appear to be for cash may mean **inadequate documentation** is kept. The level of cash on site can be decreased by **daily rather than weekly bankings**. In addition the need for cash on site can be decreased by paying wages by cheque, and by paying all but the smallest payments by cheque.

The cash book should obviously still be maintained but **cheque stubs** should also show **details of amounts paid**. The cash book should be supported by invoices and other supporting documentation, and should be cross-referenced to the general ledger (see below).

Cash reconciliations

There is no indication of the **till-rolls** that are kept being reconciled to cash takings.

There should be a **daily reconciliation** of cash takings and till rolls; this should be reviewed if not performed by the shop manager.

Bank reconciliations

There is no mention of bank reconciliations taking place.

Bank reconciliations should be carried out at least **monthly** by the shop manager, and reviewed by the owner.

Purchases

There is no formal system for **recording purchases**. Invoices do not appear to be filed in any particular way. It would be difficult to see whether accounting records were complete, and hence it would be difficult to prepare a set of accounts from the accounting records available.

In addition the way records are maintained means that accounts would have to be **prepared on a cash basis**, and not on an accruals basis.

A purchase day book should be introduced. Invoices should be recorded in the purchase day book, and filed in a logical order, either by date received or by supplier.

General ledger

There is **no general ledger**, and again this means that annual accounts cannot easily be prepared (and also management accounts).

A general ledger should be maintained with entries made from the cash book, wages records and purchase day book. This will enable accounts to be prepared on an accruals basis.

Supervision

Jonathan does not take a very active part in the business, only signing cheques over $250, and visiting the shops only half a day each week. This may mean that assets can easily go missing, and Jonathan cannot readily see whether the business is performing as he would wish.

Jonathan should **review wage/sales tax/cash book reconciliations**. Management accounts should also be prepared by shop managers for Jonathan.

6 Revenue and capital expenditure

FAST FORWARD

Most of the key controls over **capital and revenue expenditure** are the general purchase controls.

It is also important that **non-current assets** are **recorded correctly**, so that profit/loss and assets are not misstated.

6.1 Controlling non-current assets

As with inventory, organisations have to make sure that they maintain **safe custody** over non-current assets; the financial consequences of loss or pilferage could be much more serious than the loss of the odd item of inventory. Similarly assets must be guarded against the risk of **excessive loss of value** or their not being fully utilised. The nature of a balance sheet and income statement means that it is also important to classify capital and revenue expenditure correctly, or profit will be over or under-stated.

The aims of controls, controls and audit tests will be the same over non-current asset purchases as over other sorts of purchases, which we discussed in Section 2. However the auditor may test a higher proportion of non-current asset purchases, and may indeed look at all the purchases in a year if they are few in number but for large amounts individually.

6.2 Risks

- **Asset acquisitions** and **disposals not** being **authorised**
- **Asset acquisitions** and **disposals not** being **recorded**
- Asset records including items which have been **disposed** of, are of **negligible value** or **do not exist**
- **Misappropriation** of assets
- Assets being used for **private benefit**
- **Deterioration in condition** or obsolescence of assets
- **Depreciation** being **charged** at too high or too low a rate
- **Depreciation** being **calculated** incorrectly
- **Income from assets** not being **received** or recorded
- **Revenue and capital expenditure** are accounted for **incorrectly**

6.3 Aims of controls

6.3.1 Authorisation

- All **acquisitions** are **authorised**
- All **disposals and scrappings** are **authorised**

6.3.2 Security

- **Non-current assets** are **safeguarded** against loss, pilferage or damage

6.3.3 Valuation

- **Non-current assets** are **valued correctly**
- **Depreciation** is **calculated correctly**
- **Adjustments** are made for write-downs in the value of assets

6.3.4 Recording

- All **asset movements** are **recorded**
- **Asset records** only **include items** that belong to the organisation
- **Asset records** include **assets that exist** and are held by the client
- **All expenditure** is **classified correctly** in the accounts as capital or revenue expenditure

6.4 Controls

As we've mentioned all the controls over purchases discussed in Section 2 will be relevant, and the organisation should also have similar controls over asset security as it does over inventory security.

In addition, the organisation should consider ways of marking ownership on the assets (for example on computer equipment), and should maintain a **non-current asset register**. All capital items should be written up in this register, including identification details. The non-current asset register should be regularly reconciled to the general ledger.

6.5 Tests of controls

The tests over **purchases** and **inventory security** will also be relevant here.

The auditors may also wish to review the following:

- **Board minutes** for authorisation of capital purchases
- **Sensitive codes** in the general ledger such as non-current assets and repairs and maintenance to confirm revenue and capital expenditure is being allocated correctly
- **Budgeted capital purchases** with **actual purchases** and enquire why there are significant differences
- **Reconciliations of the general ledger** with the **non-current asset register**. There should be evidence that these have taken place on a regular basis and that discrepancies have been investigated and cleared

Chapter Roundup

- Tests of controls of the **sales system** will be based around:
  - **Selling** (authorisation)
  - **Goods outwards** (custody)
  - **Accounting** (recording)
- **Purchases systems** tests will be based around:
  - **Buying** (authorisation)
  - **Goods inwards** (custody)
  - **Accounting** (recording)
- Key controls over **wages** cover:
  - **Documentation** and **authorisation** of staff changes
  - **Calculation** of wages and salaries
  - **Payment** of wages
  - **Authorisation** of **deductions**
- Key controls over **receipts** include:
  - Proper **post-opening** arrangements
  - **Prompt recording**
  - **Prompt banking**
  - **Reconciliation** of records of cash received and banked
- Key controls over **payments** include:
  - **Restriction of access** to cash and cheques
  - Procedures for **preparation and authorisation** of payments
- A further important control is **regular independent bank reconciliations**
- **Inventory controls** are designed to ensure safe custody. These include:
  - **Restriction of access** to inventory
  - **Documentation** and **authorisation** of movements
- Other important controls over inventory include regular **independent inventory counting** and **review of inventory condition.**
- Most of the key controls over **capital and revenue expenditure** are the general purchase controls.
- It is also important that **non-current assets** are **recorded correctly**, so that profit/loss and assets are not misstated.

Quick Quiz

1 Complete the table, putting the sales system control considerations under the correct headings.

Ordering/credit approval	Dispatch/invoicing	Recording/accounting

(a) All sales that have been invoiced have been put in the general ledger
(b) Orders are fulfilled
(c) Cut off is correct
(d) Goods are only supplied to good credit risks
(e) Goods are correctly invoiced
(f) Customers are encouraged to pay promptly

2 Name five controls relating to the ordering and granting of credit process.

3 When checking sales invoicing the auditor should verify ………………………., ……………….. ,……………. and …………………………., ………………………., correct analysis in the sales ledger and correct posting and that sales tax has been dealt with.

4 Complete the table, putting the purchase system control considerations under the correct headings.

Ordering	Receipt/invoices	Accounting

(a) Orders are only made to authorised suppliers
(b) Liabilities are recognised for all goods and services received
(c) Orders made at competitive prices
(d) All expenditure is authorised
(e) Cut off is correctly applied
(f) Goods and services are only accepted if there is an authorised order

5 Name six procedures auditors should carry out if wages are paid in cash.

6 Name the five key aims of controls of the cash system.

7 Give five examples of tests to be performed on the cash payments book.

8 Three important controls over the protection of inventories are:

- Restriction of access to stores
- Regular inventory counts
- Reconciliation of book inventory to physical inventory

True ☐

False ☐

Answers to Quick Quiz

1

Ordering/credit approval	Dispatch/invoicing	Recording/accounting
(b) (d) (f)	(e)	(a) (c)

2
- **Segregation** of duties; credit control, invoicing and inventory dispatch
- **Authorisation** of **credit terms** to customers
  - References/credit checks obtained
  - Authorisation by senior staff
  - Regular review
- **Authorisation** for changes in **other customer data**
  - Change of address supported by letterhead
  - Deletion requests supported by evidence balances cleared/customer in liquidation
- **Orders** only **accepted** from **customers** who have no credit problems
- **Sequential numbering** of blank pre-printed order documents
- **Correct prices quoted** to **customers**
- **Matching** of **customer orders** with production orders and dispatch notes and querying of orders not matched
- **Dealing** with **customer queries**

3 quantities, prices, calculations, additions, discounts

4

Ordering	Receipt/invoices	Accounting
(a) (c)	(b) (f)	(d)

5
- **Arrange to attend** the **pay-out** of wages to confirm that the official procedures are being followed
- Before the wages are paid **compare payroll** with **wage packets** to ensure all employees have a wage packet
- **Examine receipts** given by employees; **check unclaimed wages** are recorded in unclaimed wages book
- **Check** that **no employee receives more than one wage packet**
- **Check entries** in the **unclaimed wages book** with the entries on the payroll

- **Check that unclaimed wages** are **banked regularly**
- **Check** that unclaimed wages books shows **reasons** why wages are unclaimed
- **Check pattern** of **unclaimed wages** in unclaimed wages book; variations may indicate failure to record
- **Verify** a sample of holiday pay **payments** with the **underlying records** and **check** the **calculation** of the amounts paid

6
- **All monies received** are **recorded**
- **All monies received** are **banked**
- **Cash and cheques** are **safeguarded** against loss or theft
- **All payments** are **authorised**, **made** to the **correct payees** and **recorded**
- **Payments** are **not made twice** for the same liability

7 For a sample of payments:

- **Compare** with paid cheques to ensure payee agrees
- **Note** that **cheques** are **signed** by the **persons authorised** to do so within their authority limits
- **Check** to **suppliers' invoices** for goods and services. Verify that supporting documents are signed as having been **checked** and **passed for payment** and have been stamped 'paid'
- **Check** to **suppliers' statements**
- **Check** to **other documentary evidence**, as appropriate (agreements, authorised expense vouchers, wages/salaries records, petty cash books etc)

8 True

Now try the question below from the Exam Question Bank

Number	Level	Marks	Time
Q13	Introductory	N/a	45 mins

14

Types of audit

Introduction

In this chapter we focus on the audit of areas other than the accounting system. With operational audits again rather than learning lists, you should focus on the main **risks** of each area, see how **controls** can address these risks and how internal audit can test that these risks have in fact been addressed.

Value for money and management audits have a somewhat different focus. Auditors are seeking to measure how **well** the organisation or management has performed, although auditors may focus on areas or personnel whose performance is, or it is felt might be, particularly poor.

Social and environmental audits can both seek to ascertain whether risks (particularly the risks of non-compliance with legislation and hence legal action) have been addressed, and also that the organisation's performance is improving (reduced emissions, more recycling etc).

Topic list	Learning outcomes	Syllabus references	Ability required
1 Operational audits	C(ii),(iii)	C(7)	Evaluation
2 Value for money audits	C(ii),(iii),(v)	C(7)	Evaluation
3 Management audits	C(ii),(iii),(v)	C(7)	Evaluation
4 Social and environmental audits	C(ii),(iii)	C(7)	Evaluation

1 Operational audits

FAST FORWARD

Controls over operations are designed to ensure that **customer requirements** are taken into account. **assets and resources** are made **available when required**, **assets** are **safeguarded**, **legislation** and **internal guidelines** are followed, and **operations** are **monitored** and **reviewed** by management.

Operational audits are a vital part of the **operational control process**, designed to confirm **adequacy and implementation** of control and risk management policies.

Key term

Operational audits are audits of the operational processes of the organisation. They are also known as management or efficiency audits. Their prime objective is the monitoring of management's performance, ensuring the organisation's policies are complied with.

1.1 Risks and controls in operations

In this section we shall examine a number of the most significant types of operational audits. You may be asked about one or more of these in the exam, but it is possible that you may be asked to recommend the audit approach for an area that we haven't covered. However as you work through this section you will see that the operational audits have many significant elements in common, and these are summarised below.

1.1.1 Risks

Risks that affect many areas of operations include the following:

- Assets, resources and facilities are **not available** when required
- **Sales** are **lost** because of operational difficulties or weaknesses
- **Assets** are **damaged** or **misappropriated**
- **Business** is **interrupted**
- The organisation fails to **comply with internal guidelines** or **external legislation**

1.1.2 Aims of controls

Clearly controls will be designed with the aims of combating the main risks. Significant aims are likely to include:

- **Internal procedures** are **sufficient** to meet risks and are complied with
- **Operational functions** are **properly resourced**
- **Customer requirements** are **identified** and taken into account
- **Assets and facilities** are **available** when required
- **Assets** are **managed effectively**
- **Back-up resources** and **facilities** are **available** in the event of disruption

1.1.3 Controls

Adequate controls and risk management processes should exist, and it is also important that managers are able to assure themselves that their controls and risk assessments are adequate, including of course operational audits.

Important controls in many areas will include:

- **Regular review of resources** and **assets** to ensure they are available, adequate and have not been misappropriated
- **Quality checks** on resources and products
- Procedures such as competitive tendering and review of alternative supply sources are in place to ensure **resources** are **obtained** at a reasonable price
- **Planning and forecasting procedures**
- **Comparison of actual results** with **plans**
- **Regular reports** to senior management
- **Security procedures** for safeguarding assets
- **Contingency plans** are in place and resources will be made available if the organisation suffers serious disruption

1.2 Approaching operational audit assignments

There are two aspects of an operational assignment:

- Ensure policies are **adequate**
- Ensure policies **work effectively**

1.2.1 Adequacy

The internal auditor will have to review the policies of a particular department by:

- **Reading** them
- **Discussion** with members of the department

Then the auditor will have to assess whether the policies are adequate, and possibly advise the board of improvements which could be made.

1.2.2 Effectiveness

The auditor will then have to examine the effectiveness of the controls by:

- **Observing them** in operation
- **Testing them**

1.3 Logistics audit

Key term

Logistics are the processes by which materials or goods are brought into the business, transferred between locations and delivered to customers.

1.3.1 Risks

- **Inventory** is **not delivered** at the right time to the right place in the right condition
- **Inventory** is **stolen**

- Poor quality products result in **lost sales** or **damage** or **injury**
- Business is **interrupted**

1.3.2 Aims of controls

- **Inventory** is **available** when needed to meet business requirements
- **Assets** are **safeguarded**
- **Logistics** is being **managed effectively**

1.3.3 Controls

- Computerised **planning and forecasting systems**
- Orders over a given size being **authorised** by an experienced manager
- **Inventory counts** and other security measures
- **Checks on quality** of stock
- Detailed analysis of **volume requirements**
- Availability of **alternative facilities** at short notice
- Proper arrangements for **vehicle maintenance**

1.3.4 Tests of controls

- **Observe movements** of **inventory** from one location to another
- **Compare book inventory** with physical quantities
- **Review records** used for logistics forecasts for accuracy and relevance, and confirm managers are monitoring these forecasts
- **Determine adequacy of maintenance arrangements** by reviewing adequacy of contracts and organisation's policy on maintenance, and check whether organisation's policy on maintenance is being followed.
- **Review security measures** to confirm their adequacy
- **Review contingency plans** to confirm adequate back-up facilities will be available

1.4 Procurement audit

Key term

Procurement is the process of **purchasing** for the business.

A procurement audit will concentrate on the systems of the purchasing department(s). The internal auditor will be checking that the system achieves key objectives and that it operates according to the organisation's guidelines. Many of the controls will be the same as in the purchases cycle.

A procurement system is likely to have many systems within it (for example, tendering, placing orders, checking goods inwards), which the internal auditor would probably approach separately.

1.4.1 Risks

- Goods and services are **not available** when required
- The organisation **pays too much** for goods and services
- Employees or suppliers **defraud** the organisation

1.4.2 Aims of control

- Procurement policy is in line with **organisation guidelines** and the **demands of relevant legislation**
- The organisation has **goods and services** when it needs them
- The organisation pays **reasonable prices** for those goods and services
- The organisation does **not make short-term savings** on goods and services which lead to longer term inflated costs

1.4.3 Controls

- The business always **invites tenders** for goods and services
- **Research** is conducted on **potential suppliers** before they are invited to tender
- **Requirements** for goods and services are always put in **writing**
- Use is made of **discounting and calculations** of long term costs where service is for a prolonged period
- **No transactions** are carried out with **employees** and connected persons

1.4.4 Tests of control

- Review a sample of contracts to confirm **research and tender** process
- **Check back a sample of invoices** to written requisitions
- For a sample of long term contracts, **check long term calculations** exist and are correct
- **Review central database of suppliers** to ensure that none are connected parties

1.5 Marketing audit

Key term

Marketing is the **process of assessing and enhancing demand for the company's products.**

Marketing and its link with sales is very important for the business. An audit may be especially critical for a marketing department which may be complex with several different teams, for example:

- Research
- Advertising
- Promotions
- After sales

It is vital to ensure that **information** is **passed properly** within the department, and activities are streamlined.

It is important for the internal auditor to review the marketing processes to ensure:

- The process is **managed efficiently**
- **Information is freely available** on manager demand
- **Risks** are being **managed** correctly

1.5.1 Risks

- **Customer requirements** are not taken into account
- Customers **do not know about products**
- Prices are **not competitive**
- Goods are **priced** at **too low a level**, promotion considerations resulting in excessive discounts

1.5.2 Aims of controls

- **Customer demand** should be **understood** and met
- Customers should be **made aware** of products
- Products are **competitive** in terms of price and quality
- Goods and services are sold for **valuable consideration**

1.5.3 Controls

Some of the controls will be similar to those discussed in the sales cycle in the last chapter. The following controls might be used to meet the above objectives:

- **Market research** should be commissioned or carried out
- **Actual sales** should be **compared to budgets**
- **Advertising** is **targeted**
- Promotions are **timed to coincide** with periods historically linked with sales, eg Christmas
- **Competitor prices** are **monitored**
- **Terms and conditions** are **made known** to customers
- **Credit checks** are made

1.5.4 Tests of control

Some of the tests, particularly those in relation to credit, will be the same as those discussed in the sales system in the last chapter

- **Review adequacy of company policy** on commissioning market research
- For a sample of major promotions, **check** that **research** was **commissioned** and used
- **Check that actual sales are compared** to budgeted sales and that **variances** are **investigated**
- For a sample of major promotions, **ensure** that **timing** has been considered
- Ensure that **records are maintained** of **competitor pricing policy**
- **Review terms and conditions** to ensure that they comply with company policy
- **Check a sample of contracts/sales** to ensure **terms and conditions** were **highlighted**

1.6 Treasury audit

Key term

Treasury is a function within the finance department of a business. It **manages the funds of a business**.

It is vital for an organisation that funds are managed so that cash is available when required.

There are risks associated with treasury, in terms of interest rate risk and foreign currency risk, and the auditor must ensure that the **risk is managed in accordance with company procedures**.

As with marketing audits, it is vital to ensure that **information is available** to the treasury department, so that they can **ensure funds are available when required**.

1.6.1 Risks

The most important risks affecting the treasury function are as follows.

- **Business activities** have to be **curtailed** due to lack of funds
- Hedging results in **losses** over time
- **Exposures** are **not communicated** to the board

1.6.2 Aims of controls

- Treasury policies are carried out in accordance with **organisation policies**
- **Money is available** to the organisation when it is required
- **Risks** in relation to foreign currency and interest rates are **managed effectively**
- **Transactions** do **not lose** the **organisation** money over time
- **Exposures** are **highlighted** and reported on, on a timely basis
- **Treasury activities** are **fully** and completely **recorded** in the accounts

1.6.3 Controls

- Cash flow **forecasting**
- **Arrangements with the bank** in the event of cash emergencies
- **Contingency funds** available
- Clear policy on **tolerated risk**
- **Regular review of investment**
- Frequent **two-way communication**

1.6.4 Tests of controls

- **Reviewing cash flow forecasts**
- **Read correspondence** with the bank
- **Read contingency plans** and assessing them for realism
- **Discuss review** of investments with investment managers
- **Seek evidence** of **such reviews** being made (reports, memos)
- **Seek evidence** of **communication with board**

We shall look in detail about the ways in which organisations deal with hedging and accounting for financial risks, particularly currency and interest rate risks, in Part D of this Text.

1.7 Human resources audit

Key term

The **human resources** department on one hand **procures a human resource** (employee) for the operation of the business and on the other **supports those employees in developing the organisation**.

The processes need to ensure that people are available to work as the business requires them and that the overall development of the business is planned and controlled.

Again, **ensuring company policies are maintained and information is freely available** are key factors for internal audit to assess.

As well as carrying out specific human resource audits, internal auditors should also consider human resource issues on a range of other operational audits, for example considering whether the treasury function is staffed by employees with sufficient experience of the financial markets.

1.7.1 Risks

- **Inadequate staffing**, either in terms of staff numbers or in terms of expertise
- **Over-reliance** on certain key personnel
- Excessive staff **turnover**
- **Staff** are paid the **wrong amounts**
- The **correct deductions** are not made for taxes
- **Industrial action** disrupts the organisation
- The organisation is subject to **actions for wrongful dismissal**
- Failure to comply with **employment laws**

1.7.2 Aims of controls

- Sufficiently qualified and capable staff **are available** when required
- Staff are paid the **correct remuneration** on a timely basis
- Staff are **content** and not prone to industrial action or seeking alternative employment
- **Employment laws** are **complied** with
- The **human resource** is **handled considerately**
- There is **adequate contingency planning** to overcome staff shortages should they arise

1.7.3 Controls

- The business has a **long term human requirement plan**
- **Salary** is **benchmarked** against the market
- **Performance** of staff is regularly and formally **appraised**
- Staff are given **adequate training**
- **Key personnel** are not put at risk together
- **Long term succession planning** is undertaken
- **Payroll controls** as discussed in Chapter 12
- **Relationships with trade unions** are well maintained
- Human resources managers receive **training in employment law**

1.7.4 Tests of control

- **Obtain a copy** of the **long term human resource plan** and review it
- **Obtain evidence** that the HR department **monitors pay levels** in the market
- **Review of appraisal procedure**, check that a sample of employees have had appraisals
- **Review training records** to ensure that training is in accordance with the organisation;s policy
- **Review long term succession plan** and any 'apprenticing' schemes are in operation
- **Review training procedures** within department by discussion with staff

1.8 Research and development audit

Key terms

The UK's standard SSAP 13 defines research and development expenditure as falling into one or more of the following categories.

(a) **Pure research** is original research to obtain new scientific or technical knowledge or understanding. There is **no clear commercial end** in view and such research work does not have a practical application. Companies and other business entities might carry out this type of research in the hope that it will provide new knowledge which can subsequently be exploited.

(b) **Applied research** is original research work which also seeks to obtain new scientific or technical knowledge, but which has a specific practical aim or application (for example research on improvements in the effectiveness of toothpastes or medicines). Applied research may develop from 'pioneering' pure research, but many companies have full-time research teams working on applied research projects.

(c) **Development** is the use of existing scientific and technical knowledge to produce new (or substantially improved) products or systems, prior to starting commercial production operations.

There are a number of elements in research and development processes; they need to be consistent with **business marketing strategy** and procedures are needed over both research projects and development.

1.8.1 Risks

- **Research and development effort** is **wasted** on projects that will provide no benefits for the company in terms of sales or are not in line with corporate strategy
- **Resources are wasted** on duplicated projects
- Projects do **not deliver** the **planned benefits**, are late or over budget
- **Loss of data** interrupts research and development

1.8.2 Aims of controls

- The **best-quality** and **technically advanced goods and services** are available to customers in the short and long-term
- **Research and development** is **properly planned**, **budgeted**, **monitored and reported**
- Research and development complies with **internal standards** and with **all relevant legislation**
- **Accounting requirements** for research and development are **fulfilled** without distorting their true objectives

1.8.3 Controls

- **Research and development strategy** is **decided** and **reviewed** by the board
- Research and development activities are **co-ordinated centrally**
- Procedures exist for **communicating the results** of research and development
- Research and development activities follow a **common project methodology**
- **Progress on projects** is **reported regularly** against plans and forecasts
- **Post implementation reviews** are carried out on research and development projects
- Research and development staff keep **full, backed-up records** of their findings

1.8.4 Tests of controls

- **Review** and consider adequacy of **organisation guidelines** for research and development projects
- **Test sample of projects** to see whether they have been following guidelines
- **Review budgets** to determine whether they are accurate and check that actual figures have been compared with budgets
- **Check to see** that **results** of research and development have been regularly **communicated** to management
- **Review results** of **post implementation reviews** and confirm that points arising have been actioned
- **Check sample of research and development projects** to accounting records and financial accounts to **confirm fairness of accounting treatments**
- **Check** that **adequate back-up facilities** have been arranged should research and development be interrupted

2 Value for money audits

FAST FORWARD

Value for money audits focus on whether organisations have achieved **economy, efficiency and effectiveness** in their operations. Auditors will review specific areas.

2.1 Measurement of economy, efficiency and effectiveness

A 1990 Audit brief on VFM audit defined the three Es as follows.

(a) **Economy**

Attaining the **appropriate quantity and quality** of physical, human and financial resources (**inputs**) at **lowest cost**. An activity would not be economic, if, for example, there was over-staffing or failure to purchase materials of requisite quality at the lowest available price.

(b) **Efficiency**

This is the relationship between **goods or services produced** (**outputs**) and the **resources** used to produce them. An efficient operation produces the maximum output for any given set of resource inputs; or it has minimum inputs for any given quantity and quality of product or service provided.

(c) **Effectiveness**

This is concerned with how well an **activity** is **achieving its policy objectives** or other intended effects.

The internal auditors will **evaluate these three factors** for any given business system or operation in the company. Value for money can often only be judged by **comparison**. In searching for value for money, present methods of operation and uses of resources must be **compared with alternatives**.

2.2 Example

A good example of value for money is a bottle of Fairy Liquid. If we believe the advertising, Fairy is good 'value for money' because it washes half as many plates again as any other washing up liquid. Bottle for

bottle it may be more expensive, but plate for plate it is cheaper. Not only this but Fairy gets plates 'squeaky' clean. To summarise, Fairy gives us VFM because it exhibits the following characteristics.

- Economy (more clean plates per pound)
- Efficiency (more clean plates per squirt)
- Effectiveness (plates as clean as they should be)

These are the three Es of VFM.

2.3 Measurement of value for money

Economy, efficiency and effectiveness can be studied and measured with reference to the following.

Inputs	Economy
Inputs means money or resources - the labour, materials, time and so on consumed, and their cost. For example, a VFM audit into state secondary education would look at the efficiency and economy of the use of resources for education (the use of schoolteachers, school buildings, equipment, cash) and whether the resources are being used for their purpose: what is the pupil/teacher ratio and are trained teachers being fully used to teach the subjects they have been trained for?	Economy is concerned with the cost of inputs, and it is achieved by obtaining those inputs at the lowest acceptable cost. Economy does not mean straightforward cost-cutting, because resources must be acquired which are of a suitable quality to provide the service to the desired standard. Cost-cutting should not sacrifice quality to the extent that service standards fall to an unacceptable level. Economising by buying poor quality materials, labour or equipment is a 'false economy'.
Outputs	**Efficiency**
Outputs mean the results of an activity, measurable as the services actually produced, and the quality of the services. In the case of a VFM audit of secondary education, outputs would be measured as the number of pupils taught and the number of subjects taught per pupil; how many examination papers are taken and what is the pass rate.	Efficiency means the following. (a) Maximising output for a given input, for example maximising the number of transactions handled per employee or per £1 spent (b) Achieving the minimum input for a given output
Impacts	**Effectiveness**
Impacts are the effect that the outputs of an activity or programme have in terms of achieving policy objectives. Policy objectives might be to provide a minimum level of education to all children up to the age of 16, and to make education relevant for the children's future jobs and careers. This might be measured by the ratio of jobs vacant to unemployed school leavers.	Effectiveness means ensuring that the outputs of a service or programme have the desired impacts; in other words, finding out whether they succeed in achieving objectives, and if so, to what extent. In a profit-making organisation, objectives can be expressed financially in terms of target profit or return. In NFP (not for profit) organisations, effectiveness cannot be measured this way, because the organisation has non-financial objectives. The effectiveness of performance in NFP organisations could be measured in terms of whether targeted non-financial objectives have been achieved.

2.4 Selecting areas for investigation

Value for money can focus on organisation, process or activity. Each of these should be reviewed within individual organisations, with a view to assessing its economy, efficiency and effectiveness.

- Service delivery (the actual provision of a public service)
- Management process
- Environment

An alternative approach is to look at areas of spending. A value for money assessment of economy, efficiency, and effectiveness would look at whether:

- **Too much money** is being spent on certain items or activities, to achieve the targets or objectives of the overall operation.
- Money is being spent to **no purpose**, because the spending is not helping to achieve objectives.
- Changes could be made to **improve performance**.

An illustrative list is shown below of the sort of spending areas that might be looked at, and the aspects of spending where value for money might be improved.

- Employee expenses
- Premises expenses
- Supplies and services
- Establishment expenses
- Capital expenditure

2.5 Auditing value for money

Audit procedures testing **efficient** and **economic use** of **resources** and **processes** can focus on **internal procedures**, including the **adequacy** of the **plans and standards** to be achieved, **comparison of actual performance** against **plans and standards** and also how performance is directed, the **sort of feedback** that is **obtained** by managers and whether this **feedback** is acted upon.

Alternatively the internal audit department can take an investigative approach, focussing on **high-risk areas**. An investigative approach may focus away from compliance with systems and towards other measures of achievement, for example **external benchmarking**.

At the heart of auditing effectiveness is a definition of the **target** to be **achieved**. Auditors will be concerned to measure whether performance is acceptable in relation to the target, and if it isn't how far it has fallen short. One way of measuring effectiveness is to obtain external opinions, either expert opinions or the opinions of the **users** of the services.

2.6 Problems with VFM auditing

Problems with VFM auditing	
Measuring outputs	For example, the outputs of a fire brigade can be measured by the number of call-outs, but it is not satisfactory to compare a call-out to individuals stuck in a lift with a call-out to a small house fire or a major industrial fire or a road accident etc.
Defining objectives	In not for profit organisations the quality of the service provided will be a significant feature of their service. For example, a local authority has, amongst its various different objectives, the objective of providing a rubbish collection service. The effectiveness of this service can only be judged by establishing what standard or quality of service is required.

Problems with VFM auditing	
Sacrifice of quality	Economy and efficiency can be achieved by **sacrificing quality**. Neither outputs nor impacts are necessarily measured in terms of quality. For example, the cost of teaching can be reduced by increasing the pupil:teacher ratio in schools, but it is difficult to judge the consequences of such a change on teaching standards and quality.
Measuring effectiveness	For example, the effectiveness of the health service could be said to have improved if hospitals have greater success in treating various illnesses and other conditions, or if the life expectancy of the population has increased, but a consequence of these changes will be overcrowded hospitals and longer medical waiting lists.
Overemphasis in cost control	There can be an **emphasis** with VFM audits on **costs and cost control** rather than on achieving more benefits and value, so that management might be pressurised into 'short term' decisions, such as abandoning capital expenditure plans which would create future benefits in order to keep current spending levels within limits.
Measuring efficiency	In profit-making organisations, the efficiency of the organisation as a whole can be measured in terms of return on capital employed. Individual profit centres or operating units within the organisation can also have efficiency measured by relating the quantity of output produced, which has a market value and therefore a quantifiable financial value, to the inputs (and their cost) required to make the output. In NFP organisations, output does not usually have a **market value**, and it is therefore more difficult to measure efficiency. This difficulty is compounded by the fact that, since NFP organisations often have many different activities or operations, it is difficult to compare the efficiency of one operation with the efficiency of another. For example, with the police force, it might be difficult to compare the efficiency of a serious crimes squad with the efficiency of the traffic police.

2.7 Best value

'Best value' is a new performance framework introduced into local authorities by the government. They are required to publish annual best value performance plans and review all of their functions over a five year period.

As part of 'Best value' authorities are required to strive for continuous improvement by implementing the '4 Cs':

- **Challenge**. How and why is a service provided?
- **Compare**. Make comparisons with other local authorities and the private sector.
- **Consult**. Talk to local taxpayers and services users and the wider business community in setting performance targets.
- **Compete**. Embrace fair competition as a means of securing efficient and effective services.

2.7.1 Internal auditors and best value

One of internal audit's **standard roles** in an organisation is to **provide assurance that internal control systems are adequate to promote the effective use of resources and that risks are being managed properly**.

In relation to best value, **this role can be extended** to ensure that the authority has arrangements in place to achieve best value, that the risks and impacts of best value are incorporated into normal audit testing and that the authority keeps abreast of best value developments.

As best value depends on assessing current services and setting strategies for development, **internal audit can take part in the 'position audit'**, as they should have a good understanding of how services are currently organised and relate to each other.

As assurance providers, they key part internal audit will play is in **giving management assurance that their objectives and strategies in relation to best value are being met**.

Question

Value for money

Learning outcome: C(v)

(a) Outline the basic principles of value for money auditing.

(b) Give examples of the factors which may be quantified in a VFM investigation.

Answer

(a) VFM audit is also known as performance auditing and effectiveness auditing. Traditionally this focused on the elimination of waste and extravagance but today the role is much wider. VFM auditing is concerned with **economy, efficiency** and **effectiveness**.

Economy is taken to mean the achievement of a given result with the least expenditure of money, manpower or other resources. **Efficiency** extends the idea to that of converting resources into a desired product or service in the most advantageous ratio. **Effectiveness** brings into account the goals and objectives which the activity under audit is intended to meet.

The auditor must assess the effectiveness of activities without questioning the policy decisions made and the objectives they serve. He may give advice on improved management or more effective services but must leave policy decisions to elected councillors, members of Parliament or appointed board members.

The VFM auditors may make use of various 'performance indicators' and comparisons to help him to assess whether the organisation matches up to criteria of economy, efficiency and effectiveness. Do proper arrangements (eg appropriate departmental management information systems) exist for securing economy, efficiency and effectiveness? Are these arrangements operating satisfactorily in practice?

(b) The following are examples of the factors which may be quantified in a VFM investigation.

(i) **Productivity**

Measures of work performed per unit of staff time can be compared at different times. Skilled or professional work is more difficult to measure by this criteria than routine and repetitive tasks. For example, it will be relatively easy to measure the productivity of an invoice processing clerk in terms of the number of invoices processed per hour, but it would be more difficult to apply productivity measures to casework carried out by a social worker.

(ii) **Costs**

Unit costs may be compared over time, or between organisations, or in comparison to budget. Care must be taken in making inter-authority comparisons to ensure that like is being compared with like.

(iii) **Service volume**

An example might be the number of hospital beds provided or the number of operations of a particular type carried out.

(iv) **Public demand**

Waiting lists will provide an indication of potential demand, and trends over time will show whether the organisation is meeting those demands.

(v) **Utilisation of services provided**

Percentages of services may be monitored: a typical example is that of bed occupancy rates.

3 Management audits

FAST FORWARD

Management audit is a method of examining the performance of managers without concentrating exclusively on financial matters.

Key term

Management audit is an objective and independent appraisal of the effectiveness of managers and the corporate structure in the achievement of entity objectives and policies. Its aim is to identify existing and potential management weaknesses and to recommend ways to rectify them.

(CIMA *Official Terminology*)

3.1 Purpose of management audit

A management audit might be thought of as a **non-routine investigation** into the performance of a manager or group of managers which, unlike financial audits by internal or external auditors, attempts to look at all aspects of the management performance, and does not concentrate solely on financial matters.

3.2 Carrying out a management audit

Like any other audit, a management audit involves deciding the **audit objectives** (which managers to audit, what aspects of their work and so on), **carrying out an investigation**, **gathering evidence and reporting the results**. The difficulty here is the subjective nature of the audit objectives, which are to do with management policy decisions, rather than just transactions and systems.

It is therefore imperative early on in the audit planning to consider the areas the audit will cover, and what will be the end product of the audit - what forms **reports** will take.

Management audits can cover a wide variety of situations, for example to consider whether management policies are being applied to purchase of company cars, promotions and the sale of fixed assets no longer in use.

3.3 Management audit and the three Es

Auditing of a manager's efficiency and economy calls for obtaining evidence on whether the manager has used his or her **resources** (labour, materials, fixed assets, other assets, and management information) in the **best way** and without overspending and waste.

These findings are reported, with suitable recommendations, to the person to whom the manager is accountable (for example to the manager's superior, or a higher authority, such as the board of directors.

Similarly, auditing of a manager's **effectiveness** in his or her job calls for obtaining evidence on whether a manager has had a **clear objective** (or objectives) and **sufficient authority** and **resources** to achieve that **objective**, and whether the objective (or objectives) have in fact been **achieved**.

An assessment of efficiency, economy and effectiveness can be achieved by financial measures, many of them routine. Examples are as follows.

- **Setting a budgeted expenditure limit** for a manager, and expecting the manager not to overspend this limit
- **Setting a target for achievement** (eg completion of a project) and then measuring the cost of the work done and whether the benefits have justified the costs
- **Budgetary control** variance reporting
- **Profit centre profitability**
- **An investment centre's ROI**

Audits of **economy** can also be much more detailed. The auditors can look into the items of expenditure incurred by a manager, to assess whether they have been excessive, or perhaps inadequate. For example, an investigation might look into spending on office computer systems by a manager. Has there been too much spending on equipment that is too unsophisticated for the job in hand? Has the price paid been excessive? Is the usage of magnetic files and printer stationery excessive? Is the manager reluctant to computerise office procedures?

3.4 What weaknesses might a management audit reveal?

The following examples are illustrative of what weaknesses a management audit might find.

(a) Weaknesses among members of the **board of directors.** In particular, directors might be found to give insufficient attention to planning for the future (for example, refusing to fund research and development).

(b) A lack of awareness among directors and managers of the **objectives** of the organisation, and the extent to which these are being achieved; a failure to define clearly the objectives and responsibilities of individual managers.

(c) Standards or **targets** are not being **met**.

(d) Inadequate steps are being taken to provide **adequate finance** for the company.

(e) The **wrong sort of managers** are being recruited and employed; and managers have insufficient technical competence to do their job, or are not up-to-date with the current technology to do their job as well as they should.

(f) Managers are **unwilling to delegate**, and retain authority for matters which ought to be delegated.

(g) There is a **lack** of any clear and identifiable **management style** in the organisation.

(h) There is not **enough staff/management training**.

(i) Managers do **not** do enough to **measure** and **assess** the **performance** of their subordinates.

(j) **Methods of work** have been **inadequately defined**; or procedures have been laid down but are not properly enforced.

(k) Managers **waste too much** of their **time**.

(l) The **management information systems** in the company are **inadequate**, and managers do not get the sort of information they need at the right time.

(m) Management audits at branch/local unit level may discover where the **local unit** is making decisions which are **sub-optimal** to the organisation as a whole, because the local unit has not followed company policy but instead 'gone its own way'.

4 Social and environmental audits

FAST FORWARD

Social and environmental audits are designed to ascertain whether the organisation is complying with codes of best practice or internal guidelines or is fulfilling the wider requirements of being a good corporate citizen.

4.1 Social audits

The process of checking whether an organisation has achieved set targets may fall within a social audit that a company carries out.

Social audits will involve:

- Establishing whether the organisation has a **rationale** for engaging in socially responsible activity
- Identifying that all current environment programmes are **congruent** with the mission of the company
- **Assessing objectives and priorities** related to these programmes
- **Evaluating company involvement** in such programmes past, present and future

Whether or not a social audit is used depends on the degree to which social responsibility is part of the **corporate philosophy**. A cultural awareness must be achieved within an organisation in order to implement environmental policy, which requires Board and staff support.

4.1.1 Targets and indicators

The targets and indicators that social audits are designed to consider will **vary** from **organisation to organisation**, depending on what the issues are. To illustrate the point, a case study based on the 2000 annual report of Shell is given below.

Case Study

Measuring Social Performance

Shell is a large multi-national company that deals in oil, gas and chemicals. There are various issues which make social and environmental issues important to this company:

- It deals in the earth's natural resources
- The business is heavily environmentally legislated
- It employs a significant number of people
- Some employees work in risky environments
- It operates in areas of the world where Human Rights issues are not given sufficient priority

Targets

In response to the social and environmental issues raised above, the company have set targets of social and environmental performance which they evaluate and report on to shareholders on an annual basis.

The following are examples of targets which the company has set:

Environmental

- Reduce emissions of carbon dioxide from refinery activity
- Continue to develop cleaner fuels
- Reduce emissions of nitrogen oxides from burning fuel in our operations
- Eliminate spills of crude oil, oil and chemicals

Social

- Zero employee fatalities in work-related incidents
- Not exploit children in any country where child labour exists, by
  - Employing children under the legal age of employment
  - Dealing with other companies who employ children illegally
- Pursue equal opportunities for men and women in all countries that this is legally possible

Sustainability principles

The company has also set general sustainability principles which all staff should apply in daily business:

- Respect and safeguard people
- Engage and work with stakeholders
- Minimise impact on the environment
- Use resources efficiently
- Maximise profitability
- Maximise benefits to the community

Reporting

The company reports on all these issues to its shareholders, and where-ever possible, the facts included within this report are verified by independent verifiers.

The case study shows a number of targets and sustainability indicators. Some can be measured in mathematical terms, for example:

- Emissions
- Spills
- Elimination of work-related fatalities
- Employment of children

However, some of the targets are not specific enough to be able to measure in that way. For example, it is more difficult to identify whether the company is in relation to achieving a target of developing cleaner fuels until the cleaner fuel appears. Such a development target cannot have a prescribed timescale.

Equally, it is difficult to measure the effect of the general principles which the company has included within the culture of the company.

4.2 Environmental audits

Key term

Environmental audits seek to assess how well the organisation performs in safeguarding the environment in which it operates, and whether the company complies with its environmental policies.

An environmental audit might be undertaken as part of obtaining or maintaining the BSI's ISO 14001 standard.

Auditors will mainly be concerned with the following:

- Board and management having **good understanding** of the environmental impact and related legislation of the organisation's activities in areas such as buildings, transport, products, packaging and waste
- Adoption and communication of adequate policies and procedures to ensure **compliance with relevant standards and laws**
- Adoption and **review of progress** against quantifiable targets
- Assessment of whether **progress** is being made **economically and efficiently**
- **True, fair and complete reporting** of environmental activities

The auditor will carry out the following steps:

- Obtain a copy of the organisation's environmental policy
- Assess whether the policy is likely to achieve objectives:
  - Meet **legal requirements**
  - Meet **environmental standards**
  - Satisfy key **customers/suppliers' criteria**
- **Test implementation and adherence** to the policy by:
  - Discussion
  - Observation
  - 'Walk-though tests' where possible

Chapter Roundup

- Controls over operations are designed to ensure that **customer requirements** are taken into account. **Assets and resources** are made **available when required**, **assets** are **safeguarded**, **legislation** and **internal guidelines** are followed, and **operations** are **monitored** and **reviewed** by management.
- **Operational audits** are a vital part of the **operational control process**, designed to confirm **adequacy and implementation** of control and risk management policies.
- **Value for money audits** focus on whether organisations have achieved **economy, efficiency and effectiveness** in their operations. Auditors will review specific areas.
- **Management audit** is a method of examining the performance of managers without concentrating exclusively on financial matters.
- **Social and environmental audits** are designed to ascertain whether the organisation is complying with codes of best practice or internal guidelines or is fulfilling the wider requirements of being a good corporate citizen.

Quick Quiz

1 Fill in the blank.

.... are the processes by which materials or goods are brought into the business, transferred between locations and delivered to customers.

2 Which other systems would be included within a procurement system?

3 What are the most important aims of controls over the treasury function?

4 What are the most important risks affecting an organisation's research and development?

5 Link the value for money 'E' with its definition.

(a) Economy
(b) Efficiency
(c) Effectiveness

(i) The relationships between the goods and services produced (outputs) and the resources used to produce them.

(ii) The concern with how well an activity is achieving its policy objectives or other intended effects.

(iii) Attaining the appropriate quantity and quality of physical, human and financial resources (inputs) at lowest cost.

6 In the context of best value audits what are the four Cs?

7 Management audits will normally be designed to measure a manager's performance in financial terms

True ☐

False ☐

8 What sort of areas might be covered by a social audit?

Answers to Quick Quiz

1 **Logistics** are the processes by which materials or goods are brought into the business, transferred between locations and delivered to customers.

2
- Tendering
- Placing orders
- Checking goods inwards

3
- Treasury policies are carried out in accordance with company policies
- Money is available to the company when it is required
- Risks in relation to foreign currency and interest rates are managed effectively
- Transactions do not lose the company money over time
- Exposures are highlighted and reported on, on a timely basis
- Treasury activities are fully and completely recorded in the accounts

4
- Research and development effort is wasted on projects that will provide no benefits for the company in terms of sales or are not in line with corporate strategy
- Resources are wasted on duplicated projects
- Projects do not deliver the planned benefits, are late or over budget
- Loss of data interrupts research and development

5 (a) (iii), (b) (i), (c) (ii)

6
- Challenge
- Compare
- Consult
- Compete

7 False. Not necessarily. The audit may focus on non-financial issues such as ability to delegate, adequacy of training and so forth.

8
- Sustainable use of resources
- Compliance with health and safety
- No exploitation of labour, particularly child labour
- Equal opportunities

Now try the question below from the Exam Question Bank

Number	Level	Marks	Time
Q14	Examination	25	45 mins

15

Fraud

Introduction

In this chapter we consider the various types of fraud that internal audit may have to investigate. The exam may require discussion of a variety of types of fraud, but may well give most importance to fraud related to sources of finance, hence we discuss these in more detail in section 2. It is important that you are able to identify signs of fraud in different circumstances, so work carefully through Section 3. You also need to have a good knowledge of both how fraud is prevented **and** detected. Remember that although there may be significant costs involved in implementing a good system of fraud prevention, the **consequences** of successful fraud may be very serious, both for the **reputation** of the organisation and the position of its directors.

Topic list	Learning outcomes	Syllabus references	Ability required
1 Types of fraud	C(iii),(iv)	C(3)	Evaluation
2 Fraud related to sources of finance	C(iii),(iv)	C(3)	Evaluation
3 Fraud risks	C(iii),(iv)	C(3)	Evaluation
4 Prevention of fraud	C(iii),(iv)	C(3)	Evaluation
5 Detection of fraud	C(iii),(iv)	C(3)	Evaluation

1 Types of fraud

FAST FORWARD

Common frauds include **payroll frauds**, **conspiracy with other parties** and **stealing assets**.

Key term

In a famous court case, **fraud** was defined as:

'a false representation of fact made with the knowledge of its falsity, or without belief in its truth, or recklessly careless, whether it be true or false.'

1.1 Incidence of fraud

While the vast majority of employees are honest, some employees may decide to **act dishonestly**. The incidence of financial fraud, particularly in a computer environment, is increasing. This presents a challenge to management and to internal (and external) auditors.

The mere presence of internal auditors should discourage fraudsters for fear of being discovered. The widely-held general perception that auditors should be expected to uncover all fraud is unrealistic, as it is not feasible to check every transaction and entry.

However, it is not unreasonable to expect fraud involving amounts that are **material** to be detected.

Internal auditors will best be able to detect frauds if they are knowledgeable about the most common methods of fraud (but not experienced in them!). These are described in the following paragraphs.

1.2 Ghost employees

These are **imaginary employees** whose 'wages' are paid and distributed amongst the fraudsters. This type of fraud is easier to perform if there is extensive reliance on casual workers, and minimal record keeping for such workers.

A detection tool that may indicate this type of fraud is a **review of the numbers of employees** required to achieve a standard amount of work. If at some times of the year a larger number appear to be required, there may be something amiss.

Scrutiny of signatures given as proof of receipt of wages should be made, together with an examination of bank direct credit schedules.

1.3 Miscasting of the payroll

This fraud involves **'skimming' a very small amount** off each genuine wage or salary payment. For example, an employee who has earned £210.95 would receive only £210.90 in their bank account – the other £0.05 being skimmed off into the fraudster's account! The fraud relies on employees either not noticing or not complaining about the very small discrepancy. Over a large number of employees this can lead to substantial payments.

1.4 Stealing unclaimed wages

This is effectively confined to **wages paid in cash** and can occur when an employee leaves without notice or is away sick.

1.5 Collusion with external parties

This could involve **suppliers**, **customers** or their staff. Possible frauds are overcharging on purchase invoices, undercharging on sales invoices or the sale of confidential information (eg customer lists, expansion plans) to a competitor. Management should watch out for unusual discounts or commissions being given or taken, or for an excessive zeal on the part of an employee to handle all business with a particular company.

1.6 Altering cheques and inflating expense claims

These are self-explanatory. They can include **claiming expenses** more than once, **claiming on personal expenses** but paying on a **company credit card**, **inflated car mileage claims** and **private entertaining** billed to the organisation.

1.7 Stealing assets

Using the **organisation's assets for personal gain and stealing inventory or fully-depreciated assets** are both encountered in practice. Whether or not the private use of company telephones and photocopiers is a serious matter is up to the organisation to judge, but it may still be fraudulent.

1.8 Issuing false credit notes

Another way of avoiding detection when cash and cheques received from customers have been misappropriated is to **issue a credit note that is not sent to the customer** (who has paid his account) but is recorded in the books. The issue of itemised statements monthly may show this up, as the customer should query the credit note. A similar tactic is to write a debt off as bad to cover up the disappearance of the payment.

1.9 Sales fraud

Failing to record all sales may be perpetrated in a business with extremely **poor controls over sales recording** and minimal segregation of duties. In such circumstances, a dishonest bookkeeper may **invoice customers** but **fail to record the invoices** so that the customer's payments never have to be recorded.

This type of fraud can occur where a customer is receiving large numbers of invoices from the business every month and so the bookkeeper's failure to record one or two invoices (if detected by auditors or his superiors) is simply put down to incompetence rather than fraud. A warning sign here is the perception by customers that 'your accounts department is a mess ... always getting things wrong ... we've given up trying to get our account right '.

Other sales frauds include **overcharging**, **not delivering the quantity ordered** and **bribery of customers**.

2 Fraud related to sources of finance

FAST FORWARD

Examples of financial fraud include **teeming and lading**, **manipulation of accounts**, **advance fee frauds** and **pyramid schemes**.

2.1 Types of fraud

Some methods of fraud relating to sources of finance are described briefly in the following paragraphs.

2.2 Teeming and lading

This is a 'rolling' fraud rather than a 'one-off' fraud. It occurs when a clerk has the chance to misappropriate payments from customers or to suppliers.

(a) Cash received by the company is **'borrowed'** by the **cashier** rather than being kept as petty cash or banked.

(b) When the cashier knows that a **reconciliation** is to be performed, or audit visit planned, he **pays the money back** so that everything appears satisfactory at that point, but after the audit the teeming and lading starts again.

Surprise visits by auditors and **independent checking** of cash balances should discourage this fraud.

Another common fraud may arise when one employee has sole control of the sales ledger and recording debtors' cheques.

(a) The employee **pays cheques** into a **separate bank account**, either by forged endorsement or by opening an account in a name similar to the employer's.

(b) The clerk has to **allocate cheques or cash received** from other customers against the account of the customer whose payment was misappropriated. This prevents other staff from asking why the account is still overdue or from sending statements etc to the customers. However, the misallocation has to continue as long as the money is missing.

This fraud, therefore, never really stops. It can be detected by **independent verification** of debtors balances (eg by circulation) and by **looking at unallocated payments**, if the sales ledger is organised to show this. In addition, sending out **itemised monthly statements** to debtors should act as a deterrent.

2.3 Manipulation of accounts

While **employee fraud** is usually undertaken purely for the employee's financial gain, **management fraud** is often undertaken to **improve** the company's apparent **performance**, to **reduce tax liabilities** or to **improve managers' promotion prospects**. Managers are often in a position to override internal controls and to intimidate their subordinates into collusion or turning a blind eye. This makes it difficult to detect such frauds.

This clash of interest between loyalty to an employer and professional integrity can be difficult to resolve. Management manipulation of results often comes to light after a takeover or on a change of internal audit staff or practices. Its consequences can be far reaching for the employing company in **damaging its reputation** or because it **results in legal action**. Because management usually have access to much larger sums of money than more lowly employees, the financial loss to the company can be immense.

2.4 Advance fee fraud

This type of fraud involves the fraudster taking a fee or deposit up-front, promising to **deliver in the future** goods and services that never materialise.

Many companies have been **exposed to such frauds** from international sources. In recent years, for example, the highest incidence of such fraud led to the Central Bank of Nigeria publishing warnings around the world. Hopefully, wide publicity about the details of such fraud schemes will mean that fewer such frauds will be perpetrated successfully.

Advance fee fraud in Nigeria

The advance fee fraud is normally perpetrated by the sending of a letter that promises to transfer million of US dollars to the addressee's bank account. In order to gain access to the funds, the addressee is requested to assist in paying various 'taxes' and 'fees' that will allow the funds to be processed. The fraudsters often make use of fake Government, Central Bank and Nigerian National Petroleum Corporation documents and go to considerable lengths to give the scam the appearance of a legitimate offer. They request confidentiality about the transaction.

The gathering of advance fees, made up of supposed legal fees, registration fees, VAT and so on, is the actual objective of the scam.

Two recent variants of the scam have been reported. The first, normally directed at religious and charitable organisations, is the request for fees to process bogus inheritances from a will. The second is an offer to use chemicals to transform paper into US dollar bills with the proceeds being shared by both parties.

2.5 Pyramid scheme frauds

Pyramid scheme frauds can take various forms. The schemes are based on the idea that the scope of the scheme **continually widens** to **involve more people**. People (or firms) newly recruited to the scheme may be **induced to invest money** that is not actually invested but goes towards paying returns to others already in the scheme. While the membership of the scheme multiplies, it appears that those in the scheme cannot lose.

However, such a scheme is destined to fail eventually as the flow of potential recruits dries up. Those setting up the scheme may have made themselves rich, at the expense of those recently recruited to the scheme.

3 Fraud risks

FAST FORWARD

Signs of high fraud risk include indications of **lack of integrity**, **excessive pressures**, **poor control systems**, **unusual transactions** and **lack of audit evidence**.

3.1 Signs of fraud risk

Internal auditors should be alert for signs of fraud risk during **any** work that they carry out. A list of examples of conditions or events that may increase the risk of either fraud or error or both and indicate that they may exist. The list is partly based on a list given in the UK Auditing Practices Board's auditing standard SAS 110 *Fraud and error.*

Fraud and error	
Previous experience or incidents which call into question the integrity or competence of management	Management dominated by one person (or a small group) and no effective oversight board or committee Complex corporate structure where complexity does not seem to be warranted High turnover rate of key accounting and financial personnel Personnel (key or otherwise) not taking holidays Personnel lifestyles that appear to be beyond their known income Significant and prolonged under-staffing of the accounting department Poor relations between executive management and internal auditors Lack of attention given to, or review of, key internal accounting data such as cost estimates Frequent changes of legal advisors or auditors History of legal and regulatory violations
Particular financial reporting pressures within an entity	Industry volatility Inadequate working capital due to declining profits or too rapid expansion Deteriorating quality of earnings, for example increased risk taking with respect to credit sales, changes in business practice or selection of accounting policy alternatives that improve income The entity needs a rising profit trend to support the market price of its shares due to a contemplated public offering, a takeover or other reason Significant investment in an industry or product line noted for rapid change Pressure on accounting personnel to complete financial statements in an unreasonably short period of time Dominant owner-management Performance-based remuneration
Weaknesses in the design and operation of the accounting and internal controls system	A weak control environment within the entity Systems that, in their design, are inadequate to give reasonable assurance of preventing or detecting error or fraud Inadequate segregation of responsibilities in relation to functions involving the handling, recording or controlling of the entity's assets Poor security of assets Lack of access controls over IT systems Indications that internal financial information is unreliable Evidence that internal controls have been overridden by management Ineffective monitoring of the operation of system which allows control overrides, breakdown or weakness to continue without proper corrective action Continuing failure to correct major weakness in internal control where such corrections are practicable and cost effective

Fraud and error	
Unusual transactions	Unusual transactions, especially near the year end, that have a significant effect on earnings Complex transactions or accounting treatments Unusual transactions with related parties Payments for services (for example to lawyers, consultants or agents) that appear excessive in relation to the services provided Large cash transactions Transactions dealt with outside the normal systems Investments in products that appear too good to be true, for example low risk, high return products
Problems in obtaining sufficient appropriate audit evidence	Inadequate records, for example incomplete files, excessive adjustments to accounting records, transactions not recorded in accordance with normal procedures and out-of-balance control accounts Inadequate documentation of transactions, such as lack of proper authorisation, supporting documents not available and alternation to documents (any of these documentation problems assume greater significance when they relate to large or unusual transactions) An excessive number of differences between accounting records and third party confirmations, conflicting audit evidence and unexplainable changes in operating ratios Evasive, delayed or unreasonable responses by management to audit inquires Inappropriate attitude of management to the conduct of the audit, eg time pressure, scope limitation and other constraints
Some factors unique to an information systems environment which relate to the conditions and events described above	Inability to extract information from computer files due to lack of, or non-current, documentation of record contents or programs Large numbers of program changes that are not documented, approved and tested Inadequate overall balancing of computer transactions and data bases to the financial accounts

Question — Procurement fraud

Learning outcomes: C(ii)

Give examples of indicators of fraud in the tendering process.

Answer

(a) **Suppliers**

Examples include **disqualification of suitable suppliers**, a very **short list of alternatives** and **continual use** of the **same suppliers** or a single source. The organisation should also be alert for any signs of personal relationships between staff and suppliers.

(b) **Contract terms**

Possible signs here include **contract specifications** that do not make commercial sense and contracts that include special, but unnecessary specifications, that only one supplier can meet.

(c) **Bid and awarding process**

Signs of doubtful practice include **unclear evaluation criteria**, **acceptance of late bids** and **changes in the contract specification** after some bids have been made. Suspicions might be aroused if reasons for awarding the contract are unclear or the contract is awarded to a supplier with a **poor performance record** or who appears to **lack the resources** to carry out the contract.

(d) **After the contract is awarded**

Changes to the contract after it has been awarded should be considered carefully, also a large number of **subsequent changes in contract specifications** or **liability limits**.

4 Prevention of fraud

FAST FORWARD

In order to prevent fraud, managers must be aware of the **risks** and **signs** of fraud.

Exam focus point

Questions on fraud are likely in this paper. The emphasis may be on how management control systems can **prevent fraud**.

4.1 Prioritising prevention

Prevention of fraud must be an **integral** part of **corporate strategy**. Managing the risk of fraud is a key part of managing business risks in general, and if the company's risk management procedures are poor, management of fraud risk is also likely to be unsuccessful.

Certain recent developments, notably downsizing, have however meant that certain controls that are designed to prevent fraud, for example segregation of duties, may not be possible. Hence it is equally important the control system is designed so as to **detect and investigate** fraud.

4.2 Reasons for fraud

Management must have an understanding of how and why frauds might arise Examples include:

(a) The risk of fraud may be increased by factors that are specific to the **industry**. Lower profit margins due to increased competition may be a temptation to manipulate results.

(b) Factors specific to the **business** may also increase the risk of fraud.

  (i) **Personnel** factors such as extensive authority given to dominant managers.

  (ii) **Organisation** factors such as unclear structure of responsibility or lack of supervision of remote locations.

  (iii) **Strategy** factors such as a lack of a business strategy or great emphasis being placed on reward by results.

(c) **Changes in circumstances** may also increase the risk of fraud. Often a control system may become inadequate as a result of changes in the business, particularly changes in technology or internal organisation.

(d) Certain areas, for example cash sales are **normally high risk**.

4.3 Reasons for poor controls

Management also need to understand factors that may prevent controls from operating properly.

(a) Controls will not function well if there is a **lack of emphasis** on compliance or a **lack of understanding** of why the controls are required, how they should operate and who should be operating them.

(b) **Staff problems** such as understaffing, poor quality or poorly motivated staff can impede the operation of controls.

(c) **Changes in senior personnel** can lead to a lack of supervision during the transition period.

(d) **Emphasis on the autonomy of operational management** may lead to controls being bypassed.

4.4 General prevention policies

FAST FORWARD

Prevention policies include emphasis on **ethics** and **personnel and training procedures**. Controls within particular business areas such as **segregation of duties** and **documentation requirements** are also significant.

Management can implement certain general controls that are designed to prevent fraud.

(a) **Emphasising ethics** can decrease the chances of fraud. Several businesses have formal codes of ethics which employees are required to sign covering areas such as gifts from customers. Management can also ensure that they set 'a good example'.

(b) **Personnel controls** are a very important means of preventing fraud. Thorough **interviewing** and **recruitment procedures** including obtaining references can be an effective screening for dishonest employees. **Appraisal** and grievance systems can prevent staff demotivation.

(c) **Training and raising awareness** can be important. There are many examples of frauds taking place where people who were unwittingly close were shocked that they had no idea what was happening. **Fraud awareness education** should therefore be an integral part of the training programme, particularly for managers and staff in **high risk areas** such as procurement, and staff with key roles in fraud prevention and detection, for example human resources.

4.5 Prevention of fraud in specific business areas

Controls will also be needed in specific areas of the business where a high risk of fraud has been identified.

(a) **Segregation of duties** is a key control in fraud prevention. Ultimately operational pressures may mean that segregation is incomplete. Management should nevertheless identify certain functions that must be kept separate, for example separating the cheque signing function from the authorisation of payments.

(b) **Appropriate documentation** should be required for all transactions.

(c) **Limitation controls** such as only allowing staff to choose suppliers from an approved list, or limiting access to the computer network by means of passwords can reduce the opportunities for fraud.

(d) Certain actions should be **prohibited** such as leaving a computer terminal without logging off.

(e) **Internal audit** work should **concentrate** on these areas.

5 Detection of fraud

FAST FORWARD

Managers and staff should be aware of their **responsibilities** to help in detecting fraud. Fraud detection is also helped by having **information readily available** and allowing **whistleblowing**.

5.1 Manager and staff responsibilities

If fraud is to be detected, it is important that everyone involved in detection should be aware of their responsibilities.

(a) **Operational managers** should be **alert for signs** of petty fraud, as well as checking the work staff have done and also being aware of what staff are doing.

(b) **Finance staff** should be alert for **unusual items** or **trends** in accounting data, also incomplete financial information.

(c) **Personnel staff** should be alert for **signs of discontent** or **low morale**, and also should(if possible) be aware of close personal relationships between staff who work together.

(d) **Internal audit staff** have responsibility for ensuring **systems** and controls are thoroughly **reviewed**. One off exercises such as surprise visits may be undertaken alongside annual audit work.

(e) **External audit staff** are required to **assess** the **risk** that fraud may have a **material impact** on a company's accounts when planning their audit work. They are required to **report** all instances of fraud found to management, unless they suspect management of being involved in the fraud. The external auditors should also report to management any material weaknesses in the accounting and internal control systems.

(f) **Non-executive directors** should **act** on **signs** of **dishonesty** by senior executive management. The **audit committee** should **review the organisation's performance** in fraud prevention and report any suspicious matters to the board.

5.1.1 Fraud officer

Many large organisations have appointed a fraud officer, who is responsible for **initiating** and **overseeing fraud investigations**, **implementing the fraud response plan**, and for **any follow-up actions**. The fraud officer should be able to **talk to staff confidentially** and be able to **provide advice** without consulting senior management.

5.2 Availability of information

It is of course important that information should be available to enable management to identify signs of actual fraud, or of an environment where fraud may occur.

(a) **Cost and management accounting systems** should **provide** promptly **information** with sufficient detail to enable management to identify parts of the business whose performance is out of line with expectations. Actual results should be compared with budgeted results and explanations sought for significant variances.

(b) **Personnel procedures** such as **staff meetings**, **appraisals** and **exit interviews** may indicate low morale or staff who are under undue pressure.

(c) **Lines of reporting** should be **clear**. Staff should know to whom they should report any suspicions of fraud.

5.3 Whistleblowing

The likelihood of fraud detection may have been increased by recent legislation in a number of countries that provides **employment protection rights** to 'whistleblowers', employees who reveal fraud or malpractice in a workplace. The legislation covers disclosure of certain 'relevant failures', including committal of a criminal offence, failure to comply with legislation, endangering health and safety or damaging the environment.

Some employers are introducing a formal concerns procedure, which sets out how potential whistleblowers should communicate their concerns.

5.4 Investigation of fraud

FAST FORWARD

Organisations should establish a **fraud response plan**, setting out how the **method** and **extent** of the fraud and **possible suspects** should be investigated.

If the worse does happen there should be a **fraud response plan**, a strategy for **investigating** and **dealing with the consequences** of frauds that have occurred.

Certain actions might have to be taken as soon as the fraud comes to light. There may include **ensuring the security of the records** that will be used to investigate what has happened, and also the **securing of assets** that may be vulnerable to theft. Procedures may have to include suspending staff, changing passwords and so on.

Investigation procedures should be designed with the following aims in mind:

(a) **Establishing** the **extent** of the loss, ascertain on whom it fell and assess how it may be recovered

(b) **Establishing how** the fraud **occurred**

(c) Considering **who else** may have been **implicated** in the fraud

(d) Assessing whether the **fraud** was not detected because **existing controls** were not operating properly, or whether existing controls would have been unlikely to prevent or identify the fraud

Key decisions in fraud investigation will include who will be **carrying out the investigation** and also whether the investigation will be **undercover**. Guidance produced by the accountancy firm KPMG has highlighted the importance of obtaining quickly a picture of the **activities** of the suspected fraudster by reviewing his personal paperwork (diaries, files, expense claims etc.) and also contacting the people who worked with him.

Ultimately the detection and prevention of fraud requires not only a **clear strategy** but also a **willingness to enforce controls**. One of the 'Big Four' accountancy firms, Ernst and Young undertook an international survey called '*Fraud- the unmanaged risk*' The interesting results of this survey are summarised below.

Fraud - the unmanaged risk: Ernst & Young

- 1 in 4 businesses had lost over US$1m through fraud in the last 5 years.
- 2 out of 5 businesses had suffered more than 5 frauds in the last 5 years. Some had detected more than 50.
- More than half the fraud were discovered by chance.
- More than three quarters of the frauds were committed by employees. Only financial institutions were hit mainly by outsiders.
- Businesses were most concerned about computer and purchasing frauds.
- Over three quarters of the respondents believed the worst fraud they had experienced was preventable. But lack of prevention policies and inadequate controls meant that over half believed it could happen again.
- 88% of respondents felt that organisations were as much or more at risk from fraud than 5 years ago.
- 3 out of 5 growing businesses expand first and put the controls in place later.
- Nearly half of the respondents thought that their organisation's directors had a less than good understanding of their core business and that their understanding of overseas operations was even lower.
- Significantly fewer frauds are suffered by businesses whose directors retain full responsibility for instituting and implementing fraud prevention controls.
- 3 out of 4 businesses thought that their internal controls could be overridden by senior managers intent on fraud.
- Nearly half believed that the courts do not understand major fraud cases.

Chapter Roundup

- Common frauds include **payroll frauds**, **conspiracy with other parties** and **stealing assets**.
- Examples of financial fraud include **teeming and lading**, **manipulation of accounts**, **advance fee frauds** and **pyramid schemes**.
- Signs of high fraud risk include indications of **lack of integrity**, **excessive pressures**, **poor control systems**, **unusual transactions** and **lack of audit evidence**.
- In order to prevent fraud, managers must be aware of the **risks** and **signs** of fraud.
- Prevention policies include emphasis on **ethics** and **personnel and training** procedures. Controls within particular business areas such as **segregation of duties** and **documentation requirements** are also significant.
- Managers and staff should be aware of their **responsibilities** to help in detecting fraud. Fraud detection is also helped by having **information readily available** and allowing **whistleblowing**.
- Organisations should establish a **fraud response plan**, setting out how the **method** and **extent** of the fraud and **possible suspects** should be investigated.

Quick Quiz

1 What factors might indicate fraudulent collusion with external parties?

2 What is teeming and lading?

3 Fill in the blank.

.... continually widen to involve more people.

4 Give three examples of problems in obtaining audit evidence that might indicate fraud.

5 What are the main factors that might prevent controls operating properly?

6 What are the main personnel controls that can be used to limit the risk of fraud?

7 Define whistleblowing.

8 How is the audit committee involved in fighting fraud?

Answers to Quick Quiz

1 Unusual discounts or commissions, or excessive eagerness to handle certain clients by oneself

2 Misappropriation of funds and their temporary repayment when an audit takes place.

3 **Pyramid schemes** continually widen to involve more people.

4
- Inadequate records
- Inadequate documentation of transactions
- Differences between accounting records and third party confirmations
- Lack of response by management to enquiries
- Unreasonable time pressures from management

5
- Lack of emphasis on compliance
- Lack of understanding of why controls are required
- Staff problems
- Changes in senior personnel
- Excessive emphasis on the authority of line management

6
- Rigorous recruitment procedures including interviews and references
- Appraisals
- Procedures to deal with grievances

7 Reporting fraud and malfeasance in the workplace

8 As well as being a possible recipient of allegations by whistleblowers and being alert for signs of fraud by executive management, the audit committee should review the organisation's fraud policies and any instance of actual fraud as part of their annual review of internal control.

Now try the questions below from the Exam Question Bank

Number	Level	Marks	Time
Q15	Introductory	N/a	30 mins

16

Ethics

Introduction

In the last chapter in this section we deal with the ethical issues that affect how the auditors conduct internal reviews and how auditors report their findings.
We begin by a brief consideration of what ethics are; although this might seem theoretical, the issue of whether ethical behaviour is obeying a series of rules or striving towards best practice is fundamental and has various practical implications.
We then consider the main external and internal guidelines that internal auditors should follow, and then we shall examine how you should approach the kind of situation that you will encounter in your exam.

Topic list	Learning outcomes	Syllabus references	Ability required
1 Ethics	C(vii)	C(8)	Evaluation
2 CIMA guidelines	C(vii)	C(8)	Evaluation
3 Organisational guidelines and corporate codes	C(vii)	C(8)	Evaluation
4 Practical situations	C(vii)	C(9)	Evaluation
5 Examination questions: an approach	C(vii)	C(9)	Evaluation

1 Ethics

FAST FORWARD

Ethics, a set of moral principles, are manifest in various ways, for example CIMA's code. Ethics can be approached by following rules, or striving for the best possible standards of behaviour.

1.1 What do ethics mean?

Key term

Ethics are a set of moral principles to guide behaviour

Ethics in organisations relates to **social responsibility** and **business practice.**

Organisations contain a variety of ethical systems.

(a) **Personal ethics** (eg deriving from a person's upbringing, religious or non-religious beliefs, political opinions, personality). People have different ethical viewpoints at different stages in their lives. Some will judge situations on 'gut feel'. Some will consciously or unconsciously adopt a general approach to ethical dilemmas, such as 'the end justifies the means'.

(b) **Professional ethics** (eg CIMA's code of ethics, medical ethics).

(c) **Organisation cultures** (eg 'customer first').Culture, in denoting what is normal behaviour, denotes what is the right behaviour in many cases.

(d) **Organisation systems**. Ethics might be contained in a formal code, reinforced by the overall statement of values. A problem might be that ethics do not always save money, and there is a real cost to ethical decisions. Besides, the organisation has different ethical duties to different stakeholders. Who sets priorities?

1.2 Compliance vs integrity based approaches

Lynne Paine (*Harvard Business Review*, March-April 1994) suggests that there are two approaches to the management of ethics in organisations.

- **Compliance**-based
- **Integrity**-based

1.2.1 Compliance-based approach

A compliance-based approach is primarily designed to ensure that the company **acts within the letter of the law**, and that violations are prevented, detected and punished. Some organisations, faced with the legal consequences of unethical behaviours, take legal precautions such as those below.

- Compliance procedures to detect misconduct
- Audits of contracts
- Systems for employees to report criminal misconduct without fear of retribution
- Disciplinary procedures to deal with transgressions

Corporate compliance is limited in that it relates only to the law, but legal compliance is 'not an adequate means for addressing the full range of ethical issues that arise every day'. Furthermore, mere compliance with the law is no guide to **exemplary** behaviour.

1.2.2 Integrity-based programmes

'An integrity-based approach combines a concern for the law with an **emphasis on managerial responsibility** for ethical behaviour. Integrity strategies strive to define companies' guiding values, aspirations and patterns of thought and conduct. When integrated into the day-to-day operations of an organisation, such strategies can help prevent damaging ethical lapses, while tapping into powerful human impulses for moral thought and action.

An integrity-based approach to ethics treats ethics as an issue of organisation culture.

Ethics management has several tasks.

- To **define** and give life to an **organisation's defining values**.
- To **create an environment** that supports **ethically sound behaviour**
- To **instil a sense** of **shared accountability** amongst employees.

The table below indicates some of the differences between the two main approaches.

	Compliance	Integrity
Ethos	Knuckle under to external standards	Choose ethical standards
Objective	Keep to the law	Enable legal and responsible conduct
Originators	Lawyers	Management, with lawyers, HR specialists etc
Methods (both includes education, and audits, controls, penalties)	Reduced employee discretion	Leadership, organisation systems
Behavioural assumptions	People are solitary self-interested beings	People are social beings with values
Standards	The law	Company values, aspirations (including law)
Staffing	Lawyers	Managers and lawyers
Education	The law, compliance system	Values, the law, compliance systems
Activities	Develop standards, train and communicate, handle reports of misconduct, investigate, enforce, oversee compliance	Integrate values *into* company systems, provide guidance and consultation, identify and resolve problems, oversee compliance

In other words, an integrity-based approach **incorporates** ethics into corporate culture and systems.

A similar approach considers ethics from two points of view.

Key terms

Utilitarianism says that the promotion of the best long-term interest of everyone concerned should be the moral standard: we should take those actions that lead to the greatest balance of good versus bad consequences.

Deontology emphasises maxims, duties, rules and principles that are so important that they should be followed whatever the consequences. 'Thou shalt not kill' is an example.

Note that the two views are not necessarily opposing ones. Very often the same conclusion is reached from both points of view.

2 CIMA guidelines

FAST FORWARD

CIMA's Ethical Guidelines are founded on a number of **objectives and fundamental principles**.

2.1 CIMA's ethical guidelines

CIMA issued its *Ethical Guidelines* in March 1992. The preface to the *Guidelines* explains that the Council of the Institute have adopted the International Federation of Accountants' (IFAC) *Guidelines on Ethics for Professional Accountants*, with some changes and modifications.

The guide gives the **basic principles** which members should follow in their professional lives. There are **serious consequences for failing to do so**, quite apart from the unacceptability of failure. Whenever a complaint is made against a member, failure to follow the contents of the ethical guide will be taken into account when a decision is made as to whether a *prima facie* case exists of professional misconduct.

'Members' include registered students, and this means you. If you are doing anything unethical it might help your understanding of this chapter, but we suggest you stop it at once!

2.2 Definitions

The introduction to the guide concentrates on defining the **general characteristics** and **skills** of the professional, the most important being: skills acquired by training and education; acceptance of duties to society as a whole; an objective outlook; high standards of conduct and performance.

2.2.1 Public interest

Key term

Public interest is 'the collective well-being of the community of people and institutions the professional accountant serves'.

The professional accountant's duty is **not** just that given to an individual client or employer, but extends to the public as a whole.

2.2.2 Objectives

The objectives of the profession can only be achieved if four basic needs are met.

- **Credibility** (of information and information systems)
- Professionalism
- Quality of services
- Confidence (in a framework of professional ethics)

2.2.3 Fundamental principles

The fundamental principles which must be observed by all members are as follows.

- Integrity
- Objectivity
- Professional competence and due care
- Confidentiality
- Professional behaviour
- Professional and technical standards
- Freedom from conflicts of interest

2.3 Fundamental principles

Let's look at the fundamental principles in more detail.

2.3.1 Integrity

Integrity is the important principle of honesty and requires that you are not to be party to the supply of false or misleading information.

> 'Professional accountants should not be party to the falsification of any record or knowingly or recklessly supply any information or make any statement which is misleading, false or deceptive in a material particular.'

2.3.2 Objectivity

Objectivity is a combination of impartiality, intellectual honesty and a freedom from conflicts of interest. Members should act fairly and not allow prejudice or bias or the influence of others to override objectivity.

2.3.3 Professional competence and due care

Professional competence and due care means you should refrain from performing any services that you cannot perform with reasonable care, competence and diligence. You have a duty to remain technically up-to-date.

2.3.4 Confidentiality

You have a duty to respect an employer's or client's confidentiality unless there is a legal or professional right or duty to disclose. It also means not using information obtained in the course of work for personal advantage.

2.3.5 Professional behaviour

Professional behaviour means, in essence, not doing anything that might bring discredit to the profession.

2.3.6 Professional and technical standards

This means presenting financial information fully, honestly and professionally .This also means keeping your accounting skills up to scratch and performing your job in accordance with relevant standards, both technical and professional. This includes conforming to standards of bodies such as IFAC, IASC, national professional bodies, national regulatory bodies and relevant international and national legislation.

2.3.7 Resolution of ethical conflicts

There are many situations which could cause ethical conflicts, ranging from the trivial to the very serious (such as fraud or illegal acts). The situations mentioned in the guide include the following.

- Pressure from an overbearing colleague or from family or friends
- Members asked to act contrary to technical and/or professional standards
- Divided loyalties between colleagues and professional standards
- Publication of misleading information
- Members having to do work beyond the degree of expertise or experience they possess

The guide suggests the following route to **resolve such complaints.**

- Use the organisation's complaints procedure.
- If (i) fails report the problem to an immediate superior or, if this is inappropriate, to a higher level of management.
- During or prior to (i) or (ii), discuss the problem with an objective adviser (but maintain confidentiality).
- If nothing comes of (i) to (iii) above, then resignation may be the only alternative. If the member does resign he should submit an information memorandum to a representative of his employer.
- Keep a record of all the actions you have taken in (i) to (iv).
- Do not divulge information to third parties, unless seeking advice from the Institute, or unless you are legally obliged to do so.

2.4 Other guidelines

(a) **Employment**

The **employment** part of the guide is concerned with making sure that you behave legally with respect to your employment. For example, you are permitted to join a union, and to go on strike, as long as it is lawful.

(b) **Tax practice**

This part of the guide is mainly concerned with making sure that the client knows that he or she is responsible for a return; that you do not falsify returns; and that clients know that tax returns and tax advice could be challenged by the tax authorities.

Difficulties may arise if there is a material omission or error in a tax return or a failure to file a required tax return. If this happens, the member should recommend that disclosure be

made to the revenue authorities, but should not inform the revenue authorities without permission.

(c) **Cross border activities**

The ethical requirements which are the most strict should be used when different ones might be applied.

(d) **Agency**.

This covers you if you are contemplating acceptance of an appointment as an agent.

(e) **Publicity and solicitation**

This part of the guide is concerned with ensuring that you obtain publicity in a 'dignified' manner, that direct mail is used appropriately and so on.

Part B of the Guide is applicable to all members in public practice and covers **independence, fees and commission, activities incompatible with the practice of public accountancy, clients' monies, relations with other professional accountants in public practice** and **advertising.**

2.5 Ethics for internal auditors

The Institute of Internal Auditors in the UK and Ireland has issued a code of guidance. It is along similar lines to CIMA's although it lays more stress on the importance of not engaging in **activities or relationships** that may be in **conflict** with the **interests** of the **organisation.**

The guidance also requires internal auditors to perform internal auditing services in accordance with the International Standards for the Professional Practice of Internal Auditing. These standards deal with:

(a) **Assurance services**. The internal auditors' objective assessment of evidence to provide an independent opinion or conclusion regarding a process, system or other subject matter. The nature and scope of assurance services are determined by the internal auditor.

(b) **Consulting services.** These are advisory in nature and generally performed at the **specific request** of an **engagement client.**

2.5.1 Objectivity

The International Standards contain specific guidance on objectivity:

(a) Internal auditors should **not provide assurance services** on operations for which they were previously responsible.

(b) Assurance work on functions over which the **chief audit executive** has responsibility should be overseen by someone outside the internal audit activity.

(c) However internal auditors can provide **consulting services** on operations for which they have had previous responsibilities.

2.5.2 Due professional care

The guidance stresses the need for auditors to consider the **adequacy** and **effectiveness** of **risk management, control** and **governance** processes as well as the significance of the items and the probability of errors. The **costs versus** the **benefits** of doing work should also be considered carefully.

The guidance lays particular stress on auditor involvement in the governance process, suggesting that the auditors should be making recommendations for:

- **Promoting appropriate ethics and values** within an organisation

- **Ensuring effective organisational performance** and accountability
- **Communicating risk** and **control information**
- **Coordinating the activities of** and communicating information among, the board, internal and external auditors and management

3 Organisational guidelines and corporate codes

FAST FORWARD

Organisations are coming under pressure from various sources to act ethically, and have responded by publishing **ethical codes**, setting out their **values** and **responsibilities** towards stakeholders.

3.1 Ethical principles

Organisations are coming under increasing pressure from a number of **sources** to behave more ethically.

- **Government**
- UK and European **legislation**
- **Treaty obligations** (such as the Rio Summit)
- **Consumers**
- **Employers**
- **Pressure groups**

These sources of pressure expect an ethical attitude towards the following.

- **Stakeholders** (employees, customers, competitors, suppliers and society at large)
- **Animals**
- **Green issues** (such as pollution and the need for recycling)
- **The disadvantaged**
- Dealings with **unethical companies or countries**

3.2 Corporate codes and corporate culture

Case Study

British Airways got caught in 1993 waging a 'dirty tricks' campaign against its competitor **Virgin Atlantic**. British Airways maintained that the offending actions (essentially, the poaching of Virgin's customers) were those of a small group of employees who overstepped the bounds of 'proper' behaviour in their eagerness to foster the interests of their employer.

An alternative view digs a little deeper. Some observers believed that the real villain of the piece was **British Airways' abrasive corporate culture**, inspired by the then chairman of BA, Lord King.

One of **BA's** responses to its defeat in the courts against Virgin and the bad publicity arising from the case was to **introduce a code of ethics**.

Many commentators would argue that the introduction of a code of ethics is **inadequate** on its own. To be effective a code needs to be accompanied by **positive attempts to foster guiding values, aspirations and patterns of thinking that support ethically sound behaviour** - in short a **change of culture**.

Increasingly organisations are responding to this challenge by devising **ethics training programmes** for the entire workforce, instituting comprehensive **procedures for reporting and investigating ethical concerns** within the company, or even setting up an **ethics office** or department to supervise the new measures. About half of all major companies now have a formal code of some kind.

Exam focus point

An examination question may include an extract from a set of corporate guidelines on which candidates were expected to comment. Even if you are not given specific information about a company's policy, though, remember that all organisations have ethical standards and there will almost certainly be something in the information that you are given that will enable you to infer at least some of the values held by the people or departments involved.

Question

Code of ethics

Learning outcome C (vii)

Here are some extracts from an article that appeared in the *Financial Times* in April 1995.

> 'Each company needs its own type of code: to reflect the national culture, the sector culture, and the exact nature of its own structure.
>
> The nature of the codes is changing. NatWest's code, for example, tries to do much more than simply set out a list of virtues. Its programme involves not only the production of a code, but a dedicated effort to teach ethics, and a system by which the code can be audited and monitored.
>
> For example, it has installed a 'hot-line' and its operation is monitored by internal auditors. The board of NatWest wanted it to be confidential - within the confines of legal and regulatory requirements - and the anonymity of 'whistle-blowers' has been strictly maintained.
>
> The code contains relevant and straightforward advice. For example: 'In recognising that we are a competitive business, we believe in fair and open competition and, therefore, obtaining information about competitors by deception is unacceptable. Similarly, making disparaging comments about competitors invariably invites disrespect from customer and should be avoided.' Or: 'Employment with NatWest must never be used in an attempt to influence public officials or customers for personal gain or benefit.'
>
> Jonathan Bye, manager of public policy at NatWest, says the bank is continually looking at ways of refreshing the code and measuring its effectiveness.

How would you suggest that the effectiveness of a company's policy on ethics could be measured?

Answer

Some ideas that you might think through are: **training effectiveness measures; breaches of the code dealt with; activity in the ethics office; public perceptions of the company**. Try to flesh them out and think of some other ideas. The extract above should suggest some.

3.3 Company code of conduct

An **Ethical code** typically contains a **series of statements setting out the organisation's values and explaining how it sees its responsibilities towards stakeholders.**

Typical statements in a corporate code

- The company conducts all of its business on **ethical principles** and expects staff to do likewise.
- **Employees** are seen as the most important component of the company and are expected to work on a basis of trust, respect, honesty, fairness, decency and equality. The company will only employ people who follow its ethical ideals.
- **Customers** should be treated courteously and politely at all times, and the company should always respond promptly to customer needs by listening, understanding and then performing to the customer requirements.
- The company is dedicated to complying **with legal or regulatory standards** of the industry, and employees are expected to do likewise.
- The company's relationship with **suppliers and subcontractors** must be based on mutual respect. The company therefore has responsibilities including ensuring fairness and truthfulness in all of its dealings with suppliers, including pricing and licensing, fostering long-term stability in the supplier relationship, paying suppliers on time and in accordance with agreed terms of trade and preferring suppliers and subcontractors whose employment practices respect human dignity.
- The company has a responsibility to: foster open markets for trade and investment; promote **competitive behaviour** that is socially and environmentally beneficial and demonstrates mutual respect among competitors; and refrain from either seeking or participating in questionable payments or favours to secure competitive advantages.
- A business should protect and, where possible, improve **the environment**, promote sustainable development, and prevent the wasteful use of natural resources.
- The company has a responsibility in **the community** to: respect human rights and democratic institutions, and promote them wherever practicable; recognise government's legitimate obligation to the society at large and support public policies and practices that promote human development through harmonious relations between business and other segments of society; collaborate with those forces in the community dedicated to raising standards of health, education, workplace safety and economic well-being; respect the integrity of local cultures; and be a good corporate citizen through charitable donations, educational and cultural contributions and employee participation in community and civic affairs.

Employee behaviour

Learning outcome: C(vii)

How can an organisation influence employee behaviour towards ethical issues?

Answer

Here are some suggestions.

- Recruitment and selection policies and procedures
- Induction and training
- Objectives and reward schemes
- Ethical codes
- Threat of ethical audit

3.4 The impact of a code of conduct

A code of conduct can set out the company's expectations, and in principle a code such as that outlined above addresses many of the problems that the organisations may experience. However, **merely issuing a code is not enough**.

(a) The **commitment of senior management** to the code needs to be real, and it needs to be very clearly communicated to all staff. Staff need to be persuaded that expectations really have changed.

(b) Measures need to be taken to **discourage previous behaviours** that conflict with the code.

(c) **Staff need to understand** that it is in the **organisation's best interests** to change behaviour, and become committed to the same ideals.

(d) Some employees – including very able ones - may find it very difficult to buy into a code that they **perceive may limit their own earnings** and/or restrict their freedom to do their job.

(e) In addition to a general statement of ethical conduct, **more detailed statements** (codes of practice) will be needed to set out formal procedures that must be followed.

4 Practical situations

FAST FORWARD

Exam questions are often founded on what should be done if breaches of laws, regulations or ethical guidelines occur. **Close relationships** between the parties or other **conflicts of interest** are often a complication.

4.1 Examination questions

Examination questions will expect you to be able to apply your understanding of ethical issues to practical problems arising in organisations. Later in this chapter we are going to suggest an approach that you may find helpful in dealing with such questions, but first we are going to take the bare bones of a situation and see how it might be built up into the kind of scenario you will have to face.

4.2 The problem

The exam will present you with a scenario, typically containing an array of detail much of which is potentially relevant. The problem, however, will be one or other of two basic types.

(a) **A wishes B to do C which is in breach of D**

where

A	=	a situation, person, group of people, institution or the like
B	=	you/a management accountant, the person with the ethical dilemma
C	=	acting, or refraining from acting, in a certain way
D	=	an ethical principle, quite possibly one of the CIMA's fundamental principles

(b) Alternatively, the problem may be that A has done C, B has become aware of it and D requires some kind of response from B.

4.3 Example: the problem

A management accountant joined a manufacturing company as its Finance Director. The company had acquired land on which it built industrial units. The Finance Director discovered that, before he had started at the company, one of the units had been sold and the selling price was significantly larger than the amount which appeared in the company's records. The difference had been siphoned off to another company - one in which his boss, the Managing Director, was a major shareholder. Furthermore, the Managing Director had kept his relationship with the second company a secret from the rest of the board.

The Finance Director confronted the Managing Director and asked him to reveal his position to the board. However, the Managing Director refused to disclose his position to anyone else. The secret profits on the sale of the unit had been used, he said, to reward the people who had secured the sale. Without their help, he added, the company would be in a worse position financially.

The Finance Director then told the Managing Director that unless he reported to the board he would have to inform the board members himself. The Managing Director still refused. The Finance Director disclosed the full position to the board.

The problem is of the **second basic type. B** is of course the easiest party to identify. Here it is the **Finance Director**. **A** is clear, as well: it is the **Managing Director**. **C** is the **MD's breach of his directorial duties** regarding related party transactions not to obtain any personal advantage from his position of director without the consent of the company for whatever gain or profit he has obtained. **D** is the **principle that requires B not to be a party to an illegal act**. (Note that we distinguish between ethical and legal obligations. B has legal obligations as a director of the company. He has ethical obligations not to ignore his legal obligations. In **this** case the two amount to the same thing.)

4.4 Relationships

You may have a feeling that the resolution of the problem described in Paragraph 4.3 is just too easy, and you would be right. This is because A, B, C and D are either people, or else situations involving people, who stand in certain relationships to each other.

- A may be B's boss, B's subordinate, B's equal in the organisational hierarchy, B's husband, B's friend.
- B may be new to the organisation, or well-established and waiting for promotion, or ignorant of some knowledge relevant to the situation that A possesses or that the people affected by C possess.
- C or D, as already indicated, may involve some person(s) with whom B or A have a relationship - for example the action may be to misrepresent something to a senior manager who controls the fate of B or A (or both) in the organisation.

Question **Relationships**

Learning outcome: C(vii)

Identify the relationships in the scenario above. What are the possible problems arising from these relationships?

Answer

The MD is the Finance Director's boss. He is also a member of the board and is longer established as such than B the Finance Director.

In outline the problems arising are that **by acting ethically the Finance Director will alienate the MD**. Even if the problem were to be resolved the episode would sour all future dealings between these two parties. Also, **the board may not be sympathetic to the accusations of a newcomer**. The Finance Director may find that he is ignored or even dismissed.

Relationships should never be permitted to affect ethical judgement. If you knew that your best friend at work had committed a major fraud, for example, **integrity** would demand that **in the last resort** you would have to bring it to the attention of somebody in authority. But note that this is only in the last resort. Try to imagine what you would do in practice in this situation.

Surely your **first course** would be to try to **persuade your friend** that what they had done was wrong, and that they themselves had an ethical responsibility to own up. Your **second option**, if this failed, might be to try to get **somebody** (perhaps somebody outside the organisation) that you knew could **exert pressure** on your friend to persuade him or her to own up.

There is obviously a limit to how far you can take this. The important point is that just because you are dealing with a situation that involves ethical issues, this **does not mean that all the normal principles of good human relations and good management have to be suspended**. In fact this is the time when such business principles are most important.

4.5 Consequences

Actions have consequences and the consequences themselves are quite likely to have their own ethical implications.

In the case study given above, for example, we can identify the following further issues.

(a) The MD's secret transaction appears to have been made in order to secure the sale of an asset the proceeds of which are helping to prop up the company financially. Disclosure of the truth behind the sale may mean that the company is pursued for compensation by the buyer of the site. The **survival of the company** as a whole may be jeopardised.

(b) If the truth behind the transaction becomes public knowledge this could be highly damaging for the company's **reputation**, even if it can show that only one black sheep was involved.

(c) The board may simply rubber stamp the MD's actions and so the Finance Director may still find that he is expected to be party to dishonesty. (This assumes that the **company as a whole is amoral** in its approach to ethical issues. In fact the MD's refusal to disclose the matter to the board suggests otherwise.)

In the last case we are back to square one. In the first two cases, the Finance Director has to consider the ethicality or otherwise of taking action that could lead to the collapse of the company, extensive redundancies, unpaid creditors and shareholders and so on.

4.6 Grey areas

Sometimes prescribed rules and principles may appear to conflict with the promotion of the best long-term interests of everyone concerned. As a result there are **grey areas where it is not at all clear what to do for the best.**

4.7 Example: grey areas

Suppose, for example, that Richard, one of your company's highly valued employees, stole some money a year ago at a time of exceptional need arising due to personal circumstances beyond his control. He approached the company for a temporary loan at the time, but was refused. He has now owned up to you voluntarily, and presented you with a cheque made out to the company for the missing funds. His personal circumstances are now in order.

The company's code clearly states that any employee discovered to be acting dishonestly will be instantly dismissed. It is doubtful whether the board could be persuaded to make an exception.

You know that the cost of finding and training a replacement for Richard is likely to exceed the amount of money stolen and now repaid.

The **utilitarian** view is clear: **Richard should not be sacked**. The **deontological** view is also clear: **Richard should be dismissed instantly**.

Question

Theft

Learning outcome: C(vii)

Richard has asked you not to tell anybody about his earlier indiscretion.

What do you do?

Answer

The problem with **Richard** is extremely difficult, but it is **not just a matter of keeping quiet**. If you keep quiet and **accept the cheque** on the company's behalf, the **accounting records would have to be falsified**. **Keeping quiet and not accepting the cheque implicates you in the theft**. If Richard will not put the matter in writing to the board himself, you will have to speak up and let them decide Richard's fate. One of the main issues is that the **theft was not previously discovered.** Is this your fault? What extra controls are needed?

Other points that you might have made are that the board must notify the company's auditors and explain its decision (whatever that may be). If the **corporate code** is waived in this case, openness is the best policy: perhaps the code should be less extreme or the particular circumstances of this case should be made widely known to prevent rumour and dissatisfaction spreading through the company.

Grey areas also emerge when, on the one hand, there are **many different interests involved**, and it is **difficult to know what weight to attach to each**, so that it is impossible to decide what the utilitarian view actually is, and on the other hand there are no clear rules that apply to the situation or else there are

several rules or principles that conflict with one another (for example, being fair to Richard and being honest in your dealings with the company in the example above).

Andrew Stark ('What's the Matter with Business Ethics', HBR, May-June 1993) identifies two particularly challenging ethical situations.

(a) 'identifying ethical courses of action in difficult gray-area situations ... "not issues of right versus wrong," but **"conflicts of right versus right"**;

(b) 'navigating those situations where the **right course is clear**, but real-world **competitive and institutional pressures** lead even well-intentioned managers astray'.

4.8 Actions

In spite of the difficulties, your aim will usually be to reach a satisfactory resolution to the problem. **The actions that you recommend** will often include the following.

- **Informal discussions** with the parties involved.
- **Further investigation** to establish the full facts of the matter. What extra information is needed?
- The **tightening up of controls or the introduction of new ones**, if the situation arose due to laxity in this area. This will often be the case and the principles of professional competence and due care and of technical standards will usually be relevant.
- **Attention to organisational matters** such as changes in the management structure, improving communication channels, attempting to change attitudes.

The last two items, for example, are clearly relevant to the situation that has arisen in the case study in Paragraph 4.3.

5 Examination questions: an approach

5.1 Dealing with questions

FAST FORWARD

In a situation involving ethical issues, there are **practical steps** which should be taken.

- Establish the facts of the situation by further investigation and work.
- Consider the alternative options available for action.
- Consider whether any professional guidelines have been breached.
- State the best course of action based on the steps above.

An article in *CIMA Student* in February 1993 ('Learning and thinking about ethics') contained the following advice for candidates who wish to achieve good marks in ethics questions. (The emphasis is BPP's.)

'The precise question requirements will vary, but in general marks will be awarded for:

- **analysis of the situation;**
- **a recognition of ethical issues;**
- **explanation if appropriate of relevant part of *Ethical Guidelines***, and **interpretation** of its relevance to the question;
- making clear, logical, and appropriate **recommendations** for action. Making inconsistent recommendations does not impress examiners;

- **justifying recommendations** in practical business terms and in ethical terms.

As with all case study based questions there is likely to be **more than one acceptable answer**, and marks will depend on how well the case is argued, rather than for getting the 'right' answer.

> However, questions based on ethical issues tend to produce a range of possible solutions which are, on the one hand, consistent with the *Ethical Guidelines* and acceptable, and on the other hand, a range of clearly inadmissible answers which are clearly in breach of the *Ethical Guidelines* and possibly the law.'

5.2 Step-by-step approach

We suggest, instead, that:

(a) **You use the question format to structure your answer**

(b) **You bear in mind what marks are being awarded for** (see above)

(c) **That you adhere to the following list of do's and don'ts**. Be sure to read the notes following.

DO	Note	DON'T
Identify the key facts as briefly as possible (one sentence?)	1	Merely paraphrase the question
Identify the major principle(s) at issue	2	Regurgitate the entire contents of the Ethical Guidelines
Consider alternative actions and their consequences	3	List every single possible action and then explain how all the unsuitable ones can be eliminated
Make a decision and recommend action as appropriate	4	Fail to make a decision or recommend action. Propose actions in breach of the *Ethical Guidelines* or the law
Justify your decision	5	Be feeble. 'This should be done because it is ethical' is not terribly convincing

Notes

1 **One sentence** is an ideal to aim for.

2 (a) **Use the terminology of the *Ethical Guidelines*, but not *ad nauseam*.** 'Integrity' is often more clearly described as 'honesty' (although the two words are not synonymous). Don't forget the words 'fairness', 'bias', and 'influence' when discussing 'objectivity'.

(b) **Don't torture the case study to make it fit a fundamental principle**: if, say, 'justice' is the most persuasive word for a situation don't be afraid of using it.

(c) If the law is involved, don't get carried away - this is **not a law exam**. 'The director has a statutory duty to ...' is sufficient: there is no need to go into legal detail.

3 Useful ways of generating alternatives are:

(a) To **consider the problem from the other side of the fence**: imagine you are the guilty party

(b) To **consider the problem from the point of view of the organisation** and its culture and environment

4 Making a decision is often very hard, but if you cannot do this you are simply not ready to take on the responsibilities of a qualified accountant. There are usually a number of decisions that could be justified, so **don't be afraid of choosing the 'wrong' answer.**

5 This is not actually as hard as you might think, as we shall show you in a moment.

5.3 Regurgitating the question

Possibly the most **common fault** in students' answers to questions on ethics is that they include large **amounts of unanalysed detail copied out from the question** scenarios in their answers. This earns no marks.

You can very easily avoid the temptation to merely paraphrase the question. Simply **begin your answer by stating that you are referring to 'issues'** (by which you mean all the details contained in the question) **discussed at a previous meeting, or set out in full in 'appended documents'.** If you do this you will be writing your report to someone already in possession of the same facts as you have.

5.4 Justifying your decision

The *CIMA Student* article quoted above says that **marks will be awarded for 'justifying recommendations in practical business terms and in ethical terms'.** We shall conclude by examining a passage from a CIMA model solution to a question on ethics to see how this can be done.

> 'Perhaps the first thing to do is to report the whole matter, in confidence and informally, to the chief internal auditor with suggestions that a tactful investigation is undertaken to verify as many of the facts as possible. The fact that the sales manager has already been tackled (informally) about the matter may be a positive advantage as he/she may be recruited to assist in the investigation. It could however be a problem as the information needed for further investigation may have already been removed. Tact is crucial as handling the matter the wrong way could adversely influence the whole situation. An understanding of who participants are and how they are implicated can be used positively to bring about change with the minimum of disruption.'

Here is the same passage with some of the *practical* justifications in italics and **ethical** justifications in bold.

> 'Perhaps the first thing to do is to **report** the whole matter, **in confidence** and **informally**, to the chief internal auditor with suggestions that a **tactful investigation** is undertaken to **verify as many of the facts** as possible. The fact that the sales manager has already been tackled (informally) about the matter may be a positive advantage as **he/she may be recruited** to assist in the investigation. It could however be a problem as the information needed for further **investigation** may have already been removed. **Tact** is crucial as handling the matter the wrong way could adversely influence the whole situation. An understanding of who participants are and how they are implicated can be used positively to bring about change with the **minimum of disruption**.'

Note that by suggesting reporting, investigating and verifying facts and so on you are exhibiting **professional competence** and **due care**. Tact avoids bringing discredit on the profession; it is also a sound approach to dealing with people in business, as is the informality of the suggested approach. Recruiting the sales manager to help is managerially sound as it is an effective use of resources.

The key to this approach is **using the right language**, and to a large extent you cannot help doing so if you have sensible suggestions to make. The real problem that many students experience with questions of this type is lack of confidence in their own judgement. If you have sound business and managerial sense and you know your *Ethical Guidelines* there is every reason to suppose that an answer that you propose will be acceptable, so don't be shy of expressing an opinion.

5.5 Practical situations

In an internal company role, ethical problems could be in the following forms.

- Conflict of duties to different staff superiors
- Discovering an illegal act or fraud perpetrated by the company (ie its directors)
- Discovering a fraud or illegal act perpetrated by another employee
- Pressure from superiors to take certain viewpoints, for example towards budgets (pessimistic/optimistic etc)

Question — Internal audit and director of finance

Learning outcome: C(vii)

Discuss the potential problems of the internal audit function reporting systems weaknesses to the chief finance officer and indicate how these problems might be resolved.

Answer

Problem of reporting

The potential problem of reporting to the chief finance officer is that the chief finance officer's position and rewards may **depend** upon sound financial systems. Any criticisms of the chief finance officer may be seen as affecting his personal welfare, and the chief finance officer may be tempted to suppress the criticisms or fight them. If there is conflict it is likely that the board will back the chief finance officer as he is seen as a key member of the corporate management team.

The following steps can reduce the potential for conflict and protect the position of internal audit.

Audit planning

The audit plan should be drawn up on the basis of **tackling key risks** and having **undertaken consultation** across the organisation. A formal plan cannot easily be disputed.

Resourcing

The resources for tackling the main internal audit work should be **allocated separately** from the resources for tackling one-off projects, so that the internal audit team's attention is not diverted from the main audit.

Segregation of duties

The chief finance officer should have a **supervisory role**, with responsibilities for the systems delegated to line managers. Alternatively the audit manager or head of internal audit should not have line reporting responsibility to the chief finance officer.

In addition internal audit should ideally not also have responsibility for **developing controls** or **reporting compliance**.

Audit committee

Having the head of internal audit **report** on a **regular basis directly** to an audit committee made up of independent non-executive directors is the most important means of maintaining internal auditor independence. The head of internal audit should also be able to report concerns directly to the chief executive.

Chapter roundup

- **Ethics**, a set of moral principles, are manifest in various ways, for example CIMA's code. Ethics can be approached by following rules, or striving for the best possible standards of behaviour.
- **CIMA's Ethical Guidelines** are founded on a number of **objectives and fundamental principles.**
- Organisations are coming under pressure from various sources to act ethically, and have responded by publishing **ethical codes**, setting out their **values** and **responsibilities** towards stakeholders.
- Exam questions are often founded on what should be done if breaches of laws, regulations or ethical guidelines occur. **Close relationships** between the parties or other **conflicts of interest** are often a complication.
- In a situation involving ethical issues, there are **practical steps** which should be taken.
  - Establish the facts of the situation by further investigation and work.
  - Consider the alternative options available for action.
  - Consider whether any professional guidelines have been breached.
  - State the best course of action based on the steps above.

Quick quiz

1 Explain the difference between utilitarianism and deontology as approaches to ethics.

2 _______ ________ is the collective well-being of the community of people and interest that the professional accountant serves.

3 What are the four basic needs that underlie professional objectives?

4 What fundamental principles should be observed by all CIMA members?

5 Give three examples of situations that could cause ethical conflicts.

6 What sort of statements might be included in an organisation's ethical code?

7 How can you seek to resolve ethical situations that are not clearcut?

8 List five dos for exam questions on ethics.

Answers to quick quiz

1 Utilitarianism is based on the promotion of the best long-term interest of everyone concerned; deontology is based on adherence to maxims, duties, rules and principles whatever the consequences.

2 **Public interest** is the collective well-being of the community of people and interest that the professional accountant serves.

3
- Credibility (of information and information systems)
- Professionalism
- Quality of services
- Confidence (in a framework of professional ethics)

4
- Integrity
- Objectivity
- Professional competence and due care
- Confidentiality
- Professional behaviour
- Professional and technical standards
- Freedom from conflicts of interest

5
- Pressure from an overbearing colleague or from family or friends
- Members being asked to act contrary to technical and/or professional standards
- Divided loyalties between colleagues and professional standards
- Publication of misleading information
- Having to do work beyond one's degree of experience or expertise

6
- Organisation conducts business on ethical principles
- Employees expected to live up to ethical principles
- Fair and courteous dealing with customers
- Commitment to comply with legal and regulatory standards
- Fair dealings with suppliers
- Responsible competitive behaviour
- Environmentally friendly policies
- Community responsibilities

7
- Informal discussions with parties
- Further investigation
- Tightening of controls or introduction of new controls

8
- Identify key facts as briefly as possible
- Identify major principles at issue
- Consider alternative actions and their consequences
- Make a decision and recommend actions
- Justify your decision

Now try the questions below from the Exam Question Bank

Number	Level	Marks	Time
Q16	Introductory	N/a	20 mins

Part D
Management of financial risk

17

Financial and international risk

Introduction

Part D will cover the risks that organisations face from changes in economic indicators and from dealings abroad. The obvious link here is the risk of changes in exchange rates having an adverse effect on the organisation's position. We shall cover how businesses can deal with the impact of exchange rates, and also interest rates, in later chapters in this section.

In this chapter we shall concentrate on other financial and international risks. Although most of these can be dealt with more briefly than interest or exchange rate risks, do not underestimate their importance. A business will clearly be concerned if it has made significant returns in an overseas country, but there is a (political) risk that it will be blocked from taking those monies out of that country.

Financial risk is a major area in this syllabus, being weighted at 30%. The examiners have indicated that financial risk hedging will be covered in the majority of papers, and that the promised 25% numerical content of the paper will mainly be found in questions on financial risk.

Topic list	Learning outcomes	Syllabus references	Ability required
1 Trading and credit risks	B(i),(iv) D(i),(ii)	B(1),(2),D(1)	Evaluation
2 Political risks	B(i),(iv) D(i),(ii)	B(1),(2),D(1),(3)	Evaluation
3 Legal risks	B(i),(iv) D(i),(ii)	B(1),(2),D(1)	Evaluation
4 Cultural risks	B(i),(iv) D(i),(ii)	B(1),(2),D(1)	Evaluation

1 Trading and credit risks

FAST FORWARD

The risks faced by businesses include those arising from **general business and trading conditions**.

1.1 Trading risks

Both domestic and international traders will face trading risks, although those faced by the latter will generally be greater due to the increased distances and times involved. The types of trading risk include:

(a) **Physical risk** – the risk of goods being lost or stolen in transit, or the documents accompanying the goods going astray

(b) **Credit risk** – the possibility of payment default by the customer. This is discussed further below

(c) **Trade risk** – the risk of the customer refusing to accept the goods on delivery (due to sub-standard/inappropriate goods), or the cancellation of the order in transit

(d) **Liquidity risk** – the inability to finance the credit

Such risks may be reduced with the **help** of **banks, insurance companies, credit reference agencies** and government agencies, such as the UK's Export Credit Guarantee Department (ECGD).

Other ways to reduce these risks include risk **transfer.** A business shipping parcels overseas may agree a contract obligating the courier to pay for losses in excess of its statutory liability.

1.2 Credit risks

FAST FORWARD

Management of **credit risk** is of particular importance to exporters and various instruments and other arrangements are available to assist in this, such as documentary credits, bills of exchange, export credit insurance, export factoring and forfaiting.

Key term

Credit risk is the possibility that a loss may occur from the failure of another party to perform according to the terms of a contract. *(OT 2000)*

You may well have covered the elements of a basic credit risk or debtor management strategy in some detail in your earlier studies. Briefly these are:

- Assess the **creditworthiness** of new customers before extending credit, by obtaining trade, bank and credit agency references and making use of information from financial statements and salesmen's reports.
- Set **credit limits** and **credit periods** in line with those offered by competitors, but taking account of the status of individual customers.
- Set up a system of **credit control** that will ensure that credit checks and terms are being adhered to.
- Set out clear **debt collection procedures** to be followed.
- **Monitor** the efficiency of the system by the regular production and review of **reports** such as age analysis, credit and bad debt ratios and statistical analyses of incidences and causes of default and bad debts amongst different types of customer and trade.

- Consider the use of a **debt factor** to assist in the management, collection and financing of debts where this is cost effective.

1.3 International credit risk management

Where a company trades overseas, the risk of bad debts is potentially increased by the lack of direct contact with, and knowledge of, the overseas customers and the business environment within which they operate. Whilst the basic methods of minimising foreign credit risk will be as set out above, we shall here consider the additional options available to the exporter.

There are a number of methods of reducing the risks of bad debts in foreign trade.

1.3.1 Export factoring

Export factoring is essentially the same as factoring domestic trade debts. Factoring, as compared with forfaiting which we discuss below, is widely regarded as an appropriate mechanism for trade finance and collection of receivables for small to medium-sized exporters, especially where there is a flow of small-scale contracts.

A factoring service typically offers prepayment of up to 80% against approved invoices. Service charges vary between around 0.75% and 3% of total invoice value, plus finance charges at levels comparable to bank overdraft rates for those taking advantage of prepayment arrangements.

1.3.2 Forfaiting

Key term

Forfaiting is the purchase of financial instruments such as bills of exchange or letters of credit on a non-recourse basis by a forfaiter, who deducts interest (in the form of a discount) at an agreed rate for the period covered by the notes. The forfaiter assumes the responsibility for claiming the debt from the importer (buyer) who initially accepted the financial instrument drawn by the seller of the goods. Traditionally forfaiting is fixed-rate medium-term (one to five year) finance. *(OT 2000)*

Forfaiting is a method of providing **medium-term** (say, three to five years) **export finance,** which originated in Switzerland and Germany where it is still very common. It has normally been used for export sales involving capital goods (machinery etc), where payments will be made over a number of years. Forfaiting is also used as a short-term financing tool.

The following diagram should help to clarify the procedures.

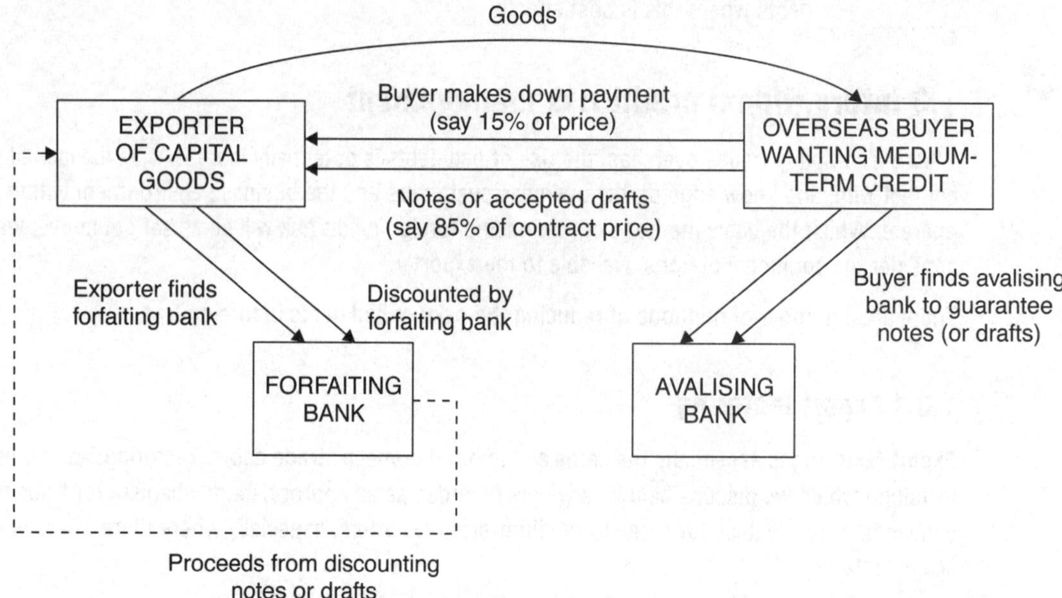

Forfaiting can be an **expensive choice** and **arranging it** takes time. However, it can be a useful way of enabling trade to occur in cases where other methods of ensuring payment and smooth cash flow are not certain, and in cases where trade may not be possible by other means.

1.3.3 Documentary credits

Documentary credits ('letters of credit') provide a method of payment in international trade which gives the exporter a risk-free method of obtaining payment.

At the same time, documentary credits are a method of obtaining **short-term finance** from a bank, for **working capital**. This is because a bank might agree to discount or negotiate a bill of exchange.

(a) The exporter receives **immediate payment** of the amount due to him, less the discount, instead of having to wait for payment until the end of the credit period allowed to the buyer.

(b) The buyer is able to get a **period of credit** before having to pay for the imports.

Banks may advance **pre-shipment finance** to help with manufacture.

The buyer (a foreign buyer, or a UK importer) and the seller (a UK exporter or a foreign supplier) first of all agree a contract for the sale of the goods, which provides for payment through a documentary credit. The **buyer** then requests a bank in his country to issue a **letter of credit** in favour of the exporter. This bank that issues the letter of credit is known as the **issuing bank.** The buyer is known as the **applicant** for the credit and the exporter is known as the **beneficiary** (because he receives the benefits).

The issuing bank, by issuing its letter of credit, **guarantees payment** to the beneficiary. Banks are involved in the credits, not in the underlying contracts. The cost of issuing a letter of credit is usually borne by the buyer.

A documentary credit arrangement must be made between the exporter, the buyer and participating banks **before the export sale takes place**. Documentary credits are slow to arrange, and administratively cumbersome; however, they might be considered essential where the risk of non-payment is high, or when dealing for the first time with an unknown buyer.

1.3.4 International credit unions

International credit unions are organisations or associations of finance houses or banks in different countries (in Europe). The finance houses or banks have reciprocal arrangements for providing instalment credit finance.

Suppose, for example, that an exporter in Spain wishes to sell some capital goods to a customer in Germany and the customer wants to pay for the goods by instalment.

(a) The exporter can **approach a member of an international credit union** in Spain, and ask for the necessary instalment finance to be arranged through a German member of the credit union.

(b) Details of the **proposed sale** will be **given to the German finance house** or bank, which will then decide on the terms of instalment credit it will offer to the German buyer (in accordance with the German laws and practice).

(c) The Spanish finance house will **receive full payment** for the goods from the German finance house and pay the exporter. The German finance house is then left with a normal hire purchase agreement with the German buyer.

This type of scheme has **advantages** for **small exporters** who cannot afford to allow lengthy credit periods to its overseas customers. Examples of international credit unions are the European Credit Union and Eurocredit.

1.3.5 Export credit insurance

Export credit insurance is insurance against the risk of non-payment by foreign customers for export debts. Not all exporters take out export credit insurance because premiums are very high and the benefits are sometimes not fully appreciated; but, if they do, they will obtain an insurance policy from a private insurance company that deals in export credit insurance.

(a) If a **credit customer defaults on payment**, the task of pursuing the case through the courts will be lengthy, and it might be a long time before payment is eventually obtained.

(b) There are various reasons why non-payment might happen. Export credit insurance provides insurance against non-payment for a **variety of risks** in addition to the buyer's failure to pay on time.

Case Study

Gerling NCM provides credit insurance for short-term export credit business. A credit insurance policy for export trade on short-term credit (up to 180 days) or on cash terms is known as a short-term guarantee.

Exporters can choose to obtain credit insurance:

- For all their export business on a regular basis
- For selected parts of their export business
- For occasional, high-value export sales

However, Gerling NCM prefers to provide comprehensive insurance for an exporter's entire export business.

1.3.6 Bills of exchange

Bills of exchange are often **sold to banks**, who **collect payment** from **the importer**. If the importer defaults, the exporter must bear the loss.

1.3.7 Acceptance credits

Acceptance credits provide **short-term finance** for the **exporter** by a **bank agreeing** to **accept bills of exchange drawn on itself**. Once accepted, the bills can be discounted to provide immediate finance.

1.3.8 Export merchants

Export merchants **buy goods** from **manufacturers** and then **export them**. The manufacturer receives payment quickly and the export merchant bears the **risk of bad debts**.

1.3.9 Government departments

Government departments supply **support for banks** who are **providing finance** to exporters of **generally expensive capital goods**.

2 Political risks

FAST FORWARD

Multinationals can take various measures to combat the risks of **political interference** or **turbulence** including agreements with governments, insurance, and location elsewhere of key parts of the production process.

2.1 Political risks for multinationals

Key term

Political risk is the risk that political action will affect the position and value of a company.

When a multinational company invests in another country, by setting up a subsidiary, it may face a **political risk** of action by that country's government which restricts the multinational's freedom. The government of a country will almost certainly want to encourage the development and growth of commerce and industry, but it might also be suspicious of the motives of multinationals which set up subsidiaries in their country, perhaps fearing exploitation.

2.2 Methods of government action

If a government tries to prevent the exploitation of its country by multinationals, it may take various measures.

(a) Import **quotas** could be used to limit the quantities of goods that a subsidiary can buy from its parent company and import for resale in its domestic markets.

(b) Import **tariffs** could make imports (such as from parent companies) more expensive and domestically produced goods therefore more competitive.

(c) Legal standards of safety or quality (**non-tariff barriers**) could be imposed on imported goods to prevent multinationals from selling goods through a subsidiary which have been banned as dangerous in other countries.

(d) **Exchange control regulations** could be applied (see below).

(e) A government could **restrict** the ability of foreign companies to buy domestic companies, especially those that operate in politically sensitive industries such as defence contracting, communications, energy supply and so on.

(f) A government could **nationalise** foreign-owned companies and their assets (with or without compensation to the parent company).

(g) A government could insist on a **minimum shareholding** in companies by residents. This would force a multinational to offer some of the equity in a subsidiary to investors in the country where the subsidiary operates.

2.3 Assessment of political risk

There are a large number of factors that can be considered to assess political risk, for example government stability, remittance restrictions and assets seized. Measurement is often by **subjective weighting** of these factors. **Industry specific factors** are also important.

2.4 Dealing with political risk

There are various strategies that multinational companies can adopt to limit the effects of political risk.

(a) **Negotiations with host government**

The aim of these negotiations is generally to obtain a **concession agreement**. This would cover matters such as the transfer of capital, remittances and products, access to local finance, government intervention and taxation, and transfer pricing. The main problem with concession agreements can be that the initial terms of the agreement may not prove to be satisfactory subsequently. Companies may have different reasons for choosing to set up initially and choosing to stay, whilst the local government may be concerned if profits are too high.

(b) **Insurance**

In the UK the Export Credits Guarantee Department (ECGD) provides protection against various threats including **nationalisation, currency conversion problems**, war and revolution.

(c) **Production strategies**

It may be necessary to strike a balance between **contracting out to local sources** (thus losing control) and **producing directly** (which increases the investment and hence increases the potential loss.) Alternatively it may be better to locate key parts of the production process or the distribution channels abroad. Control of patents is another possibility, since these can be enforced internationally.

(d) **Contacts with markets**

Multinationals may have **contacts with customers** that interventionist governments cannot obtain.

(e) **Financial management**

If a multinational **obtains funds** in **local investment markets**, these may be on terms that are less favourable than on markets abroad, but would mean that local institutions suffered if the local government intervened. However governments often limit the ability of multinationals to obtain funds locally.

Alternatively guarantees can be obtained from the government for the investment that can be enforced by the multinational if the government takes action.

(f) **Management structure**

Possible methods include **joint ventures** or **ceding control** to local investors and obtaining profits by a management contract.

If governments do intervene, multinationals may have to make use of the advantages they hold or **threaten withdrawal**. The threat of expropriation may be reduced by negotiation or legal threats.

2.5 Blocked funds

Exchange controls restrict the flow of foreign exchange into and out of a country, usually to defend the local currency or to protect reserves of foreign currencies. Exchange controls are generally more restrictive in developing and less developed countries although some still exist in developed countries. Typically, a government might enforce regulations:

(a) **Rationing the supply of foreign exchange**. Anyone wishing to make payments abroad in a foreign currency will be restricted by the limited supply, which stops them from buying as much as they want from abroad.

(b) **Restricting the types of transaction** for which payments abroad are allowed, for example by suspending or banning the payment of dividends to foreign shareholders, such as parent companies in multinationals, who will then have the problem of **blocked funds**.

Exam focus point

Discussion of methods of dealing with blocked funds is often a weakness in students' answers.

Ways of overcoming blocked funds include the following.

(a) The parent company could **sell goods or services** to the subsidiary and obtain payment. The amount of this payment will depend on the volume of sales and also on the transfer price for the sales.

(b) A parent company that grants a subsidiary the right to make goods protected by patents can charge a **royalty** on any goods that the subsidiary sells. The size of any royalty can be adjusted to suit the wishes of the parent company's management.

(c) If the parent company makes a **loan** to a subsidiary, it can set the interest rate high or low, thereby affecting the profits of both companies. A high rate of interest on a loan, for example, would improve the parent company's profits to the detriment of the subsidiary's profits.

(d) **Management charges** may be levied by the parent company for costs incurred in the management of international operations.

Political risk

Learning outcomes: B(i), (iv)

Your company has purchased the following data which provide scores of the political risk for a number of countries in which the company is considering investing in a new subsidiary.

	Total	*Economic performance*	*Debt in default*	*Credit ratings*	*Government stability*	*Remittance restrictions*	*Access capital*
Weighting	100	25	10	10	25	15	15
Gmala	37	13	4	5	5	10	0
Forland	52	5	10	9	16	8	4
Amapore	36	12	2	3	9	5	5
Covia	30	9	3	2	15	1	0
Settia	39	15	4	3	11	4	2

Countries have been rated on a scale from 0 up to the maximum weighting for each factor (eg 0-15 for remittance restrictions). A high score for each factor, as well as overall, reflects low political risk.

A proposal has been put before the company's board of directors that investment should take place in Forland.

Required

Prepare a brief report for the company's board of directors discussing whether or not the above data should form the basis for:

(a) The measurement of political risk, and

(b) The decision about which country to invest in

Answer

To: Board of directors
From: Accountant
Date: 17 December 20X8
Subject: The evaluation of political risk in investment decisions

The measurement of political risk

Political risk in foreign investment could be defined as the threat that a foreign government will change the rules of the game after the investment has been made. There are various agencies that can provide risk scores for different countries, but the key problem for all such approaches is that the scores that they use will always be subjective. The best example of the limitations of this approach is the case of Iran. Most commentators believed the regime under the Shah to be inherently stable, but as it turned out, this belief was completely wrong.

Weaknesses of approach

Considering the data that is being used in this case in more detail, there are a number of weaknesses that should be recognised.

(a) **Economic performance** is one of the most heavily weighted factors. However it can be argued that this is not really a component of political risk.

(b) There is **no information** as to how the **weightings have been arrived** at.

(c) A number of factors that could have been included have been ignored. These include:

(i) Cultural homogeneity

(ii) Quality of infrastructure
(iii) Legal system
(iv) Record on nationalisation
(v) Currency stability

Other methods of evaluation

The directors should also consider some of the other approaches to the evaluation of political risk. These include:

(a) Seeking the **views of individuals** with direct experience of the countries in question, such as academics, diplomats and journalists

(b) **Social** as well as **economic analysis**

The decision about which country to invest in

The evaluation of political risk must obviously form some part of the decision about which country to invest in. However, the use of this type of data to evaluate political risk in this context can be misleading for the following reasons:

(a) **Microrisks**

These scores are valid at the macro level, but they do not **measure the risk** that is faced at the **micro level** by the industry or firm. Certain industries, such as mining and agriculture are more prone to political risk than are others. Some activities will be welcomed by countries due to the perceived benefits that their presence can bring. Examples of this can be seen in the UK economy where the activities of the multinational biotechnology companies are being severely restricted, while investment by Japanese microchip companies is welcomed and assisted.

(b) **Emphasis on political features**

It can lead to an **over-emphasis** on the **political features** of the host country while neglecting other **vital considerations** such as the **strategic fit** of the new investment with the company's other operations.

Conclusion

This type of data therefore has relevance to the investment decision, but should not form the sole basis on which the decision is made. Although Forland comes out best in the overall scores, it has the **worst level** of **economic performance**. If the subsidiary is being developed with a view to serving primarily the local market, then this factor should receive a higher weighting in the overall decision making process since it will have a significant impact on the expected cash flow that will be generated.

3 Legal risks

FAST FORWARD

Legal risk can be reduced by keeping abreast of changes, acting as a good corporate citizen and lobbying.

3.1 Legal impacts

Companies may face government legislation or action in any jurisdiction that extend over its whole range of activities. Important areas may include:

(a) **Export and import controls** for political, environmental, or health and safety reasons. Such controls may not be overt but instead take the form of bureaucratic procedures designed to discourage international trade or protect home producers.

(b) **Favourable trade status** for particular countries, eg EU membership, former Commonwealth countries.

(c) **Monopolies and mergers legislation**, which may be interpreted not only within a country but also across nations. Thus the acquisition of a company in country A, by company B, which both sell in country C may be seen as a monopolistic restraint of trade.

(d) **Law of ownership**. Especially in developing countries, there may be legislation requiring local majority ownership of a firm or its subsidiary in that country, for example.

(e) **Taxation law** may be used to encourage or discourage particular import/export activities. For example, freeports may be set up, or generous tax incentives for inward investment may be offered.

(f) **Acceptance of international trademark, copyright and patent conventions**. Not all countries recognise such international conventions.

(g) Determination of minimum **technical standards** that the goods must meet, eg noise levels, contents and so on.

(h) **Standardisation measures** such as packaging sizes.

(i) **Pricing regulations**, including credit (eg, some countries require importers to deposit payment in advance and may require the price to be no lower than those of domestic competitors).

(j) **Restrictions on promotional messages**, methods and media.

(k) **Product liability**. Different countries have different rules regarding product liability (ie the manufacturer's/retailer's responsibility for defects in the product sold and/or injury caused). US juries are notoriously generous in this respect.

Bear in mind that organisations may face legal risks from lack of legislation (or lack of enforcement of legislation) designed to protect them.

Case Study

The lax enforcement of intellectual property legislation can cause problems for companies trading in certain markets. Britain's Imperial Tobacco group has had difficulties with its operations in Indonesia. A provincial trader, Sumatra stole the trademark of its premier cigarette brand, Davidoff, and Imperial Tobacco had major problems enforcing its rights.

The problem lay not in the law, which was strengthened about 10 years ago, but in the reluctance of the courts to enforce the law. Eventually Imperial needed a decision by the Indonesian Supreme Court to enforce its rights. The lower courts had refused to consider evidence that the sale of the trademark to Sumatra was fraudulent, and ignored claims that Sumatra was not actively using the trademark as it was required to do by Indonesian law.

Imperial Tobacco's problems could have had serious consequences for the Indonesian economy as a whole. Not only had Imperial Tobacco planned to invest in a hi-tech factory generating hundreds of jobs, but Imperial's problems might have deterred other companies from investing even though 2003 was designated by the Indonesian government as the year of investment.

Far Eastern Economic Review 22 May 2003

3.2 Dealing with legal risks

3.2.1 Consequences of non-compliance

Businesses that fail to comply with the law run the risk of **legal penalties** and accompanying **bad publicity**. Companies may also be forced into legal action to counter claims of allegedly bad practice that is not actually illegal; as the McDonalds case demonstrates, even a victory in such an action cannot prevent much bad publicity.

The issues of legal standards and costs have very significant implications for companies that trade internationally. Companies that meet a strict set of standards in one country may face accusations of **hypocrisy** if their practices are laxer elsewhere. Ultimately higher costs of compliance, as well as costs of labour may mean that companies **relocate** to countries where costs and regulatory burdens are lower.

3.2.2 The legislative process

Policy in many areas only changes slowly over time. Industries and organisations must however be alert for **likely changes in policy.** Managers must be political realists and understand politicians' hidden agendas that may be quite different to their stated objectives. They must also be aware of the **wider implications** of policy shifts. Although John Major's Citizen's Charter was ridiculed in some quarters, it helped draw more attention to the importance of consumer interests in the UK.

Businesses also need to consider the impact of changes in how powers are **devolved** outside central government. In America state legislatures have been described as 'the forum for the ideas of the nation.'. Directly elected mayors also wield considerable power in major cities.

Businesses need to be aware of the wider social consequences of legislation changes and how they affect issues that are discussed in other chapters in this book. For example legislation against sexual discrimination has had an impact on the opportunities women are offered, and through its effect on their working lives, has had wider impacts on their lifestyle choices.

3.2.3 Good citizenship

One aspect of minimising problems from governmental intervention is social and commercial good citizenship, complying with best practice and being responsive to ethical concerns. Often what is considered good practice at present is likely to acquire some regulatory force in the future. In addition, compliance with voluntary codes, particularly those relating to best practice or relations with consumers, can be marketed positively.

3.2.4 Other steps

Companies may wish to take all possible steps to avoid the bad publicity resulting from a court action. This includes implementing systems to make sure that the company **keeps abreast** of **changes in the law**, and staff are kept fully informed. Internal procedures may be designed to minimise the risks from legal action, for example human resource policies that minimise the chances of the company suffering an adverse judgement in a case brought by a disgruntled ex-employee. Contracts may be drawn up requiring **binding arbitration** in the case of disputes. Ultimately businesses may prefer the costs of settling cases out of court, rather than the direct and indirect consequences of court action.

Of course compliance with legislation may involve **extra costs**, including the extra procedures and investment necessary to conform to safety standards, staff training costs and legal costs. However these costs may also act as a **significant barrier to entry**, benefiting companies that are already in the industry.

4 Cultural risks

FAST FORWARD

Cultural risk affects the products and services produced and the way organizations are managed and staffed. Businesses should take cultural issues into account when deciding where to sell abroad, and how much to **centralise** activities.

4.1 Challenges of different cultures

Where a business trades with, or invests in, a foreign country additional uncertainty is introduced by the existence of different customs, laws and language. Communication between parties can be hindered, and potential deals put into jeopardy by ignorance of the expected manner in which such transactions should be conducted.

Case Study

Assumptions about particular cultures can also be dangerous. *Accountancy* magazine ran a series a few years ago about the major cultural issues involved in dealing with particular countries. Its article on Greece suggested that 'unorthodox' methods might be required to be successful there:

'The concept of a bribe is one that is well understood in Greece.'

Unsurprisingly the magazine received a number of complaints about this article.

The following areas may be particularly important.

(a) The **cultures and practices of customers** and consumers in individual markets

(b) The **media and distribution systems** in overseas markets

(c) The **different ways of doing business** (eg it is reputed that Japanese companies are concerned to avoid excessive legalism) in overseas markets

(d) The degree to which **national cultural differences matter** for the product concerned (a great deal for some consumer products, eg washing machines where some countries prefer front-loading machines and others prefer top-loading machines, but less so for products such as gas turbines)

(e) The degree to which a firm can use its own '**national culture**' as a selling point

4.2 Dealing with cultural risk

4.2.1 Deciding which markets to enter

Making the right choices about which markets to enter is a key element in dealing with cultural risk. When deciding what types of country it should enter (in terms of environmental factors, economic development, language used, cultural similarities and so on), the major criteria for this decision should be as follows.

(a) **Market attractiveness**. This concerns such indicators as GNP/head and forecast demand.

(b) **Competitive advantage**. This is principally dependent on prior experience in similar markets, language and cultural understanding.

(c) **Risk**. This involves an analysis of political stability, the possibility of government intervention and similar external influences.

Some products are extremely sensitive to the **environmental differences**, which bring about the need for adaptation; others are not at all sensitive to these differences, in which case standardisation is possible. A useful way of analysing products internationally is to place them on a continuum of **environmental sensitivity**. The greater the environmental sensitivity of a product, the greater the necessity for the company to understand the way in which its products interact with economic, socio-cultural and other environmental variables.

Environmentally sensitive	Environmentally insensitive
Adaptation necessary	Standardisation possible
• Fashion clothes	• Industrial and agricultural products
• Convenience foods	• World market products, eg jeans

4.2.2 Use of control systems

Local conditions and the scale of operations will influence the organisation structure of companies trading internationally. Conglomerates with widely differing product groups may organise globally by product, with each operating division having its own geographic structure suited to its own needs.

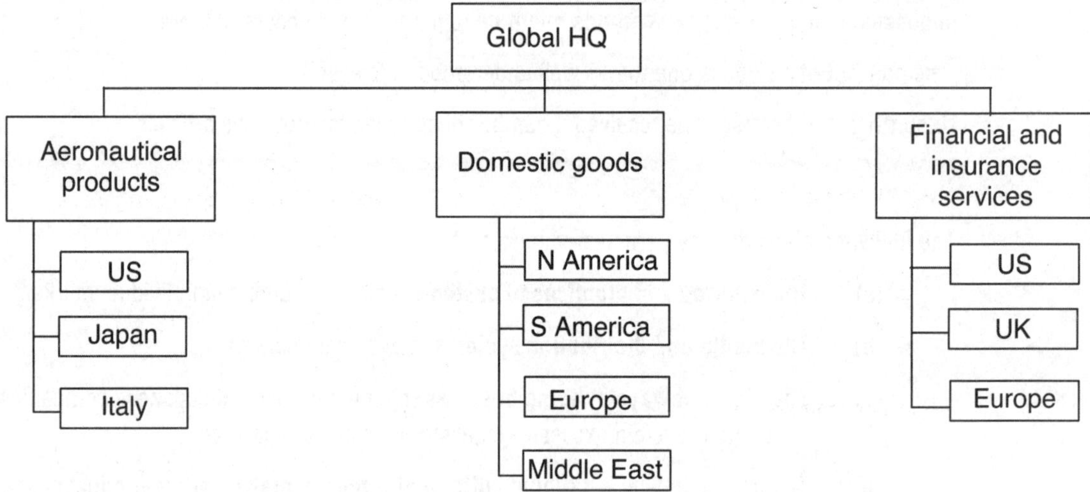

Companies with more integrated operations may prefer their top-level structure to be broken down **geographically** with product management conducted locally.

Very large and complex companies may be organised as a **heterarchy,** an organic structure with significant local control.

(a) **Some headquarters functions are diffused geographically**. For example, R&D might be in the UK, marketing in the US. Or again certain products will be made in one country, and others elsewhere. (Motor manufacturers do not make every model of car at each factory.) Some central functions might be split up: many firms are experimenting with having several centres for R&D.

(b) **Subsidiary managers have a strategic role for the corporation as a whole** (eg through bargaining and coalition forming).

(c) **Co-ordination is achieved through corporate culture and shared values** rather than a formal hierarchy. Employees with long experience might have worked in a number of different product divisions.

(d) **Alliances** can be formed with other company parts and other firms, perhaps in joint ventures or consortia.

A variety of factors influence **management methods** in the international setting; they pull in different directions and it may be that compromise is necessary.

Central control may be appropriate if the volume of international business or the company's experience in international operations is low. Centralisation can **promote efficiency** and prevent duplication of effort between regions. Even when operations are on a limited scale, when conformity with demanding technical standards is required, **functional representation** in international management may be necessary. Thus, a largely autonomous foreign subsidiary may have to accept supervision of its quality assurance or financial reporting functions.

If business is done globally, a form of **regional organisation** may be appropriate if there is some measure of social and economic integration within regions. The need for rapid response to local opportunities and threats may be served by a significant measure of **decentralisation**. National political and cultural sensitivities may reinforce this, but a shortage of local talent may limit it.

4.2.3 Management of human resources

The balance between local and expatriate staff must be managed. There are a number of influences.

- The availability of technical skills such as financial management
- The need for control
- The importance of product and company experience
- The need to provide promotion opportunities
- Costs associated with expatriates such as travel and higher salaries
- Cultural factors

For an international company, which has to think globally as well as act locally, there are a number of problems.

- Do you employ mainly **expatriate staff** to control local operations?
- Do you employ **local managers**, with the possible loss of central control?
- Is there such a thing as the **global manager**, equally at home in different cultures?

Expatriate staff are sometimes favoured over local staff.

(a) Poor **educational opportunities** in the market may require the import of skilled technicians and managers. For example, expatriates have been needed in many western firms' operations in Russia and Eastern Europe, simply because they understand the importance of profit.

(b) Some senior managers believe that a business run by expatriates is easier to **control** than one run by local staff.

(c) Expatriates might be better able than locals to **communicate** with the corporate centre.

(d) The expatriate may **know more about the firm** overall, which is especially important if he or she is fronting a sales office.

The use of expatriates in overseas markets has certain disadvantages.

(a) They **cost** more (eg subsidised housing, school fees).

(b) **Culture shock**. The expatriate may fail to adjust to the culture (eg by associating only with other expatriates). This is likely to lead to poor management effectiveness, especially if the business requires personal contact.

(c) A substantial training programme might be needed.

(i) **Basic facts** about the country will be given with basic language training, and some briefings about cultural differences.

(ii) **Immersion training** involves detailed language and cultural training and simulation of field social and business experiences. This is necessary to obtain an intellectual understanding and practical awareness of the culture.

Employing local managers raises the following issues.

(a) A **glass ceiling** might exist in some companies. Talented local managers may not make it to board level if, as in many Japanese firms, most members of the board are drawn from one country.

(b) In some cases, it may be hard for locals to **assimilate** into the **corporate culture**, and this might led to communication problems.

(c) Locals will **have greater knowledge of the country**, but may find it difficult to understand the wider corporate picture.

Those firms that export sporadically might employ a home-based sales force. Their travel expenses will of course be high, and it might not always be easy to recruit people willing to cope with the pace.

The following issues may also be important.

(a) **Recruitment and training**. In countries with low levels of literacy, more effort might need to be spent on basic training.

(b) **Career management**. Can overseas staff realistically expect promotion to the firm's highest levels if they do well?

(c) **Appraisal schemes**. These can be a minefield at the best of times, and the possibilities for communications failure are endless. For example, in some cultures, an appraisal is a two way discussion whereas in others arguing back might be considered a sign of insubordination.

(d) Problems associated with the **status of women**.

(e) **Communications**. Human Resources Management tries to mobilise employees' commitment to the goals of the organisation. In far-flung global firms, the normal panoply of staff newsletters and team briefings may be hard to institute but are vital. Time differences also make communication difficult.

Chapter roundup

- The risks faced by businesses include those arising from **general business and trading conditions**.
- Management of **credit risk** is of particular importance to exporters and various instruments and other arrangements are available to assist in this, such as documentary credits, bills of exchange, export credit insurance, export factoring and forfaiting.
- Multinationals can take various measures to combat the risks of **political interference** or **turbulence** including agreements with governments, insurance, and location elsewhere of key parts of the production process.
- **Legal risk** can be reduced by keeping abreast of changes, acting as a good corporate citizen and lobbying.
- **Cultural risk** affects the products and services produced and the way organizations are managed and staffed. Businesses should take cultural issues into account when deciding where to sell abroad, and how much to **centralise** activities.

Quick quiz

1 What is physical trading risk?

2 Define forfaiting.

3 What is an international credit union?

4 Give three examples of restrictions that may be defined as political risk.

5 By what methods do governments impose exchange controls?

6 Give four examples of ways companies can overcome exchange controls.

7 Give five examples of types legislation that may impact upon an organisation's operations

8 What are the main disadvantages in using expatriates in senior management roles?

Answers to quick quiz

1 The risk of goods being lost or stolen in transit, or the documents accompanying the goods going astray

2 A method of export finance where a bank purchases from a company a number of sales invoices or promissory notes, usually obtaining a guarantee of payment.

3 An organisation or association of finance houses or banks in different countries in Europe

4 Exchange controls, tax regulations, regulations on the use of local resources

5
- Rationing the supply of foreign exchange
- Restricting the types of transaction for which payments abroad are allowed

6
- Selling goods or services to subsidiary
- Charging a royalty on goods sold by subsidiary
- Interest rate manipulation
- Management charges

7
- Monopolies and mergers legislation
- Law of ownership
- Tax law
- Trademark and copyright law
- Standardisation (marketing and technical) laws
- Pricing laws
- Product liability laws
- Marketing and advertising legislation

8
- Greater cost
- Failure to adjust to culture
- Training requirements
- Limits opportunities for local managers

Now try the question below from the Exam Question Bank

Number	Level	Marks	Time
Q17	Examination	25	45 mins

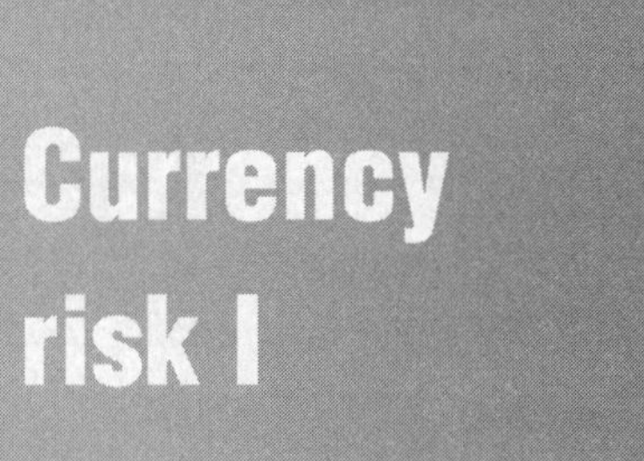

Currency risk I

Introduction

In this chapter and the next, we look at risks relating in particular to **exchange rate fluctuations**.

The temptation with currency risk is to go very quickly through the topics covered in this chapter and spend more time on the more difficult techniques covered in the next chapter, Chapter 19. However a number of the topics covered in this chapter will certainly be covered in exam questions.

Topic list	Learning outcomes	Syllabus references	Ability required
1 Exchange rates	D(iv),(v)	D(7)	Comprehension
2 Factors influencing exchange rates	D(iv),(v)	D(7)	Application
3 Currency risks	D(i),(ii),(iii)	D(1)	Evaluation
4 Management of economic risk	D(i),(ii),(iii)	D(2)	Evaluation
5 Management of translation risk	D(i),(ii),(iii)	D(2)	Evaluation
6 Management of transaction risk	D(i),(ii),(iii)	D(10)	Evaluation
7 Forward exchange contracts	D(i),(ii),(iii)	D(8)	Evaluation
8 Money market hedging	D(i),(ii),(iii)	D(8)	Evaluation
9 Choosing a hedging method	D(i),(ii),(iii),(vi)	D(4),(8)	Evaluation

1 Exchange rates

FAST FORWARD

Currencies are quoted at Term currency X units: Base currency 1 unit.

The **spot rate** is the rate at which currencies are currently quoted on the foreign exchange markets. The **forward rate** is the rate at which currencies will be exchanged on a set future date.

1.1 Spot rates

Key term

The **spot rate** is the exchange or interest rate currently offered on a particular currency or security.

The **spot rate** is the rate of exchange in currency for **immediate delivery.**

If an importer has to pay a foreign supplier in a foreign currency, he might ask his bank to sell him the required amount of the currency. For example, suppose that a bank's customer, a trading company, has imported goods for which it must now pay US$10,000.

(a) The company will ask the bank to sell it US$10,000. If the company is buying currency, the bank is selling it.

(b) When the bank agrees to sell US$10,000 to the company, it will tell the company what the spot rate of exchange will be for the transaction. If the bank's selling rate (known as the **'offer'**, or **'ask'** price) is, say $1.7935 for €1, the bank will charge the company:

$$\frac{\$10,000}{\$1.7935 \text{ per } £1} = €5,575.69$$

Similarly, if an exporter is paid, say, US$10,000 by a customer in the USA, he may wish to exchange the dollars to obtain euros. He will therefore ask his bank to buy the dollars from him. Since the exporter is selling currency to the bank, the bank is buying the currency.

If the bank quotes a buying spot rate (known as the **'bid'** price) of, say $1.8075, for the currency the bank will pay the exporter:

$$\frac{\$10,00}{\$1.8075 \text{ per } €1} = €5,532.50$$

1.2 Currency quotes

A bank expects to make a profit from selling and buying currency, and it does so by offering a rate for selling a currency which is different from the rate for buying the currency.

Key term

If a currency is quoted at $1.50:£, the $ is the **term currency** (the **reference currency**), the £ is the **base currency**.

When considering the prices banks are using, remember that the bank will **sell** the **term/reference currency low**, and **buy** the **term/reference currency high**. For example if a UK bank is buying and selling dollars, the selling (offer) price may be $1.41, the buying (bid) price may be $1.43.

Question

Exchange of currency

Learning outcomes D(iv), (v)

Calculate how much sterling exporters would receive or how much sterling importers would pay, ignoring the bank's commission, in each of the following situations, if they were to exchange currency and sterling at the spot rate.

(a) A UK exporter receives a payment from a Danish customer of 150,000 kroners.

(b) A German importer buys goods from a Japanese supplier and pays 1 million yen.

Spot rates are as follows.

	Bank sells (offer)		Bank buys (bid)
Denmark Kr/£	9.4340	-	9.5380
Japan Y/€	203.65	-	205.78

Answer

(a) The bank is being asked to buy the Danish kroners and will give the exporter:

$$\frac{150,000}{9.5380} = £15,726.57 \text{ in exchange}$$

(b) The bank is being asked to sell the yen to the importer and will charge for the currency:

$$\frac{1,000,000}{203.65} = €4,910.39$$

1.2.1 Direct and indirect currency quotes

Key term

A **direct quote** is the amount of **domestic** currency which is equal to **one foreign currency unit**. An **indirect quote** is the amount of **foreign** currency which is equal to **one domestic currency unit**.

Currencies may be quoted in either direction. In most countries, direct quotes are more common although in the UK indirect quotes are invariably used.

For example the US dollar and Swiss Franc may be quoted as SFr/$ = 1.723 or $/SFr = 0.580. In other words, SFr1.723 = $1 and $0.580 = SFr1. One rate is simply the reciprocal of the other.

A further complication to be aware of is that the offer rate in one country becomes the bid rate in the other. For example, Malaysian Ringgit (MR) are quoted in London like this:

	Bank sells (offer)		*Bank buys (bid)*
MR/£	4.0440	-	4.0910

However, in Kuala Lumpur you would see:

	Bank sells (offer)		*Bank buys (bid)*
MR/£	4.0910	-	4.0440

Exam focus point

Exchange rates given in the examination could be as quoted in any countries. Because of these complications you should always double-check which rate you are using when choosing between the bid or offer rate. One sure method is to recognise that the bank makes money out of the transaction and will therefore offer you the worse of the two possible rates!

1.3 Forward rates

Key term

Forward exchange rate is an exchange rate set for the exchange of currencies at some future date.

(OT 2000)

For reasons discussed later, a forward exchange rate might be higher or lower than the spot rate. If it is higher, the quoted currency will be cheaper forward than spot. For example, if in the case of Swiss Francs against sterling (i) the spot rate is 2.156 - 2.166 and (ii) the three months forward rate is 2.207 – 2.222:

(a) A bank would sell 2,000 Swiss Francs:

(i) At the spot rate, now, for £927.64 $\left(\frac{2,000}{2.156}\right)$

(ii) In three months time, under a forward contract, for £906.21 $\left(\frac{2,000}{2.207}\right)$

(b) A bank would buy 2,000 Swiss Francs:

(i) At the spot rate, now, for £923.36 $\left(\frac{2,000}{2.166}\right)$

(ii) In three months time, under a forward contract, for £900.09 $\left(\frac{2,000}{2.222}\right)$

In both cases, the quoted currency (Swiss Franc) would be worth less against sterling in a forward contract than at the current spot rate. This is because it is quoted **forward, at a lower rate, cheaper**, or 'at a **discount'**, against sterling. If the forward rate is a **higher rate, more expensive** than the spot rate, then it is 'at a **premium'** to the spot rate.

2 Factors influencing exchange rates

2.1 Currency supply and demand

FAST FORWARD

Factors influencing the exchange rate include the comparative rates of inflation in different countries (**purchasing power parity**), comparative interest rates in different countries (**interest rate parity**), the underlying balance of payments, speculation and government policy on managing or fixing exchange rates.

The exchange rate between two currencies - ie the buying and selling rates, both 'spot' and forward - is determined primarily by **supply and demand** in the foreign exchange markets. Demand comes from individuals, firms and governments who want to buy a currency and supply comes from those who want to sell it.

Supply and demand for currencies are in turn influenced by:

- The rate of inflation, compared with the rate of inflation in other countries
- Interest rates, compared with interest rates in other countries
- The balance of payments
- Sentiment of foreign exchange market participants regarding economic prospects
- Speculation
- Government policy on intervention to influence the exchange rate

Other factors influence the exchange rate through their relationship with the items identified above. For example:

(a) **Total income and expenditure** (demand) in the domestic economy determines the demand for goods, including:

- Imported goods
- Goods produced in the country which would otherwise be exported if demand for them did not exist in the home markets

(b) **Output capacity** and the **level of employment** in the domestic economy might influence the balance of payments, because if the domestic economy has full employment already, it will be unable to increase its volume of production for exports.

(c) The **growth in the money supply** influences interest rates and domestic inflation.

2.2 Interest rate parity (International Fisher Effect)

Key term

Interest rate parity method is a method of predicting foreign exchange rates based on the hypothesis that the difference between the interest rates in the two countries should offset the difference between the spot rates and the forward foreign exchange rates over the same period. *(OT 2000)*

The difference between spot and forward rates reflects differences in interest rates. If this were not so, then investors holding the currency with the lower interest rates would switch to the other currency for (say) three months, ensuring that they would not lose on returning to the original currency by fixing the exchange rate in advance at the forward rate. If enough investors acted in this way (known as **arbitrage**), forces of supply and demand would lead to a change in the forward rate to prevent such risk-free profit making.

The principle of **interest rate parity** links the foreign exchange markets and the international money markets. The principle can be stated as follows.

Exam formula

$$\text{Forward rate US\$/£} = \text{Spot US\$/£} \times \frac{1+\text{nominal US interest rate}}{1+\text{nominal UK interest rate}}$$

This equation is based on US dollar/sterling exchange and interest rates as shown in the formulae provided in the exam, but of course can be generalised to other cases. It shows that:

Difference in interest rates determines the difference between forward and spot rates

2.2.1 Example: interest rate parity

Exchange rates between two currencies, the Northland florin (NF) and the Southland dollar (S$) are listed in the financial press as follows.

Spot rates	4.7250	NF/$S
	0.21164	$S/NF
90 day rates	4.7506	NF/$S
	0.21050	$S/NF

The money market interest rate for 90 day deposits in Northland florins is 7.5% annualised. What is implied about interest rates in Southland?

Assume a 365-day year. (*Note.* In practice, foreign currency interest rates are often calculated on an alternative **360-day** basis, one month being treated as 30 days.)

Solution

Today, $S1.000 buys NF4.7250.

NF4.7250 could be placed on deposit for 90 days to earn interest of NF(4.7250 × 0.075 × 90/365) = NF0.0874, thus growing to NF(4.7250 + 0.0874) = NF4.8124.

This is then worth $S 1.0130 at the 90 day exchange rate.

This tells us that the annualised expected interest rate on 90-day deposits in Southland is 0.013 × 365/90 = 5.3%.

Alternatively, applying the formula given earlier, we have the following.

Northland interest rate on 90 day deposit = r_n = 7.5% × 90/365 = 1.85%

Southland interest rate on 90 day deposit = r_s

90-day forward exchange rate = $f_{s/n}$ = 0.21050

Spot exchange rate = $s_{s/n}$ = 0.21164

$$\frac{1+r_s}{1+0.0185} = \frac{0.21050}{0.21164}$$

$1 + r_s$ = 1.0185 × 0.21050 ÷ 0.21164 = 1.013

r_s = 0.013, or 1.3%

Annualised, this is 0.013 × 365/90 = 5.3%

2.3 Purchasing power parity

Key term

Purchasing power parity theory states that the exchange rate between two currencies is the same in equilibrium when the purchasing power of currency is the same in each country. *(OT 2000)*

Interest rate parity should not be confused with **purchasing power parity**. Purchasing power parity theory predicts that the exchange value of foreign currency depends on the relative purchasing power of each currency in its own country and that **spot exchange rates will vary over time according to relative price changes.**

Formally, purchasing power parity can be expressed in the following formula.

Exam formula

$$\text{Forward rate US\$/£} = \text{Spot US\$/£} \times \frac{1+\text{US inflation rate}}{1+\text{UK inflation rate}}$$

Note that the term 'forward rate' is used here as meaning the expected future spot rate and will not necessarily coincide with the 'forward exchange rate' currently quoted.

2.4 Example: Purchasing power parity

The exchange rate between UK sterling and the Danish kroner is £1 = 8.00 kroners. Assuming that there is now purchasing parity, an amount of a commodity costing £110 in the UK will cost 880 kroners. Over the next year, price inflation in Denmark is expected to be 5% while inflation in the UK is expected to be 8%. What is the 'expected spot exchange rate' at the end of the year?

Using the formula above:

$$\text{Future (forward) rate, } S_t = 8 \times \frac{(1.05)}{1.08}$$

$$= 7.78$$

This is the same figure as we get if we compare the inflated prices for the commodity. At the end of the year:

UK price	=	£110 × 1.08 = £118.80
Denmark price	=	Kr880 × 1.05 = Kr924
S_t	=	924 ÷ 118.80 = 7.78

In the real world, exchange rates move towards purchasing power parity only over the **long term**. However, the theory is sometimes used to predict future exchange rates in **investment appraisal problems** where forecasts of relative inflation rates are available.

2.5 The Fisher effect

The term **Fisher effect** is sometimes used in looking at the relationship between **interest** rates and expected rates of **inflation**.

The rate of interest can be seen as made up of two parts: the real required rate of return plus a premium for inflation. Then:

Exam formula

[1 + nominal (money) rate] = [1 + real interest rate] [1 + inflation rate]

Countries with relatively high rates of inflation will generally have high nominal rates of interest, partly because high interest rates are a mechanism for reducing inflation, and partly because of the Fisher effect: higher nominal interest rates serve to allow investors to obtain a high enough real rate of return where inflation is relatively high.

According to the **international Fisher effect**, interest rate differentials between countries provide an unbiased predictor of future changes in spot exchange rates. The currency of countries with relatively high interest rates is expected to depreciate against currency's with lower interest rates, because the higher interest rates are considered necessary to compensate for the anticipated currency depreciation. Given free movement of capital internationally, this idea suggests that the real rate of return in different countries will equalise as a result of adjustments to spot exchange rates.

The Fisher effect can be expressed as:

$$\frac{1+r_f}{1+r_{uk}} = \frac{1+i_f}{1+i_{uk}}$$

where

r_f is the nominal interest rate in the foreign country, with inflation rate i_f

r_{uk} is the nominal interest rate in the home country, with inflation rate i_{uk}

3 Currency risk

FAST FORWARD

Currency risk occurs in three forms: **transaction exposure** (short-term), **economic exposure** (effect on present value of longer term cash flows) and **translation exposure** (book gains or losses).

Currency risk arises from unexpected movements in exchange rates. A company may become exposed to **currency risk** (or **'exchange rate risk'**) in a number of ways, including the following.

- As an exporter of goods or services
- Through having an overseas subsidiary
- Through being the subsidiary of an overseas company
- Through transactions in overseas capital markets

The following different types of foreign exchange risk (or 'currency risk') may be distinguished.

(a) **Economic risk** refers to the effect of exchange rate movements on the **international competitiveness** of a company. For example, a UK company might use raw materials which are priced in US dollars, but export its products mainly within the European Union. A depreciation of sterling against the dollar or an appreciation of sterling against other EU currencies will both erode the competitiveness of the company. **Diversification of the supplier and customer base** across different countries may reduce this kind of exposure to risk.

(b) **Transaction risk** is the risk of adverse exchange rate movements occurring in the course of **normal international trading transactions**. This arises when export prices are fixed in foreign currency terms, or imports are invoiced in foreign currencies. Below, we discuss various methods for reducing this type of exposure to risk.

(c) **Translation risk** arises from differences in the currencies in which **assets and liabilities** are denominated. If a company has different proportions of its assets and liabilities denominated in particular currencies, then exchange rate movements are likely to have varying effects on the value of these assets and liabilities. This could influence investors' and lenders' attitudes to the financial worth and creditworthiness of the company. Such risk can be reduced if assets and liabilities denominated in particular currencies can be **held in balanced amounts**.

Case Study

In the 2002 Annual Report of the **Hilton Group plc,** the Group's management of its exposure to currency risk was reviewed as following.

'Due to the international nature of its core activities, the group's reported profits, net assets and gearing are all affected by movements in foreign exchange rates. The group seeks to mitigate the effect of any structural currency exposure that may arise from the translation of the foreign currency assets by borrowing in foreign currencies to match at least 75% of the foreign currency assets.... Although the group carries out operations through a number of foreign enterprises, group exposure to currency risk at a transactional level is minimal. The day-to-day transactions of overseas subsidiaries are carried out in local currency.'

4 Management of economic risk

FAST FORWARD

Economic exposure can be hedged by **matching assets and liabilities** and **diversification**.

4.1 Economic exposure

Key Term

Economic exposure is the risk that exchange rate movements might reduce the international competitiveness of a company. It is the risk that the present value of a company's future cash flows might be reduced by adverse exchange rate movements.

Economic exposure reveals itself in many different ways, as shown in the following examples.

4.2 Example: Economic exposure

Suppose a UK company invests in setting up a subsidiary in Eastern Europe. The currency of the Eastern European country depreciates continuously over a five year period. The cash flows remitted back to the UK are worth less in sterling terms each year, causing a reduction in the value of the investment project.

Another UK company buys raw materials which are priced in US dollars. It converts these materials into finished products which it exports mainly to Spain. Over a period of several years, the pound depreciates against the dollar but strengthens against the euro. The sterling value of the company's income declines while the sterling cost of its materials increases, resulting in a drop in the value of the company's cash flows.

The value of a company depends on the **present value** of its **expected future cash flows**. If there are fears that a company is exposed to the sort of exchange rate movements described above, this may reduce the company's value. Protecting against economic exposure is therefore necessary to protect the company's share price.

A company need not even engage in any foreign activities to be subject to economic exposure. For example if a company trades only in the UK but the pound strengthens appreciably against other world currencies, it may find that it loses UK sales to a foreign competitor who can now afford to charge cheaper sterling prices.

None of these examples are as simple as they seem, however, because of the compensating actions of economic forces. For example, if the exchange rate of an Eastern European country depreciates significantly, it is probably because of its high inflation rate.

So if the Eastern European subsidiary of a UK company **increases its prices** in line with inflation, its cash flows in the local currency will increase each year. These will be converted at the depreciating exchange rate to produce a fairly constant sterling value of cash flows. Alternatively, if the subsidiary does not increase its prices, it may increase its sales volume by selling at more competitive prices.

4.3 Hedging economic exposure

Various actions can reduce economic exposure, including the following.

(a) **Matching assets and liabilities**

A foreign subsidiary can be financed, so far as possible, with a loan in the currency of the country in which the subsidiary operates. A depreciating currency results in reduced income but also reduced loan service costs. A multinational will try to match assets and liabilities in each currency so far as possible.

(b) **Diversifying the supplier and customer base**

For example, if the currency of one of the supplier countries strengthens, purchasing can be switched to a cheaper source.

(c) **Diversifying operations world-wide**

On the principle that countries which confine themselves to one country suffer from economic exposure, international diversification is a method of reducing economic exposure.

5 Management of translation risk

FAST FORWARD

Translation exposure, the risk of apparent losses appearing when accounting results are translated, probably does not need to be hedged.

5.1 Translation exposure

Key term

Translation exposure is the risk that the organisation will make **exchange losses** when the **accounting results** of its foreign branches or subsidiaries are **translated** into the **home currency**.

Translation losses can result, for example, from restating the book value of a foreign subsidiary's assets at the exchange rate on the balance sheet date. Such losses will not have an impact on the firm's cash flow unless the assets are sold.

There are opposing arguments as to whether translation exposure is important. The arguments centre on whether the reporting of a translation gain or loss will affect the company's share price.

(a) There is a powerful argument that, to the extent that cash flows are not affected, **translation exposure** can be **ignored.**

(b) On the other hand, those who believe that accounting results are an important determinant of share price argue that translation losses should be reduced to a minimum.

The argument can be perhaps resolved by saying that it is important to consider potential losses arising from changes to the **economic value** of assets whereas changes to their **book values** are unimportant if there is no change to the economic value. In other words, **translation exposure** is unimportant to the extent that it does not represent **economic exposure**. Following this argument, translation exposure does not need to be specifically managed if economic exposure is being properly managed. For example, the matching of assets and liabilities in each currency will hedge translation exposure as well as economic exposure.

5.2 Example: Economic and translation risk

Lundrill is a UK company with a subsidiary in the East Asian People's Republic (EAPR). The current exchange rate between the EAPR $ and sterling is 30 EAPR $:£1. However the financial director of Lundrill Ltd believes that the EAPR may devalue by up to 20% over the next six months.

Summarised financial data for the EAPR subsidiary, Lundo EAPR is as follows.

	$'000	$'000
Turnover		60,000
Non-current assets		65,500
Current assets		
Inventory	6,000	
Receivables	4,500	
Cash	2,000	
		12,500
Current liabilities		(3,500)
Long-term loans		(750)
		73,750
Shareholders' equity		73,750

(i) All sales from the EAPR are denominated in £, and all debts are payable in £.

(ii) Long-term loans consist of a debt owed in sterling to Lundrill Ltd (25%) and a loan from a bank in the EAPR, denominated in EAPR $ with interest payable at 10% per annum.

(iii) The cost of goods sold and other operating expenses (excluding interest) for Lundo EAPR are 80% of turnover. 30% of this is payable in sterling and 70% in EAPR dollars.

Required

(a) Calculate the balance sheet translation exposure of Lundrill and the potential profit or loss on exposure of the balance sheet using the closing rate method where all exposed assets and liabilities are translated at the current exchange rate.

(b) Calculate the economic exposure (the impact on the £ value of Lundo EAPR's annual cash flow in the first full year after devaluation). Ignore the time value of money.

Solution

(a)

	$'000	*Exposed*	*£'000 at current rate*	*£'000 if $ devalues*
Fixed assets	65,500	Yes	2,183	1,819
Current assets				
Inventory	6,000	Yes	200	167
Receivables	4,500	No	150	150
Cash	2,000	Yes	67	56
	12,500		417	373
Current liabilities	(3,500)	Yes	(117)	(97)
Long-term loans	(750)	75%	(25)	(22)
	73,750		2,458	2,073
Shareholder's equity	73,750	Residual	2,458	2,073

Balance sheet exposure = (65,500,000 + 6,000,000 + 2,000,000 – (3,500,000 + 562,500)
= $69,437,500

Expected loss on translation exposure = 69,437,500 £/EAPR $ exchange rate change
= 69,437,500 (0.0333 – 0.0277)
= £385,764 (rounded down to £385,000)

which is the change in the shareholders' equity.

6 Management of transaction risk

FAST FORWARD

Basic methods of hedging risk include **matching receipts and payments**, **invoicing in own currency**, and **leading and lagging** the times that cash is received and paid.

6.1 Hedging transaction risk

Key term

Hedge is a transaction to reduce or eliminate an exposure to risk. *(OT 2000)*

We shall now look at the various means by which a business can hedge or manage the risk that has a direct effect on immediate cash flows – transaction risk. This risk is illustrated in the following question.

Question — **Exchange rate movements**

Learning outcomes: D(i),(ii),(iii)

Bulldog Ltd, a UK company, buys goods from Redland which cost 100,000 Reds (the local currency). The goods are re-sold in the UK for £32,000. At the time of the import purchase the exchange rate for Reds against sterling is 3.5650 - 3.5800.

Required

(a) What is the expected profit on the re-sale?

(b) What would the actual profit be if the spot rate at the time when the currency is received has moved to:

(i) 3.0800 - 3.0950

(ii) 4.0650 - 4.0800?

Ignore bank commission charges.

Answer

(a) Bulldog must buy Reds to pay the supplier, and so the bank is selling Reds. The expected profit is as follows.

	£
Revenue from re-sale of goods	32,000.00
Less cost of 100,000 Reds in sterling (÷ 3.5650)	28,050.49
Expected profit	3,949.51

(b) (i) If the actual spot rate for Bulldog to buy and the bank to sell the Reds is 3.0800, the result is as follows.

	£
Revenue from re-sale	32,000.00
Less cost (100,000 ÷ 3.0800)	32,467.53
Loss	(467.53)

(ii) If the actual spot rate for Bulldog to buy and the bank to sell the Reds is 4.0650, the result is as follows.

	£
Revenue from re-sale	32,000.00
Less cost (100,000 ÷ 4.0650)	24,600.25
Profit	7,399.75

This variation in the final sterling cost of the goods (and thus the profit) illustrates the concept of transaction risk.

6.2 Direct risk reduction methods

The **forward exchange contract** is perhaps the most important method of obtaining cover against risks, where a firm decides that it does not wish to speculate on foreign exchange. Another frequently used method is employing market investments and loans to hedge against risk. However, there are **other methods of reducing risk** which we shall consider first:

- Currency of invoice
- Matching receipts and payments
- Leads and lags
- Matching long term assets and liabilities
- Money market hedges

6.3 Currency of invoice

One way of avoiding exchange risk is for an exporter to **invoice his foreign customer in his own domestic currency**, or for an importer to arrange with his foreign supplier to be invoiced in his domestic currency.

(a) If an exporter is able to quote and invoice an overseas buyer in sterling, then **the foreign exchange risk is in effect transferred to the overseas buyer.**

(b) Similarly, an importer may be able to persuade the overseas supplier to invoice in sterling rather than in a foreign currency.

Although either the exporter or the importer avoids exchange risk in this way, only one of them can. The other must accept the exchange risk, since there will be a period of time elapsing between agreeing a contract and paying for the goods (unless payment is made with the order).

An alternative method of achieving the same result is to negotiate contracts expressed in the foreign currency but specifying **a fixed rate of exchange** as a condition of the contract.

There is a possible **marketing advantage** to be obtained by proposing to **invoice in the buyer's own currency**, when there is competition for the sales contract. The foreign buyer, invoiced in his own currency, will not have the problem of deciding whether to protect himself against exchange risks.

(a) If the exporter believes that he is in danger of not winning the contract, owing to competition from other sellers overseas, and if the buyer's own currency is weak and likely to depreciate against sterling, the exporter might offer to invoice the buyer in his own (weak) currency in order to win the contract. The exporter would in effect be offering the buyer a **price discount** due to the probability of a movement in exchange rates favourable to the buyer and therefore unfavourable to the exporter.

(b) In some export markets, foreign currency (often the US dollar) is the **normal trading** currency, and so exporters might have to quote prices in that currency for customers to consider buying from them. By arranging to sell goods to customers in a foreign currency, a exporter might be able to obtain a loan in that currency at a lower rate of interest than in his own currency, and at the same time obtain cover against exchange risks by arranging to repay the loan out of the proceeds from the sales in that currency.

There are certain other aspects to the currency of invoicing that an exporter might wish to consider.

6.3.1 Pricing and price lists

If the exporter issues price lists in foreign currency, he should be aware of the need to revise price lists as the value of his domestic currency fluctuates against the value of the foreign currency.

6.3.2 Customer relations

A switch from invoicing in a foreign currency to invoicing in sterling might not be easy to achieve, at least not without giving adequate warning to the customer. The ability of an exporter to make a change might be thwarted by the resistance of a customer with bargaining strength.

6.3.3 Accounting systems

Accounting procedures for invoicing in foreign currency, or borrowing in a foreign currency, are a little more complex than for invoicing and borrowing in sterling.

Exam focus point

You may be asked in the exam how invoicing policy might change if financing arrangements change.

6.4 Matching receipts and payments

A company can reduce or eliminate its foreign exchange transaction risk exposure by matching receipts and payments. Wherever possible, a company that expects to make payments and have receipts in the same foreign currency should plan to **offset its payments against its receipts in the currency.**

The process of matching is made simpler by having **foreign currency accounts** with a bank. Residents of a lot of countries are allowed to have bank accounts in any foreign currency. Receipts of foreign currency can be credited to the account pending subsequent payments in the currency. (Alternatively, a company might invest its foreign currency income in the country of the currency - for example it might have a bank deposit account abroad - and make payments with these overseas assets/deposits).

Offsetting (matching payments against receipts) will be **cheaper** than arranging a forward contract to buy currency and another forward contract to sell the currency, provided that receipts occur before payments, and the time difference between receipts and payments in the currency is not too long. Any **differences** between the amounts receivable and the amounts payable in a given currency may be covered by a forward exchange contract to buy/sell the amount of the difference.

6.5 Leads and lags

Companies might try to use:

- **Lead payments:** payments in advance, or
- **Lagged payments:** delaying payments beyond their due date

in order to take advantage of foreign exchange rate movements. With a lead payment, paying in advance of the due date, there is a finance cost to consider. This is the interest cost on the money used to make the payment.

6.5.1 Example: leads and lags

A company owes $30,000 to a US supplier, payable in 90 days. It might suspect that the US dollar will strengthen against sterling over the next three months, because the US dollar is quoted forward at a premium against sterling on the foreign exchange market. The spot exchange rate is $1.50 = £1.

(a) The company could pay the $30,000 now, instead of in 90 days time. This would cost £20,000 now, which is a payment that could have been delayed by 90 days.

(b) The cost of this lead payment would be interest on £20,000 for 90 days, at the company's borrowing rate or its opportunity cost of capital.

(c) This cost needs to be compared against the potential benefit derived from saving an increased sterling cost that would have arisen if the $ had strengthened against the £.

6.6 Netting

Unlike matching, netting is not technically a method of managing exchange risk. However, it is conveniently dealt with at this stage. The objective is simply to save transactions costs by netting off inter-company balances before arranging payment. Many **multinational groups** of companies engage in **intra-**

group trading. Where related companies located in different countries trade with one another, there is likely to be inter-company indebtedness denominated in different currencies.

Key term

Netting is a process in which credit balances are netted off against debit balances so that only the reduced net amounts remain due to be paid by actual currency flows.

In the case of **bilateral netting,** only two companies are involved. The lower balance is netted off against the higher balance and the difference is the amount remaining to be paid.

6.6.1 Example: bilateral netting

A and B are respectively UK and US based subsidiaries of a Swiss based holding company. At 31 March 20X5, A owed B SFr300,000 and B owed A SFr220,000. Bilateral netting can reduce the value of the intercompany debts: the two intercompany balances are set against each other, leaving a net debt owed by A and B of SFr 80,000 (SFr300,000 – 220,000).

6.7 Multilateral netting

As you will have guessed, **multilateral netting** is a more complex procedure in which the debts of more than two group companies are netted off against each other. There are different ways of arranging multilateral netting. The arrangement might be co-ordinated by the company's own central treasury or alternatively by the company's bankers.

The **common currency** in which netting is to be effected needs to be decided upon, as does the method of establishing the exchange rates to use for netting purposes. So that it is possible to agree the outstanding amounts in time but with minimum risk of exchange rate fluctuations in the meantime, this may involve using the exchange rates applying a few days before the date at which payment is to be made.
Netting has the following advantages.

(a) **Foreign exchange purchase** costs, including commission and the spread between selling and buying rates, and money transmission costs are **reduced**.

(b) There is **less loss in interest** from having money in transit.

Local laws and regulations need to be considered before netting is used, as netting is restricted by some countries. In some countries, bilateral netting is permitted but multinational netting is prohibited; in other cases, all payments can be combined into a single payment which is made on a 'gross settlements' basis.

6.7.1 Example: multilateral netting

A group of companies controlled from the USA has subsidiaries in the UK, South Africa and Denmark. Below, these subsidiaries are referred to as UK, SA and DE respectively. At 30 June 20X5, inter-company indebtedness is as follows.

Debtor	*Creditor*	*Amount*
UK	SA	1,200,000 South African rand (R)
UK	DE	480,000 Danish kroners (Kr)
DE	SA	800,000 South African rand
SA	UK	£74,000 sterling
SA	DE	375,000 Danish kroners

It is the company's policy to net off inter-company balances to the greatest extent possible. The central treasury department is to use the following exchange rates for this purpose.

US$1 equals R 6.126 / £0.6800 / Kr 5.880.

You are required to calculate the net payments to be made between the subsidiaries after netting off of inter-company balances.

Solution

The first step is to convert the balances into US dollars as a common currency.

Debtor	*Creditor*	*Amount in US dollars*
UK	SA	1,200,000 ÷ 6.126 = $195,886
UK	DE	480,000 ÷ 5.880 = $81,633
DE	SA	800,000 ÷ 6.126 = $130,591
SA	UK	£74,000 ÷ 0.6800 = $108,824
SA	DE	375,000 ÷ 5.880 = $63,776

	Paying subsidiaries			
Receiving subsidiaries	*UK*	*SA*	*DE*	*Total*
	$	$	$	$
UK	-	108,824	-	108,824
SA	195,886	-	130,591	326,477
DE	81,633	63,776	-	145,409
Total payments	(277,519)	(172,600)	(130,591)	580,710
Total receipts	108,824	326,477	145,409	
Net receipt/(payment)	(168,695)	153,877	14,818	

The UK subsidiary should pay $153,877 to the South African subsidiary and $14,818 to the Danish subsidiary.

6.8 Matching long-term assets and liabilities

When an international company has an operating subsidiary abroad, it may try to **finance the subsidiary's long-term assets with a matching long-term loan in the same currency.** For example, suppose that a US company with a French subsidiary decides to purchase extra premises in France which must be paid for in euros. The company may try to finance the purchase by raising a loan in euros, which it would then repay out of the operating profits (in euros) from the use of the French premises.

7 Forward exchange contracts

FAST FORWARD

A **forward contract** specifies in advance the rate at which a specified quantity of currency will be brought and sold.

7.1 Forward exchange contracts

Key term

A **forward exchange contract** is:

(a) An immediately firm and binding contract between a bank and its customer

(b) For the purchase or sale of a specified quantity of a stated foreign currency

Key term (Cont'd)

(c) At a rate of exchange fixed at the time the contract is made

(d) For performance (delivery of the currency and payment for it) at a future time which is agreed upon when making the contract (This future time will be either a specified date, or any time between two specified dates.)

Forward exchange contracts hedge against transaction exposure by allowing a trader who knows that he will have to buy or sell foreign currency at a date in the future, to make the purchase or sale at a predetermined rate of exchange. The trader will therefore know in advance either how much local currency he will receive (if he is selling foreign currency to the bank) or how much local currency he must pay (if he is buying foreign currency from the bank).

7.2 Forward rates and future exchange rate movements

Interest rate parity predicts that the forward rate is the spot price ruling on the day a forward exchange contract is made plus or minus the interest differential for the period of the contract. **It is wrong to think of a forward rate as a forecast of what the spot rate will be on a given date in the future**, and it will be a coincidence if the forward rate turns out to be the same as the spot rate on that future date.

It is however likely that the spot rate will move in the direction indicated by the forward rate. Currencies with high interest rates are likely to depreciate in value against currencies with lower interest rates: the attraction of higher interest persuades investors to hold amounts of a currency that is expected to depreciate.

7.3 Expectations theory of forward exchange rates

On the assumption that risk is absent, the **expectations theory of forward exchange rates** predicts that **the percentage difference between forward and spot rates now equals the expected change in spot rates over the period.**

Thus, given expectations of interest rates and inflation rates, the spot rate three months from now is expected to equal the three-months forward rate quoted now, for example. Because on average the forward rate equals the future spot rate, and overestimates it about as often as it underestimates it, the forward market is said to be an **unbiased predictor** of exchange rates.

7.4 Fixed and option contracts

A forward exchange contract may be either **fixed** or **option**.

(a) **'Fixed'** means that performance of the contract will take place on a specified date in the future. For example, a two months forward **fixed** contract taken out on 1 September will require performance on 1 November.

(b) **'Option'** means that performance of the contract may take place, at the option of the customer, either

   (i) At any date from the contract being made up to and including a specified final date for performance, or

   (ii) At any date between two specified dates

They can be used bit by bit.

Option forward exchange contracts are different from **currency options**, which are explained later. Option forward exchange contracts must be performed at some time.

7.5 Example: forward exchange contracts (1)

A UK importer knows on 1 April that he must pay a foreign seller 26,500 Swiss francs in one month's time, on 1 May. He can arrange a forward exchange contract with his bank on 1 April, whereby the bank undertakes to sell the importer 26,500 Swiss francs on 1 May, at a fixed rate of, say, 2.64.

The UK importer can be certain that whatever the spot rate is between Swiss francs and sterling on 1 May, he will have to pay on that date, at this forward rate,

$$\frac{26{,}500}{2.64} = £10{,}037.88.$$

(a) If the spot rate is lower than 2.64, the importer would have successfully protected himself against a weakening of sterling, and would have avoided paying more sterling to obtain the Swiss francs.

(b) If the spot rate is higher than 2.64, sterling's value against the Swiss franc would mean that the importer would pay more under the forward exchange contract than he would have had to pay if he had obtained the francs at the spot rate on 1 May. He cannot avoid this extra cost, because a forward contract is binding.

7.6 What happens if a customer cannot satisfy a forward contract?

A customer might be unable to satisfy a forward contract for any one of a number of reasons.

(a) An **importer** might find that:

  (i) His supplier **fails to deliver the goods as specified**, so the importer will not accept the goods delivered and will not agree to pay for them

  (ii) The **supplier sends fewer goods** than expected, perhaps because of supply shortages, and so the importer has less to pay for

  (iii) The supplier is late with the delivery, and so the importer does not have to pay for the goods until later than expected

(b) An **exporter** might find the same types of situation, but in reverse, so that he does not receive any payment at all, or he receives more or less than originally expected, or he receives the expected amount, but only after some delay.

7.7 Close-out of forward contracts

If a customer cannot satisfy a forward exchange contract, the bank will make the customer fulfil the contract.

(a) If the customer has arranged for the bank to **buy** currency but then cannot deliver the currency for the bank to buy, the bank will:

  (i) **Sell currency** to the customer **at the spot rate** (when the contract falls due for performance)

  (ii) Buy **the currency back**, under the terms of the forward exchange contract

(b) If the customer has contracted for the bank to **sell** him currency, the bank will:

  (i) **Sell the customer** the **specified amount of currency** at the forward exchange rate

  (ii) **Buy back the unwanted currency** at the spot rate

Thus, the bank arranges for the customer to perform his part of the forward exchange contract by either selling or buying the 'missing' currency at the spot rate. These arrangements are known as **closing out** a forward exchange contract.

7.8 Example: forward exchange contracts (2)

Shutter arranges on 1 January with a US supplier for the delivery of a consignment of goods costing US$96,000. Shutter will have to pay for the goods in six months time, on 1 July. The company therefore arranges a forward exchange contract for its bank to sell it US$96,000 six months hence.

In the event, the size of the consignment is reduced and, on 1 July, Shutter only needs US$50,000 to pay its supplier. The bank will therefore arrange to close out the forward exchange contract for the US$46,000 which Shutter does not need. This is called a **partial close-out**.

Exchange rates between the US dollar and sterling are as follows.

1 January	
Spot	$1.5145 - 1.5155
6 months forward	$1.5050 - $1.5070
1 July	
Spot	$1.5100 - 1.5110

Compute the cost to Shutter of the whole transaction, ignoring commission.

Solution

On 1 July the bank will sell Shutter US$96,000, to fulfil the original forward contract. The bank will then buy back the unwanted US$46,000 at the prevailing spot rate, thus closing out the contract.

	£
Sale of US$96,000 at $1.5050	63,787.38
Purchase of US$46,000 at $1.5110	30,443.41
Cost to Shutter	33,343.97

Exam focus point

It may seem a pedantic point, but don't confuse forward contracts (currency risk management) with forward rate agreements (interest risk management). The examiner has criticised candidates for confusing the two.

7.9 Extensions of forward contracts

When a forward exchange contract reaches the end of its period, a customer might find that he has not yet received the expected currency from an overseas buyer, or does not yet have to pay an overseas seller. The customer still wants to buy or sell the agreed amount of currency in the forward exchange contract, but he wants to **defer the delivery date** for the currency under the contract. The customer can then ask the bank to close out the old contract at the appropriate spot rate, and ask for a new contract for the extra period, with the rate being calculated in the usual way.

8 Money market hedging

FAST FORWARD

Money market hedging involves borrowing in one currency, converting the money borrowed into another currency and putting the money on deposit until the time the transaction is completed, hoping to take advantage of favourable interest rate movements.

8.1 Using the money market

Because of the close relationship between forward exchange rates and the interest rates in currencies, it is possible to 'manufacture' a forward rate by using the spot exchange rate and money market lending or borrowing. This technique is known as a **money market hedge** or **synthetic forward**.

8.2 Hedging payments

Suppose a British company needs to **pay** a Swiss creditor in Swiss francs in three months time. It does not have enough cash to pay now, but will have sufficient in three months time. Instead of negotiating a forward contract, the company could:

Step 1. Borrow the appropriate amount in pounds now

Step 2. Convert the pounds to francs immediately

Step 3. Put the francs on deposit in a Swiss franc bank account

Step 4. When the time comes to pay the creditor:

(a) Pays the creditor out of the franc bank account

(b) Repays the pound loan account

The effect is exactly the same as using a forward contract, and will usually cost almost exactly the same amount. If the results from a money market hedge were very different from a forward hedge, speculators could make money without taking a risk (see *Covered interest arbitrage* which follows). Therefore market forces ensure that the two hedges produce very similar results.

8.3 Example: money market hedge

A UK company owes a Danish creditor Kr3,500,000 in three months time. The spot exchange rate is Kr/£ 7.5509 - 7.5548. The company can borrow in sterling for 3 months at 8.60% per annum and can deposit kroners for 3 months at 10% per annum. What is the cost in pounds with a money market hedge and what effective forward rate would this represent?

Solution

The interest rates for 3 months are 2.15% to borrow in pounds and 2.5% to deposit in kroners. The company needs to deposit enough kroners now so that the total including interest will be Kr3,500,000 in three months' time. This means depositing:

Kr3,500,000/(1 + 0.025) = Kr3,414,634.

These kroners will cost £452,215 (spot rate 7.5509). The company must borrow this amount and, with three months interest of 2.15%, will have to repay:

£452,215 × (1 + 0.0215) = £461,938.

Thus, in three months, the Danish creditor will be paid out of the Danish bank account and the company will effectively be paying £461,938 to satisfy this debt. The effective forward rate which the company has 'manufactured' is 3,500,000/461,938 = 7.5768. This effective forward rate shows the kroner at a discount to the pound because the kroner interest rate is higher than the sterling rate.

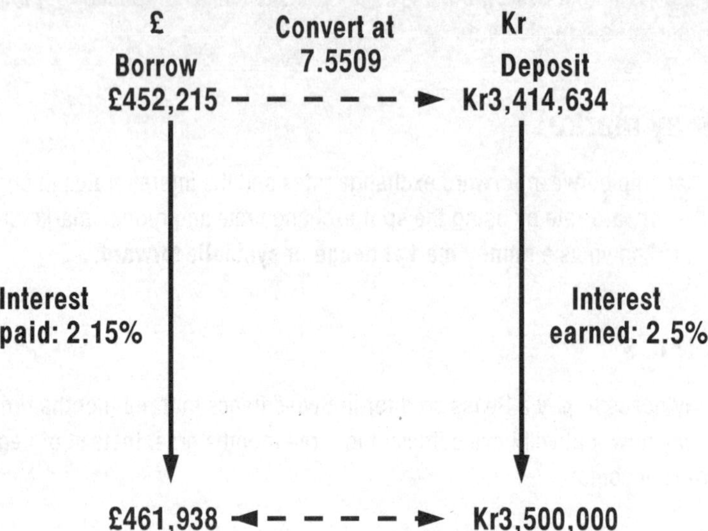

8.4 Hedging receipts

A similar technique can be used to cover a foreign currency **receipt** from a debtor. To manufacture a forward exchange rate, follow the steps below.

Step 1. Borrow an appropriate amount in the foreign currency today

Step 2. Convert it immediately to home currency

Step 3. Place it on deposit in the home currency

Step 4. When the debtor's cash is received:

(a) Repay the foreign currency loan
(b) Take the cash from the home currency deposit account

Exam focus point

Variations on these money market hedges are possible.

8.5 Forward exchange contracts versus money market hedge

Is one of these methods of cover likely to be cheaper than the other? The answer is perhaps, but not by much. There will be very little difference between borrowing in foreign currency and repaying the loan with currency receivables and borrowing in sterling and selling forward the currency receivables. This is because the premium or discount on the forward exchange rate reflects the interest differential between the two countries, as explained in the next section.

9 Choosing a hedging method

FAST FORWARD

In the exam you may be asked to see what the results are of using a number of different hedging methods, and identify the cheapest.

9.1 Choice of methods

When a company expects to receive or pay a sum of foreign currency in the next few months, it can choose between using the **forward exchange market** and the **money market** to hedge against the foreign exchange risk. Both of these methods were introduced in the previous chapter. The cheaper option available is the one that ought to be chosen. Other methods may also be possible, such as making **lead payments**.

9.2 Example: choosing the cheapest method

Trumpton has bought goods from a US supplier, and must pay $4,000,000 for them in three months time. The company's finance director wishes to hedge against the foreign exchange risk, and the three methods which the company usually considers are:

- Using forward exchange contracts
- Using money market borrowing or lending
- Making lead payments

The following annual interest rates and exchange rates are currently available.

	US dollar		*Sterling*	
	Deposit rate	*Borrowing rate*	*Deposit rate*	*Borrowing rate*
	%	%	%	%
1 month	7	10.25	10.75	14.00
3 months	7	10.75	11.00	14.25

	\$/£ exchange rate (\$ = £1)
Spot	1.8625 - 1.8635
1 month forward	1.8565 – 1.8577
3 months forward	1.8445 – 1.8460

Which is the cheapest method for Trumpton? Ignore commission costs. (The bank charges for arranging a forward contract or a loan.)

Solution

The three choices must be compared on a similar basis, which means working out the cost of each to Trumpton either **now** or **in three months time**. Here the cost to Trumpton now will be determined.

Choice 1: the forward exchange market

Trumpton must buy dollars in order to pay the US supplier. The exchange rate in a forward exchange contract to buy $4,000,000 in three months time (bank sells) is $1.8445/£.

The cost of the $4,000,000 to Trumpton in three months time will be:

$$\frac{\$4{,}000.000}{1.8445} = £2{,}168{,}609.38$$

This is the cost **in three months**. To work out the cost **now**, we could say that by deferring payment for three months, the company is:

(a) Saving having to borrow money now at 14.25% a year to make the payment now, or

(b) Avoiding the loss of interest on cash on deposit, earning 11% a year

The choice between (a) and (b) depends on whether Trumpton plc needs to borrow to make any current payment (a) or is cash rich (b). Here, assumption (a) is selected, but (b) might in fact apply.

At an annual interest rate of 14.25% the rate for three months is approximately 14.25/4 = 3.5625%. The 'present cost' of £2,168,609.38 in three months time is:

$$\frac{£2,168,609.38}{1.035625} = £2,094,010.27$$

Choice 2: the money markets

Using the money markets involves:

(a) Borrowing in the foreign currency, if the company will eventually receive the currency

(b) Lending (depositing) in the foreign currency, if the company will eventually pay the currency

Here, Trumpton will pay $4,000,000 and so it would **lend** US dollars.

It would lend enough US dollars for three months, so that the principal repaid in three months time plus interest will amount to the payment due of $4,000,000.

(a) Since the US dollar deposit rate is 7%, the rate for three months is approximately 7/4 = 1.75%.

(b) To earn $4,000,000 in three months time at 1.75% interest, Trumpton would have to lend now:

$$\frac{\$4,000,000}{1.0175} = \$3,931,203.93$$

These dollars would have to be purchased now at the spot rate of (bank sells) $1.8625. The cost would be:

$$\frac{\$3,931,203.93}{1.8625} = £2,110,713.52$$

By lending US dollars for three months, Trumpton is matching eventual receipts and payments in US dollars, and so has hedged against foreign exchange risk.

Choice 3: lead payments

Lead payments should be considered when the currency of payment is expected to strengthen over time, and is quoted forward at a premium on the foreign exchange market.

Here, the cost of a lead payment (paying $4,000,000 now) would be $4,000,000 ÷ 1.8625 = £2,147,651.01.

In this example, the present value of the costs are as follows.

	£
Forward exchange contract	2,094,010.27 (cheapest)
Money markets	2,110,713.52
Lead payment	2,147,651.01

Question — Hedging

Learning outcome D(ii),(iii),(vi)

Weft is an importer/exporter of textiles and textile machinery. It is based in the UK but trades extensively with countries throughout Europe, particularly in the eurozone. It has a small subsidiary based in Germany. The company is about to invoice a customer in Germany for 750,000 euros, payable in three months' time. Weft's treasurer is considering two methods of hedging the exchange risk. These are:

Method 1

Borrow €750,000 for three months, convert the loan into sterling and repay the loan out of eventual receipts. The interest payable on the loan will be purchased in the forward exchange market.

Method 2

Enter into a 3-month forward exchange contract with the company's bank to sell €750,000.

The spot rate of exchange is €1.6006 to £1.

The 3-month forward rate of exchange is €1.5935 to £1.

Annual interest rates for 3 months' borrowing are: euro 3%, sterling 5%.

Required

(a) Which of the two methods is the most financially advantageous for Weft?

(b) What are the other factors to consider before deciding whether to hedge the risk using the foreign currency markets?

Answer

(a) **Method 1**

Weft borrows €750,000.

Three months interest is €750,000 × 3% × 3/12 = €5,625.

The customer pays €750,000 in three months' time, which is sufficient to repay the loan principal but not the interest. The interest must be **paid** by **converting pounds into euros**. Since the amount of interest payable is known in advance, the euros can be purchased on the forward market at a cost of 5,625/1.5935 = £3,530.

The borrowed €750,000 will presumably be converted into sterling at the spot rate of €1.6006, to obtain £468,574. This money will be used somehow. Using the information available, it will be assumed that the company can invest the money at the sterling three-month interest rate of 5%.

Interest earned will be £468,574 × 5% × 3/12 = £5,857.

So, at the end of three months, the net sterling cash from the transaction is:

£468,574 + £5,857 – £3,530 = £470,901.

Method 2

The exchange rate is fixed in advance at €1.5935 by the forward contract. Cash received in three months is converted to produce €750,000/1.5935 = £470,662.

Conclusion

On the basis of the above calculations, Method 1 gives a slightly higher receipt. However, the difference is quite small, and banker's commission has been excluded from the calculation.

(b) **Factors to consider before deciding whether to hedge foreign exchange risk using the foreign currency markets**

Defensive strategy

The company should have a clear strategy concerning how much foreign exchange risk it is prepared to bear. A highly risk-averse or 'defensive' strategy of hedging all transactions can be **expensive** in terms of **commission costs**, but recognises that exchange rates are unpredictable, can be volatile and so can cause severe losses unless the risk is hedged.

Predictive strategy

An alternative **'predictive' strategy** recognises that if all transaction exposures are hedged, the chance of making gains from favourable exchange rate movements is lost. It might be possible to predict the future movement in an exchange rate with some confidence. The company could therefore **attempt** to **forecast foreign exchange movements** and only hedge those transactions where **losses from currency exposures** are **predicted**. For example, if inflation is high in a particular country, its currency will probably depreciate, so that there is little to be gained by hedging **future payments** in that currency. However, **future receipts** in a weak currency would be hedged, to provide protection against the anticipated currency loss.

A predictive strategy can be a risky strategy. If exchange rate movements were certain, **speculators** would almost certainly force an **immediate fall** in the exchange rate. However, some corporate treasurers argue that, if predictions are made sensibly, a predictive strategy for hedging should lead to higher profits within acceptable risk limits than a risk-averse strategy of hedging everything. Fewer hedging transactions will also mean lower commission costs payable to the bank. The risk remains, though, that a single large uncovered transaction could cause severe problems if the currency moves in the opposite direction to that predicted.

Maximum limit

A sensible strategy for a company could be to set a **maximum limit**, in money terms, for a **foreign currency exposure**. Exposures above this amount should be hedged, but below this limit a predictive approach should be taken or, possibly, all amounts could be left unhedged.

Offsetting

Before using any technique to hedge foreign currency transactions, **receipts and payments** in the same currency at the same date should be **offset**. This technique is known as matching. For example, if the company is expecting to receive €750,000 on 31 March and to pay €600,000 at about the same time, only the net receipt of €150,000 needs to be considered as a currency exposure.

Matching can be applied to receipts and payments which do not take place on exactly the same day by simply hedging the period and amount of the difference between the receipt and payment, or even by using a currency bank account. A company that has many receipts and payments in a single currency such as the euro should consider **matching assets with liabilities** in the same currency.

Chapter roundup

- Currencies are quoted at Term currency X units:Base currency 1 unit.
- The **spot rate** is the rate at which currencies are currently quoted on the foreign exchange markets. The **forward rate** is the rate at which currencies will be exchanged on a set future date.
- Factors influencing the exchange rate include the comparative rates of inflation in different countries (**purchasing power parity**), comparative interest rates in different countries (**interest rate parity**), the underlying balance of payments, speculation and government policy on managing or fixing exchange rates.
- **Currency risk** occurs in three forms: **transaction exposure** (short-term), **economic exposure** (effect on present value of longer term cash flows) and **translation exposure** (book gains or losses).
- **Economic exposure** can be hedged by **matching assets and liabilities** and **diversification**.
- **Translation exposure,** the risk of apparent losses appearing when accounting results are translated, probably does not need to be hedged.
- Basic methods of hedging risk include **matching receipts and payments**, **invoicing in own currency**, and **leading and lagging** the times that cash is received and paid.
- A **forward contract** specifies in advance the rate at which a specified quantity of currency will be brought and sold.
- **Money market hedging** involves borrowing in one currency, converting the money borrowed into another currency and putting the money on deposit until the time the transaction is completed, hoping to take advantage of favourable interest rate movements.
- In the exam you may be asked to see what the results are of using a number of different hedging methods, and identify the cheapest.

Quick quiz

1 Identify the three types of currency risk.

2 Which factors influence the supply and demand for currencies?

3 The principle of purchasing power parity must always hold.

True ☐

False ☐

4 A company might make payments earlier or later in order to take advantage of exchange rate movements. What is this called?

5 Define a 'forward exchange rate'.

6 Fill in the boxes in the diagram with (A) to (E), to indicate which factors are linked by which theory.

(A) Purchasing powering parity theory

(B) Expectations theory

(C) Fisher effect

(D) International Fisher effect

(E) Interest rate parity

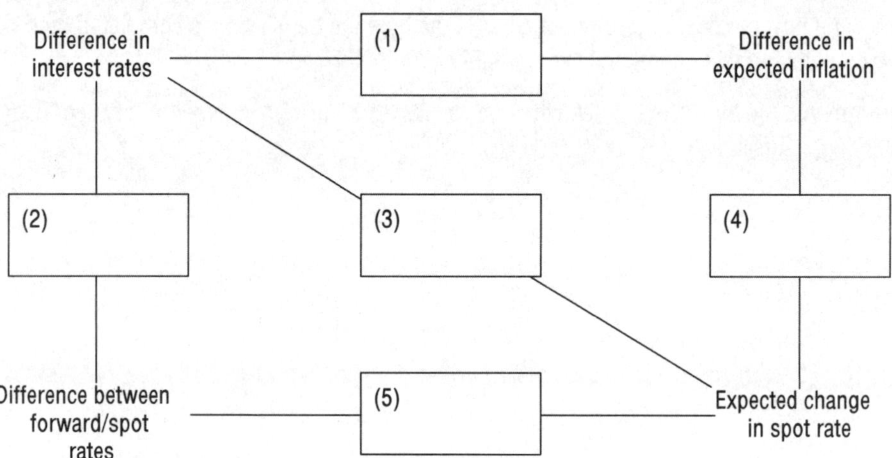

7 Fill in the blanks

(a) Forward rate cheaper quoted at ______________________

(b) Forward rate more expensive quoted at ______________________

8 What steps can be taken in money markets to cover a foreign currency receipt from a debtor?

Answers to quick quiz

1 (a) Transaction risk
(b) Translation risk
(c) Economic risk

2 (a) Relative rates of inflation
(b) Relative interest rates
(c) The balance of payments position
(d) Market sentiment
(e) S peculation
(f) Government policy

3 False. In reality, prices of commodities do differ significantly in different countries.

4 Leading and lagging

5 An exchange rate set for the exchange of currencies at some future date

6 (1) C Fisher effect
(2) E Interest rate parity
(3) D International Fisher effect
(4) A Purchasing power parity effect
(5) B Expectations theory

7 (a) Discount
(b) Premium

8 (a) Borrow an appropriate amount in the foreign currency today
(b) Convert it immediately to home currency
(c) Place home currency on deposit
(d) When the debtor's cash is received, repay the foreign currency loan and take the cash from the home currency deposit account

Now try the questions below from the Exam Question Bank

Number	Level	Marks	Time
Q18	Examination	25	45 mins

Currency risk II

Introduction

In this chapter, we extend our discussion of **currency risk management** and consider some of the variety of **financial instruments** which are now available for managing **financial risks** of various kinds.

Using the method described in this chapter for dealing with futures and options will ensure that you set out your workings clearly and should be able to gain marks for the straightforward areas easily. Don't neglect swaps as currency swaps are frequently set in exams. Foreign exchange calculations are often highlighted as weaknesses.

Topic list	Learning outcomes	Syllabus references	Ability required
1 Currency futures	D(ii),(iii),(vi)	D(8)	Evaluation
2 Currency options	D(ii),(iii),(vi)	D(8)	Evaluation
3 Currency swaps	D(ii),(iii),(vi)	D(8)	Evaluation

1 Currency futures

FAST FORWARD

Currency futures are contracts for the sale or purchase at a set future date of a set quantity of currency. A step-by-step approach can be used to deal with complications.

Transaction on future date		Now		On future date	
Receive	currency	Sell	currency futures	Buy	currency futures
Pay	currency	Buy	currency futures	Sell	currency futures
Receive	$	Buy	currency futures	Sell	currency futures
Pay	$	Sell	currency futures	Buy	currency futures

1.1 What is a future?

A future represents a **commitment** to an **additional transaction** in the future that limits the risk of existing commitments.

1.1.1 Example: futures

1 January

(a) On 1 January the price (the spot price) of a consignment of cocoa beans is $1,000.

(b) You have already agreed to buy a consignment of cocoa beans for $1,200 on 28 February.

(c) You buy a three-month cocoa futures contract at $1,100 that expires on 31 March. This means you are committing to buying an additional consignment of cocoa beans, not at today's spot price, but at the **futures price** of $1,100. $1,100 represents what the market thinks the spot price will be on 31 March.

28 February

(a) You buy the consignment of cocoa beans at $1,200.

(b) You are still committed to buying the consignment at $1,100 on 31 March, but that will mean that you have two consignments of cocoa beans rather than just the one you need. You therefore sell the futures contract you bought on 1 January to eliminate this additional commitment. The futures contract is now priced at $1,233, as the market now believes that $1,233 will be the spot price on 31 March.

(c) Because you have sold the contract for more than the purchase price, you have made a gain on the futures contract of 1,233 – 1,100 = $133 This can be set against the purchase you made.

Net cost = 1,200 – 133 = $1,067

1.2 Types of futures

Key terms

Futures contract is a contract relating to currencies, commodities or shares that obliges the buyer (issuer) to purchase (sell) the specified quantity of the item represented in the contract at a pre-determined price at the expiration of the contract.

Unlike forward contracts, which are entered into privately, futures contracts are traded on organised exchanges, carry standard terms and conditions, have specific maturities, and are subject to rules concerning margin requirements. *(OT 2000)*

A **financial future** is a futures contract which is based on a financial instrument, rather than a physical commodity. There are financial futures for interest rates, currencies and stock market indices.

A **currency future** is a futures contract to buy or sell a currency.

Currency futures are not nearly as common as forward contracts, and their market is much smaller.

1.3 Trading in futures

Key term

Futures market is an exchange-traded market for the purchase or sale of a standard quantity of an underlying item such as currencies, commodities or shares, for settlement at a future date at an agreed price. *(OT 2000)*

On the currency futures markets, currencies such as the pound, euro, yen and Swiss franc are all priced in US dollars. There is no contract for the US dollar itself.

Key term

The **contract size** is the fixed minimum quantity of commodity which can be bought or sold using a futures contract.

In general, dealing on futures markets must be in a whole number of contracts.

Key term

The **contract price** is the price at which the futures contract can be bought or sold.

For all currency futures the contract price is in US dollars (e.g. $/SFr 0.5800 as used in the last example). The contract price is the figure which is traded on the futures exchange. It changes continuously and is the basis for computing gains or losses.

Key term

The **settlement date** (or delivery date, or expiry date) is the date when trading on a particular futures contract stops and all accounts are settled.

On the International Monetary Market (IMM), the settlement dates for all currency futures are at the end of March, June, September and December. The period for which a currency contract is traded before the settlement date is normally a **maximum of nine months**. This means that for each currency there will be three contracts being traded at any time, each to a different settlement date.

POSITIONS	
Buyer of futures contract	Long position
Seller of futures contract	Short position

Key term

When futures contracts are bought or sold, a **deposit** known as the **initial margin** must be advanced.

The size of this margin depends on the actual contract but might typically amount to about 5% of the value of contracts dealt in. This deposit is refunded when the contract is closed out.

Key term

A future's price may be different from the spot price, and this difference is the **basis**.

Basis = spot price – futures price

(Some books show it the other way round, so that the basis is the amount by which the futures price exceeds the spot price.) The basis will move towards zero at the delivery date.

1.4 Tick sizes

Key term

One tick (or the **tick size**) is the smallest measured movement in the contract price. For currency futures this is a movement in the fourth decimal place.

The value of one tick = contract size × tick size. A movement in the price of the Swiss Franc contract from $/SFr 0.5800 to 0.5801 is a one-tick movement. The **value of a tick** is the gain or loss which is made if there is one tick price movement. This value depends on the contract size. Examples of tick values and contract sizes are shown in the following table.

Currency future	Contract size	Tick	Value of one tick
Swiss franc	SFr 125,000	$0.0001 per SFr	$12.50
Japanese yen	Y 12.5 million	$0.0001 per Y100	$12.50
Sterling	£62,500	$0.0001 per £	$6.25
Euro	€125,000	$0.0001 per €	$12.50

Market traders will compute gains or losses on their futures positions by reference to the number of ticks by which the contract price has moved. For instance, the futures market gain in the previous example could have been computed as follows.

Bought at	0.5800
Sold at	0.6000
Gain	0.0200 = 200 ticks.

8 contracts × 200 ticks × $12.50 = $20,000.

The futures markets have grown rapidly as more and more speculators have become involved and this has increased short-term volatility. The only risk to hedgers is that the futures market does not always provide a perfect hedge. This can result from two causes.

(a) Amounts must be **rounded to a whole number of contracts**, causing inaccuracies.

(b) **Basis risk** is the risk that the futures contract price may move by a different amount from the price of the underlying currency or commodity. The actions of speculators may increase basis risk.

When deciding to use futures to hedge currency risk, you need to consider the following things when **setting up** the hedge.

- **Which contract** out of a number of contracts with different settlement dates?
- **What type** of futures contract - are you looking for a **buy** or **sell** contract?
- **Which settlement date**?

1.5 Which contract settlement date?

Currency futures are traded for a period of about nine months before the settlement date is reached. This means that at any time there will be a choice of three settlement dates to choose from. To hedge currency receipts and payments a futures contract must have a settlement date **after** the date that the actual currency is needed. Usually the best hedge is achieved by selecting the contract which matures **next after** the actual cash is needed.

1.6 Which type of contract?

One of the limitations of currency futures is that currencies can only be bought or sold for US dollars. The basic rules are given below.

(a) If you need to **buy** a currency on a future date with US dollars, take the following action.

Step 1. Buy the appropriate currency futures contracts now

Step 2. Close out by selling the same number of futures contracts on the date that you buy the actual currency

(b) If you need to **sell** a currency on a future date for US$, take the following steps.

Step 1. Sell the appropriate currency futures contracts now

Step 2. Close out by buying the same number of futures contracts on the date that you sell the actual currency

1.7 Dealing with a futures question

A number of possible stages are involved.

Step 1. The setup process

This may involve the following steps.

(a) **Choose which contract**

You must chose an expiry date after the underlying exposure.

(b) **Choose type of contract**

A €125,000 contract will be to buy or sell €. If the company owes €, it will wish to buy € so will **buy € futures**. However a UK company receiving $ will wish to sell $ or buy £. As the contract size is quoted in £, £62,500, the company will **buy £ futures**.

(c) **Choose number of contracts**

You need to divide the amount being hedged by the size of contract, rounding to the nearest whole contract.

You may also need to calculate how much of the currency of the future is needed. You do this by using today's price for the futures contract to convert the amount being hedged into the currency of the futures contract, and then divide by the size of the futures contract.

(d) **Calculate tick size**

Tick size = Minimum price movement × standard contract size

Remember that the minimum price has to be calculated to the **fourth** decimal place, for example $0.0001 per £.

Step 2. **Estimate the closing futures price**

You should be given this in the question.

Step 3. **Hedge outcome**

(a) **Calculate futures market outcome**

This will be

Tick movement × tick value × number of contracts

(b) **Calculate net outcome**

Spot market payment or receipt translated at closing rate
+ Futures market profit/(loss)

The currency used for this calculation will be the opposite to the currency of the receipt/payment being hedged. Ultimately therefore, a dollar receipt or payment is

being hedged, the value of the futures profit or loss will also have to be converted using the **closing spot rate**.

The gain or loss on the future will accrue during the contract. For exam purposes you will take this gain or loss when the contract is terminated.

1.8 Example: futures contract

A US company buys goods worth €720,000 from a German company payable in 30 days. The US company wants to hedge against the € strengthening against the dollar.

Current spot is 0.9215 – 0.9221 $/€ and the € futures rate is 0.9245 $/€.

The standard size of a 3 month € futures contract is €125,000.

In 30 days time the spot is 0.9345 – 0.9351 $/€.

Closing futures price will be 0.9367.

Evaluate the hedge.

Solution

Step 1. Setup

(a) **Which contract?**

We assume that the three month contract is the best available.

(b) **Type of contract**

We need to buy € or sell $.

As the futures contract is in €, we need to buy futures.

(c) **Number of contracts**

$\frac{720{,}000}{125{,}000}$ = 5.76, say 6 contracts

(d) **Tick size**

Minimum price movement × contract size = 0.0001 × 125,000 = $12.50

Step 2. Closing futures price

We're told it will be 0.9367

Step 3. Hedge outcome

(a) **Outcome in futures market**

Opening futures price	0.9245	Buy at low price
Closing futures price	0.9367	Sell at high price
Movement in ticks	122 ticks	Profit
Futures profit/loss	122 × $12.50 × 6 contracts = $9,150	

(b) **Net outcome**

	$
Spot market payment (720,000 × 0.9351 $/£)	673,272
Futures market profit	(9,150)
	664,122

Remember the following table.

Transaction on future date		Now		On future date	
Receive	currency	Sell	currency futures	Buy	currency futures
Pay	currency	Buy	currency futures	Sell	currency futures
Receive	$	Buy	currency futures	Sell	currency futures
Pay	$	Sell	currency futures	Buy	currency futures

1.9 Non-dollar receipts and payments

We have already made the point that futures can only be bought or sold as a whole number of contracts. When hedging, there is no necessary advantage in rounding **up** because futures trading can produce a loss as regularly as a profit. The problem which has not yet been covered is what to do when a company outside America is hedging a receipt or payment that isn't in dollars. The method normally used is to convert to the other currency using the exchange rate implicit in the futures contract (i.e. today's contract price) and then divide by the futures contract size.

1.10 Example: currency futures

Great Eastern, a British company, has purchased steel worth Y100 million from Japan and needs to pay for this in 90 days' time. How can it hedge the cost of the purchase by using currency futures? On IMM the Japanese yen future is trading at $0.8106 per 100 yen and the Sterling future is trading at $1.6250 per pound.

Solution

The company must buy yen futures and sell sterling futures. The size of the Japanese yen futures contract is Y12.5 million. The number of yen futures to buy is 100/12.5 = 8.

8 contracts represent $\frac{8 \times 12{,}500{,}000 \times \$0.8106}{100} = \$810{,}600.$

$810,600, converted at the sterling futures price, gives £ 810,600/1.6250 = £498,831. The sterling contract size is £62,500. The company should sell £498,831/£62,500 = 7.98 contracts, rounded to 8 contracts.

Summary. Today, buy 8 yen contracts and sell 8 sterling contracts. In 90 days, close out by selling 8 yen contracts and buying 8 sterling contracts.

1.11 Choosing between forward contracts and futures contracts

A futures market hedge attempts to achieve the same result as a forward contract, that is to fix the exchange rate in advance for a future foreign currency payment or receipt. As we have seen, hedge inefficiencies mean that a futures contract can only fix the exchange rate subject to a margin of error.

Forward contracts are agreed 'over the counter' between a bank and its customer. Futures contracts are standardised and traded on futures exchanges. This results in the following advantages and disadvantages.

1.11.1 Advantages of futures over forward contracts

(a) **Transaction** costs should be **lower**.

(b) The **exact date** of **receipt** or **payment** of the currency does **not have to be known**, because the futures contract does not have to be closed out until the actual cash receipt or payment is made. In other words, the futures hedge gives the equivalent of an 'option forward' contract, limited only by the expiry date of the contract.

1.11.2 Disadvantages of futures compared with forward contracts

(a) The **contracts cannot be tailored** to the user's exact requirements.

(b) **Hedge inefficiencies** are **caused** by having to deal in a whole number of contracts and by basis risk.

(c) **Only a limited number of currencies** are the subject of futures contracts (although the number of currencies is growing, especially with the rapid development of Asian economies).

(d) The **procedure for converting** between two currencies neither of which is the US dollar is twice as complex for futures as for a forward contract.

In general, the disadvantages of futures mean that the market is much smaller than the currency forward market.

2 Currency options

FAST FORWARD

Currency options protect against **adverse exchange rate movements** while allowing the investor to take advantage of favourable exchange rate movements. They are particularly useful in situations where the cash flow is not certain to occur (eg when tendering for overseas contracts).

2.1 The nature of an option

Key term

An **option** is a right of an option holder to buy (call) or sell (put) a specific asset on predetermined terms on, or before, a future date. *(OT 2000)*

We looked at the use of interest rate options in Chapter 11. Now, we turn to currency options.

2.2 Currency options

There is a major drawback to forward exchange contracts as a means of managing foreign exchange risk. A forward exchange contract is an agreement to buy or sell a given quantity of foreign exchange, which **must be carried out** because it is a binding contract. Some exporters might be uncertain about the amount of currency they will earn in several months time. They would be unable to enter forward exchange contracts without the risk of contracting to sell more or less currency to their bank than they will actually earn when the time comes.

An alternative method of obtaining foreign exchange cover, which overcomes much of the problem, is the **currency option**.

Key term

A **currency option** is an agreement involving an option, but not an obligation, to buy or to sell a certain amount of currency at a stated rate of exchange (the exercise price) at some time in the future.

The exercise price for the option may be the same as the current spot rate, or it may be more favourable or less favourable to the option holder than the current spot rate.

Companies can choose whether to buy:

(a) A tailor-made currency option from a bank, suited to the company's specific needs. These are **over-the-counter** (OTC) or **negotiated** options, or

(b) A standard option, in certain currencies only, from an options exchange. Such options are **traded** or **exchange-traded** options.

As with other types of option, buying a currency option involves paying a premium, which is the most the buyer of the option can lose.

Currency options are not the same as forward exchange option contracts, although the similarity in names might seem confusing. Unlike a forward exchange contract (option or otherwise), a currency option **does not have to be exercised**. Instead, when the date for exercising the option arrives, the importer or exporter can either exercise the option or let the option lapse.

2.3 The purpose of currency options

The purpose of currency options is to reduce or eliminate exposure to currency risks, and they are particularly useful for companies in the following situations:

(a) Where there is **uncertainty** about **foreign currency receipts or payments**, either in timing or amount. Should the foreign exchange transaction not materialise, the option can be sold on the market (if it has any value) or exercised if this would make a profit.

(b) To **support the tender** for an **overseas contract**, priced in a foreign currency

(c) To allow **the publication of price lists** for its goods in a foreign currency

(d) To protect the import or export of **price-sensitive goods**.

In both situations (b) and (c), the company would not know whether it had won any export sales or would have any foreign currency income at the time that it announces its selling prices. It cannot make a forward exchange contract to sell foreign currency without becoming exposed in the currency.

2.4 Example: currency options

Tartan plc has been invited to tender for a contract in Blueland with the bid priced in Blues (the local currency). Tartan thinks that the contract would cost £1,850,000. Because of the fierce competition for the bid, Tartan is prepared to price the contract at £2,000,000, and since the exchange rate is currently B2.80 = £1, it puts in a bid of B5,600,000. The contract will not be awarded until after six months.

What can happen to Tartan with the contract? Consider the following possible outcomes.

(a) Tartan plc decides to hedge against the currency risk, and on the assumption that it will be awarded the contract in six months time, it enters into a **forward exchange contract** to sell B5,600,000 in six months time at a rate of B2.8 = £1.

As it turns out, the company fails to win the contract and so it must buy B5,600,000 spot to meet its obligation under the forward contract. The exchange rate has changed, say, to B2.5 = £1.

	£
At the outset:	
Tartan sells B5,600,000 forward at B2.8 to £1	2,000,000
Six months later:	
Tartan buys B5,600,000 spot to cover the hedge, at B2.5 to £1	(2,240,000)
Loss	(240,000)

(b) Alternatively, Tartan plc might decide not to make a forward exchange contract at all, but to **wait and see** what happens. As it turns out, Tartan is awarded the contract six months later, but by this time, the value of the Blue has fallen, say, to B3.2 = £1.

Question

Hedging decision

Learning outcomes: D(ii),(iii)

Have a go at calculating the outcome, before looking at the calculation below.

	£
Tartan wins the contract for B5,600,000, which has a sterling value of (B3.2 = £1)	1,750,000
Cost of the contract	(1,850,000)
Loss	(100,000)

(c) A **currency option** would, for a fixed cost, eliminate these risks for Tartan plc. When it makes its tender for the contract, Tartan might purchase a currency option to sell B5,600,000 in six months time at B2.8 to £1, at a cost of £40,000.

The worst possible outcome for Tartan plc is now a loss of £40,000.

(a) If the company **fails to win the contract,** Tartan will **abandon** the option (unless the exchange rate has moved in Tartan's favour and the Blue has weakened against sterling so that the company can make a profit by buying B5,600,000 at the spot rate and selling it at B2.8 = £1).

(b) If the company **wins the contract** and the exchange rate of the Blue has **weakened** against sterling, Tartan will **exercise** the option and sell the Blues at 2.80.

	£	£
Proceeds from selling B5,600,000		2,000,000
Cost of contract	1,850,000	
Cost of currency option	40,000	
		1,890,000
Net profit		110,000

(c) If the Blue has **strengthened** against sterling, Tartan will **abandon** the option. For example, if Tartan wins the contract and the exchange rate has moved to B2.5 = £1, Tartan will sell the B5,600,000 at this rate to earn £2,240,000, and will incur costs, including the abandoned currency option, of £1,890,000.

	£	£
Proceeds from selling B5,600,000		2,240,000
Cost of contract	1,850,000	
Cost of currency option	40,000	
		1,890,000
Net profit		350,000

2.5 Comparison of currency options with forward contracts and futures contracts

In the last chapter, we saw that a hedge using a currency future will produce approximately the same result as a currency forward contract, subject to hedge inefficiencies. When comparing currency options with forward or futures contracts we usually find the following.

(a) If the currency movement is adverse, the option will be exercised, but the hedge will not normally be quite as good as that of the forward or futures contract; this is because of the **premium cost of the option**.

(b) If the currency movement is favourable, the option will not be exercised, and the result will normally be better than that of the forward or futures contract; this is because the option allows the holder to **profit from the improved exchange rate**.

These points are illustrated by the next series of examples.

2.6 Example: currency options (2)

Crabtree is expecting to receive 20 million Westland shillings (Sh) in one month's time. The current spot rate is Sh/£ 19.3383 - 19.3582. Compare the results of the following actions.

(a) The receipt is hedged using a forward contract at the rate 19.3048.

(b) The receipt is hedged by buying an over-the-counter (OTC) option from the bank, exercise price Sh/£ 19.30, premium cost 12 pence per 100 shillings.

(c) The receipt is not hedged.

In each case compute the results if, in one month, the exchange rate moves to:

(a) 21.00
(b) 17.60

Solution

The target receipt at today's spot rate is 20,000,000/19.3582 = £1,033,154.

(a) The receipt using forward contract is fixed with certainty at 20,000,000/19.3048 = £1,036,012. This applies to both exchange rate scenarios.

(b) The cost of the option is 20,000,000/100 × 12/100 = £24,000. This must be paid at the start of the contract.

The results under the two scenarios are as follows.

Scenario	(a)	(b)
Exchange rate	21.00	17.60
Exercise price	19.30	19.30
Exercise option?	YES	NO
Exchange rate used	19.30	17.60
	£	£
Pounds received	1,036,269	1,136,364
Less option premium	24,000	24,000
Net receipt	1,012,269	1,112,364

(c) The results of not hedging under the two scenarios are as follows.

Scenario	(a)	(b)
Exchange rate	21.00	17.60
Pounds received	£952,381	£1,136,364

Summary. The option gives a result between that of the forward contract and no hedge. If the Westland shilling weakens to 21.00, the best result would have been obtained using the forward market (£1,036,012). If it strengthens to 17.60, the best course of action would have been to take no hedge (£1,136,364). In both cases the option gives the second best result, being £24,000 below the best because of its premium cost.

2.7 Example: currency options (3)

In **Example: currency options (2)**, by how much would the exchange rate have moved if the forward and option contracts gave the same result? Comment on your answer.

Solution

The forward contract gives a receipt of £1,036,012 whatever the movement in exchange rate. If the option is to give a net receipt of £1,036,012, it must give a gross amount (before deducting the premium) of £1,036,012 + £24,000 = £1,060,012. This implies that the exchange rate has moved to 20,000,000/1,060,012 = 18.87 shillings to the pound.

The option will not be exercised at this exchange rate. It is allowed to lapse, giving an exchange gain which just covers the premium cost. The option becomes advantageous over a forward contract if the exchange rate strengthens beyond 18.87 shillings to the pound.

2.8 Types of options

FAST FORWARD

- A currency **call** option is a right to **buy** the underlying instrument.
- A currency **put** option is a right to **sell** the underlying instrument.

Transaction on future date		Now		On future date	
Receive	currency	Buy	currency put	Sell	currency
Pay	currency	Buy	currency call	Buy	currency
Receive	$	Buy	currency call	Buy	currency
Pay	$	Buy	currency put	Sell	currency

Key terms

There are two types of currency option, both of which can be bought and sold.

(a) **Call options** give the **buyer** of the option the **right** to **buy** the underlying **currency** at a **fixed rate of exchange** (and the **seller** of the option would be **required** to **sell** the underlying **currency** at that rate).

(b) **Put options** give the **buyer** of the option the **right** to **sell** the underlying **currency** at a **fixed rate of exchange** (and the **seller** of the option would be **required** to **buy** the underlying **currency** at that rate).

2.8.1 Choosing the correct type of option

The vast majority of options examples which we consider are concerned with **hedgers** who **purchase** options in order to reduce risk. We are seldom concerned with option writers who sell options.

So, given that we are normally going to *purchase* options, should we **purchase puts or calls**? With OTC options there is usually no problem in making this decision. If, for example, we may need to buy US dollars at some stage in the future, we can hedge by purchasing a US dollar call option. With traded options, however, we run into the same problem as with futures. Only a limited number of currencies are available and there is no US dollar option as such. We have to **rephrase the company's requirements**, as we did with futures.

For example, a UK company wishing to sell US dollars in the future can hedge by purchasing £ sterling call options (ie options to buy sterling with dollars). Similarly, a German company which needs to buy US dollars can hedge by purchasing Euro put options.

Transaction on future date		Now		Option on future date	
Receive	currency	Buy	currency put	Sell	currency
Pay	currency	Buy	currency call	Buy	currency
Receive	$	Buy	currency call	Buy	currency
Pay	$	Buy	currency put	Sell	currency

2.9 Choosing the strike price and the number of contracts to be used

If an American company wished to sell say £3.75 million, the computation of the number of contracts was easy (£3,750,000/£31,250 = 120 option contracts). A problem arises when a non-US company wishes to buy or sell US dollars using traded options. The amount of US dollars must first be converted into the home currency. For this purpose the best exchange rate to use is the **exercise price**, which means that the number of contracts may vary according to which exercise price is chosen.

2.10 Surplus cash when the number of contracts is rounded

Assume that a company chooses to hedge the receipt of $10 million by purchasing 229 June £ call option contracts, exercise price 1.400 $/£. Demonstrate the result if the spot rate on June 30 is (i) 1.55; (ii) 1.35.

The premium cost is 229 × $0.0574 × 31,250 = $410,769. This must be purchased at today's spot $/£ rate, which is 1.4461, giving a cost of £284,053.

Scenario (i)

The option will be exercised and £31,250 × 229 = £7,156,250 will be purchased with 7,156,250 × 1.40 = $10,018,750. The customer provides $10,000,000, but $18,750 has to be purchased at the June 30 spot rate of 1.55 $/£, giving an additional cost of £12,097.

The total sterling amount received from the sale of $10 million is:

	£
Option premium paid	(284,053)
£ purchased by exercising option	7,156,250
Purchase of surplus $ on 30 June	(12,097)
Net £ received	6,860,100

Scenario (ii)

The option is abandoned. $10,000,000 is converted at the spot rate 1.35, giving £7,407,407. After subtracting the option premium of £284,053, the net receipt is £7,123,354.

By way of comparison, a forward contract would have yielded 10,000,000/1.4101 = £7,091,696.

2.11 Closing out when traded options still have time to run

The above example assumes that the traded option is at its expiry date when the decision needs to be made between exercising or abandoning. In practice, most traded options are **closed out**, like futures contracts, because the date when the cash is required does not match the option expiry date.

Suppose that the company in the above example was due to receive $10 million on 10 June. Then June option contracts would still be used, but on 10 June the decision that needs to be made is whether to **close out the option**, to **exercise it** or to allow it to **lapse**. Closing out will be more beneficial than exercising or allowing to lapse if the option still has a positive time value.

Assume that the company purchased 229 June sterling call option contracts, exercise price 1.400, and that on 10 June spot rate is 1.55 and the 1.400 call option premium has risen to 15.35 cents per pound

The intrinsic value of the option is $(1.55 - 1.40) = 15 cents. If the option is exercised, a gain of 15 cents per £ will be made, as opposed to a gain of 15.35 cents per £ if the call option is sold and the company **receives the premium** (as it is selling the option). Consequently the contracts will be sold for a premium of $0.1535 × 31,250 × 229 = $1,098,484.

	$	£
Option premium paid at start		(284,053)
Option premium received at end	1,098,484	
Cash from customer	10,000,000	
Total dollars received	11,098,484	
Converted to sterling at 1.55:		7,160,312
Net sterling received		6,876,259

2.12 Option calculation

Because of the complications, it is best to use a similar method to the method we used for futures to assess the impact of options.

Step 1. Set up the hedge

(a) Choose contract date
(b) Decide whether put or call option required
(c) Decide which strike price applies
(d) How many contracts
(e) Tick size
(f) The premium may need to be converted using the spot rate

Step 2. Ascertain closing price

You should be given this.

Step 3. Calculate outcome of hedge

You may have to calculate the outcome under more than one closing spot rate.

(a) Outcome in options market. This will include deciding whether to exercise the option

(b) Net outcome

2.13 Example: currency options (6)

A UK company owes a US supplier $2,000,000 payable in July. The spot rate is 1.5350-1.5370 $/£ and the UK company is concerned that the $ might strengthen.

The details on the Philadelphia Stock Exchange for $/£ £31,250 options (cents per £1) are as follows.

	Calls			Puts		
Strike price	June	July	August	June	July	August
1.4750	6.34	6.37	6.54	0.07	0.19	0.50
1.5000	3.86	4.22	4.59	0.08	0.53	1.03
1.5250	1.58	2.50	2.97	0.18	1.25	1.89

Show how traded $/£ currency options can be used to hedge the risk at 1.525. Calculate the sterling cost of the transaction if the spot rate in July is:

(a) $1.46-$1.4620

(b) $1.61-$1.6120

Solution

Step 1. Set up the hedge

(a) Which date contract? July

(b) Put or call? Put, we need to put (sell) pounds in order to generate the dollars we need

(b) Which strike price? 1.5250

(d) How many contracts

$$\frac{2{,}000{,}000 \div 1.525}{31{,}250} \approx 42 \text{ contracts}$$

(e) Tick size = 31,250 × 0.0001 = $3.125

(f) Premium $= \frac{1.25}{100} \times 31{,}250 \times 42$

= $16,406 @ 1.5350

= £10,688

We need to pay for the option in $ now. Therefore the bank sells low at 1.5350.

Step 2. Closing spot and futures prices

Case (a) $1.46

Case (b) $1.61

Assume here the price to use for options calculation is the same as the closing spot rate.

Step 3. Outcome

(a) **Options market outcomes**

Strike price put (sell at)	1.5250	1.5250
Closing price (buy at)	1.46	1.61
Exercise?	Yes	No
If exercised, tick movement	650	–
Outcome of options position	650 × 42 × \$3.125 = \$85,313	–

(b) **Net outcome**

	\$	\$
Spot market payment	(2,000,000)	(2,000,000)
Option market	85,313	-
	(1,914,687)	(2,000,000)
	£	£
Translated at closing spot rate 1.46/1.61	(1,311,429)	(1,242,236)
Premium (remember premium has to be added in separately as translated at the **opening** spot rate)	(10,688)	(10,688)
	(1,322,117)	(1,252,924)

2.14 Drawbacks of currency options

- The **cost** depends on the **expected volatility** of the **exchange rate**.
- **Options** must be paid for **as soon** as they are **bought**.
- **Tailor-made** options **lack negotiability**.
- **Traded options** are **not available** in **every currency**.

2.15 Graphical illustration of currency options

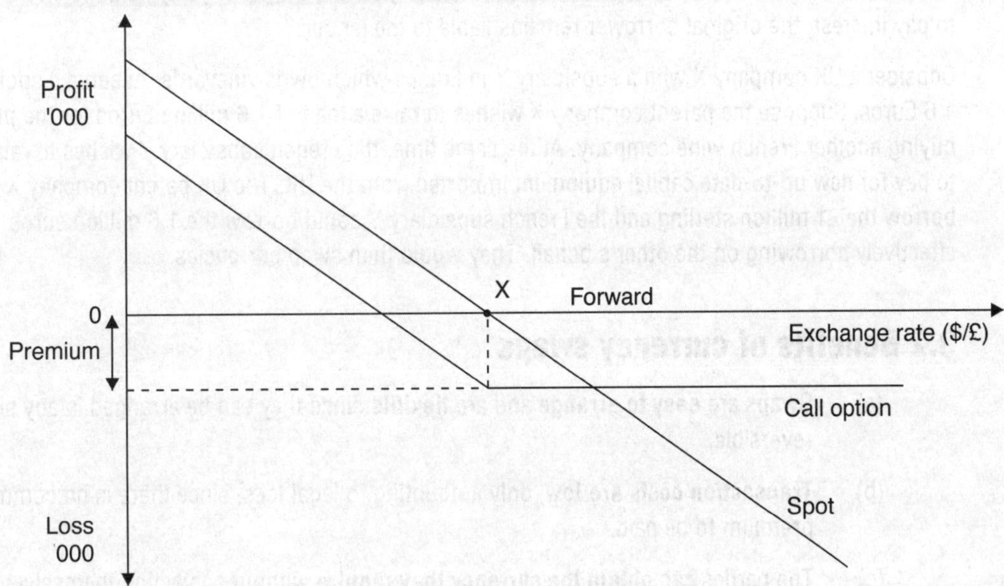

Figure 1 Currency call option, forward and spot markets: profit/loss profile

Suppose that a UK-based company expects to receive an amount of export income in dollars (\$) in three months' time. Figure 1 illustrates the profit/loss profile of different st ategies.

(a) Selling dollars and buying sterling in the **forward market** eliminates all uncertainty. The outcome is represented by a horizontal line.

(b) Relying on the **spot market** results in a net gain or loss compared with the forward market if the spot exchange rate in three months' time turns out to be below or above $X per pound respectively.

(c) If a **call option** is used, it will not be exercised if the exchange rate is less than $X per pound. A currency call option reduces the potential gain compared with the spot market strategy (b) by the amount of the premium on the option, but has the advantage that potential losses are contained as they will not exceed the value of the premium.

3 Currency swaps

FAST FORWARD

Currency swaps effectively involve the exchange of debt from one currency to another.

Currency swaps can provide a **hedge** against exchange rate movements for longer periods than the forward market, and can be a means of obtaining finance from new countries.

3.1 Swap procedures

Key term

A **swap** is 'an arrangement whereby two organisations contractually agree to exchange payments on different terms, eg in different currencies, or one at a fixed rate and the other at a floating rate' .(*OT 2000*)

In a **currency swap**, the parties agree to swap equivalent amounts of currency for a period. This effectively involves the exchange of debt from one currency to another. Liability on the main debt (the principle) is not transferred and the parties are liable to **counterparty risk**: if the other party defaults on the agreement to pay interest, the original borrower remains liable to the lender.

Consider a UK company X with a subsidiary Y in France which owns vineyards. Assume a spot rate of £1 = 1.6 Euros. Suppose the parent company X wishes to raise a loan of 1.6 million Euros for the purpose of buying another French wine company. At the same time, the French subsidiary Y wishes to raise £1 million to pay for new up-to-date capital equipment imported from the UK. The UK parent company X could borrow the £1 million sterling and the French subsidiary Y could borrow the 1.6 million euros, each effectively borrowing on the other's behalf. They would then swap currencies.

3.2 Benefits of currency swaps

(a) Swaps are **easy to arrange** and are **flexible** since they can be arranged in any size and are reversible.

(b) **Transaction costs are low**, only amounting to legal fees, since there is no commission or premium to be paid.

(c) The parties can **obtain the currency they require** without subjecting themselves to the **uncertainties** of the foreign exchange markets.

(d) The company can gain **access to debt finance in another country** and currency where it is little known, and consequently has a poorer credit rating, than in its home country. It can therefore take advantage of lower interest rates than it could obtain if it arranged the currency loan itself.

(e) Currency swaps may be used to **restructure the currency base** of the company's liabilities. This may be important where the company is trading overseas and receiving revenues in foreign currencies, but its borrowings are denominated in the currency of its home country. Currency swaps therefore provide a means of reducing exchange rate exposure.

(f) At the same time as exchanging currency, the company may also be able to **convert fixed rate debt** to **floating rate or vice versa**. Thus it may obtain some of the benefits of an interest rate swap in addition to achieving the other purposes of a currency swap.

(g) A currency swap could be used to **absorb excess liquidity** in one currency which is not needed immediately, to create funds in another where there is a need.

In practice, most currency swaps are conducted between banks and their customers. An agreement may only be necessary if the swap were for longer than, say, one year.

3.3 Example: hedging strategy using a swap

Adventurer, a UK company, is considering a contract to supply a telephone system to Blueland Telecom. All operating cash flows would be in the local currency, the Blue, as follows.

Time from start	*Cash flow*
	Blues
0	(700,000)
6 months	(400,000)
12 months	1,800,000

Because of high inflation in Blueland, the directors of Adventurer Ltd are very concerned about foreign exchange risk. However, the only available form of cover is a currency swap at a fixed rate of 9 Blues to the pound, for 1,100,000 Blues, to take effect in full at the start of the project and to last for a full year. The interest rate chargeable on the Blues would be 18% a year. This compares to a UK opportunity cost of capital for Adventurer Ltd of 22%.

The alternative to the swap is to convert between sterling and Blues at the spot rate, currently 10 Blues to the pound. The Blue floats freely on world currency markets. Two possible scenarios have been forecast for inflation in Blueland and the UK over the year for which the project will last is forecast to be as follows.

UK	*Blueland*
%	%
2	10
4	70

Required

Show whether or not Adventurer should use the available swap. Do not discount receipts and payments to a single time.

Solution

The first step is to calculate the exchange rate in each of the different inflation scenarios. The rates can be found if we assume **purchasing power parity** between the two countries. Then, with inflation rates expressed as decimals:

$$\text{Exchange rate after a year} = \text{current spot rate} \times \frac{1+\text{Blueland inflation rate}}{1+\text{UK inflation rate}}$$

Now as our flows are six monthly, we need to convert this to an equivalent relationship over 1/2 year, which is achieved taking the **square root** of the inflation factor:

$$\text{Exchange rate after six months} = \text{current spot rate} \times \sqrt{\frac{1+\text{Blueland inflation rate}}{1+\text{UK inflation rate}}}$$

Month	*Inflation* *Blueland*	*UK*	*Exchange rate B/£*
0			10.00
6	0.10	0.02	10.38
12	0.10	0.02	10.78
0			10.00
6	0.70	0.04	12.79
12	0.70	0.04	16.35

The swap will be evaluated by comparing the results of the swap to the results using the currency markets **for each scenario**. It is assumed that Adventurer will have to borrow funds in the UK to finance the deal, and therefore interest will be calculated at the opportunity cost of funds, 22%. The interest rate for six months will be $\sqrt{1.22} - 1 = 0.1045 = 10.45\%$.

(a) **Using the currency swap**

Adventurer Ltd will have to borrow sterling funds in the UK to finance the swap. The sterling investment required before interest is £1,100,000/9 = £122,222.

The cost of funds in the UK is 22%. However, swaps involve the transfer of interest rate liabilities as well as of principal, and therefore the interest cost will be calculated at the swap rate of 18%. This means that the interest charge will ne 1,100,000 × 0.18 = 198,000 Blues.

It is assumed that no interest will be earned on the 400,000 Blues which will be lying idle until month 6.

At the year end 1,100,000 Blues will be at the swap rate of 9 Blues to the pound, yielding £122,222, equal to the initial sterling outlay at the end of the year. The surplus funds (1,800,000 – 1,100,000 = 700,000 Blues) will be converted at the prevailing year end spot rate. The sterling value of the interest payments of 198,000 Blues will also be converted at the spot rate. It is assumed that no interest will be paid until the end of the year.

Inflation rates	*Spot rate receipts*	*Interest*	*Profit*
	£	£	£
2% and 10%	64,935	18,367	46,568
4% and 70%	42,813	12,110	30,703

(b) **Using the currency markets**

(i) Inflation rates 2% and 10%:

	Blues	£	*Interest at 22%* £
Investment - month 0	(700,000)	(70,000)	(15,400)
Investment - month 6	(400,000)	(38,536)	(4,027)
		(108,536)	(19,427)
Interest		(19,427)	
Total cost		(127,963)	
Price received	1,800,000	166,976	
Net profit/(loss)		39,013	

(ii) Inflation rates 4% and 70%:

	Blues	£	*Interest at 22%* £
Investment - month 0	(700,000)	(70,000)	(15,400)
Investment - month 6	(400,000)	(31,274)	(3,268)
		(101,274)	(18,668)
Interest		(18,668)	
Total cost		(119,942)	
Price received	1,800,000	110,092	
Net profit/(loss)		(9,850)	

Whatever the inflation rates, Adventurer Ltd will be better off with the swap than without it. It should therefore use the swap.

Chapter roundup

- **Currency futures** are contracts for the sale or purchase at a set future date of a set quantity of currency. A step-by-step approach can be used to deal with complications.

Transaction on future date		Now		On future date	
Receive	currency	Sell	currency futures	Buy	currency futures
Pay	currency	Buy	currency futures	Sell	currency futures
Receive	$	Buy	currency futures	Sell	currency futures
Pay	$	Sell	currency futures	Buy	currency futures

- **Currency options** protect against **adverse exchange rate movements** while allowing the investor to take advantage of favourable exchange rate movements. They are particularly useful in situations where the cash flow is not certain to occur (eg when tendering for overseas contracts).
- A currency **call** option is a right to **buy** the underlying instrument.
- A currency **put** option is a right to **sell** the underlying instrument.

Transaction on future date		Now		On future date	
Receive	currency	Buy	currency put	Sell	currency
Pay	currency	Buy	currency call	Buy	currency
Receive	$	Buy	currency call	Buy	currency
Pay	$	Buy	currency put	Sell	currency

- **Currency swaps** effectively involve the exchange of debt from one currency to another.
- Currency swaps can provide a **hedge** against exchange rate movements for longer periods than the forward market, and can be a means of obtaining finance from new countries.

Quick quiz

1 What does *CIMA Official Terminology* define as 'a right of an option holder to buy or sell a specific asset on predetermined terms on, or before, a future date'.

2 In the context of currency options, a put option gives the option buyer the right to buy the underlying currency at a fixed rate of exchange.

True ☐

False ☐

3 What are the main variables determining the value of a share (call) option?

4 In a currency swap, the parties agree to swap equivalent amounts of currency for a period.

True ☐

False ☐

5 **Fill in the blank**.

_______________ is 'a form of financing whereby money borrowed in one country or currency is covered by lending an equivalent amount in another.' *(OT 2000)*

6 What is the difference between a direct quote and an indirect quote?

7 What is the significance of a settlement date in futures?

8 If you need to sell a currency on a future date for US dollars, what steps should you take?

Answers to quick quiz

1 An option

2 False. This is true of a call option, not a put option.

3
- The current value of the share
- The exercise price of the option
- The time to expiry of the option
- Variability of the price of the share
- The risk-free rate of interest

4 True

5 A back-to-back loan

6
- A direct quote is the amount of domestic currency that is equal to one foreign currency unit.
- An indirect quote is the amount of foreign currency that is equal to one domestic currency unit.

7 A settlement date is the date when trading on a futures contract stops and all accounts are settled.

8 (a) Sell the appropriate currency futures contracts now
(b) Buy the same number of futures contracts on the same day you sell the actual currency

Now try the question below from the Exam Question Bank

Number	Level	Marks	Time
Q19	Examination	25	45 mins

Interest rate risk

Introduction

Here we consider **interest rate risk** and some of the financial instruments which are now available for managing financial risks, including **'derivatives'** such as **options** and **swaps**. The risk of interest rate changes is however less significant in most cases than the risk of currency fluctuations which, in some circumstances, can fairly easily wipe out profits entirely if it is not hedged.

So far with this syllabus the examiner has shown a particular interest in swaps, so don't neglect this topic. The Black-Scholes model for valuing options is also an increasingly important area; although you will not have to use the formula, you need an understanding of its components.

In the last section we deal with the wider issue for how financial instruments are valued for management and financial reporting purposes, concentrating on controls that ensure that appropriate accounting methods are used.

In the exam numerical questions will not be set on interest rate futures, options and forward rate agreements. They may however be set on swaps.

Topic list	Learning outcomes	Syllabus references	Ability required
1 Interest rate risk	D(ii)	D(5)	Evaluation
2 Interest rate futures	D(ii)	D(5)	Evaluation
3 Interest rate options	D(ii)	D(5)	Evaluation
4 Interest rate swaps	D(ii)	D(5),(6)	Evaluation
5 Hedging strategy alternatives: example	D(iii)	D(5)	Evaluation
6 Valuing financial instruments	D(i)	D(9)	Evaluation

1 Interest rate risk

FAST FORWARD

Factors influencing **interest rate risk** include the following.

- Fixed rates versus floating rate debt
- The term of the loan

1.1 Managing a debt portfolio

The corporate treasurers will be responsible for managing the company's **debt portfolio**, that is, in deciding how a company should obtain its short-term funds so as to:

(a) Be able to **repay debts** as they mature

(b) **Minimise any inherent risks**, notably invested foreign exchange risk, in the debts the company owes and is owed

There are a number of situations in which a company might be exposed to risk from interest rate movements.

1.2 Risks from interest rate movements

(a) **Fixed rate versus floating rate debt**

A company can get caught paying **higher interest rates** by having fixed rather than floating rate debt, or floating rather than fixed rate debt, as market interest rates change.

(b) **Currency of debt**

This is also a foreign currency exposure. A company can face higher costs if it borrows in a currency for which exchange rates move adversely against the company's domestic currency. The treasurer should seek to **match the currency of the loan** with the **currency of the underlying operations**/assets that generate revenue to pay interest/repay the loans.

(c) **Term of loan**

A company can be exposed by having to **repay a loan earlier** than it can afford to, resulting in a need to re-borrow, perhaps at a higher rate of interest.

(d) **Term loan or overdraft facility**

A company might prefer to **pay for borrowings only when it needs the money** as with an overdraft facility: the bank will charge a commitment fee for such a facility. Alternatively, a term loan might be preferred, but this will cost interest even if it is not needed in full for the whole term.

1.3 Analysis of interest rate risk

Some of the interest rate risks to which a firm is exposed may **cancel each other out**, where there are both assets and liabilities with which there is exposure to interest rate changes. If interest rates rise, more interest will be payable on loans and other liabilities, but this will be compensated for by higher interest received on assets such as money market deposits.

The effect of interest rate changes depends upon whether interest rates for the assets and liabilities are floating or fixed.

(a) **Floating** interest rates, of course, move up and down according to general market conditions.

(b) With **fixed** interest rates, the interest on the asset or liability will only be repriced at the date of maturity in the light of prevailing market conditions. If a fixed interest rate liability matures at the same time as a fixed rate asset, then the interest rate risks arising from the repricing of the two instruments will cancel each other out.

The degree to which a firm is exposed to interest rate risk can be identified by using the method of **gap analysis**. Gap analysis is based on the principle of **grouping together** assets and liabilities which are sensitive to interest rate changes according to their maturity dates. Two different types of 'gap' may occur.

(a) **A negative gap**

A negative gap occurs when a firm has a **larger amount of interest-sensitive liabilities** maturing at a certain time or in a certain period than it has interest-sensitive assets maturing at the same time. The difference between the two amounts indicates the net exposure.

(b) **A positive gap**

There is a positive gap if the amount of interest-sensitive assets maturing in a particular time exceeds the amount of interest-sensitive liabilities maturing at the same time.

With a **negative** gap, the company faces exposure if interest rates **rise** by the time of maturity. With a **positive** gap, the company will lose out if interest rates **fall** by maturity. The company's interest rate hedge should be based on the size of the gap.

1.4 Interest rate risk management

Where the magnitude of the risk is **immaterial** in comparison with the company's overall cash flows, one option is to **do nothing** and to accept the effects of any movement in interest rates which occur.

Exam focus point

Bear in mind this possibility - the decision *not* to take action to reduce interest rate risk - when answering questions in the exam.

Alternatively the company can seek to hedge the risk.

Question — Hedging

Learning outcome: D(ii)

Explain what is meant by hedging in the context of interest rate risk.

Answer

Hedging is a means of reducing risk. Hedging involves coming to an agreement with another party who is prepared to take on the risk that you would otherwise bear. The other party may be willing to take on that risk because he would otherwise bear an opposing risk which may be 'matched' with your risk; alternatively, the other party may be a speculator who is willing to bear the risk in return for the prospect of making a profit. In the case of interest rates, a company with a variable rate loan clearly faces the risk

that the rate of interest will increase in the future as the result of changing market conditions which cannot now be predicted.

Many financial instruments have been introduced in recent years to help corporate treasurers to hedge the risks of interest rate movements. These instruments include forward rate agreements, financial futures, interest rate swaps and options.

Case Study

In its 2002 annual report, **Kingfisher** discussed its management of interest rate risk: 'The interest rate exposure of the group arising from its borrowing and deposits is managed by the use of fixed and floating rate debt and investment, interest rate swaps, cross currency interest rate swaps, interest rate options and interest rate futures. Against the backdrop of market conditions which prevailed during the year, the majority of the Group's borrowings and investments have remained at floating rates of interest.'

Tate and Lyle noted in its 2002 annual report that: 'The Groups policy is that no interest rate fixings are undertaken for more than 12 years and between 30% and 75% of Group net debt is fixed for more than one year ... If the interest rates applicable to the Group's floating rate debt rise from the levels at the end of March 2002 by an average of 1% over the year to March 2003, this would reduce Group profit before tax by £3 million.

1.5 Interest rate risk management

Methods of reducing interest rate risk include:

- Forward rate agreements (FRAs)
- Pooling
- Interest rate futures
- Interest rate options (or interest rate guarantees)
- Interest rate swaps

In the remainder of this section, we look at FRAs and pooling, before considering interest rate futures, swaps and options.

1.6 Forward rate agreements (FRAs)

FAST FORWARD

Forward rate agreements hedge risk by **fixing the interest rate** on future borrowing.

Key term

Forward rate agreements (FRAs) are agreements, typically between a company and a bank, about the interest rate on future borrowing or bank deposits.

A company can enter into a FRA with a bank that fixes the rate of interest for borrowing at a certain time in the future. If the actual interest rate proves to be higher than the rate agreed, the bank pays the company the difference. If the actual interest rate is lower than the rate agreed, the company pays the bank the difference.

One **limitation** on FRAs is that they are usually only available on loans of at least £500,000. They are also likely to be **difficult to obtain for periods of over one year**.

An **advantage** of FRAs is that, for the period of the FRA at least, they **protect the borrower** from adverse market interest rate movements to levels above the rate negotiated for the FRA. With a normal variable rate loan (for example linked to a bank's base rate or to LIBOR) the borrower is exposed to the risk of such adverse market movements. On the other hand, the borrower will similarly not benefit from the effects of favourable market interest rate movements.

The **interest rates** which banks will be willing to set for FRAs will reflect their **current expectations** of **interest rate movements**. If it is expected that interest rates are going to rise during the term for which the FRA is being negotiated, the bank is likely to seek a higher fixed rate of interest than the variable rate of interest which is current at the time of negotiating the FRA.

1.6.1 Example: forward rate agreement

It is 30 June. Lynn will need a £10 million 6 month fixed rate from 1 October. Lynn wants to hedge using an FRA. The relevant FRA rate is 6% on 30 June.

What is the result of the FRA and the effective loan rate if the 6 month FRA benchmark rate has moved to

(a) 5%

(b) 9%

Solution

(a) At 5% because interest rates have fallen, Lynn plc will pay the bank:

	£
FRA payment £10 million × (6% – 5%) × $^6/_{12}$	(50,000)
Payment on underlying loan 5% × £10 million × $^6/_{12}$	(250,000)
Net payment on loan	(300,000)
Effective interest rate on loan	6%

(b) At 9% because interest rates have risen, the bank will pay Lynn plc

	£
FRA receipt £10 million × (9% – 6%) × $^6/_{12}$	150,000
Payment on underlying loan at market rate 9% × £10 million × $^6/_{12}$	(450,000)
Net payment on loan	(300,000)
Effective interest rate on loan	6%

Exam focus point

This example is shown for illustration; in the exam you will not be expected to carry out interest rate risk calculations.

1.7 Pooling of subsidiaries' cash balances

FAST FORWARD

Pooling can help avoid paying higher interest rates on borrowing and can make management of interest rate risk easier.

If an organisation, for example a group of companies, has a large number of different bank accounts with the same bank, it can ask the bank to pool balances when considering interest and overdraft limits.

1.7.1 Benefits of pooling

(a) **Netting surpluses and deficits**

For the parent company, the main benefit of pooling cash balances is that **surpluses** can **be netted off** against deficits, thus reducing the amount of interest payable. Because borrowing rates are higher than deposit rates, it is better to use surplus cash to **reduce borrowing** than to put it on deposit. A central treasury could lend funds to subsidiaries at better rates than they would be able to borrow.

Unfortunately when cash balances are in different currencies this tactic does not necessarily work. If the **forward rates** are **not in equilibrium** with the interest rates, then there may be opportunities for making gains by keeping cash in other currencies.

(b) **Greater control**

Pooling balances means that it is easier for a central treasury department to exercise control over funds, and use its **expertise** to ensure risks are managed and opportunities exploited effectively.

(c) **Greater investment opportunities**

Better rates may be available for pooled funds, and the central treasury function that holds the pooled funds may have **access to markets** such as offshore markets that are not available to local operations.

(d) **Elimination of exchange risk**

Another benefit to the parent company of pooling all resources in the home currency is that **currency exchange risk** is **eliminated** for the net surplus.

1.7.2 Drawbacks of pooling of subsidiaries' cash balances

(a) **Need for cash**

Operating subsidiaries need **cash balances** as part of their working capital in order to make payments. If these payments are higher than expected, there may be insufficient cash in the subsidiaries. Local managers may try to ensure that they have the maximum amount of cash possible to make the payments, leading to disharmony within the group.

(b) **Local decision-making**

Local managers may feel **demotivated** if the responsibility for investing funds is taken away from them. They may not therefore provide **full co-operation** to the centralised department.

(c) **Transaction costs**

Transferring cash surpluses to the parent company and then back to the subsidiary again when required incurs **unnecessary transaction costs**, which can be relatively high compared with any interest saving, particularly when interest rates are low.

(d) **Matching**

Good currency risk management will attempt to **minimise risk** by **matching receipts and payments**, and assets and liabilities, in the same currency. Pooling might conflict with this principle.

2 Interest rate futures

FAST FORWARD

Interest rate futures can be used to hedge against interest rate changes between the current date and the date at which the interest rate on the lending or borrowing is set. Borrowers **sell futures** to hedge against **interest rate rises;** lenders **buy futures** to hedge against **interest rate falls.**

2.1 Futures contracts

Most futures contracts involve interest rates (**interest rate futures**), and these offer a means of hedging against the risk of interest rate movements. Such contracts are effectively a gamble on whether interest rates will rise or fall.

Interest rate futures are similar in effect to FRAs, except that the terms, amounts and periods are **standardised**. For example, a company can contract to buy (or sell) £100,000 of a notional 30-year Treasury bond bearing an 8% coupon, in say, 6 months time, at an agreed price. The basic principles behind such a decision are:

(a) The futures price is likely to vary with changes in interest rates, and this acts as a **hedge** against adverse interest rate movements. We shall see how this works in a later example.

(b) The outlay to buy futures is much less than for buying the financial instrument itself, and so a company can hedge large exposures of cash with a relatively **small initial employment of cash.**

Borrowers will wish to hedge against an interest rate rise by **selling futures now** and **buying futures** on the day that the interest rate is fixed.

On the other hand lenders will wish to hedge against the possibility of falling interest rates by **buying futures now** and **selling futures** on the date that the actual lending starts.

2.2 Pricing futures contracts

The **pricing** of an interest rate futures contract is determined by prevailing interest rates. For example, if three month eurodollar time deposit interest rates are 8%, a three month eurodollar futures contract will be priced at 92 (100 – 8). If interest rates are 11%, the contract price will be 89 (100 – 11). This decrease in price, or value, of the contract, reflects the reduced attractiveness of a fixed role deposit in time of rising interest rates.

A **tick** or **basis point of price** has a known, measurable value. Here are some examples.

(a) In the case of 3-month eurodollar futures, the **amount** of the **underlying instrument** is a **3-month deposit** of \$1,000,000. As a tick is 0.01% (or one-hundredth of one per cent), the value of a tick is \$25 (0.01% × \$1,000,000 × 3/12).

(b) In the case of long gilt futures, the **underlying instrument** is **£100,000 of notional gilts.** Given that a tick is 1/32 of one per cent, the value of one tick is £10 (0.01% × £100,000).

Interest rate futures are not all priced in the same way.

(a) Prices of **short-term interest rate futures**, which, as already indicated, reflect the interest rates on the underlying financial instrument, are quoted at a **discount to a par value of 100**. For example, a price of 93.40 indicates that the underlying money market deposit is being traded at a rate of 6.6% (100 – 93.40).

(b) Pricing for **long-term bond futures** is as a **percentage of par value**, similarly to the pricing of bonds themselves.

(i) In the case of US Treasury bond futures, prices are quoted in 32nds of each full percentage point of price. The number of 32nds is shown as a number following a hyphen. For example, 91-23 denotes a price of $91^{23}/_{32}$ per 100 nominal value and 91-16 denotes a price of $91^{1}/_{2}$ per 100 nominal value.

(ii) For other types of bond future, decimal pricing is used, so that if Italian government bond futures are quoted at 92.75, this indicates a price of $92^{3}/_{4}$ per 100 nominal value.

2.2.1 Example: futures price movements (1)

June 3-month euro futures fell in price on a particular day from 96.84 to 96.76. Privet plc has purchased June futures, having a 'long' position on five contracts ie they have bought now to sell later. Calculate the change in value of the contracts on the day concerned, given the value of one tick is 25 euros (size 0.01%).

Solution

The fall in price represents 8 ticks (96.84 – 96.76 = 0.08 and the tick size is 0.01%). The value of one tick is 25 euros. Each contract has fallen in value by 25 × 8 = 200 euros. Privet plc has bought five contracts and so the day's price movement represents for the company a loss on the contracts of 200 × 5 = 1,000 euros.

2.2.2 Example: futures price movements (2)

September long gilts sterling futures fell in price on a particular day from 99-9 to 98-27. Privet plc has sold September futures, having a 'short' position of 10 contracts, ie they have sold now to match with a later purchase. Calculate the change in value of the contract on the day concerned, given that the tick size is 1/32 of 1%.

Solution

The fall in price represents 14 ticks ($99^{9}/_{32} - 98^{27}/_{32} = {}^{14}/_{32}$ and the tick size is $^{1}/_{32}$ of 1%). The value of one tick for long gilts sterling futures is £15.625. Each contract has fallen in value by £15.625 × 14 = £218.75. For Privet plc, which has sold 10 contracts, the day's price movement represents a profit of £218.75 × 10 = £2,187.50, (ie it will cost them less to purchase the contracts to sell).

Question

Interest rate futures

Learning outcome: D(ii)

The following futures price movements were observed during a week in October.

Contract	*Price at start of week*	*Price at end of week*
December short sterling	90.40	91.02
December US Treasury bonds	92.16	92.06
December Japanese government bond	93.80	94.25

Hawthorn has the following positions in these contracts:

(a) A short position (seller) of ten December short sterling contracts (tick value = £12.50, size 0.01%)

(b) A long position (buyer) of six December US Treasury bonds contracts (Tick value = $31.25, size 1/32 of 1%)

(c) A long position of eight December Japanese government bonds contracts (tick value = Y10,000, size 0.01%)

Required

Calculate the profit or loss to the company on the futures contracts.

Answer

Short sterling

Increase in price (91.02 – 90.40 = 0.62)	62 ticks
Value per tick	£12.50
Increase in value of one contract (62 × £12.50)	£775

The company is a seller of ten contracts and would lose £7,750 (£775 × 10)

US Treasury bond futures

Fall in price ($92^{16/32}$ – $92^{6/32}$ = 10/32)	10 ticks
Value per tick	$31.25
Fall in value of one contract (10 × $31.25)	$312.50

The company is a buyer of six contracts and would lose $1,875 ($312.50 × 6)

Japanese government bonds

Increase in price (94.25 – 93.80 = 0.45)	45 ticks
Value per tick	Y10,000
Increase in value of one contract (45 × Y10,000)	Y450,000

The company is a buyer of eight contracts and would gain Y3,600,000 (Y450,000 × 8)

2.3 Example: interest rate hedge using futures

Yew has taken a 3 month $1,000,000 eurodollar loan with interest payable of 8%, the loan being due for rollover on 31 March. At 1 January, the company treasurer considers that interest rates are likely to rise in the near future. The futures price is 91 representing a yield of 9%. Given a standard contract size of $1,000,000 the company **sells** a eurodollar three month contract to hedge against interest on the three month loan required at 31 March (to **sell** a contract is to commit the seller to take a deposit). At 31 March the spot interest rate is 11%.

What is the cost saving to Yew?

Solution

The company will **buy back** the future on 31 March at 89 (100 – 11). The cost saving is the **profit on the futures contract**.

$1,000,000 × (91 – 89) × 3/12 = $5,000

The hedge has effectively reduced the new annual interest cost by 2%. Instead of a cost of 11% at 31 March ($27,500) for a three month loan, the net cost is $22,500 ($27,500 – $5,000), a 9% annual cost.

2.4 Use of interest rate futures

The **standardised nature** of interest rate futures is a limitation on their use by the corporate treasurer as a means of hedging, because they **cannot always be matched** with specific interest rate exposures. However, their use is growing. Futures contracts are frequently used by banks and other financial institutions as a means of hedging their portfolios: such institutions are often not concerned with achieving an exact match with their underlying exposure.

The seller of a futures contract does not have to own the underlying instrument, but may need to deliver it on the contract's delivery date if the buyer requires it. Many, but not all, interest rate contracts are **settled for cash** rather than by delivery of the underlying instrument.

Interest rate futures offer an attractive means of **speculation** for some investors, because there is no requirement that buyers and sellers should actually be lenders and borrowers (respectively) of the nominal amounts of the contracts. A relatively small investment can lead to substantial gains, or alternatively to substantial losses. The speculator is in effect 'betting' on future interest rate movements.

2.5 Basis risk

There are two reasons why it is often not possible to achieve a perfect (100%) hedge with futures, as follows.

(a) The fact that futures are available only in certain standard sizes means that the contracts may not fit exactly the company's needs.

(b) There is also **basis risk,** arising from the fact that the price of the futures contract may not move as expected in relation to the value of the instrument which is being hedged. There are two main reasons for basis risk.

  (i) **Cashflow requirements** may differ, altering the relative values of the underlying financial instrument and the derivative futures contract. This is because usually no payment is required when a forward contract is entered into, while an initial margin must be deposited for a futures contract.

  (ii) The **financial instrument** which the firm is seeking to hedge may be different from the financial instrument which underlies the futures contract. For example, a firm may wish to hedge interest rates which are linked to bank base interest rates using a futures contract which is based on the London Inter-Bank Offered Rate (LIBOR). This type of hedge is called **cross hedging**, and there will be basis risk because LIBOR will not always move exactly in line with bank base interest rates.

The basis risk can be calculated as the difference between the futures price and the current price (**'cash market' price**) of the underlying security.

3 Interest rate options

FAST FORWARD

Interest rate options allow an organisation to limit its exposure to adverse interest rate movements, while allowing it to take advantage of favourable interest rate movements.

Borrowers can set a **maximum** on the interest they have to pay by buying **put** options.

Lenders can set a **minimum** on the interest they receive by buying **call** options.

3.1 Interest rate options (guarantees)

Key term

An **interest rate option** grants the buyer of it the right, but **not the obligation**, to deal at an agreed interest rate (strike rate) at a future maturity date. On the date of expiry of the option, the buyer must decide whether or not to exercise the right.

Clearly, a buyer of an option to borrow will not wish to exercise it if the market interest rate is now below that specified in the option agreement. Conversely, an option to lend will not be worth exercising if market rates have risen above the rate specified in the option by the time the option has expired.

Key term

An **interest rate guarantee (IRG)** is an interest rate option which hedges the interest rate for a **single period** of up to **one year**.

Tailor-made **'over-the-counter' interest rate options** can be purchased from major banks, with specific values, periods of maturity, denominated currencies and rates of agreed interest. The cost of the option is the **'premium'**. Interest rate options offer more flexibility than and are more expensive than FRAs.

3.2 Caps, floors and collars

FAST FORWARD

Caps set a ceiling to the interest rate; a **floor** sets a lower limit. A **collar** is the simultaneous purchase of a cap and floor.

Various **cap** and **collar** agreements are possible.

Key term

An interest rate **cap** is an option which sets an interest rate ceiling.

A **floor** is an option which sets a lower limit to interest rates.

Using a **'collar'** arrangement, the borrower can buy an interest rate cap and at the same time sell an interest rate floor which fixes the cost for the company.

The cost is lower than for a cap alone. However, the borrowing company forgoes the benefit of movements in interest rates below the floor limit in exchange for this cost reduction.

A **zero cost collar** can even be negotiated sometimes, if the **premium** paid for buying the cap equals the premium received for selling the floor.

3.2.1 Example: cap and collar

Suppose the prevailing interest rate for a company's borrowing is 10%. The company treasurer considers that a rise in rates above 12% will cause serious financial difficulties for the company. How can the treasurer make use of a 'cap and collar' arrangement?

Solution

The company can buy an interest rate cap from the bank. The bank will reimburse the company for the effects of a rise in rates above 12%. As part of the arrangements with the bank, the company can agree that it will pay at least 9%, say, as a 'floor' rate. The bank will pay the company for agreeing this. In other words, the company has sold the floor to the bank, which partly offsets the costs of the cap. The bank benefits if rates fall below the floor level.

3.3 A graphical approach to options

A graphical approach to options may help you to understand options more fully and may provide a means of illustrating options in answers to exam questions. The examples illustrated below generally refer to **share prices**. In the case of other types of option (eg interest rate options or currency options), then it will be the value or price of the particular underlying investment (eg the interest rate or the currency) which is relevant.

Figure 1 shows the position of a **call option holder**.

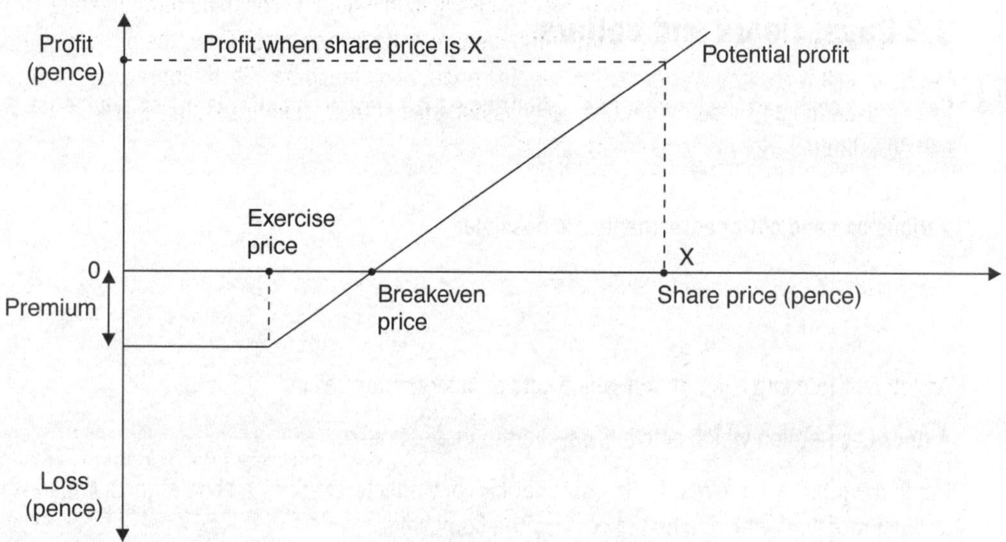

Figure 1 Call option holder ('long call position')

The holder of the call option will not exercise the option unless the share price is at least equal to the **exercise price** (or **strike price**) at the exercise date. If the share price is above that level, he can cut his losses (up to the break-even price) or make profits (if the share price is above the break-even price). Holding a call option is called having a **long position** in the option.

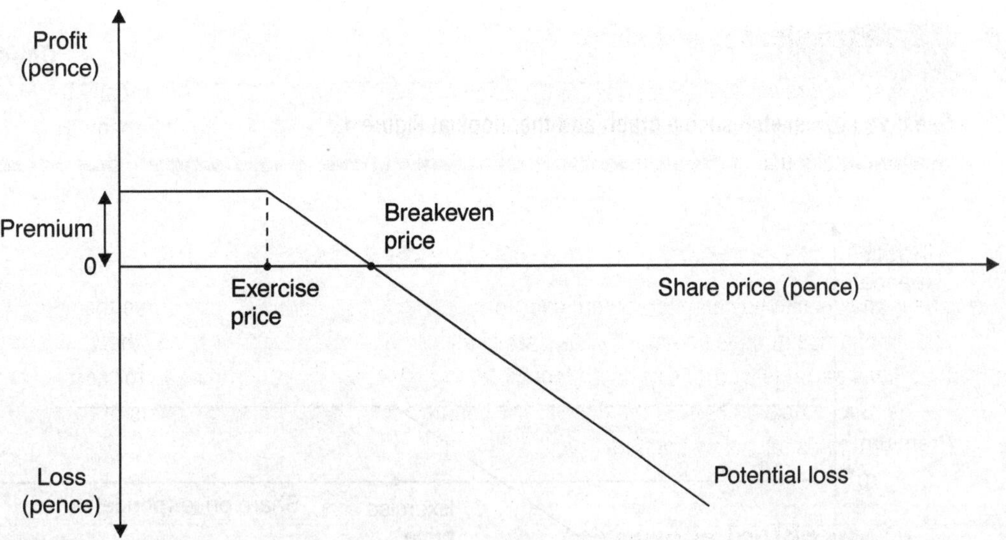

Figure 2 Call option writer ('short call position')

Any profit made by the holder of the option is reflected by the loss of the other party to the transaction - the writer of the option. Accordingly, Figure 2, illustrating the potential outcomes for the writer of the option, looks like a 'mirror image' of Figure 1. Selling or writing a call option is called taking a **short call position**. It can be seen from Figure 2 that the writer of the call option is exposed to potentially unlimited losses.

The position of the **buyer of a put option** is illustrated in Figure 3. The maximum potential profit is equal to the exercise price, which is the position if the share price falls to zero. Then, the put option holder has the option to sell worthless shares at the exercise price. You should be able to appreciate that the put option can be used to protect a holder of shares against a fall in their value. As Figure 3 shows, the loss on the option is limited to the size of the premium.

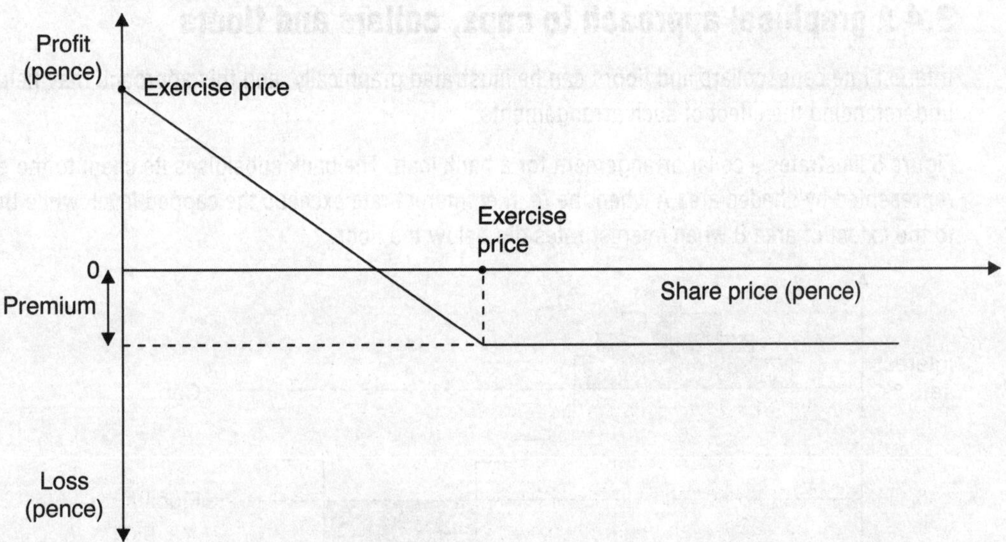

Figure 3 Put option holder ('long put position')

You will probably by now be able to guess what a graph illustrating the position of a put option writer will look like.

Question — **Option graphs**

See if you can sketch such a graph and then look at Figure 4.

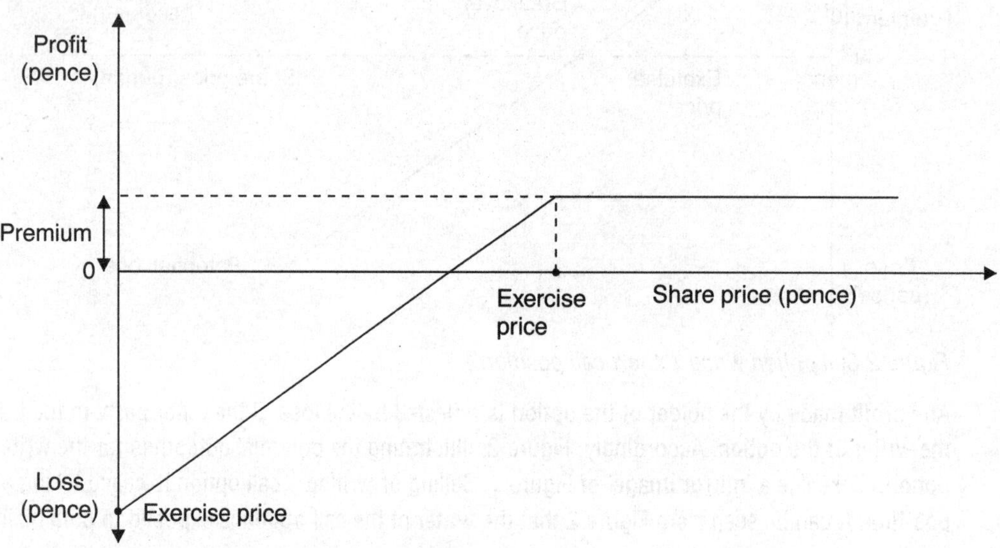

Figure 4 Put option writer ('short put position')

Figures 1 to 4 illustrate the basic positions which can be taken in options. It is also possible to combine different option positions in various ways, depending on the combination of risks and returns which are sought from different outcomes.

3.4 A graphical approach to caps, collars and floors

Interest rate caps, collars and floors can be illustrated graphically, and this approach may help in understanding the effect of such arrangements.

Figure 5 illustrates a collar arrangement for a bank loan. The bank subsidises its client to the extent represented by shaded area A when the market interest rate exceeds the capped level, while the bank gains to the extent of area B when interest rates dip below the floor.

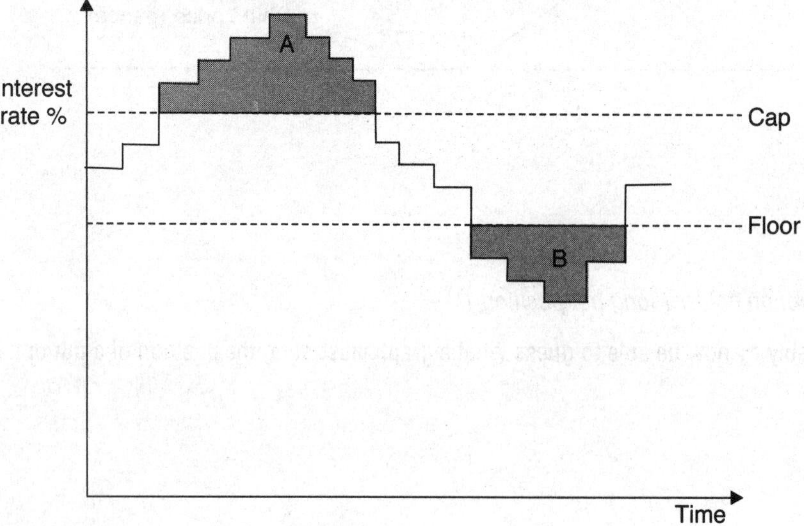

Figure 5 Interest rate collar through time

In the example shown in Figure 6, a company has a loan at LIBOR (London Inter-Bank Offered Rate). Suppose that for an annual cost of 1% of principal, it can buy a cap at 8%. When LIBOR is between 6% and 8%; the vertical distance between the two lines on the graph represents the cost of the cap. The cap begins to pay off when LIBOR rises above 8%, with a break-even point where LIBOR is 9%.

Part or all of the cost of the cap may be set off by agreeing to an interest rate floor, thus making a collar. In the case of a **zero cost collar**, the cost of the cap is fully offset by the proceeds of the floor.

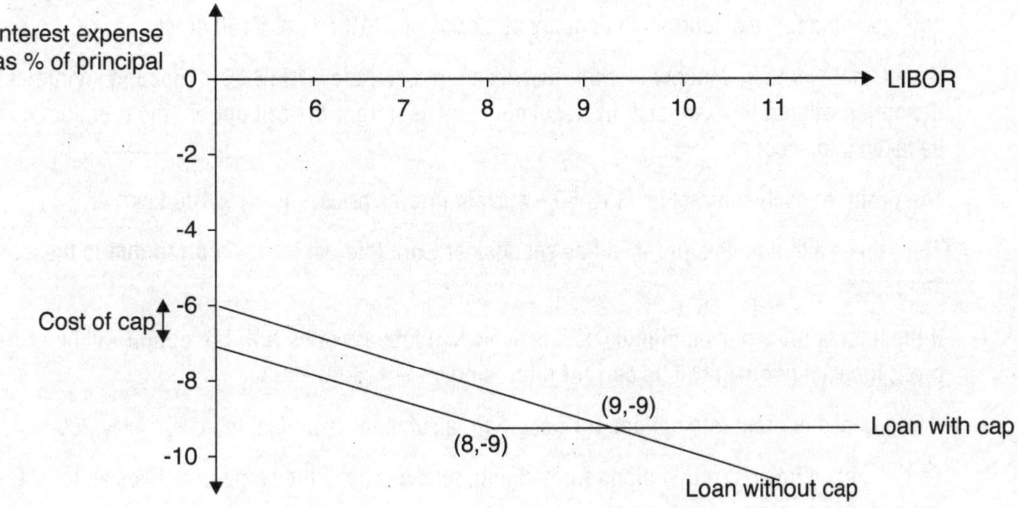

Figure 6 Loan with Interest rate cap

Figure 7 illustrates the profit/loss profile for a zero cost collar. This might be achieved by combining a floor with the arrangement illustrated in Figure 6. The interest expense cannot exceed 8% and cannot be less than 5%. Between 5% and 8%, the interest expense matches LIBOR.

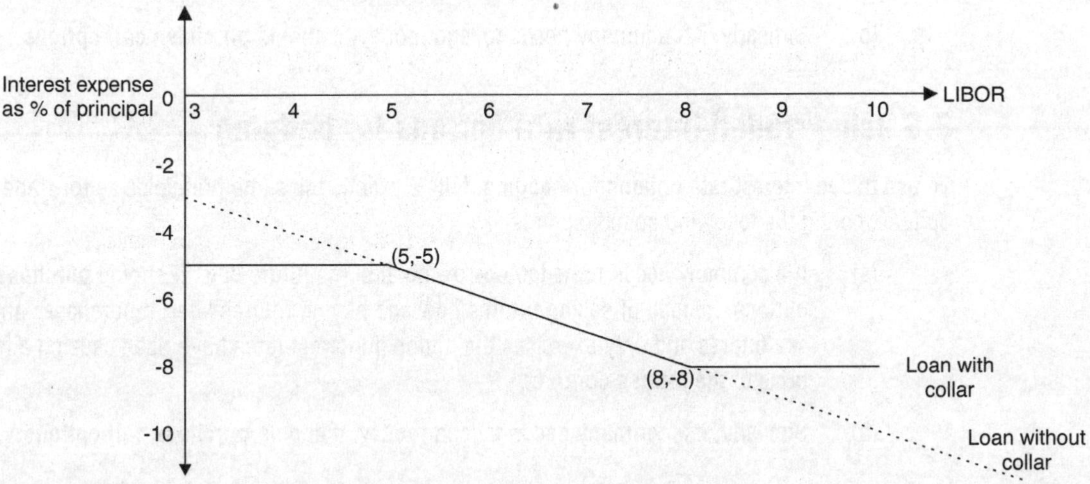

Figure 7 Loan with interest rate collar

3.5 Traded interest rate options

Exchange-traded interest rate options are available as **options on interest rate futures,** which give the holder the right to buy (call option) or sell (put option) one futures contract on or before the expiry of the option at a specified price. The best way to understand the pricing of interest rate options is to look at a schedule of prices. The schedule below (from the *Financial Times*) is for 12 October.

UK long gilt futures options (LIFFE) £100,000 100ths of 100%

Strike	*Calls*			*Puts*		
Price	*Nov*	*Dec*	*Jan*	*Nov*	*Dec*	*Jan*
£113.50	0.87	1.27	1.34	0.29	0.69	1.06
£114.00	0.58	0.99	1.10	0.50	0.91	1.32
£114.50	0.36	0.76	0.88	0.77	1.18	1.60

This schedule shows that an investor could pay 1.34/100 × £100,000 = £1,340 to purchase the right to buy a sterling futures contract in January at a price of £113.50 per £100 stock.

If, say, in December, January sterling futures are priced **below** £113.50 (reflecting an interest rate **rise**), the option will not be exercised. In calculating any gain from the call option, the premium cost must also be taken into account.

The profit for each contract is: (113.50 – current futures price – 1.34) × 100 ticks

To evaluate a hedge, this profit will be set against extra interest costs incurred due to the interest rate increase.

If the futures price moves **higher,** as it is likely to if interest rates **fall,** the option will be exercised. The profit for each contract will be current futures prices – 113.50 – 1.34.

Using traded interest rate options for hedging (calculations examinable only in May 2004)

To use traded interest rate options for hedging, follow exactly the same principles as for traded currency options, noting the following specific points.

(a) If a company needs to hedge borrowing at some future date, it should **purchase put** options. Instead of selling futures now and buying futures later, it purchases an option to sell futures and only exercises the option if interest rates have risen causing a fall in the price of the futures contract.

(b) Similarly, if a company needs to lend money, it should **purchase call options.**

3.6 Using traded interest rate options for hedging

To use traded interest rate options for hedging, follow exactly the same principles as for traded currency options, noting the following specific points.

(a) If a company needs to hedge borrowing at some future date, it should **purchase put** options. Instead of selling futures now and buying futures later, it purchases an option to sell futures and only exercises the option if interest rates have risen causing a fall in the price of the futures contract.

(b) Similarly, if a company needs to lend money, it should **purchase call options.**

3.7 Collars using traded interest rate options

When we used OTC interest rate options to make collars, we saw that a **collar for borrowing** is made by buying a cap and selling a floor at a lower interest rate., and a **collar for lending** is made by selling a cap and buying a floor at a lower interest rate. Converting this into the language of traded options, buying a **cap**, which fixes our maximum borrowing rate, means buying a traded **put** option. When we buy a **floor**, we are buying a **call** option.

Remembering that lower interest rates mean higher futures prices and higher option strike prices, we can deduce that when we use traded options the floor must be at a **higher** strike price than the cap. Thus a **collar for borrowing** is made by **buying a put** and **selling a call** at a higher strike price, and a **collar for lending** is made by **selling a put** and **buying a call** at a higher strike price.

3.8 Example: collars using traded interest rate options

Panda wishes to borrow £4 million fixed rate in June for 9 months and wishes to protect itself against rates rising above 6.75%. It is 11 May and the spot rate is currently 6%. The data is as follows:

SHORT STERLING OPTIONS (LIFFE)

£500,000 points of 100%

Strike price		*Calls*			*Puts*	
	June	*Sept*	*Dec*	*June*	*Sept*	*Dec*
9325	0.16	0.03	0.03	0.14	0.92	1.62
9350	0.05	0.01	0.01	0.28	1.15	1.85
9375	0.01	0.01	0.01	0.49	1.39	2.10

Panda negotiates the loan with the bank on 12 June (when the £4m loan rate is fixed for the full nine months) and closes out the hedge.

Using the above data, show how Panda can use a collar to hedge its £4million loan.

Solution

There are many possible collars that Panda could use. However, let us assume that Panda wishes to cap its interest rate at 6.75%, but wishes to reduce the premium it will pay to do so by using a collar.

FLOOR: at various strike prices			Cap at 6.75%	
Call option strike price	Interest rate	Premium	Premium	Net premium cost/(benefit)
9325	6.75%	0.16%	0.14%	(0.02%)
9350	6.50%	0.05%	0.14%	0.09%
9375	6.25%	0.01%	0.14%	0.13%

This table shows that if the cap is fixed at 6.75% and the floor at 6.25% (strike price 9375), the net cost of the resultant collar is 0.13%. Effectively, the company will pay between (6.75 + 0.13) = 6.88% and (6.25 + 0.13) = 6.38%.

If the maximum/minimum rates are the same at 6.75%, there is a net benefit of 0.02%. The company is certain to pay 6.75% – 0.02% = 6.73%. If interest rates fall the company does not enjoy this reduced cost however.

3.9 Valuation of options

FAST FORWARD

The value of an option depends on:

- The current price of the asset
- The exercise price
- The volatility (standard deviation) of the asset value
- The time period to expiry
- The risk-free rate of interest

The widespread use of derivatives involving options has resulted in much attention being paid to the **valuation of options**. The share option is a common form of option, giving the right but not the obligation to buy or to sell a quantity of a company's shares at a specified price within a specified period.

The value of a share option is made up of:

- 'Intrinsic value'
- 'Time value'

The **intrinsic value** of an option depends upon:

- Share price
- Exercise price

The **time value** of an option is affected by:

- Time period to expiry
- Volatility of the underlying security
- General level of interest rates

In this section we will use a share call option to illustrate how the factors listed affect an option's value. We will then describe in outline the Black-Scholes model for valuing options.

3.9.1 Time to expiry

The value of all options will increase with the length of the expiry period, because in this period the underlying security has time to rise and create a gain for the option holder. If the underlying security falls in value, the option holder makes no loss other than the initial premium cost.

3.9.2 Volatility of the underlying security

Options on volatile securities will be more valuable than options on securities whose prices do not change much. This is because volatile securities will either show large increases or large decreases in value. The holder of a call option will gain a lot from a large increase in the value of the security but will lose nothing if it falls in value.

3.9.3 The general level of interest rates

The intrinsic value of an in-the-money call option is equal to the share price minus the exercise price. If the option has time to run before expiry, the exercise price will not have to be paid until the option is exercised.

(a) The option's value will therefore depend on the current share price minus the **present value of the exercise price.**

(b) If interest rates increase, this present value will decrease and **the value of the call option will increase**.

3.10 The Black-Scholes model

The **Black-Scholes** model for the valuation of **European call options** was developed in 1973. (**European options** are options that can only be exercised on the expiry date, as opposed to **American options**, which can be exercised on any date up till the expiry date.) The model is based on the principle that the equivalent of an investment in a call option can be set up by **combining an investment in shares** with **borrowing the present value of the option exercise price.**

The model requires an estimate to be made of the variation in return on the shares. One way of making such an estimate is to measure the variation in the share price in the recent past and to make the assumption that this variability will apply during the life of the option.

Variants of the model are applied by practitioners in the field, who often make use of programmed electronic calculators or computers to determine option prices. Alternatively, option tables based on the model can be used.

In order to incorporate **volatility** and the **probabilities** of option prices into the model, the following assumptions are needed:

- **Returns** are **normally distributed.**
- **Share price changes** are **lognormally distributed**.
- Potential price changes follow a **random** (Brownian motion) model.
- **Volatility** is constant over the life of the option.

The Black-Scholes formula is also based on the following other important assumptions:

- Traders can trade **continuously.**
- **Financial markets** are perfectly **liquid.**
- **Borrowing** is possible at the **risk-free rate.**
- There are **no transaction costs.**
- Investors are **risk-neutral.**

The Black-Scholes model has three main elements to it.

(a) The share price

(b) A **measure** of how **option prices vary** with share prices (discussed below)

(c) The **borrowing element** that must be combined with the share investment to produce an option equivalent

Within the model:

(a) The difference between the share price and the option exercise price is the **intrinsic value** of the option.

(b) A **time differential** factor, reflecting the fact that the option will be exercised in the future., is included.

(c) The model is very dependent upon the **share price volatility**. This is likely to be calculated on the basis of historical movements, and different conditions may apply in the future.

3.10.1 Using the Black-Scholes model to value share options

The value of the option depends upon:

(a) **Current share price**

If the share price rises, the value of a call option will increase. For currency options, the relevant 'price' is the spot exchange rate.

(b) **Exercise price of the option**

The higher the exercise price, the lower is the value of a call option.

(c) **Share price volatility or standard deviation of return on underlying share**

The higher the standard deviation of the return, the higher is the value of a call option, because there is more likelihood that the share price will rise above the option price.

(d) **Time to expiration of the option**

The longer the period to expiration, the higher is the value of a call option because there is more time for the share price to rise above the option price.

(e) **Risk-free rate of interest**

The higher the risk-free rate of interest, the higher is the value of a call option. As the exercise price will be paid in the future, its present value diminishes as interest rates rise. This reduces the cost of exercising and thus adds value to the option.

SUMMARY OF DETERMINANT OF OPTION PRICES		
↑ in	*Call price*	*Put price*
Share price	↑	↓
Exercise price	↓	↑
Volatility	↑	↑
Time to expiry	↑	↑
Risk-fee rate of return	↑	↓

3.11 Applications of options theory

Options theory can be applied to business decisions beyond the areas of financial instruments such as traded share options, currency options and interest rate options. The following are examples from the range of possible applications.

(a) **Convertible loan stock** provides a combination of a conventional loan with a call option. If the option is exercised, the loan is exchanged for a specified number of shares in the company.

(b) **Share warrants** provide the holder with an option to purchase shares from the company at a specified exercise price during a specified time period.

(c) **Government loan guarantees** effectively provide a put option to holders of risky loans, giving the holders an opportunity to exercise an option of obtaining reimbursement from the government if a borrower defaults.

(d) **Insurance** more generally is a form of put option which is exercised when an insurance claim is made.

(e) **Share purchase** at the prevailing market price can be seen as equivalent to the purchase of a call option combined with the sale of a put option, while putting the remaining amount on deposit at a risk-free rate of return over the option period.

(f) Option valuation theory which is used in valuing share options can be extended to various options which financial managers may meet in making **capital investment decisions.**

4 Interest rate swaps

FAST FORWARD

Interest rate swaps are where two parties agree to exchange interest rate payments.

Interest rate swaps can act as a means of **switching** from paying one type of interest to another, raising **less expensive loans** and **securing better** deposit **rates**.

Interest rate swaps are transactions that exploit different interest rates in different markets for borrowing, to **reduce interest costs** for either **fixed or floating rate loans**.

4.1 Arranging a swap

An **interest rate swap** is an arrangement whereby two companies, or a company and a bank, swap interest rate commitments with each other. In a sense, each simulates the other's borrowings, with the following effects.

(a) A company which has **debt at a fixed rate of interest** can make a **swap** so that it ends up paying **interest at a variable rate**.

(b) A company which has **debt at a variable rate of interest** (floating rate debt) ends up paying a **fixed rate of interest**.

Note that the parties to a swap retain their obligations to the original lenders. This means that the parties must accept **counterparty risk**. An example is illustrated in Figure 1.

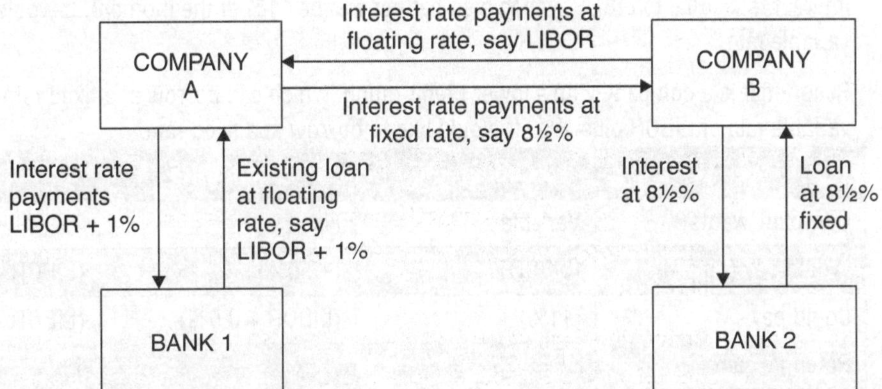

Figure 1 *Interest rate swap*

In this example, company A can use a swap to change from paying interest at a floating rate of LIBOR + 1% to one of paying fixed interest of (8½% + 1%) = 9½%.

A swap may be arranged with a bank, or a counterparty may be found through a bank or other financial intermediary. Fees will be payable if a bank is used. However a bank may be able to find a **counterparty more easily**, and may have **access to more counterparties** in **more markets** than if the company seeking the swap tried to find the counterparty itself.

4.2 Interest rate and currency swaps

FAST FORWARD

A **fixed to floating rate currency swap** is a combination of a currency and interest rate swap.

Interest rate swaps could be arranged in different currencies, for example between a fixed rate in US dollars and a floating rate in sterling. Where this happens, the swaps are normally reversed with the principal eventually swapped back at the original exchange rate. For example, a UK company and a US company can arrange a back-to-back loan and currency swap (Figure 2).

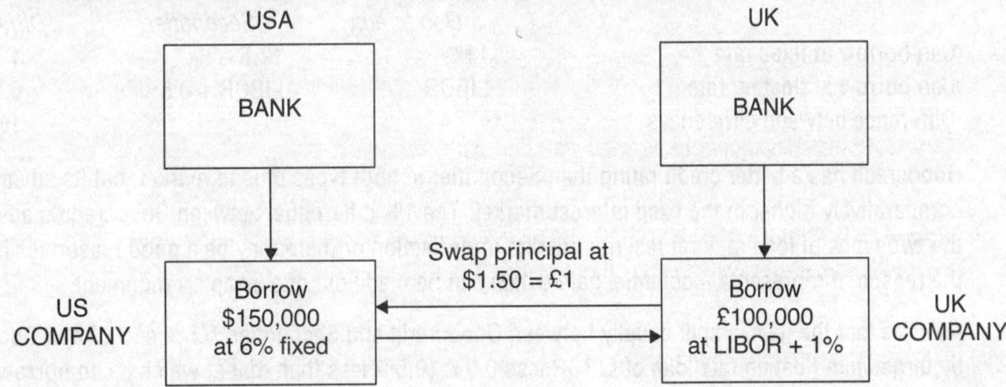

Figure 2 Interest loan and currency swap

The companies can service each other's debt (interest rate swap) and also exchange the principal, with the UK company taking $150,000 and the US company taking £100,000 (currency swap). Each company will eventually repay the principal on each other's loans at a rate of $1.50 = £1.

4.3 Example: interest rate swaps

Goodcredit has been given a high credit rating. It can borrow at a fixed rate of 11%, or at a variable interest rate equal to LIBOR, which also happens to be 11% at the moment. It would like to borrow at a variable rate.

Secondtier is a company with a lower credit rating, which can borrow at a fixed rate of 12½% or at a variable rate of LIBOR plus ½%. It would like to borrow at a fixed rate.

	Goodcredit	Secondtier	Sum total
Company wants	Variable	Fixed	
Would pay (no swap)	(LIBOR)	(12.5%)	(LIBOR + 12.5%)
Could pay	(11%)	(LIBOR + 0.5%)	(LIBOR + 11.5%)
Potential gain			1%
Split evenly	0.5%	0.5%	
Expected outcome	(LIBOR – 0.5%)	(12%)	(LIBOR + 11.5%)
Swap terms			
Could pay	(11%)	(LIBOR + 0.5%)	(LIBOR + 11.5%)
Swap floating	(LIBOR + 0.5%)	LIBOR + 0.5%	
Swap fixed	12%	(12%)	
Net paid	(LIBOR – 0.5%)	(12%)	(LIBOR + 11.5%)
Would pay	(LIBOR)	(12.5%)	(LIBOR + 12.5%)
Gain	0.5%	0.5%	1%

The results of the swap are that Goodcredit ends up paying variable rate interest, but at a lower cost than it could get from a bank, and Secondtier ends up paying fixed rate interest, also at a lower cost than it could get from investors or a bank.

If both parties ended up paying interest at a lower rate than was obtainable from the bank, where did this gain come from? To answer this question, set out a table of the rates at which both companies could borrow from the bank.

	Goodcredit	*Secondtier*	*Difference*
Can borrow at fixed rate	11%	12.5%	1.5%
Can borrow at floating rate	LIBOR	LIBOR + 0.5%	0.5%
Difference between differences			1%

Goodcredit has a better credit rating than Secondtier in both types of loan market, but its advantage is comparatively higher in the fixed interest market. The 1% differential between Goodcredit's advantage in the two types of loan may represent a market imperfection or there may be a good reason for it. Whatever the reason, it represents a potential gain which can be made out of a swap arrangement.

Assume that the gain is split equally between Goodcredit and Secondtier, 0.5% each. Then Goodcredit will be targeting a floating rate loan of LIBOR less 0.5% (0.5% less than that at which it can borrow from the bank). Similarly, Secondtier will be targeting a fixed interest loan of 12.5% – 0.5% = 12%. These are precisely the rates which are obtained by the swap arrangement illustrated above. Note that for the swap to give a gain to both parties:

(a) Each company must borrow in the loan market in which it has **comparative advantage**. Goodcredit has the greatest advantage when it borrows fixed interest. Secondtier has the least disadvantage when it borrows floating rate.

(b) The parties must actually **want** interest of the opposite type to that in which they have comparative advantage. Goodcredit wants floating and Secondtier wants fixed.

Once the target interest rate for each company has been established, there is an infinite number of swap arrangements which will produce the same net result. The example illustrated above is only one of them.

Question — Swap terms

Learning outcome: D(ii)

We illustrated above one way in which the swap could work. (Swap fixed 12%, swap floating (LIBOR + 0.5%). Suggest an alternative arrangement for the swap by entering swap interest payments into this *pro-forma* to move from the original interest paid to the desired result.

	Goodcredit	*Secondtier*
Could pay	(11%)	(LIBOR + 0.5%)
Swap floating		
Swap fixed		
Net interest cost	(LIBOR – 0.5%)	(12%)

Answer

Enter any figure into any slot of the pro-forma and the other figures must automatically balance out. Here is one of many possible solutions.

	Goodcredit	*Secondtier*
Could pay	(11%)	(LIBOR + 0.5%)
Swap floating	(LIBOR – 0.5%)	LIBOR – 0.5%
Swap fixed	11%	(11%)
Net interest cost	(LIBOR – 0.5%)	(12%)

Question — Swaps

Learning outcome: D(ii),(iii)

Seeler Muller wishes to borrow 300 million euros for five years at a floating rate to finance an investment project in Germany. The cheapest rate at which it can raise such a loan is Euro LIBOR + 0.75%.

The company's bankers have suggested that one of their client companies, Overath Maier, would be interested in a swap arrangement. This company needs a fixed interest loan at €300 million. The cheapest rate at which it can arrange the loan is 10.5% per annum. It could, however, borrow in euros at the floating rate of euro LIBOR + 1.5%.

Seeler Muller can issue a fixed interest 5 year bond at 9% per annum interest. The banker would charge a swap arrangement fee of 0.15% per year to both parties. You are required to devise a swap by which both parties can benefit.

Answer

	Seeler Muller	Overath Maier	Sum total
Company wants	Floating	Fixed	
Would pay (no swap)	(LIBOR + 0.75%)	(10.5%)	(LIBOR + 11.25%)
Could pay	(9%)	(LIBOR + 1.5%)	(LIBOR + 10.5%)
Commission	(0.15%)	(0.15%)	(0.3%)
Potential gain			0.45%
Split evenly	0.225%	0.225%	
Expected outcome	(LIBOR + 0.525%)	(10.275%)	(LIBOR + 10.8%)
Swap terms			
Could pay	(9%)	(LIBOR + 1.5%)	(LIBOR + 10.5%)
Swap floating	(LIBOR + 1.5%)	LIBOR + 1.5%	
Swap fixed	10.125%	(10.125%)	
Commission	(0.15%)	(0.15%)	(0.3%)
Net paid	(LIBOR + 0.525%)	(10.275%)	(LIBOR + 10.8%)
Would pay	(LIBOR + 0.75%)	(10.5%)	(LIBOR + 11.25%)
Gain	0.225%	0.225%	0.45%

Both companies make a net gain of 0.225%. The swap proceeds as follows.

Step 1. Seeler Muller raises a fixed interest 5 year loan for €300 million at 9% interest.

Step 2. Overath Maier raises a floating rate €300 million loan at LIBOR + 1.5%.

Step 3. The companies swap loan principals.

Step 4. Each year, each company pays its own loan interest and the interest to the counter-party, and receives interest from the counter-party.

Step 5. At the end of 5 years, the loan principals are swapped back and the companies repay their original loans.

4.4 Other advantages of swaps

Interest rate swaps have several further attractions.

- They are **easy to arrange**.
- They are **flexible**. They can be arranged in any size and, if required, reversed.
- The **transaction** costs **are low**, limited to legal fees.

As with all hedging methods, interest rate swaps can alternatively be used as a means of financial speculation. In cases receiving much publicity, local authority treasurers in the UK have engaged in such speculation with disastrous results.

Exam focus point

Note that the financial advantages of a swap are not necessarily shared equally; it depends on the relative bargaining power of the two parties involved.

5 Hedging strategy alternatives: example

FAST FORWARD

If you have to discuss which instrument should be used to hedge interest rate risk, consider **cost**, **flexibility**, **expectations** and **ability to benefit** from favourable interest rate movements.

5.1 Hedging instruments

Different hedging instruments often offer alternative ways of managing risk in a specific situation. In this section, after initial discussion of three possible hedging methods, we work through an example in which different ways in which a company can hedge interest rate risk are evaluated, covering both interest rate futures and interest rate options (interest rate guarantees).

5.2 Example: hedging alternatives

It is 31 December. Octavo plc needs to borrow £6 million in three months' time for a period of six months. For the type of loan finance which Octavo would use, the rate of interest is currently 13% per year and the Corporate Treasurer is unwilling to pay a higher rate.

The treasurer is concerned about possible future fluctuations in interest rates, and is considering the following possibilities:

(a) Forward rate agreements (FRAs)
(b) Interest rate futures
(c) Interest rate guarantees or short-term interest rate caps

Required

Explain briefly how each of these three alternatives might be useful to Octavo plc.

Solution

Forward rate agreements (FRAs)

Entering into a FRA with a bank will allow the treasurer of Octavo plc to **effectively lock in an interest rate** for the six months of the loan. This agreement is independent of the loan itself, upon which the prevailing rate will be paid. If the FRA were negotiated to be at a rate of 13%, and the actual interest rate paid on the loan were higher than this, the bank will pay the difference between the rate paid and 13% to Octavo plc. Conversely, if the interest paid by Octavo turned out to be lower than 13%, they would have to pay the difference to the bank. Thus the cost of Octavo will be 13% regardless of movements in actual interest rates.

Interest rate futures

Interest rate futures have the same effect at FRAs, in effectively **locking in an interest rate**, but they are standardised in terms of size, duration and terms. They can be **traded on an exchange** (such as LIFFE in London), and they will generally be **closed out before the maturity date**, yielding a profit or loss that is offset against the loss or profit on the money transaction that is being hedged. So, for example, as Octavo is concerned about rises in interest rates, the treasurer can sell future contracts now; if that rate does rise, their value will fall, and they can then be bought at a lower price, yielding a profit which will compensate for the increase in Octavo's loan interest cost. If interest rates fall, the lower interest cost of the loan will be offset by a loss on their futures contracts.

There may not be an **exact match** between the **loan and the future contract** (100% hedge), due to the standardised nature of the contracts, and margin payments may be required whilst the futures are still held (see Chapter 13), where margins are discussed the context of currency futures).

Interest rate guarantees

Interest rate guarantees (or short term interest rate options) give Octavo the opportunity to **benefit from favourable interest rate movements** as well as protecting them from the effects of adverse movements. They give the holder the **right** but not the **obligation** to deal at an agreed interest rate at a future maturity date. This means that if interest rates rise, the treasurer would exercise the option, and 'lock in' to the predetermined borrowing rate. If, however, interest rates fall, then the option would simply lapse, and Octavo would feel the benefit of lower interest rates.

The main disadvantage of options is that a premium will be payable to the seller of the option, whether or not it is exercised. This will therefore add to the interest cost. The treasurer of Octavo will need to consider whether this cost, which can be quite expensive, is justified by the potential benefits to be gained form favourable interest rate movements.

Exam focus point

When considering interest rate or currency risk hedging, don't discuss every possible technique that you can recall. Marks will only be awarded for techniques that are **appropriate** to the circumstances described in the question.

6 Valuing financial instruments

FAST FORWARD

IASs 32 and 39 hay have major impacts upon organisations using complex financial instruments. They may have to review their **accounting systems** and **risk management strategies**.

6.1 IASs 32 and 39

Whether you studied the UK or international version of old syllabus Paper 7 *Financial Reporting*, you should have come across IAS 32 *Financial instruments: presentation and disclosure* and IAS 39 *Financial instruments: recognition and measurement.* The details of the standards are summarised below.

6.1.1 IAS 32 *Financial instruments: presentation and disclosure*

- The definitions of financial asset, financial liability and equity instrument are fundamental to IAS 32.
- A **financial asset** is cash, an equity instrument, a contractual right to receive cash or other financial assets, or a contractual right to exchange financial instruments under potentially favourable conditions.
- A **financial liability** is a contractual obligation to deliver cash or other financial assets, or a contractual obligation to exchange financial instruments under potentially unfavourable conditions.
- A financial liability can also be a contract settled in the entitys own instruments, and is a non-derivative for which a variable number of equity instruments is to be delivered, or a derivative settled other than by the exchange of a fixed amount of cash or other instrument in return for a fixed number of the entity's own shares.
- An **equity instrument** is a contract that evidences a residual interest in the assets of an enterprise after deducting all its liabilities.

- Financial instruments include:
  - **Primary** instruments
  - **Derivative** instruments
- A financial instruments must be classified as a **financial liability**, **financial asset** or **equity instrument**.
- The **substance** of the financial instrument is more important than its **legal form.**
- The **critical feature of a financial liability** is the contractual obligation to deliver cash or another financial instrument.
- **Compound instruments** are split into equity and liability parts and presented accordingly.
- **Interest, dividends, losses and gains** are treated according to whether they relate to a financial liability or an equity instrument.
- There are different types of **risk**
  - **Price risk** (three types - currency risk, interest rate risk and market risk)
  - **Credit risk**
  - **Liquidity risk**
  - **Cash flow risk**
- Risk disclosures include descriptions of hedges including **hedging instruments** and **risks** being hedged. They also include asset and liability exposure, contractual repricing/maturity dates and effective interest rates for **interest rate risk**, and maximum to, and significant concentrations of, **credit risk.**
- Disclosures will be **numerical** and **narrative**
- The **level of detail** of disclosure depends on management judgement
- **Terms, conditions**, **accounting policies** and **fair values** must be disclosed

6.1.2 IAS 39 *Financial instruments: recognition and measurement*

- The standard suggests four categories of financial instrument:
  - **Financial asset** or **financial liability** held at **fair value through profit or loss** (designated at fair value or **held for trading)**
  - **Held to maturity investments** (non-derivative financial assets with fixed or determinable payments and fixed maturity)
  - **Loans and receivables**, that are non-derivative financial assets with fixed or determinable payments that are not quoted in an active market
  - **Available for sale financial assets**
- **Derivatives** are defined as having four components: an underlying index or variable, the notional amount or payment provision, little or no initial net investment and future settlement.
- **Embedded derivatives** are contractually attached to a host contract, for example a convertible bond with a host debt contract and an equity conversion option embedded in it. Although they are attached, embedded derivatives must be accounted for separately if their economic characteristics and risks are not closely related to the host contract's economic characteristics and risks, they would be classified as a derivative if they were a separate

instrument and the hybrid instrument is not accounted for at fair value in the profit and loss account.

- **All financial assets and liabilities** should be **recognised on the balance sheet**, including **derivatives.**
- They should be **initially recognised at fair value**, and thereafter also measured at **fair value**, except for **loans and receivables** (amortised costs), **held to maturity investments** (amortised costs), **equity instrument investments and related derivatives** that lack an active market price and reliably measured fair value (cost).
- IAS 39 establishes conditions for determining when **control** over a financial asset or liability has been **transferred** to another party including transfers of the right to receive cash and transfers of the risks and rewards of ownership.
- At each balance sheet date, assessment is required of whether a financial asset or group of assets have been **impaired**, through financial difficulty, breach of contract, disappearance of active market or decline in future contracts.
- **Hedge accounting** is permitted in certain circumstances, provided the hedging relationship is clearly defined, measurable and actually effective and its cash flows are highly probable.
- **Fair value hedge accounting** means including the gain or loss from remeasuring the hedging instrument at fair value in the income statement, and also taking to the income statement gains or losses on hedged items attributable to hedged risks.
- **Extensive disclosures** are required.

The significant requirements imposed by IASs 32 and 39 have placed major demands on the systems of many organisations. Organisations will need to be able to:

- Value all assets, liabilities and derivatives
- Produce documentation of hedging strategies
- Provide testing of effectiveness
- Manage hedging relationships
- Generate the information necessary to fulfil accounting requirements
- Accommodate modifications to new IAS requirements

6.2 Accounting issues

Organisations will have to pay particular attention to the following issues.

6.2.1 Classification of instruments

Correct classification of **hedges** will be particularly important. Other classifications will also require judgement's. Whether an asset is **held for trading** will depend on the organisations intentions when entering contracts and also whether it makes extensive use of credit techniques such as **leveraging** and **credit enhancement** and is mainly dealing with banks, traders and fund managers.

Similarly whether an asset is **held to maturity** will also depend on management intent. It may be doubted whether assets are held to maturity if the organisation's investment policy states that the investment policy is being managed to meet short-term liquidity needs.

6.2.2 Measurement of fair value

The presumption in IAS 39 is that fair values can be reliably determined even for complex derivatives. In some cases valuation techniques may require complicated assumptions or large amounts of detail, and

this may lead to the organisation incurring significant costs. The decision-making process will require informed judgement of which **methods, formulae and assumptions** to use and also **sensitivity analysis** on responsiveness to change in key variables.

6.2.3 Hedging

It may be difficult to determine the pattern of **income recognition** for hedged accounting adjustments.

6.2.4 Embedded derivatives

A very significant judgement will be how closely a derivative is **related to the host contract** and hence whether it is an embedded derivative that needs to be accounted for separately from the host contract. Organisations will also need to identify contracts that are **outside the scope of IAS 39,** but contain embedded derivatives that are within the scope of the standard.

6.2.5 Recognition and derecognition

It may be difficult to decide when precisely assets and liabilities should be derecognised. IAS 39 indicates that an organisation should consider both the **substance of control** and who bears the **risks and returns,** and that the evaluation of the transfer of risks and rewards should precede the evaluation of the transfer of control.

6.3 Accounting systems

In order to deal effectively with the accounting issues, the accounting system should be able to produce **journal updates** and **accounting entries** for IAS 39 significant events such as hedge termination.

Organisations will also need to consider carefully how IAS 39 requirements impact upon the statements they have to produce for various regulatory bodies.

6.4 Business processes and systems

Organisations will need to make sure that their systems are robust enough to be able to **process** a trade or hedge from trading through risk management to accounting entry generation. The **market data** and **models** used must be consistent; inaccuracies may result in unnecessary income volatility.

The systems must also be able to **link assets and liabilities, derivatives** and **accommodate changes in hedge allocations** and **measure hedge effectiveness.**

Because of the requirements to measure instruments at fair value, **sources of fair value information** will need to be identified.

Organisations will also have to consider their **communication strategies.** Users will be examining a range of disclosures on fair value, hedging and gains and losses, and they need to receive a clear view of what is happening.

6.5 Risk management strategies

As well as needing to understand the new rules, treasury departments must also consider whether **risk management strategies** will need to be **modified. Monitoring procedures** will have to be **strengthened**. Risk officers may have to employ **different management techniques, limiting** the **hedging strategies used** or **specifying different effectiveness assessment methods for different structures**, so that the arrangements qualify as hedges under the standard.

Organisations may also provide means of allowing users to **select and test hedges** from a pre-approved set of hedge strategies.

The IAS may also impact upon **funding arrangements** with certain funding structures (debt factoring or securitisations) requiring review to ensure compliance with the IAS.

6.6 The future of IAS 39

Recent revisions to IAS 39 have proved to be controversial. Banks in particular have been unhappy with the changes, claiming that the new rules will introduce misleading volatility into their accounts. They claim that the hedging rules in the standard do not match what the banks are trying to do when they hedge risk. It is possible that endorsement of the standard by the European Commission will be delayed by a year from its planned 2005 implementation date.

For the medium to longer-term the International Accounting Standards Board has set up a working party to examine the fundamentals of the standard, with a view to replacing it.

Chapter roundup

- Factors involving **interest rate risk** include the following.
  - Fixed rates versus floating rate debt
  - The term of the loan
- **Forward rate agreements** hedge risk by **fixing the interest rate** on future borrowing.
- **Pooling** can help avoid paying higher interest rates on borrowing and can make management of interest rate risk easier.
- **Interest rate futures** can be used to hedge against interest rate changes between the current date and the date at which the interest rate on the lending or borrowing is set. Borrowers **sell futures** to hedge against **interest rate rises;** lenders **buy futures** to hedge against **interest rate falls.**
- **Interest rate options** allow an organisation to limit its exposure to adverse interest rate movements, while allowing it to take advantage of favourable interest rate movements.
- **Borrowers** can set a **maximum** on the interest they have to pay by buying **put** options.
- **Lenders** can set a **minimum** on the interest they receive by buying **call** options.
- **Caps** set a ceiling to the interest rate; a **floor** sets a lower limit. A **collar** is the simultaneous purchase of a cap and floor.
- The **value of an option** depends on:
  - The current price of the asset
  - The exercise price
  - The volatility (standard deviation) of the asset value
  - The time period to expiry
  - The risk-free rate of interest
- **Interest rate swaps** are where two parties agree to exchange interest rate payments.
- Interest rate swaps can act as a means of **switching** from paying one type of interest to another, raising **less expensive loans** and **securing better** deposit **rates**.
- A **fixed to floating rate currency swap** is a combination of a currency and interest rate swap.
- If you have to discuss which instrument should be used to hedge interest rate risk, consider **cost**, **flexibility**, **expectations** and **ability to benefit** from favourable interest rate movements.
- IASs 32 and 39 hay have major inputs upon organisations using complex financial instruments. They may have to review their **accounting systems** and **risk management strategies**.

Quick quiz

1. Identify three aspects of a debt in which a company may be exposed to risk from interest rate movements. (Example: Fixed rate *versus* floating rate debt.)

2. What are 'FRAs'?

3. Apart from FRAs, identify three other types of financial instrument which might be used to reduce interest rate risk.

4. What name is given to the degree or percentage to which risk exposure is covered?

5. Complete the following definition of a futures contract (from *OT 2000*).

   'A contract relating to currencies, commodities or shares that obliges the buyer/issuer to __________'

6. Complete the following (from *OT 2000*).

   'Unlike (1) __________, which are entered into privately, futures contracts are traded on (2) __________,carry standard (3) __________, have specific (4) __________, and are subject to rules concerning (5) __________requirements.'

7. Fill in the blanks in the following definition of a *swap*, from *OT 2000*.

   'An arrangement whereby two (1) __________ contractually agree to exchange (2) __________ on different terms, eg in different (3) __________, or one at a (4) __________rate and the other at a (5) __________ rate.

8. Fill in the blanks.

   With a *collar*, the borrower buys (1) __________and at the same time sells (2) __________.

Answers to quick quiz

1 Any **three** of :

- Fixed rate *versus* floating rate debt
- Debt in different currencies
- Different terms of loan
- Term loan or overdraft facility

2 Forward interest rate agreements.

3
- Interest rate futures
- Interest rate options
- Interest rate swaps

Other answers may also be valid.

4 Hedge efficiency.

5 '... purchase/sell the specified quantity of the item represented in the contract at a predetermined price at the expiration of the contract.'

6
- Forward contracts
- Organised exchanges
- Terms and conditions
- Maturities
- Margin

7
- Organisations
- Payments
- Currencies
- Fixed
- Floating

8
- An interest rate cap
- An interest rate floor

Now try the questions below from the Exam Question Bank

Number	Level	Marks	Time
Q20	Examination	25	45 mins

Part E
Risk and control in information systems

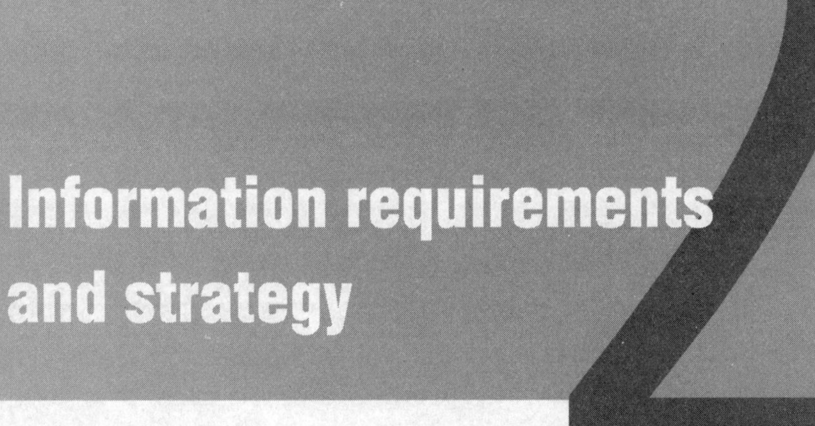

Information requirements and strategy

Introduction

In the last section of this text we concentrate on the role of information systems in supporting the risk control environment. We start by demonstrating how important information is to organisations, and how organisations develop information strategies that support management and internal control requirements. In later chapters we shall be looking at the systems that organisations implement, how the information technology function is organised, the risks information systems face, and the controls designed to deal with those risks.

Topic list	Learning outcomes	Syllabus references	Ability required
1 Information requirements	E(i)	E(1)	Evaluation
2 The value of information	E(i)	E(1)	Evaluation
3 Information strategy	E(i)	E(2)	Evaluation
4 Developing an information strategy	E(i)	E(2)	Evaluation

1 Information requirements

FAST FORWARD

Organisations **require information for** recording transactions, measuring performance, making decisions, planning and controlling.

Strategic planning, management control and operational control may be seen as a **hierarchy** of planning and control decisions.

1.1 Needs for information

Key terms

Data is the raw material for data processing. Data consists of numbers, letters and symbols and relates to facts, events, and transactions.

Information is data that has been processed in such a way as to be meaningful to the person who receives it.

An **information system** is 'an organisational and management solution, based on information technology, to any challenge posed by the environment'.

All organisations require information for a range of **purposes**. These can be categorised as follows.

- Information for **planning**
- Information for **controlling**
- Information for **recording transactions**
- Information for **performance measurement**
- Information for **decision making**

1.1.1 Planning

Planning requires a knowledge of the available resources, possible time-scales and the likely outcome under alternative scenarios. Information is required that helps **decision making**, and how to implement decisions taken.

1.1.2 Controlling

Once a plan is implemented, its actual performance must be controlled. Information is required to assess **whether it is proceeding as planned** or whether there is some unexpected deviation from plan. It may consequently be necessary to take some form of corrective action.

1.1.3 Recording transactions

Information about **each transaction or event** is required. Reasons include:

(a) Documentation of transactions can be used as **evidence** in a case of dispute.

(b) There may be a **legal requirement** to record transactions, for example for accounting and audit purposes.

(c) **Operational information** can be built up, allowing control action to be taken.

1.1.4 Performance measurement

Just as individual operations need to be controlled, so overall performance must be measured. **Comparisons against budget or plan** are able to be made. This may involve the collection of information on, for example, costs, revenues, volumes, time-scale and profitability.

1.1.5 Decision making

Strategic planning, management control and operational control may be seen as a hierarchy of planning and control decisions. (This is sometimes called the Anthony hierarchy, after the writer Robert Anthony.)

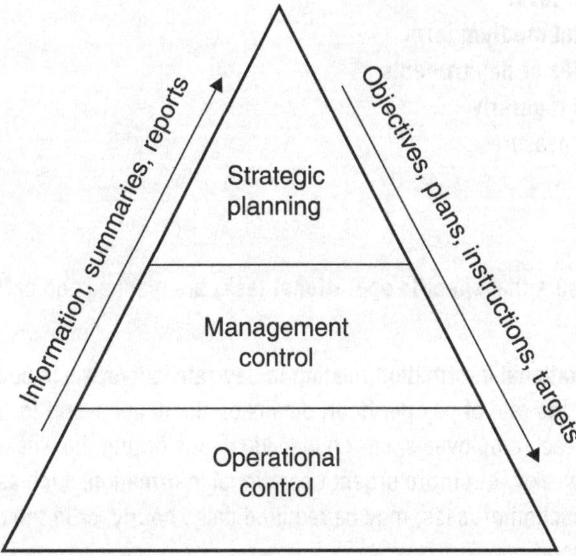

1.2 Types of information

FAST FORWARD

Strategic information is used to **plan** the **objectives** of the organisation, and to **assess** whether the objectives are being met in practice.

Tactical information is used to decide **how the resources of the organisation should be employed**, and to **monitor** how they are being and have been employed.

Operational information is used to ensure that **specific operational tasks** are planned and carried out as intended.

1.2.1 Strategic information

Strategic information is used to **plan** the **objectives** of the organisation, and to **assess** whether the objectives are being met in practice. Such information includes overall profitability, the profitability of different segments of the business, future market prospects, the availability and cost of raising new funds, total cash needs, total manning levels and capital equipment needs.

Strategic information is:

- Derived from both **internal and external** sources
- **Summarised** at a high level
- Relevant to the **long term**
- Concerned with the **whole organisation**
- Often prepared on an **'ad hoc'** basis
- Both **quantitative and qualitative**
- **Uncertain**, as the future cannot be accurately predicted

1.2.2 Tactical information

Tactical information is used to decide **how the resources of the business should be employed**, and to **monitor** how they are being and have been employed. Such information includes productivity measurements (output per hour) budgetary control or variance analysis reports, and cash flow forecasts, staffing levels and profit results within a particular department of the organisation, labour turnover statistics within a department and short-term purchasing requirements.

Tactical information is:

- Primarily generated internally (but may have a limited external component)
- **Summarised at a lower level**
- Relevant to the **short and medium term**
- Concerned with **activities or departments**
- Prepared **routinely and regularly**
- Based on **quantitative** measures

1.2.3 Operational information

Operational information is used to ensure that **specific operational tasks** are planned and carried out as intended.

In the payroll office, for example, operational information relating to day-rate labour will include the hours worked each week by each employee, the rate of pay per hour, details of deductions, and for the purpose of wages analysis, details of the time each employee spent on individual jobs during the week. In this example, the information is required weekly, but more urgent operational information, such as the amount of raw materials being input to a production process, may be required daily, hourly, or in the case of automated production, second by second.

Operational information is:

- Derived from **internal** sources
- **Detailed**, being the processing of raw data
- Relevant to the **immediate term**
- **Task-specific**
- Prepared very **frequently**
- Largely **quantitative**

It may help to clarify the above to consider it in terms of how well **structured** the problem situation is. Examples of unstructured and structured decisions at the different levels of management are given below.

	Example of a structured decision	Example of a semi-structured decision	Example of an unstructured decision
Operational level	Devising stock control procedures	Selecting a new supplier	Employing a supervisor
Tactical level	Selecting products to discount	Budget calculation and allocation	Expanding into a new design
Strategic level	Major investment decisions	Entering a new market; producing a new product line	Restructuring the organisation

1.3 The qualities of good information

FAST FORWARD

'Good' information **aids understanding**. ACCURATE is a handy mnemonic for the qualities of good information.

'Good' information is information that adds to the understanding of a situation. The qualities of good information are outlined in the following table.

Quality		Example
A	ccurate	Figures should add up, the degree of rounding should be appropriate, there should be no typos, items should be allocated to the correct category, assumptions should be stated for uncertain information.
C	omplete	Information should includes everything that it needs to include, for example external data if relevant, or comparative information.
C	ost-beneficial	It should not cost more to obtain the information than the benefit derived from having it. Providers or information should be given efficient means of collecting and analysing it. Presentation should be such that users do not waste time working out what it means.
U	ser-targeted	The needs of the user should be borne in mind, for instance senior managers need summaries, junior ones need detail.
R	elevant	Information that is not needed for a decision should be omitted, no matter how 'interesting' it may be.
A	uthoritative	The source of the information should be a reliable one (**not**, for instance, 'Joe Bloggs Predictions Page' on the Internet unless Joe Bloggs is known to be a reliable source for that type of information).
T	imely	The information should be available when it is needed.
E	asy to use	Information should be clearly presented, not excessively long, and sent using the right medium and communication channel (e-mail, telephone, hard-copy report etc).

Exam focus point

You will **not be asked simply to produce a list** of the qualities of good information in the exam. Exam questions will expect you to be able to identify **the information problems** that a company is having, and to **suggest solutions**.

1.4 Improvements to information

The table on the following page contains suggestions as to how poor information can be **improved**.

Feature	Example of possible improvements
Accurate	Use computerised systems with automatic input checks rather than manual systems. Allow sufficient time for collation and analysis of data if pinpoint accuracy is crucial. Incorporate elements of probability within projections so that the required response to different future scenarios can be assessed.
Complete	Include past data as a reference point for future projections. Include any planned developments, such as new products. Information about future demand would be more useful than information about past demand. Include external data.
Cost-beneficial	Always bear in mind whether the benefit of having the information is greater than the cost of obtaining it.
User-targeted	Information should be summarised and presented together with relevant ratios or percentages.
Relevant	The purpose of the report should be defined. It may be trying to fulfil too many purposes at once. Perhaps several shorter reports would be more effective. Information should include exception reporting, where only those items that are worthy of note – and the control actions taken by more junior managers to deal with them – are reported.
Authoritative	Use reliable sources and experienced personnel. If some figures are derived from other figures the method of derivation should be explained.
Timely	Information collection and analysis by production managers needs to be speeded up considerably, probably by the introduction of better information systems
Easy-to-use	Graphical presentation, allowing trends to be quickly assimilated and relevant action decided upon. Alternative methods of presentation should be considered, such as graphs or charts, to make it easier to review the information at a glance. Numerical information is sometimes best summarised in narrative form or vice versa. A 'house style' for reports should be devised and adhered to by all. This would cover such matters as number of decimal places to use, table headings and labels, paragraph numbering and so on.

1.5 Information requirements in different sectors

The following table provides examples of the typical information requirements of organisations operating in different sectors.

Sector	Information type	Example(s)	General comment
Manufacturing	Strategic	Future demand estimates New product development plans Competitor analysis	The information requirements of commercial organisations are influenced by the need to make and monitor profit. Information that contributes to the following measures is important: • Changeover times • Number of common parts • Level of product diversity • Product and process quality
	Tactical	Variance analysis Departmental accounts Stock turnover	
	Operational	Production reject rate Materials and labour used Stock levels	
Service	Strategic	Forecast sales growth and market share Profitability, capital structure	Organisations have become more customer and results-oriented over the last decade. As a consequence, the difference between service and other organisation's information requirements has decreased. Businesses have realised that most of their activities can be measured, and many can be measured in similar ways regardless of the business sector.
	Tactical	Resource utilisation such as average staff time charged out, number of customers per hairdresser, number of staff per account Customer satisfaction rating	
	Operational	Staff timesheets Customer waiting time Individual customer feedback	
Public	Strategic	Population demographics Expected government policy	Public sector (and non-profit making) organisations often don't have one overriding objective. Their information requirements depend on the objectives chosen. The information provided often requires interpretation (eg student exam results are not affected by the quality of teaching alone). Information may compare actual performance with: • Standards • Targets • Similar activities • Indices • Activities over time as trends
	Tactical	Hospital occupancy rates Average class sizes Percent of reported crimes solved	
	Operational	Staff timesheets Vehicles available Student daily attendance records	

Sector	Information type	Example(s)	General comment
Non-Profit / charities	Strategic	Activities of other charities Government (and in some cases overseas government) policy Public attitudes	Many of the comments regarding Public Sector organisations can be applied to not-for-profit organisations. Information to judge performance usually aims to assess economy, efficiency and effectiveness. A key measure of efficiency for charities is the percentage of revenue that is spent on the publicised cause (eg rather than on advertising or administration).
	Tactical	Percent of revenue spent on admin Average donation 'Customer' satisfaction statistics	
	Operational	Households collected from / approached Banking documentation Donations	

2 The value of information

FAST FORWARD

The **cost and value** of information are often not easy to quantify – but attempts should be made to do so.

2.1 Factors that make information a valuable commodity

Information is now recognised as a valuable resource, and a **key tool in the quest for a competitive advantage.**

Easy **access** to information, the **quality** of that information and **speedy methods of exchanging** the information have become essential elements of business success.

Organisations that make **good use of information** in decision making, and which use new technologies to access, process and exchange information are likely to be **best placed to survive** in increasingly competitive world markets.

Unlike certain commodities the value of **information in general** is **not** based on **scarcity**: indeed the most frequent complaint of many modern managers is that there is **far too much of it** about.

Moreover, the value of information is **in the eyes of the beholder** to some extent: information about a new type of plastic may be of keen interest and value to a car manufacturer, but of no value whatsoever to a software house.

The **factors which make information valuable** are as follows.

(a) The **source of the information**

If the information comes from a source that is widely known and respected for quality, thoroughness and accuracy (Reuters, say, or the BBC) it will be more valuable to users than information from an unknown or untested source, because it can be relied upon with confidence.

(b) The **ease of assimilation**

Modern methods of presentation can use not only words and figures but also **colour, graphics, sound and movement**. This makes the receipt of information a richer (and so more valuable) experience, and it means that information can be more easily, and therefore more quickly, understood: again a feature that people will be willing to pay for.

(c) **Accessibility**

If information can be made available in an easily accessible place (such as the **Internet**) users do not have to commit too much time and effort to retrieve it. If just a few sentences of information is required, and they can find these (for instance using an Internet search engine) without having to buy a whole book or newspaper, then they should be willing to pay for this convenience.

2.2 The value of obtaining information

In spite of its value in a general sense, information which is **obtained but not used** has no actual value to the person that obtains it. A decision taken on the basis of information received also has no actual value. It is only the **action taken** as a result of a decision which realises actual value for a company. The cost of collecting information bears no relation to its value. An item of information which leads to an actual increase in profit of £90 is not worth having if it costs £100 to collect.

Question — Assessing the value of information

Learning outcome: E(i)

The value of information lies in the action taken as a result of receiving it. What questions might you ask in order to make an assessment of the value of information?

Answer

(a) What information is provided?
(b) What is it used for?
(c) Who uses it?
(d) How often is it used?
(e) Does the frequency with which it is used coincide with the frequency of provision?
(f) What is achieved by using it?
(g) What other relevant information is available which could be used instead?

An assessment of the value of information can be derived in this way, and the cost of obtaining it should then be compared against this value. On the basis of this comparison, it can be decided whether certain items of information are worth having. It should be remembered that there may also be intangible benefits which may be harder to quantify.

Deciding whether it is worthwhile having more information should depend on the **marginal benefits** expected from getting it and the **extra costs** of obtaining it. The benefits of more information should be measured in terms of the difference it would make to management decisions if the information were made available. Since the incremental cost of obtaining extra quantities of information will eventually exceed the marginal benefits derived from them, there will inevitably be **a limit to the economic size of a management information system**.

2.3 Information management

Information must be managed just like any other organisational resource.

Key term

Information Management refers to the basic approach an organisation has to the management of its information systems, including:

- Planning IS/IT developments
- Organisational environment of IS
- Control
- Technology

Information management should ensure that **information** is **provided to users** and that **redundant information** is not being produced. It entails the following **tasks**.

- Identifying current and future **information needs**
- Identifying information **sources**
- **Collecting** the information
- **Storing** the information
- Facilitating existing methods of **using** information and identifying new ways of using it
- Ensuring that information is **communicated** to those who need it, and is **not communicated** to those who are not entitled to see it

Developments in technology provide new sources of information, new ways of collecting it, storing it and processing it, and new methods of communicating and sharing it.

Although computing and telecommunications technology provide fabulous tools for carrying out the information management tasks listed above, they are not always the best tools; nor are they always available.

2.4 Information systems

Key terms

Strategic information systems are systems at any level of an organisation that change goals, processes, products, services or environmental relationships with the aim of gaining competitive advantage.

Strategic-level systems are systems used by senior managers for long-term decision making.

Information Systems (IS) strategy refers to the long-term plan concerned with exploiting information systems either to support business strategies or create new strategic options. It needs to ensure that information is obtained, retained, distributed and made available for implementing strategy in all areas of an organisation's activities.

2.5 Information technology

Key term

Information technology describes the interaction of computer technology and data transmission technology in order to operate systems that satisfy the information needs of the organisation, including hardware, software and operating systems.

Information technology strategy involves deciding how information needs will be met by balancing supply and demand of funds and facilities, and the development of programmes to supply IT.

3 Information strategy

FAST FORWARD

A **strategy for information** management, systems and technology is justified on the grounds that IS/IT is costly and is vital for many organisations.

Key term

The **Information strategy (IS)** refers to the long-term plan concerned with exploiting IS and IT either to support business strategies or create new strategic options.

3.1 Why have an information strategy?

A strategy for information systems and information technology is **justified** on the grounds that IS/IT:

- Involves **high costs**
- Is **critical to the success** of many organisations
- Is now used as part of the commercial strategy in the battle for **competitive advantage**
- Impacts on **customer service**
- Affects **all levels of management**
- Affects the way **management information** is created and presented
- **Requires effective management** to obtain the maximum benefit
- Involves many **stakeholders** inside and outside the organisation

3.2 IS/IT/IM is a high cost activity

Many organisations invest large amounts of money in IS, but not always wisely.

The unmanaged proliferation of IT is likely to lead to expensive mistakes. Two key benefits of IT, the ability to **share** information and the **avoidance of duplication**, are likely to be lost.

All IT expenditure should therefore require approval to ensure that it enhances rather than detracts from the overall information strategy.

3.3 IS/IT/IM is critical to the success of many organisations

When developing an IS/IT/IM strategy a firm should assess **how important IT is** in the provision of products and services. The role that IT fills in an organisation will vary depending on the type of organisations. IS/IT could be:

- A **support** activity
- A **key** operational activity
- **Potentially** very important
- A **strategic** activity (without IT the firm could not function at all)
- A source of **competitive advantage**

Ultimately a failure of computer systems to work can result in a failure of some organisations to function at all.

3.4 Information and competitive advantage

It is now recognised that information can be used as a source of competitive advantage. Many organisations have recognised the importance of information and developed an **information strategy**, covering IS, IT and IM.

Information systems should be tied in some way to **business objectives**.

(a) The **corporate strategy** is used to plan functional **business plans** which provide guidelines for information-based activities.

(b) On a year-by-year basis, the **annual plan** would try to tie in business plans with information systems projects for particular applications, perhaps through the functioning of a steering committee.

IT can be used as a strategic weapon to gain competitive advantage for the organisation

(a) It can **improve productivity** and **performance** (eg in design and manufacturing).

(b) It can be used to **alter** the **management and organisational structure** of the business (eg electronic mail, telecommuting).

(c) It can lead to the **development of entirely new businesses** (eg Reuters created an electronic market place where subscribers could trade via Reuter terminals).

3.5 IT can impact significantly on the business context

IT is an **enabling** technology, and can produce dramatic changes in individual businesses and whole industries. For example, the deregulation of the airline industry encouraged the growth of computerised seat-reservation systems. IT can be both a **cause** of major changes in doing business and a **response** to them.

3.6 IT affects all levels of management

IT has become a routine feature of office life, **a facility for everyone to use**. IT is no longer used solely by specialist staff.

3.7 IT and its effect on management information

The use of IT has permitted the design of a range of information systems, which we shall look at in the next chapter.

IT permeates the different layers of management, as a routine feature of office life and a facility for everyone to use.

(a) Senior managers can see **more precisely** what goes on at operational level.

(b) Operational management can be **empowered by IT** (eg expert systems) to take decisions, which computers can support.

(c) **Delayering**. IT renders redundant the information processing role of middle managers.

(d) Use of IT requires so-called **intellective** skills, the ability to analyse and manipulate abstract data. These used to be management's concern.

(e) Email systems and diary planning systems enable managers to **co-ordinate** their activities better. 63% of UK companies in a recent survey by the DTI use email.

IT has also had an effect on **production processes**. For example, Computer Integrated Manufacturing (CIM) changed the methods and cost profiles of many manufacturing processes. The techniques used to **measure and record costs** have also adapted to the use of IT.

3.8 IT and stakeholders

Parties interested in an organisation's use of IT are as follows.

(a) **Other business users** – for example to facilitate Electronic Data Interchange (EDI).

(b) **Governments** – eg telecommunications regulation, regulation of electronic commerce.

(c) **IT manufacturers** looking for new markets and product development. User-groups may be able to influence software producers.

(d) **Consumers** – for example as reassurance that product quality is high, consumers may also be interested if information is provided via the Internet.

(e) **Employees** – as IT affects work practices.

3.9 Information systems and corporate/business strategy

It is widely accepted that an organisation's information system should **support** corporate and business strategy. In some circumstances an information system may have a greater influence and actually help **determine** corporate / business strategy. For example:

(a) IS/IT/IM may provide a possible source of competitive advantage. This could involve new technology not yet available to others or simply using existing technology in a different way.

(b) The information system may help in formulating business strategy by **providing information** from internal and external sources.

(c) Developments in IT may provide **new channels** for distributing and collecting information, and /or for conducting transactions eg the Internet.

Some common ways in which IS/IT/IM have had a major impact on organisations are explained below.

(a) **The type of products or services that are made and sold**

For example, consumer markets have seen the emergence of home computers, compact discs and satellite dishes for receiving satellite TV; industrial markets have seen the emergence of custom-built microchips, robots and local area networks for office information systems. Technological changes can be relatively minor, such as the introduction of tennis and squash rackets with graphite frames, fluoride toothpaste and turbo-powered car engines.

(b) **The way in which products are made**

There is a continuing trend towards the use of automation and computer aided design and manufacture. The manufacturing environment is undergoing rapid changes with the growth of advanced manufacturing technology. These are changes in both apparatus and technique.

(c) **The way in which services are provided**

High-street banks encourage customers to use 'hole-in-the-wall' cash dispensers, or telephone or Internet banking. Most larger shops now use computerised **Point of Sale terminals** at cash desks. Many organisations use **e-commerce**: selling products and services over the Internet.

(d) **The way in which markets are identified**

Database systems make it much easier to analyse the market place.

(e) **The way in which employees are mobilised**

Technology encourages workforce empowerment. Using technology frequently requires changes in working methods. This is a change in organisation.

(f) **The way in which firms are managed**

An empowered workforce often leads to the 'delayering' of organisational hierarchies (in other words, the reduction of management layers).

(g) The means and extent of **communications** with customers.

Benefits of technological change might therefore be as follows.

- To **cut production costs** and so (probably) to **reduce sales prices** to the customer
- To develop **better quality** products and services
- To develop products and services that **did not exist before**
- To **provide** products or services to customers **more quickly or effectively**
- To **free staff** from repetitive work and to tap their creativity

An important role of the information technology and finance functions is to help ensure the agreed strategy is proceeding according to plan. The table below outlines the rationale behind this view.

	Traditional view	Strategic implications
Cost	The finance and information technology functions can be relatively expensive	Shared services and outsourcing could be used to capture cost savings
IT	IT has traditionally been transaction based	IT/IS should be integrated with business strategy
Value	The finance and IT functions do not add value	Redesign the functions
Strategy	Accountants and IT managers are seen as scorekeepers and administrators rather than as a business partner during the strategic planning process	Change from cost-orientated to market-orientated ie development of more effective strategic planning systems

4 Developing an information strategy

FAST FORWARD

There are a range of methodologies and frameworks for establishing the information requirements of an organisation including **Enterprise Analysis**, **Critical Success Factors** (**CSFs**), and **Earl's three leg analysis**.

4.1 Context of information strategy

An information strategy should be developed with the aim of ensuring IS/IT is utilised as efficiently and effectively as possible in the pursuit of organisational goals and objectives.

The inputs and outputs of the IS/IT strategic planning process are summarised on the following diagram.

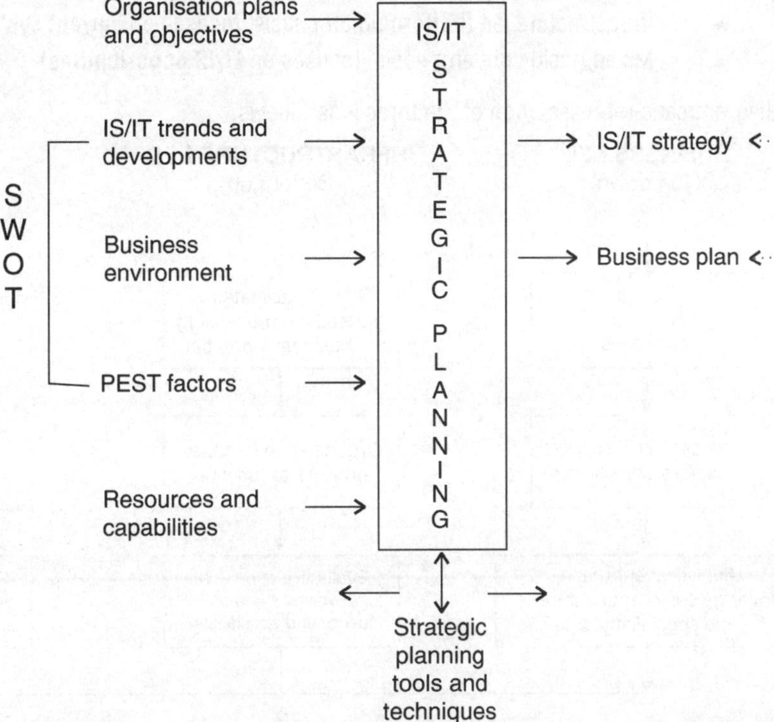

An IS strategy therefore deals with the integration of an organisation's information requirements and information systems planning with its **long-term overall goals** (customer service etc). IS strategy deals with what applications should be developed and where resources should be deployed.

The **information technology (IT) strategy** leads on from the IS strategy above. It deals with the **technologies** of:

- Computing
- Communications
- Data
- Application systems

This provides a framework for the analysis and design of the **technological infrastructure** of an organisation. This strategy indicates how the information systems strategies that rely on technology will be **implemented**.

4.2 Establishing organisational information requirements

The identification of organisational information needs and the information systems framework to satisfy them is at the heart of a strategy for information systems and information technology.

The IS and IT strategies should complement the overall strategy for the organisation. It follows therefore that the IS/IT strategy should be considered whenever the organisation prepares other long-term strategies such as marketing or production.

4.3 Earl's three leg analysis

The writer Earl devised a method for the development of IS strategies. His method identified three legs of IS strategy development.

- Business led (top down emphasis, focuses on **business plans and goals**)
- Infrastructure led (bottom up emphasis, focuses on **current systems**)
- Mixed (inside out emphasis, focuses on **IT/IS opportunities**)

A diagrammatic representation of the three legs follows.

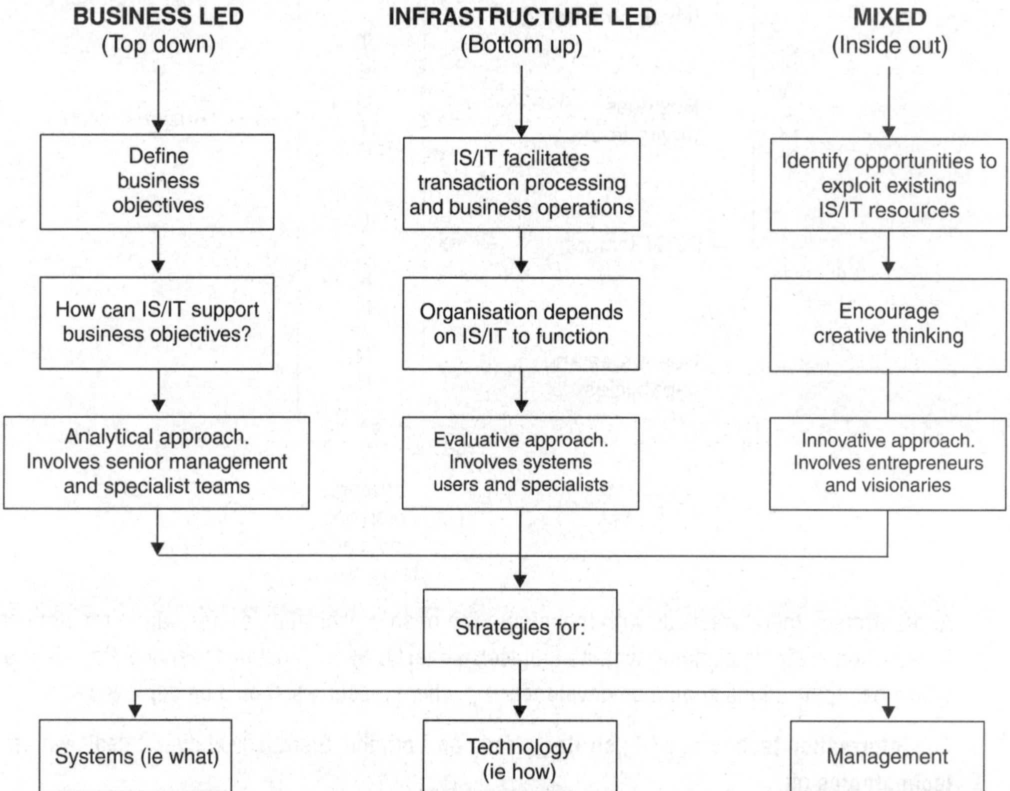

Earl's three leg analysis is explained in the following table.

Leg or approach	Comment
Business led (top down)	The overall objectives of an organisation are identified and then IS/IT systems are implemented to enable these objectives to be met. This approach relies on the ability to break down the organisation and its objectives to a series of business objectives and processes and to be able to identify the information needs of these. This is an analytical approach. The people usually involved are senior management and specialist teams.

Leg or approach	Comment
Infrastructure led (bottom up)	Computer based transaction systems are critical to business operations. The organisation focuses on systems that facilitate transactions and other basic operations. This is an evaluative approach. The people usually involved are system users and specialists.
Mixed (inside out)	The organisation encourages ideas that will exploit existing IT and IS resources. Innovations may come from entrepreneurial managers or individuals outside the formal planning process. This is an innovative/creative approach. The people involved are entrepreneurs and/or visionaries.

We will now look at a number of other methodologies and frameworks that may be used as part of the information systems strategy development process.

4.4 Enterprise analysis

Key term

Enterprise analysis involves examining the entire organisation in terms of structure, processes, functions and data elements to identify the key elements and attributes of organisational data and information.

Enterprise analysis is sometimes referred to as **business systems planning**. This approach involves the following steps.

Step 1 Ask a large sample of managers about:

- How they use information
- Where they get information
- What their objectives are
- What their data requirements are
- How they make decisions
- The influence of the environment

Step 2 Aggregate the findings from *Step 1* into subunits, functions, processes and data matrices. Compile a Process/data class matrix to show:

- What data classes are required to support particular organisational processes
- Which processes are the creators and users of data

Step 3 Use the matrix to identify areas that information systems should focus on, eg on processes that create data.

Enterprise analysis approach – strength	Comment
Comprehensive	The enterprise analysis approach gives a comprehensive view of the organisation and its use of data and systems.

Enterprise analysis approach – weaknesses	Comment
Unwieldy	The enterprise analysis approach results in a mountain of data that is expensive to collect and difficult to analyse.
Focussed on existing information	Survey questions tend to focus on how systems and information are currently used, rather than on how information that is needed could be provided. The analysis has tended to result in existing systems being automated rather than looking at the wider picture.

4.5 Critical success factors

The use of **critical success factors (CSFs)** can help to determine the information requirements of an organisation. CSFs are operational goals. If operational goals are achieved the organisation should be successful.

Key term

Critical success factors are a small number of key operational goals vital to the success of an organisation. CSFs are used to establish organisational information requirements.

The CSF approach is sometimes referred to as the **strategic analysis** approach. The philosophy behind this approach is that managers should focus on a small number of objectives, and information systems should be focussed on providing information to enable managers to monitor these objectives.

Two separate types of critical success factor can be identified. A **monitoring** CSF is used to keep abreast of existing activities and operations. A **building** CSF helps to measure the progress of new initiatives and is more likely to be relevant at senior executive level.

- **Monitoring** CSFs are important for **maintaining** business
- **Building** CSFs are important for **expanding** business

One approach to **determining the factors** which are critical to success in performing a function or making a decision is as follows.

- List the organisation's corporate objectives and goals
- Determine which factors are critical for accomplishing the objectives
- Determine a small number of key performance indicators for each factor

4.5.1 Example

One of the **objectives** of an organisation might be to maintain a high level of service direct from stock without holding uneconomic stock levels. This is first quantified in the form of a **goal**, which might be to ensure that 95% of orders for goods can be satisfied directly from stock, while minimising total stockholding costs and stock levels.

CSFs might then be identified as the following.

- **Supplier performance** in terms of quality and lead times
- Reliability of **stock records**
- **Forecasting** of demand variations

The determination of **key performance indicators** for each of these CSFs is not necessarily straightforward. Some measures might use **factual**, objectively verifiable, data, while others might make use of **'softer' concepts**, such as opinions, perceptions and hunches.

For example, the reliability of stock records can be measured by means of physical stock counts, either at discrete intervals or on a rolling basis. Forecasting of demand variations will be much harder to measure.

Where measures use quantitative data, performance can be measured in a number of ways.

- In **physical quantities**, for example units produced or units sold
- In **money terms**, for example profit, revenues, costs or variances
- In **ratios** and **percentages**

4.5.2 Data sources for CSFs

In general terms *Rockart* identifies four **general sources** of CSFs.

(a) The **industry** that the business is in.

(b) The **company** itself and its situation within the industry.

(c) The **environment**, for example consumer trends, the economy, and political factors of the country in which the company operates.

(d) Temporal organisational factors, which are **areas of corporate activity** which are currently **unacceptable** and represent a cause of concern, for example, high stock levels.

More specifically, possible internal and external data sources for CSFs include the following.

(a) **The existing system**. The existing system can be used to generate reports showing **failures to meet CSFs.**

(b) **Customer service department**. This department will maintain details of **complaints** received, **refunds** handled, **customer enquiries** etc. These should be reviewed to ensure all failure types have been identified.

(c) **Customers**. A survey of customers, provided that it is properly designed and introduced, would reveal (or confirm) those areas where **satisfaction** is high or low.

(d) **Competitors**. Competitors' operations, pricing structures and publicity should be closely monitored.

(e) **Accounting system**. The **profitability** of various aspects of the operation is probably a key factor in any review of CSFs.

(f) **Consultants**. A specialist consultancy might be able to perform a detailed review of the system in order to identify ways of satisfying CSFs.

The CSF approach to IS/IT planning is illustrated in the following diagram.

The critical success factor approach to IS/IT planning

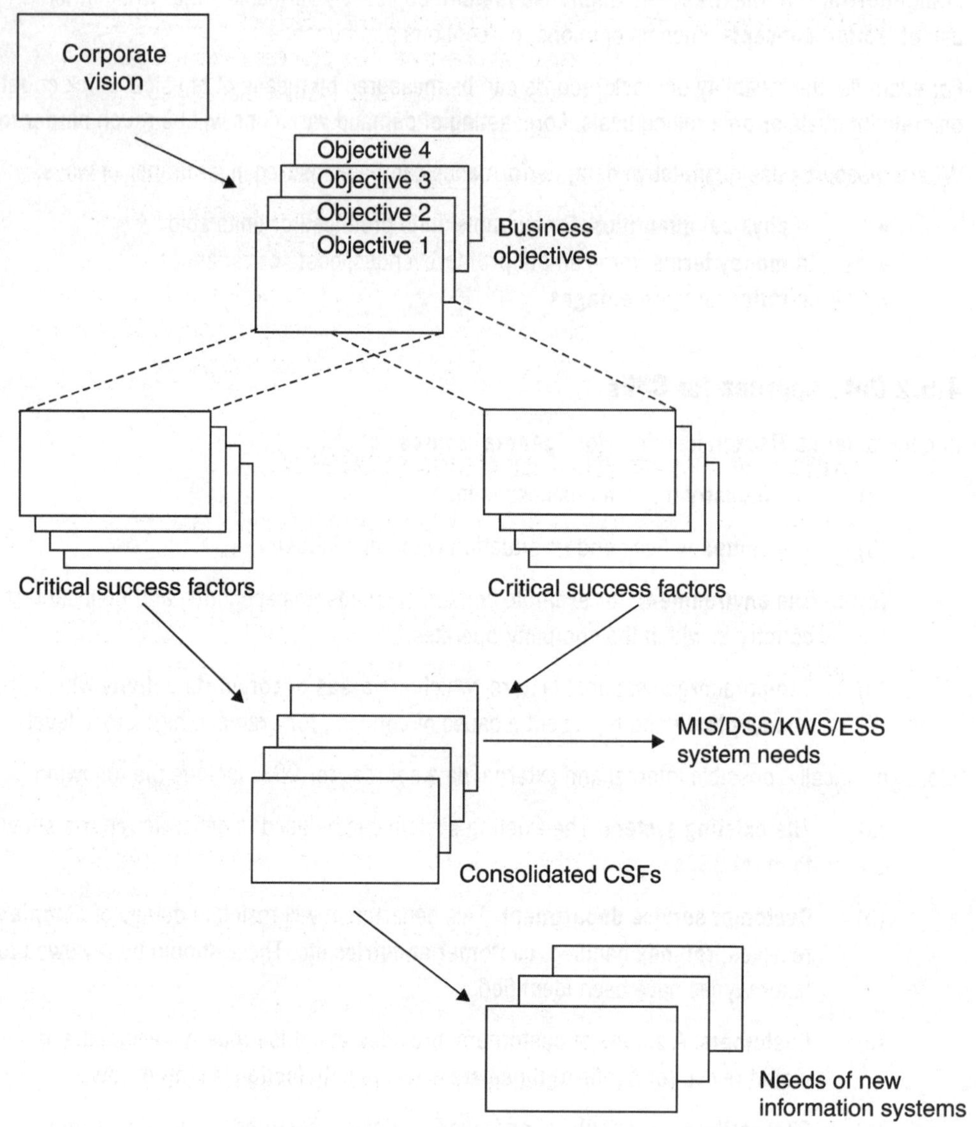

Source: IT Strategy for Business, Joe Peppard
Chapter 4, Garret Hickey

4.5.3 CSF approach: strengths and weaknesses

CSF approach – strengths	Comment
Takes into account environmental changes	The CSF approach requires managers to examine the environment and consider how it influences their information requirements.
Focuses on information	The approach doesn't just aim to establish organisational objectives. It also looks at the information and information systems required to establish and monitor progress towards these objectives.
Facilitates top management participation in system development	The clear link between information requirements and individual and organisational objectives encourages top management involvement in system (DSS, ESS) design.

CSF approach – weaknesses	Comment
Aggregation of individual CSFs	Wide-ranging individual CSFs need to be aggregated into a clear organisational plan. This process relies heavily on judgement. Managers who feel their input has been neglected may be alienated.
Bias towards top management	When gathering information to establish CSFs it is usually top management who are interviewed. These managers may lack knowledge of operational activities.
CSFs change often	The business environment, managers and information systems technology are subject to constant change. CSFs and systems must be updated to account for change.

4.6 Parsons' six information systems strategies

The writer Parsons identified six possible generic Information System (IS) strategies. These are outlined in the following table.

Generic strategy for IS	Comment
Centrally planned	The logic of this approach is that those planning IS developments should have an understanding of the overall strategic direction. Business and IS strategy are viewed as being closely linked.
Leading edge	There is a belief that innovative technology use can create competitive advantage, and therefore that risky investment in unproven technologies may generate large returns. The organisation must have the motivation and ability to commit large amounts of money and other resources. Users must be enthusiastic and willing to support new initiatives.
Free market	This strategy is based on the belief that the market makes the best decisions. The IS function is a competitive business unit, which must be prepared to achieve a return on its resources. The department may have to compete with outside providers.
Monopoly	The direct opposite to the free market strategy. This strategy is based upon the belief that information is an organisational asset that should be controlled by a single service provider.
Scarce resource	This strategy is based on the premise that information systems use limited resources, and therefore all IS development requires a clear justification. Budgetary controls are in place and should be adhered to. New projects should be subject to Cost Benefit Analysis (CBA).
Necessary evil	IS/IT is seen as a necessary evil of modern business. IS/IT is allocated enough resource only to meet basic needs. This strategy is usually adopted in organisations that believe that information is not important to the business.

Chapter roundup

- Organisations **require information for** recording transactions, measuring performance, making decisions, planning and controlling.
- **Strategic information** is used to **plan** the **objectives** of the organisation, and to **assess** whether the objectives are being met in practice.
- **Tactical information** is used to decide **how the resources of the organisation should be employed**, and to **monitor** how they are being and have been employed.
- **Operational information** is used to ensure that **specific operational tasks** are planned and carried out as intended.
- 'Good' information **aids understanding**. ACCURATE is a handy mnemonic for the qualities of good information.
- The **cost and value** of information are often not easy to quantify – but attempts should be made to do so.
- A **strategy for information** management, systems and technology is justified on the grounds that IS/IT is costly and is vital for many organisations.
- There are a range of methodologies and frameworks for establishing the information requirements of an organisation including **Enterprise Analysis**, **Critical Success Factors** (**CSF**s), and **Earl's three leg analysis**.

Quick quiz

1 List five uses of information.

2 List five characteristics of strategic information.

3 List five characteristics of tactical information.

4 List five characteristics of operational information.

5 What are the main factors that make information valuable?

6 Give three examples of the benefits of technological change.

7 List four general sources of CSFs.

8 List Parsons' six information strategies.

Answers to quick quiz

1 Planning, controlling, recording transactions, measuring performance and making decisions.

2
- Derived from both internal and external sources
- Summarised at a high level
- Relevant to the long term
- Concerned with the whole organisation
- Often prepared on an 'ad hoc' basis
- Both quantitative and qualitative
- Uncertain, as the future cannot be predicted accurately

3
- Primarily generated internally (but may have a limited external component)
- Summarised at a lower level
- Relevant to the short and medium term
- Concerned with activities or departments
- Prepared routinely and regularly
- Based on quantitative measures

4
- Derived from internal sources
- Detailed, being the processing of raw data
- Relevant to the immediate term
- Task-specific
- Prepared very frequently
- Largely quantitative

5
- Source of information
- Ease of assimilation
- Accessibility

6
- Cut production costs and reduce sales prices to the customer
- Develop better quality products and services
- Develop products and services that did not exist before
- Provide products or services to customers more quickly or effectively
- Free staff from repetitive work and to tap their creativity

7
- The industry that the business is in
- The company itself and its situation within the industry
- The environment, for example consumer trends and the economy
- Specific internal measures, for example inventory levels

8
- Centrally planned
- Leading edge
- Free market
- Monopoly
- Scarce resource
- Necessary evil

Now try the question below from the Exam Question Bank

Number	Level	Marks	Time
Q21	Examination	25	45 mins

Information systems

Introduction

Having dealt with the factors determining information strategy, in this chapter we go on to consider how organisations evaluate the information systems that are available to them and choose the right one. We discuss examples of information systems in Section 1 including transaction processing, decision support and executive information systems which are all mentioned in your syllabus. In the second section we consider how organisations identify the systems that best fulfil their needs for operational and control management.

Topic list	Learning outcomes	Syllabus references	Ability required
1 Types of information systems	E(ii)	E(3)	Evaluation
2 Evaluating information systems	E(ii)	E(1),(3)	Evaluation

1 Types of information system

FAST FORWARD

- Organisations require different **types of information system** to provide **different levels** of information in a range of **functional areas**.
- There are six major types of Information Systems: Executive Support Systems (**ESS**), Management Information Systems (**MIS**), Decision Support Systems (**DSS**), Knowledge Work Systems (**KWS**), Office Automation Systems (**OAS**) and Transaction Processing Systems (**TPS**).

1.1 Systems requirements

A modern organisation requires a **wide range of systems** to hold, process and analyse information. We will now examine the various information systems used to serve organisational information requirements.

Organisations require different **types of information system** to provide different **levels of information** in a range of **functional areas**. One way of portraying this concept is shown on the following diagram (taken from *Laudon* and *Laudon, Management Information Systems*).

Types of information systems

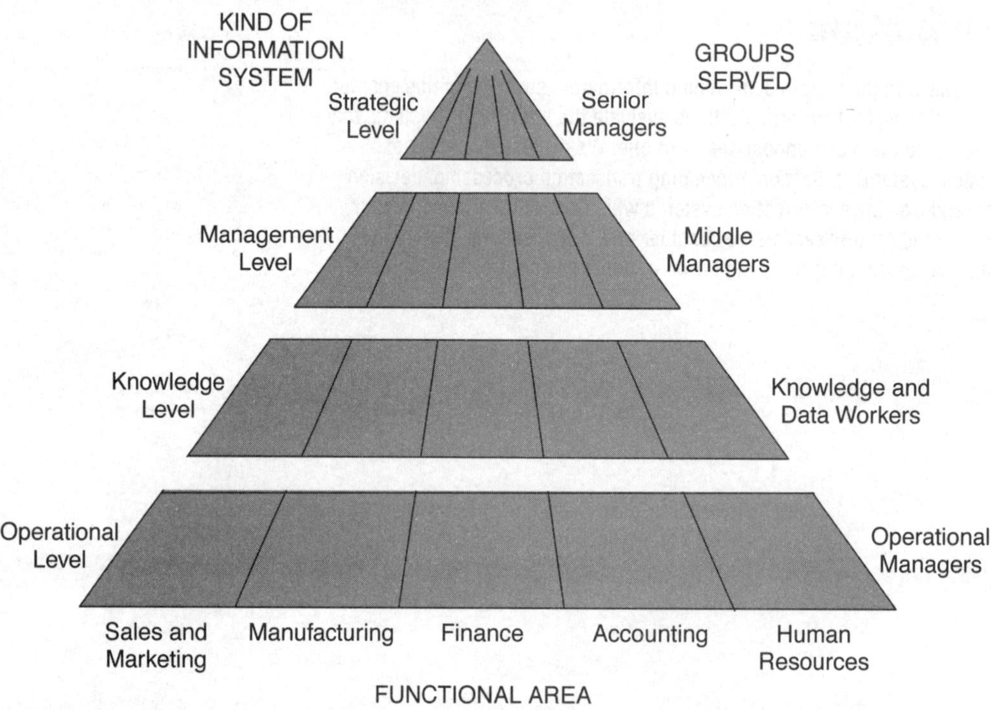

System level	System purpose
Strategic	To help senior managers with long-term planning. Their main function is to ensure changes in the external environment are matched by the organisation's capabilities.
Management	To help middle managers monitor and control. These systems check if things are working well or not. Some management- level systems support non-routine decision making such as 'what if?' analyses.
Knowledge	To help knowledge and data workers design products, distribute information and perform administrative tasks. These systems help the organisation integrate new and existing knowledge into the business and to reduce the reliance on paper documents.

System level	System purpose
Operational	To help operational managers track the organisation's day-to-day operational activities. These systems enable routine queries to be answered, and transactions to be processed and tracked.

There are six **types of information system**:

- Executive Support Systems (ESS)
- Management Information Systems (MIS)
- Decision-Support Systems (DSS)
- Knowledge Work Systems (KWS)
- Office Automation Systems (OAS)
- Transaction Processing Systems (TPS)

1.2 Executive Support Systems (ESS)

Key term

An **Executive Support System (ESS)** or **Executive Information System (EIS)** pools data from internal and external sources and makes information available to senior managers in an easy-to-use form. ESS help senior managers make strategic, unstructured decisions.

An ESS should provide senior managers with easy access to key **internal and external** information. The system summarises and tracks strategically critical information, possibly drawn from internal MIS and DSS, but also including data from external sources eg competitors, legislation, external databases such as Reuters.

An ESS is likely to have the following **features**.

- Flexibility
- Quick response time
- Sophisticated data analysis and modelling tools

A model of a typical ESS is shown below.

An Executive Support System (ESS)

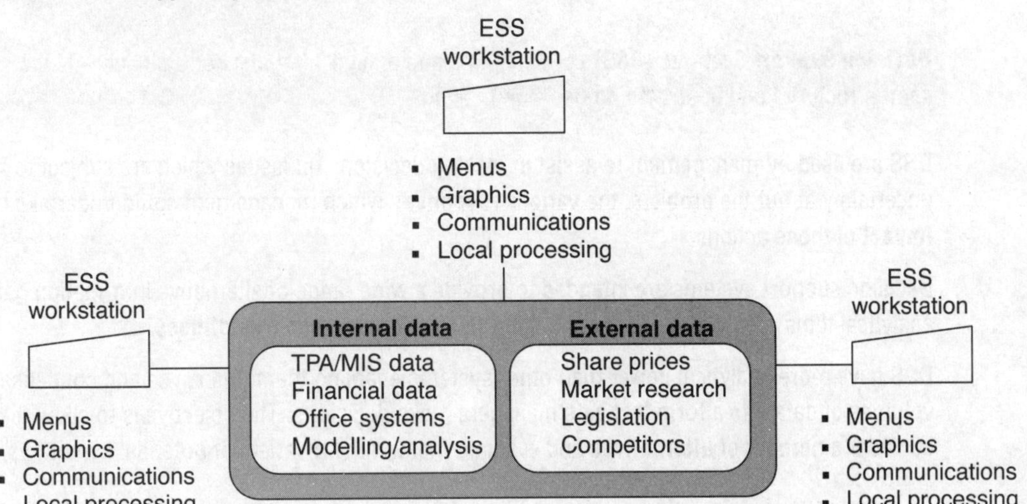

Other more specialist systems include **Enterprise Resource Planning Systems (ERP)** which capture accounting, operational, customer and supplier data. They produce tailored reports and can also be used to update performance measures, for strategic planning and customer and supply chain management as well as identifying and planning the **enterprise-wide resources required**.

1.3 Management Information Systems (MIS)

Key term

Management Information Systems (MIS) convert data from mainly internal sources into information (eg summary reports, exception reports). This information enables managers to make timely and effective decisions for planning, directing and controlling the activities for which they are responsible.

An MIS provides regular reports and (usually) on-line access to the organisation's current and historical performance.

MIS usually transform data from underlying transaction processing systems into summarised files that are used as the basis for management reports.

MIS have the following characteristics:

- Support **structured** decisions at operational and management control levels
- Designed to report on **existing** operations
- Have little analytical capability
- Relatively **inflexible**
- Have an **internal** focus

Exam Focus Point

Some texts use the term **Management Information System** as an umbrella term for **all information systems** within an organisation.

1.4 Decision Support Systems (DSS)

Key term

Decision Support Systems (DSS) combine data and analytical models or data analysis tools to support semi-structured and unstructured decision making.

DSS are used by management to assist in making decisions on issues which are subject to high levels of uncertainty about the problem, the various **responses** which management could undertake or the likely **impact** of those actions.

Decision support systems are intended to provide a wide range of alternative information gathering and analytical tools with a major emphasis upon **flexibility** and **user-friendliness**.

DSS have more analytical power than other systems enabling them to analyse and condense large volumes of data into a form that aids managers make decisions. The objective is to allow the manager to consider a number of **alternatives** and evaluate them under a variety of potential conditions.

1.5 Knowledge Work Systems (KWS)

Key terms

Knowledge Work Systems (KWS) are information systems that facilitate the creation and integration of new knowledge into an organisation.

Knowledge Workers are people whose jobs consist of primarily creating new information and knowledge. They are often members of a profession such as doctors, engineers, lawyers and scientists.

Knowledge Work Systems (KWS) are information systems that facilitate the creation and integration of new knowledge into an organisation. They provide knowledge workers with tools such as:

- Analytical tools
- Powerful graphics facilities
- Communication tools
- Access to external databases
- A user-friendly interface

The workstations of knowledge workers are often designed for the specific tasks they perform. For example, a design engineer would require sufficient graphics power to manipulate 3-D Computer Aided Design (**CAD**) images; a financial analyst would require a powerful desktop computer to access and manipulate a large amount of financial data (an **investment workstation**).

The components of a KWS are shown in the following diagram.

Knowledge work system

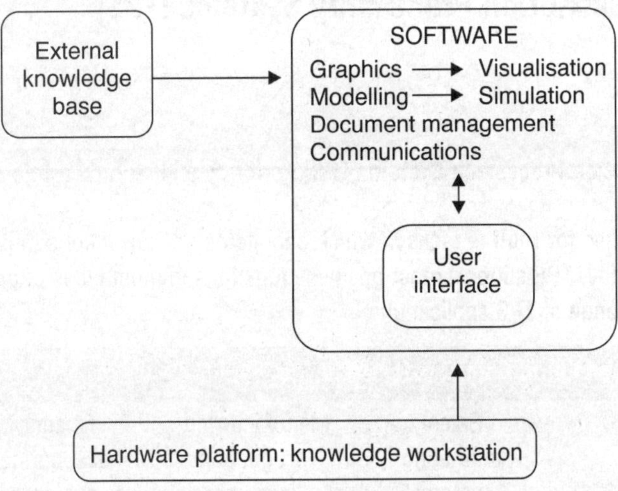

Virtual reality systems are another example of KWS. These systems create computer generated simulations that emulate real-world activities. Interactive software and hardware (eg special headgear) provide simulations so realistic that users experience sensations that would normally only occur in the real world.

Case Study

Virtual reality

Burger King have used virtual reality stores to test new store designs.

Volvo have used virtual reality test drives in vehicle development.

1.6 Office Automation Systems (OAS)

Key term

Office Automation Systems (OAS) are computer systems designed to increase the productivity of data and information workers.

OAS support the major activities performed in a typical office such as document management, facilitating communication and managing data. Examples include:

- Word processing, desktop publishing, and digital filing systems
- E-mail, voice mail, videoconferencing, groupware, intranets, schedulers
- Spreadsheets, desktop databases

1.7 Transaction Processing Systems (TPS)

Key term

A **Transaction Processing System (TPS)** performs and records routine transactions.

TPS are used for **routine tasks** in which data items or transactions must be processed so that operations can continue. TPS support most business functions in most types of organisations. The following table shows a range of TPS applications.

Transaction processing systems					
	Sales/ marketing systems	Manufacturing/ production systems	Finance/ accounting systems	Human resources systems	Other types (eg university)
Major functions of system	• Sales management • Market research • Promotion Pricing • New products	• Scheduling • Purchasing Shipping/ receiving • Engineering • Operations	• Budgeting • General ledger • Billing • Management accounting	• Personnel records • Benefits • Salaries • Labour relations • Training	• Admissions • Student academic records • Course records • Graduates

Transaction processing systems					
	Sales/ marketing systems	Manufacturing/ production systems	Finance/ accounting systems	Human resources systems	Other types (eg university)
Major application systems	• Sales order information system • Market research system • Pricing system	• Materials resource planning • Purchase order control • Engineering • Quality control	• General ledger • Accounts receivable /payable • Budgeting • Funds management	• Payroll • Employee records • Employee benefits • Career path systems	• Registration • Student record • Curriculum/ class control systems • Benefactor information system

1.7.1 Batch processing and On-line processing

A TPS will process transactions using either **batch** processing or **on-line** processing.

Batch processing involves transactions being **grouped** and **stored** before being processed at regular intervals, such as daily, weekly or monthly. Because data is not input as soon as it is received the system will not always be up-to-date.

The lack of up-to-date information means batch processing is usually not suitable for systems involving customer contact. Batch processing is suitable for internal, regular tasks such as payroll.

On-line processing involves transactions being input and processed immediately. An airline ticket sales and reservation system is an example.

The workings of both processing methods are shown in the following diagram.

Batch processing and on-line processing

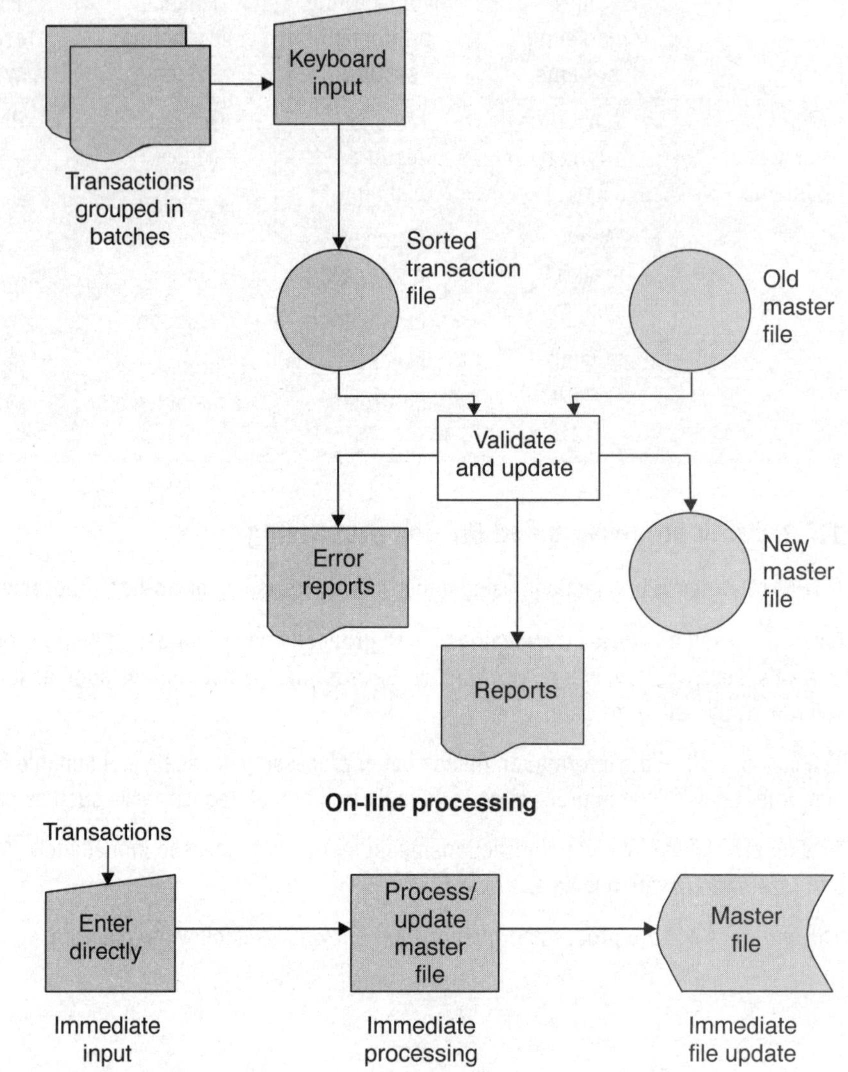

On-line processing

Transactions
Enter directly
Process/ update master file
Master file
Immediate input
Immediate processing
Immediate file update

1.8 System dependencies and integration

The six types of system we have identified exchange data with each other. The ease with which data flows from one system to another depends on the extent of **integration** between systems.

The level of integration will depend on the nature of the organisation and the systems involved. The cost of integrating systems (eg programmer time) should be considered against benefits of integration (quicker availability of information, less time spent inputting information).

Interrelationships between systems are shown in the following diagram from *Loudon and Loudon*.

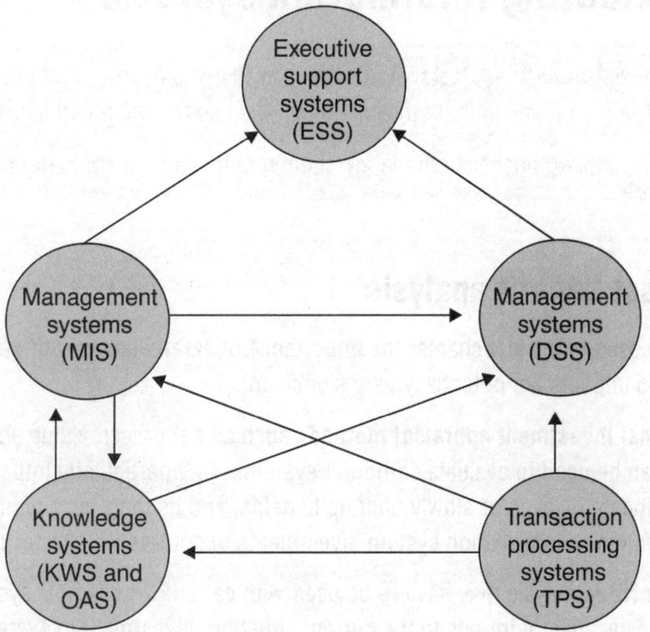

1.9 Information systems: levels, types and functions

Examples of the levels and types of information system we have discussed in this section are shown in the following diagram.

TYPES OF SYSTEMS					
	Strategic-Level Systems				
Executive Support Systems (ESS)	5-year sales trend forecasting	5-year operating plan	5-year budget forecasting	Profit planning	Human resource planning
	Management-Level Systems				
Management Information Systems (MIS)	Sales management	Inventory control	Annual budgeting	Capital investment analysis	Relocation analysis
Decision Support Systems (DSS)	Sales region analysis	Production scheduling	Cost analysis	Pricing/profitability analysis	Contract cost analysis
	Knowledge-Level System				
Knowledge Work Systems (KWS)	Engineering workstations	Graphics workstations	Managerial workstations		
Office Automation Systems (OAS)	Word processing	Document imaging	Electronic calendars		
	Operational-Level Systems				
Transaction Processing Systems (TPS)		Machine control	Securities trading	Payroll	Compensation
	Order tracking	Plant scheduling		Accounts payable	Training & development
	Order processing	Material movement control	Cash management	Accounts receivable	Employee record keeping
	Sales and Marketing	**Manufacturing**	**Finance**	**Accounting**	**Human Resources**

2 Evaluating information systems

FAST FORWARD

Although **cost-benefit analysis** should be used to evaluate information systems, the **wider operational and control issues** mean that other methods such as the **balanced scorecard** should also be used.

As well as fulfilling financial criteria, systems must also be **technically and operationally viable.**

2.1 Cost benefit analysis

We discussed in the last chapter the importance of careful analysis of developing information systems, as costs and impacts are potentially very significant.

Traditional investment appraisal methods such as net present value, internal rate of return and payback period can be used to evaluate computer systems. One particularly important feature of NPV is that it can accommodate delayed or slowly built up benefits, and its long-term nature is thus particularly suited to assessing major information system investments in contrast to shorter term methods such as payback.

However NPV analysis may have to be used with care. If for example systems development is being proposed because of threats to the current situation, investment in systems should be compared not with the current situation but the projected situation if the threats are realised.

It is also important to **collect all the costs** involved including programming, training, **maintenance** and employee costs.

Cost benefit analysis is most appropriate when **direct improvements** in productivity and performance are being sought. It should be possible to quantify benefits if efficiency and effectiveness are being pursued.

2.2 Problems with cost benefit analysis

The main problem with using traditional cost-benefit analysis to evaluate systems is that the costs and benefits tend to be derived from the accounting system. However a most important aspect of investment in systems is **improving the quality** of **operational and control information** and this cannot **easily be measured in accounting terms**. For example what can be placed on not having information? Other benefits such as improved **responsiveness** and **flexibility** may also be very difficult to measure.

The indirect benefits, **often strategic**, of better information are also very difficult to quantify. Organisations may find it very difficult to assess how much better information about customers has impacted upon customer service, or improved information about competitors yielded a competitive advantage. Internal benefits might include **improving the linkages** between **processes and activities**, and **improved organisational performance** in areas other those where the new systems are introduced

Dealing with **risk** may be very problematic. The discount rates used can be adjusted for risk. However even with simple projects deciding what this adjustment might be is problematic; as information technology projects carry a number of different risks, some of which may not be apparent immediately, it may be impossible to make a confident adjustment to the rate.

Possible methods for dealing with unquantifiable benefits include:

(a) Carry out the NPV analysis using alternative values for intangibles

(b) Treat intangibles as options

(c) Calculate the NPV for the quantifiable cash flows. If it is positive, accept the investment. If it is negative, calculate the value of intangibles to make the net present value zero and assess whether these values appear to be realistic.

2.3 Other methods

Along with financial analysis methods, other investment appraisal methods can be appropriate in different circumstances.

(a) **Balanced scorecard**

A balanced scorecard approach covering multiple goals is likely to be most appropriate if systems are meant to change fundamentally the way the organisation is **managed**, by for example removing constraints or increasing flexibility. If improvements are to result in better forecasting or planning, changes in the organisational structure may also be required.

(b) **Strategic analysis**

Use of Porter's model to assess the impact of systems on competitive forces should be used if information systems are designed to help the organisation achieve **competitive advantage.**

Strategy	How IS/IT can support the strategy
Cost-leadership	By facilitating reductions in cost levels, for example by reducing the number of administration staff required. Allowing better resource utilisation, for example by providing accurate stock information allowing lower 'buffer' inventories to be held. Using IT to support just-in-time and advanced manufacturing systems.
Differentiation	Differentiation can be suggested by IT, perhaps in the product itself or in the way it is marketed. The publishing example quoted earlier provides evidence of this – with the move from paper-based products to electronic.
Focus	IT may enable a more customised or specialised product/service to be produced. IT also facilitates the collection of sales and customer information that identifies targetable market segments.

IT can also keep competitors away by raising the costs of entry, or improved IT can be an entry mechanism. IT can help tie in customers by raising the costs of switching.

(c) **Business case analysis**

Business case analysis is helpful if systems are being used to **generate new business**. It needs to cover financial consequences, marketing and operational issues.

2.4 Technical and operational viability

As well as assessing viability in terms of financial value or benefits to the business, technical and operational issues must also be considered carefully.

Key **technical issues** might include:

- Availability of technology
- Skills necessary to use technology
- Changes in risk profile
- Compatibility with existing systems
- The systems' number of users and transaction/data volumes

Important **operational issues** include:

- Availability and reliability of data
- Strong operational procedures
- Level of support and commitment
- Human resource implications
- Impacts on external stakeholders

Question

New information system

Learning outcome: E(ii)

NEST is a national furniture retailer operating from twelve large showrooms on retail parks close to the principal motorways. The present management information system was set up in 20X0 and since that time the business has expanded rapidly. A new project for the design and implementation of a new system to meet current and future needs will commence soon. There is some urgency as the present system frequency 'crashes' leaving staff with the problem of explaining delays to dissatisfied customers. Staff turnover among systems personnel is high.

Required

Write a memorandum to the Head of Systems to explain the need for a cost-benefit assessment of the proposed new system.

Answer

MEMORANDUM

To: Head of systems
From: Accountant
Date: 24 July 20X4
Re: Cost benefit assessment of the proposed new system

The primary purpose of the cost benefit assessment is to ensure that the **benefits are greater** than the **costs**.

It is important to include both **capital and revenue costs** and to cover all of the setting up, running and maintenance expenses. Costs should include the following.

(a) **Hardware, software, computer room modifications, cabling and ancillary equipment** (for example modems).

(b) **Set-up costs** for analysis, design, specification, programming etc, file conversion; to training implementation and testing, staff recruitment.

(c) **Ongoing costs**: wages of systems staff, telecoms costs, power, consumables, further training, fallback facilities.

(d) **Investment in training** will be particularly important as part of a strategy to reduce staff turnover.

Benefits are much harder to express quantitatively but there are some that will be of particular value to Nest.

(a) **Improved customer satisfaction**: a higher level of reliability of the system will increase customer confidence and goodwill and reduce customer complaints.

(b) **Higher staff morale** resulting from improved self-esteem and teamworking with the new reliable system.

(c) The **saving of valuable time** spent resolving the consequences of current 'crashes'. This in turn may bring the further benefits of higher sales and improved inventory control.

(d) **Improved decision making** based on high quality information.

Capital investment appraisal techniques can help to evaluate the project, using payback period, accounting rate of return or discounted cash flow methods.

Whilst it is impossible to eliminate the risks associated with the project entirely, careful assessment of the costs and benefits will give the company confidence to proceed with the required new system.

Chapter roundup

- Organisations require different **types of information system** to provide **different levels** of information in a range of **functional areas**.
- There are six major types of Information Systems: Executive Support Systems (**ESS**), Management Information Systems (**MIS**), Decision Support Systems (**DSS**), Knowledge Work Systems (**KWS**), Office Automation Systems (**OAS**) and Transaction Processing Systems (**TPS**).
- Although **cost-benefit analysis** should be used to evaluate information systems, the **wider operational and control issues** mean that other methods such as the **balanced scorecard** should also be used.
- As well as fulfilling financial criteria, systems must also be **technically and operationally viable.**

Quick quiz

1 What is a system that facilitates the creation and integration of new knowledge into an information management system called?

2 A system that pools data from internal and external sources and makes information available to senior managers in an easy to use form is called an executive support system.

True ☐

False ☐

3 What sorts of information system are designed to increase the productivity of data and information workers?

4 __________ ______________ ___________ are systems that combine data and analytical models or data analysis tools to support semi-structured and unstructured decision-making.

5 Management information systems are systems designed to perform and record routine transactions.

True ☐

False ☐

6 Match the following examples of systems to the types of system they are

A	Inventory control	1	ESS
B	Electronic calendars	2	MIS
C	Engineering work stations	3	DSS
D	Order tracking	4	KWS
E	Sales region analysis	5	OAS
F	Human resource planning	6	TPS

7 Name three methods other than cost-benefit analysis, that can be used to appraise information systems.

8 Give three examples of technical issues that should be considered when assessing the viability of a system.

Answers to quick quiz

1 A knowledge information system.

2 True

3 Office automation systems

4 **Decision support systems** are systems that combine data and analytical models or data analysis tools to support semi-structured and unstructured decision-making.

5 False. Transaction processing systems are systems designed to perform and record routine transactions Management information systems are systems that convert data, mainly from internal systems into information.

6 A2
B5
C4
D6
E3
F1

7
- Balanced scorecard
- Strategic analysis
- Business case analysis

8
- Availability of technology
- Skills needed to use technology
- Changes in risk profile
- Compatibility with existing systems
- Performance criteria based on usage and volumes

Now try the question below from the Exam Question Bank

Number	Level	Marks	Time
Q22	Examination	25	45 mins

23

Organising the information technology function

Introduction

As with any business function, the way in which the **information technology function** is organised will impact significantly on the service able to be offered and delivered.

We begin this chapter by looking at the different ways of **structuring** the information systems function. We then move on to explore wider organisational issues, including the options available to account for the costs associated with information systems.

The chapter concludes with the pros and cons of **outsourcing**. The syllabus and learning outcomes relevant to this chapter emphasise the criteria for selecting outsourcing partners and for managing ongoing relationships. Among the major issues covered are service level agreements, discontinuation/change of supplier and hand-over considerations.

Topic list	Learning outcomes	Syllabus references	Ability required
1 Information systems department	E(iii)	E(4)	Evaluation
2 Centralisation and decentralisation	E(iii)	E(4)	Evaluation
3 Accounting issues	E(iii)	E(4)	Evaluation
4 Other organisational issues	E(iii)	E(4)	Evaluation
5 Outsourcing	E(iii)	E(5),(6)	Evaluation

1 Information systems department

FAST FORWARD

The **IS/IT manager** and the **IS/IT director** is responsible for strategy development, risk management and infrastructure

The IS/IT **steering committee** makes decisions relating to the future use and development of IS/IT.

The **database administrator** is responsible for all data and information held within an organisation.

An **Information Centre** (IC) provides support for computer users within the organisation.

1.1 Directing information systems

Most organisations choose have an information systems department, or team responsible for the tasks and responsibilities associated with information systems. In some organisations this department may be referred to as the information technology department – as information systems increasingly utilise information technology.

In a small company, information systems may be the responsibility of the finance director or the company secretary or simply an office manager. In larger organisations there may be an **information systems director** and/or an **information systems manager**.

The IS/IT director or manager would have responsibility for the following areas.

IS/IT director responsibility	Comment
IS/IT strategy development	The IS/IT strategy must compliment the overall strategy of the organisation. The strategy must also be achievable given budgetary constraints. Returns on investments in IS/IT should be monitored.
IS/IT risk management	This is a wide ranging area including legal risks, such as ensuring compliance with relevant data protection legislation, ensuring adequate IS/IT security measures and disaster recovery arrangements.
Steering committee	The IS/IT director should play a key role in a steering committee set up to oversee the role of IS/IT within the organisation. There is more on steering committees later in this chapter.
IS/IT infrastructure	Standards should be set for the purchase and use of hardware and software within the organisation.
Ensuring employees have the IS/IT support and tools the require	Efficient links are required between IS/IT staff and the rest of the organisation. Technical assistance should be easily obtainable.

An IS/IT director therefore requires a wide range of skills. The ideal person would possess technical know-how, excellent general management ability, a keen sense of business awareness and a good understanding of the organisations' operations.

In the following paragraphs we explain some of the key personnel and roles that may be present in an information systems department.

1.2 IS/IT steering committee

Organisations may set up a **steering committee** to oversee all information system development. A steering committee might also be set up for a 'one-off' computer-related project. The steering committee's tasks may include the following.

(a) To **approve (or reject) projects** whose total budgeted cost is below a certain limit and so within their authorisation limit.

(b) To **recommend projects** to the board of directors for acceptance when their cost is high enough to call for approval at board level.

(c) To establish **company guidelines** within the framework of the IT strategy for the development of computer-based processing and management information systems.

(d) The **co-ordination and control** of the work of the study group(s) and project development groups, in respect of the development time, the cost and the technical quality of the investigations.

(e) The **evaluation** of the feasibility study reports and system specifications. The steering committee must be satisfied that each new system has been properly justified.

(f) To monitor and **review each new system after implementation** to check whether the system has met its objectives. If it hasn't, to investigate the reasons for the system's failure, and take any suitable control or remedial measures.

(g) In an organisation which has a continuing programme of new DP projects, assessing the contribution of each project to the long-term **corporate objectives** of the organisation, ranking projects in order of **priority** and assigning resources to the most important projects first, and taking decisions to defer projects when insufficient resources are available.

The steering committee might include the following.

- The **information director**, or a senior IS staff member
- **Accountants** for advice relating to costs and benefits
- Senior **user management**

1.3 Database administrator

A key information systems role is that of database administrator. A database administrator is responsible for all data and information held within an organisation. Key tasks include:

- Preparing and maintaining a record of all data held within the organisation (the data dictionary)
- Co-ordinating data and information use to avoid duplication and maximise efficiency
- Analysing the data requirements of new applications
- Implementing and controlling procedures to protect data integrity
- Recording data ownership

1.4 Operations control

Operations control is concerned with ensuring IS/IT systems are working and available to users. Key tasks include:

- Maintaining the IS/IT infrastructure
- Monitoring network usage and managing network resources
- Keeping employees informed, eg advance warning of service interruptions
- Virus protection measures eg ensuring anti-virus software updates are loaded
- Fault fixing

1.5 Systems development staff

In medium to large organisations in is likely that the IS department will include staff with programming and systems analysis skills. Key tasks for staff involved in systems development include:

- Systems analysis
- Systems design and specification
- Systems testing
- Systems evaluation and review

1.6 Data processing staff

Over the past two decades the traditional centralised data processing department has become less common. Most departments now process their own data using on-line systems, rather than batching up transactions and forwarding paper copies of them to a centralised department for processing.

Staff involved in data processing today are spread throughout the organisation, for example a call centre employee may input an order, an accounts clerk may process journal entries etc. Accurate data entry skills and an understanding of the task they are performing are key skills.

1.7 Information centre staff

Key term

An **Information Centre (IC)** is a small unit of staff with a good technical awareness of computer systems, whose task is to provide a support function to computer users within the organisation.

Information centres, sometimes referred to as **support centres**, are particularly useful in organisations which use distributed systems and so are likely to have hardware, data and software scattered throughout the organisation.

1.7.1 Help

An IC usually offers a **Help Desk** to solve IT problems. Help may be via the telephone, e-mail, through a searchable knowledge base or in person.

Remote diagnostic software may be used which enables staff in the IC to take control of a computer and sort out the problem without leaving their desk.

The help desk needs sufficient staff and technical expertise to respond quickly and effectively to requests for help. IC staff should also maintain good relationships with hardware and software suppliers to ensure their maintenance staff are quickly on site when needed.

1.7.2 Problem solving

The IC will **maintain a record of problems** and identify those that occur most often. If the problem is that users do not know how to use the system, training is provided.

Training applications often contain **analysis software**, drawing attention to trainee progress and common problems. This information enables the IC to identify and address specific training needs more closely.

If the problem is with the system itself, a solution is found, either by modifying the system or by **investment in new hardware or software**.

1.7.3 Improvements

The IC may also be required to consider the **viability of suggestions** for improving the system, and to bring these improvements into effect.

1.7.4 Standards

The IC is also likely to be responsible for setting, and encouraging users to conform to, common **standards**.

(a) **Hardware standards** ensure that all of the equipment used in the organisation is compatible and can be put into use in different departments as needed.

(b) **Software standards** ensure that information generated by one department can easily be shared with and worked upon by other departments.

(c) **Programming standards** ensure that applications developed by individual end-users (for example complex spreadsheet macros) follow best practice and are easy to modify.

(d) **Data processing standards** ensure that certain conventions such as the format of file names are followed throughout the organisation. This facilitates sharing, storage and retrieval of information.

1.7.5 Security

The IC may help to preserve the security of data in various ways.

(a) It may develop **utility programs** and **procedures** to ensure that back-ups are made at regular intervals.

(b) The IC may **help to preserve the company's systems** from attack by computer viruses, for instance by ensuring that the latest versions of anti-virus software are available to all users, by reminding users regularly about the dangers of viruses, and by setting up and maintaining 'firewalls', which deny access to sensitive parts of the company's systems.

1.7.6 End-user applications development

An IC can help applications development by providing **technical guidance** to end-user developers and to encourage comprehensible and well-documented programs. Understandable programs can be maintained or modified more easily. Documentation provides a means of teaching others how the programs work. These efforts can greatly extend the usefulness and life of the programs that are developed.

2 Centralisation and decentralisation

FAST FORWARD

A **centralised IS/IT department** has the advantages of the **same information** being used, **better security and control**, and possibly **greater expertise**.

A **decentralised IS/IT department** has the advantages of **greater knowledge** of **local requirements** and **quicker responsiveness**.

2.1 Organising the IT department

We now look at how the IS/IT department could be structured. There are two main options - centralised or decentralised. (Note that in this section we are discussing the structure of a department – rather than the information system architecture structure we covered in Chapter 3.)

Key terms

A **centralised** IS/IT department involves all IS/IT staff and functions being based out at a single central location, such as head office.

A **decentralised** IS/IT department involves IS/IT staff and functions being spread out throughout the organisation.

There is no single 'best' structure for an IS/IT department – an organisation should consider its IS/IT requirements and the merits of each structure.

2.2 Centralisation of IS/IT department

2.2.1 Advantages of a centralised IS/IT department

(a) Assuming centralised processing is used, there is only one set of files. Everyone uses the **same data and information**.

(b) It gives **better security/control** over data and files. It is easier to enforce standards.

(c) Head office is in a **better position** to know what is going on.

(d) There may be **economies of scale** available in purchasing computer equipment and supplies.

(e) Computer staff are in a **single location**, and **more expert staff** are likely to be employed. Career paths may be more clearly defined.

2.2.2 Disadvantages of a centralised IS/IT department

(a) Local offices might have to **wait** for IS/IT services and assistance.
(b) **Reliance on head office**. Local offices are less self-sufficient.
(c) A **system fault** at head office will impact across the organisation.

2.3 Decentralisation of IS/IT department

2.3.1 Advantages of a decentralised IS/IT department

(a) IS/IT staff will be **more aware** of **local business requirements**.

(b) Each office is **more self-sufficient**.

(c) Offices are likely to have **quicker access** to IS/IT support/advice.

(d) A decentralised structure is more likely to **facilitate accurate IS/IT cost/overhead allocations**.

2.3.2 Disadvantages of a decentralised IS/IT department

(a) **Control** may be more **difficult** - different and uncoordinated information systems may be introduced.

(b) Self-sufficiency may encourage a **lack of co-ordination** between departments.

(c) **Increased risk of data duplication**, with different offices holding the same data on their own separate files.

3 Accounting issues

FAST FORWARD

There are three broad possibilities when **accounting for costs** related to information systems.

- IS costs are treated as an administrative **overhead**
- IS costs are **charged out at cost**
- IS costs are **charged out at market rates**

Some organisations establish IT as a **separate company,** which may lead to **greater profits** and **better opportunities** for staff, but may result in a worse service to the main organisation

3.1 Costs of IS/IT department

Providing and maintaining information systems to deliver good quality information involves significant expenditure. The costs incurred are summarised in the following table.

Capital costs	Revenue costs (one-off)	Revenue costs (ongoing)
Hardware purchase Cabling System installation	System development costs eg programmer and analyst fees, testing costs, file conversion costs etc Initial training costs Any redundancy costs attributable to the new system	IS/IT staff costs Communication and transmission costs Power System maintenance and support Ongoing training Consumables such as paper, printer ink, floppy disks, CDs etc

The organisation must account for the costs incurred providing and maintaining information systems. The IS charging system should encourage the efficient use of IS/IT resources. There are three broad possibilities when accounting for costs related to information systems.

- IS costs are treated as an **administrative overhead**
- IS costs are **charged out at cost**
- IS costs are **charged out at market rates**

3.2 Information technology as an administrative overhead

Under this system IT/IS costs are treated as a general administrative expense, and are not allocated to user departments.

Advantages of this approach are:

(a) It is **simple and cheap to administer**, as there is no charge out system to operate.

(b) It may **encourage innovation and experimentation** as user-departments are more likely to demand better quality systems if they will not bear any cost.

(c) The relationship between IS staff and user departments is **not subject** to **conflict over costs**.

Disadvantages of this approach are:

(a) User departments may make **unreasonable** (and economically unjustifiable) **demands**.

(b) Any **inefficiencies** within the IS/IT department are **less likely to be exposed** - as user departments will not be monitoring cost levels.

(c) User departments may **accept sub-standard service**, as it is 'free'.

(d) A **true picture** of **user departments financial performance** is **not obtained** - as significant costs attributable to that department are held in a central pool.

3.3 Information technology charged out at cost

A cost-based charge out involves IS/IT costs being allocated to user departments. Costs may be allocated according to methods such as: cost per transaction processed; cost per page; cost per hour of programmer's and/or analyst's time; cost per number of terminals/workstations; cost per unit of processing time.

However, collecting and analysing the detailed information required to allocate costs using these indicators can be time-consuming, and therefore costly. For the sake of simplicity therefore, the allocation across user departments may be based on a relatively simple measure such as an estimate of IS/IT use.

The **advantages** of re-charging IS/IT costs to user departments, at cost, are:

(a) **Simpler** than **charging at market value** - the amount recharged is the total IS/IT costs incurred.

(b) **User departments** are **encouraged** to **consider the cost** of their usage of IT services.

(c) **It encourages efficiency** within the IS/IT department as excessive recharges are likely to result in complaints from other departments.

Disadvantages exist, too.

(a) **Inefficiencies in the IS/IT department** are merely **passed on to users**. This could be avoided if the department is only permitted to recharge budgeted or standard costs.

(b) The **basis for recharging** must be **realistic** - or users will feel that costs recharged are unfair which could lead to conflict.

(c) It may be **difficult to choose** a **realistic basis** to allocate the costs.

Under both the central overhead approach and the charge-out-at-cost approach the IS function is treated as a cost centre. This can influence the way in which information systems and technology are viewed within an organisation – it encourages the view that they are a drain on resources rather than tools in the quest for competitive advantage.

3.4 Market-based charge out methods

Under market-based methods, the IS/IT department acts as a profit centre. It sets its own prices and charges for its services with the aim of making a profit.

Advantages of the market-based charge out method include:

(a) User departments have the **right to demand external standards** of service. If the service provided by the IT department is sub-standard, it should be given the chance to improve - with the ultimate sanction of users choosing an outside supplier.

(b) It encourages an **entrepreneurial attitude**. IT managers are in charge of a department that could make a profit - this should help motivation.

(c) **Efficiency and innovation** within the IS/IT department is encouraged, as the more efficient the department is, and the more services users buy, the greater the profit will be. Bonuses for IT staff could be based on departmental profit.

(d) A **true picture** of user departments **financial performance** is able to be obtained - as the IS/IT costs charged to each department are based on market-rates.

Disadvantages of the market-based charge out method include:

(a) It can be **difficult to decide** on the **charge out rate**, particularly if there is no comparable service provider outside the organisation.

(b) If users feel rates are excessive, they may **reduce their usage** to below optimal levels, and **relationships** between the **IS/IT department** and **user departments** may become **strained**.

(c) Even if the service provided is poor, it may **not** be in the **organisation's interest** for user departments to buy from outsiders: the IS function's fixed costs still have to be covered, and there may result an under-use of resources available within the organisation. Also, a coherent approach to IS/IT should be taken - this would be difficult if a range of suppliers were used across the organisation.

3.5 Establishing the IS/IT function as a separate company

The concept of establishing the IS/IT department as a profit centre can be taken a step further; The IS/IT function could become a separate company, with a separate legal entity.

User departments within the 'main' company would **purchase IS/IT services** from the separate IS/IT company, and ideally should be free to change suppliers if service or value levels are sub-standard.

The new IS/IT company can also offer its services to **other organisations** with the aim of increasing revenue and profit.

The advantages and disadvantages of market-based charge out methods covered earlier also apply to situations where a separate company has been set up.

Additional advantages include:

(a) The **opportunity for increased revenue** and **profit**.
(b) **Increased career opportunities** for IS/IT staff.
(c) **Opportunities for economies of scale** if the company grows.

Additional disadvantages include:

(a) IS/IT staff **may lose touch** with main **company operations**.

(b) **Increased administration** required for the additional company.

(c) The **standard of service provided** to the **main company** may suffer, as the focus switches to new clients.

(d) **Setting appropriate prices** for new clients may be difficult. Tasks may not be similar to those undertaken within the original company.

4 Other organisational issues

FAST FORWARD

A **legacy system** is an old outdated system that continues to be used, but no longer meets the information requirements of the organisation.

4.1 Organisation structure

The structure of the organisation and the structure of the organisation's information systems are related issues. Organisations that disperse decision making power to local offices will require an effective local management information system.

4.2 Constant change

A reliance on IS/IT commits an organisation to **continual change**. The pace of technological change is rapid. Computer systems - both hardware and software - are likely to be superseded after a few years.

4.3 Interoperability

Interoperability refers to the ability of systems to **share and exchange information** and facilities with other systems regardless of the technology platform or service provider. Interoperability implies an ability to cope with a variety of data structures, and the easy transfer of skills between applications and technologies.

4.4 Backward compatibility

A new version of a program is said to be backward compatible if it can **use files and data created with an older version** of the same program. Computer hardware is said to be backward compatible if it can run the same software as previous models.

Backward compatibility is important because it **eliminates the need to start afresh** when upgrading. In general, manufacturers try to keep their products backward compatible. Sometimes, however, it is necessary to sacrifice backward compatibility to take advantage of new technology.

4.5 Legacy system

A legacy system is an old outdated system which continues to be used, but no longer meets the information requirements of the organisation. The main reason(s) legacy systems continue to be used often include the **cost of replacing** it, and the significant time and effort involved in introducing a new system.

Legacy systems often require **specialised knowledge** to **maintain them** in a condition suitable for operation. This may leave an **organisation exposed** should certain staff leave the organisation.

Legacy systems may also require data to be in a **specific, maybe unusual format**. This can cause compatibility problems if other systems are replaced throughout an organisation.

File conversion issues are common when replacing legacy systems, for example:

- Establishing the formats of data files held on the legacy system
- Assessing the data held for accuracy and completeness

- Automated file conversion procedures may not be applicable due to system compatibility and data issues
- Ensuring transferred data is available in the required format for all applications that access it

4.6 Open systems

Organisations develop computerised systems over a period of time, perhaps focusing on different functions at different times. The ease with which systems interact with each other is important for organisation efficiency. Examples of inefficiencies caused by systems incompatibility include:

(a) **Hardware** supplied by **different manufacturers** that cannot interact.

(b) **Data duplicated** in **different areas** of the business as separate systems can not use the same source.

(c) **Software** that is **unable to interact** with other packages.

Open systems aim to ensure compatibility between different systems. An open systems infrastructure supports organisation-wide functions and allows interoperability of networks and systems. Authorised users are able to access applications and data from any part of the system.

5 Outsourcing

FAST FORWARD

Outsourcing is the contracting out of operations or services. There are various outsourcing options available, with different levels of control maintained 'in-house'. Outsourcing has **advantages** (eg use of highly skilled people) and **disadvantages** (eg lack of control).

Key term

Outsourcing is the contracting out of specified operations or services to an external vendor.

5.1 Types of outsourcing

There are four **broad classifications** of outsourcing, as described in the following table.

Classification	Comment
Ad-hoc	The organisation has a short-term requirement for increased IS/IT skills. An example would be employing programmers on a short-term contract to help with the programming of bespoke software.
Project management	The development and installation of a particular IS/IT project is outsourced. For example, a new accounting system. (This approach is sometimes referred to as **systems integration.**)
Partial	Some IT/IS services are outsourced. Examples include hardware maintenance, network management or ongoing website management.
Total	An external supplier provides the vast majority of an organisation's IT/IS services; eg third party owns or is responsible for IT equipment, software and staff.

5.2 Levels of service provision

The degree to which the provision and management of IS/IT services are transferred to the third party varies according to the situation and the skills of both organisations.

(a) **Time-share**.

The vendor charges for access to an external processing system on a time-used basis. Software ownership may be with either the vendor or the client organisation.

(b) **Service bureaux**

Service bureaux usually focus on a specific function. Traditionally bureaux would provide the same type of service to many organisations eg payroll processing. As organisations have developed their own IT infrastructure, the use of bureaux has decreased.

(c) **Facilities management (FM)**.

The terms 'outsourcing' and 'facilities management' are sometimes confused. Facilities management traditionally involved contracts for premises-related services such as cleaning or site security.

In the context of IS/IT, facilities management involves an outside agency managing the organisation's IS/IT facilities. All equipment usually remains with the client, but the responsibility for providing and managing the specified services rests with the FM company. FM companies operating in the UK include Accenture and Cap Gemini.

The following table shows the main features of each of the outsourcing arrangements described above.

	Outsourcing arrangement		
Feature	**Timeshare**	**Service bureaux**	**Facilities Management (FM)**
Management responsibility	Mostly retained	Some retained	Very little retained
Focus	Operational	A function	Strategic
Timescale	Short-term	Medium-term	Long-term
Justification	Cost savings	More efficient	Access to expertise; higher quality service provision. Enables management to concentrate on the areas where they do possess expertise.

5.3 Organisations involved in outsourcing

5.3.1 Facilities management companies

FM arrangements have been covered in paragraph 5.2(c).

5.3.2 Software houses

Software houses concentrate on the provision of 'software services'. These services include feasibility studies, systems analysis and design, development of operating systems software, provision of application program packages, 'tailor-made' application programming, specialist systems advice, and so on. For example, a software house might be employed to write a computerised system for the London Stock Exchange.

5.3.3 Consultancy firms

Some consultancy firms work at a fairly high level, giving advice to management on the general approach to solving problems and on the types of system to use. Others specialise in giving more particular systems advice, carrying out feasibility studies and recommending computer manufacturers/software houses that will supply the right system. When a consultancy firm is used, the terms of the contract should be agreed at the outset.

The use of consultancy services enables management to learn directly or indirectly from the experience of others. Many larger consultancies are owned by big international accountancy firms; smaller consultancies may consist of one- or two-person outfits with a high level of specialist experience in one area.

The following categories of **consulting activity** have been identified by *Beaumont* and *Sutherland*.

(a) **Strategic studies**, involving the development of a business strategy or an IS strategy for an organisation.

(b) **Specialist studies**, where the consultant provides a high level of expertise in one area, for example Enterprise Resource Management software.

(c) **Project management**, involving supervision of internal and external parties in the completion of a particular project.

(d) **Body-shopping**, where the necessary staff, including consultants, project managers, systems analysts and programmers, for a project are identified.

(e) **Recruitment**, involving the supply of permanent or temporary staff.

5.3.4 Hardware manufacturers and suppliers

Computer manufacturers or their designated suppliers will provide the **equipment** necessary for a system. They will also provide, under a **maintenance contract**, engineers who will deal with any routine servicing and with any breakdown of the equipment.

Case Study

The retailer Sears outsourced the management of its vast information technology and accounting functions to Accenture. First year *savings* were estimated to be £5 million per annum, growing to £14 million in the following year, and thereafter. This is clearly considerable, although re-organisation costs relating to redundancies, relocation and asset write-offs are thought to be in the region of £35 million. About 900 staff were involved: under the transfer of undertakings regulations (which protect employees when part or all of a company changes hands), Accenture was obliged to take on the existing Sears staff. This provided new opportunities for the staff who moved, while those who remained at Sears are free to concentrate on strategy development and management direction.

5.4 Developments in outsourcing

Outsourcing arrangements are becoming increasingly flexible to cope with the ever-changing nature of the modern business environment. Three trends are:

(a) **Multiple sourcing**.

This involves outsourcing different functions or areas of the IS/IT function to a range of suppliers. Some suppliers may form alliances to present a stronger case for selection.

(b) **Incremental approach**.

Organisations progressively outsource selected areas of their IT/IS function. Possible problems with outsourced services are solved before progressing to the next stage.

(c) **Joint venture sourcing**.

This term is used to describe an organisation entering into a joint venture with a supplier. The costs (risks) and possible rewards are split on an agreed basis. Such an arrangement may be suitable when developing software that could be sold to other organisations.

(d) **Application Service Providers (ASP)**.

ASPs are third parties that manage and distribute software services and solutions to customers across a Wide Area Network. ASPs could be considered the modern equivalent of the traditional computer bureaux.

5.5 Managing outsourcing arrangements

Managing outsourcing arrangements involves deciding what will be outsourced, choosing and negotiating with suppliers and managing the supplier relationship.

When considering whether to outsource a particular service the following questions are relevant.

(a) Is the system of **strategic importance**? Strategic IS are generally not suited to outsourcing as they require a high degree of specific business knowledge that a third party IT specialist can not be expected to possess.

(b) Can the system be **relatively isolated**? Functions that have only limited interfaces are most easily outsourced eg payroll.

(c) Do we know **enough about the system** to manage the outsourced service agreement? If an organisation knows very little about a technology it may be difficult to know what constitutes good service and value for money. It may be necessary to recruit additional expertise to manage the relationship with the other party.

(d) Are our requirements likely to change? Organisations should avoid tying themselves into a long-term outsourcing agreement if requirements are likely to change.

5.6 The tendering process

The organisation needs to make certain specifications about what it requires when inviting tenders for outsourcing. The most important decision is the **nature of the relationship** between the **organisation** and the **service provider**. This will depend on the **service** that has been **outsourced**.

(a) If full facilities management is involved, and almost all management responsibility for IT/IS lies with the entity providing the service, then a close relationship between the parties is necessary (a '**partnership**'). The relationship is likely to be founded on broadly drawn, incentive-based contracts with the expectation that the customer and supplier will do business over many years.

(b) On the other hand, if a **relatively simple function** such as payroll were outsourced, such a close relationship with the supplier would not be necessary. A 'typical' supplier - customer relationship is all that is required. (Although issues such as confidentiality need to be considered with payroll data.) Contracts here are likely to be very detailed.

When inviting applications for tender, the organisation also needs to consider:

- Whether to have an open tendering process or whether to invite applications from selected suppliers. Selecting potential suppliers in advance is more likely if a close relationship is being sought and the tendering organisation is seeking the partner best able to understand the **philosophy** and **objectives** of the organisation, especially in the area of development.
- Whether to **outsource other activities** at the same time. If a business is shifting its focus significantly, it might well seek outsourcing partners who possess the relevant experience and skills in the areas in which it seeks to develop.
- Whether to seek a **single partner** or a **number of partners**. Large organisations may decide they need different partners for different skills.

Requests for tender need to make clear the **required product delivery**, the **present** and **planned hardware** and **software configuration** and the **history and future expectations** of the organisation. The potential suppliers must understand how the bids will be **evaluated**.

5.6.1 Service level agreement

A key factor when choosing and negotiating with external vendors is the contract offered and subsequently negotiated with the supplier. The contract is sometimes referred to as the **Service Level Contract** (SLC) or **Service Level Agreement** (SLA).

The key elements of the contract are described in the following table.

Contract element	Comment
Timescale	When does the contract expire? Is the timescale suitable for the organisation's needs or should it be renegotiated?
Service level	The contract should clearly specify **minimum levels of service** to be provided. Penalties should be specified for failure to meet these standards. Relevant factors will vary depending on the nature of the services outsourced but could include: Response time to requests for assistance/information System 'uptime' percentage Deadlines for performing relevant tasks
Exit route	Arrangements for an exit route, addressing how transfer to another supplier, or the move back in-house, would be conducted.
Software ownership	Relevant factors include: Software licensing and security If the arrangement includes the development of new software who owns the copyright?
Dependencies	If related services are outsourced the level of service quality agreed should group these services together.
Employment issues	If the arrangement includes provision for the organisation's IT staff to move to the third party, employer responsibilities must be specified clearly.

5.6.2 Dealing with the supplier

The organisation also needs to decide the roles of the staff who will deal with the outsourcing supplier. **The managers** and **staff involved** will be **responsible** for **managing service level** and **delivery** and business development. They will need to have the **technical capability** to assess the performance of the provider, but will also need to have the necessary **contract management skills**.

The **degree of monitoring** required will also need to be considered carefully. Heavy monitoring could mean internal costs are high, as a lot of specialists will be checking all aspects of the service provision at regular stages in the process, but on the other hand risk will be low as problems should be identified early. Loose monitoring focused on end results will have lower costs, but problems will not be picked up until the end of the process or, worst of all, picked up by customers.

Another important decision in the organisation is whether its staff should deal directly with the suppliers or whether it should operate through an internal intermediary. Using the remaining internal IT department as the intermediary has the advantages of providing a **single focus** for the relationship, **better control of costs** (as the demands other users make directly may incur extra charges) and **better monitoring** of usage of service. An internal intermediary is probably essential in larger organisations where there are multiple IT suppliers.

5.6.3 Changeover arrangements

Over time the services outsourced may be re-tendered and the supplier changed. The changeover may present certain problems that need to be anticipated, with the initial contract including the necessary provisions. Possible problems include:

(a) **Loss of copyright** on **own software** run by vendor. Explicit contract clauses should cover the **ownership of the software**, its **security** and its **confidentiality**

(b) **Loss of copyright** on **software** vendor develops as part of outsourcing. Again the contract needs to be clear, although here considerations of cost, product value and exclusivity will influence who holds the copyright

(c) **Dependence on supplier** for IT for which supplier has **exclusive rights**. To avoid this the organisation should only use what they own, have right to, is publicly available or easily replaced.

(d) **Partial transfer** to another supplier. **Separate contracts** for separate services should be drawn up to minimise problems when the original supplier is still supplying some services, but others have been transferred to a new supplier.

Question

Outsourcing

Learning outcome: E(iii)

Do any organisations with which you are familiar use outsourcing? What is the view of outsourcing in the organisation?

Answer

One view is given below.

The PA Consulting Group's annual survey of outsourcing found that 'on average the top five strategic outsourcers out-performed the FTSE by more than 100 per cent over three years; the bottom five under-performed by more than 66%'.

However the survey revealed that of those organisations who have opted to outsource IT functions, only five per cent are truly happy with the results. A spokesman for the consultants said that this is because most people fail to adopt a proper strategic approach, taking a view that is neither long-term nor broad enough, and taking outsourcing decisions that are piecemeal and unsatisfactory.

This lack of prescience is compounded by a failure to take a sufficiently rigorous approach to selection, specification, contract drafting and contract management.

The survey found that a constant complaint among many of those interviewed is the lack of ability of outsourcing organisations to work together.

Twenty-five per cent of those asked would bring the functions they had outsourced back in-house if it were possible.

5.7 Advantages of outsourcing arrangements

The **advantages** of outsourcing are as follows.

(a) Outsourcing can remove uncertainty about **cost**, as there is often a long-term contract where services are specified in advance for a **fixed price**. If computing services are inefficient, the costs will be borne by the FM company. This is also an incentive to the third party to provide a high quality service.

(b) Long-term contracts (maybe up to ten years) encourage **planning** for the future.

(c) Outsourcing can bring the benefits of **economies of scale**. For example, a FM company may conduct research into new technologies that benefits a number of their clients.

(d) A specialist organisation is able to retain **skills and knowledge**. Many organisations would not have a sufficiently well-developed IT department to offer IT staff opportunities for career development. Talented staff would leave to pursue their careers elsewhere.

(e) New skills and knowledge become available. A specialist company can **share** staff with **specific expertise** between several clients. This allows the outsourcing company to take advantage of new developments without the need to recruit new people or re-train existing staff, and without the cost.

(f) **Flexibility** (contract permitting). Resources may be able to be scaled up or down depending upon demand. For instance, during a major changeover from one system to another the number of IT staff needed may be twice as large as it will be once the new system is working satisfactorily.

An outsourcing organisation is more able to arrange its work on a **project** basis, whereby some staff will expect to be moved periodically from one project to the next.

5.8 Disadvantages of outsourcing arrangements

Some possible **drawbacks** are outlined below.

(a) It is arguable that information and its provision is an **inherent part of the business** and of management. Unlike office cleaning, or catering, an organisation's IT services may be too important to be contracted out. Information is at the heart of management.

(b) A company may have highly **confidential information** and to let outsiders handle it could be seen as **risky** in commercial and/or legal terms.

(c) If a third party is handling IS/IT services there is no onus upon internal management to keep up with new developments or to suggest new ideas. Consequently, opportunities to gain **competitive advantage** may be missed. Any new technology or application devised by the third party is likely to be available to competitors.

(d) An organisation may find itself **locked in** to an unsatisfactory contract. The decision may be very difficult to reverse. If the service provider supplies unsatisfactory levels of service, the effort and expense the organisation would incur to rebuild its own computing function or to move to another provider could be substantial.

(e) The use of an outside organisation does not encourage awareness of the potential **costs** and benefits of IS/IT within the organisation. If managers cannot manage in-house IS/IT resources effectively, then it could be argued that they will not be able to manage an arrangement to outsource effectively either.

5.9 Insourcing

FAST FORWARD

Insourcing involves recruiting IS/IT staff internally, from other areas of the business, and teaching these business-savvy employees about technology.

Supporters of **insourcing** believe it is easier (and cheaper) to teach technical skills to business people than to teach business skills to technical people.

Outsourcing involves purchasing information technology expertise from outside the organisation. Several factors have led some to believe this is not the best solution in today's environment.

(a) Many organisations have found there is a shortage of qualified **candidates** with the skills they require.

(b) The **cost** of acquiring people with high-tech expertise and business skills, whether employing or outsourcing, fluctuates due to factors affecting supply and demand.

(c) Third, there is increasing recognition that to do a good job, IT professionals must understand the **business principles** behind the systems that they develop and manage.

Insourcing involves recruiting IS/IT staff internally, from other areas of the business, and teaching these business-savvy employees about technology. The logic behind the idea is that it is easier (and cheaper) to **teach technical skills to business people** than to teach business skills to technical people.

Supporters of insourcing believe it has the potential to:

(a) Create a better quality workforce that combines both technical and business skills.
(b) Reduce costs.
(c) Improve relationships and communication between IT staff and other departments.
(d) Increase staff retention - through providing an additional career path.

Possible disadvantages include:

(a) The risk that non-technical employees will not pick up the IS/IT skills required.
(b) Finding staff willing to make the change.
(c) Replacing staff who do make the switch.

INSOURCING: IS DEPARTMENTS BECOMING MORE EFFICIENT AND IMAGINATIVE

IS managers find themselves caught between the proverbial rock and a hard place. While facing increasing pressure from management to launch development initiatives, they must somehow cope with backlogs of change requests to existing systems.

In the past, the solution might have been to throw more money at the problem, and hire more programmers. However, as companies tighten their belts to survive in a tremendously competitive marketplace, they are trying to meet these challenges by becoming more efficient and more imaginative.

How does an organisation reduce the number of programmers working on legacy applications and increase the number working on new development initiatives, while holding maintenance-level productivity at a constant, or even improved, level?

One option open to MIS is to bite the bullet and outsource maintenance tasks. But this is not an attractive solution to many IS managers. 'There's no way I'm going to turn over applications that are critical to the everyday running of the business,' said a director of a major company. 'Once you farm out these apps, they're gone. You've lost control of your own destiny.'

This loss of control over applications critical to the company's business is a major disadvantage of outsourcing. Once applications are maintained outside the IS department, the understanding of how to work on them is lost to the company; these systems gradually, but inevitably, become the possession of the outsourcer.

There is an alternative to outsourcing - 'insourcing'. Insourcing is based on the old maxim that it is far more effective to teach someone to fish than to fish for them. That is, rather than outsourcing maintenance, and then reengineering processes to free up resources, the company either uses existing staff with key skills to train other staff, or hires an outsider to facilitate the Insourcing process by improving the capabilities of existing staff.

For insourcing to work, staff must be capable and prepared to set aside the necessary time and resources, and management must be prepared to actively support and resource the process.

Chapter Roundup

- The **IS/IT manager** and the **IS/IT director** is responsible for strategy development, risk management and infrastructure.
- The IS/IT **steering committee** makes decisions relating to the future use and development of IS/IT.
- The **database administrator** is responsible for all data and information held within an organisation.
- An **Information Centre** (IC) provides support for computer users within the organisation.
- An **Information Centre** (IC) provides support for computer users within the organisation.
- A **centralised** IS/IT department has the advantages of the **same information** being used, **better security and control**, and possibly **greater expertise**.
- A **decentralised** IS/IT department has the advantages of **greater knowledge** of **local requirements** and **quicker responsiveness**.
- There are three broad possibilities when **accounting for costs** related to information systems.
  - IS costs are treated as an administrative **overhead**
  - IS costs are **charged out at cost**
  - IS costs are **charged out at market rates**
- Some organisations establish IT as a **separate company,** which may lead to **greater profits** and **better opportunities** for staff, but may result in a worse service to the main organisation.
- A **legacy system** is an old outdated system that continues to be used, but no longer meets the information requirements of the organisation.
- **Outsourcing** is the contracting out of operations or services. There are various outsourcing options available, with different levels of control maintained 'in-house'. Outsourcing has **advantages** (eg use of highly skilled people) and **disadvantages** (eg lack of control).
- **Insourcing** involves recruiting IS/IT staff internally, from other areas of the business, and teaching these business-savvy employees about technology.
- Supporters of **insourcing** believe it is easier (and cheaper) to teach technical skills to business people than to teach business skills to technical people.

Quick quiz

1 List four possible responsibilities of an IS/IT steering committee.

2 List three advantages of a decentralised IS/IT department.

3 List three disadvantages of a decentralised IS/IT department.

4 Define 'legacy system'.

5 'Information systems that are strategically important should be outsourced to ensure those working with these systems have excellent technical knowledge'.

True ☐

False ☐

6 List four advantages of outsourcing the IS/IT function.

7 List four disadvantages of outsourcing the IS/IT function.

8 What would a SLA contain?

Answers to quick quiz

1
- Ensuring IS/IT activities comply with IS/IT strategy
- Ensuring IS/IT activities compliment the overall organisation strategy
- Ensuring resources committed to IS/IT are used effectively
- Monitoring IS/IT projects
- Providing leadership and guidance on IS/IT

2
- Each office can introduce an information system specially tailored for its individual needs.
- Local offices are more self-sufficient.
- Offices are likely to have quicker access to IS/IT support/advice.
- A decentralised structure is more likely to facilitate accurate IS/IT cost/overhead allocations.

3
- Control may be more difficult - different and uncoordinated information systems may be introduced.
- Self-sufficiency may encourage a lack of co-ordination between departments.
- Increased risk of data duplication, with different offices holding the same data on their own separate files.
- Increased risk of errors and inconsistencies between systems.

4 A legacy system is an old outdated system which continues to be used, but no-longer meets the information requirements of the organisation.

5 False. Strategic IS are generally not suited to outsourcing as they require a high degree of specific business knowledge that a third party IT/IS specialist can not be expected to possess.

6
- Cost control - services are specified in advance for a fixed price.
- Certainty - long-term contracts allow greater certainty in planning for the future.
- Economies of scale. Several organisations will employ the same company.
- Skills and knowledge are retained within the specialist company who can offer staff career development.

- New skills and knowledge become available. A specialist company can share staff with specific expertise between several clients.
- Flexibility - resources employed can be scaled up or down depending upon demand.

7
- An organisation's IS services may be too important to be contracted out. Information is at the heart of management.
- Risky – confidential or commercially sensitive information could be leaked.
- Opportunities may be missed to use IS/IT for competitive advantage - there is no onus upon internal management to keep up with new developments and have new ideas.
- Locked in - an organisation may be locked into a contract with a poor service provider.
- Hard to reverse - the effort and expense an organisation would have to incur to rebuild its own computing function and expertise would be enormous.
- Outsourcing does not encourage an awareness of the potential costs and benefits of IT amongst managers.

8 The Service Level Agreement (SLA). It should specify minimum levels of service, arrangements for an exit route, transfer arrangements and dispute procedures.

Now try the question below from the Exam Question Bank

Number	Level	Marks	Time
Q23	Examination	25	45 mins

Information technology risks and controls

Introduction

In this chapter we shall be looking at the main risks that organisations face through using information technology and the main controls that they can use to deal with them. Some of the material may be familiar from your earlier studies, but it is worth looking at again. The starting point for most questions in this area is what risks are involved. You then need to be able to select the controls that are relevant to counter the issues.

Although this chapter covers the main general threats that the use of information technology systems can create, new specific threats are being publicised all the time so it is certainly worth reading IT supplements in newspapers or specialist magazines to gain further understanding of how best to tackle threats to systems.

Topic list	Learning outcomes	Syllabus references	Ability required
1 Risks of information technology	E(iv),(v)	E(7),(9),(10)	Evaluation
2 Organisational controls	E(iv),(v)	E(8),(11)	Evaluation
3 Contingency controls and disaster planning	E(iv),(v)	E(7),(11)	Evaluation
4 Access controls	E(iv),(v)	E(8),(11)	Evaluation
5 Integrity and backup controls	E(iv),(v)	E(8),(11)	Evaluation
6 Theft and fraud prevention	E(iv),(v)	E(8), (11)	Evaluation
7 Internet and e-mail	E(iv),(v)	E(10),(11)	Evaluation
8 Data protection	E(iv),(v)	E(8), (11)	Evaluation

1 Risks of information technology

FAST FORWARD

Risks to data and systems include **physical risks** such as fire and water, **risks** through **human error or fraud**.

Internet links have resulted in additional risks including **hacking** and **viruses**.

1.1 Risks of physical damage

1.1.1 Natural threats

Fire is the **most serious hazard** to computer systems. Destruction of data can be even more costly than the destruction of hardware.

Water is a serious hazard. In some areas flooding is a natural risk, for example in parts of central London and many other towns and cities near rivers or coasts. Basements are therefore generally not regarded as appropriate sites for large computer installations.

Wind, rain and storms can all cause substantial **damage to buildings**. In certain areas the risks are greater, for example the risk of typhoons in parts of the Far East. Many organisations make heavy use of prefabricated and portable offices, which are particularly vulnerable. Cutbacks in maintenance expenditure may lead to leaking roofs or dripping pipes.

Lightning and electrical storms can play havoc with power supplies, causing power failures coupled with power surges as services are restored. Minute adjustments in power supplies may be enough to affect computer processing operations (characterised by lights which dim as the country's population turns on electric kettles following a popular television program).

1.1.2 Human threats

Organisations may also be exposed to physical threats through the actions of humans. **Political terrorism** is the main risk, but there are also threats from individuals with **grudges.** Staff are a physical threat to computer installations, whether by spilling a cup of coffee over a desk covered with papers, or tripping and falling doing some damage to themselves and to an item of office equipment.

1.2 Risks to data and systems integrity

The **risks** include

- Human error
  - Entering incorrect transactions
  - Failing to correct errors
  - Processing the wrong files
  - Failing to follow prescribed security procedures
- Technical error such as malfunctioning hardware or software and supporting equipment such as communication equipment, normal and emergency power supplies and air conditioning units.
- Commercial espionage
- Malicious damage
- Industrial action

These risks may be particularly significant because of the nature of computer operations. The **processing** capabilities of a computer are **extensive**, and enormous quantities of data are processed without human intervention, and so without humans knowing what is going on. Information on a computer file **can be changed** without leaving any physical trace of the change. In comparison, a change to a manual file would often involve leaving a trace - eg crossing out data on a card file to insert new data etc

1.3 Risks of fraud

Computer fraud usually involves the theft of funds by **dishonest use** of a computer system. The type of computer fraud depends on the point in the system at which the fraud is perpetrated.

(a) **Input fraud**

Data input is falsified; good examples are putting a **non-existent employee** on the salary file or a non-existent supplier to the purchases file.

(b) **Processing fraud**

A programmer or someone who has broken into this part of the system may **alter a program**. For example, in a large organisation, a 'patch' might be used to change a program so that 10 pence was deduced from every employee's pay cheque and sent to a fictitious account to which the perpetrator had access. A 'patch' is a change to a program which is characterised by its speed and ease of implementation.

(c) **Output fraud**

Output documents may be **stolen or tampered with** and control totals may be altered. Cheques are the most likely document to be stolen, but other documents may be stolen to hide a fraud.

(d) **Fraudulent use of the computer system**

Employees may feel that they can use the computer system for their **own purposes** and this may take up valuable processing time. This is probably quite rare, but there was a case of a newspaper publisher's computer system being used by an employee to produce another publication!

1.3.1 Recent developments increasing the risk of fraud

Over the last few years there have been rapid developments in all aspects of computer technology and these have increased the opportunities that are available to commit a fraud. The most important of the recent developments are as follows.

(a) **Computer literacy**

The proportion of the population which is computer literate is growing all the time. Once people know how to use a computer, the dishonest ones among them may attempt computer fraud.

(b) **Communications**

The use of telephone links and other public communication systems has increased the ability of people outside the organisation to break into the computer system. These 'hackers' could not have operated when access was only possible on site.

(c) **Reduction in internal checks**

The more computers are used, the fewer the tasks left to personnel to carry out. A consequence of this is often a **reduction** in the number of **internal checks** carried out for any transaction.

(d) **Technical change**

Improvements in the **quality of software** and the increase in **implementation of good software** has not kept pace with the improvements in hardware. Distributed systems and networked PCs have become very common but this has caused the control over central databases and programs to be relaxed.

1.3.2 Other deliberate actions

Data and/or systems may be threatened by deliberate actions other than fraud, for example **commercial espionage**, **malicious damage** or **industrial action**.

1.4 Internet risks

Establishing organisational links to the Internet brings numerous security dangers.

(a) Corruptions such as **viruses** on a single computer can spread through the network to all of the organisation's computers. (Viruses are described at greater length later in this section.)

(b) Disaffected employees have much greater potential to do **deliberate damage** to valuable corporate data or systems because the network could give them access to parts of the system that they are not really authorised to use.

(c) If the organisation is linked to an external network, persons outside the company (**hackers**) may be able to get into the organisation's internal network, either to steal data or to damage the system.

(d) Employees may **download inaccurate information** or imperfect or **virus-ridden software** from an external network. For example 'beta' (free trial) versions of forthcoming new editions of many major packages are often available on the Internet, but the whole point about a beta version is that it is not fully tested and may contain bugs that could disrupt an entire system.

(e) Information transmitted from one part of an organisation to another may be **intercepted**. Data can be 'encrypted' (scrambled) in an attempt to make it unintelligible to eavesdroppers, this is covered later in this section.

(f) The **communications link itself may break down or distort data**. The worldwide telecommunications infrastructure is improving thanks to the use of new technologies, and there are communications 'protocols' governing the format of data and signals transferred.

1.4.1 Hacking

Hacking involves attempting to gain unauthorised access to a computer system, usually through telecommunications links.

Hackers require only limited programming knowledge to cause large amounts of damage. The fact that billions of bits of information can be transmitted in bulk over the public telephone network has made it **hard to trace** individual hackers, who can therefore make repeated attempts to invade systems. Hackers, in the past, have mainly been concerned to **copy** information, but a recent trend has been their desire to **corrupt it**.

Phone numbers and passwords can be guessed by hackers using **electronic phone directories** or number generators and by software which enables **rapid guessing** using hundreds of permutations per minute.

Default passwords are also available on some electronic bulletin boards and sophisticated hackers could even try to 'tap' messages being transmitted along phone wires (the number actually dialled will not be scrambled).

1.4.2 Viruses

Key term

A **virus** is a piece of software which infects programs and data and possibly damages them, and which replicates itself.

Viruses need an **opportunity to spread**. The programmers of viruses therefore place viruses in the kind of software which is most likely to be copied. This includes:

- Free software (for example from the Internet).
- Pirated software (cheaper than original versions).
- Games software (wide appeal).
- **E-mail attachments**. E-mail has become the most common means of spreading the most destructive viruses. The virus is often held in an attachment to the e-mail message. Recent viruses have been programmed to send themselves to all addresses in the user's electronic address book.

The main types of viruses (and related programs) are explained in the following table.

Type of virus/program	Explanation/Example
File viruses	File viruses infect program files. When you run an infected program the virus runs first, performs an unauthorised act and copies itself to another file or to another location (replicating itself).
Boot sector or 'stealth' viruses	The boot sector is the part of every hard disk and diskette which is read by the computer when it starts up. These 'stealth' viruses hide from virus detection programs by hiding themselves in boot records or files. If the boot sector is infected, the virus runs when the machine starts.
Trojan	A Trojan (or Trojan Horse) is a small program that performs an unexpected function. The trojan is hidden inside a 'valid' program. Trojans therefore act like a virus, but they aren't classified as a virus as they don't replicate themselves.
Logic bomb	A logic bomb is a program that is executed when a specific act is performed. The logic bomb then performs an unexpected function, often designed to cause damage.
Time bomb	A time bomb is a logic bomb activated at a certain time or date, such as Friday the 13th or April 1st.
Worm	A worm is a type of virus that can replicate (copy) itself and use memory, but cannot attach itself to other programs.
Dropper	A dropper is a program that installs a virus while performing another function.

Type of virus/program	Explanation/Example
Macro viruses	A macro virus is a piece of self-replicating code written in an application's 'macro' language. Many applications have macro capabilities including all the programs in Microsoft Office. The distinguishing factor which makes it possible to create a virus with a macro is the existence of auto-execute events. Auto-execute events are opening a file, closing a file, and starting an application. Once a macro is running, it can copy itself to other documents, delete files, and create general havoc. Melissa was a well publicised macro virus.

1.4.3 Denial of service attack

A fairly new threat, relating to Internet websites and related systems is the 'Denial of Service (DoS)' attack. A denial of service attack is characterised by an attempt by attackers to prevent legitimate users of a service from using that service. Examples include attempts to:

- 'Flood' or bombard a site or network, thereby preventing legitimate network traffic (major sites, such as Amazon.com and Yahoo! have been targeted in this way)
- Disrupt connections between two machines, thereby preventing access to a service
- Prevent a particular individual from accessing a service

1.5 Combating risks and security

Key term

Security, in information management terms, means the **protection of data** from accidental or deliberate threats which might cause unauthorised modification, disclosure or destruction of data, and the **protection of the information system** from the degradation or non-availability of services.

Security refers to **technical** issues related to the computer system, psychological and **behavioural** factors in the organisation and its employees, and protection against the unpredictable occurrences of the **natural world**.

Security can be subdivided into a number of aspects.

(a) **Prevention**. It is in practice impossible to prevent all threats cost-effectively.

(b) **Detection**. Detection techniques are often combined with prevention techniques: a log can be maintained of unauthorised attempts to gain access to a computer system.

(c) **Deterrence**. As an example, computer misuse by personnel can be made grounds for disciplinary action.

(d) **Recovery procedures**. If the threat occurs, its consequences can be contained (for example checkpoint programs).

(e) **Correction procedures**. These ensure the vulnerability is dealt with (for example, by instituting stricter controls).

(f) **Threat avoidance**. This might mean changing the design of the system.

The international security standard, ISO 7799 groups its recommendations under the following headings

(a) **Business continuity planning**. This means that there should be measures to ensure that if major failures or disasters occur, the business will not be completely unable to function.

(b) **Systems access control.** This includes protection of information, information systems, networked services, detection of unauthorised activities and security when using the systems.

(c) **Systems development and maintenance**. This includes security measures and steps to protect data in operational and application systems and also ensuring that IT projects and support are conducted securely.

(d) **Physical and environmental security.** Measures should be taken to prevent unauthorised access, damage and interference to business premises, assets, information and information facilities and prevention of theft

(e) **Compliance** with any relevant legal requirements and also with organisational policies in standards. There is no point in having them if they are not enforced.

(f) **Personnel security**. This covers issues such as recruitment of trustworthy employees, and also reporting of security-related incidents. Training is particularly important, with the aim that users are aware of information security threats and concerns and are equipped to comply with the organisation's security policy.

(g) **Security organisation**. It should be clear who has responsibility for the various aspects of information security. Additional considerations will apply if facilities and assets are accessed by third parties or responsibility for information processing has been outsourced.

(h) **Computer and network management**. This include ensuring continuity of operations and minimising the risk of systems failures, also protecting the integrity of systems and safeguarding information, particularly when exchanged between organisations. Particularly important is protection from viruses.

(i) **Asset classification and control**. Information is an asset, just like a machine, building or a vehicle, and security will be improved if information assets have an 'owner', and are classified according to how much protection they need.

(j) **Security policy**. A written document setting out the organisation's approach to information security should be available to all staff.

2 Organisational controls

FAST FORWARD

Organisations need to develop a **security policy**, make **responsibility** for **information systems** an integral part of the manager's role, and have appropriate **segregation of duties**.

2.1 Developing a security policy

Information security is an important responsibility for all levels of management. A security policy is needed, not simply a collection of measures adopted ad hoc. Developing security policy would involve normal risk management procedures including **identification**, **quantification** and **prioritisation** of risks, **costing, selection** and **implementation** of **counter measures** and drawing up of contingency plans

The International Federation of Accountants in its Information Technology Guideline 1 *Managing security of information* included an example Information Security Policy statement.

INFORMATION SECURITY POLICY STATEMENT EXAMPLE

- The purpose of the Information Security Policy is to protect the organization's information assets from all types of threats, whether internal or external, deliberate, or accidental. Information systems security is critical to the organization's survival.
- The Chief Executive Officer supports and has approved the Information Security Policy.
- It is the Policy of the organization to ensure that:
  - Assets will be classified as to the level of protection required;
  - Information will be protected against unauthorized access;
  - Confidentiality of information will be assured;
  - Integrity of information will be maintained;
  - Personnel security requirements will be met;
  - Physical, logical, and environmental security (including communications security) will be maintained;
  - Legal, regulatory, and contractual requirements will be met;
  - Systems development and maintenance will be performed using a life cycle methodology;
  - Business continuity plans will be produced, maintained, and tested;
  - Information security awareness training will be provided to all staff;
  - All breaches of information systems security, actual or suspected, will be reported to, and promptly investigated by Information Systems Security; and
  - Violations of Information Security Policy will result in penalties or sanctions.
- Standards, practices, and procedures will be produced, and measures implemented to support the Information Security Policy. These may include, but are not limited to, virus protection, passwords, and encryption.
- Business requirements for the availability of information and information systems will be met.
- The roles and responsibilities regarding information security are defined for:
  - Executive management;
  - Information systems security professionals;
  - Data owners;
  - Process owners;
  - Technology providers;
  - Users; and
  - Information systems auditors.
- The Information Systems Security function has direct responsibility for maintaining the Information Security Policy and providing guidance and advice on its implementation.
- All managers are directly responsible for implementing the Information Security Policy within their areas of responsibility, and for adherence by their staff.
- It is the responsibility of each employee to adhere to the Information Security Policy.

2.2 Management responsibilities

Responsibility for information technology should be clearly set down within the remit of every layer of management.

Organisation level	Examples of responsibilities
Top management	Establish **ownership of security and continuity.** Specify work of **audit committee** and **internal and external auditors.** Initiate and approve **contingency plan**. Act on all incidents of known **violation** of management **security policy** (such as illegal and unethical transactions).
User management	Establish **security function and strategy** Establish **procedures** (for example, segregation of duties or authorisation procedures). Strive to employ, train and develop **competent** and **trustworthy personnel** with clear lines of authority and responsibility. Establish **risk assessment procedures**, **monitor system weaknesses** and **assess contingency plans.** Ensure **information security audits** are carried out and recommendations actioned. Establish **physical and access controls** to assets and data. Establish and maintain checkpoints and balances. Monitor compliance with controls through scheduled and unscheduled audits.
Data processing manager	Ensure that hardware, software and computer operations **meet security requirements.**
Personnel departments	Establish **terms of employment** and screening procedures consistent with company and department security aims Include security in **job performance appraisals** and apply appropriate rewards and disciplinary measures.

2.3 Personnel security planning

Certain employees will always be placed in a position of trust, for example senior systems analysts, the database administrator and the computer security officer. With the growth of networks, almost all employees may be in a position to do damage to a computer system.

Although most employees are honest and well-intentioned, if they wish to do so, it may be relatively easy for individuals to compromise the security of an organisation.

The types of measure that can be used to control personnel people as follows.

- Careful recruitment including taking up of references
- Job rotation
- Supervision and observation by a superior
- Review of computer usage (for example via systems logs)
- Enforced vacations

Termination procedures, restricting their access to sensitive data, are required for employees about to leave an organisation. Management should also consider the possible effects of industrial action directed at computer processing.

2.4 Division of responsibilities in the DP department

If the organisation has a separate the DP department, the principle of division of responsibilities states that work is divided between systems analysts, programmers and operating staff, and that operations jobs are divided between data control, data preparation and computer room operations etc. The functions of an organisation structure, as far as control is concerned, are twofold.

(a) To **assign** the **responsibility** for certain tasks to specific jobs and individuals. A person in a given job has the responsibility for ensuring that certain controls are applied. Some jobs are specifically control jobs. These are the jobs of the data control clerks and, to a large extent, of the file librarian.

(b) To **prevent deliberate error**. It is easier for a person to commit fraud if he can input data, write programs and operate the computer all by himself. By dividing up the work, it is more difficult to commit fraud or tamper with data, except in collusion with others.

Organisation controls can be applied by creating a **division of duties** into at least three parts.

- Data capture and the authorisation of data processing work
- Computer operations work
- Systems analysis and programming work

In addition, within the computer operations section, the computer operators should ideally not be given responsibilities for data control, nor should they be given responsibility for looking after the computer file library.

Note that these controls are hard to implement in an environment of end-user computing.

2.5 Computer support department

In environments where there is a lot of end-user computing, the computer will be more of a support service than having responsibility for processing data itself. The services provided might include **user** and **software support**, **change and configuration management**, **backups, documentation** and **maintenance.** The controls over this department should ensure that its activities **enhance security.**

2.6 End-user computing

In the case of PC, end user-based operations it is difficult to apply **segregation of duties**. The same person who operates the computer also **inputs data**, and may even **write his** or **her own programs** for it.

In these cases, however, it is still essential that the data being processed is not such as to have a bearing on the assets of the business. For example, if a PC were to be used for a sales ledger system or payroll system, the person responsible for data input and operating the PC must not be allowed to **design the system** nor **write its programs**, and there must also be suitable internal (and external) **audit checks** of the system.

3 Contingency controls and disaster planning

FAST FORWARD

Organisations should have systems in place for dealing with the **most common natural threats** of fire, water and weather interruptions.

Contingency plans for major disruptions should include **standby and recovery** procedures.

3.1 Minimsing physical threats

Physical security comprises two sorts of controls.

- Protection against **natural** and man made **disasters**, such as fire, flood or sabotage
- Protection against **intruders** gaining physical access to the system (discussed in the next section

A proper **fire safety plan** is an essential feature of security procedures, in order to prevent fire, detect fire and put out the fire. Fire safety includes:

- **Site preparation** (for example, appropriate building materials, fire doors)
- **Detection** (for example, **smoke detectors**)
- **Extinguishing** (for example, **sprinklers**)
- **Training** for staff in observing **fire safety procedures** (for example, no smoking in computer room)

Flooding and water damage can be countered by the use of **waterproof ceilings and floors** together with the provision of **adequate drainage**.

Keeping up maintenance programmes can counter the leaking roofs or dripping pipes that result from **adverse weather conditions**. The problems caused by power surges resulting from lightning can be countered by the use of **uninterrupted (protected) power supplies**. This will protect equipment from fluctuations in the supply. Power failure can be protected against by the use of a **separate generator**.

Threats from terrorism can be countered by **physical access controls** and consultation with police and fire authorities.

Accidental damage can be avoided by **sensible attitudes to office behaviour** and **good office layout** .

3.2 Contingency planning

Key term

A **contingency** is an unscheduled interruption of computing services that requires measures outside the day-to-day routine operating procedures.

The preparation of a contingency plan (also known as a disaster recovery plan) is one of the stages in the development of an organisation-wide security policy. A contingency plan is necessary in case of a major **disaster,** or if some of the **security measures** discussed elsewhere **fail**.

A **disaster** occurs where the system for some reason breaks down, leading to potential **losses** of equipment, data or funds. The system **must recover as soon as possible** so that further losses are not incurred, and current losses can be rectified.

Question — Systems breakdown

Learning outcome: E(v)

What actions or events might lead to a system breakdown?

Answer

System breakdowns can occur in a variety of circumstances, for example:

(a) Fire destroying data files and equipment.
(b) Flooding.
(c) A computer virus completely destroying a data or program file or damaging hardware.
(d) A technical fault in the equipment.
(e) Accidental destruction of telecommunications links (eg builders severing a cable).
(f) Terrorist attack.
(g) System failure caused by software bugs which were not discovered at the design stage.
(h) Internal sabotage (eg logic bombs built into the software).

Any disaster recovery plan must therefore provide for:

(a) **Standby procedures** so that some operations can be performed while normal services are disrupted.

(b) **Recovery procedures** once the cause of the breakdown has been discovered or corrected.

(c) **Personnel management** policies to ensure that (a) and (b) above are implemented properly.

3.3 Contents of a disaster recovery plan

The contents of a disaster recovery (or contingency plan) will include the following.

Section	Comment
Definition of responsibilities	It is important that somebody (a manager or co-ordinator) is designated to take control in a crisis. This individual can then delegate specific tasks or responsibilities to other designated personnel.
Priorities	Limited resources may be available for processing. Some tasks are more important than others. These must be established in advance. Similarly, the recovery program may indicate that certain areas must be tackled first.
Backup and standby arrangements	These may be with other installations, with a company that provides such services (eg maybe the hardware vendor); or reverting to manual procedures.
Communication with staff	The problems of a disaster can be compounded by poor communication between members of staff.
Public relations	If the disaster has a public impact, the recovery team may come under pressure from the public or from the media.
Risk assessment	Some way must be found of assessing the requirements of the problem, if it is contained, with the continued operation of the organisation as a whole.

The contingency plan is dependent on effective **back-up procedures** for data and software, and arrangements for replacement – and even alternative premises.

The plan must cover all activities from the initial response to a 'disaster', through to damage limitation and full recovery. Responsibilities must be clearly spelt out for all tasks.

3.4 Hardware duplication

Hardware duplication may be required permit a system to function in case of breakdown.

The provision of **back-up computers** tends to be quite costly, particularly where these systems have no other function. Many organisations will use **several smaller computer systems** and find that a significant level of protection against system faults can be provided by **shifting operations** to one of the systems still functioning.

Where an organisation has only a single system to rely recourse to a backup facility is unavailable. In these instances one response would be to negotiate a **maintenance contract** which provides for backup facilities.

3.4.1 Available standby hardware facilities

(a) **Computer bureaux** can agree to make their own systems available in the event of an emergency. Such an arrangement has to be specified in advance, as there might be other demands on a bureau's resources.

(b) Co-operating with **other organisations** in the locality, through a mutual aid agreement, may be a way of pooling resources. However, these other organisations themselves might not, in the event, be able to spare the computer time.

(c) **Disaster standby companies** (operating specially set up computer rooms only used for the purpose) are becoming more widespread as computer users are made more aware of the potential dangers of a major disaster.

These companies offer **office premises** with desks, telephones and storage space which are equipped with hardware, including terminals, of the same type as that used by their customers. In the event of a disaster, the customer can 'invoke' standby procedures and load backups of software to carry on essential business.

Disaster standby companies generally offer services to users of one hardware manufacturer's equipment only, and clearly require a number of subscribers if they are to offer a cost effective service. The upper limit on subscribers is governed by the probability that two customers require facilities at once; this is determined by insurers.

4 Access controls

FAST FORWARD

Physical access control attempts to stop **intruders** or other unauthorised persons getting near to computer equipment or storage media. Important aspects are **door locks** and **card entry systems**

4.1 Access risks and controls

Access controls are designed to prevent intruders getting near to computer equipment and/or storage media.

(a) **Personnel**, including receptionists and, outside working hours, security guards, can help control human access.

(b) **Door locks** can be used where frequency of use is low. (This is not practicable if the door is in frequent use.)

(c) Locks can be combined with:

   (i) A **keypad system**, requiring a code to be entered.
   (ii) A **card entry system**, requiring a card to be 'swiped'.

(d) **Intruder alarms are vital**.

(e) Even if intruders get past the physical controls a system of **effective passwords** should prevent their being able to access the systems.

The best form of access control would be one which **recognised** individuals immediately, without the need for personnel or cards. However, machines which can identify a person's fingerprints or scan the pattern of a retina are **expensive**, so are used only in highly sensitive industries, eg defence.

It may not be cost effective or practical to use the same access controls in all areas. The **security requirements of different departments** should be estimated, and appropriate measures taken. Some areas will be very restricted, whereas others will be relatively open.

4.2 Personal identification numbers (PINs)

In some organisations staff are allocated an individual **personal identification number**, or PIN, which identifies him or her to the system. Based on the security privileges allocated, the person will be **allowed** access to certain parts of a building, but prevented from accessing other areas.

4.3 Door locks

Conventional door locks are of value in certain circumstances, particularly where users are only required to pass through the door a **couple of times a day**. If the number of people using the door increases and the frequency of use is high, it will be difficult to persuade staff to lock a door every time they pass through it.

A 'good' lock must be accompanied by a **strong door**. Similarly, other points of entry into the room/complex must be as well protected, otherwise the intruder will simply use a **window** to gain access.

One difficulty with conventional locks is the matter of **key control**. Each person authorised to use the door will need a key. Cleaners and other contractors might also be issued with keys. Practices such as lending out keys or taking duplicate keys may be difficult to prevent.

One approach to this is the installation of **combination locks**, where a numbered keypad is located outside the door and access allowed only after the correct 'code', or sequence of digits has been entered. This will only be fully effective if users ensure the combination is kept confidential, and the combination is **changed** frequently.

4.4 Card entry systems

Card entry systems are a more sophisticated means of control than the use of locks, as **cards can be programmed** to allow access to certain parts of a building only, between certain times.

Cards allow a high degree of monitoring of staff movements; they can for example be used instead of clock cards to record details of time spent on site. Such cards can be incorporated into **identity cards**, which also carry the photograph and signature of the user and which must be 'displayed' at all times.

4.5 Passwords

FAST FORWARD

Passwords are an important access control, although they can be ineffective if the system is simple or if users are careless.

Key term

Passwords are a set of characters which may be allocated to a person, a terminal or a facility which are required to be keyed into the system before further access is permitted.

Unauthorised persons may **circumvent physical access controls.** A **logical access system** can prevent access to data and program files, by measures such as the following.

- Identification of the user
- Authentication of user identity
- Checks on user authority

Passwords can be applied to data files, program files and to parts of a program.

(a) One password may be **required to read** a **file**, but another to **write new data** to it.

(b) The terminal user can be **restricted** to the **use of certain files** and programs (eg in a banking system, junior grades of staff are only allowed to access certain routine programs).

If what is entered matches a password issued to an authorised user or valid for that particular terminal the system permits access. Otherwise the system does **not allow access,** the terminal may **lock** and should **record the attempted unauthorised access.**

Keeping track of **failed attempts** can alert managers to repeated efforts to break into the system; in these cases the culprits might be caught, particularly if there is an apparent pattern to their efforts.

The restriction of access to a system with passwords is effective and widely used but the widespread and growing use of PCs and networks is making physical isolation virtually impossible. The wider use of information systems requires that access to the system becomes equally widespread and easy. **Requirements for system security** must be balanced by the operational requirements for access: a rigidly enforced isolation of the system may significantly reduce the value of the system.

4.5.1 Problems with using passwords

Passwords ought to be effective in keeping out unauthorised users, but they are by no means foolproof.

(a) By **experimenting with possible passwords**, an unauthorised person can gain access to a program or file by guessing the correct password. This is not as difficult as it may seem when too many computer users specify 'obvious' passwords for their files or programs.

(b) Someone who is **authorised to access** a data or program file may **tell an unauthorised person** what the password is, perhaps through carelessness.

(c) Many password systems come with **standard passwords** as part of the system, such as LETMEIN. It is essential for these to be removed if the system is to be at all secure. Such common passwords become widely known to people in the industry using similar packages.

(d) Password systems may rely upon users to use them conscientiously. Users can be extremely sloppy with their security control. Passwords are often **left in plain view** or **'hidden' beneath keyboards** or inside desk drawers where virtually anyone could readily find them. A password system requires both a software system and strong organisational policies, including disciplinary sanctions for disclosure of passwords, if it is to be effective.

Case Study

The following is a good example of the sort of code that organisations might issue on use of passwords.

Best Password Practice

Here is a checklist of points to be observed by computer users to whom passwords have been allocated.

- Keep your password secret. Do not reveal it to anyone else.
- Do not write it down. The second easiest way of revealing a password is to write it on an adhesive label and stick this to the VDU, the desk beneath the keyboard, the inside of a desk drawer or the underside of an overhead filing cabinet.
- Change your password regularly.
- Change and use your password discreetly. Even though a password does not show up on screen, it is easy for onlookers to see which keys are being used. (FRED is a popular password for this reason; the relevant keys are close together on a QWERTY keyboard.)
- Do not use an obvious password. (FRED is an obvious password. Your name or nickname is another)
- Change your password if you suspect that anyone else knows it.

4.5.2 Securing the password system

As well as personal codes of practice, steps can be taken to make the password system more sophisticated and hence lessen the chances of correct guessing by intruders.

- **Regular changes** enforced through the system; users could be required to change their passwords every week or month and not be allowed to use a previous password
- Password **not being shown** on the screen
- Password following a **standard format**, for example having a minimum number of characters and having a combination of letters and numbers

5 Integrity and backup controls

FAST FORWARD

Integrity controls include **input controls** (accuracy, completeness and validity), **processing controls** (accuracy and completeness) and **output controls** (accuracy, security and completeness).

5.1 Integrity controls

Key terms

Data integrity in the context of security is preserved when data is the same as in source documents and has not been accidentally or intentionally altered, destroyed or disclosed.

Systems integrity refers to system operation conforming to the design specification despite attempts (deliberate or accidental) to make it behave incorrectly.

Data will maintain its **integrity** if it is **complete** and **not corrupted**. This means that:

(a) The original **input** of the data must be controlled in such a way as to ensure that the results are complete and correct.

(b) Any **processing and storage** of data must maintain the **completeness** and **correctness** of the data captured.

(c) That reports or other **output** should be set up so that they, too, are complete and correct.

5.1.1 Input controls

Input controls should ensure the **accuracy, completeness and validity** of input.

(a) **Data verification** involves ensuring data entered matches source documents.

(b) **Data validation** involves ensuring that data entered is not incomplete or unreasonable. Various checks can be used, depending on the data type.

(i) **Check digits**. A digit calculated by the program and added to the code being checked to validate it eg modulus 11 method.

(ii) **Control totals**. For example, a batch total totalling the entries in the batch.

(iii) **Hash totals**. A system generated total used to check the reasonableness of numeric codes entered.

(iv) **Range checks**. Used to check the value entered against a sensible range, eg balance sheet account number must be between 5,000 and 9,999.

(v) **Limit checks**. Similar to a range check, but usually based on a upper limit eg must be less than 999,999.99.

Data may be **valid** (for example in the **correct format**) but still **not match source documents**.

Processing controls should ensure the **accuracy and completeness of processing**. Programs should be subject to development controls and to rigorous testing. Periodic running of test data is also recommended.

5.1.2 Output controls

Output controls should ensure the **accuracy, completeness** and **security of output**. The following measures are possible.

- Investigation and follow-up of error reports and exception reports
- Batch controls to ensure all items processed and returned
- Controls over distribution/copying of output
- Labelling of disks/tapes

5.2 Backup controls

FAST FORWARD

Critical data should be regularly **backed-up** and stored separately. An **archiving policy** should ensure that data is preserved in the long-term.

Key term

Back-up means to make a copy in anticipation of future failure or corruption. A back-up copy of a file is a duplicate copy kept separately from the main system and only used if the original fails.

The **purpose of backing up data** is to ensure that the most recent usable copy of the data can be recovered and restored in the event of loss or corruption on the primary storage media.

Back-up controls aim to maintain system and data integrity. We have classified back-up controls as an integrity control rather than a contingency control because back-ups should be part of the **day-to-day procedures** of all computerised systems.

A related concept is that of **archiving.** Archiving data is the process of moving (by copying) data from primary storage, such as a hard disk, to tape or other portable media for long-term storage.

Archiving provides a legally acceptable **business history**, while freeing up **hard disk space**. If archived data is needed, it can be restored from the archived tape to a hard disk. Archived data can be used to recover from site-wide disasters, such as fires or floods, where data on primary storage devices is destroyed.

How long data should be retained will be influenced by:

- Legal obligations
- Other business needs

Data stored for a long time should be tested periodically to ensure it is **still restorable** – it may be subject to **damage** from environmental conditions or mishandling.

In a well-planned data back-up scheme, a copy of backed up data is delivered (preferably daily) to a secure **off-site** storage facility.

A **rotation scheme** can provide a restorable history from one day to several years, depending on the needs of the business.

A well-planned **back-up and archive strategy** should include:

(a) A plan and schedule for the **regular back-up of critical data**.
(b) Archive plans.
(c) A **disaster recovery plan** that includes off-site storage.

As with archiving, regular tests should be undertaken to **verify that data backed up can be successfully restored**.

The **intervals** at which back-ups are performed must be decided. Most organisations back up their data daily, but back-ups may need to be performed more frequently, depending on the nature of the data and of the organisation.

Even with a well planned back-up strategy some re-inputting may be required. For example, if after three hours work on a Wednesday a file becomes corrupt, the Tuesday version can be restored – but Wednesday's work will need to be re-input.

5.3 Audit trail

The original concept of an audit trail is to enable a manager or auditor to follow transactions stage-by-stage through a system to ensure that they had been processed correctly. The intention is to:

- **Identify errors**
- **Detect fraud**

Modern integrated computer systems have cut out much of the time-consuming stage-by-stage working of older systems, but there should still be some **means of identifying individual records** and the **input and output documents** associated with the processing of any individual transaction.

Key term

An **audit trail** is a record showing who has accessed a computer system and what operations he or she has performed. Audit trails are useful both for maintaining security and for recovering lost transactions. Accounting systems include an audit trail component that is able to be output as a report.

In addition, there are separate audit trail software products that enable network administrators to monitor use of network resources.

An audit trail should be provided so that every transaction on a file contains a **unique reference** (eg a sales system transaction record should hold a reference to the customer order, delivery note and invoice).

Typical contents of an accounting software package audit trail include the following items.

(a) A system generated **transaction number.**
(b) A meaningful reference number eg invoice number.
(c) Transaction type eg reversing journal, credit note, cashbook entry etc.
(d) Who input the transaction (user ID).
(e) Full **transaction details** eg net and gross amount, customer ID and so on.
(f) The **PC or terminal** used to enter the transaction.
(g) The **date** and **time** of the entry.
(h) Any additional reference or **narration** entered by the user.

6 Theft and fraud prevention

FAST FORWARD

Organisations should ensure **detailed records** are kept of all computer equipment and software and **theft prevention measures** such as locking items away are in place.

Important **fraud prevention methods** include **security policy, training** and **internal audit.**

6.1 Computer theft

As computer equipment becomes **smaller** and **more portable**, it can be 'smuggled' out of buildings with greater ease. Indeed much equipment is specifically **designed for use off-site**.

A **log of all equipment** should be maintained. This may already exist in basic form as a part of the fixed asset register. The log should include the **make, model** and **serial number** of each item, together with some other organisation-generated code which identifies the **department** which owns the item, the **individual** responsible for the item and its **location**. Anyone taking any equipment off-site should book it out and book it back in.

Smaller items of equipment, such as laptop computers and floppy disks, should always be **locked securely away**. Larger items cannot be moved with ease and one approach adopted is the use of **bolts** to secure them to desks. This discourages 'opportunity' thieves. Larger organisations may also employ site security guards and install closed circuit camera systems.

Question

Theft prevention

Learning outcome: E(v)

You are the chief accountant at your company. Your department, located in an open-plan office, has five networked desktop PCs, a laser printer and a dot matrix printer.

You have just read an article suggesting that the best form of security is to lock hardware away in fireproof cabinets, but you feel that this is impracticable. Make a note of any alternative security measures which you could adopt to protect the hardware.

Answer

(a) **'Postcode'** all pieces of hardware. Invisible ink postcoding is popular, but visible marking is a better deterrent. Soldering irons are ideal for writing on plastic casing.

(b) **Mark the equipment** in other ways. Some organisations spray their hardware with permanent paint, perhaps in a particular colour (bright red is popular) or using stencilled shapes.

(c) Hardware can be **bolted to desks**. If bolts are passed through the desk and through the bottom of the hardware casing, the equipment can be rendered immobile.

(d) Ensure that the organisation's **standard security procedures** (magnetic passes, keypad access to offices, signing in of visitors etc) are followed.

6.1.1 Software piracy

An organisation can face problems through **unlicensed use** of software by staff on its own machines, or its staff illegally making copies for their own use of the software it owns itself.

Record keeping is the most important control **preventing** the **unlicensed use** of software:

- **Maintaining records** of **software purchase and licensing**, identifying the software being used on each machine
- Maintaining a **central secure store** of **disks**
- **Spot checks** to confirm that all software being used is licensed

6.2 Computer fraud

We have seen that **computer fraud usually involves the theft of funds by dishonest use of a computer system**.

The management of every company must be conscious of the possibility and costs of computer fraud and everything must be done to prevent it. Employees (including directors) are the most likely perpetrators of fraud. A dishonest employee will be rare, but temptation should be avoided by giving **no opportunity or motive** to staff.

6.2.1 Fraud prevention

The UK's Audit Commission suggested six measures as being particularly important in the prevention and detection of fraud:

- **Involvement of internal audit**
- **Computer audit skills** in the internal audit function
- Rigorously implemented **computer security policy**
- All staff being given **computer awareness training**
- **Risk analysis** focusing on activities and functions most prone to abuse
- **Staff being employed** to **ensure compliance** with the organisation's computer security policy

In addition, organisations can take additional steps.

(a) **Instigate stringent controls** at the **periphery of the financial system**, at all points where money leaves the company.

(b) Program the computers to **change the controls** operated over **specific transactions.**

It is possible to **use expert systems** to monitor fraud. Barclaycard has installed an expert system to monitor credit card transactions. It has been fed with information relating to credit card frauds perpetrated over a twenty year period. The expert system can therefore 'recognise' suspicious buying patterns.

7 Internet and e-mail

FAST FORWARD

To combat risks from using the Internet, organisations should have **virus protection software** and **encryption procedures**, and also take measures against the security and legal risks of using **Email**.

7.1 Risks of Internet

We discussed in Section 1 the possible dangers of establishing links to the Internet, which are amongst the most serious risks that organisations face.

(a) Corruptions such as **viruses** on a single computer can spread through the network to all of the organisation's computers.

(b) Disaffected employees have much greater potential to do **deliberate damage** to valuable corporate data or systems.

(c) If the organisation is linked to an external network, persons outside the company (**hackers**) may be able to get into the company's internal network, either to steal data or to damage the system.

(d) Employees may **download inaccurate information** or imperfect or **virus-ridden software** from an external network.

(e) Information transmitted from one part of an organisation to another may be **intercepted**.

(f) The **communications link itself may break down or distort data**.

7.2 Protecting against viruses

The main protection against viruses is **anti-virus software**. Anti-virus software, such as McAfee or Norton's searches systems for viruses and removes any that are found. **On-access virus scanning** prevents infection by disallowing access to infected items.

Anti-virus programs include an **auto-update feature** that enables the program to **download profiles** of new viruses, enabling the software to check for all **known** or existing viruses. Very new viruses may go undetected by anti-virus software (until the anti-virus software vendor updates their package - and the organisation installs the update).

Additional precautions include **disabling floppy disk drives** to prevent viruses entering an organisation via floppy disk. However, this can disrupt work processes. At the very least, organisations should ensure **all files received via floppy disk** and e-mail are virus checked.

Dirty PCs can also be useful. A dirty PC is a machine that is not connected to any networks, which can be used for any task that it would be **dangerous** to do on a machine used for everyday work. Employees should use this machine when trying out any external software, including demonstration disks and games. No work should be done on the machine, and no disks used on the dirty machine should be used on any other machine.

Personnel policies are also important in dealing with viruses.

- Staff's **information technology training** should include dealing with viruses
- **Disciplinary procedures** should be used against staff who use unauthorised software on the network.

External e-mail links can be protected by way of a **firewall** that may be configured to virus check all messages, and may also prevent files of a certain type being sent via e-mail (eg .exe files, as these are the most common means of transporting a virus).

Controls we have discussed in other contexts can also be used to **combat viruses**.

(a) **Backups.** All software including operating system software should be write-protected and stored in a safe place.

(b) **Contingency plans.** Plans should specify how the virus should be **contained**. The infected terminals may have to be disconnected from the network and disk interchange between PCs suspended. **Recovery procedures** may include restoration of hard disks, checking data to see whether it has been corrupted and thoroughly checking all infected objects.

Case Study

COMPUTER VIRUS TIMELINE

1981 Apple Viruses 1, 2, and 3 are some of the first viruses in the public domain. Found on the Apple II operating system, the viruses spread via pirated computer games.

1983 Fred Cohen, while working on his dissertation, formally defines a computer virus as 'a computer program that can affect other computer programs by modifying them in such a way as to include a (possibly evolved) copy of itself.'

1986 Two programmers replace the executable code in the boot sector of a floppy disk with their own code designed to infect each floppy accessed on any drive.

1988 One of the most common viruses, Jerusalem, is unleashed. Activated every Friday the 13th, the virus affects both .EXE and .COM files and deletes any programs run on that day.

1990 Symantec launches Norton AntiVirus, one of the first anti-virus programs developed by a large company.

1991 Tequila is the first polymorphic virus to cause significant damage. Polymorphic viruses make detection difficult for virus scanners by changing their appearance with each new infection.

1992 1300 viruses are in existence, an increase of 420% from December 1990. The Michelangelo scare predicts 5 million computers will crash, but only 5,000–10,000 actually do crash.

1994 The 'Good Times' e-mail hoax is widespread. The hoax warns of a malicious virus that will erase an entire hard drive by opening an email with the subject line 'Good Times'. The hoax, or a modified version, often resurfaces.

1999 The Melissa virus executes a macro in a document attached to an e-mail, which forwards the document to 50 addresses from the user's Outlook address book. The virus also infects other Word documents and subsequently mails them out as attachments. Melissa spread faster than any other previous virus.

2000 In May The Love Bug worm shut down e-mail systems around the world. The 'Stages' virus, disguised as a joke email about the stages of life, spreads across the Internet. Unlike previous viruses, Stages is hidden in an attachment with a false '.txt' extension, making it easier to lure recipients into opening it.

2001 The Anna Kournikova virus which masquerades as a picture of tennis star Anna Kournikova, operates in a similar manner to Melissa and The Love Bug. It spreads by sending copies of itself to the entire address book in Microsoft Outlook. It is believed that this virus was created with a so-called virus creation kit, a program which can enable even a novice programmer to create these malicious programs. The Code Red worm attacked computer networks in July and August, affecting over 700,000 computers. Code Red took advantage of a vulnerability in Microsoft's Windows 2000 and Windows NT server software.

2002 Early in January LFM showed up as the first virus to infect Shockwave Flash (.SWF) files. It was named for the message it displays while it's infecting: 'Loading.Flash.Movie...'. In May the Javascript worm SQLSpider was released. It was unique in that it attacked installations running Microsoft SQL Server (and programs that use SQL Server technology).

7.3 Encryption and other safety measures

Key term

Encryption involves scrambling the data at one end of the line, transmitting the scrambled data, and unscrambling it at the receiver's end of the line.

Encryption aims to ensure the security of data during transmission. It involves the translation of data into secret code. To read an encrypted file, you must have access to a secret key or password that enables you to decrypt it. Unencrypted data is called plain text; encrypted data is referred to as cipher text.

Encryption is the only secure way to **prevent eavesdropping** (since eavesdroppers can get round password controls, by tapping the line or by experimenting with various likely passwords).

More sophisticated encryption techniques include:

- **Digital signature.** This is **encryption** by means of private keys, ensuring the senders are who they claim to be and providing evidence should the sender later claim the order was never made.
- **Digital envelope.** This involves sending the key used to encrypt the message separately from the encrypted message.

Authentication is a technique for making sure that a message has come from an authorised sender. Authentication involves adding an extra field to a record, with the contents of this field derived from the remainder of the record by applying an algorithm that has previously been agreed between the senders and recipients of data.

Systems can have **firewalls** (which disable part of the telecoms technology) to prevent unwelcome intrusions into company systems, but a determined hacker may well be able to bypass even these.

Dial-back security operates by requiring the person wanting access to the network to dial into it and identify themselves first. The system then dials the person back on their authorised number before allowing them access.

7.4 E-mail

We indicated in Section 1 that E-mail can impose **legal** and **security** problems, and is often the gateway through which viruses can enter systems. To combat these risks, organisations should enforce strict policies.

(a) **Limits** should be imposed on the personal use of e-mail. A blanket prohibition may not work, as employees will use web services instead. A possible solution would be to provide a secondary personal e-mail address, usable from desk computers, but with limitations such as a prohibition on attachments.

(b) The policy should prohibit the sending of **defamatory**, abusive, sexist or racist **messages**, or downloading offensive material.

(c) E-mails to external customers should give the **company's name, address, telephone number** and **fax number** and full name of the person sending the e-mail. They should include a disclaimer.

(d) The sending of **confidential information** to external sources should be **prohibited** as far as possible. If confidential information has to be sent, it should be encrypted or password-protected.

(e) Ideally **external e-mails** should contain **matters of fact** only.

(f) Employees should be advised that e-mails may have to be **disclosed** in court, and hence they should not delete sensitive e-mails from the system, and should keep hard copies of sensitive e-mails. If there is a legal dispute, employees should not discuss it over e-mail.

(g) All **attachments** to e-mails received should be **copied to disks**, and **checked** for viruses.

(h) Security software should be used to **analyse attachments** for viruses and e-mails themselves for sensitive words or abusive language. Electronic limits can also be placed on the types of attachment specific users can send out.

7.5 Benefits of Internet

Provided they have proper procedures in place for dealing with risk, the benefits to organisations of the Internet can of course be great.

(a) **The Internet reduces transaction costs and thus stimulates economic activity**. According to one US calculation, a banking transaction via the Internet costs 1 cent, 27 cents at an ATM (automated teller machine) and 52 cents over the telephone. Significant savings can be enjoyed by small-scale or even single customers.

(b) The Internet **reduces costs for vendors**. Savings can be achieved through **economies of scale** (becoming a high volume global supplier with low costs) and **economies of scope** (through product specialization). Links between vendors, intermediaries and manufacturer minimise the need for stock and ensure that delivery, installation and after-sales service can all be arranged automatically. Certain goods, for example computer software or music, can be **delivered electronically,** reducing delivery and insurance costs and increasing the timeliness of delivery.

(c) **Marketing can be targeted at selected customers** based on customer registration information or past purchase history. The internet also offers innovative marketing alternative such as product demonstrations, detailed user manuals and cross-selling of services.

(d) **The speed, range and accessibility of information on the Internet, and the low cost of capturing and distributing it, create new commercial possibilities**. Businesses can focus on **niche product/service supply issues**; by doing so, they attract specialised buyers and sellers; in turn they acquire more expertise that generates continued customer loyalty and participation.

Through websites, the Internet provides opportunities to automate tasks that would previously have required more costly interaction with the organisation. These have often been called low-touch or zero-touch approaches. Tasks which a website may automate include:

(a) **Frequently-Asked Questions (FAQs)**: carefully-structured sets of answers can deal with many customer interactions.

(b) **Status checking**: major service enquiries (Where is my order? When will the engineer arrive? What is my bank balance?) can also be automated, replacing high-cost human service processes, and also providing the opportunity to proactively offer better service and new services.

(c) **Keyword search**: the ability to search provides web users with opportunities to find information in large and complex websites.

(d) **Wizards (interview style interface) and intelligent algorithms**: these can help diagnosis, which is one of the major elements of service support.

(e) **E-mail and systems to route and track inbound e-mail**: the ability to route and/or to provide automatic responses will enable organisations to deal with high volumes of e-mail from actual and potential customers.

(f) **Bulletin boards**: these enable customers to interact with each other, thus facilitating self-activated customer service and also the opportunity for product/service referral. Cisco in particular has created communities of Cisco users who help each other - thus reducing the service costs for Cisco itself.

(g) **Call-back buttons**: these enable customers to speak to someone in order to deal with and resolve a problem; the more sophisticated systems allow the call-centre operator to know which web pages the users were consulting at the time.

(h) **Transaction processing**: the taking of orders and payment on-line.

The risks of avoiding involvement include **losing customers** who seek **new sources of supply** through the Intranet and **losing suppliers** who demand e-business capabilities and deal only with e-enabled enterprises.

7.6 Benefits of Intranets

Key term

An **intranet** is an internal network used to share information. Intranets utilise Internet technology and protocols. The firewall surrounding an internet fends off unauthorised access.

The idea behind an 'intranet' is that organisations set up their own **mini version of the Internet.** Intranets use a combination of the organisation's own networked computers and Internet technology. Each employee has a browser, used to access a server computer that holds corporate information on a wide variety of topics, and in some cases also offers access to the Internet.

Potential applications include company newspapers, induction material, online procedure and policy manuals, employee web pages where individuals post details of their activities and progress, and **internal databases** of the corporate information store.

Most of the **cost** of an intranet is the **staff time** required to set up the system.

The **benefits** of intranets are diverse.

(a) Savings accrue from the **elimination of storage**, **printing** and **distribution** of documents that can be made available to employees on-line.

(b) Documents on-line are often **more widely used** than those that are kept filed away, especially if the document is bulky (eg manuals) and needs to be searched. This means that there are **improvements in productivity** and **efficiency**.

(c) It is much **easier to update** information in electronic form.

(d) Wider access to corporate information should open the way to **more flexible working patterns**, eg material available on-line may be accessed from remote locations.

8 Data protection

FAST FORWARD

Organisations should ensure that they only **process the data** about individuals that they are **permitted to** by law, and that the data they retain on individuals is **accurate** and **up-to-date**.

8.1 Data protection legislation

In recent years, there has been a growing fear that the ever-increasing amount of **information** about individuals held by organisations could be misused.

In particular, it was felt that an individual could easily be harmed by the existence of computerised data about him or her which was inaccurate or misleading and which could be **transferred to unauthorised third parties** at high speed and little cost.

During the 1980s and 1990s individuals were therefore **given more protection** from organisations holding data about them.

The UK's data protection legislation is typical of the sorts of measures that have been enacted in recent years worldwide. The Data Protection Act 1998 includes eight principles with which users must comply.

DATA PROTECTION PRINCIPLES

Schedule 1 of the Act contains the data protection principles.

1 Personal data shall be processed fairly and lawfully and, in particular, shall not be processed unless:

   (a) At least one of the conditions in Schedule 2 is met (see paragraph 5.11 (c) later in this chapter).

   (b) In the case of sensitive personal data, at least one of the conditions in Schedule 3 is also met (see 5.11 (d)).

2 Personal data shall be obtained only for one or more specified and lawful purposes, and shall not be further processed in any manner incompatible with that purpose or those purposes.

3 Personal data shall be adequate, relevant and not excessive in relation to the purpose or purposes for which they are processed.

4 Personal data shall be accurate and, where necessary, kept up to date.

5 Personal data processed for any purpose or purposes shall not be kept for longer than is necessary for that purpose or those purposes.

6 Personal data shall be processed in accordance with the rights of data subjects under this Act.

7 Appropriate technical and organisational measures shall be taken against unauthorised or unlawful processing of personal data and against accidental loss or destruction of, or damage to, personal data.

8 Personal data shall not be transferred to a country or territory outside the European Economic Area unless that country or territory ensures an adequate level of protection for the rights and freedoms of data subjects in relation to the processing of personal data.

8.2 Consequences of failure to comply with legislation

Organisations may be subject to sanctions if they breach individuals' rights.

(a) A data subject may seek **compensation** through the courts for damage and any associated distress caused by the **loss**, **destruction** or **unauthorised disclosure** of data about himself or herself or by **inaccurate data** about himself or herself.

(b) A data subject may apply to the courts for **inaccurate data** to be **put right** or even **wiped off** the data user's files altogether. Such applications may also be made to the Registrar.

(c) A data subject may obtain **access** to personal data of which he or she is the subject. (This is known as the 'subject access' provision.) In other words, a data subject can ask to see his or her personal data that the data user is holding.

(d) A data subject can **sue** a data user for any **damage or distress** caused to him by personal data about him that is **incorrect** or **misleading** as to matter of **fact** (rather than opinion).

8.3 Compliance with data protection legislation

Measures could include the following.

- **Obtain consent from individuals** to hold any sensitive personal data you need.
- **Supply individuals** with a **copy of any personal data** you hold about them if so requested.
- Consider if you may need to **obtain consent** to **process personal data**.
- Ensure you **do not pass on personal data** to unauthorised parties.

Chapter roundup

- Risks to data and systems include **physical risks** such as fire and water, **risks** through **human error or fraud**.
- **Internet links** have resulted in additional risks including **hacking** and **viruses.**
- Organisations need to develop a **security policy,** make **responsibility for information systems** an integral part of the manager's role, and have appropriate **segregation of duties.**
- Organisations should have systems in place for dealing with the **most common natural threats** of fire, water and weather interruptions.
- **Contingency plans for major disruptions** should include **standby and recovery** procedures.
- **Physical access control** attempts to stop **intruders** or other unauthorised persons getting near to computer equipment or storage media. Important aspects are **door locks** and **card entry systems**.
- **Passwords** are an important access control, although they can be ineffective if the system is simple or if users are careless.
- **Integrity controls** include **input controls** (accuracy, completeness and validity), **processing controls** (accuracy and completeness) and **output controls** (accuracy, security and completeness).
- **Critical data** should be regularly **backed-up** and stored separately. An **archiving policy** should ensure that data is preserved in the long-term.
- Organisations should ensure **detailed records** are kept of all computer equipment and software and **theft prevention measures** such as locking items away are in place.
- Important fraud prevention methods include security policy, training and internal audit.
- To combat risks from using the Internet, organisations should have **virus protection software** and **encryption procedures**, and also take measures against the security and legal risks of using **Email**.
- Organisations should ensure that they only **process the data** about individuals that they are **permitted to** by law, and that the data they retain on individuals is **accurate** and **up-to-date**.

Quick quiz

1 List three physical access control methods.

2 List four risks to data.

3 What is the purpose of taking a back-up?

4 Why should certain duties be segregated between staff members?

5 List six possible items shown on an accounting package audit trail report.

6 Briefly describe the process of encryption.

7 What is the most common method of spreading a virus?

8 What is the purpose of input controls in a computerised information system?

Answers to quick quiz

1
- Personnel (security guards)
- mechanical devices (eg keys)
- electronic devices (eg card-swipe systems, PIN keypads).

2
- Human error
- Hardware error
- Software error
- Deliberate actions

3 To enable valid files to be restored in case of a future corruption or failure.

4 To reduce the opportunity for fraud and/or malicious damage.

5
- Transaction number
- Transaction date and time
- User ID
- Transaction type
- Amount
- Terminal/PC used to input
- User entered description or narration

6 Encryption involves scrambling data at one end of the communications link, transmitting the scrambled data, then receiving and unscrambling the data at the other end of the link.

7 E-mail.

8 To ensure the accuracy, completeness and validity of input.

Now try the question below from the Exam Question Bank

Number	Level	Marks	Time
Q24	Examination	25	45 mins

25

Systems development controls

Introduction

In this chapter we consider the process of systems development that you will have encountered in earlier studies. However we provide a somewhat different focus, by concentrating on the controls that should prevent the system being poorly designed and inadequately tested, and the staff who operate it being inadequately briefed.

Topic list	Learning outcomes	Syllabus references	Ability required
1 Systems development - revision	E(v)	D(1)	Analysis
2 Ensuring quality in systems	E(v)	D(1)	Analysis
3 Stages of testing	E(v)	D(1)	Analysis
4 Developing a testing strategy	E(i)	D(2)	Analysis
5 Training	E(v)	D(3)	Analysis
6 Documentation	E(v)	D(1)	Analysis
7 File conversion and changeover	E(v)	D(1)	Analysis
8 Post-implementation review	E(v)	D(1)	Analysis
9 Audit of systems development	E(v)	D(1)	Analysis

1 Systems development – revision

FAST FORWARD

The key stages of the **systems development lifecycle** are **feasibility study, systems investigation, systems analysis, systems design, systems implementation, systems control**.

Knowledge brought forward from earlier studies

In your previous studies you will have looked at systems development in detail. We summarise below the main points you will have covered before going on to talk about control and audit of development and implementation.

1.1 Systems development life cycle (SDLC)

The SDLC is a disciplined approach to systems upgrades intended to reduce the possibility of ending up with a system that fails to meet the needs of the organisation and wastes time and money.

There are six stages, although in practice the first three may overlap, and so may the fourth and fifth. These are outlined on the next page.

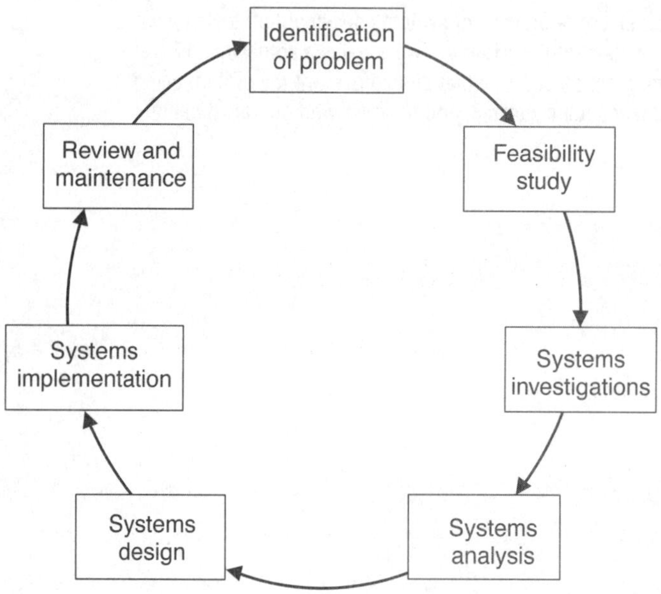

SYSTEMS DEVELOPMENT LIFE CYCLE	
Feasibility study	Briefly review the existing system Identify possible alternative solutions
Systems investigation	Obtain details of current requirements and user needs such as data volumes, processing cycles and timescales Identify current problems and restrictions
Systems analysis	Consider why current methods are used and identify better alternatives

SYSTEMS DEVELOPMENT LIFE CYCLE	
Systems design	Determine what inputs, processing and storage facilities are necessary to produce the outputs required Consider matters such as program design, file design and security Prepare a detailed specification of the new system Test system fully
Systems implementation	Write or acquire software, test it, convert files, install hardware and start running the new system
Review and maintenance	Ensure that the new system meets current objectives, and that it continues to do so

The cycle begins again when a review suggests that it is becoming difficult for an installed system to continue to meet current objectives through routine maintenance.

1.2 Risks of systems developments

If systems development is not controlled properly, the following problems could develop:

- Unauthorised changes to systems
- Poor systems being allowed to become active
- Development of systems that are not flexible enough to cope with changes in circumstances
- Loss of confidence among managers, staff and customers
- Increased risk of fraud or problems with data protection legislation
- Excessive costs

2 Ensuring quality in systems

FAST FORWARD

The **'V' model** shows the relationship between system development, testing and quality throughout a systems development project.

2.1 The 'V' model

The 'V' model shows the relationship between system **development**, **testing** and **quality** throughout a systems development project. An illustration of the V model follows. The 'V' refers to the **two legs** of the diagram – system design runs down the left leg of the V and testing runs up the right leg.

The 'V' Model

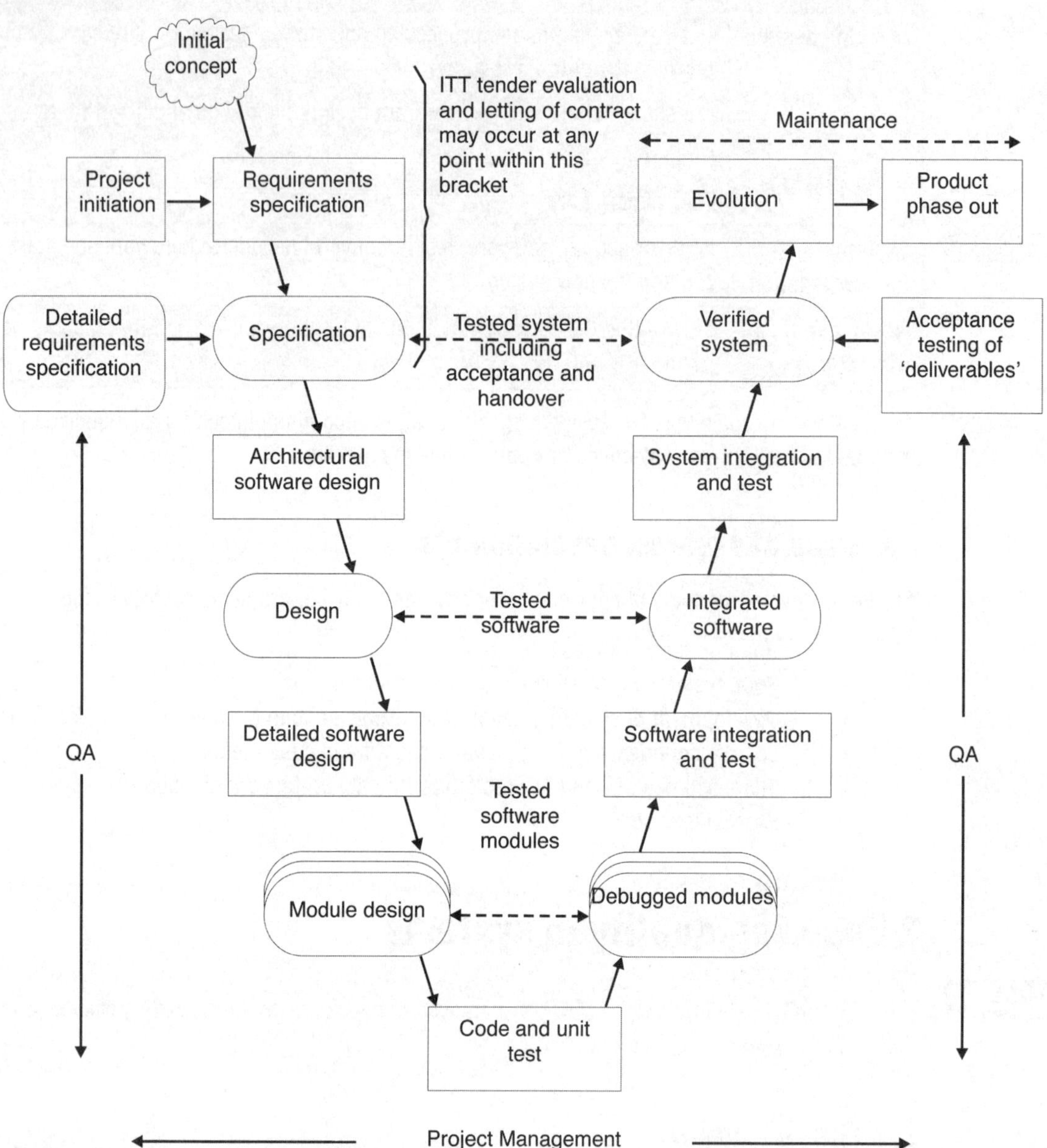

The left leg of the V shows the system development stages of analysis and design – including programming. The upward leg covers the assembly and testing phases and product delivery.

2.2 V model 'quality links'

The model shows **three links** between the left and right legs of the V. These links all refer to testing of some sort. We will look at testing in detail later in this chapter – the explanation below is provided to explain the role of the V model in system quality.

(a) Starting from the bottom point of the V travelling up the right leg, the first link is between **'debugged' modules** (sections) of the system and the **module design.** This check ensures individual modules operate as intended.

(b) The second quality link checks the **integrated software** against the **design specification** for the integrated modules (ie how the modules operate together).

(c) At the top of the V is the final test of quality. The **verified system** is checked against the **overall systems specification**. This process includes user acceptance testing and system hand-over or sign-off.

3 Stages of testing

FAST FORWARD

A system must be thoroughly **tested** to ensure it operates as intended. The nature and scope of testing will vary depending on the size and type of the system and user acceptance testing.

Four basic **stages of testing** can be identified: system logic, program testing, system testing and user acceptance testing.

3.1 Need for testing

A system must be **thoroughly tested before implementation** – a system that is not thoroughly tested may 'go live' with faults that cause disruption and prove costly. The scope of tests and trials will vary depending on the size and purpose of the system.

Four basic stages of testing can be identified:

- System logic
- Program testing
- System testing
- User acceptance testing.

3.2 Testing system logic

Before any programs are written, the **logic devised** by the **systems analyst** should be checked. This process would involve the use of flow charts or structure diagrams such as data flow diagrams.

The path of **different types of data** and **transactions** are manually plotted through the system, to ensure all possibilities have been catered for and that the processing logic is correct. When all results are as expected, programs can be written.

3.3 Program testing

Program testing involves **processing test data** through all programs. Test data should be of the type that the program will be required to process and should include invalid/exceptional items to test whether the program reacts as it should. Program testing should cover the following areas:

- Input validity checks
- Program logic and functioning
- Interfaces with related modules \ systems
- Output format and validity

The testing process should be **fully documented** – recording data used, expected results, actual results and action taken. This documentation may be referred to at a later date, for example if program modifications are required.

Two types of program testing are unit testing and unit integration testing.

3.3.1 Unit testing and unit integration testing

Key terms

Unit testing means testing one function or part of a program to ensure it operates as intended.

Unit integration testing involves testing two or more software units to ensure they work together as intended. The output from unit integration testing is a debugged module.

Unit testing involves **detailed testing** of part of a program – refer back to the V model and you will see unit testing referred to at the lowest point of the V. If it is established during unit testing that a program is not operating as intended, the cause of the error must be established and corrected. Automated diagnostic routines, which step through the program line by line, may be used to help this process.

Test cases should be developed that include **test data** (inputs), **test procedures**, **expected results** and **evaluation criteria**. Sets of data should be developed for both unit testing and integration testing. Cases should be developed for all aspects of the software.

3.4 System testing

When it has been established that individual programs and interfaces are operating as intended, overall system testing should begin. System testing has a wider focus than program testing. System testing should extend beyond areas already tested, to cover:

- **Input documentation** and the practicalities of input eg time taken
- **Flexibility of system** to allow amendments to the 'normal' processing cycle
- **Ability to produce information** on time
- Ability to cope with **peak system resource requirements** eg transaction volumes, staffing levels
- **Viability of operating procedures**

System testing will involve testing both **before installation** (known as off-line testing) and **after implementation** (on-line testing). As many problems as possible should be identified before implementation, but it is likely that some problems will only become apparent when the system goes live.

3.5 User acceptance testing

Key term

User acceptance testing is carried out by those who will use the system to determine whether the system meets their needs. These needs should have previously been stated as acceptance criteria. The aim is for the customer to determine whether or not to accept the system.

It is vital that users are involved in system testing to ensure the system operates as intended when used in its operating environment. Any problems identified should be corrected. This will improve system efficiency and should also encourage users to accept the new system as an important tool to help them in their work.

Users process test data, system performance is closely monitored and users report how they felt the system meets their needs. Test data may include some historical data, because it is then possible to check results against the 'actual' output from the old system.

4 Developing a testing strategy

FAST FORWARD

To ensure a coherent, effective approach to testing, a **testing plan** should be developed.

To ensure a coherent, effective approach to testing, a testing plan should be developed. This plan would normally form part of the overall software development quality plan.

A testing strategy should cover the following areas.

Testing strategy area	Comment
Strategy approach	A testing strategy should be formulated that details the approach that will be taken to testing, including the tests to be conducted and the testing tools/techniques that will be used.
Test plan	A test plan should be developed that states: • What will be tested • When it will be tested (sequence) • The test environment
Test design	The logic and reasoning behind the design of the tests should be explained.
Performing tests	Detailed procedures should be provided for all tests. This explanation should ensure tests are carried out consistently, even if different people carry out the tests.
Documentation	It must be clear how the results of tests are to be documented. This provides a record of errors, and a starting point for error correction procedures.
Re-testing	The re-test procedure should be explained. In many cases, after correction, all aspects of the software should be re-tested to ensure the corrections have not affected other aspects of the software.

The presence of 'bugs' or errors in the vast majority of software/systems demonstrates that even the most rigorous testing plan is unlikely to identify all errors. The limitations of software testing are outlined below.

Limitation	Comment
Poor testing process	The test plan may not cover all areas of system functionality. Testers may not be adequately trained. The testing process may not be adequately documented.
Inadequate time	Software and systems are inevitably produced under significant time pressures. Testing time is often 'squeezed' to compensate for project over-runs in other areas.
Future requirements not anticipated	The test data used may have been fine at the time of testing, but future demands may be outside the range of values tested. Testing should allow for future expansion of the system.
Inadequate test data	Test data should test 'positively' – checking that the software does what it should do, and test 'negatively' – that it doesn't do what it shouldn't. It is difficult to include the complete range of possible input errors in test data.
Software changes inadequately tested	System/software changes made as a result of testing findings or for other reasons may not be adequately tested as they were not in the original test plan.

5 Training

FAST FORWARD

Training should be targeted to ensure those involved receive training relevant to the tasks they perform.

5.1 Training requirements

Staff training in the use of information systems and information technology is essential if the return on investment in IS/IT is to be maximised.

Training is not simply an issue that affects operational staff. Training in information technology **affects all levels** in an organisation, from senior managers learning how to use an executive information system for example, to accounts clerks learning how to use an accounting package.

Training will be needed when:

- A new system is implemented
- An existing system is significantly changed
- Job specifications change
- New staff are recruited
- Skills have been forgotten

A **systematic approach** to training can be illustrated in a flowchart as follows.

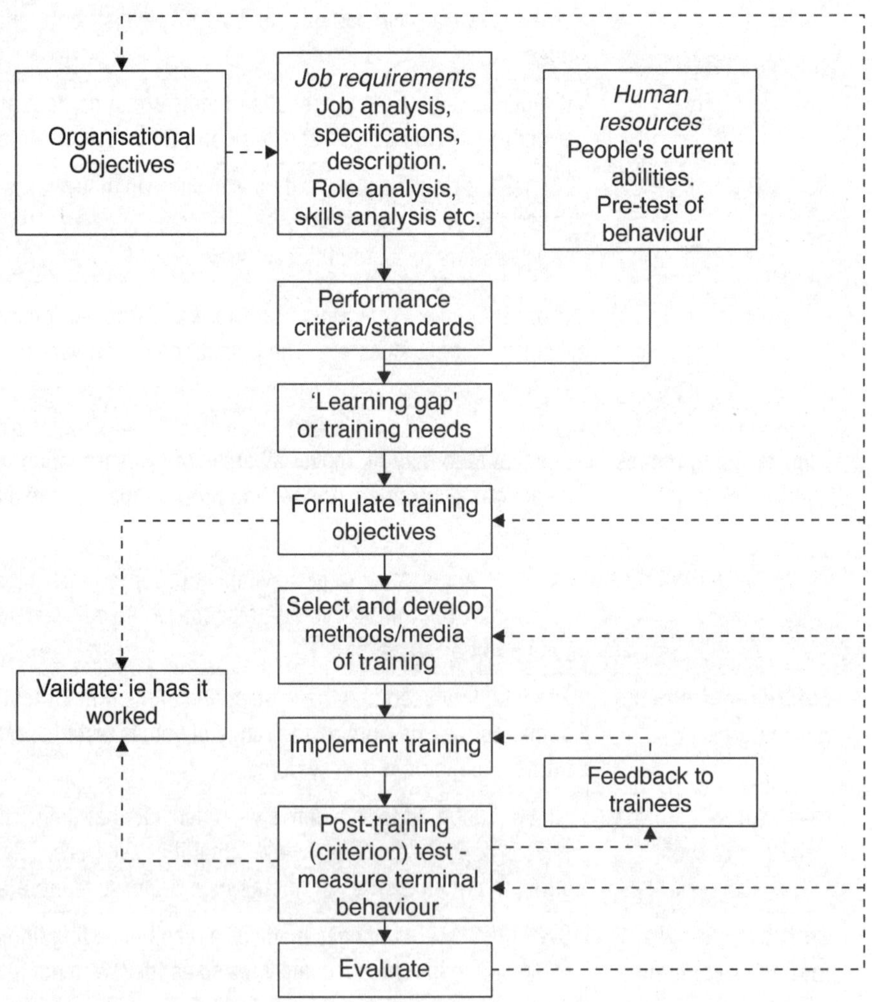

Note the following points in particular.

(a) Training is provided primarily to help the **organisation** achieve its **objectives**.

(b) An individual's **training need** is generally defined as follows.

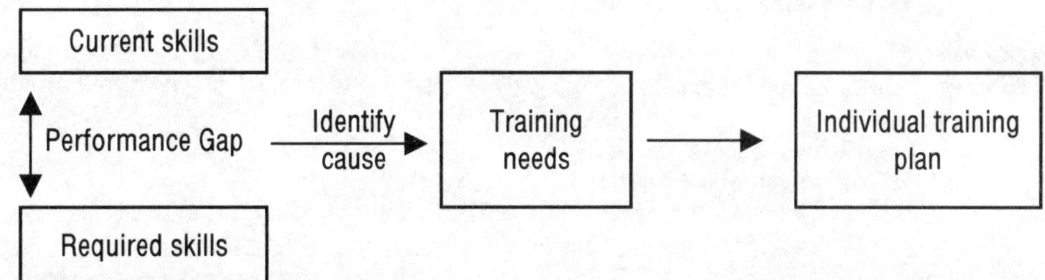

(c) Training should be **evaluated** to make sure that it has worked. If not the method may have been wrong. Whatever the cause, the training need still exists.

5.2 Senior management training

Senior managers are most likely to require training in the use of Executive Support Systems and Decision Support Systems (including spreadsheets).

Senior managers may also require an awareness of information technology in general, and **project management skills** to enable them to manage the acquisition and use of IS/IT within the organisation.

Training relevant to the management of information systems should therefore form part of a managers development plan.

5.3 Operational staff

Operational staff are most likely to be involved in processing transactions. This could involve the use of bar-code readers (eg supermarket checkout operators), or keying into a transaction processing system.

Training should focus on the **specific tasks** the user is required to perform eg entering an invoice or answering a query.

There are a range of options available to deliver training.

Training method	Comment
Individual tuition 'at desk'	A trainer could work with an employee observing how they use a system and suggesting possible alternatives
Classroom course	The software could be used in a classroom environment, using 'dummy' data.
Computer-based training (CBT)	Training can be provided using CDs, or via an interactive website.
Case studies and exercises	Regardless of how training is delivered, it is likely that material will be based around a realistic case study relevant to the user.
Software reference material	Users may find on-line help, built-in tutorials and reference manuals useful.

The training method applicable in a given situation will depend on the following factors:

- Time available
- Software complexity
- User skill levels
- Facilities available
- Budget

6 Documentation

FAST FORWARD

The **technical manual** is produced as a reference tool for those involved in producing and installing the system.

The **user manual** is used to explain the system to users.

Key term

Documentation includes a wide range of technical and non-technical books, manuals, descriptions and diagrams relating to the design, use and operation of a computer system. Examples include user manuals, hardware and operating software manuals, system specifications and program documentation.

6.1 Technical manual

The technical manual is produced as a reference tool for those involved in producing and installing the system. The technical manual should include the following.

- Contact details for the original developers
- System overview
- System specifications including performance details
- Hardware technical specification
- System objectives
- Flowcharts or Data Flow Diagrams
- Entity models and life histories
- Individual program specifications
- Data dictionary

The technical manual should be referred to when future modifications are made to the system. The technical manual should be updated whenever system changes are made.

6.2 User manual

The system should be documented from the point-of-view of **users**. User documentation is used to **explain** the system to users and in training. It provides a **point of reference** should the user have problems with the system. Much of this information **may be available on-line** using context-sensitive help eg 'Push F1 for help'.

The manual provides full documentation of the **operational procedures** necessary for the 'hands-on' running of the system. Amongst the matters to be covered by this documentation would be the following.

(a) **Systems set-up procedures**. Full details should be given for each application of the necessary file handling and stationery requirements etc.

(b) **Security procedures**. Particular stress should be placed on the need for checking that proper authorisation has been given for processing operations and the need to restrict use of machine(s) to authorised operators.

(c) **Reconstruction control procedures**. Precise instructions should be given in relation to matters such as back-up and recovery procedures to be adopted in the event of a systems failure.

(d) **System messages**. A listing of all messages likely to appear on the operator's screen should be given together with an indication of the responses which they should evoke.

(e) **Samples**, including input screens and reports.

When a system is developed in-house, the user documentation might be written by a systems analyst. However, it might be considered preferable for the user documentation to have some input from **users.** As user-documentation is intended to help users, it must be written in a way that users are able to understand. The aim is to **ensure the smooth operation of the system,** not to turn users into analysts.

As with the technical manual, the content of the user manual must be updated to reflect any system changes.

7 File conversion and changeover

FAST FORWARD

There are four approaches to **changeover**: direct changeover, parallel running, pilot operations and phased changeover. These vary in terms of time required, cost and risk.

7.1 File conversion procedures

Key term

File conversion, means converting **existing files** into a format suitable for the new system.

When a new system is introduced, files must be created that conform to the requirements of that system.

The file conversion process is shown in the following diagram, which assumes the original data is held in manual files.

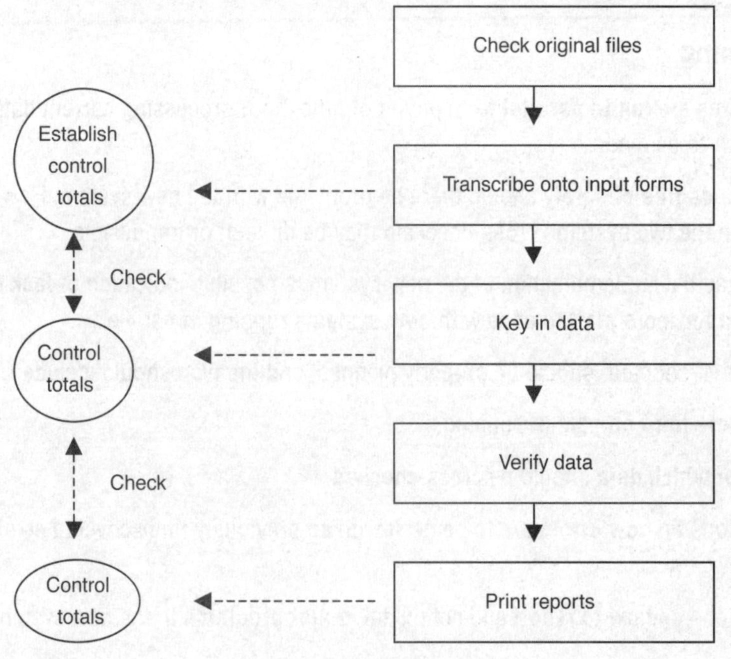

It is essential that the 'new' converted files are accurate. Various controls can be utilised during the conversion process.

(a) **One-to-one checking** between records on the old and new systems.

(b) **Sample checking**. Selecting and checking a sample of records, as there are too many to check individually.

(c) **Built-in data validation** routines in automated conversion processes.

(d) **Control totals** and **reconciliations**. These checks could include checking the total number of records, and the value of transactions.

7.2 Changeover procedures

Once the new system has been fully and satisfactorily tested the changeover can be made. This may be according to one of four approaches.

- Direct changeover
- Parallel running
- Pilot operation
- Phased or 'staged' changeover

7.2.1 Direct changeover

The old system is **completely replaced** by the new system **in one move**.

This may be unavoidable where the two systems are substantially different, or where the costs of parallel running are too great.

While this method is comparatively **cheap** it is **risky** (system or program corrections are difficult while the system has to remain operational).

The new system should be introduced during **a quiet period**, for example over a bank holiday weekend or during an office closure.

7.2.2 Parallel running

The **old and new** systems are **run in parallel** for a period of time, both processing current data and enabling cross checking to be made.

This method provides a **degree of safety** should there be problems with the new system. However, if there are differences between the two systems cross-checking may be difficult or impossible.

There is a **delay** in the actual implementation of the new system, a possible indication of **lack of confidence,** and a need for **more staff** to cope with both systems running in parallel.

This cautious approach, if adopted, should be properly planned, and the plan should include:

(a) A firm **time limit** on parallel running.

(b) Details of **which data** should be **cross-checked**.

(c) Instructions on how **errors** are to be dealt with eg previously undiscovered errors in the old system.

(d) Instructions on how to report and act on any **major problems** in the new system.

7.2.3 Pilot operation

Pilot operation involves selecting part or parts of an organisation (eg a department or branch) to operate running the new system in parallel with the existing system. When the branch or department piloting the system is satisfied with the new system, they cease to use the old system. The new system is then piloted in another area of the organisation.

Pilot operation is **cheaper** and **easier to control** than running the whole system in parallel, and provides a **greater degree of safety** than a direct changeover.

7.2.4 Phased changeover

Phased changeover involves selecting a complete section of the system for a direct changeover, for example in an accounting system the purchase ledger. When this part is running satisfactorily, another part is switched – until eventually the whole system has been changed.

A phased series of direct changeovers is less risky than a single direct changeover, as any problems and disruption experienced should be isolated in an area of operations.

The relative advantages and disadvantages of the various changeover methods are outlined in the following table.

Method	Advantages	Disadvantages
Direct changeover	Quick Minimal cost Minimises workload	Risky Could disrupt operations If fails, will be costly
Parallel running	Safe, built-in safety Provides way of verifying results of new system	Costly-two systems need to be operated Time-consuming Additional workload
Pilot operation	Less risky than direct changeover Less costly than complete parallel running	Can take a long time to achieve total changeover Not as safe as complete parallel running
Phased changeover	Less risky than a single direct changeover Any problems should be in one area – other operations unaffected	Can take a long time to achieve total changeover Interfaces between parts of the system may make this impractical

8 Post-implementation review

FAST FORWARD

A **post-implementation review** is carried out to see whether the targeted performance criteria have been met, and to review of costs and benefits. The review should culminate in the production of a **report**.

8.1 Audit objectives

A **post-implementation review** should establish whether the objectives and targeted performance criteria have been met, and if not, why not, and what should be done about it.

In appraising the operation of the new system immediately after the changeover, comparison should be made between **actual and predicted performance**. This will include:

(a) Consideration of **throughput speed** (time between input and output).
(b) Use of computer **storage** (both internal and external).
(c) The number and type of **errors/queries**.
(d) The **cost** of processing (data capture, preparation, storage and output media, etc).

A special **steering committee** may be set up to ensure that post-implementation reviews are carried out, although the **internal audit** department may be required to do the work of carrying out the reviews.

The post-implementation measurements should **not be made too soon** after the system goes live, or else results will be abnormally affected by 'teething' problems, lack of user familiarity and resistance to change.

8.2 The post-implementation audit report

The findings of a post-implementation review team should be formalised in a **report**.

(a) A **summary** of their findings should be provided, emphasising any areas where the system has been found to be **unsatisfactory**.

(b) A review of **system performance** should be provided. This will address the matters outlined above, such as run times and error rates.

(c) A **cost-benefit review** should be included, comparing the forecast costs and benefits identified at the time of the feasibility study with actual costs and benefits.

(d) **Recommendations** should be made as to any **further action** or steps which should be taken to improve performance.

9 Audit of systems development

FAST FORWARD

Auditors should monitor systems development carefully. They should confirm the **appropriate control framework** is in place over developments, that **system development standards** are being followed, and that the system contains **controls** over **completeness**, **security** and **accuracy** of data.

9.1 Role of auditors

Auditors have a very important role in the development of certainly major systems, and significant audit involvement can help ensure control procedures operate and avoid the problems discussed in Section 1. Auditors are likely to be involved in three main areas:

- Assessing adequacy of control framework
- Checking whether predetermined standards for systems development have been followed
- Reviewing effectiveness of controls

9.2 Assessing adequacy of control framework

Auditors will wish to see in advance that development will take place within a control framework.

9.2.1 Staffing

Auditors will check that the project is appropriately staffed. This will include checking that it is led by a **manager** with **appropriate IT experience** and that the **project team** represents user groups, particularly the accounting function.

9.2.2 Review

Auditors will confirm that **management review,** including **review by the board and audit committee** is built into development procedures.

9.3 Development process

Auditors will be particularly concerned with the following areas.

9.3.1 Feasibility study

Auditors will wish to confirm that the project is **justified on financial** and other **relevant grounds**, there is evidence that a **number of options** have been **considered**. They will also check that the **timescale** for **project completion** is **realistic**. Auditors should also follow the results of the **feasibility study through**, to confirm that the contract specification is based on the feasibility study.

9.3.2 Suppliers

Auditors will wish to check that **suppliers** are **reputable**, and that the contract is **tight**. They will ascertain that **delivery schedules and timetables** have been agreed.

9.3.3 System design and testing

Auditors will be concerned with controls over the data used in development, that changes to data are authorised. They should check that the programmers are **following formal program specifications**. They will also be concerned that there is a **full information trail** for the design process and that the project has been **endorsed** by the development team **and** users of the system.

The **specifications** are **unlikely** to cover every eventuality. Auditors will be concerned that the **process** for **obtaining approval** of **deviations** has been followed.

With testing, auditors will require that all aspects, not just software, are tested and **testing** is carried out by the systems development team, programmers and users.

At the testing stage auditors will also wish to carry out their own testing on controls, or at any rate obtain assurance that controls have been tested. Auditors will be primarily concerned to test the operation of controls that ensure the system is **reliable, produces accurate data and is secure**. They will also (naturally!) be concerned with how easy the system will be to audit.

9.3.4 Implementation

Auditors will check that staff have been **fully trained** and **support documentation** is complete.

Auditors will confirm in advance that **file conversion** has been properly planned, and the implementation plan allows sufficient time for implementation of each aspect of the system.

9.4 After installation

As well as checking that the **post-completion review** has been **carried out**, auditors should themselves review the system development as part of an ongoing review of the organisation's project management procedures.

Question

Testing

Learning outcome: B(v)

Two stages of computer software testing are:

- Systems testing
- User acceptance testing

Required

Briefly describe each of these two stages.

Answer

Systems testing

Computer programmes are written and tested by programmers as the first major stage in writing those programmes. Systems testing then occurs when the initial programming is complete and the software is released by the programmers for additional testing by the systems analyst or a project leader. Systems testing will seek assurance that the software **works correctly** in the following areas.

(a) To ensure that the **specification for the system has been met**. Software will be designed to meet certain features in the initial specification for a project. If these features are not met, then the software will fail to meet user expectations and at the worst the whole system may be unusable.

(b) To check that the **user interface** is understandable and usable. Software must be easy to use; additional checks will be made to ensure that screen formats are consistent and the same keys are pressed to carry out common functions such as closing dialog boxes.

(c) To ensure that data is **processed correctly**. Checks need to be made to ensure that data is transferred between individual programmes (for example the sales program updates the stock balances in the stock system). Similarly, processing within one program should operate correctly (for example the correct sales ledger account is updated when an invoice is raised). Test data will be prepared and run within the program to meet these objectives. Further work will be necessary to ensure that appropriate error messages are generated (for example no sales ledger account is available for a customer), and that these are understandable by the user.

User acceptance testing

User acceptance testing will take place **after systems testing**. It is at this stage that users are involved with the software for the first time. User acceptance testing will seek the following assurances

(a) The software **meets the systems specification** agreed by the users (this specification will normally be contained in flowcharts or entity-relationship models). Users will therefore want to check the design of the software, and in particular will check the individual screens to ensure that they are usable. Change requests may be generated where either the system has been incorrectly designed, or where users find that they need additional functionality building into the system that was not in the initial specification.

(b) The **workflow of each department is accurately reflected** in the software. Although the specification should reflect work flows, it is only when the system itself is available that a full check is possible. Again, change requests may be generated if the software does not meet the existing work practices.

(c) Appropriate **documentation** is being generated to provide training and reference material. Although this material is unlikely to be complete, users may be able to test the accuracy of draft material and provide valuable input into the important points that need to be included in both sets of material.

Chapter roundup

- The key stages of the **systems development lifecycle** are **feasibility study, systems investigation, systems analysis, systems design, systems implementation, systems control**.
- The **'V' model** shows the relationship between system development, testing and quality throughout a systems development project.
- A system must be thoroughly **tested** to ensure it operates as intended. The nature and scope of testing will vary depending on the size and type of the system and user acceptance testing.
- Four basic **stages of testing** can be identified: system logic, program testing, system testing and user acceptance testing.
- To ensure a coherent, effective approach to testing, a **testing plan** should be developed.
- **Training** should be targeted to ensure those involved receive training relevant to the tasks they perform.
- The **technical manual** is produced as a reference tool for those involved in producing and installing the system.
- The **user manual** is used to explain the system to users.
- There are four approaches to **changeover**: direct changeover, parallel running, pilot operations and phased changeover. These vary in terms of time required, cost and risk.
- A **post-implementation review** is carried out to see whether the targeted performance criteria have been met, and to review costs and benefits. The review should culminate in the production of a **report**.
- Auditors should be actively involved in systems development. They should confirm the **appropriate control framework** is in place over developments, that **system development standards** are being followed, and that the system contains **controls** over **completeness, security** and **accuracy** of data.

Quick quiz

1 Explain the three 'quality links' included in the V model.

2 List four different stages of testing applicable through a systems development project.

3 Define 'unit testing'.

4 List five situations where training is required.

5 What factors are relevant when considering how training should be delivered?

6 Which method of system changeover is probably most expensive?

7 Which method of system changeover is usually the riskiest?

8 What should the post-implementation audit establish?

Answers to quick quiz

1 Starting from the bottom point of the V travelling up the right leg, the first link is between 'debugged' modules (sections) of the system and the module design. This check ensures individual modules operate as intended.

The second quality link checks the integrated software against the design specification for the integrated modules (ie how the modules operate together).

At the top of the V is the final quality link where the verified system is checked against the overall systems specification. This process includes user acceptance testing and system hand-over or sign-off.

2
- System logic
- Program testing
- System testing
- User acceptance testing

3 Unit testing means testing one function or part of a program to ensure it operates as intended

4
- A new system is implemented
- An existing system is significantly changed
- Job specifications change
- New staff are recruited
- Skills have been forgotten

5
- The time available
- How complex the software is
- The existing user-skill level
- The training facilities available
- The cost

6 Parallel running

7 Direct changeover

8 Whether the system objectives and targeted performance criteria have been met

Now try the question below from the Exam Question Bank

Number	Level	Marks	Time
Q25	Introductory	N/a	40 mins

Appendix 1
International terminology

International Accounting Terminology and Formats

Terminology

Below is a short list of the most important terms you are likely to use or come across, together with their international equivalents.

UK term	International term
Profit and loss account	Income statement
Profit and loss reserve (in balance sheet)	Accumulated profits
Turnover	Revenue
Debtor account	Account receivable
Debtors (eg 'debtors have increased')	Receivables
Debtor	Customer
Creditor account	Account payable
Creditors (eg 'creditors have increased')	Payables
Creditor	Supplier
Debtors control account	Receivables control account
Creditors control account	Payables control account
Stock	Inventory
Fixed asset	Non-current asset (generally). Tangible fixed assets are also referred to as 'property, plant and equipment'.
Long-term liability	Non-current liability
Provision (eg for depreciation)	Allowance (You will sometimes see 'provision' used too.)
General ledger	Nominal ledger
VAT	Sales tax
Debentures	Loan notes
Preference shares/dividends	Preferred shares/dividends

Formats

Note that the financial statements are generally expressed in dollars rather than pounds.

In general the format for the income statement (international) is the same as the profit and loss account (UK) except for a couple of differences in terminology. Here is a simple example, with the differences highlighted.

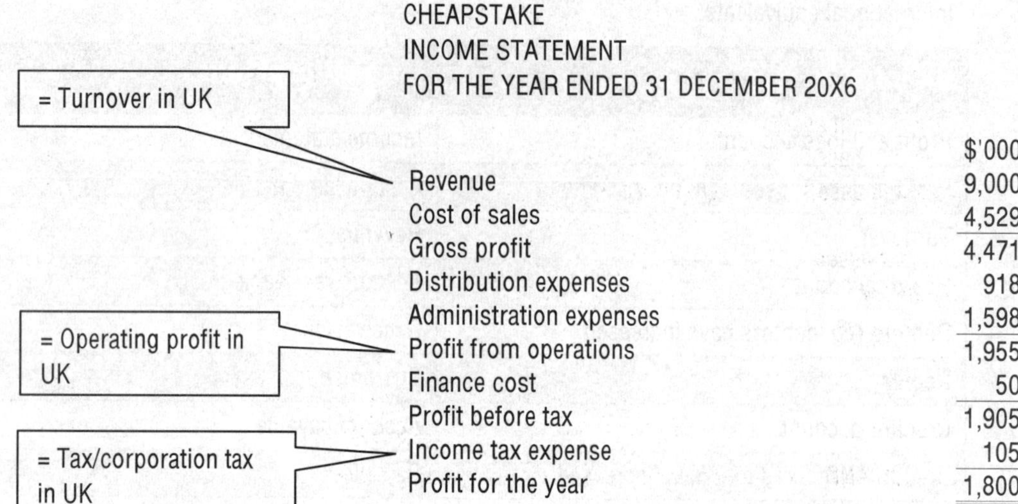

CHEAPSTAKE
INCOME STATEMENT
FOR THE YEAR ENDED 31 DECEMBER 20X6

	$'000
Revenue	9,000
Cost of sales	4,529
Gross profit	4,471
Distribution expenses	918
Administration expenses	1,598
Profit from operations	1,955
Finance cost	50
Profit before tax	1,905
Income tax expense	105
Profit for the year	1,800

The format of the balance sheet is different from the UK. **Instead of having net assets (assets less liabilities) equal to capital and reserves, it has total assets in the top half equal to equity and liabilities in the bottom half.**

CHEAPSTAKE
BALANCE SHEET AS AT 31 DECEMBER 20X6

ASSETS	$'000	$'000
Non-current assets		
Intangible asset: goodwill		270
Tangible assets: property and plant		2,720
		2,990
Current assets		
Inventory	1,950	
Receivables	1,544	
Bank	200	
		3,694
		6,684
EQUITY AND LIABILITIES		
Capital and reserves		
$1 Ordinary shares		400
10% preferred shares		600
Revaluation reserve		350
Accumulated profits		2,274
		3,624
Non-current liabilities		
5% Loan notes	1,000	
Deferred tax	120	1,120
Current liabilities		1,940
		6,684

(As you can see, assets = capital plus liabilities, rather than assets less liabilities = capital.)

Appendix 2
Mathematical tables and exam formulae

PRESENT VALUE TABLE

Present value of £1 ie $(1+r)^{-n}$ where r = interest rate, n = number of periods until payment or receipt.

Periods (n)	Interest rates (r) 1%	2%	3%	4%	5%	6%	7%	8%	9%	10%
1	0.990	0.980	0.971	0.962	0.952	0.943	0.935	0.926	0.917	0.909
2	0.980	0.961	0.943	0.925	0.907	0.890	0.873	0.857	0.842	0.826
3	0.971	0.942	0.915	0.889	0.864	0.840	0.816	0.794	0.772	0.751
4	0.961	0.924	0.888	0.855	0.823	0.792	0.763	0.735	0.708	0.683
5	0.951	0.906	0.863	0.822	0.784	0.747	0.713	0.681	0.650	0.621
6	0.942	0.888	0.837	0.790	0.746	0.705	0.666	0.630	0.596	0.564
7	0.933	0.871	0.813	0.760	0.711	0.665	0.623	0.583	0.547	0.513
8	0.923	0.853	0.789	0.731	0.677	0.627	0.582	0.540	0.502	0.467
9	0.914	0.837	0.766	0.703	0.645	0.592	0.544	0.500	0.460	0.424
10	0.905	0.820	0.744	0.676	0.614	0.558	0.508	0.463	0.422	0.386
11	0.896	0.804	0.722	0.650	0.585	0.527	0.475	0.429	0.388	0.350
12	0.887	0.788	0.701	0.625	0.557	0.497	0.444	0.397	0.356	0.319
13	0.879	0.773	0.681	0.601	0.530	0.469	0.415	0.368	0.326	0.290
14	0.870	0.758	0.661	0.577	0.505	0.442	0.388	0.340	0.299	0.263
15	0.861	0.743	0.642	0.555	0.481	0.417	0.362	0.315	0.275	0.239
16	0.853	0.728	0.623	0.534	0.458	0.394	0.339	0.292	0.252	0.218
17	0.844	0.714	0.605	0.513	0.436	0.371	0.317	0.270	0.231	0.198
18	0.836	0.700	0.587	0.494	0.416	0.350	0.296	0.250	0.212	0.180
19	0.828	0.686	0.570	0.475	0.396	0.331	0.277	0.232	0.194	0.164
20	0.820	0.673	0.554	0.456	0.377	0.312	0.258	0.215	0.178	0.149

Periods (n)	Interest rates (r) 11%	12%	13%	14%	15%	16%	17%	18%	19%	20%
1	0.901	0.893	0.885	0.877	0.870	0.862	0.855	0.847	0.840	0.833
2	0.812	0.797	0.783	0.769	0.756	0.743	0.731	0.718	0.706	0.694
3	0.731	0.712	0.693	0.675	0.658	0.641	0.624	0.609	0.593	0.579
4	0.659	0.636	0.613	0.592	0.572	0.552	0.534	0.516	0.499	0.482
5	0.593	0.567	0.543	0.519	0.497	0.476	0.456	0.437	0.419	0.402
6	0.535	0.507	0.480	0.456	0.432	0.410	0.390	0.370	0.352	0.335
7	0.482	0.452	0.425	0.400	0.376	0.354	0.333	0.314	0.296	0.279
8	0.434	0.404	0.376	0.351	0.327	0.305	0.285	0.266	0.249	0.233
9	0.391	0.361	0.333	0.308	0.284	0.263	0.243	0.225	0.209	0.194
10	0.352	0.322	0.295	0.270	0.247	0.227	0.208	0.191	0.176	0.162
11	0.317	0.287	0.261	0.237	0.215	0.195	0.178	0.162	0.148	0.135
12	0.286	0.257	0.231	0.208	0.187	0.168	0.152	0.137	0.124	0.112
13	0.258	0.229	0.204	0.182	0.163	0.145	0.130	0.116	0.104	0.093
14	0.232	0.205	0.181	0.160	0.141	0.125	0.111	0.099	0.088	0.078
15	0.209	0.183	0.160	0.140	0.123	0.108	0.095	0.084	0.074	0.065
16	0.188	0.163	0.141	0.123	0.107	0.093	0.081	0.071	0.062	0.054
17	0.170	0.146	0.125	0.108	0.093	0.080	0.069	0.060	0.052	0.045
18	0.153	0.130	0.111	0.095	0.081	0.069	0.059	0.051	0.044	0.038
19	0.138	0.116	0.098	0.083	0.070	0.060	0.051	0.043	0.037	0.031
20	0.124	0.104	0.087	0.073	0.061	0.051	0.043	0.037	0.031	0.026

CUMULATIVE PRESENT VALUE TABLE

This table shows the present value of £1 per annum, receivable or payable at the end of each year for *n* years $\frac{1-(1+r)^{-n}}{r}$.

Periods (n)	Interest rates (r) 1%	2%	3%	4%	5%	6%	7%	8%	9%	10%
1	0.990	0.980	0.971	0.962	0.952	0.943	0.935	0.926	0.917	0.909
2	1.970	1.942	1.913	1.886	1.859	1.833	1.808	1.783	1.759	1.736
3	2.941	2.884	2.829	2.775	2.723	2.673	2.624	2.577	2.531	2.487
4	3.902	3.808	3.717	3.630	3.546	3.465	3.387	3.312	3.240	3.170
5	4.853	4.713	4.580	4.452	4.329	4.212	4.100	3.993	3.890	3.791
6	5.795	5.601	5.417	5.242	5.076	4.917	4.767	4.623	4.486	4.355
7	6.728	6.472	6.230	6.002	5.786	5.582	5.389	5.206	5.033	4.868
8	7.652	7.325	7.020	6.733	6.463	6.210	5.971	5.747	5.535	5.335
9	8.566	8.162	7.786	7.435	7.108	6.802	6.515	6.247	5.995	5.759
10	9.471	8.983	8.530	8.111	7.722	7.360	7.024	6.710	6.418	6.145
11	10.368	9.787	9.253	8.760	8.306	7.887	7.499	7.139	6.805	6.495
12	11.255	10.575	9.954	9.385	8.863	8.384	7.943	7.536	7.161	6.814
13	12.134	11.348	10.635	9.986	9.394	8.853	8.358	7.904	7.487	7.103
14	13.004	12.106	11.296	10.563	9.899	9.295	8.745	8.244	7.786	7.367
15	13.865	12.849	11.938	11.118	10.380	9.712	9.108	8.559	8.061	7.606
16	14.718	13.578	12.561	11.652	10.838	10.106	9.447	8.851	8.313	7.824
17	15.562	14.292	13.166	12.166	11.274	10.477	9.763	9.122	8.544	8.022
18	16.398	14.992	13.754	12.659	11.690	10.828	10.059	9.372	8.756	8.201
19	17.226	15.679	14.324	13.134	12.085	11.158	10.336	9.604	8.950	8.365
20	18.046	16.351	14.878	13.590	12.462	11.470	10.594	9.818	9.129	8.514

Periods (n)	**Interest rates (r) 11%**	**12%**	**13%**	**14%**	**15%**	**16%**	**17%**	**18%**	**19%**	**20%**
1	0.901	0.893	0.885	0.877	0.870	0.862	0.855	0.847	0.840	0.833
2	1.713	1.690	1.668	1.647	1.626	1.605	1.585	1.566	1.547	1.528
3	2.444	2.402	2.361	2.322	2.283	2.246	2.210	2.174	2.140	2.106
4	3.102	3.037	2.974	2.914	2.855	2.798	2.743	2.690	2.639	2.589
5	3.696	3.605	3.517	3.433	3.352	3.274	3.199	3.127	3.058	2.991
6	4.231	4.111	3.998	3.889	3.784	3.685	3.589	3.498	3.410	3.326
7	4.712	4.564	4.423	4.288	4.160	4.039	3.922	3.812	3.706	3.605
8	5.146	4.968	4.799	4.639	4.487	4.344	4.207	4.078	3.954	3.837
9	5.537	5.328	5.132	4.946	4.772	4.607	4.451	4.303	4.163	4.031
10	5.889	5.650	5.426	5.216	5.019	4.833	4.659	4.494	4.339	4.192
11	6.207	5.938	5.687	5.453	5.234	5.029	4.836	4.656	4.486	4.327
12	6.492	6.194	5.918	5.660	5.421	5.197	4.988	4.793	4.611	4.439
13	6.750	6.424	6.122	5.842	5.583	5.342	5.118	4.910	4.715	4.533
14	6.982	6.628	6.302	6.002	5.724	5.468	5.229	5.008	4.802	4.611
15	7.191	6.811	6.462	6.142	5.847	5.575	5.324	5.092	4.876	4.675
16	7.379	6.974	6.604	6.265	5.954	5.668	5.405	5.162	4.938	4.730
17	7.549	7.120	6.729	6.373	6.047	5.749	5.475	5.222	4.990	4.775
18	7.702	7.250	6.840	6.467	6.128	5.818	5.534	5.273	5.033	4.812
19	7.839	7.366	6.938	6.550	6.198	5.877	5.584	5.316	5.070	4.843
20	7.963	7.469	7.025	6.623	6.259	5.929	5.628	5.353	5.101	4.870

EXAM FORMULAE

Valuation models

(i) Irredeemable preference share, paying a constant annual dividend, d, in perpetuity, where P_0 is the ex-div value:

$$P_0 = \frac{d}{k_{pref}}$$

(ii) Ordinary (equity) share, paying a constant annual dividend, d, in perpetuity, where P_0 is the ex-div value:

$$P_0 = \frac{d}{k_e}$$

(iii) Ordinary (equity) share, paying an annual dividend, d, growing in perpetuity at a constant rate, g, where P_0 is the ex-div value:

$$P_0 = \frac{d_1}{k_e - g} \text{ or } P_0 = \frac{d_0[1+g]}{k_e - g}$$

(iv) Irredeemable (undated) debt, paying annual after tax interest, i(1 – t), in perpetuity, where P_0 is the ex-interest value:

$$P_0 = \frac{i[1-t]}{k_{d\ net}}$$

or, without tax:

$$P_0 = \frac{i}{k_d}$$

(v) Total value of the geared firm, V_g (based on MM):

$$V_g = V_u + DT_c$$

(vi) Future value S, of a sum X, invested for n periods, compounded at r% interest:

$$S = X[1 + r]^n$$

(vii) Present value of £1 payable or receivable in n years, discounted at r% per annum:

$$PV = \frac{1}{[1+r]^n}$$

(viii) Present value of an annuity of £1 per annum, receivable or payable for n years, commencing in one year, discounted at r% per annum:

$$PV = \frac{1}{r}\left[1 - \frac{1}{[1+r]^n}\right]$$

(ix) Present value of £1 per annum, payable or receivable in perpetuity, commencing in one year, discounted at r% per annum:

$$PV = \frac{1}{r}$$

(x) Present value of £1 per annum, receivable or payable, commencing in one year, growing in perpetuity at a constant rate of g% per annum, discounted at r% per annum:

$$PV = \frac{1}{r - g}$$

Cost of capital

(i) Cost of irredeemable preference capital, paying an annual dividend d in perpetuity, and having a current ex-div price P_0:

$$k_{pref} = \frac{d}{P_0}$$

(ii) Cost of irredeemable debt capital, paying annual net interest i(1 – t), and having a current ex-interest price P_0:

$$k_{d\ net} = \frac{i[1 - t]}{P_0}$$

(iii) Cost of ordinary (equity) share capital, paying an annual dividend d in perpetuity, and having a current ex div price P_0:

$$k_e = \frac{d}{P_0}$$

(iv) Cost of ordinary (equity) share capital, having a current ex div price, P_0, having just paid a dividend, d_0, with the dividend growing in perpetuity by a constant g% per annum:

$$k_e = \frac{d_1}{P_0} + g \text{ or } k_e = \frac{d_0[1+g]}{P_0} + g$$

(v) Cost of ordinary (equity) share capital, using the CAPM:

$$k_e = R_f + [R_m - R_f]\beta$$

(vi) Cost of ordinary (equity) share capital in a geared firm, (no tax):

$$k_{eg} = k_0 + [k_0 - k_d]\frac{V_D}{V_E}$$

(vii) Cost of ordinary (equity) share capital in a geared firm, (with tax):

$$k_{eg} = k_{eu} + [k_{eu} - k_d]\frac{V_D[1 - t]}{V_E}$$

(viii) Weighted average cost of capital, k_0:

$$k_0 = k_{eg}\left[\frac{V_E}{V_E + V_D}\right] + k_d\left[\frac{V_D}{V_E + V_D}\right]$$

(ix) Adjusted cost of capital (MM formula)

$$k_{adj} = k_{eu}[1 - tL] \text{ or } r^* = r[1 - T^*L]$$

In the following formula, β_u is used for an ungeared β, and β_g is used for a geared β:

(x) β_u from β_g, taking β_d as zero, (no tax):

$$\beta_u = \beta_g\left[\frac{V_E}{V_E + V_D}\right]$$

(xi) β_u from β_g, taking β_d as zero, (with tax):

$$\beta_u = \beta_g \left[\frac{V_E}{V_E + V_D[1-t]} \right]$$

Other formulae

(i) Purchasing power parity (Law of one price)

$$\text{Forward rate US\$/£} = \text{Spot US\$/£} \times \frac{1 + \text{US inflation rate}}{1 + \text{UK inflation rate}}$$

(ii) Interest rate parity (International Fisher effect)

$$\text{Forward rate US\$/£} = \text{Spot US\$/£} \times \frac{1 + \text{nominal US interest rate}}{1 + \text{nominal UK interest rate}}$$

(iii) Link between nominal (money) and real interest rates

[1 + nominal (money) rate] = [1 + real interest rate][1 + inflation rate]

(iv) Equivalent annual cost

$$\text{Equivalent annual cost} = \frac{\text{PV of costs over n years}}{\text{n year annuity factor}}$$

(v) Theoretical ex-rights price

$$\text{TERP} = \frac{1}{N+1}[(N \times \text{Cum rights price}) + \text{Issue price}]$$

(vi) Value of a right

$$\text{Value of a right} = \frac{\text{Rights on price} - \text{Issue price}}{N+1}$$

or

$$\frac{\text{Theoretical ex rights price} - \text{Issue price}}{N}$$

where N = number of rights required to buy one share.

Exam question bank

1 Cybernetic control — 30 mins

Learning outcome: A(i)

One common approach to organisational control theory is to look at the model of a cybernetic system. This is often illustrated by the concept of a thermostat.

Required

Explain the limitations of the simple feedback control this model illustrates, as an explanation of the working of organisational control systems.

2 Bonus schemes — 45 mins

Learning outcome: A(ii)

It has been suggested that optimal bonus schemes for profit centre managers promise significant rewards for the achievement of challenging targets in areas they can influence. These schemes balance short-term pressure with incentives to maintain a long-term focus and protect managers from the distorting effects of uncontrollable factors.

It has also been suggested that many bonus schemes have additional features with different motivational effects.

Required

(a) The following are two possible features of bonus schemes.

- Limiting the range of performance within which rewards are linked to results, in particular ignoring losses and limiting maximum payments
- Linking incentive payments wholly or partly to the profit of the organisation as a whole

Explain why bonus schemes might include these features.

Explain the effects of incorporating these features in bonus schemes (16 marks)

Bonus schemes are normally designed to motivate full-time employees who have no other employment and are wholly dependent upon the organisation for their income. Part-time employees and short-term employees might not be included.

(b) Describe and advise on the possible features of bonus schemes which are designed to motivate non-executive directors who are part-time, remunerated by fees under contracts for a fixed number of years and required by corporate governance codes to maintain independence. (9 Marks)

(Total Marks = 25)

3 Divisionalised structures — 45 mins

Learning outcome: A(iii)

Divisionalised structures are normal in large firms, and occur even when centralised structures would be feasible.

Required

(a) Explain and discuss the arguments for divisionalised structures in large firms. (7 marks)

(b) Explain the costs and potential inefficiencies of a divisionalised structure. (8 marks)

(c) Explain how adoption of a divisionalised structure changes the role of top management and their control of subordinates. (10 marks)

(Total Marks = 25)

4 Cumbersome process 45 mins

Learning outcome: A(iv)

Budgeting has been criticised as

- a cumbersome process which occupies considerable management time;
- concentrating unduly on short-term financial control;
- having undesirable effects on the motivation of managers;
- emphasising formal organisation structure.

Required

(a) Explain these criticisms. (10 marks)

(b) Explain what changes can be made in response to these criticisms to improve the budgeting process. (15 marks)

(Total Marks = 25)

5 Risk identification 35 mins

Learning outcome: B(i)

The following statement has been made: 'Risk identification is an attempt rigorously to identify all possible events, situations or activities which could cause or enhance losses. It has three main stages:

(a) An analysis of the major types of loss affecting the individual or firm
(b) A systematic search for all the immediate causes of such losses
(c) A systematic assessment of the underlying causes and their consequences

Describe how the above stated three main stages of risk identification are carried out in practice.

6 Crashcarts (Pilot paper) 90 mins

Learning outcome: B(i),(ii)

Crashcarts IT Consultancy is a £100 million turnover business listed on the Stock Exchange with a reputation for providing world class IT consultancy services to blue chip clients, predominantly in the retail sector. In 2000, Crashcarts acquired a new subsidiary for £2 million based on a P/E ratio of 8, which it renamed Crashcarts Call Centre. The call centre subsidiary leased all of its hardware, software and telecommunications equipment over a five-year term. The infrastructure provides the capacity to process three million orders and ten million line items per annum. In addition, maintenance contracts were signed for the full five-year period. These contracts include the provision of a daily backup facility in an off-site location.

Crashcarts Call Centre provides two major services for its clients. First, it holds databases, primarily for large retail chains' catalogue sales, connected in real time to clients' inventory control systems. Second, its call centre operation allows its clients' customers to place orders by telephone. The real-time system determines whether there is stock available and, if so, a shipment is requested. The sophisticated technology in use by the call centre also incorporates a secure payment facility for credit and debit card

payments, details of which are transferred to the retail stores' own computer system. The call centre charges each retail client a lump sum each year for the IT and communication infrastructure it provides. There is a 12 month contract in place for each client. In addition, Crashcarts earns a fixed sum for every order it processes, plus an additional amount for every line item. If items are not in stock, Crashcarts earns no processing fee.

Crashcarts Call Centre is staffed by call centre operators (there were 70 in 2001 and 80 in each of 2002 and 2003). In addition, a management team, training staff and administrative personnel are employed. Like other call centres, there is a high turnover of call centre operators (over 100% per annum) and this requires an almost continuous process of staff training and detailed supervision and monitoring.

A summary of Crashcarts Call Centre's financial performance for the last three years:

	2001	*2002*	*2003*
	£'000	£'000	£'000
Revenue			
Contract fixed fee	400	385	385
Order processing fees	2,500	3,025	3,450
Line item processing fees	600	480	390
Total revenue	3,500	3,890	4,225
Expenses			
Office rent and expenses	200	205	210
Operator salaries and salary-related costs	1,550	1,920	2,180
Management, administration and training salaries	1,020	1,070	1,120
IT and telecoms lease and maintenance expenses	300	310	330
Other expenses	150	200	220
Total expenses	3,220	3,705	4,060
Operating profit	280	185	165

Non-financial performance information for the same period is as follows.

	2001	*2002*	*2003*
Number of incoming calls received	1,200,000	1,300,000	1,350,000
Number of orders processed	1,000,000	1,100,000	1,150,000
Order strike rate (orders/calls)	83.3%	84.6%	85.2%
Number of line items processed	3,000,000	3,200,000	3,250,000
Average number of line items per order	3.0	2.9	2.8
Number of retail clients	8	7	7
Fixed contract income per client	£50,000	£55,000	£55,000
Income per order processed	£2.50	£2.75	£3.00
Income per line order processed	£0.20	£0.15	£0.12
Average number of orders per operator	15,000	15,000	15,000
Number of operators required	66.7	73.3	76.7
Actual number of operators employed	70.0	80.0	80.0

Required

(a) Discuss the increase in importance of risk management to all businesses (with an emphasis on listed ones) over the last few years and the role of management accountants in risk management. (10 marks)

(b) Advise the Crashcarts Call Centre on methods for analysing its risks. (5 marks)

(c) Apply appropriate methods to identify and quantify the major risks facing Crashcarts at both parent level and subsidiary level. (20 marks)

(d) Categorise the components of a management control system and recommend the main controls that would be appropriate for the Crashcarts Call Centre. (15 marks)

(Total Marks = 50)

7 Segregation of duties 45 mins

Learning outcome: B(v)

The UK's old Auditing Practices Committee Guideline on internal control lists eight types of internal control, including organisation and segregation of duties.

Required

(a) Explain briefly what is meant by segregation of duties, why it is important in internal control, and how internal auditors can confirm its effectiveness. (7 marks)

A small branch has one manager and few managerial staff, which makes segregation of duties within the branch impossible.

Required

(b) Explain how Head Office can maintain internal control of the branch. (7 marks)

A large company has restructured. This has considerably reduced the number of managers and eliminated much of what was deemed to be unnecessary bureaucracy including many controls on stock, purchases and time recording. In a flatter structure, junior managers and supervisors have been provided with authority (empowered) to take a wide range of decisions of immediate concern, and with access to much of the company database. The new structure emphasises team work to implement rapid changes.

Required

(c) Explain how internal control can be maintained in this situation. (11 marks)

(Total Marks = 25)

8 Corporate governance (Pilot paper) 45 mins

Learning outcome: B(vii)

You have recently been appointed as head of the internal audit function for a large UK listed company that trades internationally, having worked within its finance function for two years period to your new appointment.

Your company has also appointed a new chief executive, headhunted from a large US corporation where she had held the post of vice president, finance.

Required

As part of the new chief executive's orientation programme, you have been asked to prepare a detailed report which provides key information on the principles of good corporate governance for UK listed companies.

You should address the following in your report, remembering that her background is in US governance and procedures.

(a) The role and responsibilities of the board of directors. (5 marks)
(b) The role and responsibilities of the audit committee. (10 marks)
(c) Disclosure of corporate governance arrangements. (10 marks)

(Total Marks = 25)

9 Internal audit role — 35 mins

Learning outcome: C(ii)

You have been appointed manager of internal audit in a large organisation and asked to set up an appropriate department.

Required

Write a report for the board clarifying the role of internal audit with regard to external audit and accounting systems. In your report, you should:

(a) Compare briefly the role of the external audit to that of the internal audit

(b) Describe the steps the external auditors need to take to be able to rely on specific internal audit work

(c) Discuss whether the existence of an internal audit function simplifies the job of the external auditors

10 Audit sampling — 25 mins

Learning outcome: C(iii)

It is important to recognise that audit sampling may be constructed on a non-statistical basis. If the auditors use statistical sampling, probability theory will be used to determine sample size and random selection methods to ensure each item or £1 in value of the population has the same chance of selection. Non-statistical sampling is more subjective than statistical sampling, typically using haphazard selection methods and placing no reliance upon probability theory. However, in certain circumstances statistical sampling techniques may be difficult to use. The auditors will review the circumstances of each audit before deciding whether to use statistical or non-statistical sampling.

Required

(a) List three situations where the auditors would be unlikely to use audit sampling techniques.

(b) Describe the factors which the auditors should consider when determining the size of a sample.

(c) Describe to what extent statistical sampling enhances the quality of the audit evidence.

11 Analytical review — 45 mins

Learning outcome: C(iii)

You are a senior internal auditor at Patchit, a machine tool manufacturer. A draft set of financial statements for the year have been prepared by management, and it has fallen to you to examine the figures for reasonableness and at the same time identify significant audit areas which may require further work even though your systems audit during the year has proved satisfactory. You are aware of the fact that the company is at present contemplating an issue of £2,000,000 15% loan stock (redeemable in the year 20X0) in order to assist the remodelling of its present production facilities. The majority of the directors are in favour of making the issue but a few are reluctant to do so in view of the fact that the machine tools industry is subject to wide-ranging fluctuations in sales and profits.

Abbreviated financial statements for Patchit together with typical ratios for firms in the machine tool industry are as follows.

INCOME STATEMENTS FOR THE YEARS ENDED 31 DECEMBER

	20X2		20X1	
	£'000	£'000	£'000	£'000
Sales		23,500		20,500
Cost of goods sold		16,000		14,000
Gross profit		7,500		6,500
Selling expenses	2,700		1,900	
Administration expenses	2,300		2,600	
		5,000		4,500
Profit from operations		2,500		2,000
Interest paid		500		300
Net profit before taxation		2,000		1,700
Taxation		1,200		1,020
Net profit after taxation		800		680
Dividends paid		525		280
Profit for the year retained		275		400
Retained profit brought forward		6,090		5,690
Retained profit carried forward		6,365		6,090

BALANCE SHEETS AS AT 31 DECEMBER

	20X2		20X1	
	£'000	£'000	£'000	£'000
Non-current assets (net)		6,315		5,600
Other assets		800		750
		7,115		6,350
Current assets				
Inventory	5,100		3,200	*
Receivables	2,900		1,900	**
Prepayments	100		100	
Cash and bank	600		590	
	8,700		5,790	
Payables: amounts falling due within one year	3,600		2,400	
		5,100		3,390
Total assets less current liabilities		12,215		9,740
Payables: amounts falling due after more than one year				
8% loan stock (20Y0-20Y3)		5,500		3,300
		6,715		6,440
Called up share capital				
Ordinary 50p shares authorised, issued and fully paid		350		350
Retained profits		6,365		6,090
		6,715		6,440

* (Inventory valuation at 31.12.X0 was £2,500,000)

** (Receivables' balance at 31.12.X0 totalled £1,700,000)

Typical industrial averages for 20X2 and 20X1 are as follows.

Gross profit on sales	34%	Acid test ratio	1.2:1
Net profit before tax on sales	11%	Average age of receivables	30 days
Net profit before tax on net assets employed	19.5%	Average age of inventory	73 days
Working capital ratio	2.5:1	Interest cover	8 times

Required

(a) Review the above financial statements and industry averages and explain which main features therein require most attention during your forthcoming final audit. (12 marks)

(b) With regard to those areas which may cause you some concern, describe the main matters which you would need to investigate (a detailed audit programme is not required). (13 marks)

(Total Marks = 25)

12 Management control framework 35 mins

Learning outcome: C(i)

A typical description of the framework of the management control cycle is:

(a) Defining the objectives
(b) Planning the activity necessary to achieve the objectives
(c) Organising resources and directing performance
(d) Monitoring results
(e) Regulating by reviewing and adjusting plans or directives

Required

Use the framework of the management control cycle above to explain how a board should ensure that an adequate system of internal control exists.

13 Controls over cash and cheques 45 mins

Learning outcome: C(iii)

List the types of control which may exist over the system for handling cash and cheques.

14 VFM and performance indicators 45 mins

Learning outcome: C(v)

(a) Give three specific examples of methods of analysis which may be employed in value for money audits. (6 marks)

(b) Explain the use of performance indicators and the advantages and limitations of using these indicators in a value for money audit in the public sector. Include three examples of performance indicators in your explanation. (19 marks)

(Total Marks = 25)

15 Fraud 30 mins

Learning outcome: C(v)

Explain how management control system can help to minimise the risk of fraud in purchasing.

16 Codes of conduct **25 mins**

Learning outcome: C(vii)

Some codes of conduct appear to have a double standard. One such is quoted below.

Customer and supplier relations

The company does not seek to gain any advantage through the improper use of business courtesies or other inducements. Good judgement and moderation must be exercised to avoid misinterpretation and adverse effect on the reputation of the company and its employees. Offering, giving, soliciting or receiving any form of bribe is prohibited.

Business courtesies

Gifts, favours and entertainment may be given in the following circumstances.

(i) If they are consistent with customary business practices.
(ii) If they are not excessive in value and cannot be construed as a bribe or payoff.
(iii) If they are not in contravention of applicable law or ethical standards.
(iv) If they will not embarrass the company or the employee if publicly disclosed.

Gifts, favours, entertainment or other inducements may not be accepted by employees from any person or organisation that does or seeks business with, or is a competitor of, the company, except as common courtesies usually associated with customary business practices. An especially strict standard applies when suppliers are involved. Favours or entertainment, appropriate in our sales programmes may not be appropriate or acceptable from suppliers. It is never acceptable to accept a gift in cash or cash equivalent.

Required

Comment on the acceptability of the above code of conduct. If you consider it appropriate, suggest with reasons any amendments you would wish to see in the code of conduct.

17 ZX (Pilot paper) **45 mins**

Learning outcome: D(i),(ii)

ZX is a UK-based retailer and manufacturer that also owns a limited number of outlets in the USA, but is anxious to expand internationally via the use of franchising agreements. The enterprise plans to open five franchised shops in each of France, Italy, Germany, Belgium and Holland over the course of the next twelve months. ZX will provide loan finance to assist individuals wishing to purchase a franchise, the average cost of which will be €100,000. Loans will also be available (up to a maximum of 50% of the purchase price) to cover the cost of the franchisee acquiring suitable freehold or leasehold premises. The total sum required for the property loan facility is estimated by the treasurer of ZX to equal €4.8 million. The opportunity cost of capital in the UK is 10% per annum but, in recognition of the lower rates of interest available in the Eurozone, ZX will only charge the franchisees a fixed rate of 7.0% each year on all loans. Repayments will be made in equal Euro-denominated instalments.

ZX charges commission to the franchisees at a rate of 1% of sales revenue, and also earns a net margin of 12% (of retail value) on the products supplied to the outlets from its UK manufacturing plant.

Planned sales from the new European outlets equal €26 million over the next twelve months, but the enterprise recognises that its profits are dependent upon both sales revenue and the extent of loan defaults amongst franchisees (if any). Estimates of the likelihood of a range of scenarios are detailed below.

Probability	*Sales*	*Number of loan defaults*	*Comment*
0.1	10% below plan	2	Economic difficulties reduce sales and cause problems for some franchisees
0.3	20% below plan	4	Severe economic problems lead to low sales and higher loan defaults
0.4	As per plan	0	'Base case'
0.2	As per plan	1	The weak German economy causes problems for one franchisee

Loan default is assumed to mean total write-off and ZX expects 80% of the new franchisees to take full advantage of the loan facilities offered to them.

The current Euro:Sterling exchange rate is €1.3939/£ and the Euro is expected to strengthen against Sterling by 5% over the next twelve months.

In addition to the cash required to fund the foreign loan facility, a further £3.65 million of working capital will be required for the expansion project and the treasury department of ZX requires a minimum annualised return of 15% on all overseas projects.

Required

(a) Use the table of possible scenarios given above to calculate the expected sterling value of the additional profit that ZX will earn if the store openings are completed as planned and the foreign exchange rate forecast is fulfilled. (You should use the average exchange rate over the year for the calculation.)

You should evaluate whether this profit yields the return required for international operations. (7 marks)

(b) Discuss the risks that ZX might face in choosing to expand into Europe via the use of franchising. (8 marks)

(c) Evaluate methods of managing/minimising the risks involved in granting Euro denominated loans to the franchisees. (10 marks)

(Total Marks = 25)

18 OX — 45 mins

Learning outcome: D(ii),(iii),(vi)

OX plc has export orders from a company in Singapore for 250,000 china cups, and from a company in Indonesia for 100,000 china cups. The unit variable cost to OX of producing china cups is 55. The unit sales price to Singapore is Singapore $2.862 and to Indonesia, 2,246 rupiahs. Both orders are subject to credit terms of 60 days, and are payable in the currency of the importers. Past experience suggests that there is 50% chance of the customer in Singapore paying 30 days late. The Indonesian customer has offered to OX the alternative of being paid US $125,000 in 3 months time instead of payment in the Indonesian currency. The Indonesian currency is forecast by OX's bank to depreciate in value during the next year by 30% (from an Indonesian viewpoint) relative to the US dollar.

Whenever appropriate, OX uses option forward foreign exchange contracts.

Foreign exchange rates (mid rates)

	$Singapore/$US	*$US/£*	*Rupiahs/£*
Spot	2.1378	1.4875	2,481
1 month forward	2.1132	1.4963	No forward
2 months forward	2.0964	1.5047	market exists
3 months forward	2.0915	1.5105	

Assume that any foreign currency holding in the UK will be immediately converted into sterling.

	Money market rates (% per year)	
	Deposit	*Borrowing*
UK clearing bank	6	11
Singapore bank	4	7
Euro-dollars	7½	12
Indonesian bank	15	Not available
Euro-sterling	6½	10½
US domestic bank	8	12½

These interest rates are fixed rates for either immediate deposits or borrowing over a period of two or three months, but the rates are subject to future movement according to economic pressures.

Required

(a) Using what you consider to be the most suitable way of protecting against foreign exchange risk, calculate the sterling receipts that OX can expect from its sales to Singapore and to Indonesia, without taking any risks.

All contracts, including foreign exchange and money market contracts, may be assumed to be free from the risk of default. Transactions costs may be ignored. (13 marks)

(b) If the Indonesian customer offered another form of payment to OX, immediate payment in US dollars of the full amount owed in return for a 5% discount on the rupiah unit sales price, calculate whether OX is likely to benefit from this form of payment. (7 marks)

(c) Discuss the advantages and disadvantages to a company of invoicing an export sale in a foreign currency. (5 marks)

(Total Marks = 25)

19 BS — 45 mins

Learning outcome: D(ii),(iii),(vi)

BS is an importer/exporter of heavy machinery for a variety of industries. It is based in the UK but trades extensively with the USA. Assume that you are a newly appointed management accountant with BS plc. The company does not have a separate treasury function and it is part of your duties to assess and manage currency risks. You are concerned about the recent fluctuations in the exchange rate between US$ and sterling and are considering various methods of hedging the exchange risk involved. Assume it is now the end of March. The following transactions are expected on 30 June.

Sales receipts	$450,000
Purchases payable	$250,000

Economic data

- The spot rate of exchange is US$1.6540-1.6590 to the £.
- The US$ premium on the three-month forward rate of exchange is 0.82-0.77 cents.
- Annual interest rates for three months' borrowing are: USA 6 per cent; UK 9 per cent.
- Annual interest rates for three months' lending are: USA 4 per cent; UK 6.5 per cent.
- Option prices (cents per £, contract size £12,500):

	Calls		*Puts*	
Exercise price $	*June*	*September*	*June*	*September*
1.60	-	15.20	-	-
1.65	2.65	7.75	-	3.45
1.70	1.70	3.60	-	9.32

Assume that there are three months from now to expiry of the June contracts.

Required

(a) Calculate the net sterling receipts that BS plc can expect from its transactions if the company hedges the exchange risk using each of the following alternatives:

(i) The forward foreign exchange market

(ii) The money market

Accompany your calculations with brief explanations of your approach and recommend the most financially advantageous alternative for BS plc. Assume transaction costs would be 0.2 per cent of the US$ transaction value under either method, paid at the beginning of the transaction (ie now). (8 marks)

(b) Explain the factors the company should consider before deciding to hedge the risk using the foreign currency markets, and identify any alternative actions available to minimise risk. (5 marks)

(c) Discuss the relative advantages and disadvantages of using foreign currency options compared with fixed forward contracts. To illustrate your arguments assume that the actual spot rate in three months' time is 1.6458-1.6513, and assess whether BS plc would have been better advised to hedge using options, rather than a fixed forward contract. (12 marks)

(Total Marks = 25)

20 Financial risks (Pilot paper) 45 mins

Learning outcome: D(i),(ii),(iii),(vi)

A listed services group with a UK head office and subsidiaries throughout the world reports in Sterling and shows the following liabilities in its notes to the accounts.

Liabilities All figures are in £ million	*Total liabilities*	*Floating rate*	*Fixed rate liabilities*	*Weighted average interest rate*	*Weighted average years for which rate is fixed*
£ Sterling	98	98			
$ US	41	8	33	7.25%	5
Euro	4	4			
Total	143	110	33		

Maturity All figures are in £ million	*Total*	*Maturing within 1 year*	*Within 1-2 years*	*Within 2-5 years*	*Over 5 years*
£ Sterling	98	73	3	18	4
$ US	41				41
Euro	4	1	1	1	1
Total	143	74	4	19	46

Interest rates are currently about 5%.

Required

(a) (i) Evaluate the main sources of financial risk for this group (assuming there are no offsetting assets that might provide a hedge against the liabilities).

(ii) Quantify the transaction risk faced by the group if sterling was to depreciate against the $US and Euro by 10%.

(iii) Evaluate how transaction risk relates to translation risk and economic risk in this example. (13 marks)

(b) Discuss the use of exchange traded and Over The Counter (OTC) derivatives for hedging and how they may be used to reduce the exchange rate and interest rate risks the group faces. Illustrate your answer by comparing and contrasting the main features of appropriate derivatives. (12 marks)

(Total Marks = 25)

21 IT strategy 45 mins

Learning outcome: E(i)

Explain *five* reasons why it is essential for a modern organisation to have an IT strategy. Illustrate your answer with examples of these reasons drawn from your own knowledge and experience. (25 marks)

22 Information systems strategy (Pilot paper) 45 mins

Learning outcome: E(ii)

The information systems strategy within the MG organisation has been developed over a number of years. However, the basic approach has always remained unchanged. An IT budget is agreed by the board each year. The budget is normally 5% to 10% higher than the previous year's to allow for increases in prices and upgrades to computer systems.

Systems are upgraded in accordance with user requirements. Most users see IT systems as tools for recording day-to-day transactions and providing access to accounting and other information as necessary. There is no Enterprise Resource Planning System (ERPS) or Executive Information System (EIS).

The board tends to rely on reports from junior managers to control the business. While these reports generally provide the information requested by the board, they are focused at a tactical level and do not contribute to strategy formulation or implementation.

Required

(a) Compare and contrast information systems strategy, information technology strategy and information management strategy and explain how these contribute to the business. (10 marks)

(b) Advise the board on how an ERPS and EIS could provide benefits over and above those provided by transaction processing systems. (10 marks)

(c) Recommend to the board how it should go about improving its budgetary allocations for IT and how it should evaluate the benefits of ERPS and EIS. (5 marks)

(Total Marks = 25)

23 Facilities management 45 mins

Learning outcome: E(iii)

The directors of DS are not satisfied with the GDC Ltd facilities management company which was contracted two years ago to run the IT system of the company. At that time, the existing in-house IT development and support department was disbanded and all control of IT systems handed over to GDC Ltd. The appointment of GDC Ltd was relatively rushed and although an outline contract was agreed, no detailed Service Level Agreement was produced.

Over the last few weeks the number of complaints received from staff regarding the service has been increasing and the provision of essential management reports has not been particularly timely.

A recent exchange of correspondence with GDC Ltd failed to resolve the matter. Staff at GDC Ltd recognised the fall in standards of service, but insisted that it has met its contractual obligations. DS's lawyers have confirmed that GDC Ltd is correct.

Key features of DS's contract with the GDC Ltd facilities management company:

The contract can be terminated by either party with three months' notice

GDC Ltd will provide IT services for DS, the services to include:

- Purchase of all hardware and software
- Repair and maintenance of all IT equipment
- Help desk and other support services for users
- Writing and maintenance of in-house software
- Provision of management information

Price charged to be renegotiated each year but any increase must not exceed inflation, plus 10%.

Required

(a) Explain, from the point of view of DS, why it might have received poor service from GDC Ltd, even though GDC Ltd has met the requirements of the contract. (12 marks)

(b) Explain the courses of action now available to DS relating to the provision of IT services. Comment on the problems involved in each course of action. (13 marks)

(Total Marks = 25)

24 Computer security 45 mins

Learning outcome: E(iv)

Computer security is of vital importance to all organisations. Security is the means by which losses are controlled and therefore involves the identification of risks and the institution of measures to either prevent such risks entirely or to reduce their impact.

Required

(a) Identify the main areas of risk which may arise in relation to a computer system. (12 marks)

(b) Describe the different forms of control which should be instituted to safeguard against computer security risks. (13 marks)

(Total Marks = 25)

25 Systems development project 40 mins

Learning outcome: E(v)

Identify and briefly describe the major stages in a computer systems development project.

Exam answer bank

1 Cybernetic control

Pass marks. The control model gives an obvious structure for this answer, The lack of comparability between the thermostat and the organisational control model is partly due to the complexities in the environment and results, but is also due to the factors slowing the response of organisations.

The simple feedback control model consists of five stages.

- Determine the objectives.
- Measure the actual results.
- Compare the actual results with the objectives.
- Determine the appropriate control action.
- Implement the control action.

A thermostatic control system operates by measuring the actual temperature and comparing this with the desired temperature. If it is too low or too high the heating is switched on or off as appropriate.

The analogy between this and organisational control has a number of limitations.

Operation of the system

The thermostatic control system is a **closed or semi-closed system** in which the control mechanism is self-regulating and relates to its environment in a controlled and prescribed manner. In contrast an organisation is an **open system** which is connected to and interacts with its environment.

Determining objectives

A thermostatic control system has a single objective which is to maintain the temperature within predetermined limits. An organisation may have multiple objectives, some of which may be conflicting (for example motivation and control).

In an organisation the original objectives may **cease to be appropriate** if the external environment changes. For example the original objective may have been to maximise profitability but because of changes in the external environment the objective may change to one of survival. The thermostatic control system does not change in this way. For example it cannot move from an objective of maintaining the temperature to an alternative objective of regulating the humidity.

Measuring the actual results

A thermostatic control system uses a mechanical device to measure the actual results with reasonable accuracy. Organisational control systems rely on less accurate measurement which can be subject to human error, for example in allocating expenditure to different cost centres.

A thermostatic control system monitors **results on a continuous basis** whereas many organisational systems only provide **monitoring information** at the end of each discrete feedback period. This can mean the control action is taken too late.

Comparing results

The output of a thermostatic control system is **easily measured**. Some of the outputs of organisational systems may be difficult to measure, particularly the long term or strategic effects of management actions.

Determining the appropriate control action

A thermostatic control system simply has to **determine whether to switch the heating on or off** and the effect of such action is known with a reasonable degree of certainty. In contrast there are many different types of control action which could be taken in organisations and managers may have difficulty in identifying them and in determining the likely outcomes of their actions.

A distinction between **controllable** and **uncontrollable deviations** from plan can be made fairly readily within a thermostatic control system. Such a distinction is not so easily made in an organisational system

Human involvement in organisational control systems means that the **actual results** are more likely to be misinterpreted than in thermostatic control systems.

Implementing control action

A thermostatic control system can **implement control action** rapidly but **changes in response** to feedback in an organisational system can be relatively slow, possibly rendering the control action inappropriate. In addition the thermostat will respond automatically to variances whereas in an organisational system the individual managers must be persuaded to take the correct control action.

Organisational systems can also encourage **deviations from plan** (positive feedback) or take control action in advance of deviations (feedforward control).

2 Bonus schemes

Pass marks. The biggest danger in (a) is the temptation to overrun on the time allowed for the solution, given the marks available. Bonus schemes are a recurring feature of this exam and most candidates should be able to write about them both from theoretical and personal knowledge without too much difficulty.

(b) requires much more thought – think about the key issue of independence for NEDs. As long as the features you suggest do not compromise independence or suggest awarding too generous bonuses you will be earning marks.

Examiner's comment. Common errors in part (a) were variants on failing to read the question carefully and plan an appropriate answer. Candidates were sensible to prepare for possible questions on bonus schemes but they must be prepared to answer the question actually asked, not the question on the topic they might have preferred.

(a) **Limiting the range of performance within which rewards are linked to results**

Many schemes do indeed limit the range of performance within which rewards are linked to results, in particular ignoring losses and limiting maximum payments.

Unless the organisation in question was operating in an extremely stable and predictable environment, it would be unacceptable to the vast majority of managers to be asked to participate in a remuneration system that might require them to reimburse their employer in the event of losses being incurred. In general, managers want to receive their standard salary, they do not want the threat of some of it being taken away if their organisation reports losses. If the organisation were to **impose penalties for poor performance**, managers may well **manipulate their targets to ensure that they did not suffer financially**.

Reasons for capping maximum payments include a desire by risk averse managers to **limit the organisation's maximum liability** and the **prevention of payments which shareholders might regard as excessive**. It should be noted, however, that **unexpectedly good performance could well be the result of poor planning**. There may have been a significant rise in sales demand due to a major competitor leaving the market or costs may have fallen sharply following a world-wide drop in the price of the raw material in question, perhaps following a bumper harvest. For managers to benefit from poor planning by receiving excessive bonuses would seem unfair.

Limiting range of performance within which rewards are linked to results

If **losses are excluded** from the range of performance, **full participation** in the scheme is likely as no financial penalty (or negative bonus) can be imposed on a manager if levels of performance are

particularly poor. Salaries will be viewed as fair payment for duties performed, with any bonus being regarded as a genuine reward for effort. Managers may **take unnecessary risks**, however, as they are under no financial risk themselves, and **poor levels of performance may be deliberately further depressed** to ensure easier future targets.

Capping maximum payments should ensure that managers **concentrate on improvements which will be sustainable year-on-year**. The financial incentive provided should be large enough to motivate without being excessive. Managers might feel **no incentive to improve performance beyond the cut-off level**, however, and they could be forced into **holding back for future periods profit-generating or cost-cutting strategies and ideas** once the maximum limit has been reached. A limit on maximum payments could also cause managers to feel **disempowered**, the message being sent out by the bonus system indicating that no matter how good their performance, the most they would receive is £X.

Linking incentive payments to the profits of the organisation as a whole

This is a **popular feature** in many bonus schemes for a number of **reasons**.

(i) Profit is a **widely-understood measure**, and the maximisation of organisational profit is generally accepted to be congruent with the goals of shareholders.

(ii) As **profit reporting forms** part of most organisation's **standard reporting procedures**, little additional work is required for profit to be used as the standard measure of performance (compared with more elaborate performance reward mechanisms which can generate substantial data collection costs).

(iii) It also provides a **basis for participation** in bonus schemes by service centre staff such as those of internal audit and IT departments, for whom the use of other measures can be much more problematic.

(iv) The profit reported by many profit centres will be **significantly affected** by **head office policies** on, for example, salary levels or stock valuation, and so overall organisational profit may be more objective.

(v) Rather than arguing over scarce resources, the use of organisational profit may persuade **profit centre managers** to **work together** to further the aims of the organisation as a whole.

(vi) As agents of the organisation's shareholders, **managers' rewards should be closely linked to the rewards of shareholders.**

Benefits of linking payments to organisational profits

(i) Inter-profit centre/-divisional **conflicts should be minimised**, with all parts of the organisation concentrating on group results.

(ii) Management attention should be focused on the need to **cut unnecessary expenditure.**

(iii) Management will **not be diverted from performing their regular duties** to agree on more elaborate performance-reward systems.

Drawbacks of linking payments to organisational profits

(i) If the proportion of the bonus that is linked to overall organisational performance is significant and other profit centres do not perform well, managers will get a reduced bonus payment or even no payment at all. Managers who consistently perform well and achieve their individual targets are likely to become demotivated if they receive no bonus because of poor levels of performance in other parts of the organisation.

(ii) Managers could feel that their area of responsibility is too small to have a substantial impact on group profits and may become demotivated.

(iii) Managers may **cut short-term, discretionary costs** in order to achieve current profit targets at the **expense of future profits**.

(b) **Bonus schemes for non-executive directors (NEDs)**

The design of bonus schemes for NEDs is **problematic**. If the bonus is **too small** the NEDS may **not be motivated** to do anything more than the minimum required to collect their fees. If the bonus is **too generous** they may **stop acting in the best interests of shareholders for fear of incurring the displeasure of the executive directors** and thereby jeopardizing their bonus payments.

A bonus scheme for NEDs will therefore need to include the following **features**.

(i) It should ensure that **high quality and motivated NEDs** are recruited, thereby ensuring that shareholders will benefit from the appointment of the NEDs.

(ii) The bonus should be paid either **in cash or in the companies' shares**. Such methods will motivate the NED without contravening the recommendation from the Hampel report that NEDs are not granted share options.

(iii) The bonus scheme could be **linked to the long-term performance of the company**, rather than simply to the financial performance of the current period. A **balanced range of performance measures** such as increase in market share or stock market valuation in relation to competitors over a certain period of time (depending on the NEDs' length of contract) and so on should **encourage NEDs to take a broader view of corporate governance.**

(iv) It is important that **good corporate governance is seen to be maintained**. Shareholders' prior approval of any bonus scheme should be obtained to avoid any impression that NEDs' bonuses are being offered as a *quid pro quo* for the executive directors' remuneration.

(v) Any bonus scheme should be designed to provide an incentive for the NED to achieve specific objectives or complete specific tasks outside his normal duties as a NED.

Bonuses are justified for tasks such as carrying out competitor reviews or designing staff remuneration schemes, which will enhance the NED's× understanding of the business without compromising his independence.

(vi) Any **goal-oriented bonuses** should **be paid immediately following the work to which they relate**. Rolling up of bonus payments may silence any criticism from the NED as the payment date approaches.

3 Divisionalised structures

Pass marks. Parts (a) and (b) can be answered from book knowledge, and this would have been perfectly acceptable. Part (c), however, looks at the question from a slightly different angle, which requires some thought. You will almost always find that questions in the MCS exam do this. Many candidates will leave out these parts of questions, so any sensible comments you can find to make will impress the examiner and make your paper stand out from the others. In part (c) it is very helpful to think of control as 'making sure that the right things get done by subordinates'.

Other points. Instead of repeating book knowledge, an alternative approach to part (a) might adopt Williamson's ideas about transaction cost economics. We have included both approaches. Matters that you may legitimately have mentioned in part (c) but which are not included in our answer are organisational culture and leadership style.

Examiner's comment. Common errors were: misreading part (a) and setting out the arguments for *and against* divisionalisation; writing about the *measurement* of divisional performance (marks were not available for expositions of ROI and RI); writing far too much in answer to parts (a) and (b). Marks were allowed if candidates answered part (c) from the perspective of top *divisional* management, although the question was intended to be about top *group* management.

(a) **Arguments for divisionalised structures in large firms**

(i) **Decision makers at divisional level** have **more awareness** of their markets and products and of local problems. They are closer to, and so have a better understanding of, day-to-day operational problems.

(ii) There is **greater speed of decision making** and response to changing events since there is no need to refer decisions upwards. This is valued by customers and is particularly important in a modern, rapidly changing environment.

(iii) Divisionalisation allows more **senior management** to **concentrate on strategic problems** affecting the organisation as a whole. They need not be burdened by large amounts of information that is not relevant to their role.

(iv) Divisionalisation helps more **junior managers** to **develop** in roles of responsibility. Divisional managers can be more adventurous and are better motivated.

Development of hierarchy

An alternative is to argue that the **complexity of the transactions** required for a business to operate **increases, transaction costs can be reduced by adopting some kind of hierarchy**. For example, a firm that only needs legal advice on very rare occasions will engage a firm of solicitors from outside (from the market). If, as that firm grows, it needs legal advice more and more it will eventually be cheaper to set up a full time legal department within the organisation (in an hierarchical structure).

As the **level of complexity increases** still further and we get into the realm of the 'large firms' envisaged in the question, the **cost savings are counterbalanced by the increasing costs of keeping control**. These costs arise because managers are prevented by the hierarchical division of responsibilities from taking the best decisions in their limited area of control, and because information tends to be lost or distorted as it passes through the hierarchy.

Development of M-form

This **leads to** the development of the **multi-divisional** or **M-form organisation** which, by mixing the features of both markets and hierarchies, has the following **advantages**.

(i) Each division has **quasi-autonomous** status: it is a separate business unit.

(ii) **Strategic decisions** are taken by **senior managers** (the hierarchy), while **operational decisions** are made by **divisional managers** (the market).

(iii) An **incentive mechanism** exists and is used to encourage divisional managers to share the interests of senior managers.

(iv) An **internal audit system** is in place, with performance measures to evaluate the success or otherwise of both managers and of divisions.

(v) There is a system of **allocating resources** whereby senior managers distinguish the most profitable alternatives from amongst all divisions.

(b) **The costs and potential inefficiencies of a divisionalised structure**

(i) **Duplication of functions and facilities**. It is perhaps wasteful for each division to have, say, its own management accounting department or production equipment.

(ii) In spite of Williamson's ideals, there will inevitably be some **loss of information** *needed* by the senior managers to take strategic decisions. At the extreme, for example, a divisional manager may be able to hide the truth about a division's poor performance from the top management, who would close down the division or change its manager if they were aware of the full story.

(iii) Competition between divisions *may* be healthy and encourage all divisions to do better. If divisions are dependent upon each other for input, processing or output, however, competition may cause them to take **decisions that are not in the interests of the organisation as a whole.**

(iv) **Senior management** may find that it is spending much of its **time resolving disputes between divisions** about, say, unfair transfer prices or biased allocation of capital investment, rather than concentrating on strategic issues.

As business conditions alter, the balance of power must be able to *shift* between the central authority and the divisions if the organisation as a whole is to be capable consistently of striking the optimum balance between integration and autonomy.

(c) **The role of top management and their control of subordinates**

In a centralised structure **senior managers** are responsible for both the strategic management of the organisation as a whole and for the day-to-day operations of the functions they represent. With a **divisionalised structure** these managers hand over the management of functions to their subordinates. Their role **becomes one more like that of an investor looking for a return on an investment.**

(i) They need to learn to **manage with 'hands off'**, on the basis of summary data, without getting involved in the day -to-day detail. The control system needs to develop appropriate **performance measures** that facilitate this approach. An **internal audit department** reporting directly to top management may be needed for reassurance that day to day operations are being properly managed.

(ii) Rather than fighting their own function's corner in matters such as transfer pricing and capital investment they need to be able to look at these issues from the **point of view of group interests** and **proper co-ordination** of the activities of the organisation as a whole.

(iii) They may need to develop **reward systems** for subordinates **that ensure goal congruence.**

(iv) They will manage from the point of view of the changing environment in which the business as a whole operates, but their perspective of the environment and their subordinates' perspective may be different. **Mutual sharing of environmental data** will become essential.

A useful exposition of the problems of control in large diversified companies is provided by **Goold and Campbell** who identify three different styles of central management.

(i) **Strategic planning**, which entails the centre participating in and influencing the strategies of the core businesses.

(ii) **Financial control**, which focuses on annual profit targets rather than getting involved in the detail of how these are achieved.

(iii) **Strategic control**, where the top management is concerned with the plans of its business units but believes in autonomy for business unit managers. Control is maintained through **financial targets** and **strategic objectives**, but top management do not advocate strategies or interfere in major decisions.

4 Cumbersome process

Pass marks. In this question you need to focus on the budget as a strategic tool, highlighting its impact on performance and thinking about how the organisation's structure determines the budgetary system. A wide focus on a number of different performance measures will help you answer (b) and this is also the sort of question where you can gain credit through bringing in real-life examples.

(a) **Cumbersome and time-consuming process**

Even with the arrival of spreadsheets on PCs in the 1980s, producing the budget in all but the smallest organisation is a time-consuming and laborious task. **Forecasts** have to be made, **data gathered** from a multitude of sources and a **budget drawn up** that is both achievable and appropriate to the position the manager in question perceives he has in the organisation. It is not unusual for **line mangers and their staff to spend weeks preparing budget submissions**.

Once a spreadsheet is actually set up to produce a budget, it is still quite a task to flex the figures and/or change the assumptions upon which the model is based. So **budget officers and management accountants** might then spend at least as long **coordinating** and **revising** the individual budgets, **consolidating** them into, and finally distributing, the master budget.

A benchmarking exercise by Price Waterhouse in 1995 found that budgeting costs a median of $63,000 for every $100m of base revenue within finance departments alone and that budget preparation takes an average of 110 days from start to finish.

Short-term financial control

Budgets are an expression of an organisation's plans and objectives in financial terms. Achieving these financial results can therefore take on an **overriding importance** if the management accounting control system gives signals to the effect that doing so is the only way of achieving the plans and objectives. **Longer-term aims and objectives** (increasing market share, improving levels of customer satisfaction) are often **forgotten** in the rush to hit budgeted profit. **Short-term profit levels can be manipulated**, however (and often are if managerial bonuses are based on budgeted profit), usually to the detriment of those factors which provide for the long-term success of the organisation (such as product quality, customer satisfaction and employee motivation).

Motivation of managers

Targets for bonuses tend to be **based on the figures contained in the budget** and so the budget can be seen as a **commitment** and a **constraint**. It might encourage **rigidity** and **discourage flexibility** in operational decision making since managers are likely to concern themselves simply with achieving the budgeted results. The budgeting and associated reward system might motivate employees to **manipulate results for short-term gain** (perhaps by cutting discretionary expenditure) rather than motivate them to think of ways of improving departmental efficiency, say, as a means of reducing expenditure.

The **degree of difficulty of the budget target** can also have **undesirable effects on the motivation** of managers. If the target is too difficult employees will become demotivated as they cannot achieve it. If it is too easy there will be no sense of achievement in attaining the required standard and hence no motivating force.

Formal organisation structure

Budgets tend to be **based on a system of responsibility centres organised on a departmental or functional basis**. Such organisational structures tend to be **bureaucratic**, **communication is often slow** and **responsibilities overlap**. Achieving, say, departmental targets becomes of paramount importance, regardless of the effect this might have on overall company performance. Functional hierarchies encourage functional excellence but functional departments do not work well together in meeting customers' requirements; they incur excess cost, are too slow and create quality problems.

'Traditional budgeting....strengthens the vertical chain of command and control rather than empowering the front-line. It **constrains** rather than increases flexibility and responsiveness. It **reinforces departmental barriers** rather than encouraging knowledge-sharing across the organisation. It makes people feel undervalued - as ''costs to be minimised'' rather than as assets to be developed. And it is **bureaucratic**, **internally focused** and **time-consuming**. In short, its time is up.' (Hope and Fraser, *Management Accounting*, December 1997)

(b) **Steps to reduce bureaucracy**

There are a number of steps that can be taken to reduce the bureaucracy and time associated with budgeting.

(i) The **time allowed to build the budget should be reduced**. Employees are likely to use up as much time as they are given and will continue to 'fine tune' figures until the last possible moment.

(ii) The **number of versions made of the budget should also be reduced**; the precision gained with each cycle rarely justifies the extra effort.

(iii) The **budget period should be reduced**. A system of rolling budgets will be more accurate than a conventional budget that looks 15 or 18 months into the future.

Alternatively, managers could be given **board-approved targets** which they could aim to achieve in their own way. There would be no need to submit detailed plans for approval, just planning assumptions and overall targets.

Short-term financial control

Extensive surveys conducted by the leading accounting firms indicate that 99% of all companies in Europe still operate with formal budgeting systems. Peter Bunce and Robin Fraser reported in *Management Accounting* (February 1997) of a number of Scandinavian organisations which are adopting alternative and, they hope, more effective methods of financial planning and performance measurement. IKEA, the world's largest furniture manufacturer and retailer, abandoned budgeting in 1992. Business managers now simply have to **keep costs within certain revenue ratios**.

ABB is implementing its own version of the **balanced scorecard**. This method of performance analysis considers not just financial performance but also customer knowledge, internal business processes and learning and growth. It emphasises non-financial as well as financial information, looks at the medium and long term objectives as well as short-term targets and takes into account external as well as internal information.

Volvo's new planning process focuses on **objectives** and employs **key performance indicators**.

Instead of using the budget as a means of concentrating on short-term profitability and maximising return to shareholders, other organisations are concentrating on **finding and profitably satisfying customers**. This involves adopting a programme of total quality management and establishing employee, customer and shareholder loyalty and, in the long term, maximising value creation for all of the organisation's stakeholders.

Motivation of managers

Rather than appraising managerial performance in terms of targets based on an internally-generated budget, it should be **based on external intelligence** derived from benchmarking exercises and customer feedback. **Targets** should not simply be short term and financially orientated but **cover a wide range of measures** as advocated by the balanced scorecard approach. Mangers will thus be motivated to work towards the organisation's goals and objectives rather than concentrating on departmental or personal ones.

Formal organisation structure

To cope with the demands of today's rapidly-changing and competitive business environment, organisations need to be **decentralised** to allow greater speed of decision making and response to changing events. ABB, for example, is highly decentralised, each unit managing its own finances as if it were an independent company. **Processes** and **teams** are of paramount importance. Processes offer managers a clearer view of which work should be done and, when new technology is applied, how such work can be done faster and more effectively. Svenska Handelsbanken, for example, abandoned traditional budgeting in 1979 and operates each branch like an independent business.

It is therefore evident that although the budgeting process can be criticised, many organisations are evolving ways of overcoming the problems.

5 Risk identification

> **Pass marks**. (a) offers a method of analysing losses which you may find helpful. It is important that risk analysis is wide-ranging, hence to score good marks in (c) you need to be aware of a large number of possible sources of information.

(a) **Risk analysis**

As stated in the question the first stage of risk identification is to **analyse the major types of loss** to which the party at risk is subject. To do this it will need to consider its circumstances: what it does and how it does it; what it uses in the process; who does it; and what the consequences would be of not doing it.

The types of loss affecting a business will thus be seen to fall into five main categories, although they are somewhat interlinked.

(i) **Pecuniary losses**

Pecuniary losses can arise from the **interruption of the businesses**, from the **dishonesty** of the people working in the business, or though the **default** (for example bad debts) or **wrong-doing** of external parties. A business might, for example, need to protect its secret processes, or guard against computer fraud, or put up bandit screens in its branches.

(ii) **Liability losses**

Liability losses result from **damage or injury to third parties**. A food manufacturer would be particularly concerned, as would a bus and coach operator.

(iii) **Property losses**

Property losses are perhaps the most obvious kind. The key concern here is not with financial compensation for a factory that has burnt down, but with the **reinstatement** of **the factory** so that business may continue.

(iv) **Personal losses**

Personal losses derive from **accidents** to or the **sickness or death of employees**. Any employee is a potential liability while he is at work, but a business may be particularly vulnerable if a key employee with special management or technical skills suffers some mishap.

(v) **Interruption losses**

Interruption losses can arise from any of the other causes: financial loss may cause **delay in obtaining supplies**; liability losses may involve a **stoppage of production** because a product is unsafe; property losses will **deprive the business of the tools** to do the job and personnel losses of the hands to guide the tools.

(b) The **immediate causes** of loss **are expressed** in general terms. For example a flood is an immediate cause of any of the five types of loss described above. It may in turn be caused by a variety of underlying factors - an adjoining river, a burst pipe, torrential rain, a faulty sprinkler system, and so on - and thus immediate causes must be identified first. In practise this will involve a systematic search including discussions with those who have the greatest knowledge of particular areas of the business and also outside parties such as neighbours, architects or government officers.

(c) **Underlying causes**

The underlying causes of loss can be identified and assessed in detail. Organisations will probably keep detailed records of their activities and the unit costs involved, but it is unlikely that any organisation can predict the full cost of every loss which might befall it with certainty. The calculation will involve numerous factors, of which those noted in the following paragraphs are only suggestions.

(i) **Organisation charts** will be needed if a manager is taken ill, for example to calculate which personnel will have extra work in his and other departments, how much need be paid in overtime rates and whether additional expertise may have to be brought in temporarily. The personnel department may be asked for lists of employees with appropriate skills and experience who are prepared to help out.

(ii) **Production flow charts** must be used to discover the extent to which a factory's production will be affected by one machine breaking down, and whether alternative machines can be obtained or constructed, or alternative processes used.

(iii) **Supplies flow charts** and forecasts will help to assess how long a factory can maintain some or all of its production if any particular supplier suffers a major fire, or bankruptcy, and whether there are alternative suppliers.

(iv) **Details of major customers** can be monitored to identify those whose bankruptcy could damage the organisation.

(v) **Published accounts**, internal accounts and budgets are a fertile source of information. The more carefully costs are allocated to each department, the easier it should be to calculate additional costs which would be incurred in a given emergency, which budgets will be affected and how quickly necessary funds can be made available.

(vi) **Detailed plans of site and buildings** will show potential bottlenecks in fire escape routes, obstructions which might make difficulties for fire engines and problems of access which could occur for both the site and its neighbours from fire, explosion, or escaping gas.

(vii) **Physical inspection of buildings and machines** (and perhaps of personnel, in the medical sense, and of their working practices) should take place on a regular basis.

6 Crashcarts

Pass marks. The Turnbull and COSO guidance on risk are important in this paper and you should get credit for quoting **relevant** parts. The emphasis that these reports place on accurate and relevant information has obvious implications for the management accountant, both in terms of ensuring the information is correct, and devising new measures. (b) should offer fairly easy marks, but don't run over time on it.

The calculations in (c) though long-winded are not technically difficult once you realise what drives the risk. The assumption that enquiries only fail to become orders because of shortages of inventory seems a slightly strange one and certainly worth a comment in the discussion. Otherwise the approach to questions like (c) is to work methodically through the information and assume most of it will be relevant to a discussion of risks; in some cases the risks will be obvious, in others you will need to think and make connections between different pieces of information (such as the client bases of parents and subsidiaries).

It is possible to go into a lot of technical detail about control systems in (d), but remember that this is also a practical paper, and thus suggesting appropriate controls will gain you considerable credit. The best way to emphasise that the controls you suggest are relevant is to group them under the key risk headings identified in (c).

(a) **Corporate governance guidance**

In America the COSO committee has emphasised the importance of **enterprise risk management**, in particular the links between the organisation's **strategy** and its ability to bear risks, **enhancement** of **risk responses** and **considering opportunities** as well as risks.

The UK's **Turnbull committee** suggested that review of internal controls should be an **integral part** of the **company's operations**.

Risk perspective

The Turnbull committee emphasised the importance of a risk-based perspective, in particular avoiding **unnecessary financial risks**, risks that **accounting information** may be **unreliable** and threats to the **safeguarding of assets**. Boards need also to be able to make sure that controls are not so restrictive that there is a **risk of missed opportunities**.

Role of the board

In particular the board should consider:

(i) The identification, evaluation and management of all **key risks** affecting the organisation

(ii) The **effectiveness of internal control**; again that does not just mean financial controls but also operational, compliance and risk management controls

(iii) The **action taken** if any **weaknesses** are found

The Turnbull report recommends that when assessing the **effectiveness of internal control**, boards should consider the following:

(i) The **nature** and **extent** of the **risks** which face the company and which it regards as **acceptable** for the company to bear within its particular business

(ii) The **threat** of such **risks becoming a reality**

(iii) If that happened, the company's ability to **reduce** the **incidence** and **impact** on the business

(iv) The **costs and benefits** related to operating relevant controls

Role of management accountants

Providing information

Turnbull recommends that in order to carry out their work effectively, boards need to receive and review reports on internal control. Reports by management accountants could form part of this review, particularly reports on the **operation of the budgeting systems**, **feedback** on the results of comparison between actual and budgeted figures, and details of the **action taken** if significant variances have been identified.

Management accountants can also play a key role in **risk quantification**, presenting the results of complex risk quantification techniques in a form that will enable the board to decide on the threats the organisation faces.

Management accountants must also be concerned with the **accuracy of information**.

Designing systems

Recommendations by management accountants can help ensure that risk avoidance and reduction is built into management accounting control systems. This includes specifying the key information that systems will handle; in an **uncertain environment** more use will be made of **external, non-financial** and **projected information**. COSO emphasises the importance of refining large volumes of data into **actionable information**, and changing information systems as required, to support new objectives.

(b) A formal methodology to analyse risk is made up of five stages

(i) **Risk identification**

The company needs first to identify what potential risks there might be. This can be achieved by **physical inspection** of, for example, computerised equipment, **review of documentation**, for example **correspondence with clients**, and **brainstorming** with representatives of various departments. An important part of risk identification is **identifying events** that could cause problems.

(ii) **Risk assessment**

Risk assessment involves ascertaining all the **possible consequences** of the identified risks actually occurring. **Sources of information** that might need to be reviewed include organisation and production charts, information about major customers and accounting information.

(iii) **Risk profiling**

Risk profiling involves using the results of the risk identification and assessment to group risks according to their **likelihood** and **consequences**.

(iv) **Risk quantification**

A variety of techniques such as **sensitivity analysis**, **scenarios** and **expected values** can be used to calculate the impact of risks. The company should aim to quantify:

- Average or expected results or losses
- Frequency of losses
- Chances of losses
- Largest predictable losses

(v) **Risk consolidation**

Senior management at the parent must ascertain whether there are any risks that are **common** to both the parent and subsidiary, such as problems with accounting information, and try to ascertain the impact of these risks.

(c) **Risk identification – subsidiary**

Client risk

The major risk the subsidiary faces is the loss of clients. The subsidiary has a number of large retail clients, so the loss of even a couple may have a serious impact on profits. The subsidiary may be particularly vulnerable to being **undercut** on price, with cost centres abroad having lower labour costs and hence being able to offer better terms.

Running out of inventory

As indicated below, the subsidiary faces the risk of major loss of income through its clients having insufficient inventory

Information technology risks

The subsidiary may be vulnerable to a **major breakdown in technology**. The **maintenance contract** and the **off-site back-up** should help mitigate this risk, although this may make the subsidiary vulnerable to problems with its suppliers. As the subsidiary holds a lot of sensitive data, the consequences of a successful attempt at **hacking** could be serious. In a few years time the technology will need replacing; although IT developments should mean that the subsidiary can easily find compatible technology, there may be a **risk of increased lease payments** and **further pressure on profits**.

Human resource risk

The subsidiary may be vulnerable to loss of orders due to mistakes or slowness of processing by inadequately trained or poorly motivated staff. The holding of credit and debit card information may make the subsidiary vulnerable to **fraud** by staff members.

Risk identification – parent

Investment risk

The parent faces the risk of **loss of income** if the subsidiary loses clients, and ultimately **impairment, in the value of its investment** in its accounts. However the parent will not be liable for the subsidiary's debts should the subsidiary run into financial difficulties.

Reputation risk

The parent may suffer a loss of reputation if the subsidiary is unable to provide an adequate service. This may be quite serious for the parent as there appears to be **overlap** between the **parent and subsidiary's clients** and both are providing information technology services. The parent may be more vulnerable as the services it provides seem to be more in the nature of one-off consultancy projects rather than long-term continuing operations.

Control risk

The parent may also face the risk that controls over the subsidiary fail to work, resulting in the need for expenditure of time and resources to correct difficulties.

Risk quantification

The company can use a number of **different sensitivity calculations** to assess the impact of for example price changes and loss of customers. Here we shall look at the impact of running out of inventory and of spare operator capacity.

Running out of inventory

	2001	*2002*	*2003*
Number of incoming calls received	1,200,000	1,300,000	1,350,000
Number of orders processed	1,000,000	1,100,000	1,150,000
Out of stock-orders	200,000	200,000	200,000
Average number of line items per order	3.0	2.9	2.8
Out of stock-line items	600,000	580,000	560,000
	£	£	£
Income per order processed	2.50	2.75	3.00
Income per line item processed	0.20	0.15	0.12
Lost income per order	500,000	550,000	600,000
Lost income per line item	120,000	87,000	67,200
Total lost income from running out of inventory	620,000	637,000	667,200

This calculation assumes that the sole reason for the difference between incoming calls and orders is lack of inventory, and ignores the possibility of staff problems.

Spare capacity

	2001	*2002*	*2003*
Number of operators	70	80	80
Capacity (operators x orders per operator)	1,050,000	1,200,000	1,200,000
Actual number of orders	1,000,000	1,100,000	1,150,000
Spare capacity (orders)	50,000	100,000	50,000
	£	£	£
Cost per order (operator costs/ order capacity)	1.48	1.60	1.82
Cost of spare capacity	73,810	160,000	90,833

(d) **Elements of Management Control Systems**

In common with other control systems, management accounting control systems have **inputs**, **processes** and **outputs**.

The outputs are used by managers to assure themselves that specific tasks are being carried out **efficiently and effectively** (operational control) and assuring themselves that resources have been obtained and used **efficiently and effectively** in the **accomplishment** of the **organisation's objectives**. This implies comparison of outputs with predictions/targets, so that there is a **predictive element** built into control systems. It also implies determining the cause of deviation from predictions/targets and taking corrective action if necessary.

As well as taking action based on **feedback** arising from what has happened, management accounting systems also allow **feedforward control**, the forecasting of differences between actual and planned outcomes, and the implementation of action beforehand to avoid differences.

Responsibility centres

As indicated above, there is a risk that controls over the subsidiary will fail to work and that the parent will suffer a **loss of resources**. Responsibility centres are a key component of management accounting systems, but the parent's directors need to decide how much **responsibility** the subsidiary will be allowed, and how much power will be **centralised**.

Key controls

The main controls that Crashcarts should implement are largely based round the key risks identified in (c). A few general measures for reducing risk are also relevant.

General risk reduction measures

(i) There should be procedures in place for identifying and assessing risks (see (b)) and recording risks in a **risk register**.

(ii) It may be economic to appoint a **risk manager** to monitor risk, and deal immediately with serious risks.

(iii) The board and audit committee should maintain awareness of risks, and carry out a formal **review of the company's risk management processes** at least once a year.

(iv) **Internal audit** should concentrate on the key risk areas.

Subsidiaries

Client risk

(i) The subsidiary should have formal arrangements for dealing with each client, including **someone managing the relationship** and periodically **receiving feedback** on service levels.

(ii) Senior managers should receive reports from each client service manager and be alert for any **common problems in relationships**.

(iii) **Formal tendering procedures** should be in place if contracts are periodically re-advertised. These should involve senior management and operational staff. After every tender, **debriefing procedures** should be in place to ensure lessons are learnt.

(iv) There should also be procedures in place for **monitoring trends** in the market, both in terms of identifying which **clients** might be **vulnerable** and any **opportunities** to win new business.

Running out of inventory

It may seem that clients running out of inventory is something that the subsidiary has no control over. However the subsidiary should keep full records of when **orders** are **lost** through lack of inventory and **inform the clients**; the subsidiary should not assume that the client will automatically act to deal with the problems.

Information technology risks

(i) **Supplier performance** should be **monitored** by having staff appointed to liase with the supplier.

(ii) In particular the **security** of the system needs to be kept under review and controls against outside hacking tested regularly.

(iii) **Records** should be kept of all problems that arise, how they were dealt with and what the consequences were.

(iv) Full controls should be maintained at the call centre including **passwords** and **other access controls**, **data confirmation**, **backup**, **virus protection**.

(v) **Insurance** against disasters should be taken out.

Human resource risks

(i) A **formal induction programme** and **immediate and appropriate training** should ensure that staff reach full competence as quickly as possible.

(ii) **Morale** can be **improved** by obtaining and acting upon feedback from staff (including exit interviews), appraisals and appropriate reward schemes.

(iii) Potential causes of stress should be monitored including **working conditions** and **health and safety considerations**, and **stress counselling be made available** if **required**.

Parent

Investment risk

The value of the investment is primarily dependent on **maintaining** and **expanding** the **client base**. However the value of the investment should be monitored by obtaining **performance information** on a regular basis.

Reputation risk

(i) Reputation risk will of course be much reduced if the risk measures taken by the subsidiary are successful

(ii) However the parent should also have **contingency plans** for **damage limitation** should problems arise with the subsidiary. This includes acting through news management to maintain its reputation, and also policies to preserve its own relations with specific clients who have had problems with the subsidiary.

Control risk

(i) The financial performance of the subsidiary should be compared with targets, **variances highlighted** and action taken to correct problems. The senior managers of the parent should receive information that problems have been corrected.

(ii) Similar procedures should apply to **non-financial performance measures**, in particular the calls received, orders and line items processed.

(iii) Key decisions, for example **major expenditure** by the **subsidiary**, should be **authorised** by the **parent's board**.

7 Segregation of duties

Pass marks. A temptation that must be resisted is to write too much on part (a) at the expense of the other parts. In (a) you must understand why segregation of duties is an important organisational control. Parts (b) and (c) require discussion of alternative means of achieving control when management autonomy means a lack of segregation of duties. Review of performance indicators (outputs) is particularly important in both cases; other important controls are organisation controls and internal audit.

Examiner's comment. Part (a) required a statement of why segregation of duties was important and the consequences of lack of segregation. A common error in part (b) was to suggest the imposition of very tight controls from head office; branch managers must have some autonomy if they are to manage properly. Various approaches were possible to part (c); good answers concentrated on the balancing of empowerment and control. The reduction in bureaucracy should have meant that the remaining controls were essential, not merely desirable.

(a) **Definition**

The Auditing Practice Committee's guideline on internal controls defined segregation of duties as 'the separation of those responsibilities or duties which would, if combined, enable one individual to **process** a **complete transaction**'.

Importance

The main purposes of segregation of duties are as follows.

(i) It allows **independent checking** of one person by another, thus reducing the risk of intentional discrepancies and unintentional errors.

(ii) By increasing the number of people in the transaction process, it **reduces** the **risk of collusion**.

(iii) Effective segregation means that **responsibilities are established clearly**.

Role of internal audit

Internal audit can ensure segregation is operating properly by means of the following checks.

(i) **System reviews**. These should ensure in particular that the **functions** of authorisation, execution and recording of transactions, and safeguarding of assets are **kept separate**.

(ii) **Detailed checks**. Internal audit should ensure segregation is operating as laid down, and in particular **authorisation controls** are adequate and are fully operational.

(iii) **Follow-up of other weaknesses**. Certain other failings in internal controls may imply lack of segregation of duties. Examples include **lack of documentation** of transactions or decisions and **poor controls** over the **custody** of cash and cheques.

(b) Head office can compensate for the lack of segregation of duties by use of the following controls.

(i) The branch manager should, when recruited, have been subject to a **full reference check**.

(ii) Head office should ensure that the branch manager exercises appropriate control over **day-to-day transactions**. He should for example sign all cheques for significant amounts.

(iii) **Certain decisions**, for example fixed asset or other large purchases, should be **authorised** by **head office** as well as by the branch manager.

(iv) Head office should receive **regular returns** from the branch manager and should **investigate unusual sales patterns**, and **shortages** of cash or stock. The branch's performance should be compared with the performance of other branches.

(v) **Internal audit** should visit the branch regularly. **Surprise visits** can serve as a **check on stock or cash levels**.

(vi) **Expected visits** should be used as a check that the **authorisation procedures** laid down by the company are being followed. In addition internal audit may substantively test certain transactions, particularly large or unusual payments.

(c) The company's commitment to a flatter, less bureaucratic structure means that certain controls will no longer be operating. Responsibilities will not be laid down in detail, and junior managers will not be subject to detailed supervision from the company's head office.

What the company must do to maintain control is as follows:

(i) Concentrate on effectively **implementing controls** that can work in a more **informal structure**

(ii) Ensure **goal congruence** so that junior managers have a personal interest in achieving the company's objectives

Organisation controls

(i) Although the company can no longer rely on a hierarchical structure, it can still issue a **mission statement** setting out objectives and business ethics.

(ii) There will still be **some limits** to managers' authority, for example annual budget limits.

Personnel controls

(i) Personnel controls will be of increased importance. These should include controls not just at the **recruitment** stage but also at the **key promotion stages**.

(ii) **Training** will be important as a means of developing management skills and another means of communicating the aims of the company.

Management controls

(i) Review of management performance should be achieved by **financial and non-financial indicators**.

(ii) **Management audits** either by other managers or internal audit will be a useful quality control check.

(iii) Certain traditional internal audit checks, such as checks on **custody of assets** and that **separate authorisation** is obtained on the (rare) occasions it is required, will still be used.

Reward

As well as controls, the reward system should encourage the **achievement of objectives** in accordance with the aims of the organisation. A range of measures may be required, including financial targets and total quality management.

8 Corporate governance

Pass marks. You need to know about the UK's Combined Code since it represents best practice in one of the major stock markets in the world. However whether you would get a question in the exam specifically on it is uncertain, since CIMA has indicated that questions will not be focused on one jurisdiction. This question, requiring listing of the main corporate governance requirements, appears to be very straightforward for a Strategic level paper.

To: Chief Executive
From: Accountant
Date: 2 August 20X4
Subject; Corporate Governance

The Combined Code was originally published in the UK in 1998 to bring together the recommendations of the Cadbury, Greenbury and Hampel reports. It was updated in 2003. The UK guidance in some ways is less prescriptive than guidance in America and elsewhere, being based more on companies disclosing reasons for any non-compliance with the guidelines in the Code.

(a) **Role and responsibilities of the board**

All listed companies should be led by an **effective board**. The board should meet regularly and have **certain matters** reserved for its decision such as mergers and major asset acquisitions and disposals.

The board should present a **balanced and understandable assessment** of the **company's position and prospects** in the annual accounts and other reports such as interim reports and reports to regulators.

The board should **review the effectiveness of internal control** annually and report to shareholders that they have done so. The review should cover all controls including financial, operational and compliance controls and risk management.

As part of their responsibility for ensuring that internal controls are effective, the board should appoint an **audit committee.**

(b) **Role and responsibilities of the audit committee**

The audit committee should consist of at least three independent non-executive directors, at least one of whom has relevant and recent accounting experience.

(i) **Review of financial statements and systems**

The committee should review both the **interim (if published) and annual accounts**. This should involve assessment of the judgements made about the **overall appearance** and **presentation** of the accounts, and also **any changes in accounting policies and practices, major judgmental areas** and **compliance with standards and legal requirements**.

As well as reviewing the accounts, the committee's review should cover the financial reporting and budgetary systems. This involves considering **performance indicators** and **information systems** that allow **monitoring** of the **most significant business and financial risks**, and the progress towards financial objectives.

(ii) **Liaison with external auditors**

The audit committee will be responsible for the **appointment or removal of the external auditors** as well as fixing their remuneration. They should consider whether there are threats to the **independence** of external audit, in particular whether the **provision of non-audit services may lead to a conflict of interest.**

The audit committee should also be in contact with external auditors during their audit. The committee should **discuss the scope of the external audit** prior to the start of the audit. The committee should also act as a **forum** for **liaison** between the external auditors, the internal auditors and the finance director and help **the external auditors to obtain the information** they require.

If problems arise during the audit, the audit committee should be available for **consultation,** and see that the **concerns raised by the external auditors** are **resolved.**

(iii) **Review of internal audit**

The audit committee should review on an annual basis the work of internal audit .The review should cover the following aspects.

- **Standards** including objectivity, technical knowledge and professional standards
- **Scope** including how much emphasis is given to different types of review
- **Resources**
- **Reporting arrangements**
- **Work plan**, especially review of controls and coverage of high risk areas
- **Liaison** with external auditors
- **Results**

(iv) **Review of internal control**

The audit committee should **monitor** continually the **adequacy** of **internal control systems**, focusing particularly on the control environment, management's attitude towards controls and overall management controls. Committee members should check that there are systems in place to promote compliance with legislation. They should review reports on the operation of **codes of conduct** and review violations. Each year the committee should be responsible for **reviewing the company's statement on internal controls** prior to its approval by the board.

The committee should also address the risk of **fraud**, ensuring employees are aware of risks, there are mechanisms in place for staff to report fraud, and fraud to be investigated.

(v) **Review of risk management**

The audit committee can play an important part in the review of risk recommended by the Turnbull report. This includes confirming that there is a **formal policy** in place for **risk management** and that the policy is backed and regularly monitored by the board. They should also **review** the **arrangements** for ensuring that managers and staff are aware of their responsibilities. They should also ensure that there are channels for staff to **report improprieties.**

(vi) **Investigations**

The committee will also be involved in implementing and reviewing the results of one-off investigations. Audit committees should be given specific authority to investigate matters of concern, and in doing so have access to sufficient resources, appropriate information and outside professional help.

(c) **Disclosure requirements**

The Combined Code requires the following general disclosures:

(i) A **narrative statement** of how they **applied the principles** set out in the Combined Code, providing explanations which enable their shareholders to assess how the principles have been applied.

(ii) A **statement** as to whether or not they **complied** throughout the accounting period with the **provisions** set out in the Combined Code. Listed companies that did not comply throughout the accounting period with all the provisions must specify the provisions with which they did not comply, and give reasons for non-compliance.

The directors should **explain** their **responsibility for preparing accounts**. They should **report that the business is a going concern**, with supporting assumptions and qualifications as necessary.

In addition the following further statements are required:

(i) Information about the **board of directors**: **changes in the composition** of the board in the year, the **identity of the chairman, chief executive** and **senior non-executive** director and **information about the independence** of the **non-executives**, frequency of and attendance at board meetings, how the board's performance has been evaluated.

(ii) Brief report on the **remuneration, audit and nomination committees** covering terms of reference, composition and frequency of meetings

(iii) Information about **relations with auditors** including reasons for change and steps taken to ensure auditor objectivity and independence when non-audit services have been provided

(iv) A statement that the directors have reviewed the **effectiveness** of **internal controls**, including risk management, within the framework of the Turnbull guidelines

(v) A statement on relations and **dialogue with shareholders**

(vi) A statement that the company is a **going concern**

(vii) An **operating and financial review.**

Please contact me if you have any further queries.

9 Internal audit role

Pass marks This question brings out the need to understand the difference between the different types of audit. Most of the areas considered by external auditors when they review the work of internal audit should also be considered when the audit committee carries out its annual review of internal audit.

REPORT

To: Board of directors
From: Internal audit manager
Date: 18 November 20X6
Subject: The role of internal audit

Introduction

As requested I have produced in this report a description of the role of internal audit in comparison with that of external audit, and in the context of developing a new accounting system.

(a) **Internal audit and external audit compared**

The main functions of internal audit and external audit are very different, although some of the means of fulfilling each function are the same.

Role of external auditors

The external auditors are appointed by the shareholders to report on the stewardship of the managers of the company on a **regular basis** (usually annually). The role of the external auditors is defined by statute and the report produced by the external auditors states whether the published financial statements show a true and fair view and adhere to accounting standards.

Role of internal auditors

In contrast, internal auditors are employed directly by the managers of the company. This means that they are **not independent** of the company and its managers, unlike the external auditors. The internal auditors normally work **full time** for the company and their role is much more varied and wide-ranging than that of the external auditors. As well as statutory matters the internal auditors will be concerned with **monitoring the effectiveness of all controls** within the business, whether financial or non-financial, and whether operational departments are **implementing new systems** and **company policies**. The internal auditors will normally report directly to management, but may occasionally report directly to an audit committee. The objectives of internal audit are controlled by management.

In their work, both the internal and external auditors will evaluate and test the internal control system of the business. In this overlap area, the internal auditors may aid the external auditors to avoid duplication of work and to cut costs.

(b) **Reliance on internal audit by the external auditors**

The auditors will assess the internal controls of a company in order to determine whether they may rely on the controls and thereby reduce the number of substantive procedures to be carried out. The internal audit function will be part of the system of controls and therefore the internal audit function must be assessed by the external auditors. There are several factors which must be examined.

(i) How **independently** do the internal auditors **operate** within the company and to what level of management do they report?

(ii) What are the **scope and objectives** of the internal audit department? Is it sufficiently wide-ranging and unrestricted?

(iii) What **qualifications** do the internal auditors have? Do they receive sufficient training to carry out their jobs? Are they all screened carefully and do they follow a code of conduct of some kind?

(iv) Do the internal auditors **exercise due professional care** in their work?

(v) Are the **reports** produced by internal audit of a **good standard**, sent to the appropriate senior managers, and are they acted on promptly and effectively?

(vi) What **level of resources** is the internal audit department given?

When the external auditors have considered all these points, they may feel that internal audit work can be used as part of the external audit. Any co-operation of this sort needs to be carefully negotiated to make sure that all important matters are agreed.

(c) **The impact of internal audit on external audit**

The responsibility for the external audit cannot be **reduced** or **diluted** by the presence, and reliance on, an internal audit department. The external auditors may not have to perform a great deal of testing if they rely on internal audit work, but the review of internal audit mentioned in (b) above must be carried out, and all the internal audit working papers must be reviewed by the external auditors. Thus, the amount of work might be reduced in volume, but the external auditors must exercise greater judgement.

Internal auditors will have an **in-depth knowledge** of most aspects of the company and this knowledge may be used by the external auditors and thus their work will be simplified.

There may be certain procedures which the internal auditors are much better placed to perform than the external auditors, due to the **timing of the tests** (when the external auditors did not plan to be present) and in such cases the external auditors will find it more cost effective and often simpler to use internal audit to perform the tests in question.

10 Audit sampling

Pass marks. This question is a good indication of the main areas you will need to discuss on sampling.

(a) Auditors would be unlikely to use audit sampling techniques where:

(i) Populations are too **small** so that statistical theory cannot be applied without creating unacceptable margins of error;

(ii) There are **balances or transactions** which are of great significance in terms of size, but few in number; and

(iii) Populations are **unsuitable** because they are non-homogenous which means that sorting is required before sampling can take place.

(b) The factors which the auditors should consider when determining the size of a sample are as follows.

(i) **Assurance required**

The auditors have to **accept a risk** (sampling risk) that they may reach a different conclusion by sampling than they would if they examined the entire population. The degree of assurance the auditors plan to obtain from the results of the sample has a direct effect on the sample size. The greater the degree of assurance required, the larger will be the required sample size.

(ii) **Tolerable error/deviation rate**

This is the **maximum error or deviation rate** the auditors are prepared to accept in the population and still conclude that their audit objective has been achieved. The larger the tolerable error or deviation rate, the smaller need be the sample size.

(iii) **Expected error/deviation rate**

If the auditors **expect errors or deviations** to be present before performing tests, for example because of the results of the previous year's tests or their evaluation of internal controls, they will need to take this into account in selecting an efficient sampling method and determining the sample size.

(iv) **Stratification**

This is the process of **dividing a population into sub-populations** so that items within each sub-population are expected to have similar characteristics in certain respects. This reduces the degree of variation between items. By stratifying, the auditors can devote more of their attention to those items considered most vulnerable to material error.

(c) Statistical sampling enhances the quality of the audit evidence for the following reasons.

(i) It imposes on the auditors a **more formal discipline** as regards planning the audit of a population in that they cannot perform the mechanics of selecting a statistical sample until they have decided on the tolerable error in respect of the population and the amount of audit assurance that they wish to obtain from the sample.

(ii) The **required sample** size is **determined objectively**. Once the auditors have used their judgement to decide subjectively the tolerable error and the level of assurance required, the statistical method determines the sample size required to satisfy their objectives.

(iii) The **evaluation of test results** is **made more precisely** and the **sampling risk** is **quantified**.

11 Analytical review: Practical

Pass marks. The examiners have stated that you might be asked to analyse numerical data and this is one area of the syllabus where you might have to, although obviously assessment of accounts comes up in a number of other papers. Remember that you are trying to use analytical review to identify the key risk areas, particularly areas where controls are lacking or not operating, because these are the areas of most interest to the internal auditor.

(a) **Inventory**

Inventory represents a significant proportion of current assets (59%) and the average age of inventory has increased from 74 days in 20X1 to 95 days in 20X2 compared to an industry average of 73 days.

Average age of inventory = (average inventory / cost of sales) × 365

Receivables

Receivables represent a significant proportion of current assets (33.3%) and the average age of customers has increased from 32 days in 20X1 to 37 days in 20X2 compared to an industry average of 30 days.

Average age of receivables = (average receivables / sales) × 365

Non-current assets

Of the net assets employed in the business 52% is invested in non-current assets. (Is the valuation of non-current assets reasonable in view of the need for a loan issue to enable part of the plant to be remodelled?)

Net profit before tax on net assets employed

The percentage return has declined from 17.5% in 20X1 to 16.4% in 20X2 and compares unfavourably with an industry average of 19.5%. It appears that there is a particular problem on profit margins.

Net profit and gross profit before tax on sale

The net profit before tax on sales has marginally increased from 8.3% for 20X1 to 8.5% in 20X2 but compares poorly with an industry average of 11%. The gross profit on sales barely changed, being 31.7% in 20X1 and 31% in 20X2 but the industry average is 34%.

Expenses

There has been a saving on administration expenses but selling expenses are now 11.5% on sales as compared to 9.5% in 20X1.

Other matters

An analysis of current liabilities is required so that this item can be further investigated. The interest cover was 5 times in 20X2 as against 6.7 times in 20X1 whereas the industry average is 8 times.

(b) The areas which cause particular concern are inventory, gross profit on sales, sales expenses, receivables and the proposed loan stock issue.

Inventory

The average age of inventory has shown a marked increase with a result that there are increased holding costs with the greater amount of inventory, loss of capital tied up in inventory, dangers of obsolescence, pilferage and so on. As a consequence the auditors will need to pay particular attention to **obsolete, slow moving and damaged inventory**. They must ensure that inventory is **adequately insured** and they should carefully examine the **system of inventory recording and reporting** to management of inventory movements and levels. They will also require a detailed breakdown between raw materials, work in progress, completed machines, consumables etc. In addition to the normal checks on these figures, questions need to be asked as to the **proportion of spares** held as a service to customers and company policy as to **retention of spares for obsolete machines** including their valuation.

Gross profit on sales

The reason why Patchit is earning less than the industry average could be due to a number of different factors, for example **lower sales** prices, **more costly materials**, poor materials, **higher production costs**, **poor workmanship**, inventory control or valuation problems. The internal auditors should be aware that any of these areas could lead to gross profit reductions and their work should encompass these areas.

Sales expenses

The auditors will require an analysis of this between **fixed salaries**, commission, travelling expenses, entertainment and so on, before they can investigate further. They will be particularly concerned that management are aware of the increases which have been authorised by them. During their routine audit tests they will examine the documentation relating to certain of **the payments** made.

Receivables

The average age of receivables has slightly increased but this is an area which should be tightly controlled as the firm is losing money due to the fact that customers are taking **longer to pay**. There is also a greater danger of **bad debts** being incurred. The auditors must therefore pay particular attention to the adequacy of the provision for doubtful debts and the systems of credit control.

Proposed loan stock issue

Although this is a matter for the directors to decide, the internal auditors' advice may be sought or they may feel that they ought to advise the directors in any case. It has already been pointed out that the **interest cover** is not as good as the industry average and if the further issue is made the cover could in fact be worse. This is particularly the case with an industry which it is stated is unpredictable. Is it wise to have such heavy borrowings in such an industry? There is a possibility that if business deteriorates there could be a strain on liquidity as interest payments must be met. A possible alternative could be a bonus issue by capitalisation of part of the reserves followed by a rights issue to raise the additional cash.

12 Management control framework

Pass marks. Corporate governance is central to this question, but the answer also requires an appreciation of how the board should operate.

Examiner's comment. A number of candidates failed to follow the rubric of the question which required answers to follow the control cycle model described, discuss board level action and comment on internal control. A number of candidates merely wrote a "standard" essay. Others failed to relate the framework to anything specific.

(a) **Defining the objectives**

The directors are responsible for setting the **overall objectives** of the business. These include the **organisation's commitment** to **internal controls** and related matters such as **business ethics**. The board also should be aware that other decisions they take will have a significant impact on controls. If for example one of the objectives is to give greater autonomy to remote operating units, this will mean that central controls will decrease but **overall supervision controls** such as review of budgets and variances will become more important.

The **board** should **review** the **objectives** of the control system on a regular basis to see if they still accord with the other business objectives, and also other developments within the business for example greater computerisation.

The directors should also ensure that the **control objectives** and procedures are **communicated clearly** to **employees**. The directors should also consider **enforcement mechanisms**, for example discipline mechanisms and appraisals.

(b) **Planning activity**

The board should consider what **organisational structure** will achieve the defined objectives. This means **consideration** of the **appropriate levels** of **delegation** and also **segregation of duties**, which is a key accounting control. The board should consider how **responsibility** is to be **exercised**. This will mean **defining responsibilities** for **setting budgets** and **reporting performance** against budgets. The board should also consider how to **balance accountability** with **autonomy**, that is how much scope to allow staff to take risks that are considered acceptable.

(c) **Organising resources and directing performance**

The directors should consider not just the **direct costs** of internal control (in terms of staff resources required) but also whether **controls** may **inhibit enterprise** necessary for the business's expansion.

In order to make this assessment, the board will have to consider the **business risks** the organisation faces. This will involve identification of the **resources** that may be **vulnerable** and the potential for liabilities. There should be assessment not just of existing risks but of **potential risks** including the likelihood of these risks crystallising. **High risk** to **important resources** for example cash will have to mean significant controls in that area. **Appropriate controls** must always be maintained over **areas** that are **fundamental** to the **organisation's ability to continue**, for example compliance with a statutory licence.

However the **directors** will also need to decide which **risks** can be **tolerated**, and whether **resources** would be **best used** in for example obtaining insurance rather than implementing a system of low-level controls.

(d) **Monitoring results**

In order for monitoring to be effective, comparisons must be made of actual performance against targets. Such comparisons should not only be made by the board but by **management** at all levels of the organisation. The board must determine the appropriate level of **management review** at each level.

For the board, this is likely to mean taking an **overview** of the most **important areas** of the business. Some of the comparisons will be **financial**; a review of the **results** and **assets** held of the organisation as a whole and of its most significant operating units. It also means monitoring **major expenditure** and **investment projects**.

Certain **non-financial criteria** should also be reviewed by the board on a regular basis. What is reviewed will depend on the company, but possible areas might include extent of **staff training** or progress towards **environmental objectives**.

(e) **Regulation and review**

An **audit committee** is important in regulation and review. The audit committee should be responsible for **liaison** with **external auditors** and for discussing serious problems that the external auditors have found. The committee should also be responsible for setting out the scope of the **internal audit function** and monitoring its work. The committee should also have an **ongoing** role in **monitoring** internal control systems.

13 Controls over cash and cheques

Pass marks. In the exam you are more likely to have to relate the knowledge you demonstrate answering this question to a specific scenario, but this answer is nevertheless a very good test of your knowledge of accounting controls. Note that most of the answer is based round the concepts of internal regulations (particularly important for payments), staffing (including standby arrangements), physical controls, recording, and reconciliation.

(a) **Receipts by post and cash sales**

The main control problem here is to make sure that none of the cash is stolen or 'goes missing'. Internal controls should include the following.

(i) Safeguards to minimise the risk of someone **stealing** the mail after its receipt but before it has been opened.

(ii) Wherever possible, **appointing a responsible person**, who is not the cashier, to open or supervise the opening of the mail.

(iii) Ensuring that cash and cheques received are:

(1) **Adequately protected** (for instance, by the restrictive crossing of all cheques, money orders and the like, on first handling); and

(2) **Properly accounted** for (for instance, by the preparation of pre-lists of the cash received for an independent comparison with subsequent accounting records and book entries).

(b) In establishing an adequate system of control over **cash sales and collections** the following factors should be decided.

(i) Who is to be **authorised to receive cash** (ie whether it is to be received only by cashiers or may be accepted by sales assistants, travellers, roundsmen or others).

(ii) How sales and the receipts of cash are to be **evidenced** and what checks may be used to apply some control over such transactions. For instance, serially numbered receipt forms or counterfoils, or cash registers incorporating sealed till rolls, can be used to prove that a sale has been made and that cash has been received into the company, thereby preventing the person who receives the cash from simply pocketing it.

(c) **Custody and control of money received**

There should be adequate safeguards over any money received right up to the time it is banked. Suitable internal controls might be as follows.

(i) The **appointment of suitable persons** to be responsible at different stages for the collection and handling of money received, with clearly defined responsibilities.

(ii) **Preventing cash** from building up in large quantities, by arranging to bank the cash at suitably frequent intervals.

(iii) **Suitable arrangements** for **agreeing cash collections** with **cash and sales records**. The sales department is responsible for filling customer orders, but any cash for those orders comes into the company via the postroom and cashier. The company should ensure that sales records and cash receipts recorded by the cashier are agreed with each other, otherwise it will be difficult to tell whether goods have been paid for, and whether correct cash amounts have been received.

(iv) Arrangements for dealing with, **recording and investigating any cash shortages** or **surpluses**. If the amount of cash banked does not tally with the amount of cash received, or if the amount received does not tally with sales records, then the company should ensure that there is a standard procedure for investigating such discrepancies.

(d) **Recording cash received**

Incoming cash and cheques should be recorded as soon as possible. Means of recording include (as appropriate) receipt forms and counterfoils, cash registers and prelists. Aspects of internal control would be as follows.

(i) Specifying **who is to be responsible** for maintaining records of money received.

(ii) **Limitations on the duties and responsibilities** of the receiving cashier to prevent him from dealing with such matters as other books of account, other funds, securities and negotiable instruments, sales invoices, credit. In other words, can segregation of duties be applied?

(iii) **Standby arrangement decisions** as to who will perform the receiving cashier's functions during his absence at lunch, on holiday or through sickness.

(iv) In what circumstances, if any, are **receipts to be given** and copies of receipts retained; the serial numbering of receipt books and forms; how their issue and use are to be controlled; what arrangements are to be made, and who is to be responsible for checking receipt counterfoils against cash records and against bank paying-in slips.

(e) **Paying cash into the bank**

Cash and cheques received should be banked with the minimum of delay. It is poor security to have cash lying around instead of safely banked, and it is also poor financial management, as money cannot earn interest until it is banked. Adequate internal controls over banking cash receipts will involve rules concerning the following factors.

(i) How **frequently payments** are to be made into the bank.

(ii) Who is to make up the **bank paying-in slips** (preferably this should be done by a person independent of the receiving and recording cashier) and whether there is to be any independent check of paying-in slips against post-lists, receipt counterfoils and cash book entries.

(iii) **Who is to make payments** into the bank (preferably not the person responsible for preparing the paying-in slips).

(iv) **Whether all receipts are to be banked intact**; if not, how disbursements are to be controlled.

(f) **Cash and bank balances**

Questions to be decided in connection with the control of cash balances include the following.

(i) What amounts are to be **retained as cash floats** at cash desks and registers, and whether payments out of cash received are to be permitted.

(ii) What **restrictions are to be imposed on access** to cash registers and offices.

(iii) **Rules regarding** the **size of petty cash floats** to meet expenses.

(iv) The **frequency with** which floats are to be **checked by** independent officials, that is, by employees or supervisors who do not have anything to do with the running of the cash float. Internal auditors are quite often used for this purpose.

(v) **What arrangements** are to be made for **safeguarding cash** left on the premises outside business hours.

(vi) Whether any special arrangements (such as **cash insurance**) are judged desirable having regard to the nature of the business, the sums handled, and the length of time they are kept on the premises.

(g) **Regular reconciliation of bank accounts with the cash book**

This should be performed by a responsible official and is an essential element of control over bank balances. Considerations involve deciding to whom bank statements should be issued, how frequently reconciliations should be performed and by whom, and what procedures should be followed when carrying out the **reconciliation**.

(h) **Cheque and cash payments**

The arrangements for controlling payments will depend to a great extent on the **nature of business transacted**, the **volume of payments** involved and the **size of the company**.

(i) **Cheque payments**

Amongst the internal controls to be established for the system for payments by cheque are the following.

(i) What procedure is to be adopted for **controlling the supply and issue of cheques** for use, and who is responsible for their safekeeping.

(ii) Specification of who is to be **responsible for preparing cheques**.

(iii) **Specification of the documents** to be used as **authorisation** for preparing cheques.

(iv) The **names, number and status of persons authorised** to sign cheques; limitations to their authority; the minimum number of signatories required for each cheque.

(v) **Safeguards** to be adopted if cheques are signed mechanically or carry printed signatures.

(vi) The **extent to which cheques issued should be restrictively crossed**; and the circumstances, if any, in which blank or bearer cheques may be issued.

(vii) Arrangements for the **prompt despatch of signed cheques** and precautions against interception.

(viii) The arrangements to ensure that **payments are made** within **discount periods**, if the organisation would benefit from early payment discounts.

(j) **Cash payments**

Factors to be considered include the following.

(i) The **names, number and status of persons allowed to authorise cash expenditure**, and the documentation to be presented and preserved as evidence of cash expenditure.

(ii) Arrangements to ensure that the **vouchers supporting payments** cannot be **presented for payment twice**. (The usual way of preventing this is to stamp the voucher 'paid'.)

(iii) Whether the **level of an individual payment** should be limited, for example, a company may set the rule that cash payments can be made up to £100, but anything higher has to be paid by cheque and consequently has to go through the procedures governing cheque payments.

(iv) Rules as to **cash advances to employees** and officials, IOUs and the cashing of cheques.

So far as possible the person responsible for preparing cheques should not himself be a *cheque signatory*. In turn, cheque signatories should not be responsible for recording payments. (Although, as mentioned earlier, in the circumstances of smaller companies, staff limitations often make it impossible to divide duties in this manner and in such cases considerable responsibility falls on the adequacy of managerial supervision.)

14 VFM and performance indicators

Pass marks. Our answer to (a) discusses inputs, outputs and impacts/outcomes. In part (b) note that a balanced view of performance indicators is required; the answer explains why they are necessary, but also demands a realisation of the problems of measuring quality of service.

For (a) there are several possible sets of methods you could choose. You could continue with the theme of the three E's. You could write about detailed investigations of selective parts of an organisation, more broad-based investigations of the organisation as a whole, and reviews of the organisation's standard operations.

(a) **Methods of analysis**

Three methods of VFM analysis which may be employed in value for money audits are as follows.

(i) A study of **economy, efficiency and effectiveness** (the '3 Es') with reference to **inputs**. Inputs mean the money or **resources** - ie cost - that has gone into a programme. For example, the provision of a health visitors' service could be investigated from the point of view of the cost of labour and materials etc that go into providing the service.

(ii) A study of the '3 Es' with reference to **outputs**. Outputs mean the **results** of a programme, measured either by the **type** and **quantity** of the **service** provided, or by **quality**. In the example of a home visitors' service, an audit could look at the type of services provided, the numbers of people served, and the quality of the service.

(iii) A study of the **impacts**. Impacts mean the effect that the outputs of a programme have had on the **achievement** of **policy objectives**. Again, using the example of a home visitors' service, an audit could assess to what extent the services provided, the number of people served and the quality of service are consistent with the original aim of setting up the service in the first place.

In the public sector, inputs, outputs, and impacts are all difficult to quantify in practice.

(b) **Performance indicators**

A central theme of many of the government's pronouncements on the public sector throughout the 1980s and early 1990s has been the need to improve performance. However basic control theory tells us that in order to improve we first need to know where we are going wrong and *how far* we are going wrong.

With **public sector services**, there has generally been **no market competition** and **no profit motive**. In the private sector, these two factors help to guide the process of fixing proper prices and managing resources economically, efficiently and effectively.

Since public sector organisations cannot be judged by their success against **competition** nor by **profitability**, some other methods of assessing performance have to be used. In the public sector, however, performance measures are difficult to define. Measures of output **quantity** and output **quality**, by themselves, provide **insufficient evidence** of how well the community is served by a programme.

Performance can be measured by:

(i) **Progress** towards **appropriate objectives**, for example success in cutting hospital waiting lists to a specified maximum

(ii) **Progress** in **improving efficiency**, for example increasing the number of dustbins emptied in comparison to the resources (labour and vehicles) used. Measuring efficiency in the public sector is difficult. Activities can be defined in words and inputs are often clearly measurable but expressing outputs and efficiency in numerical terms is often only possible in a crude way

(iii) **Control** over **spending**, for example keeping energy costs per square metre of public buildings to a minimum

Problems with performance indicators

Those who have an interest in the performance of public organisations (taxpayers, community charge payers, customers, the government and Parliament), seek a few **simple** and **understandable indicators** which show the trend in efficiency over time and compared with other similar organisations, both in the UK and overseas.

These groups are entitled to performance indicators and explanations of performance and results. There are however difficulties which must be appreciated by them.

(i) There are real problems of **measurement** of **output** and the **accumulation** or **attachment** of **costs** to them, without going into misleading and meaningless allocations of 'overheads'.

(ii) It is often difficult to establish a relationship between cause and effect, especially where:

(1) **several activities interact** but contribute to achieving a desired (or sometimes undesired/unanticipated) result; or

(2) where **one activity contributes** to **more than one objective**. For example, to what extent does expenditure on street lighting contribute to road safety as opposed to the reduction of street crime?

(iii) **Performance indicators**, if simple, may be **misleading**.

(iv) Members of the **public** who receive measures of performance by a public sector department may **not fully understand** the nature of the organisation and its environment and may be unable to put into proper context any information or explanation they receive. The government would argue that this is precisely the case with the widely criticised publication of league tables for schools.

In spite of the difficulties there are benefits to be gained if performance indicators can be successfully developed.

Advantages of performance indicators

(i) They **increase the accountability** of those running the organisation to those using it and paying for it.

(ii) They give the managers of the organisation **targets** to aim at.

(iii) They need **not be absolute** (unlike financial indicators). For example different parts of an organisation can be set different targets that make allowances for local conditions. Their success in achieving those targets can be expressed in percentage terms. Different London Underground lines have been set different standards for percentage of timetabled trains run.

15 Fraud

> **Pass marks**. The key point was a recognition of the risk of collusion between purchasing staff and suppliers. The answer should have concentrated on controls which minimised this risk, particularly authorisation and monitoring.

The following features of the system should help minimise the risk of fraud.

(a) **Risk assessment**

Examples of purchase fraud include **rigged tendering**, **goods being supplied** for **private purposes** and **fraudulent transactions** with **connected companies**. In setting up a control system therefore, management should be aware of what kinds of fraud the business may be at risk of experiencing.

One possible danger is **collusion** between the person authorising purchases and suppliers. Once purchases have been authorised, there may be nothing further that can be done to prevent fraud. The important controls therefore are normally those which are aimed at identifying unusual suppliers or circumstances.

(b) **Monitoring of suppliers**

The risk of collusion between suppliers and employees can be minimised in a number of ways.

(i) The person using the goods should only be able to choose suppliers from an **approved list**.

(ii) The use of new suppliers should be **authorised** by **someone other** than the person using the goods. The person authorising new suppliers should be particularly wary of any of the following:

- Abnormal terms;
- Suppliers providing goods which they would not normally supply;
- Suppliers which appear small compared with the proposed volume of purchases.

(iii) In addition these should be **regular monitoring** by management of arrangements with suppliers. Warning signs should be investigated, such as suppliers handled directly by senior staff, or suppliers handled outside the normal control systems.

(c) **Controls in the payment cycle**

(i) **Segregation of duties**

Segregation of duties can reduce certain risks. **Segregating** the **cheque-signing role** from the **payment authorisation** role can reduce the risk that payments are made out to certain types of bogus supplier, for example those with abbreviated names. Part of the process of reviewing suppliers can be carried out at the payment stage, by checking that **individual** or **total payments** do **not appear excessive**.

(ii) **Documentation**

Requirements for **full documentation** should be linked to segregation of duties. Full documentation would include **purchase requisitions**, **purchase orders** and **purchase invoices**. These can help prevent purchases for private use.

Documentation of returns is also important; **credit notes** should always be obtained from suppliers when goods are returned in order to prevent stock losses through bogus returns.

(d) **Contract management**

There are a number of different types of contract fraud including fixing the contract tendering process and undue payments in advance. Ways of preventing contract fraud include the following.

(i) An open **competitive tendering** process.

(ii) Interim payments being made on **certification** from **independent valuers**.

(iii) Any **changes to terms** being **authorised independently** of the person who deals with the contractors on a day to day basis.

(e) **Organisation and staff controls**

(i) **Personnel**

References should be obtained for all new staff, and details retained of previous employers so that possible collusion can be checked.

(ii) **Ethics**

A **business code of ethics** can remind staff of what constitutes unreasonable inducements.

(f) **Internal audit**

Internal audit can play a role in a number of the above checks, particularly the following.

(i) **Detailed checks** of documentation.

(ii) **Scrutiny** of suppliers and payments for suspicious circumstances.

16 Codes of conduct

Pass marks. We have looked at the ways in which the code can be seen as acceptable and the ways in which it can be seen as unacceptable and have then suggested ways in which it could be improved.

You may have simply concentrated on the factors within the code that required amendment and have redrafted it, or alternatively you may have defined and justified the code as it stands. Any reasonable approach will be rewarded.

Examiner's comment. Common errors included repeating the code in the question without adding any substantial commentary and commenting that it was a contentious subject, without either agreeing with the existing approach or proposing an alternative.

As with many codes of conduct adopted in practice, there are both acceptable and unacceptable aspects to the code in question.

Aspects of the code which are acceptable

(a) The organisation has adopted a code of conduct which attempts to **conform** with **customary business practices**. It wishes to behave in a manner consistent with that of others in the market.

(b) The code appears to imply that employees can take **slight risks** and go beyond behaviour that might be construed as strictly correct in order to secure sales. It would be logical and reasonable to do this in order to gain a sales advantage.

(c) The conduct of the members of the staff working in the **purchasing function** is **controllable** by the organisation and so the organisation can determine the code of conduct which should apply. The code of conduct covering the **selling operation** has to meet the **expectations** of the **market** and **customers**, however. The organisation has **no control** over its **potential customers**, who can decide whether or not they should accept any gifts, favours or entertainment offered. That part of the code of conduct relating to the purchasing activity is therefore necessarily stricter and more stringent than the part relating to the sales activity.

(d) Any **gifts**, favours and entertainment **provided** by a **supplier benefits** an **employee** whereas those provided for **customers benefit** the **customer** rather than the employee (unless the entertainment is lavish). There are therefore stricter controls over purchasing staff than sales staff.

Aspects of the code which are unacceptable

(a) The code **fails to provide sufficient guidance**. For example, it does not specify the nature of customary business practices, common courtesies and so on. Employees have no idea about whether they can offer a potential customer a glass of wine, a bottle of wine or a case of wine.

(b) The code gives **no information** about the **repercussions** for employees for contravening the code. There is therefore no indication of the seriousness with which the organisation views breaches of the code.

(c) The penultimate sentence about 'favours or entertainment, appropriate in our sales programmes' implies a **double standard** and may encourage sales personnel to adopt a position which could damage the good name of the organisation.

(d) The unclear nature of the code relating to sales means that, because **behaviour is not actually illegal**, it may be **adopted** because it increases the organisation's short-term profits (despite the fact that it might have longer-term repercussions).

(e) If **performance measures** are based on **short-term profit**, **employees** may feel **pressurised** into adopting unethical or even illegal behaviour.

Suggested amendments to the code of conduct

Given the above comments there are various amendments which could be made to the code of conduct to increase its acceptability.

(a) **Ambiguous terms** should be **clarified**.

(b) **Penalties** for contravening the code could be **included**.

(c) It could be drastically **simplified** and the entire section on business courtesies deleted since the information provided in the remaining section provides an adequate and concise code of conduct.

(d) The **code relating** to the conduct of employees working in the **sales** function could be **rewritten** with the intention of making it as **strict** and **clear** as that covering the purchasing function employees (no entertainment, no gifts and so on). There are commercial problems associated with such an approach, however; the market and customers may expect a more liberal attitude.

Such changes would produce an **unambiguous**, **clear** and **concise code of conduct** which will **protect** the **integrity** of the organisation and allow **employees** to be **confident** that their efforts for the organisation will remain within acceptable limits.

17 ZX

Pass marks. Expected values will be a key risk quantification technique in this paper, so make sure you can follow all stages of our answer. (c) covers similar ground to another question in the pilot paper (Question 20 in this text). This emphasises that currency and interest rate risks will be important topics in this paper, and also that you shouldn't be surprised to see overlap in the requirements of different questions on the same paper.

(a) **Expected sterling value of additional profit**

Total **number of franchises offered** = 5 × 5 = 25. Total value = 25 × €100,000 = €2.5m

Value of loans made for franchise costs = 80% × €2.5 million = €2 million

Value of loans made for property = €4.8 million

Note: It is assumed that this property loan figure does not need to be multiplied by 80%, as it is the treasurer's estimate.

Total value of loans made = €2 million + €4.8 million = €6.8 million

Average loan per franchisee = €6.8 million / 25 = €272,000

Annual interest cost of the loans to ZX = 10% × €6.8 million = €680,000

Annual interest charged to franchisees = 7% × €6.8 million = €476,000

Therefore, **net annual interest cost to ZX** is (680 – 476) = €204,000

ZX's income from sales made by franchisees is 1% commission + 12% margin on goods sold = 13% × sales value.

Total planned income is 13% × planned sales = 13% × €26 million = €3, 380,000

Scen -ario	Sales propor -tion	No. of loan defaults	Sales €	ZX income: 13% × sales, €	Net interest cost €	Cost of loan write-offs €	Net profit*, €	Prob	Expected value €
1	90%	2	23,400,000	3,042,000	(204,000)	(544,000)	2,294,000	0.1	229,400
2	80%	4	20,800,000	2,704,000	(204,000)	(1,088,000)	1,412,000	0.3	423,600
3	100%	0	26,000,000	3,380,000	(204,000)	0	3,176,000	0.4	1,270,400
4	100%	1	26,000,000	3,380,000	(204,000)	(272,000)	2,904,000	0.2	580,800
								1.0	2,504,200

* Net profit to ZX is ZX income – net interest cost – cost of loan write-offs.

> **Note**: This figure does not include the receipt of €2.5 million for franchise purchases paid by the franchisees. This receipt should be credited to ZX's income statements over the period of the franchise. However, the question does not say for how many years the franchise is valid.

The expected additional profit for ZX is €2.504 million.

The exchange rate at the start of the year is €1.3939:£1. This is expected to strengthen by 5% over the next year to 1.3939 / 0.95 = €1.3242: £1.

The average exchange rate for the year is approximately (1.3939 + 1.3242) / 2 = €1.3591.

The **expected profit** in £ is therefore 2,504,200 / 1.3591 = **£1.8425 million.**

The **capital invested** by ZX is loans €6.8 million + working capital £3.65 million.
Using the opening exchange rate of €1.3939, this is £4.878 million + £3.65 million = £8.528 million.

The rate of return earned is 1.8425 / 8.528 = **21.6%**, which is comfortably above the minimum required return for international operations of 15%.

> Note: If some portion of the €2.5 million receipt from franchisees were included in profit, the rate of return would be correspondingly higher.

(b) **Risks from expanding into Europe using franchising**

Franchising in foreign countries is a form of **foreign direct investment (FDI)** and is subject to the risks associated with this, namely political risk, cultural risk, and currency risk, together with increased business risks such as damage to goods in transit and credit risk.

Political risk

Because UK is also a member of the European Union (a stable political and economic union), the **political risk** associated with any of the five countries considered is **very small**. The highest risk is probably that increases in corporate or property taxation are introduced in some regions.

Cultural risk

Cultural risk is higher. It is possible that consumers in some locations are **prejudiced** against UK products where there are local alternatives. However, because of this, franchising using national owner-managers may represent a less risky form of investment than the alternative of setting up wholly owned subsidiaries. On the other hand, franchising may prove to be an **unpopular form of business model** in some regions, which is another aspect of cultural risk. In addition it is possible that ZX will **not be able** to attract **sufficient franchisees** as it is not a well-known enough concern. Most franchises are linked to globally known brands.

Cultural risk may be exacerbated by the number of countries in which ZX is trying to expand as it will have to try to cope with cultures that are different from each other, and from the UK and USA, where ZX is currently based.

Currency risk

Any form of investment in Europe will be subject to currency risk: the risk that the euro declines in value against the pound, resulting in a reduced present value of the income stream. Again, franchising suffers lower risk than investment in wholly owned subsidiaries, although ZX's decision to make euro loans to franchisees leaves it exposed (see (c)).

Credit risk

In addition to the normal risks of customers defaulting on debts, ZX bears the risk that its **franchisees will fail** and default on the repayment of the loans it has advanced to them.

Other franchising risks

Other considerations include the risks that:

(i) Franchises are **more difficult to control** than wholly owned investments; in particular they may be unwilling to accept the ZX way of doing things as regards the image projected, store design and product stocking.

(ii) Franchise sales **displace export sales** made by the UK operation or, more indirectly, **divert resources** from the UK.

(iii) If franchises are not located carefully, they may end up **competing** with each other.

Franchising will also reduce risk in other ways by requiring franchisees to bear the capital costs of the shops.

(c) **Management of risks associated with the euro loans**

ZX intends to advance fixed interest euro-denominated loans to its franchisees. This will result in three types of financial risk: credit risk, currency risk and, possibly, interest rate risk.

Credit risk

This is the risk that some of the franchisees **default** on the **loans**. In the calculations in (a), this has been accepted as a risk. It could be reduced by:

(i) **Carrying out standard credit control checks** on franchisees, to eliminate those with a poor credit history.

(ii) Requiring that **loans** are **backed with personal guarantees** by the directors of the franchisee companies.

(iii) **Taking security for the loans** (in the form of charges over the property used for operating the franchise).

However, in taking action to reduce credit risk, ZX must be prepared to negotiate a reduced margin from franchisees, or else run the risk of a lower than expected number of franchise takers.

Currency risk

Currency transaction risk is the risk that the **sterling value of loan interest and repayments** is **eroded** if the euro declines in value against the pound. Although this is not predicted to happen in the calculations, there is a substantial risk that it will. Currency risk also applies to the commission remitted by franchisees. In addition there is a translation risk in terms of translating the value of the outstanding loans at the period-end, and a longer-term economic risk that the exchange rate will be affected by trends in the Euro-zone.

The best way to reduce **currency risk** on the **loans to franchisees** is to finance these loans out of **euro (rather than sterling) borrowings**. In that way, if the euro declines, both receipts and payments are reduced. This can produce a perfect hedge until one or more of the franchisees defaults (see credit risk above), in which case any excess euro borrowings can be hedged using methods in the next paragraph. The disadvantage of borrowing in euros is that ZX may not be able to obtain such a relatively favourable interest rate as in pounds.

Alternative ways of hedging currency risk include:

(i) **Forward currency contracts** which fix the exchange rates for future receipts and/or payments. They can be tailored to suit the company's circumstances, but bind the company into a fixed price should exchange rates move in a favourable direction.

(ii) **Futures** also fix the price of a transaction in the future, but as they are only for standardised amounts, there is likely to be some transaction exposure that isn't hedged.

(iii) **Options**: which, in return for a substantial purchase price, allow the company to avoid exchange losses while taking advantage of exchange gains.

(iv) **Matching franchise receipts** with payments to short-term creditors, that is EU based suppliers. This would however reduce the output required from the UK based factory.

Interest rate risk

ZX will suffer from **interest rate risk** if it grants **fixed interest loans** to franchisees while paying **floating rate interest** on the borrowings it makes to finance them. If interest rates rise, ZX would make a loss on this financing arrangement. This could be avoided by negotiating with its bankers to exchange some of its floating rate borrowings for fixed rate borrowings (probably at a higher rate of interest). Alternatively it could **reconsider** its plans to offer fixed rate finance, and instead offer franchisees **floating rate loans**.

In summary, the company could **avoid substantial currency** and **interest rate risk** by financing its euro loans to franchisees using fixed interest euro borrowings rather than floating rate sterling borrowings.

18 OX

Pass marks. The forward rate between Singapore dollars and £ needs to be worked out in two stages. A diagram may have been a useful way of seeing what is going on in the money market hedge. You have to start though by working 'backwards;' you want to end up with $715,000 in three months time, so you need to find the present value of that amount.

In (a) (ii) the US dollars is to be used as the hard currency, so don't worry that no forward market exists between the pound and rupiah.

In (b) you need to consider whether to convert from dollars to sterling immediately or in three months time. Don't forget the conclusion.

In (c) the risk of exchange losses has to be balanced against the improved customer relations (and the possibility of exchange gains).

(a) **Receipts from export sales**

(i) Sales to Singapore

The value of the sales at the spot rate is:

$$250{,}000 \times \text{Singapore } \$2.862 \times \frac{1}{3.1800} \text{ (W1)} = £225{,}000$$

If OX enters into a contract to sell 250,000 × 2.862 = Singapore $715,000, delivery between two and three months,

Anticipated sterling proceeds = Singapore $715,500 ÷ 3.1592 = £226,481

OX can take out a **forward option contract** to sell **Singapore dollars forward**, for delivery between two and three months. This will hopefully overcome the uncertainty surrounding the timing of the receipt from Singapore. The exchange rate used is the least favourable quoted rate for delivery during the period (in this case the three month rate).

Alternatively, OX can cover its foreign exchange risk via the **money markets**, as follows.

(1) Borrow Singapore $703,194 for three months (see W2).

(2) As required, convert to sterling at spot rate of 3.18 (W1). The proceeds will be 703,194 ÷ 3.18 = £221,130.

(3) Invest sterling in the Eurosterling market for three months at 6½% pa. The Eurosterling deposit will grow to £224,723 (W3).

(ii) **Sales to Indonesia**

The value of the sales at the spot rate is $100{,}000 \times \frac{2246}{2481} = £90{,}528$.

The first alternative is to compute the eventual proceeds using the £/US $ forward market, since payment has been offered in US dollars and no forward market exists in Rupiahs/£.

Using the US $/£ forward market, the contracted receipts from selling US $ 125,000 for delivery in three months are $\frac{125{,}000}{1.5105} = £82{,}754$

The second alternative is to use the money markets, as follows.

(1) Borrow US $ 121,359 for three months (W4)

(2) Convert US $121,359 into sterling at the spot rate of US $ 1.4875/£, giving $\frac{121{,}359}{1.4875}$ = £81,586

(3) Invest the sterling proceeds of £81,586 on the Eurosterling deposit market for three months at 6½% pa, yielding £81,586 × 1.01625 = £82,912.

Conclusion. The protection should be effected through the foreign exchange market for the sale to Singapore and through the money market for the sale to Indonesia.

(b)

	Rupiahs
Sales value (100,000 × 2,246)	224,600,000
Less 5% discount	(11,230,000)
Discounted sales value	213,370,000

$$\text{Proceeds of sales} = \frac{213{,}370{,}000}{1{,}667.9\text{(W5)}} = \$127{,}927$$

The best US $ deposit rate of interest is 8% pa in a US domestic bank.

The yield after three months is $127,927 × 1.02 = $130,486.

Converted into sterling, using the three month forward market, this is $\frac{\$130{,}486}{1.5105}$ = £86,386.

Alternatively, the US dollar proceeds could be converted immediately into sterling and then invested for three months in eurosterling. The calculation is as follows.

(i) Conversion of US $127,927 (see above) into sterling

$\frac{127{,}927}{1.4875}$ = £86,001

(ii)

	£
Yield of eurosterling 3 month deposit (£86,001 × 6.5%/4)	1,398
Add principal	86,001
	87,399

Conclusion. The best yield without the offer of immediate payment was £82,912. Both the forward foreign exchange market and the money market yield better returns, with the money market's £87,399 as the better of the alternatives.

Workings

W1 **Cross rates, Singapore $/£**

	Singapore $/US$	*US $/£*	*Singapore $/£*
Spot	2.1378	1.4875	3.1800
1 month forward	2.1132	1.4963	3.1620
2 months forward	2.0964	1.5047	3.1545
3 months forward	2.0915	1.5105	3.1592

W2 **Required Singapore $ borrowings**

The interest rate in Singapore $ is 7% pa or 1.75% for three months.

Thus the maximum borrowing which can be repaid from export sale proceeds is

Singapore $ $\frac{715{,}500}{1.0175}$ = 703,194

W3 **Eurosterling deposit**

The interest rate for three months is 1.625% (6.5/4)

Thus the yield on the deposit is £221,130 × 1.01625 = £224,723.

W4 **Required US $ borrowings**

US $ interest rates (eurodollars) are 12% pa or 3% for three months.

Thus, the maximum borrowing which can be repaid from the sale proceeds is

$\frac{\$125{,}000}{1.03}$ = $121,359

W5 **Cross rate, Rupiah/£**

	US $/£	*Rupiah/US $*	*Rupiah/£*
Spot	1.4875	1667.90	2,481

(c) When a company invoices sales in a currency other than its own, the amount of 'home' currency it will eventually receive is uncertain. There may be an advantage or a disadvantage, depending on changes in the exchange rate over the period between invoicing and receiving payment. With this in mind, invoicing in a foreign currency has the following advantages.

(i) The **foreign customer** will **find the deal more attractive** than a similar one in the exporter's currency, since the customer will bear no foreign exchange risk. Making a sale will therefore be that much easier.

(ii) The exporter can **take advantage** of **favourable foreign exchange movements** by selling the exchange receipts forward (for more of the home currency than would be obtained by conversion at the spot rate).

(iii) In some countries, the **importer** may find it **difficult** or even impossible to obtain the foreign exchange necessary to pay in the exporter's currency. The willingness of the exporter to sell in the importer's currency may therefore prevent the sale falling through.

The disadvantages of making export sales in foreign currency are the reverse of the advantages.

(i) The **exporter** (rather than the foreign customer) bears the **foreign exchange risk**.

(ii) If the **exchange movement** is **unfavourable**, the exporter's profit will be reduced.

19 BS

Pass marks. This question tests your knowledge of exchange rate hedges using fixed and option forward exchange contracts, and money market hedges. The calculations are reasonably straightforward, but as always with option contracts, you will need to think through carefully the implications of different movements in exchange rates.

Don't forget **netting off** in (a) and make sure you translate the transaction cost at the correct (spot) rate.

In (b) you need to focus on the various elements of risk (what the risks are, what the company intends to do and how the company can cope with them). It's easy to forget the 'simpler methods' of dealing with risk when you have a question about futures and options.

In (c) don't confuse option forward contracts (the **date** of performance is optional, not performance) with option contracts (here the **performance** is optional). Unusually you are told one price to use in the options calculation and you have to select as the other a price above 1.70. We have chosen 1.71 but you could equally have chosen 1.75 or 1.80.

(a) (i) Since both the receipts and payments are expected to occur **on the same date**, BS plc need only hedge the net amount, ie a receipt of \$200,000 (\$450,000 – \$250,000). To hedge this transaction, a three-month forward contract to sell dollars will be required. The rate that will apply for this contract will be \$1.6590 – \$0.0077 = \$1.6513/£.

The **transaction cost** will be paid immediately in US\$. BS must therefore **buy dollars now** to cover this at the spot rate of \$1.6540/£.

The net receipt can now be calculated:

	£
Sterling proceeds in 3 months' time: \$200,000 ÷1.6513	121,117
Transaction costs: \$200,000 × 0.2% ÷ 1.6540	(242)
Net receipt	120,875

(ii) Since the company is expecting to receive dollars, to effect a money market hedge it will need to **borrow dollars now** in anticipation. The sum to be borrowed must be just enough so that the receipt in three months' time will repay the loan and the interest due for the period.

The money will be borrowed in the US at an annual rate of 6%. This equates to a three month rate of 1.5% (6%/4). The amount to be borrowed in dollars is therefore \$200,000 ÷

1.015 = \$197,044. These dollars will be sold now at the spot rate of \$1.6590/£ to realise £118,772.

This **sterling amount** can now be invested in the UK at an annual rate of 6.5%. This equates to a three-month rate of 1.625%. The value of the deposit at the end of the three month period when the dollar loan is repaid will be £118,772 × 1.01625 = £120,702.

The transaction cost will be the same as for the forward market hedge. The net receipt under this method will therefore be £120,702 – £242 = **£120,460**.

The receipts are highest if the **forward market hedge** is used, and this will therefore be the **preferred method**.

(b) **Factors to consider**

(i) The **relative costs** of the different options

(ii) The **ability of the staff** to **manage the techniques**, given that there is not a specialist treasury department

(iii) The **attitude of the company to risk**

(iv) The **size of the transaction** in relation to the company's overall operations, and therefore the scale of the risks involved

(v) The **perceived level of risk** attached to the currencies in question

Alternative options to minimise risk

(i) **Operating bank accounts in foreign currencies.** This is only an option if the company has regular transactions in the currencies in question.

(ii) The **use of multilateral netting**. This will only be possible if there are a large number of foreign currency transactions.

(iii) The company could consider the **use of swaps and option contracts**.

(iv) The company could consider the **cost and viability** of insisting that more of its contracts are denominated in sterling.

(c) **Fixed forward exchange contract**

(i) An immediately **firm and binding contract** (for example, between a bank and its customer)

(ii) For the **purchase or sale** of a **specified quantity** of a stated foreign currency

(iii) At a **rate of exchange fixed** at the time the contract is made

(iv) For **performance at a future time** which is agreed upon when making the contract

Advantages of option contracts

Option contracts are attractive when:

(i) The **date** on which the transaction being hedged will take place is **uncertain**

(ii) There is **uncertainty** about the **likely movement in exchange rates** – the company can take advantage of any favourable movements in exchange rates, while continuing to hedge any unfavourable movements

Main drawbacks to option contracts

(i) They are **more expensive** than **fixed contracts**, and the premium will have to be paid, whether or not the option is exercised

(ii) They are **traded in standard amounts**, and therefore it is difficult to hedge exactly the sum required – in practice, the company will have to carry some of the risk itself, or use two different hedges to cover the transaction fully

Option set up

(a) Contract date

June

(b) Type of option

Buy call option

(c) Strike price

$1.70 as current spot rate is greater than other prices

(d) Number of contracts

$$\frac{200{,}000 \div \$1.70}{£12{,}500} = 9.41\text{, say 9}$$

(e) Tick size

£12,500 × 0.0001 = $1.25

(f) Premium

$$\text{Premium} = \frac{9 \times 12{,}500 \times 0.017}{1.6540}$$

$$= £1{,}156$$

Closing prices

(a) $1.71

(b) $1.6513

Outcome

(a) Options market outcome

Strike price	1.71	1.6513
Closing options price	1.70	1.70
Exercise	Yes	No
If exercised, tick movement	100	
Outcome of options position	100 × 9 × 1.25 = $1,125	

(b) Net outcome

	$	$
Spot market receipt	200,000	200,000
Options position	1,125	-
	201,125	200,000
	£	£
Translated at $1.71/1.6513	117,617	121,117
Option premium	(1,156)	(1,156)
	116,461	119,961

Given the **actual movement** in exchange rates that occurred, it is clear that BS's best decision would have been to have used a fixed forward contract rather than an option, since this would have yielded a receipt of £120,875 (greater than £119,961). However, had the dollar fallen further against sterling, for example, to $1.6385/£ or below, then the option contract would have yielded a greater receipt than the fixed contract. At this exchange rate, the receipt would be as follows:

	£
$200,000 sold at $1.6385/£	122,062
Less premium	(1,156)
	120,906

The key point is that the option contract gives the company the **possibility of benefiting** from unexpected favourable movements in rates, albeit at a higher **premium cost**. The 'correct' choice can only be made once the company has specified the degree of risk that it is willing to accept in this type of situation.

20 Financial risks

Pass marks. If your answer contains most of the points that ours does, you should score well on any questions involving discussion of currency or interest rate risk. Bear in mind however that questions may contain more complex numbers than this one does.

(a) (i) **Main sources of financial risk for the group**

Based on the information given, which shows only financial liabilities, the main sources of financial risk for the group are interest rate risk, exchange rate risk, the risk that short term loans may not be renewed and the general financial risk associated with borrowing (gearing).

Interest rate risk

Most of the group's borrowings are at a **floating rate of interest** (£110 million out of £143 million, or 77%). Because floating rate loans gives the lender the right to increase interest rates in line with general interest rate movements, the company suffers substantial risk that interest rates may increase in the future.

At present the group's **fixed rate loans** (all of which are long term with maturity in more than 5 years) are at a **significantly higher interest rate** than current floating rates. Although part of this excess may be regarded as a premium for the certainty of paying a fixed interest rate, it may also indicate that floating rate interest rates are **likely to rise** in the **medium term** future (the expectations hypothesis).

Exchange rate risk

The group reports its results and pays dividends to shareholders in pounds sterling. However, £45 million (31%) of its **borrowings are in foreign currencies** (US dollars and Euros) and there is the risk that the pound will weaken in relation to these currencies, resulting in a higher sterling cost of interest payments and loan repayments.

The group will suffer **similar exchange rate risks** on **its trading transactions** and on its foreign denominated assets, on which no information is available.

Risk that short term loans are not renewed

£74m of the group's borrowings (52%) are **due for repayment** within the next year. If the company suffers financial difficulties there may be **difficulty in refinancing its operations**. Further information would be required to evaluate this risk.

Gearing

All companies that borrow suffer from the financial risk that **interest** must be **paid** regardless of whether profits are made. The effect of borrowing is to make the group's profit and cash flow stream more volatile than that of ungeared companies. No quantitative information is available to evaluate this risk.

(ii) **Exchange rate transaction risk**

The group's transactions over the next 12 months relating to its foreign currency liabilities are predicted to be:

Liabilities		*Loan*	*Rate*	*Interest / repayment*
		£m		*£m*
US $ loans: Interest	Fixed	33	7.25%	2.3925
	Floating	8	5%	0.4000
Euro loans: Interest	Floating	4	5%	0.2000
Repayment				1.0000
Total payments				3.9925

If the pound were to depreciate 10% against the US dollar and the Euro, to 90% of its current value, the cost of the payments in pounds would rise to £3.9925 / 0.9 = £4.4361 million. Additional payments suffered over the next year would therefore be (£4.4361 - £3.9925) million = **£443,600**, which would be charged directly against group profits as an exchange loss. This is referred to as transaction risk.

(iii) **How transaction risk relates to translation risk and economic risk in this example**

Applied to this example, **translation risk** is the risk that the balance sheet values of foreign currency liabilities increase as a result of a decline in the value of the pound. The current sterling value of foreign denominated liabilities is currently £45 million. If the pound depreciated by 10%, these liabilities would be valued at £45 / 0.9 = £50 million. The increase in the balance sheet value of the liabilities would be **£5 million**, which is the translation risk.

Whereas the translation risk depends entirely on what the exchange rates are at the end of the next financial period (one year), there is also the possibility that the **value of a foreign currency liability increases still further** because of longer term movements in exchange rates. This is an example of **economic risk** that, as applied to this example, can be defined as the risk that the **expected present value of foreign currency liabilities** increases as a result of a long term forecast exchange rates.

(b) **Use of derivatives for hedging**

A derivative is a security whose **value is derived** from the **price of another asset**, known as the underlying asset. In the context of the current example, the underlying assets are bonds (loan stocks) or currencies and the main types of derivative are forward rate agreements, futures, options and swaps. These can all be used to 'hedge risk', that is reduce the risk associated with using loans and/or foreign currencies.

The derivatives can be **purchased** or **sold 'over the counter'** (OTC), that is by negotiation with a financial institution (a bank), or on **formally regulated exchange markets** which bring together buyers and sellers of standard derivative contracts (futures and options exchanges).

Exchange traded derivatives

The **advantages of exchange traded derivatives** are that they can be available in **smaller contract sizes** and to **organisations with lower credit ratings**; **transaction costs are low**, and **positions** can be **closed** at any time by entering into reverse transactions (by selling a futures contract that has previously been purchased). However, because the contract sizes, currencies, time periods and due dates are **standardised** and **limited**, it is usually only possible to obtain approximate hedges.

OTC derivatives

By contrast OTC derivatives can be tailored by negotiation to the user's exact hedging requirements. However, positions cannot be so easily reversed out if situations change, regulation is lower, transaction costs can be higher and the starting size for contracts may be too high for smaller organisations.

Characteristics of the main types of derivative relevant to the example are given below.

Forward rate agreements

A **forward rate agreement** (FRA) is an OTC contract to lend or borrow a given sum of money in the future at an interest rate that is agreed today. For currencies, the equivalent is the **forward contract:** an agreement to buy or sell a given amount of currency in the future at an exchange rate that is agreed today.

These contracts can be used to **'fix' interest rates or exchange rates** on future transactions, thus **removing the risk of rate movements** in the intervening period. In the example, the company needs to repay a euro loan (of approximately £1 million) next year. The risk of the pound weakening against the euro in the period before the loan is repaid can be hedged by entering into a forward contract to buy £1 million worth of euros at an exchange rate agreed today. The money does not need to be paid until next year, but the exchange rate is fixed today.

Note that **removing risk** is **not always beneficial**. If the pound were to strengthen against the euro, the company would have lost the opportunity of making an exchange gain if it fixed its exchange rate using a forward contract.

Futures contracts

Futures contracts are exchange traded versions of forward rate agreements and are used in a similar way to hedge risk. The markets are mainly for interest rates rather than currencies.

Options

Options can be obtained for **interest rates and currencies**, for both OTC and exchange traded contracts. In contrast to forward or futures contracts, an option need only be **exercised** (used) if it is **advantageous to the user**. For example, the company has a floating rate sterling loan on which it is currently paying 5% interest. It could purchase an option to pay fixed interest of 7% on this loan. The option would only be exercised if the floating rate rose above 7%. In all other situations the option would be allowed to lapse. The option therefore offers a guaranteed maximum to the interest paid, while allowing an unlimited reduction in the interest rate. It is known as a **cap.** Because of this flexibility, options are expensive derivatives to purchase.

Swap

A **swap** involves two parties **agreeing to swap payment obligations** on their loans. For example, if the company wished to **reduce interest rate risk**, it may consider swapping its floating rate sterling payments with a party that that was making fixed rate sterling payments on the same principal value of the loan. To **reduce exchange rate risk**, it may agree to swap its interest and repayment on a US dollar loan with a party that has a sterling loan and prefers an obligation in US dollars. This is called a **currency swap.**

21 IT strategy

> **Pass marks**. This question refers to an 'IT strategy' rather than an 'IS/IT strategy'. This should not have prevented you from including material relating to information systems that utilise IT in your answer.
>
> In a question such as this ensure you structure your answer clearly - dealing with each of the five reasons you provide separately and providing sufficient information, including an example, to earn five marks for each reason.

Reasons for having an IT strategy

In this answer we identify five reasons for developing an IT strategy, using the example of a typical small firm offering domestic services such as plumbing and electrical work. For convenience we shall refer to this firm as **EG Ltd**.

(a) **Rationalising the existing investment in IT**

Because of the benefits it offers (speed, accuracy, and so on) IT has become a **key component of most aspects of modern businesses.** Most organisations have reached the stage in their IT maturity whereby IT has been used to automate tasks previously performed manually or by obsolete technology. Most organisations could **not now conceivably disinvest in IT**, and return to traditional methods of getting work done.

However, it is common in organisations, from small to large, for IT to have been **introduced piecemeal** to address specific requirements without due regard having been paid to the way that the individual systems **work together and communicate**.

Strategy adoption

Adoption of a strategy is therefore necessary to guide the direction and scope of the **whole** IT development of a firm allowing it to match the **resources available** to the changing **environment** and enable the firm to meet its **primary business objectives**. All of these matters - overall use of resources, environmental issues and overall objectives – are key issues in the formulation of business strategies.

The next stage of IT development is to **exploit the utmost that IT has to offer** by **re-engineering the processes** with the aid of IT rather than just automating current processes.

Example

EG Ltd originally invested in stand-alone PCs for basic administrative tasks such as writing letters to customers and keeping accounts. None of its systems were fully integrated, and much work still involves inefficiencies such as re-inputting of data, or manual searches for information that is held in computerised form but is not accessible by a computer search.

An **organisation-wide strategy** needs to be formulated if the **various systems are to be brought together**, enabling further gains, for instance, automatic generation of letters to debtors, proper accessible databases of customers, suppliers, materials, staff resources.

(b) **Beating competitors and enhancing relationships**

The **traditional** view of IT's role in competitive strategy is largely **reactive** - that is, a response to existing competitive strategy and business process, but not a critical factor in **shaping** that strategy and process.

A more sensible approach is to position IT in a **pro-active** role where the competitive strategy is not viewed as given, but rather as something that should be challenged, extended and perhaps modified, in light of **emerging technologies and applications**.

The perspective of IT strictly as a **support** function in competitive strategy is increasingly out-dated. Firms are now seeking ways to exploit IT to transform their basic businesses, **enhance their relationships** with suppliers and customers, and **create new market opportunities**.

Today, successful competitive st ateoy and corporate results are likely to focus on a small number of performance attributes including **speed, flexibility, quality** and **scale**. All four areas are **profoundly affected** by an organisation's **effective use of IT** to facilitate, enhance and accelerate strategic execution.

Example

EG Ltd's original investment in IT was made partly **because their competitors and suppliers** were clearly investing in such systems too, and EG's manually-produced communications with the outside world made the entire firm **look old-fashioned and inefficient**.

Greater use of technologies now available, or becoming available, could enable EG Ltd to **surpass** many competitors and **deal much more effectively** with suppliers and customers. For instance, **computerised scheduling and booking systems** could enable EG to respond more quickly to urgent call-outs and **make and honour promises** to customers about when work will be done and how long it will take (something at which the industry in general is notoriously bad). **EDI links** to suppliers could greatly simplify ordering and administration for both parties. A good **website** could generate a great deal of new business.

(c) **Getting the systems that are really needed**

In the past many organisations have found that information systems have **failed to deliver expected benefits** for reasons such as the following.

(i) There is no **commitment by the top management** of an organisation. IT strategy invariably involves some degree of **change**, and, unless top management is behind the strategy, its implementation can prove to be impossible.

(ii) The **users and providers of IT** in the organisation have not been fully enough involved. If new systems are simply imposed on such people and they are given no chance to explain their **real needs** there is a strong chance that the system will not reflect their needs.

Need for planning

The process of going through the planning stage in itself is extremely valuable as it provides a mechanism not only for determining what needs to be done but, if properly handled, it also ensures that the result is **achieved by consensus of all interested parties.** This means that the plan is far more likely to be put into effect satisfactorily. The formulation of an **IT strategy** should then result in a clear and **generally understood and agreed** document which sets out the relative priorities of each approved project together with the identification and allocation of the appropriate **resources, approval and delivery** dates, arrangements for **testing and training, and** so on.

Example

EG Ltd originally acquired computers in cases where the manager of a function wanted one and had sufficient influence in the organisation to obtain funding. Other managers were either not interested or did not have the influence. Users, therefore, either had computers imposed on them or were deprived of them.

Need for culture change

A **culture change** is needed: those who are opposed to computerisation or simply lack enthusiasm need to be persuaded of the benefits.

(d) **Continually improving the management of the organisation**

IT brings **ongoing** revolution in the way information is created, used and presented to management. After the strategy has been developed, it must be regarded as a living entity that the organisation needs to review on a regular and systematic basis as circumstances change.

Any strategic view of IT must take technical developments into account. For instance the **Internet** and **Intranet** popularity has forced many managers to rethink the direction of applications and infrastructure investments. The most popular applications use web publishing for existing documents, web forms for transaction entry or web-to-database links to access corporate data.

Example

EG Ltd could benefit from introducing an Intranet in ways such as the following.

(i) An organisation-wide phone directory that is always up-to-date, containing internal numbers and frequently used external numbers.

(ii) Sales information including price lists for jobs, staff availability for urgent call-outs, and supplier and competitor information, including links to suppliers' and competitors' web sites

(iii) A technical database for staff such as plumbers and electricians showing how various jobs are done, how the latest tools and materials should be used, legal and safety requirements and so on.

(e) **Obtaining synergies and economies of scale**

If it is not integrated to corporate strategy a business is almost certain to be **spending too much,** if only because a sizeable percentage will be **spent on the wrong things**. If this goes unchecked there is very little chance that the company will realise the economies of scale and informational synergies that the business needs.

A company's IT architecture comprises **five different component architectures**: applications, technology, data, methods and management practices, and **spending needs to keep these architectures in balance**. For instance, if a large amount is spent on new technologies, but **nothing on training and data conversion** then at best there will be a lag before the new facilities are exploited to the full. The benefits of the IT expenditure might be delayed until the skills of users are available to produce them.

Example

EG Ltd is typical in that it has only computerised its administration so far: it has not considered benefits that could arise from using technology in **other areas of its business**, such as mobile phones and portable PCs for staff such as plumbers and electricians to use on site.

22 Information systems strategy

Pass marks. (a) demonstrates the significance of the different components of information strategy. Note in (c) that you have to use knowledge about budgeting systems that you are assumed have brought forward from intermediate or management level papers.

(a) (i) **Information systems strategy**

Information systems strategy refers to the **long-term plan** concerned with **exploiting information systems** either to **support business strategies** or **create new strategic options**. It needs to ensure that information is made available for implementing strategy in all areas of an organisation's activities.

Information strategy is focused ultimately on the business's long-term objectives, with information systems being used as a means to achieve those objectives.

(ii) **Information technology strategy**

Information technology strategy involves deciding how **information needs** will be met by balancing **supply and demand of funds and facilities**, and the development of programmes to supply IT.

Information technology strategy ultimately focuses on **investing** in the **best possible technology including hardware, software** and **operating systems.** It takes into account risk attitudes, technical standards, but also ensuring that the technology supplied is in line with the organisation's **needs, style** and **structure.**

(iii) **Information management strategy**

Information management strategy refers to the basic approach that an organisation has for managing its information systems, computerised or manual. It includes planning developments, the organisational environment and control. It should ensure that the right **information** is **provided to users** and that **irrelevant information** is not being produced.

Information management is primarily concerned with the links between the information technology function and the rest of the organisation. It is also influenced by wider issues such as the **structure** of the organisation and **the businesses** that it is in, dealing with **who** should be **responsible** for managing information, **where** the information function should be **located** and **how** information should be stored.

(b) **Transaction processing systems**

Transactions processing systems are designed for the routine processing tasks that the company needs to carry out in order to continue operations. They cover **receipts**, **payments** and **inventory movements,** and are designed to fulfil the requirements to prepare financial accounts and to report profits made by the main component parts of the organisation.

Drawbacks of transaction processing systems

The main disadvantage of these systems is that their output is not summarised in ways that might help managers make decisions. They can provide excessive detail in certain ways, but fail to provide strategically useful information such as sales or profits by product or by customer.

Need for strategic information systems

Transaction processing systems are basically knowledge systems, designed to integrate knowledge and help in operational tasks. The company however also needs **strategic systems**, designed to help senior management with long-term planning and ensuring that the business develops successfully in the light of changes in the external environment, in particular developments affecting suppliers, customers and competitors.

The company therefore needs to consider its information systems strategy carefully and ensure that it invests in management support systems that enhance strategic decision-making.

Enterprise resource planning systems

Enterprise resource planning systems are used to **identify** and **plan** the enterprise-wide resources needed to record, produce, distribute and account for customer orders. They collect accounting, operational, customer and supplier data and **produce reports** and **update performance measures.**

Advantages of enterprise resource planning systems

The systems can produce reports that are tailored to managers' needs, and are sophisticated enough to be able to cope with a range of different performance measures, for example the

balanced scorecard or **activity-based measures.** Because they provide information about the wider business and competitive environment, they can be used to **develop strategy**, and also in **customer and supplier management**.

Executive information systems

Executive information or **executive support** systems **pool data** from internal and external systems and make information available to managers in an easy-to-use form.

Advantages of executive information systems

The advantages that should be built into the systems are that they can **identify**, **track** and **summarise strategically critical information** from competitors and external information as well as internal sources. They then provide key figures and trends in whatever detail and format are required, and packages can also use these figures in data analysis and models. Executive information systems should also be **flexible** to users' needs and have a **quick response time**. They should provide information in response to **one-off enquiries.**

(c) **Drawbacks of present system**

The present **incremental** budgeting system is unsatisfactory not just in terms of the information technology function but the organisation as a whole. It takes no account of changes in business strategy and the expenditure that may be required as a result, and can also perpetuate inefficiency.

Alternative methods

Zero-based budgeting involves justifying every item of expenditure, either starting from scratch or looking at all items of current expenditure to see if they are worthwhile. Zero-based budgeting can mean that purposeless expenditure and the budgeting system responds better to changes in the business environment, although it can over-emphasise short-term benefits.

Activity-based budgeting means focusing on the activities that underlie costs and allocating resources according to the importance of the activities.

Implications for IT investment

Use of either zero-based or activity-based budgeting will imply that a **business case** has to be made for information technology investment. The case should specify **organisation information requirements** in the light of an organisation's plans and objectives, in particular the **critical success factors** of the organisation. These requirements should be linked in with developments in the information technology environment to produce the recommendations for the best systems,

23 Facilities management

Tutorial note. The various forms of outsourcing are likely examination topics - particularly the advantages and disadvantages of the outsourcing approach.

'Alarm bells' should have sounded loudly when reading this scenario, particularly the statement 'The appointment of GDC Ltd was relatively rushed and although an outline contract was agreed, no detailed Service Level Agreement was produced'. Because of this, GDC Ltd is able to provide relatively poor levels of service, yet still meet the terms of the contract.

(a) GDC appears to have met its legal obligations even though the level of service it has provided to DS has been poor. There are a number of reasons for this.

Need for service agreement

DS rushed the appointment of GDC and did not insist on a **detailed Service Level Agreement (SLA)**. The contract does not specify the level of service that GDC will provide.

For example, GDC is obligated to provide 'management information', but there is no detailed definition of what this information will entail, and no deadline for the provision of the information. (eg '...within 5 working days of month-end').

Terms of management

DS handed **complete control** of its IT systems to GDC Ltd. The absence of IT expertise within DS puts it at a **disadvantage** when arguing its case with GDC Ltd.

For example, GDC could spend significant amounts of DS money on sub-standard hardware and software. DC Ltd would **not have the expertise to question** or challenge this purchase, resulting in poor use of DS funds and a poor level of service. However, even when purchasing sub-standard hardware GDC would not have breached the requirement of the contract to 'purchase all hardware and software'.

GDC is also responsible for the writing and maintenance of in-house software. **Unless GDC has a detailed understanding of DS the software written may not be suitable**. As GDC receives a set annual fee, it may be tempted to produce software as quickly and cheaply as possible. As the contract has no mention of software standards, GDC would be meeting its legal obligations.

Length of agreement

Another reason that could be contributing DS receiving poor service is that **the agreement is now two years old**. Changes could have taken place inside DS within the past two years that an outside organisation such as GDC does not understand. The nature of management information required now may be different to that required two years ago.

Service levels could also be suffering because **GDC has no financial incentive to provide a good standard of service.** GDC has the right under the contract to increase the annual fee, above the rate of inflation, without any consultation and with no reference to the satisfaction of DS.

(b) The courses of action now available to DS relating to the provision of IT services, and the problems involved in each, are outlined below.

(i) **DS could carry on under the existing agreement**, protecting the knowledge that GDC has built up on the provision of IT services to DS, **but applying 'moral' pressure** (in the form of complaints and meetings with GDC management) to obtain a better level of service.

The main problem with this course of action is that the level of service may not improve at all.

(ii) DS could terminate the existing contract by giving three months' notice, and **negotiate a new contract with GDC with a well-defined SLA**.

Possible problems include the fact that GDC may not wish to negotiate a new SLA leaving DS with no IT services, or GDC may agree a new SLA but still provide the old shoddy service.

(iii) DS could terminate the existing contract by giving three months' notice and **look for a new supplier** of all its IT services.

However, this would mean 'starting from scratch'. Even an efficient provider would take time to develop a feel for the requirements at DS, and build up their expertise. There is no guarantee the new service provider would be better than GDC, although a more detailed SLA would help.

(iv) **DS could establish its own in-house IT team**, probably using a combination of contractors and 'permanent' employees.

The main problems with this option are the time and cost of finding setting up the team and that the team would be 'starting from scratch' and may only receive limited help from GDC during the hand-over.

(v) Another option would be to include staff with a **good understanding of DS's operations**, but little IS/IT expertise, in a new in-house team (**insourcing**). If these people can be taught IT skills, they should then be able to utilise their business knowledge to ensure relevant IT services are provided.

Problems with this option include finding staff that are suitable and willing to make this dramatic career switch, and replacing any staff who do move to the IT team.

24 Computer security

Pass marks. A good test of your knowledge of a wide range of computer controls. Note that not all threats to the system are deliberate.

(a) The main areas of risk to which a computer system is exposed, and some of the factors which may lead to the exposure are as follows.

(i) **Accidental destruction** or **loss of data** by operator or software error. The auditors should pay particular attention during their audit to recovery procedures. In addition the possibility of accidental destruction of programs or hardware, particularly the dropping of a disk pack, by an operator, and the consequences thereof, should not be overlooked.

(ii) The **acceptance of inaccurate input data** due to inadequate edit or other checks is another frequent cause of loss of data.

(iii) A **complete systems failure** can lead to loss of data and may be caused by a failure in the power supply or possibly a failure of the air conditioning or other environmental controls.

(iv) **Theft of data** from a **batch processing system** by an operator copying or removing data files, particularly where these are on easily transportable media such as magnetic tapes.

(v) **Theft of data** from an **on line or real time system** by a person obtaining unauthorised access to the system via a remote terminal and either using passwords illegally or alternatively using a 'piggyback system' (in which a valid transmission is intercepted and the final 'logging off' operation stopped in transmission to permit the illegal operator to continue in operation masquerading as the authorised user).

(vi) **Theft of software** either by operators copying or removing the program file, and in the latter case possibly demanding a ransom from the rightful owner, or alternatively by programming staff copying and attempting to sell the source documentation, with or without the object program.

(vii) **Deliberate destruction of the hardware** has been known to occur, and where adequate protection has not been provided, such acts have also led to the simultaneous destruction of software and data. Similar results may occur as a result of fire or explosion either in the computer room or adjoining premises.

(b) The different forms of control which should be instituted may be sub-divided into three main headings.

Physical security

(i) **Strict control of access** to the computer area, using such devices as magnetic keys and alarm systems.

(ii) **Effective precautions** against **fire** or other **natural disruption** including alarm systems, automatic extinguishing systems and regular inspections.

(iii) Established and well-practised **emergency procedures** in the event of fire or other disorder and alternative power supply.

(iv) **Location of the computer** so that it is difficult for unauthorised personnel to have access with the minimum of entrances and exits.

(v) Possibility of **remote storage of security copies of data.**

(vi) Location of the computer room so that it is, if possible, **situated away from known hazards** such as flooding, radiation from X-Ray equipment and radio systems and fire/explosion risks in adjoining premises.

Software security

(i) **Effective control** over the **preservation of information** contained on files by ensuring that before a file is to be overwritten a check is made on the file version.

(ii) **Prevention of unauthorised access** by the use of devices such as passwords.

Systems security

(i) **Strict control and verification** of all **input data**, where possible with control totals prepared outside the computer department.

(ii) All input should pass through an **'edit' program** as the first stage in being entered on to the computer files. This program clearly indicates all items accepted and rejected, the latter to be investigated by the user department.

(iii) Adequate controls should be in force to ensure that **amendments to programs** are properly **authorised**, **checked out** and **validated** before use.

(vi) There should be **adequate recovery, restart and standby procedures** in the event of power failure or machine breakdowns, which can be facilitated by a 'log' of all work performed and by frequent dumping of files.

(v) Controls should be instituted to ensure that **computer output** is **properly distributed**, especially confidential print-outs, payments and so on.

(vi) Proper control over **storage and issue of electronic media** with manual records being kept of physical maintenance performed. Such records frequently also record current status of the media and the details of the file(s) currently stored upon it.

25 Systems development project

Pass marks. You may need to draw on knowledge from other papers to answer this question but for this paper keep focussed on risk and controls, and also bring in strategic considerations especially compatibility of development with organisational objectives.

Stages in the system development

The stages involved from the 'initial proposal' to the computer becoming 'fully operational' may comprise the following.

- The initial study
- The setting up of the steering committee
- The feasibility study
- The evaluation of the proposals
- The systems design and development (including programs design and development)
- The system installation and implementation
- The post-implementation systems evaluation

Each of these stages is described briefly in the paragraphs following.

The initial study

This need not involve trained systems analysts (unless they are available) but can be carried out by a team (if a team is necessary) of departmental representatives headed by an experienced manager (for example, the chief accountant). The purpose of the initial study is to **clarify the problems** the change is intended to solve and to outline the managerial requirements. This stage is essential so that senior management will be able to direct those involved in the detailed feasibility study. The study, sometimes called a job specification, should quantify the disadvantages of the existing system so that a true comparison of costs and benefits can be made with the proposed solution.

The steering committee

The steering committee will normally include representatives of top management from each department affected by the project. Its function is to appoint and control the feasibility study group and it will bear the **responsibility of evaluating results** of the feasibility study and of making the final recommendation to the board of directors. In a small organisation the feasibility study team or systems analyst may be directly responsible to the board of directors.

The feasibility study

The steering committee, with the board of directors' approval, must **establish the terms of reference** within which the systems analyst and his team will work in carrying out the feasibility study. The aim of such a study is to assess the **data processing requirements** of the organisation, to **investigate and recommend possible solutions** and to provide management with information on which a decision can be based. This information should include the advantages and disadvantages of each suggestion from the technical, economic, organisational and social points of view. A plan should be made for the development, implementation and control of the recommended scheme.

When defining the new system the analyst must consider any **legal, accounting and auditing requirements**, especially the level of systems control. He should also produce a new cost/benefit analysis study of the proposed system, as part of the complete feasibility study report.

The evaluation of proposals

Once the feasibility study is completed the steering committee has the task of evaluating the proposals in the report and submitting final recommendations to the board of directors.

The steering committee, or board of directors, must **relate the feasibility study proposals** to the **original objectives** laid down. If these objectives are met, and the acquisition of a computer is approved, then the more specific details in the proposal should be considered and approved.

The systems design and development

Once the feasibility report's recommendations for the computerisation of an application have been accepted, it is the task of the systems analyst(s) to design and then to develop and implement the new system. To design and develop a larger system may, of course, require a number of analysts and programmers, and so a **project team** has to be formed (a computer consultancy or bureau may provide one). The analysts should work closely with user department representatives and it must not be forgotten that a potential user is the auditor. He should be asked to specify any additional control, auditing and print-out requirements.

Once the system has been accepted by management the development team will produce a **full systems specification**. This is a complete documentation of the whole system and must always be **properly maintained** (ie kept up to date) as parts of the system are changed or added to. The specification is the analysts' means of communicating with management, programmers, operations staff, user departments and auditors; and the documentation should cover reports to management on each part of the system; specifications to programmers; instructions to users (re inputs/outputs); instructions to computer staff.

Programmers will have to **develop, and test** the **specified programs** prior to the system becoming operational. Standard programs may be adapted to the proposed system. All work has to be fully documented.

The systems installation and implementation

This involves **planning all the stages of design, installation and implementation** (eg by the use of network analysis, critical path analysis, Gantt charts, etc). Once there is some idea of the equipment that will be used the installation planning involves the selection of site for the computer and peripherals, and other data processing department offices. Then comes the preparation of the site (eg air conditioning, strengthened flooring, electricity supplies, fire protection etc); and finally, the installation of all equipment and delivery of tapes, disks etc.

Implementation of the new system involves **planning in detail the change-over procedures**, the detailed testing of new computer files from the old systems files (with detailed checks on this file conversion). When every detail appears to be satisfactorily covered and tested, the staff have the considerable task of carrying out the actual change-over (direct, parallel or pilot operations - as decided by the systems analyst).

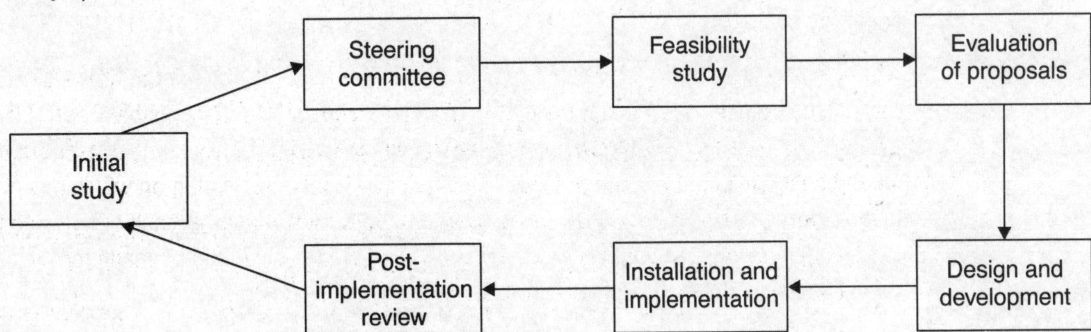

The post-implementation evaluation

In **appraising the operation of the new system** immediately after the change-over, comparison should be made between actual and predicted performance. This will include (amongst other items) consideration of throughput speed (time between input and output), use of computer storage (both internal and external), the number and type of errors/queries, the cost of processing (data capture, preparation, storage and output media, etc). It is important that the system should be reviewed periodically so that any unforeseen

problems may be solved and to confirm that it is achieving and will continue to achieve the desired results. Indeed in most systems there is a constant need to maintain and improve applications and to keep up to date with technological advances and changing user requirements.

Index

Note: **Key Terms** and their **references** are given in bold

Access control, 592
Access risks, 591
Accidental damage, 580
Accounting controls, 184
Accounting measures, 63
Accounts, 220
Adaptability culture, 95
Adaptive systems, 15
Adhocracy, 89
Administrative controls, 184
Advance fee fraud, 380
Agency, 397
Agency (in structuration theory), 28
Agency theory, 62, 202
AGM, 222
Altering cheques, 379
Analysis of errors, 266
Analytical review, 288
Anomalous error, 267
Anti-virus software, 599
Application controls, 185
Application Service Providers (ASP), 570
Applied research, 363
Appraisal, 54
Appraisal and pay, 56
Appraisal as annual event, 56
Appraisal as bureaucracy, 56
Appraisal as chat, 56
Appraisal as confrontation, 55
Appraisal as judgement, 55
Appraisal as unfinished business, 56
Appraisal barriers, 55
Appraisal cost, 126
Appraisal schemes, 428
Arbitrage, 435
Archiving, 596
Argyris, 116
Arithmetical and accounting, 186
Armstrong, 41, 53
Ashby, 16
Audit committee, 210, 220, 226
Audit evaluation, 312
Audit planning, 306
Audit risk, 286
Audit sampling, 262
Audit trail, 597
Authentication, 602
Authorisation and approval, 186
Automated controls, 185
Automated working papers, 271

Back-up, 596
Backup controls, 594
Backward compatibility, 566
Base currency, 432
Basis risks, 492
Basis, 464
Batch processing, 549
Bayes' strategy, 157
Behaviour control, 38
Behavioural factors, 116
Beliefs systems, 106
Best value, 367
Beta versions, 582
Bilateral netting, 446
Black-Scholes model, 500
Blocked funds, 420
Board, 204, 222, 227
Board committees, 228
Board composition, 227
Board meetings, 228
Board membership, 205
Board of directors, 220
Boot sector viruses, 583
Bottom up, 535
Boundary systems, 106
British Standard Code of Practice for Information Security Management (BS 7799), 585
BS 7799, 585
Budget, 36
Budget centre, 113
Budget centre selection, 112
Budget slack, 119
Budgets, 141
Bulletin boards, 603
Bureaucracy, 35, 93
Bureaucratic control, 35
Business context, 530
Business led, 534
Business Process Re-engineering (BPR), 88
Business risk, 133, **282, 286**
Business system, 7

Cadbury Committee, 199
Cadbury report, 200, 220
Call-back buttons, 603
Capital expenditure, 348
Caps, 493
Captive insurer, 146

Card entry systems, 592
Career management, 428
Cash system, 339
Centralisation, 79, 80, 561
Centralised, 562
Certainty-equivalent approach, 156
Chain of command, 75
Chairman and Chief Executive, 223
Change, 566
Changeover arrangements, 572
Chargeout rates, 564
Chargeout techniques, 564
Check digits, 595
Clan control, 36
Closed loop systems, 19
Closed system, 14
COCO framework, 182
Collars, 493
Collusion with external parties, 379
Combined Code, 222
Commitment, 43
Common methods of fraud, 378
Communication, 75
Communications, 428
Company code of conduct, 400
Company secretary, 228
Competency frameworks, 59
Competitive advantage, 425, 531, 564
Completeness, 253
Compliance, 43
Computer assisted audit techniques (CAATs), 258
Computer bureaux, 591
Computer fraud, 598
Computer literacy, 581
Computer manufacturers, 569
Computer support department, 588
Computer theft, 597
Confidentiality, 395
Configurations, 72
Confirmation, 255
Consistency culture, 94
Consultancy firms, 569
Consulting activity, 569
Content theories, 46
Contingency, 589
Contingency approach, 46
Contingency control models, 37
Contingency planning, 145, 589
Contingency plans, 176
Contingency theory, 101, 108
Contingent variables, 102
Continuous improvement, 56
Contract price, 463
Contract size, 463
Contracts of employment, 44
Control, 29
 dialectic of, 29
Control environment, 181, 183
Control of internal audits, 313
Control procedures, 181, 184
Control risk, 286
Control self assessment, 192
Control systems, 426
Control totals, 595
Controllability, 62
Controlling, 520
Convertible loan stock, 502
Core businesses, 107
Corporate codes, 398
Corporate culture, 398
Corporate governance, 198, 226
Corporate philosophy, 371
Corporate strategy, 530
Correct controls, 185
Cost of conformance, 125
Cost of non-conformance, 125
Cost of quality, 125
Counterparty risk, 503
Coupling, 13
Credit risk, 414
Criteria for evaluating appraisal schemes, 56
Critical incidents, 59
Critical success factors (CSFs), **536**
Cross border activities, 397
Culture, 70, **92**
Cultural control, 36, 95
Cultural differences, 425
Cultural risks, 425
Culture shock, 427
Culture, 104, 393
 and attitudes to risk, 93
Cumulative probability tables, 160
Currency future, 463
Currency of invoice, 444
Currency option, 470
Currency risk, 135, 438
Current ratio, 291
Cybernetic model, 34
Cybernetics, 18

Data, 520
Data dictionary, 559, 566

Data integrity, 595
Data processing, 560
Data protection, 604
Database administrator, 559
Deal and Kennedy, 94
Decentralisation, 79, 80, 84
Decentralised, 562
Decision making, 521
Decision matrix, 172
Decision Support System (DSS), 546
Decision trees, 166
Decision-making, 75
Decoupling, 13
Denial of service attack, 584
Deontology, 394
Departmentation, 78, 79
Design of the sample, 263
Designing a management accounting system, 110
Detect controls, 185
Detection of fraud, 386
Detection risk, 286
Deterministic system, 16
Development, 363
Diagnostic control systems, 106
Diagnostic software, 560
Dial-back security, 602
Direct changeover, 620
Direct quote, 433
Directors' remuneration, 208
Disaster recovery plan, 590
Disaster standby companies, 591
Discretionary controls, 185
Distribution systems, 425
Diverse businesses, 107
Divisionalisation, 83
Documentary credits, 416
Documentation, 618
Domination structures, 28
Door locks, 592
Double loop feedback, 20
DP department, 588
Dropper, 583
Duality of structure, 29
Due care, 395

Earl, 534
Earl's three leg analysis, 534
E-commerce, 532
Economic exposure, 439
Economic risk, 438
Economy, 365
Economy, efficiency and effectiveness, 364
Effectiveness, 365
Efficiency, 365
E-mail tracking systems, 603
E-mail, 602
Emmanuel et al, 115
Employee reward, 49
Empowerment, 38, 77
Encryption, 601
End-user computing, 588
Enron Corporation, 4
Enron, 4, 30
Enterprise analysis, 535
Enterprise risk management, 137
Environment, 11, 15, 103
Environmental audits, 372
Environments, 72
Ernst & Young: Fraud - the unmanaged risk, 388
Error, 263
Ethical conflicts, 396
Ethical Guidelines, 394
Ethics, 392
Evaluation, 60
Event identification, 140
Exchange control regulations, 419
Exchange controls, 420
Exchange-traded options, 470
Executive directors, 220
Executive Information System (EIS), 545
Executive Support System (ESS), 545
Existence, 253
Expatriate staff, 427
Expatriate, 427
Expectancy element in motivation, 63
Expectancy theory, 47
Expectations theory of forward exchange rates, 448
Expected cash flows, 163
Expected error, 263, 266
Expected value, 157
Expert opinion, 255
Export credit insurance, 417
Export factoring, 415
Exposure of financial assets, 152
Exposure of human assets, 152
Exposure of physical assets, 152
External audit, 237
External auditors, 212
External failure cost, 126
External networks, 90
Ezzamel, 62

Facilities Management (FM), 568
Federal decentralisation, 84
Feedback, 19, 20
Feedback control, 21
Feedback loop, 24
Feedforward control, 22
File conversion procedures, 619
File conversion, 619
File viruses, 583
Filtering, 13
Financial audit, 239
Financial control style, 107
Financial control, 107
Financial future, 463
Financial records and reporting risks, 135
Financial reporting, 224
Financial risks, 134
Financial statement assertions, 253
Fire, 580
Firewall, 600, 602
Fisher effect, 437
Flat organisation, 76
Flexible network, 91
Flooding, 580, 589
Floors, 493
Floppy disks, 598
Flowcharts, 141, 272
Foreign exchange risk, 438
Forfaiting, 415
Forward exchange contract, 447
Forward exchange rate, 434
Forward rate agreements (FRAs), 486
Foucault, 29
Framework for internal control, 236
Fraud and error, 382
Fraud officer, 386
Fraud risk, 137
Fraud, 378, 581, 598
Fraudulent use of the computer system, 581
Frequently-Asked Questions (FAQs), 603
Functional boards, 208
Fundamental principles, 395
Fundamental risks, 132
Futures contract, 463
Futures market, 463

Gap analysis of interest rate risk, 484
Gap analysis, 485
General and application controls, 185
General controls, 185
Ghost employees, 378
Goal congruence, 25, 116
Goal theory, 118
Goold and Campbell, 107
Government loan guarantees, 502
Greenbury report, 200, 220
Grey areas, 404
Gross profit margins, 291
Group incentive schemes, 65
Guest, 43

Hackers, 582, 599
Hacking, 582
Hampel report, 200, 203, 222
Handy, 93
Haphazard selection, 263
Hard HRM, 41
Hard model, 41
Hash totals, 595
Hedge, 442
Help desk, 560
Hierarchical subsystem, 13
Hierarchy, 74
Higgs report, 201
Hofstede, 118
Hold harmless agreements, 148
Hollow network, 91
Homeostasis, 16
Homeostatic system, 16
Hopwood, 100
Horizontal organisation, 88
Human behaviour and budgetary planning and control, 116
Human relations, 118
Human resources, 361, 427
Human resources audit, 361
Human threats, 580

IAS 32 Financial instruments: presentation and disclosure, 508
IAS 39 Financial instruments: recognition and measurement, 509
Import quotas, 418
Incremental approach, 570
Independent person (the auditor), 369
Indirect quote, 433
Inflating expense claims, 379
Information as a commodity, 526
Information centre (IC), 560
Information management (IM) strategy, 528
Information management, 528
Information society, 526

Information strategy, 529
Information system audit, 239
Information system, 520
Information systems (IS) strategy, 528, 529
Information systems department, 558
Information systems director, 558
Information systems manager, 558
Information systems strategy, 529, 530
Information systems, 8, 528
Information technology, 529
Information technology strategy, 533
Information value, 526
Information, 520
Infrastructure led, 535
Inherent risk, 282, 286
Initial margin, 464
Input controls, 595
Input fraud, 581
Inputs, 9
Inside out, 535
Insourcing, 574
Instability, 24
Institute of Internal Auditors, 234, 314
Institutional shareholders, 224
Insurance, 502
Integrated approach, 240
Integrated internal audit department, 241
Integration, 550
Integrity controls, 595
Integrity, 395
Interactive control systems, 107
Interactive management control, 106
Interest rate guarantee, 493
Interest rate option, 493
Interest rate parity, 435, 436
Interest rate risk, 135
Interest rate swap, 502
Internal accounts, 141
Internal audit, 212, 228, **234, 249**
assessing the performance of internal audit, 244
Internal control, 180, 210, 213, 224
Internal Control Evaluation Questionnaires (ICEQs), 273
Internal control frameworks, 181
Internal Control Questionnaires (ICQs), 272
Internal control system, 107, **181**
Internal customers, 124
Internal failure cost, 126
Internal networks, 89
International credit unions, 417
International Fisher effect, 438
Internet risks, 582
Internet, 531, 582, 599, 603
Interoperability, 566
Intranets, 604
Inventory system, 344
Investigation of fraud, 387
Investment centres, 35
Investment workstation, 547
Involvement culture, 94
IS/IT Strategy, 529
ISA 230 Documentation, 269
ISA 500 Audit evidence, 252
ISA 520 Analytical procedures, 288
ISA 530 Audit sampling, 262
ISO 14001, 373
Issuing false credit notes, 379
IT chargeout, 564
IT cost allocation, 563

Job evaluation, 49
Joint captives, 147
Joint venture sourcing, 570
Judgement of outsiders, 63

Kaplan, 115
Keyword search, 603
King report, 198, 201, 204, 226
Knowledge Work Systems (KWS), 547
Knowledge Workers, 547
Knowledge, 70
KPIs, 537

Laptop, 598
Law of requisite variety, 16
Leads and lags, 445
Legacy system, 566
Legal risks, 135, 422
Legitimation structures, 28
Letters of credit, 416
Liability, limitation of, 148
Lightning and electrical storms, 580
Limit checks, 595
Liquidity risk, 136
Lobbying, 5
Local managers, 427, 428
Lockett, 55
Locks, 592
Logic bomb, 583
Logistics audit, 357
Loss reduction, 145

Macintosh, 118
Macro viruses, 584
Macropyramid, 427
Manageable businesses, 107
Management accounting and control, 100
historical development, 100
Management accounting system, 109
Management audit, 369
Management charges, 420
Management control information, 111
Management control, 100
Management development, 75
Management fraud, 380
Management Information Systems (MIS), 544, 546
Management information, 530
Management involvement, 116
Management of internal audit, 243
Management performance measures, 63
Management style, 116
Management, 186, 530
Managerial performance, 61
Mandated controls, 185
Manual controls, 185
Market control, 35
Market testing, 35
Marketing, 359
Marketing audit, 359
Maslow's hierarchy of needs, 46
Matching receipts and payments, 445
Materiality, 309
Mathematical models, 256
Matrix organisation, 81
Measurement, 253
Media, 425
M-form, 74
Miles and Snow, 93
Mintzberg, 71, 89
Miscasting of the payroll, 378
Mission culture, 94
Mixed approach, 535
Money market hedge, 451
Monocratic boards, 208
Motivation, 45, 46, 65
Multilateral netting, 446
Multiple sourcing, 570
Multi-tier boards, 207

Narrative notes, 272
Natural threats, 580
Need theories, 46
Negative feedback, 21
Netting, 445, **446**
Networks and co-ordination, 89
Networks of contacts, 89
Networks, 89
Nomination committee, 204
Non-audit services, 225
Non-discretionary controls, 185
Non-executive directors, 205, 220
Non-financial measures, 63
Non-integrated internal audit department, 240
Non-sampling risk, 265
Non-tariff barriers, 419
Notebook, 598

OAS, 548
Objectives of internal audit, 234
Objectives of systems, 8
Objectives, 395
Objectivity, 395
Occurrence, 253
Off balance sheet transactions, 226
Office Automation System (OAS), 548
Off-line testing, 614
On-line processing, 549
On-line testing, 614
Open loop systems, 19
Open systems, 14, 567
Operational audit planning, 309
Operational audits, 356
Operational control information, 112
Operational control, 100
Operational information, 112, 522
Operational planning, 100
Operations control, 559
Opportunity loss, 173
Option forward exchange contracts, 449
Option, 469
Options theory, 502
Organisation charts, 141
Organisation culture, 92
Organisation structure, 113, 118, 566
Organisation, 186
Organisational information requirements, 534
Outputs, 10
Output controls, 595
Output fraud, 581
Outsourcing, 35, 92, **567**
Outsourcing internal audit, 246
Over the counter (OTC) options, 470

PA Consulting Group, 572
Parallel running, 620
Parsons generic strategies for IS, 539
Participation in budgeting, 118
Particular risks, 133
Partner rotation, 225
Passwords, 593
Payoff, 172
Payoff table, 172
Performance agreements, 53
Performance and rewards, 63
Performance indicators, 537
Performance management activities, 53
Performance measurement, 521
Performance review, 54
Performance-related rewards, 63
Personal identification numbers (PINs), 592
Personnel, 186
Phased changeover, 621
Physical access control, 591
Physical damage, 580
Physical inspection, 142
Physical risk, 136
Physical threats, 589
Physical, 186
Pilot operation, 620
Planning, 520
Plans of site and buildings, 142
Policies, 35
Policy boards, 208
Political risk, 136, 418
Political, 136
Population, 262
Portable, 598
Positive feedback, 21
Post-implementation review report, 622
Post-implementation review, 621
Power culture, 93
Predictive model, 23
Presentation and disclosure, 253
Prevent controls, 184
Prevention cost, 126
Prevention of fraud, 384
Price mechanism, 35
Probabilistic or stochastic, 16
Probabilistic system, 16
Probability distribution, 163
Procedures, 36, 255
Process theories, 46
Processes, 9
Processing controls, 595
Processing fraud, 581
Procurement audit, 358
Procurement, 358
Professional behaviour, 396
Professional competence, 395
Professional guidelines, 394
Profit centres, 35
Profit-related pay scheme, 64
Profit-sharing schemes, 64
Program testing, 613
Project teams, 81
Project-based culture, 82
Projected errors, 312
Projection of errors, 267
Public interest, 394
Public Oversight Board, 225
Public sector, 66
Publicity and solicitation, 397
Published accounts, 141
Purchases and expenses system, 329
Purchasing power parity, 437, 479
Pure research, 363
Pure risks, 133
Pyramid scheme frauds, 381

Qualitative aspects of errors, 266
Quality control, 283
Quality of control, 283
Questionnaires, 256

Random selection, 263
Range checks, 595
Ratios, 537
Reassessing sampling risk, 267
Receiving the service, 255
Reconciliation, 255
Recruitment and training, 428
Recruitment, 51
Reference currency, 432
Relationship between external and internal audit, 238
Remote diagnostic software, 560
Remuneration, 222, 227
Remuneration committee, 208, 220
Remuneration policy, 209, 221, 223
Report Systems auditability and control, 314
Reporting on corporate governance, 215
Requisite variety, 16
Research and development audit, 363
Research, 255
Resolution of ethical conflicts, 396
Return on capital employed, 291

Revenue expenditure, 348
Reward system, 56
Rights and obligations, 253
Risk, 132, 143, 173
Risk analysis, 141, 140, 159
Risk avoidance, 144
Risk consolidation, 142
Risk diversification, 149
Risk hedging, 149
Risk identification, 140
Risk management, 228
Risk manager, 143
Risk policy statement, 143
Risk pooling, 149
Risk profiling, 142
Risk quantification, 142, 152
Risk reduction, 144
Risk retaining, 145
Risk sharing, 148
Risk specialists, 143
Risk transfer, 148
Risks of fraud, 581
Robertson, 48
Rockart, 536
Role culture, 93
Royalty, 420
Rule, 36

Sales fraud, 379
Sales system, 324
Sample size, 265
Sampling risk, 265
Sampling units, 263
Sarbanes-Oxley Act, 201, 225
Scalar chain, 75
Scenario building, 176
Scientific management, 35
Scope of internal audit, 239
Security, 584, 589
Security policy, 585
Segregation of duties, 186
Selection, 51
Self-appraisals, 56
Self-insurance, 146
Self-organising system, 16
Semi-closed system, 14
Sensitivity analysis, 153
Service bureaux, 568
Service contracts, 221, 223
Service industries, 34
Service Level Agreement (SLA), 571
Service Level Contract (SLC), 571
Settlement date, 463
Share warrants, 502
Shared personal goals, 26
Shareholders, 214
Shell, 371
Short-termism, 65
Signification structures, 28
Simon, 100
Simons, 105
Simulation model, 174
Single loop control, 19
Size, 104
Smith report, 201
Social audits, 371
Social systems, 8, 14
Soft HRM, 42
Soft systems methodology (SSM), 24
Soft systems, 24
Software houses, 568
Software piracy, 598
Span of control, 75
Specific control procedures, 185
Speculative risks, 133
Spot rate, 432
Staff appraisal system, 54
Stakeholder theory, 202
Stakeholders, 214, 531
Standby hardware facilities, 591
Stark, 405
Statistical sampling, 262
Status checking, 603
Stealing assets, 379
Stealing unclaimed wages, 378
Stealth viruses, 583
Steering committee, 530, 558
Stewardship theory, 201
Stochastic system, 16
Stock Exchange requirements, 225
Storey, 41
Strategic analysis approach, 535, 536
Strategic audit planning, 307
Strategic control style, 107
Strategic control, 107
Strategic information, 521
Strategic level information system, 544
Strategic planning, 100, 107, 111
Strategic planning information, 111
Strategic planning style, 107
Strategic uncertainties, 106
Strategy, 105
Structuration, 29
Structures, 28

Subjective measures, 63
Substantive procedures, 252, 305
Subsystems, 11
Sufficient appropriate audit evidence, 252
Supervision, 186
Support centre, 560
Sustainability, 229
Swap, 478, 502
Synthetic forward, 451
System, 7
System boundary, 10
System objectives, 8
System testing, 614
Systematic selection, 263
Systems audit, 302
Systems development staff, 560
Systems development, 610
Systems integration, 567, 571
Systems integrity, 580, **595**
Systems testing, 624
Systems theory, 7

Tactical audit planning, 308
Tactical information, 112, 522
Tactical planning, 100
Tactics, 100
Tall and flat organisations, 76
Tall organisation, 76
Target costing, 35
Tariffs, 418
Task culture, 93
Technical manual, 618
Technical standards, 396
Technical systems, 8
Technology, 103
Teeming and lading, 380
Tendering, 570
Term currency, 432
Terms of reference for an internal audit department, 236
Test of controls, 252
Testing plan, 615
Testing strategy, 615
Tests of control, 303
Three Es, 365, 369
Three leg analysis, 534
Three legs of IS strategy development, 534
Tick size, 464
Tight and loose HRM, 43
Time bomb, 583
Time share, 568
Tolerable error, 265, 311
Top down, 534
Trade risk, 136
Traded interest rate options, 497
Trading risks, 136
Training, 58, 616
Training and learning, 57
Training needs analysis, 58
Training objectives, 59
Training plan, 616
Training programme, 427
Training system, 58
Transaction costs, 73, 602
Transaction exposure, 439
Transaction Processing System (TPS), 548
Transaction risk, 439
Transactions, 520
Transfer prices, 85
Translation exposure, 441
Translation risk, 439
Treasury audit, 360
Treasury, 360
Trojan, 583
Turbulence, 91
Turnbull Committee, 210, 317
Turnbull report, 180, 201
Types of information system, 545

U-form, 74
Unachievable budgets, 120
Unit integration testing, 614
Unit testing, 614
Upward appraisal, 57, 63
User acceptance testing, 614, 624
User manual, 618
User satisfaction surveys, 256
Utilitarianism, 394

V model, 611
Valence, 47
Validating a training scheme, 60
Valuation, 253
Value for money, 364
Value-added network, 91
Victor Vroom, 47
VIE theory, 47
Virtual network, 91
Virtual reality systems, 547
Virus, 582, **583**, 599
Voluntary and mandated controls, 185
Voluntary controls, 185

Wages system, 333
Water damage, 589
Water, 580
Whistleblowing, 226, 387
Wizards (interview style interface), 603
Working papers, 269
Worms, 583

Zero cost collar, 493

Review Form & Free Prize Draw – Paper P3 Management Accounting Risk and Control Strategy

All original review forms from the entire BPP range, completed with genuine comments, will be entered into one of two draws on 31 January 2005 and 31 July 2005. The names on the first four forms picked out on each occasion will be sent a cheque for £50.

Name: ______________________ **Address:** ______________________

____

____

How have you used this Interactive Text?
(Tick one box only)

☐ Home study (book only)

☐ On a course: college ______________

☐ With 'correspondence' package

☐ Other ______________

Why did you decide to purchase this Interactive Text? *(Tick one box only)*

☐ Have used BPP Texts in the past

☐ Recommendation by friend/colleague

☐ Recommendation by a lecturer at college

☐ Saw advertising

☐ Other ______________

During the past six months do you recall seeing/receiving any of the following?
(Tick as many boxes as are relevant)

☐ Our advertisement in *CIMA Insider*

☐ Our advertisement in *Financial Management*

☐ Our advertisement in *Pass*

☐ Our advertisement in *PQ*

☐ Our brochure with a letter through the post

☐ Our website www.bpp.com

Which (if any) aspects of our advertising do you find useful?
(Tick as many boxes as are relevant)

☐ Prices and publication dates of new editions

☐ Information on Text content

☐ Facility to order books off-the-page

☐ None of the above

Which BPP products have you used?

Text	☑	*MCQ cards*	☐	*i-Learn*	☐
Kit	☐	*CD/Tape*	☐	*i-Pass*	☐
Passcard	☐	*Big Picture Poster*	☐	*Virtual Campus*	☐

Your ratings, comments and suggestions would be appreciated on the following areas.

	Very useful	*Useful*	*Not useful*
Introductory section (Key study steps, personal study)	☐	☐	☐
Chapter introductions	☐	☐	☐
Key terms	☐	☐	☐
Quality of explanations	☐	☐	☐
Case studies and other examples	☐	☐	☐
Questions and answers in each chapter	☐	☐	☐
Fast forwards and chapter roundups	☐	☐	☐
Quick quizzes	☐	☐	☐
Exam focus points	☐	☐	☐
Question bank	☐	☐	☐
Answer Bank	☐	☐	☐
Index	☐	☐	☐
Icons	☐	☐	☐

Overall opinion of this Study Text *Excellent* ☐ *Good* ☐ *Adequate* ☐ *Poor* ☐

Do you intend to continue using BPP products? *Yes* ☐ *No* ☐

On the reverse of this page are noted particular areas of the text about which we would welcome your feedback.

The BPP author of this edition can be e-mailed at: nickweller@bpp.com

Please return this form to: Nick Weller, CIMA Range Manager, BPP Professional Education, FREEPOST, London, W12 8BR

Review Form & Free Prize Draw (continued)

TELL US WHAT YOU THINK

Free Prize Draw Rules

1. Closing date for 31 January 2005 draw is 31 December 2004. Closing date for 31 July 2005 draw is 30 June 2005.
2. Restricted to entries with UK and Eire addresses only. BPP employees, their families and business associates are excluded.
3. No purchase necessary. Entry forms are available upon request from BPP Professional Education. No more than one entry per title, per person. Draw restricted to persons aged 16 and over.
4. Winners will be notified by post and receive their cheques not later than 6 weeks after the relevant draw date.
5. The decision of the promoter in all matters is final and binding. No correspondence will be entered into.